# YOGI

ALSO BY JON PESSAH

*The Game*

# YOGI

## A LIFE
## BEHIND
## THE MASK

# JON PESSAH

LITTLE, BROWN AND COMPANY

*New York  Boston  London*

Little, Brown and Company
Hachette Book Group
1290 Avenue of the Americas, New York, NY 10104
littlebrown.com

First Edition: April 2020

Little, Brown and Company is a division of Hachette Book Group, Inc. The Little, Brown name and logo are trademarks of Hachette Book Group, Inc.

The publisher is not responsible for websites (or their content) that are not owned by the publisher.

The Hachette Speakers Bureau provides a wide range of authors for speaking events. To find out more, go to hachettespeakersbureau.com or call (866) 376-6591.

ISBN 978-0-316-31099-4
LCCN 2019951030

10 9 8 7 6 5 4 3 2 1

LSC-C

Printed in the United States of America

*In memory of David,*
*who started the ball rolling,*
*and Dave and Steve,*
*and little Sammy,*
*baseball fans all.*

# Contents

# YOGI

# Wait 'Til You See Yogi!

The visitors clubhouse in Fenway Park is hot and steamy, even on this October day of 1946. The low ceiling and exposed pipes make the cramped room feel especially small. But none of that bothers the St. Louis Cardinals, who have just drubbed the heavily favored home team, 12–3, in Game 4 of the World Series.

Every one of the youthful Cardinals is shouting and laughing, pushing and shoving, or jumping over benches. Just a year ago, many of these men had been getting their discharge papers after years of service in World War II. Now they're throwing gloves and hats at each other, happy to be back home, alive, and playing for the biggest prize in the game they love.

At the center of the celebration is one of the youngest players in the game, 20-year-old catcher Joe Garagiola, who has just tied a World Series record with four hits in a game while driving in a game-high three runs. The lanky, good-looking Garagiola whoops it up while getting pulled into one photo after another.

"It's still hard to believe I am wearing a Cardinals uniform. What a game to win!"

St. Louis finished in a tie with Brooklyn for the NL flag, then swept two games to win the NL's first-ever best-of-three playoff. Stan Musial, who batted .365 and drove in 103 runs this season, is the engine of this Cardinal team. But you don't reach a World Series without a catcher who can handle a pitching staff. And if he can hit like Joey hit the last month—.314 batting average, 10 RBI in 16 games—you have something special.

"That little Garagiola looked great behind the plate, didn't he?" manager Eddie Dyer shouts. Two of the final three games of this thrilling World Series will now be played at Sportsman's Park—the Cardinals' home field, all of eight miles from Joe's house—where St. Louis will go on to win its second title in the last three seasons. Management had put the rookie's locker next to that of captain Terry Moore, another St. Louis native. Now both men find themselves cornered by writers hunting down a *local boy makes good* story.

"Tell them about The Hill, Joey!" Moore shouts over the heads of the reporters encircling the pride of St. Louis' Italian community— mostly immigrant families who live on what's commonly called Dago Hill. "I bet the vino is really rolling up there tonight."

A New York writer asks if there are other good players up in the old neighborhood.

"Haven't you ever seen Yogi?" a surprised Garagiola asks.

Indeed, Joey still wonders why Cardinal GM Branch Rickey refused to sign Yogi when the two best friends tried out for the Cardinals a few years ago. Joey received a $500 bonus and left for the Cardinals' minor league team in Springfield in '42, leaving Berra playing American Legion ball and wondering about his future.

There isn't a day in Joey's life when he didn't know Lawdie Berra, as he's known on Dago Hill. They have lived in the same small but neatly kept houses across the street from each other ever since Joey was four years old and Lawdie was five. And Garagiola also knows Lawdie—or Larry or Yogi or whatever you call him—is the best athlete Joey's ever seen in every sport they've played, especially baseball.

So he wasn't at all surprised when the Yankees came to St. Louis and scooped up Yogi in the fall of '42. Nor was he surprised at how well his friend played for New York's top minor league team in Newark this year, which earned him a seven-game audition as a Yankee in the season's final week. And of course Yogi hit .364 with two home runs in his seven-game debut.

"Why," Garagiola tells the crowd of reporters, "he's a much better catcher than I am."

Garagiola looks at the New York writers, seeking support. "You've seen Yogi," he says. "Tell them how good he is."

"The Yankees were so far out of the pennant race that I stopped covering them in the middle of September," *New York Daily News* writer Joe Trimble explains. "I switched over to cover your race with the Dodgers."

"He's better than I am," Garagiola repeats. "He can hit homers like a big slugger. Plus he can run faster than any catcher you ever saw."

The writers return to asking about the World Series, now dead-locked at two games apiece, but Joey is undeterred. "Berra will be the best catcher in the American League in a couple of years," Garagiola tells the national media.

"Wait 'til you see Yogi!"

# PART I

**AMERICAN DREAM**

1925–1946

# CHAPTER 1

# Decisions, Decisions

## 1939–1940

Lawdie Berra has always thought he was going to be a major league baseball player. And why not? It's early in the summer of 1939, he's a few weeks past his 14th birthday, and he's always been the best player among the hundreds of boys playing ball on Dago Hill, the Italian quarter of St. Louis.

There's not much the youngest of four Berra boys can't do on a baseball field. Lawdie—the name derived from his Italian-speaking mother's struggle to pronounce "Lawrence"—is so quick and agile he can handle any infield position. He's fast enough to play all three outfield posts and has a rifle of a throwing arm. Most times, he alternates between catcher and pitcher with his best friend, Joey Garagiola, the second-best player on The Hill.

Lawdie doesn't look much like a baseball player. He stands just under five foot eight, with a large head atop big, muscular shoulders that make his neck almost invisible. He has short, muscular legs, long arms with thick wrists, and meaty hands with stubby fingers. But put a bat in those hands, and he'll hit anything thrown to him—in the strike zone or out—and hit it hard from either side of the plate. A while back, his older brothers—all good ballplayers themselves—convinced Lawdie that hitting left-handed gave him an edge. So Lawdie, a natural right-handed hitter, simply switched sides.

Nothing seems to faze this kid. Not even the taunts about his looks he always hears when he faces a team for the first time. A double with the bases loaded usually takes care of that, and there are plenty of those, too. When there's a tough pitcher on the mound? "So what?" Berra says, his toothy grin seeming to stretch from one big ear to the other. "I got a bat. I swing. That's all." Playing baseball is all Lawdie Berra wants to do, and he's sure he'll be a major leaguer one day.

There's just one problem.

Lawdie Berra's father is against the whole idea.

And that's nothing new.

Pietro Berra was against it when his oldest son Tony was invited to try out for the Cleveland Indians. Lefty, as Tony was known on the ball fields on The Hill, smacked line drives to all fields, had a strong arm, possessed plenty of speed, and could field every infield position superbly. Pietro said no to the tryout. "Out of the question," he thundered in Italian. A man's job is to provide for his family, and a man can't be a provider by playing a little boy's game. Tony, now 26, has been working in one of The Hill's many bakeries ever since.

Pietro was against it when second-born son Mike was asked to try out a few years later by the hometown Browns—the city's other and decidedly second-favorite major league team. "Baseball players are bums!" Pietro bellowed, and Mike found a job working at the Johansen Bros. shoe factory. Both young men now play semipro ball on weekends against factory teams or teams from another town, picking up a few bucks and dreaming about what might have been.

"Men don't make a living playing *a game*," Pietro Berra says each time the subject of playing professional baseball is raised.

And that is what he is saying again now. Which is why Lawdie is sitting against the kitchen wall, arms folded across his chest, a hard stare frozen on his normally smiling face. His parents have convened a family meeting to discuss their youngest son's decision to quit school now that he's made it through the eighth grade. Tony and Mike are here, listening to the same speech Pop has given so many times before. So is Pietro and Paulina's third son John, three and a half years older than Lawdie and already waiting tables for several years at Ruggeri's, one of the finest restaurants in St. Louis.

Pietro and Paulina have also asked Father Anthony Palumbo from St. Ambrose Church, the beating heart of The Hill's overwhelmingly Italian-Catholic community, to help guide their decision. The principal of Lawdie's school is there, too. For years, Lawdie has begged his parents to let him quit school, where he's spent most of his time staring out the window while waiting for the bell signaling the end of classes. He performed so poorly in his first six years that he was shifted to Wade School, an "opportunity school" for underachieving and struggling students, to get a second chance and perhaps learn a trade.

But Lawdie wasn't interested in any of that, and he played hooky more days than he'd care to admit. All he wanted to do was get outside and play ball.

Pietro isn't against his son's leaving school after the eighth grade. After all, once a boy learns how to read, write, and do basic arithmetic, what else does he need to know to find work as a laborer and one day provide for a family of his own? Like most boys on The Hill during the Depression, none of Pietro's older sons finished school before going out and finding work.

But Pietro is convinced Lawdie's poor performance in school is wrapped up in this obsession with playing ball—especially baseball. And that's what has Pietro so damn angry with his youngest son. Lawdie isn't begging to leave school so he can find a job, earn some money, and help the family. No, he wants to quit school so he can spend all his time playing ball. And that's just not acceptable.

"Baseball is for bums—a waste of time!" says Pietro, fixing a hard glare at Lawdie. "You should have a job and work like your brothers. The family needs your help."

Lawdie looks around the room for support. Both the priest and the principal agree that Lawdie doesn't really belong in school. "Not everyone is a born scholar," Father Palumbo says. But the priest and the principal think it's time for Berra to stop playing ball and find a job.

Lawdie catches the eye of his mother, who hasn't said a word. Paulina, a short, stocky woman with a big heart, only wants her son to be happy. Mom's the one who sews up the tears in his one pair of not-for-church pants after another rough game so her son might escape his father's wrath. And she's the one who tells him whether Pietro is asleep when Lawdie comes home late so he can slip in the back door and avoid another punishment. Lawdie knows his mother would do anything for him, but expecting her to go against Pop is far too much.

And that's when his three brothers step up.

"Dad, I'll work extra hours at the bakery so Lawdie can get the chance to see if he can really play," says Tony, who knows baseball scouts start tracking local players by the time they're 13. "I think he can be a great player."

"Pop, I'll do the same," Mike says. "Things are picking up. I can get more hours at the shoe factory."

By the time John makes the same pledge, Lawdie can feel his parents' resolve beginning to soften. "I'll pick up jobs around playing baseball and bring in some money," Lawdie promises, working hard to control his excitement when he sees his parents slowly nodding their heads in agreement. This meeting is working out far better than he had any reason to hope it would. His father agrees to allow him to quit school without finding a full-time job. Instead, he can do what Pietro forbade his three older sons from doing—continue to play baseball.

And he has his three brothers to thank.

Almost as relieved is Lawdie's little sister Josie, who is listening to this drama play out from another room. Thank God they're finally letting Lawdie leave school, Josie says to herself. If they didn't, she's pretty sure her brother Lawdie was going to lose his mind.

There is one school Lawdie Berra truly loves: the one run by the Works Progress Administration. The New Deal government program employs millions of Americans, who build and operate everything from schools and museums to parks and ball fields. Many of the teachers in this school are scouts from the St. Louis Cardinals and Browns. And there's a rotating band of players that includes star Cardinal outfielders Enos Slaughter, Terry Moore, and—best of all—Joe Medwick, Lawdie's favorite player.

This school's classroom: the baseball fields of Sherman Park, an hour's walk from Lawdie's house.

The lessons: hitting, pitching, fielding, and base running.

Now, *these* are the lessons, Berra tells himself, that are going to help me get the only job I've ever wanted.

Berra doesn't miss a day of this school, which runs from mid-June to mid-July of the summer of 1940. Neither does his best friend Joe Garagiola, who lives directly across the street on Elizabeth Avenue and rarely leaves his friend's side. The pair are among the first to show up each morning and the last to leave, and several of the players and scouts are beginning to notice that there's something special about these two kids. Cardinal scout Dee Walsh takes a liking to Garagiola, and one day invites him to work out at Sportsman's Park, the home field for both St. Louis teams.

Lawdie couldn't be happier for his friend. As for him? Well, he's just thrilled with the chance to hear Medwick talk about hitting a baseball. Medwick burst onto the scene in 1933 as a 21-year-old .300 hitter with home run power. One season later he was an All-Star and an important cog in a World Series winner. He led the National League in home runs (31), runs batted in (154), and batting average (.374)—baseball's Triple Crown—in 1937, and next month he'll play in his seventh straight All-Star Game.

Best of all, he is a bad-ball hitter: Medwick will swing at anything, in or out of the strike zone, as long as he thinks—he *knows*—he can hit it. Just like Berra, who rarely sees a pitch he doesn't think he can hit, no matter where it's thrown. It's little wonder Medwick is his idol.

By 1940, Berra and Garagiola are the best players in the two leagues run by the WPA and sponsored by the two St. Louis baseball teams. Lawdie, now 15 and a full eight months older than his friend, plays in the Junior League, for boys 15 to 17; Joey plays in the Midget League, for 12- to 14-year-olds. Both lead their teams to championship games played at Sportsman's Park on July 10.

The day begins with Lawdie and Joey standing in a major league dugout, watching the Columbia School drum and bugle corps march out to center field for the flag-raising ceremony. The games are announced over the public address system, and the first is all about Garagiola. Playing catcher and right field, Joe raps out four hits and drives in three runs to lead his team to an easy 12–5 victory.

Then it's Berra's turn.

"Now batting third and playing second base for the Johnny Brocks, Larry Berra," booms a voice over the PA system as Lawdie steps in and smacks a single, then comes around to score the first run in the second title game. Berra picks up another single, scores another run, and plays a flawless second base. When the game is over, the Johnny Brocks have a 7–5 win, the city title, and there's Lawdie, standing on the field, clutching the championship trophy.

When all the cheering stops, the WPA officials announce they are extending the season another four weeks. Berra is thrilled and conflicted. It seems he is as uninterested in working as he was in school, and in the year since he left school he's lost one job after another, all for the same reason—as soon as the morning turns into the afternoon and his friends are out playing ball, Lawdie simply walks off his job to find them.

He knew he'd catch a beating from his father each time, and he knew it would hurt, too. Pietro might only be five foot three and lean, but years of hard labor in the brickyard have made him powerfully strong, with hands that feel like stone when he's meting out punishment. That's the way discipline is enforced in every home on The Hill, and rarely does a father have to punish a son more than once for any given transgression.

But Lawdie is nothing if not stubborn. He remains convinced his future lies in baseball, by far the most popular game in all of America. Four more weeks playing WPA ball doesn't leave much time to find or hold down a job. But Berra's willing to take the beatings if it means he can still play ball.

The only question is how much longer Pietro Berra is willing to trade beatings for baseball. Sure, Lawdie is a local star, but that means little to his father. Tony, Mike, and John can go to bat for their little brother all they want. Sooner or later, the father of the house will decide it's time for Lawdie Berra to grow up, forget this baseball nonsense, and get—and *hold*—a real job.

And as far as Papa Berra is concerned, that day is rapidly approaching.

# CHAPTER 2

# Dago Hill
## 1925–1941

The legend of Lorenzo Pietro Berra—Lawdie's proper name in Italian, the language of the Berra household—grew as he began to roam the playing fields of Dago Hill in southwest St. Louis.

As an athlete, he was unmatched. His classmates in grade school begged the left-handed Berra to bat right-handed in their baseball games because they only had one baseball and didn't want to lose it on the roof of the Henry Shaw School, 250 feet away. Lawdie obliged—and hit the ball for homers anyway.

Former boxer Frank Mariani spotted the 13-year-old Lawdie, put the athletic youngster in the ring with older club fighters, and watched him win eight of nine matches, each for a prize of $5 to $10. Berra even avenged his one loss in a rematch. Paulina Berra worried about her young son in a boxing ring, but he kept coming home uninjured with money for the family.

It may have been an exaggeration that a teacher once asked Lawdie how he liked school and Lawdie replied, "Closed," but it rang true. The kid was a genius on any playing field, a leader and a fierce competitor, but he often played hooky from school and doubted publicly that math would matter in his life.

Of course he didn't get the big hit in every baseball game—it just felt that way—but he was a head-turning talent in almost any sport.

Joey Garagiola swore that one night the two friends wandered into the local YMCA and found a Ping-Pong tournament under way. Lawdie, who had never held a paddle, picked one out, hit a few balls, and proceeded to reach the tournament final. Joey loved to tell these and other stories about Lawdie, who rarely told them himself.

Lawdie wasn't even the star of his favorite story. At 13, he and pal Charlie Riva used to earn three-quarters of a cent per paper by selling the *St. Louis Globe-Democrat* on a corner for three cents. One afternoon, Lawdie sold a paper to a young athletic man who gave him a nickel and told him to keep the change. It was Joe Medwick, famous left fielder for the St. Louis Cardinals and eventual Hall of Famer. The star and the charming kid talked baseball for a few minutes, and when Medwick said goodbye to him by name, Lawdie's reputation soared. Medwick and his extra two-cent tip became regulars on Lawdie's corner.

Nor did the unflappable Berra seem to mind getting razzed for everything from his favorite sandwich—a banana hero with mustard—to his slightly oversized head, especially in the summer, when all the boys were buzzed to the scalp. He just grinned when the other boys kidded his mangled English, the product of his Italian-language household and his uneasy relationship with school.

If ever someone felt comfortable in his skin, it was Lawdie Berra, beloved youngest son of a large, loyal Italian family. No teasing undercut those bonds. All kids on The Hill just belonged.

Still, Lawdie was different—a sparkling athlete in a strangely proportioned body, with a round face dominated by a big nose, heavy brow, and toothy grin. He and his affable, handsome buddy Joey were almost always together—teasing and punching each other playfully. Born exactly eight months apart—Lawdie on May 12, 1925, Joey the following February, at the height of the Roaring Twenties—they came of age together in the Great Depression. Their fathers kept steady jobs at the clay products factory, but money was short, and the boys sometimes shoplifted a little extra food with a simple scam: Joey chatted with a manager while Lawdie and the others stuffed their pockets.

They also knew how to pick off a real football to sell or trade. On game day at St. Louis University, Lawdie would wait outside the wall at one end of the field until an extra-point kick sailed into his arms. Turning and punting it 40 yards or more to a friend, the buddies relayed the ball away before anyone could come to retrieve it.

More often they scavenged, following the 39th Street market truck with its rotting vegetables and fruit to the town dump. Pocketknives in hand, they sifted the detritus for salvageable bits. Few of these boys went hungry at home, but good fruit and vegetables were jewels.

Lawdie was a quiet kid, but somehow also the neighborhood peacemaker and chief organizer, and in 1937 he convinced Joey and other friends to start a new sports club—the Stags Athletic Club. Just about every block had its own club, which competed fiercely—baseball, softball, street hockey, or soccer, a sport Lawdie loved almost as much as baseball and played with the same skill and joy. Their equipment was all used or improvised and shared with opposing teams—broomhandle hockey sticks and old-magazine shin guards. As long as Lawdie and his friends were playing sports, they were happy.

The Stags rented an abandoned garage as a neighborhood clubhouse for 12 cents a month. Their allowances couldn't cover the rent, so they devised schemes to raise money. One was paying a dime for a pack of 20 cigarettes and selling them for a penny apiece. They also bagged manure dropped on the street by horses pulling merchant wagons, which they sold for 10 or 15 cents each to the neighborhood men to use as vegetable-garden fertilizer. If an adult tried to cut out the middleman, Lawdie and his friends formed a wall around their prize until it was whisked away by whoever drew the short straw that day.

Scrounging for cast-off couches and tables for their clubhouse, they talked for hours about the Cardinals—especially the "Gashouse Gang" of Dizzy Dean and Joe Medwick, which won the World Series in 1934. They played cards, talked about movies and radio programs like *The Shadow, The Green Hornet,* and *Superman.* On lucky days when they could buy—or pilfer—potatoes, they sat outside around a fire roasting them.

Some Saturday mornings, a neighborhood woman named Dominica Beltrami assembled the boys for a bus ride to Sportsman's Park and free promotional seats—first come, first served—in the left field grandstand.

As they grew older, their conversations often turned to girls. These conversations rarely included the bashful Berra, who would cross the street to avoid talking to any young lady he might know.

All these adventures took place in the security of The Hill—crossing to the Irish neighborhood of Dogtown or to Dutchtown, where Germans had settled in the 1830s, invited brawls. All the boys in St. Louis might be Cardinals or Browns fans—but in the 1930s and '40s, ethnic rivalries mattered most.

Soccer was still the only game the Italian fathers of The Hill understood, so Lawdie entered the Stags in the soccer tournament at the South Side YMCA. The Hill's Southwestern drugstore gave them T-shirts, the closest thing to a uniform they'd ever had. The Stags won the Y's soccer title and YMCA director Joe Causino always remembers the sound of Berra's voice cutting through the whoops and hollers. "Now let's go out and get the baseball trophy," Lawdie shouted. Which they did.

There were three constants for the Stags: sports, church, and beer for their dads. Saturday was the day for a bath and Confession at St. Ambrose Church. They all attended Sunday Mass at 9 a.m. with their fathers, then Sunday school with Father Charles Koester—everyone's favorite priest—while their mothers prepared the family's Sunday feast. And once Prohibition ended in 1933, the boys were expected to meet their fathers at the end of every working day with a bucket of cold beer. When Lawdie, Joey, and their friends heard the 4:30 p.m. whistle at the Liggett & Myers tobacco factory—signaling the end of the day shift for factories across the city—they stopped whatever game they were playing and ran home, grabbed 15 cents and an ice bucket, and rushed down to Fassi's Tavern to fill the buckets with ice and bottles of beer.

That bucket and beer had better be waiting for their fathers after a hard day's work or there was hell to pay. Not even the game of baseball could compete with that.

*　　*　　*

In 1908, Pietro Berra was 22 and scratching out a living as a tenant farmer in the small village of Malvaglio, Italy, about 25 miles west of Milan. A year later he left Paulina, the woman he loved, boarded a steamer to America, and chased the American Dream from California to Colorado and finally to St. Louis, where he found work stoking the red-hot kilns that produced bricks at the Laclede-Christy Clay Products Company. He sent for Paulina, married, and started his family.

Pietro is proud of the life he's carved out for his wife and their five children here on The Hill. (The couple's daughter Josie arrived in 1930.) Money's always been tight, but even in the worst year of the seemingly endless Great Depression, Pietro Berra has been a good provider—food on the table, a roof over their heads, and clothes, shoes, and coats to wear. Their quiet, tight-knit family has always been happy.

Pietro and his friend Giovanni Garagiola grew up in Italy together and arrived at The Hill about the same time, moving into shotgun houses across from each other on Elizabeth Avenue. By 1941, they had lived the same routine for a decade: standing together for the 7 a.m. truck that would take them and their neighbors to the Laclede-Christy factory, put in nine hours of hard labor, then pay another nickel to take the same truck back home.

Sometimes after work they would take carts made from bicycle parts and go to Forest Park—a huge, sprawling swath of land that is St. Louis' version of New York's Central Park—and salvage from the remains of the 1904 World's Fair for parts to use on their houses on The Hill. Locals figure about 90 percent of the houses had parts from the World's Fair.

By their mid-40s Pietro and Giovanni were still laboring hard and had talked for 10 years about almost everything—surviving the bank failures of the Great Depression by putting money in cans and burying them in their vegetable gardens, their fast-growing families (six sons and a daughter combined), and who won the previous night's bocce games. But two things began to dominate their daily talks: their sons' inexplicable fascination with baseball and the wave of worry among Italian-Americans as their adopted country moved closer to war in Europe.

Pietro and Giovanni knew all about the love affair St. Louis has with its baseball teams, especially the Cardinals. But they could never fathom the strong hold the game had on their sons. They heard their boys talk endlessly about Joe DiMaggio as if he were a god, but the cultural significance of this Italian ballplayer escaped them. The two men did not understand baseball offered the very path to American acceptance they craved for their families until Lawdie and Joe were well into their professional careers.

It hadn't been easy being an Italian in America for Pietro Berra, Giovanni Garagiola, or many of the almost four million Italians who immigrated to the United States after the 1880s—the largest influx of immigrants from a single European nation in American history. They were greeted with suspicion at best, a lynch mob at worst. Many had darker complexions than the English, Irish, and German immigrants who had preceded them. They spoke a different language, enjoyed different food and customs, and practiced only one religion.

Their work ethic and strong arms and backs were sought to build a rapidly growing America, but Italian workers were often both underpaid and resented by other Americans looking for jobs. At the turn of the century, a public notice printed in New York City newspapers offered the following pay for laborers at the Croton Reservoir in Westchester County, New York:

Common labor, White    $1.30–$1.50 a day
Common labor, Colored  $1.25–$1.40 a day
Common labor, Italian  $1.15–$1.25 a day

On March 14, 1891, an angry mob had stormed a jail in New Orleans, pulled out nine Italian men accused of murdering the chief of police, grabbed two more off the street, and hanged them all, the largest mass lynching in American history. Another five Italians were lynched in New Orleans eight years later. Between 1880 and 1920, at least 50 Italians were lynched, and during his Memorial Day speech in St. Louis in 1917, former President Teddy Roosevelt insisted that all immigrants must speak English and become "Americans," not people with hyphenated identities like Italian-Americans.

The Hill's 52 square blocks had been a safe haven for Italians since they first arrived in 1880 to work in the numerous St. Louis clay mines. Most immigrants were working poor, like other Americans in the 1930s and '40s, but Dago Hill was no high-rise tenement slum. Its tiny front lawns and shotgun houses—15 feet wide and three rooms long, a bargain for about $2,500—were fastidiously kept. Vegetables and fruit grew in side yards, an outhouse sat in back, and most painted front porches sheltered carved-stone Catholic icons. There were plenty of trees but no telephone lines until the mid- to late 1940s—more than 40 years after the telephone came to St. Louis.

Like Pietro and Giovanni, many of The Hill's men worked in one of the clay products factories or in tobacco factories making cigarettes and cigars. When Prohibition was repealed, most of the hidden stills disappeared and St. Louis' Anheuser-Busch company equipped and trained new tavern owners on The Hill. Fine neighborhood restaurants dotted the community, and a handful—like Biggie's Steak House and Ruggeri's—were known nationwide.

Customs brought from Italy defined The Hill. Dinner in the Berra household didn't start until Pop had finished his beer and his plate was full. Spaghetti, bread, and salad always accompanied the meat, and any special occasion included ravioli. Sunday's feast lasted almost all day—antipasto, risotto, salads, and pasta before the main course of chicken and beef. There was always food on the Berra table.

But wasting nothing was an article of faith, sometimes learned the hard way. In his customary seat at his father's side, young Lawdie one evening ate most but not all of the bread he took, a mistake he'd made before. But this night, as he pulled away from the dinner table, his father's strong right hand flashed across Lawdie's face, almost lifting him from his seat.

"What did I do?"

"What do you think I buy bread for?" answered Pietro. "To eat, not to waste." Indeed, Pietro wasted nothing. He made his own red wine in the basement kitchen like other men on The Hill, then used the grape skins to make salad vinegar. Everything was used. And Paulina, Lawdie's mother, always ate last, after her husband and children had had enough.

Like every woman on The Hill, Paulina went daily to 5:30 a.m. Mass at St. Ambrose Church, passing the seven-foot bronze statue of a young Italian couple, suitcase in hand, commemorating their community's immigrant experience. On her way home she bought milk, coffee, and seven loaves of bread a day for the seven Berras.

Despite being diagnosed with diabetes in 1939 (requiring three daily insulin shots), Paulina did all the shopping, cooking, cleaning, and child care. Both parents tirelessly embraced their roles with pride, and sometimes Pietro spread his weekly earnings, as much as $50, across the kitchen table for the family to appreciate.

The Berra and Garagiola families led happy lives in their adopted country, but by 1940 the war in Europe turns ominous. America—quick to claim neutrality in 1939 when Hitler invaded Poland and England and France declared war on Germany—responds to the fall of France in June of 1940 with its first peacetime draft. All men ages 21 to 36 are eligible. And by March of 1941, America is shipping supplies to the Allies and President Franklin Roosevelt is pushing congress and the nation to join the fight.

Pietro and Paulina had become American citizens in 1923, unequivocally loyal to the United States. But they worry about family and friends living in Italy, especially after Italian Prime Minister Benito Mussolini joined forces with Hitler and declared war on the Allies on June 10, 1940. As America inches toward war with Italy, the Italian families on The Hill fear for their future.

# CHAPTER 3

# Rickey's Mistake
## 1941

It's another hot and humid St. Louis summer in July 1941. But that's not what 16-year-old Lawdie Berra is thinking about right now. He's sitting in the back seat of Cardinal General Manager Branch Rickey's big black Lincoln on his way to Forest Park with his friend Joe Garagiola up front and some kid named Schoendienst fidgeting in the seat next to him. Poor guy is covered with angry red bites all over his arms and neck. Lawdie heard someone call him Red at the tryout camp in Sportsman's Park just a few minutes ago, but these bites can't be the reason.

Lawdie saw right away that Schoendienst can hit—from both sides of the plate—smacking line drives to all fields when it was his turn at bat. And he wasn't bad at shortstop, either, though the Cardinal scouts kept asking him to shift over to second base. Albert, that's his first name. Albert Schoendienst.

Schoendienst is one of the many out-of-town boys who saw the same Cardinal advertisement for an open tryout at Sportsman's Park in the newspaper that also caught the attention of Lawdie and Joey. Anyone who wasn't the property of a major league team was invited to try out for the Cardinals' minor league system. Damn, there must have been 400, maybe 500 boys who showed up yesterday, chasing the dream of playing baseball in the major leagues.

That was far too many to judge in one afternoon, so Rickey told all the St. Louis kids to go home and come back the following day. The Cardinal GM wanted to see what the out-of-town kids could do first.

Red is one of a few boys Rickey told to come back. He'd hitched a ride from Germantown, about 39 miles away in neighboring Illinois, and had reached St. Louis in the back of a milk truck. Since he didn't have any money, a secretary in Cardinal owner Sam Breadon's office gave him 25 cents, which he was going to use for food until his plan to sleep in the park ended with a heavy rain. So he spent five cents for a room in a fleabag hotel and woke up covered with bedbug bites.

But Schoendienst had another good performance today, and that's why he's sitting in Rickey's car now, on his way for a third tryout, this one with just seven other boys.

Garagiola already looks the part of a baseball star. Still only 15, he moved easily from catcher to first base to the outfield in today's tryout, performing well in each position. They didn't give any of the boys too much time to hit, but Joey showed a smooth left-handed swing that had the scouts nodding their heads.

None of the baseball men really knew what to make of the kid who came with Garagiola. Squat and thick, Berra didn't look anything like a baseball player—until he took the field. Berra showed surprising quickness behind the plate and equally surprising speed in the outfield. He also showed off his powerful right arm, though accuracy was clearly not his strong suit.

But it's when he came to the plate that the scouts truly took notice. Berra swung a big bat with his unusually long arms, almost attacking the ball more than swinging at it. And he attacked almost every pitch thrown his way—high or low, a strike or a ball—and hit it hard. The crack of the bat on ball shouted real power.

And that's why Rickey told his scouts to get Berra in his car along with Garagiola and Schoendienst. Like every Cardinal fan in St. Louis, the three boys all know the baseball legend's story. Rickey was a mediocre catcher for the Browns and New York Highlanders—he hit .239 in 120 games spread over four seasons before quitting in 1914—and was an average manager. But he all but invented the minor league system when he became the Cardinal GM, and now every team in baseball is playing catch-up. It's Rickey who built the pedestrian St. Louis franchise into a perennial contender, winning five National League pennants and three World Series since 1926.

Quite simply, there's no better judge of talent than the Great Mahatma, as the writers like to call him. Rickey has the uncanny ability to look at a young player and project how big, strong, and fast he'll be when he matures into a man—something even the best scouts can't do on a consistent basis. Even better, he has a knack for knowing which players will be average major leaguers, which boys will be good, and which boys could be great.

Once Rickey reaches the ball fields at Forest Park, the boys take turns hitting and pitching while the Cardinal GM and his scouts watch and take notes. Garagiola performs well. So does Schoendienst—who will go on to a Hall of Fame career as a second baseman for the Cardinals, Giants, and Braves. Both show good plate discipline and strike the ball with authority. They are clearly talented.

Schoendienst takes the mound when it's Berra's turn to hit. At 18, Schoendienst is older than most of the boys here and has a good, live arm, but he simply can't get a ball past Berra. As always, Lawdie goes after just about every pitch, and the results are the same as they were in Sportsman's Park—one ball after another rocketing deep into the outfield. The sound of his bat hitting the ball is unlike that of any of the other seven players. And when Schoendienst is told to stop pitching, he's convinced the odd-looking kid at the plate is the best hitter he's seen all day. Maybe any day.

Berra knows he performed well, which makes the events of the next few days so perplexing. The Cardinals offer Garagiola a contract and a $500 bonus—not a penny less, the young player says, because that's what Pop needs to pay off his mortgage. Joey is not yet 16, so Giovanni signs the contract for him. The deal: Joey will take a paying job as a groundskeeper this summer in Springfield, Missouri, 215 miles away, then play for the Class C minor league team next season, when he is 16. In essence, the Cards are hiding Joey in Springfield so no other team can lure him away.

The Cardinals are not nearly as interested in Berra. Their first offer is a contract with no bonus—not a single dollar—and Lawdie is stunned, then immediately rejects it. He knows once his father hears about Joey's bonus, Pietro will be convinced he's been right all along—playing baseball is a complete waste of his son's time. He'll tell Lawdie it's time to find a real job and keep it, and that will be it for baseball.

And that's still how Berra feels when the Cardinals come back and offer him a $250 bonus. "Son, what I'm going to say to you is for your own good," Rickey tells him. "I don't think you are going to make it to the majors. You'll be a minor leaguer, no more than Triple-A. We're looking for players who can go all the way."

That hurt, badly, especially coming from Rickey. Berra is happy for his best friend but bewildered by Rickey's indifference toward him. Whenever they play, Joey bats third and Lawdie bats fourth, the spot reserved for the team's most powerful hitter. All the kids say Lawdie is the better player—even Joey says it. Why couldn't Rickey see what everyone else sees?

Jack Maguire sees it. A part-time Cardinal scout, Maguire welcomed Berra onto his American Legion team a few weeks back and is already convinced the kid is going to be a star. So Maguire works hard to change Rickey's mind over the next few days. He insists Berra will turn out to be a better player than Garagiola and begs Rickey to spend just $250 more to find out.

Absolutely not, Rickey says.

"It's $250, and he's not worth a dollar more," he bellows at his scout.

There's no way he can accept the Cardinals offer, Berra tells his coach. "I'm happy the Cardinals like Joey," Berra says to Maguire, "but I don't understand why they aren't interested in me. Thanks for everything Mr. Maguire, but I want the same as Joey is getting. Tell Mr. Rickey my answer is still no."

Maguire has one more idea. His friend Lou McQuillen is a scout for the Browns, and the American League doormat can certainly use a hard-hitting prospect like Lawdie. But McQuillen's pitch to his bosses is brushed aside. If the Cardinals didn't sign Berra, the Browns management reasoned, how good could he be? We'll offer him a contract, a disappointed McQuillen tells Maguire, but there's no bonus. Maguire knows what Berra's answer is even before he relays the news.

All Lawdie can do is thank Maguire again and wonder about his future. For the first time since he was old enough to dream of becoming a baseball player, he has doubts. Big doubts. Indeed, it's like someone just ripped out the underpinning of his positive outlook on life. He's used to the other boys making fun of the way he looks and the way he talks, but he's always been able to silence their taunts by outplaying them on the ball field. Now the most renowned executive in all of baseball is telling him he's not good enough. *Even the lowly Browns aren't interested!*

Berra knows his parents are not going to be happy with this development, especially since the news across the street is so dramatically different. Sure enough, his parents call another family meeting to determine what the future holds for their youngest son. And as the day of the meeting approaches, Lawdie can't help but wonder if his days of playing baseball are rapidly coming to an end.

Once again, Lawdie Berra finds himself sitting with his arms folded at a meeting in his parents' kitchen with his dream of playing major league baseball hanging in the balance. Father Charles Koester, the popular young priest from St. Ambrose Church, is here. So is Joe Causino, the director of the South Side YMCA all the kids call Uncle Joe. Lawdie and his friends hitch two miles to play ball at Uncle Joe's Y and swim in one of the area's few indoor pools.

Tony and Mike are here, too. They might not agree with their father's dim view of baseball, but their patience with their little brother is beginning to run thin. Lawdie is now 16; by this age both brothers were holding down full-time jobs and playing ball when they could find the time—not the other way around.

"Respectable men do not play games for a living!" Pietro keeps repeating as the meeting gets under way. And this time there is no pushback from Tony and Mike.

Pietro doesn't know who Branch Rickey is, but Father Koester does, and he knows what Rickey's words mean for Lawdie. Father Koester is a big Browns fan, and all the boys love it when his Sunday school lessons turn into long talks about baseball. The priest knows Lawdie is a fine ballplayer, but maybe Lawdie's just not good enough.

"Baseball is a good thing, a fine thing," Father Koester tells Lawdie, "but in moderation. What you are doing is beyond all reason. No wonder your good father and mother are afraid you're going to turn into a bad boy."

A *bad boy*.

Those are words no parents on The Hill want to hear. They all acknowledge there is a small but well-known criminal element living among them, and everyone on Berra's block of Elizabeth Avenue knows the trouble they cause firsthand. A few years back, Charles Garavaglia—whose wife Ann gives Paulina insulin shots for her diabetes—was running a successful food store on The Hill when a gang of young men told him he should buy insurance from them. Garavaglia refused, and one morning he found his store burned to the ground.

If Lawdie's parents told Father Koester they're worried their youngest son might become a bad boy, this meeting is a lot more serious than he imagined.

And it doesn't help that Lawdie continues to lose one job after another. Uncle Joe was the first to set up Lawdie with employment, getting him a job as a shipping clerk with an old friend. But Causino got a call from his friend that very first afternoon. Seems the young lad Joe brought to him had gone missing.

"What happened?" Causino asked.

"Well," his friend said, "he worked like a beaver all morning. Then about noon he looked out the window. It was a wonderful day. He said, 'I'm sorry, mister, I'm quitting. But thanks for the opportunity.' Then he opened a package I thought was lunch. But it wasn't his lunch. It was a baseball glove."

Lawdie next found work in a coal yard, working in the area that pressed and stamped coal dust into bricks that people on The Hill used to fire up their stoves to cook their food and heat their homes. Lawdie wrapped the bricks with brown paper, a job that left him covered in dust by day's end. He could make as much as $25 a week—all of which went to Momma, who gave him an allowance of a dollar or two, a small fortune for a kid used to getting 15 cents a week.

Lawdie hated being covered in dirt, but he liked having money for Superman comic books, candy, soft drinks, and movies—especially westerns. But when winter turned to spring, he once again answered the call of the ball fields, and that position disappeared, too. Pietro found him another job working on a Pepsi truck, but he lost that one as well, just as he lost the good-paying position Mike found for him at the shoe factory. Could that be why Father Koester said his parents are worried he would turn out bad?

Lawdie let everyone in the room talk, not saying a word as one after another delivered the same message: he's 16, and it's time for him to grow up. But now the moment has come for him to respond. He sought out Causino to make his case for what might just be his last chance.

"Uncle Joe, you always told us that the thing a man is most interested in is what he ought to spend his life doing," Lawdie says. "I remember you said if you like something so much you eat and sleep and think it, then that's what you ought to do."

Causino takes a deep breath. Lawdie is one of his favorites—heck, Lawdie is the favorite of many of the folks on The Hill. And Causino recognizes he's a terrific ballplayer. But there are only 16 major league baseball teams. That's 400 players. As good as Lawdie is, the odds are staggering. Especially after what Branch Rickey had to say.

"That's the whole point," Joe says. "All we're trying to say is that you've got to make up your mind to be something. Pick out whatever it's going to be and work at it."

Everyone is staring at him now, and Lawdie knows no one is going to be happy with what he is about to say.

"Baseball," he tells them. "Baseball is what I want."

The room is silent for a moment, and then a flurry of conversations follow. There are many reasons for Berra's parents to say enough is enough, no more baseball, and only one reason for Lawdie to keep playing. Lawdie's performance in the government-sponsored Works Progress Administration league caught the eye of a successful oil and gas dealer named Leo Browne, who brought American Legion baseball to St. Louis in the mid-'20s. With so many boys leaving school for work throughout the Depression, high school baseball programs were decimated, turning American Legion baseball into the nation's premier amateur league. Some think it is as good as baseball's low minor leagues, and there are already a handful of major leaguers who got their start in Legion ball.

Browne recruited Lawdie earlier this summer to play for the Fred Stockham Post 245, a team loaded with top players and steeped in success. Browne thought bringing in Berra would give Stockham an even better chance at winning the city title. And that meant qualifying for the national American Legion tournament and a chance to win a national title. This was a real team, with uniforms and equipment Lawdie had only dreamed about.

For the second time in two years, Pietro Berra makes a surprising decision. Maybe it was his son's chance to travel to states halfway across the nation if his new baseball team was successful. Maybe Pietro regretted not giving his older sons the same chance to play baseball and see America outside the boundaries of St. Louis. Or maybe it was the sympathetic look on Paulina's face that melted Pietro's heart.

Whatever the reason, Pietro tells Lawdie he can keep playing baseball with Mr. Browne's team as long as he finds some kind of work at night and contributes to the family's finances. But if this doesn't work out…

His father did not have to finish his sentence for his son to understand. The clock is now ticking on his chance to make it in baseball. And Lawdie Berra knows that time is running short.

Leo Browne is surprised and confused by Branch Rickey's decision not to sign Lawdie—he's certain Berra has a future in baseball—but he's thrilled to have Lawdie playing for his Stockham Junior American Legion team. And it doesn't take Berra long to establish himself as one of the league's best players. With Berra playing right field and batting cleanup, Stockham races through the rest of the season, wins the city title handily, and then travels to Trenton, Missouri, where Berra pounds out 12 hits in 20 at-bats to power Post 245 to the state title.

Berra's bat stays hot the rest of the month of August as Stockham takes the regional title in Gaston, North Carolina, to advance to the national semifinals in Columbia, South Carolina. That's where Stockham's run ends, but it's hard for Lawdie to be too disappointed. He's an important player on a highly talented team, one that gave him the first real glove and uniform he's ever owned. More important, he excelled against topflight competition, renewing his faith that one day he would wear a major league uniform.

And he has a new nickname: Yogi.

Stockham's star second baseman Bobby Hofman—a future infielder for the New York Giants—tagged that one on him after a bunch of teammates saw a movie featuring yogis in India. These yogis sat with their arms and legs crossed, just as Lawdie does when he's sitting on the sideline waiting to hit. "You look just like one of those yogis in the movie," Hofman tells Berra. "So that's what I'm going to call you—Yogi."

The name stuck. Berra's still Lawdie on The Hill, but he's Yogi to his Stockham teammates, and he kinda likes it. Good thing, too, because he would be Yogi to just about everyone—save family and friends on The Hill—from that moment on. And one day that nickname would translate into money—big money.

★　　★　　★

It's September 11, 1941, and Lawrence (Yogi) Berra—as the *St. Louis Star-Times* reports his name the following day—is with 13 teammates at the Hotel York in downtown St. Louis, where they are being honored for their sparkling season. What a night it is for Yogi and his friends. Great food, accolades from three Cardinal scouts and the manager of their archrivals, the Aubuchon-Dennison Post, and a lively debate about who's having the more impressive season—Joe DiMaggio, with his 56-game hitting streak and .353 batting average, or Ted Williams, who is hitting .413 with 34 homers. Each Stockham player receives a jacket with the team insignia on one sleeve, a team photo, and—best of all—a baseball autographed by Dizzy Dean himself.

Yogi's parents have to admit they loved seeing their son's name in the newspapers. But the news on the next day's front page of the *St. Louis Star-Times*—and every front page in the nation—is most troubling.

## ANOTHER AMERICAN SHIP TORPEDOED
*Shooting War Seen Unless Axis Backs Down*

The newspaper is dominated with reports of a German submarine that torpedoed the American-owned freighter *Montana* sailing under a Panama flag off the waters of Iceland. The crew of 26 was saved. This followed an attack on another American-owned freighter on August 17 that cost the lives of all but three of the crew of 27. No Americans were on either ship. Both were carrying lumber and other raw materials on their way to England and the Allies for the war against the Germans and Italians.

President Franklin Roosevelt had addressed the nation while Yogi and his teammates were celebrating their 24-win season. Calling Nazi subs "the rattlesnakes of the Atlantic," FDR told the radio audience in America and around the world, "It is now clear that Hitler has begun his campaign to control the seas by ruthless force and by wiping out every vestige of international law, every vestige of humanity."

From this day forward, the President said, German and Italian warships sighted in American waters—which the President declared would extend to Iceland—enter "at their own peril." American ships and warplanes were to shoot these warships on sight.

The news doesn't get any better in the weeks that follow, and Italians on The Hill grow worried as immediate calls for a military buildup pour in from around the nation. By June, US Attorney General Francis Biddle had already classified all immigrants who had not yet become American citizens—including 600,000 Italians—as enemy aliens. Now they are required to register with the government and get a photo ID to be carried at all times.

The drumbeat to war only gets louder as autumn fades into winter. Harvard President James Bryant Conant, a chemist who would work on the atomic bomb project, is just one of many prominent figures calling for the United States to join the fight against the Axis powers. By October 25, more than 10,000 Americans are fighting for Canada. On October 29, Italy's Premier Benito Mussolini pushes back, warning that he will "crush the U.S." Like everyone on The Hill, Pietro Berra worries about his sons being sent off to war—or arrested for being Italian.

On November 11, 1941, FDR warns the country that Germany might force the United States into the war in Europe. Then the unthinkable happens in Hawaii. The Japanese launch an attack on Pearl Harbor on December 7, sending wave after wave of warplanes that tear apart the Honolulu base with bombs and machine-gun fire before the US forces can react. The five-hour-long onslaught destroys or damages eight battleships, 10 smaller warships, and 230 aircraft. The death toll of American military and civilians will reach 2,403.

The headline on the first page of the *St. Louis Post-Dispatch* is both succinct and terrifying.

## CONGRESS DECLARES WAR ON JAPAN
*1500 Killed in Attack on Hawaii*

Cleveland star pitcher Bob Feller enlists the next day, and other major leaguers will soon follow. Everyone on The Hill—everyone in the nation — is riveted to their radios that afternoon when Roosevelt addresses the nation. Telling Americans that December 7 would be "a date which will live in infamy," Roosevelt announces the United States is now at war with Japan. The next day, the FBI arrests 900 Japanese immigrants, along with 400 Germans and Italians. Internment camps are being built for all three groups. On December 11, both Hitler and Mussolini declare war on America, and FDR announces America is at war with the Axis powers within the hour.

Suddenly and for very different reasons, Lawrence (Yogi) Berra once again has no idea what his future holds.

# CHAPTER 4

# Yogi's Luck
## 1942–1943

**W**ould there even be a baseball season for Yogi Berra—or any fan of America's Pastime—to follow in 1942?

That's the question the owners of the sport's 16 teams are asking each other soon after the attack on Pearl Harbor. Able-bodied men are rapidly being drafted and rationing of essential materials—from gasoline to milk, cheese to nylon—will soon begin. The country's priorities are changing, and even though baseball provided much-needed relief during the Great Depression, the owners wonder about the future of their business in wartime America.

On January 14, 1942, baseball Commissioner Kenesaw Mountain Landis sends a handwritten letter to President Franklin Delano Roosevelt asking for direction. "The time is approaching when, in ordinary conditions, our teams would be heading for spring training camps," Landis writes. "However, inasmuch as these are not ordinary times, I venture to ask what you have in mind as to whether professional baseball should continue to operate."

Landis receives the President's written answer the very next day. "I honestly feel it would be best for the country to keep baseball going," writes FDR in what quickly becomes known as the Green Light Letter. "There will be fewer people unemployed and everybody will work longer hours and harder than ever before. And that means that they ought to have a chance for recreation and for taking their minds off their work even more than before."

It's a clear recognition of the special place baseball occupies in America. The President has only one request: he'd like baseball to play more night games so Americans working the day shift could see a game. Baseball owners, greatly relieved, schedule more night games, move spring training camps north to cut down on travel and the use of fuel, and prepare for a full season, albeit without many of its stars. More than 70 major league players will go to war in 1942, a number that would reach 384 by 1945. Thousands of minor leaguers will go to war as well.

One player who does not leave is Joe DiMaggio, who as a father of an infant son with his singer–movie star wife Dorothy Arnold is exempt from the draft. But the swift and negative reaction to Joe's decision not to sign up is a reminder that Italians—even baseball stars—are still not completely welcome in America, especially with the old country now the enemy. When DiMaggio stages a well-publicized holdout, the star receives a telegram from a group of soldiers at Camp Blanding, in Florida: "In the event the Yankees don't kick in with more than $37,000," they write, "we cordially invite you to a tryout with the 143rd Infantry, 36th Division, the fightingest regiment in this man's Army."

DiMaggio faces an avalanche of boos from the moment the season starts. He even hears them in Yankee Stadium, where the Italian flags that dotted the stands throughout his historic '41 season—when he hit in a record 56 straight games—are nowhere to be seen. His mail is filled with hateful letters with the same theme: *Go back to Italy with the rest of the cowardly wops.* Or worse.

DiMaggio, who is also grappling with marital problems, gets off to a slow start and endures the worst season in his brilliant career. Weary of the constant criticism, he'll enlist next February. Like many in baseball, the 27-year-old star will lose three years of his prime to the war.

Life is worse for DiMaggio's parents, Rosalia and Giuseppe—two of the 600,000 Italians in America who are not US citizens—back home in San Francisco. They're classified as "enemy aliens" and have to register with the government, which means being fingerprinted and receiving a photo identification card. They cannot travel outside a five-mile radius from home without their ID cards. They live under an 8 p.m.–6 a.m. curfew, and can no longer own a shortwave radio, camera, or gun. Unbeknownst to Giuseppe, the FBI considers arresting him just to prove that parents of a celebrity won't get special treatment, then decide against it.

Giuseppe's fishing boat is confiscated—like those of his fellow Italian fishermen—and San Francisco Bay, where they've all fished for a living for decades, is off-limits. The bay is now the site of a naval shipyard, so Giuseppe isn't even allowed to visit Joe's restaurant on Fisherman's Wharf. Enemy aliens—and even many Italian-Americans—aren't allowed near long stretches of California's coast, where Japanese subs attacked eight American merchant ships, sinking two, in the weeks after Pearl Harbor. Still, the DiMaggios are thankful they're not among the 10,000 Italians deemed security risks and forced from their homes on the California coast to housing inland.

Things are not quite as bad for Italians on The Hill in St. Louis, though Pietro and Paulina Berra have plenty of neighbors who are classified as enemy aliens. Anxiety runs high as FBI agents comb the neighborhoods for weeks before they're convinced the Italian community of The Hill poses no threat. What they don't uncover is the small band of young men from southern Italy who knock on doors asking for gold wedding bands to melt down and send back home to help support Italy's fight against the Allies. Like all their friends, Pietro and Paulina slam the door when these men come calling. They are Americans and want no doubts about where their loyalties lie.

Everyone on The Hill has heard about the tens of thousands of Japanese immigrants and their children—including some born in America—who've been sent to internment camps in remote parts of the nation and worry about suffering the same fate. That worry only grows worse in March of 1942, after the FBI arrests renowned Metropolitan Opera star Ezio Pinza in his Westchester County, New York home. Pinza is interrogated without a lawyer and held in an Ellis Island detention center for 11 weeks, a story that receives heavy play nationwide.

The opera star was four months shy of becoming an American citizen. If the government locks up someone as widely known as Pinza, how can any Italian in America feel safe? Indeed, by June the FBI announces more than 1,500 Italian "enemy aliens" have been arrested.

Parents on The Hill also worry about their sons going off to war, but that's not on the minds of the Berras' youngest son and his good friend across the street, who are both too young for the draft. In midspring of 1942, Joey Garagiola hugs his family, says goodbye to his best friend, and boards a train to Springfield to begin his professional baseball career. Garagiola's departure is bittersweet for Yogi, now 17, who is still puzzled that the Cardinals don't want him, too.

But he's excited to be back in a Stockham uniform when the American Legion season begins in June, and this time he starts the season behind the plate. "No one else wanted to do it," Berra tells friends, and he remains there until midseason, when he breaks a finger and splits his time between third base and right field. But no matter where Yogi plays—and Yogi is what all his teammates call him—Berra is hitting the ball even better than last season, broken finger and all.

That's what American Legion director Leo Browne tells sportswriter Bob Burnes on one of his frequent visits to the sports department of the *St. Louis Globe-Democrat*. "I've got a ballplayer out there I'd like you to see," Browne tells Burnes, perhaps the city's top sportswriter. "He does everything wrong, yet it comes out right! We've tried him at every position except pitching, and he looks as good at one as he does at the others. He swings at everything in sight. His form is all wrong and coaches can't make him wait at the plate, but he's the best hitter I've ever seen.

"His name is Yogi something or other."

Burnes turns up at Forest Park a few days later to see the player his friend is so excited about. "Yogi, this here is Bob Burnes from the *Globe-Democrat*," Browne tells Berra, who shakes hands with the writer while watching the pregame action on the field. It's batting practice, and given Yogi's scowl, it's obvious to Burnes the somewhat odd-looking young man standing before him would prefer to be in the batting cage rather than meeting a sportswriter. A few awkward minutes later, Berra returns to the field and Burnes takes a seat, ready to be impressed.

But after five innings, Burnes strolls over to Browne. Berra had trouble with almost everything hit his way at third base, wrestling the ball to the ground rather than catching it. He had one solid hit, but it was the strikeout on a pitch over his head that stuck with Burnes. "Leo, I think you've oversold this kid," says Burnes, who walks away, never thinking one day he and Berra would become fast friends.

Yogi has precious few bad days as Stockham once again rolls to the city and state titles, winning a spot in the American Legion national tournament. Wearing old uniforms borrowed from the Cardinals, Stockham opens by crushing East Chicago, Indiana, 25–0, in St. Joseph, four hours away in the northwest corner of the state. Berra astounds everyone in Phil Welch Stadium right from the start, blasting a three-run first-inning homer over the 345-foot sign in right field and clear out of the stadium. No teenager has ever done that. By the regional title game's end, Yogi's hit for the cycle—knocking out a single, double, and triple to go along with his home run—and batted in 10 runs.

Berra is just as lethal in the Legion sectionals in Russell, Kansas, the following week, slamming four doubles, a triple, and another home run as Stockham sweeps both games to reach the national final four in Hastings, Nebraska, for the second straight season. And that's where Stockham's season ends again, losing two of three games to a team from Los Angeles led by star shortstop Gene Mauch, who would become a journeyman infielder for nine major league seasons before embarking on a 26-year managerial career. Los Angeles goes on to win the national title, but many fans leave talking about Berra's steal of home, which Yogi managed without a slide.

Berra heads back to The Hill with both his reputation and his awareness of the world outside St. Louis blossoming. After two seasons, he's grown close to many of his teammates, the first non-Italian friends he's ever had. He heard some ethnic slurs from the stands in Kansas and Nebraska, but he also met people from different backgrounds he liked very much. His father might still think baseball is a lazy man's game, but Yogi's travels with Stockham have given him a glimpse of the world outside The Hill. And he's intrigued.

He's eager to trade stories with his best friend when Garagiola returns from Springfield, where he hit .254 in 67 games, playing catcher well enough to earn a promotion to Double-A ball for next season. The two friends fall back into their regular pattern, playing cards with their pals, taking in movies, and keeping a close watch on the Cardinals, who are having a great season while rumors swirl that GM Branch Rickey will soon be leaving. Rickey's squabbles with owner Sam Breadon have spilled onto the pages of the local papers, and the Dodgers, whose current GM Larry MacPhail is rejoining the Army as a lieutenant colonel, are said to be interested. Neither Yogi nor Joe knows what to make of the Rickey rumors.

Despite the loss of players to the military, it had been an interesting baseball season. Major league baseball held many fund-raisers for the war effort, the most memorable coming in August when Babe Ruth, now 48 years old, donned a uniform for the first time in seven years and faced 54-year-old Hall of Fame pitcher Walter Johnson at Yankee Stadium. The Babe had enough left to send a ball sailing into the right field stands, tipping his cap repeatedly as he rounded the bases to thunderous applause. The game raised $80,000 for the Army-Navy relief fund.

There were also signs all around the fences telling fans where they should go if their stadium came under attack. While baseball did indeed schedule more night games, as FDR had asked, teams along the Eastern Seaboard played most of their games during the day. They were concerned their stadium lights would create silhouettes of nearby shipyards, making them easy targets for German submarines lurking off the US coast.

Ted Williams puts up a Triple Crown season—leading the American League with 36 home runs, 137 runs batted in, and a .356 batting average—but his Red Sox finish nine games behind the Yankees, and he soon leaves to train as a fighter pilot in the Navy. Future Hall of Famer Paul Waner raps his 3,000th hit. And African-Americans Jackie Robinson and pitcher Nate Moreland have a one-day tryout with the Chicago White Sox during spring training that's kept secret for years.

Despite Joe DiMaggio's subpar season—his 21 home runs, 114 RBI, and .305 batting average are all the lowest totals of his career to date—the Yankees won 103 games, clinching the American League pennant early. They were favored to win the World Series against the Cardinals, who won 43 of their last 51 games to overtake the Brooklyn Dodgers for the NL pennant in the final two weeks of the season. The Cardinals lost the first game of the Series at Sportsman's Park, won the next day, then stunned all of baseball by sweeping three games in New York to take the title. Cardinal rookie Johnny Beazley, a 21-game winner during the season, hurled two complete-game wins against New York, then left to enlist in the Army Air Corps.

"Dig that cowbell out of the whatnot closet, neighbor, and dust off that horn," writes Roy Stockton, who's covered the Cardinals for the *St. Louis Post-Dispatch* since 1918. "Those Cardinal baseball players are coming home and they are champions of the world. Think of it. Ten games behind the Dodgers in early August. Conquerors of the fabulous Yankees in early October. What strange things can happen."

What strange things, indeed. Unbeknownst to Yogi, Leo Browne has sent a letter to his old friend George Weiss, whom the Yankees hired to build a farm system to rival that of the Cardinals. And that is what Weiss has done. The two men go back to Browne's days as an umpire decades earlier in the Eastern League, where Weiss owned and ran a team in New Haven, Connecticut.

"He's better than the Garagiola kid the Cardinals signed," Browne wrote to Weiss. "All he wants is a $500 bonus. Whatever you want to pay him a month, he'll take it."

Weiss, a smart, driven man who battles his weight and maintains an indifference to the feelings of others, is the rising star of the Yankee organization. He tells bullpen coach John Schulte, a resident of St. Louis, to sign Berra to a minor league contract—with a $500 bonus—if Browne's story checks out. Schulte talks to Browne, Stockham manager Jack Maguire, and a few other St. Louis friends and learns that Browne's take on Berra is shared by all. In late October, he knocks on the door at 5447 Elizabeth Avenue, introduces himself, and tells Yogi the Yankees want to offer him a contract to play for their minor league team in Norfolk, Virginia.

"We'll pay you $90 a month," the Yankee coach says, "with a $500 bonus."

Yogi can hardly believe this is happening. These are the Yankees, the team of Babe Ruth, Lou Gehrig, and, of course, Joe DiMaggio, the most famous Italian in all of baseball. Fact is, the Yankees have a long history of signing Italian players, starting with second baseman Tony Lazzeri in 1925, then shortstop Frankie Crosetti five years later. The two infielders were known as the Big Dago and the Little Dago for the six seasons they anchored the Yankee infield. DiMaggio was simply the Dago. Up-and-coming shortstop Phil Rizzuto has played in Yankee pinstripes the last two seasons and will soon leave for the Navy. If Pietro doesn't quite appreciate baseball and its role in America, he understands his son will be among many of his own people.

And he understands the value of what the Yankees are offering. Most of the houses on The Hill still cost about $2,500. The bonus New York has just put on the table will pay off most of the mortgage remaining on Pietro's home. Maybe there is something to playing this game of baseball after all.

Pietro signs the contract—Yogi is still underage—not noticing the terms for the bonus are *make good:* Berra has to be on the Norfolk roster at season's end to get the $500. But there's nothing that will distract Yogi now. He knows he'll turn 18 on May 12 of the 1943 season and will have to sign up for the selective service, but he'll deal with that when the time comes. Right now, his American Dream is about to become a reality.

Yogi goes back to his job as a tack puller for women's shoes at Johansen Bros. shoe factory for the winter, and this time there is no wandering off and getting fired. Berra knows he'll be leaving for spring training in a few months, and his parents can use the money. The job is easy enough: the tacks are there to hold the sole in place until the cement used to attach it to the shoe has dried. His job is to pull out the tacks when the shoe is ready, and he gets paid for each shoe he completes. Yogi makes $35 a week when he starts and $45 by the time he leaves, all of it going to his mother. At least Paulina increases his allowance a full dollar, to $3 a week.

Berra and Joe Garagiola slip outdoors when the temperature permits just to throw the ball around and keep their arms in shape. They hang out with their friends on Elizabeth Avenue, playing cards, talking about the latest radio episode of *The Adventures of Superman,* and, of course, reliving the Cardinals' World Series win over the Yankees.

They also listen to the adults worry about the war that many of the older boys on The Hill are already fighting. Yogi's two oldest brothers, both family men, are exempt. His older brother John is one of several recruits from The Hill who enlist in the Army Air Corps and are stationed at nearby Lambert Field for the duration of the war.

America's entry into World War II has been rough. In the first 10 months of 1942, German submarines sank more than 500 American merchant ships. In the South Pacific, the Japanese captured the Philippines and controlled most of the western Pacific and large parts of eastern and southern Asia. Rumors that Hitler has ordered the mass killing of Jews in Auschwitz and other death camps spread by the summer and are confirmed by year's end. For three years, the Allies would never develop a strategy to prevent the Holocaust.

One piece of good news: on October 12, 1942—Columbus Day—Attorney General Francis Biddle announces that Italian nationals are no longer considered enemy aliens. Many on The Hill are relieved but still wary. Things are changing fast: gas is now being rationed—three gallons a week; auto manufacturers stop making cars and start making machines for war; and the draft age soon drops from 21 to 18.

As the days grow warmer, Yogi and Joe have their minds set on baseball. Occasionally Joe would be off on a date; he is very popular with the girls. Yogi is still too shy for dating. But who cares? All he wants to do is count down the weeks and days before his first training camp and listen to his friend describe the quality of players he will face.

"Don't worry, Lawdie, it'll be just like the neighborhood," Joey tells him. "You'll be the best player on the field."

And then, a week or so before Berra's set to leave, there's a knock on the front door. It's a man with a telegram from the new Brooklyn Dodger GM, Branch Rickey. *Mr. Larry Berra,* the telegram reads, *the Dodgers request that you report to our spring training camp in Bear Mountain, N.Y.* There is a contract with an unspecified bonus to play for the Dodger organization.

*Well, don't that beat all?* First no one wants to sign him. Now he has a second offer—from Mr. Rickey, no less. Guess old Branch needs players, with even more minor leaguers than major league players drafted or enlisting in the armed services—more than 4,000 in all. But Rickey is too late. Larry "Yogi" Berra is about to start his career in the Class B Piedmont League, a New York Yankee prospect playing for the Norfolk Tars.

Timing, it appears, is everything. What a difference two years make.

★   ★   ★

A tired but excited Yogi arrives from St. Louis to the Norfolk Tars' stadium, finds his way to the clubhouse and then the equipment room. "Hi, I'm Yogi Berra," he tells the equipment man. "I need my uniform." The man gives the 17-year-old Berra a quick once-over, then digs out an old, beat-up uniform, cleats, and a rumpled hat. Yogi looks at the well-worn clothes and asks if this is the best he can get. "That's what we give kids here for a tryout," the man tells him.

Berra shakes his head and explains he's the team's new catcher. The equipment man gives Yogi another look, thinks for a moment, then presents him with a fresh uniform.

The scent of war is everywhere in this small town along the coast of the Chesapeake Bay, which is now home to a wartime Atlantic Fleet and the Fifth Naval District. Both the shipyards and the airfield are expanded, and in a blink Norfolk's gone from a town of 180,000 to a home for almost 800,000, putting a strain on resources, services, pocketbooks, and sanity.

Hundreds of thousands of young men are here, some building the ships of war, many training to fight the Axis powers and wondering if they will return home alive. German U-boats lurk off the coast of Virginia; two were sunk and its prisoners held at the naval base only weeks before Yogi arrives. A depth charge goes off in a shipyard accident and dozens more ignite, leaving 40 dead—including Elizabeth Korensky, the first WAVE killed in the line of duty—and 18 buildings leveled. The explosion shatters windows in buildings seven miles away.

Restaurants—good and bad—are filled around the clock, and so are the taverns. The town's buses and trolley cars are so packed that conductors often give up fighting through the crowd to collect tickets. The sidewalks of Granby Street, the town's main drag, are barely passable, and with all the alcohol flowing in the town's bars, Yogi is witness to plenty of drunken brawls.

Berra soon finds he can hold his own on the baseball field. Still a

46

month shy of 18, he's the team's youngest player, but he's not bashful about taking charge and plays with such enthusiasm and intensity he often startles his teammates. And sometimes his eagerness amuses them, like the time he crouched behind the plate before realizing he'd forgotten his catcher's mask. He took good-natured ribbing about that one for weeks.

Same with the foul pop in his very first game. Berra tosses his mask and calls for the ball, circles under it, then watches it fall 10 feet away. But he soon learns how to track a pop-up in the stadium lights against a night sky, and Tars manager Shaky Kain is the latest to marvel how this raw kid can do everything so wrong but have it all turn out so right. It's not long before Kain makes Berra his starting catcher and a middle-of-the-lineup hitter.

It's the business of baseball that is Berra's true education. First is the lesson of his bonus. After a few weeks pass and there's no mention of his $500, he asks Tars GM Jim Dawson when he'll get the money. Dawson is surprised. Don't you know you have to be on the roster at season's end to collect? he asks Berra, who is clearly surprised—and upset. That's not what John Schulte told him, he's sure of that, but it's right there on the first page of the contract his father signed. This is the last time he'll ever trust management.

Berra's not worried about lasting the season, but that $500 sure would have come in handy. The flood of defense workers into this town has sent the price of everything soaring, further than his $90-a-month paycheck—about $75 after taxes—can stretch. He splits a boardinghouse room with pitcher Bob Sucky for $7 a week and eats at luncheonettes and hot dog wagons outside the stadium. But he still finds himself hitting up first baseman Jack Phillips, who always seems to have some extra money, for a few bucks before their twice-monthly payday just so he can eat.

Thank the Lord for women. An older woman comes to every Sunday home game and presents Yogi with a big Italian hero filled with lunch meats and cheese. He has to resist gobbling it down too fast.

And he can always count on Momma, worried that her son is going hungry, to send $10 or $15 every few weeks. Paulina never fails to include a note.

"Don't let your father know about this," she writes in Italian, "or he'll make you come home."

Still, Yogi gets so desperate one night he decides to stage a strike. Knowing the team's two other catchers are injured and cannot play, Berra rolls on the clubhouse floor and moans until his manager rushes over to find out what's wrong.

"It's my stomach; it hurts," Yogi says. "I don't think I can play tonight."

Shaky Kain reaches into his pocket, pulls out a few dollars, and stuffs them into Berra's hand. Yogi rushes out, buys a few burgers at the first stand he finds, and wolfs them down between gulps from two bottles of Coke. Fully sated, he belts out a couple of hits in a Norfolk win.

Yogi is convinced the league is using a deadened ball—more than once he swings, connects, and thinks the ball is headed over the fence only to see it settle into an outfielder's glove. And that makes a two-game stretch against Roanoke almost unexplainable. Berra takes a wrecking ball to the Roanoke pitching staff, belting two home runs, two doubles, and two singles in seven at-bats in the first game, knocking in 13 runs. The next day he goes 5-for-5—a homer, two doubles, two singles—and knocks in 10 more runs. That's 23 RBI in two games. His bonus never looked more secure.

About the only thing that could keep him from finishing the season is the war, which continues to rage in both Europe and South Asia. Berra turns 18 on May 12, but the St. Louis draft board is able to fill its quota without ending the first baseball season of a favorite son. They'll wait until the season is all but over before sending Yogi's paperwork to Virginia, and if he's lucky, maybe he can play exhibition baseball for the troops, as so many major leaguers are doing.

Indeed, President Roosevelt's belief in the benefits of baseball extends to all branches of the military, which are instructed to form teams of pro baseball players under their command and stage exhibition games to entertain the troops. And one of the very best teams is playing right up the road at the Norfolk Naval Training Station. Base commander Captain Henry McClure wasn't much of a baseball fan when the war started, but he recognized straightaway how much the game lifted the spirits of the 16,000 officers and sailors under his command. McClure puts Chief Warrant Officer Gary Bodie in charge of finding any professional ballplayer in a Navy uniform and bringing him to Norfolk to play ball for the Bluejackets, the base team.

And Bodie doesn't disappoint. He brings in Yankee Phil Rizzuto to play shortstop and Red Sox star Dom DiMaggio—Joe D's younger brother—to man center field. Cleveland's Eddie Robinson arrives to play first base, and Bodie gets Cardinal catcher Don Padgett to handle a pitching staff that features Detroit's Freddie Hutchinson. The Bluejackets are good enough to beat many of the major league teams who come down to Norfolk to play exhibition games and raise money for the war. Oftentimes, the 3,500-seat brick-walled stadium cannot handle the demand for tickets.

Berra and the Tars play three exhibition games against the Bluejackets at McClure's stadium in the early spring of '43. After the final game, Bodie seeks out Yogi. "Son, when are you going to be eligible for the draft?" Bodie asks him.

"My birthday is May 12, but I'm hoping not to be drafted until after the season," Yogi answers. "I asked them to send the paperwork here to Virginia."

"Tell them you want to join the Navy," Bodie says. "I may be losing some of my players and you could have a chance to play ball."

Yogi almost floats back to the boardinghouse that day, but there is one more lesson to be learned in Norfolk. The better Berra plays, the harder the opposing bench jockeys—and the loudest and most foul-mouthed fans—go after him. He's used to being mocked for his looks, but this is different. These taunts are directed at his heritage. *Wop, dago,* and *guinea* are about the kindest things he hears.

Kain watches his prized player's frustration rise as the slurs grow louder, nastier, and more frequent. Too often, Berra's face is flushed with rage, and he's slamming bats when he returns to the dugout. It doesn't help that the Piedmont League's six ballparks are cozy, with oh-so-close-to-the-field stands, so everyone can hear the verbal assaults. Many in this part of the country still consider Italians nonwhite; only blacks and Jews are held in lower regard.

Finally, Kain decides to intervene. "Look, this is going to happen, more to you than others because you're Italian," Kain says, "and in language worse than what you've already heard." Kain tells Yogi the more he reacts, the worse it's going to get. "They're the characters who pay your salary. Let 'em holler all they want. Figure they're entitled.

"If you ever show them, or show anyone, that they're getting to you, you're dead. Ignore it. That's what you gotta do. Ignore it."

Berra grits his teeth and heeds his manager's advice. The Tars finish third, good enough to make the playoffs, and Yogi hits .253 in 111 games, with seven home runs—one behind teammate and league leader Jack Phillips—and 17 doubles. He shows off his speed with eight triples and a strong but scattershot arm, which accounts for most of his league-high 16 errors. He adds four home runs in the 10 games it takes Norfolk to win the league's two-round playoff. It's a performance that stamps Yogi as a bona fide prospect—and gets him that $500 check, too.

Soon after the playoffs end, Berra receives a letter instructing him to report to Richmond for his preinduction physical. His number has come up, and it's time to serve in a different uniform. But at least he won't have to fight against the country of his ancestors. Italy formally surrendered on September 8, 1943—Mussolini fled to lead the resistance against the Allies in German-held northern Italy—and on October 13 the new Italian government declares war on Germany.

Yogi remembers Bodie's advice when the admitting officer in Richmond asks what branch of the military he wants to join.

"The Navy," Yogi answers quickly. But wait. Berra asks when he has to report back to Norfolk. One week, he's told. How long would it be if he joins the Army? "Four weeks," the officer says.

Four weeks of Momma's cooking—and all that time with his family—is just too hard to turn down. Baseball can wait.

"Well, I changed my mind," Yogi says, "I want to join the Army."

Alas, it's already too late.

"Sorry son," the officer tells him.

"You're in the Navy now."

# CHAPTER 5

# War
## 1944–1945

**C**hief Warrant Officer Gary Bodie was right. By the spring of 1944 he'd lost several top players from his Norfolk Naval Training Station baseball team, including Phil Rizzuto, Dom DiMaggio, and Eddie Robinson. All three were shipped out to the South Pacific for active duty. But Yogi's call from Bodie never comes.

Instead, Yogi receives a phone call from the Red Cross during his six-week basic training in Bainbridge, Maryland—his mother is in the hospital, about to have surgery related to her ever-worsening diabetes. The Red Cross makes arrangements for Yogi to travel back to St. Louis; he arrives a day after the surgery and stays until Paulina is able to return to her home on The Hill. It's hard to know who worries more about the well-being of the other, mother or son. Paulina sends Berra's little sister Josie over to St. Ambrose Church every few days to pay $5 and light a candle in front of a statue of Jesus.

"She prays hard for that boy every day," Josie tells her friends.

Berra returns to Bainbridge, then goes to the expeditionary base at Little Creek, eight miles down the road from Norfolk, to train for amphibious landings. He wonders why he doesn't hear from Bodie, but mostly he wonders how to fill the hours when he's not training. It's a classic case of military hurry up and wait, and Berra spends most of his free time reading his comic books and going to the base movie theater at night. The only saving grace: he gets a good seat at the base movie house, his favorite spot, instead of battling the long lines in jam-packed Norfolk.

Yogi is enjoying *Boom Town,* starring Clark Gable and Spencer Tracy, when the screen goes blank, the lights go on, and all the enlisted men are instructed to report to their barracks. Their commanding officer has an important announcement. Minutes later, Yogi is standing at attention when his CO asks for volunteers for a secret mission—manning new "rocket boats" that will surprise the Nazis in the long-awaited invasion in Europe. Yogi's hand shoots up instantly.

"I want to join," Berra says. The rocket boats sound exciting. Bodie and baseball have disappeared from life, and this new assignment would mean the end of the mind-numbing boredom. "All this hangin' around is driving me crazy," he tells a fellow seaman. "I just hate it."

Berra is shipped out to a base just below Baltimore, where he's told more about his mission. He's there to learn about a speedy 36-foot wooden-hulled flat-bottom boat called a Landing Craft Small Support—LCSS, in naval parlance. About half the ship is covered by a steel deck—the only cover for the crew of five seamen and one officer. Three machine guns on ball turrets are mounted on the deck, and there are two rocket launchers, each holding 12 rockets, bolted to each side of the boat's stern. Yogi is assigned to the twin 50-caliber machine guns and tasked with loading the rocket launchers as fast as he can.

The seamen are instructed to talk to no one—not family, not girl-friends, not anyone!—about their mission. Just to make sure, the Navy censors all mail leaving the base. Berra doesn't mind, he tells his new shipmates. Working on a top-secret mission means you're important.

But it also means you're expendable. The rocket boats will be the leading edge of the massive D-Day invasion, setting up 300 yards from the beach. Their job: lob rockets into embankments along the shore to draw the fire of Nazi machine-gun nests so Allied warplanes can take them out, clearing the way for ground forces arriving in hundreds of transport ships. "We're cannon fodder," Berra jokes with a nervous laugh. The seamen come up with a new name for their LCSS: Landing Craft Suicide Squad.

Berra and his team train hard for five weeks, then leave to join a convoy in Halifax, Nova Scotia, for the 20-day journey to England. Berra is aboard the USS *Buckley,* a destroyer escort that is little more than a giant scooped-out hull topped by a steel deck. Eight rocket boats are loaded into the hold along with their crews, who are housed in bunks stacked four high along the walls.

Berra thinks of all the tales his father told of his tough voyage from the old country to America in steerage—the belly of the boat—but Yogi is sure those were luxury accommodations compared to this flat-bottom ship that sways from side to side even in calm seas. One sailor or another is vomiting at all hours. Even when Yogi doesn't feel sick he'll go topside to escape the stench.

Sleep on this voyage is all but nonexistent. There's the constant "Now hear this: clean sweep down fore and aft" blaring over the loudspeakers. Worse is the near-regular beep-beep-beep of the general quarters alarm, which every sailor responds to at full speed. After spending so much time staring at the walls down below, imagining a torpedo tearing through and all that water rushing in to drown them, Yogi and every other sailor jumps when they hear that alarm, never questioning if it's a training exercise or the real thing.

The convoy loses two of its 74 ships to German U-boat torpedoes: Berra and his crew arrive safely in Glasgow in early May, and the entire unit is soon on a train to Portsmouth in southern England, where they join more than two million men who have amassed for the invasion of Normandy. Yogi's never seen so many military men in one place. No one has. Operation Overlord, the code name for the invasion of Normandy's five beaches along a 50-mile stretch of France's coastline, will be the largest amphibious military strike in history. Almost 5,000 ships will cross the English Channel, including scores of transport ships carrying more than 150,000 ground troops. More than 1,000 aircraft will provide cover.

Berra and his shipmates train intensely for days, spending hours at the firing range, hours more on physical conditioning. Ground troops practice exiting transport ships and crawling under barbed wire with live fire passing overhead. Army Rangers practice scaling cliffs while paratroopers make jumps day and night.

Everyone is on edge when word finally comes: the invasion, almost a year in planning, is set for June 5. Berra and his team climb into their LCSS on board the USS *Bayfield* the night of June 4. At 5 a.m., bad weather convinces General Dwight Eisenhower, Supreme Allied Commander of the Allied Expeditionary Force in Europe, to postpone the invasion one day. Berra and his mates remain aboard their boat for the next 24 hours, cramped and tense, endlessly reviewing their instructions. There will be no sleep this night.

"Now hear this, now hear this," a voice blares over loudspeakers at 4:15 a.m. on D-Day. The next words come from Eisenhower. "You are about to embark upon the Great Crusade, toward which we have striven these many months," he tells the Allied troops. "The eyes of the world are upon you. The hopes and prayers of liberty-loving people everywhere march with you."

It is still dark when 20,000 men parachute behind enemy lines. Their mission: take out bridges and seize control of the roads to cut off escape routes and prevent Nazi reinforcements from entering the battle zone.

At precisely 5 a.m., Berra's rocket boat is lowered over the side of the *Bayfield* and into the French side of the English Channel, where they rendezvous with 11 other rocket boats and race off to Utah Beach. A dozen more rocket boats are heading to Omaha Beach; battleships, destroyers, and transport ships follow close behind. There are so many ships in the water that one pilot flying cover overhead will later say it appeared as if he could walk across the channel stepping from one boat to another.

The assault starts at Utah Beach. Berra loads one rocket after another into his boat's launcher, each one searching for Nazi machine-gun nests. One connects, and after an onslaught of rockets lets loose from all 12 boats, the Germans return fire. Everyone on Berra's boat is ordered below, but Yogi can't resist poking his head above deck.

He almost can't comprehend what he sees. Shells from warships are soaring overhead and exploding up and down the beach. The air is thick with Allied warplanes, which meet almost no resistance from Luftwaffe aircraft and are firing on dozens of Nazi positions. One ship gets too close to a German mine and is flipped right out of the water. All the flashing lights and thunder of guns give Berra a sense of Fourth of July fireworks gone out of control.

"Get your damn head down," Yogi hears his officer shout over the explosions, "before you get it shot off."

Small transport ships rush by and pull right onto the sand at 6:30 a.m., unloading wave after wave of American GIs. Utah will suffer the fewest casualties of all five beaches, but 197 of the 21,000 men who storm this beach will never see their loved ones again. Soon enough it will be the rocket-boat crews who scoop the wounded and the dead out of the water here and at Omaha Beach and bring them back to the *Bayfield*.

The Allies secure their first beachhead at Utah, with British and Canadian forces securing beaches code-named Gold, Juno, and Sword next. Allied forces face the heaviest resistance at Omaha Beach. Transports cannot quite reach this beach, so soldiers—those not killed by enemy fire the moment the doors of their transports drop—wade through water, at some points shoulder high, and go ashore. GIs drive jeeps submerged underwater by sitting atop seat backs, their heads barely above the sea.

Tanks that are supposed to provide support are let out in water that is too deep and sink instead. The sand is heavily fortified with mines, barbed wire, and trenches, and German guns are positioned on hard-to-reach bluffs high above the beach. It's not until nightfall that American forces gain control at Omaha Beach, but the cost is high: Berra and his shipmates soon learn that almost 3,000 men have lost their lives. In all, 4,500 Allied men die in this assault, with at least as many injured.

More troops arrive the next day; the fighting in Normandy will continue for months, but the Nazis are clearly on the run. No one knows it at this moment, but Hitler, slowly realizing all is lost, will shoot himself in a bunker the following April 30. The Germans will surrender the next week.

Hitler's Luftwaffe has been all but absent, but Berra's crew is instructed to shoot every enemy plane it sees, and when an aircraft finally breaks through the clouds, Yogi and his mates open fire and bring it down. There's just one problem: it's an Allied plane. They speed over to pluck the pilot from the water and find him both unharmed and livid.

"If you sonsabitches shot down as many German planes as you do ours," he screams, "the war would have been over long ago!"

A storm hits on the third day, and Berra's boat flips over in the rough seas; all the men are rescued and taken back to the *Bayfield*. There they remain, working almost nonstop the next 10 days, shuttling messages between Utah and Omaha Beaches, checking for mines, carefully escorting ships through the channel. On the 13th day the crews of the rocket boats are told to stand down, but no sooner does an exhausted Berra slide into his bunk than the general quarters alarm sounds.

"The hell with it," Yogi says to a shipmate. "It if hits, it hits. I ain't moving."

A bomb does drop toward the stern of the *Bayfield,* but does little damage. Yogi knows he's been lucky—today and every day during this critical mission. The things he's seen—the men killed, others who leave the beach without an arm or a leg or worse—will stay buried in his mind the rest of his life.

Yogi sees action again when the Allies take Marseilles in the south of France in late August of 1944. The rocket boats are tasked with taking out a big hotel overlooking the Mediterranean Sea that serves as a Nazi command post. It's protected by soldiers armed with machine guns and mortars, but the Allies fire one rocket after another, smashing giant holes in the stately structure. A bullet nicks Yogi in his left hand. It won't affect his ability to play ball, and he won't put in for a Purple Heart until he returns home—he doesn't want to worry his mother.

Berra is one of many manning machine guns, cutting down the Nazis as they flee the burning building. It's hard to know who kills each German soldier as the men rush to escape; it's knowledge no one is eager to have. When the fighting is done, Berra and his shipmates go ashore, where they're greeted by villagers who seemingly come out of nowhere, all carrying flowers and wine, smiling, cheering, and singing. It's good to see this side of life after all the dying Berra just witnessed.

His next port is Naples, where his entire squadron—40 enlisted men, eight officers—takes up residence in an old inn on a hill overlooking the Bay of Naples. It amounts to an extended leave. Weeks go by without orders, so Yogi tours in the country of his parents, exploring Naples and the island of Capri, discovering his dialect of Italian isn't spoken anywhere in southern Italy. He bumps into a friend from the neighborhood, Bob Cocaterra, who's driving an Army jeep on his way to Milan.

"Can you take me to Rome?" says Berra, whose commanding officer tells him he can leave, but it's his neck if their boat leaves before he returns. Yogi would love to visit Milan and the surrounding villages where he has family, but the Allies are still fighting German forces in northern Italy.

Besides, how often do you get a chance to see Vatican City and St. Peter's Basilica? Yogi reaches Rome and wanders the city, even seeing the Pope on the balcony one day; he knows instantly how happy this will make his mother. He has no need for money; Americans are so welcome that chocolate and a few cigarettes pay for just about anything.

Berra is back in time for the squadron's trip to North Africa, where he spends Christmas of 1944 in the historic Algerian port city of

Oran, which dates back to 900 AD. There's a depressing rumor they'll be shipped out to the South Pacific to fight the Japanese, but news comes right before year's end that they're all going back to the States. Champagne corks are popped aboard the transport on New Year's Eve as they begin 1945 with the three-week voyage home. When he reaches Norfolk, Yogi stays just long enough to get a train ticket for a monthlong leave in St. Louis.

Paulina loses her fight to hold back tears when her youngest son walks through the door, and the family feast begins almost immediately. Plates full of ravioli, lasagna, spaghetti, stufato—and, of course, bread and salad—never run out. Lawdie—it's never Yogi at home—tells his parents all about the Pope and Vatican City, but very little about the carnage he saw. He shows off the medals and ribbons he's won: two battle stars, a European Theater of Operations ribbon, a Distinguished Unit Citation, and a Good Conduct Medal. The Purple Heart, which he put in for once he was back—and safe—in the States, will arrive soon.

Berra returns to Norfolk and is hit with a blizzard of questions and paperwork. He meets with a Navy psychologist several times, each session centering on the same question: was he afraid out there in combat? No, Yogi keeps saying, there was no time to be scared, but deep down, he knows just how frightened he really was. Now that he's back, he tells the psychologist, the feeling of dread about what he lived through sometimes seeps into his mind.

Another doctor pushes and probes, checking his reflexes. All is well, and he's told to write down what he wants to do next on the many forms he's ordered to fill out. Sports and recreation, he writes over and over again.

Berra soon learns he's been assigned to the submarine base in New London, Connecticut. Subs? Going into combat was bad enough; squeezing into a submarine and going below the surface is as bad as it gets. And didn't you have to volunteer for subs?

But when he arrives at the New London base, he discovers he has it all wrong. The Navy actually granted his wish. His new job: sweep out the movie theater after each show and make sure no knuckleheads make trouble. Great! He's not back in St. Louis yet, but his days in combat are over.

And best of all—the submarine base has a baseball team.

# CHAPTER 6

# Looks Are Deceiving
## 1945

Lieutenant Jimmy Gleeson can only shake his head and laugh as he watches the opposing catcher argue with the home plate umpire. It's the middle of the summer of 1945, and by now the manager of the New London submarine base baseball team is convinced there isn't much Seaman 2nd Class Yogi Berra can't do with a baseball bat in his hands.

It was just a few moments ago that one of Gleeson's players was dancing off second base with Berra at the plate. Convinced the Raider runner was going to attempt to steal third, Quonset Point Naval Air Station catcher Gus Niarhos—who played two years in the Yankee organization before the war—called for a pitch out. And his pitcher delivered the ball exactly where Niarhos wanted it—high and outside to the left-handed-hitting Berra.

But the ball never reached Niarhos. Just as the catcher was rising from his crouch, Berra stepped across the plate and slapped the pitch on a line off the left field wall. The runner scored easily as Berra pulled into second base with one of his four hits for the day, sending his future Yankee teammate into a frenzy.

"Hey, ump; hey, ump!" Niarhos is shouting at umpire Joe Rafferty. "He can't do that."

And why not? Rafferty asks.

"Because that was a pitch out," an exasperated Niarhos says.

"Yeah," Rafferty replies calmly, "but you didn't tell that to Yogi."

The double stands. And Gleeson—a journeyman outfielder for the Reds, Cubs, and Indians before entering the Navy three years ago—adds another item to the growing list of things he's never seen anyone do on a baseball field.

Not that Gleeson has always been convinced Berra was a player, much less a star in the making. It was only this past January when Yogi walked into the Raider manager's office and confidently announced he wanted to play for New London's baseball team. Gleeson, who already had two major league pitchers and a former backup catcher for the Yankees on his roster, thought the five-foot-eight, 185-pound kid looked more like a wrestler.

But Berra kept insisting he played one season for the Yankee farm team in Norfolk in the Piedmont League before being drafted. So Gleeson and his assistant coach Ray Volpi, who pitched in the Yankee chain for several years, quizzed Berra on the Piedmont League's managers and top players. Berra got every question right. The New London manager still wasn't convinced but told Berra to come back in April and he'd take a look.

Gleeson didn't have to look long once Yogi stepped into the batting cage to know he had something special. Everything his pitchers threw—fastballs or curves, high or low, off the plate or high over Yogi's head—Berra drove on a line to every part of New London's ballpark. And now Yogi is firmly planted in the middle of Gleeson's lineup, the best hitter for the best team in each of the two leagues in which New London competes.

With victory over Japan seeming inevitable and the country able to see an end to years of war, playing baseball in New London is a joy. Splitting his time between catcher and left field, Yogi hits better than .400 in both the Southern New England Service League—composed of teams from the many military bases in Connecticut and Rhode Island—and the Morgan League, a five-team collection of the area's best semipro ballplayers.

Berra is also one of the many pro ballplayers who play for semipro teams under assumed names. The military frowns on this, and every league's rules prohibit the use of ringers. But men who have just risked their lives fighting a war can pick up $50 a game—more than half their monthly pay—so everyone just looks the other way. Berra plays for the Cranston Chiefs under the name Joe Cusano and thrills fans by regularly belting homers over the right field fence. Legend has it the city leaders in Cranston decided to update their stadium, raising its outfield fences to 30 feet, after a Berra blast hit the Cranston Bible Chapel—500 feet away in dead center field.

As July winds down, talk on the New London submarine base centers on why Japan continues to fight when all appears to be lost. Japan's six largest cities are close to ruins—an immense bombing of Tokyo alone left 100,000 dead and 267,000 buildings flattened—and almost five million Japanese are now homeless. On July 26, the Allies issue an ultimatum, warning Japan to surrender or face "utter devastation of the Japanese homeland." Japan rejects the ultimatum two days later.

There will be no further warnings.

At 8:15 a.m. on August 6, 1945, the doors on the bay of the American B-29 bomber *Enola Gay* swing open and the world's first atomic bomb floats by parachute toward the Japanese industrial city of Hiroshima. When it falls to just 2,000 feet above the city of 350,000, the bomb is detonated, unleashing a blast equal to 15,000 tons of TNT, which immediately kills 80,000 people and destroys almost everything standing within five square miles. Tens of thousands more Japanese citizens—at least half of them children under 10—will die from severe burns, injuries, or radiation poisoning within weeks.

This is what utter devastation now looks like.

The decision to drop the bomb was made by President Harry Truman, who's been commander in chief since the death of Franklin Roosevelt 16 weeks ago. Continuing conventional bombing and then invading the Japanese mainland would cost as many as one million

American lives, Truman was told by his military experts, which the new President found unacceptable. Truman hoped using the "Cosmic Bomb," the result of work by an international team of scientists five years in the making, would bring an end to war.

"The force from which the sun draws its power has been loosed against those who brought the war to the Far East," President Truman told the nation the next morning in a radio address. "Let there be no mistake; we shall completely destroy Japan's power to make war."

Truman's decision, made over the objections of several key advisers, including General Dwight Eisenhower, will be debated for decades to come. But Japan does not surrender, and Truman approves a second bomb, this one even more powerful than the first. At 11:02 a.m. on August 9, the bomb called Fat Man is detonated 1,650 feet over the port city of Nagasaki, and 40,000 people—a quarter of the city's population—are killed instantly. Like Hiroshima, Nagasaki will see tens of thousands more Japanese die from their wounds.

The leaders of Japan have finally been through enough. With America readying yet another bomb—and others in the works—Japan surrenders on August 14. Like all of America, Berra and the rest of the sailors on the New London submarine base cheer the news and celebrate the end of the war. The Army and Army Air Corps began discharging troops after Germany surrendered, but the Navy and Marines were waiting for the end of fighting in the Pacific before releasing their men.

New London was closing in on titles in its two leagues when the news of the atomic bombs arrived and everything was put on hold. But Berra and his teammates have other things on their minds than baseball. Yogi can now check in with the base commander and find out when his service time will end—and his professional baseball career can resume.

Jimmy Gleeson is leaning against the backstop of his Raiders' baseball field, watching his team take batting practice before a game in late August. Standing next to Gleeson is Mel Ott, the legendary player-manager of today's opponent, the New York Giants. Now 33, Gleeson is hoping to find a managing or coaching job somewhere in pro ball after he leaves the Navy.

The player he's telling Ott about is certainly helping Gleeson's prospects. Yogi Berra's already won two batting titles, hitting .429 in the Service League and .449 in the Morgan League, leading his team to first place in both leagues. And Yogi's hit better than .300 against the first three major league teams—the Boston Braves, Washington Senators, and Philadelphia A's—to face New London this summer.

"He doesn't look much like a baseball player," Gleeson tells Ott, whose own squat body and unusually high leg kick have produced 507 home runs since 1926, the most in NL history. "But he has the finest swing you'll ever see."

Ott is spellbound as Yogi lashes one line drive after another. The future Hall of Famer sees Berra's quick wrists and his ability to reach and drive an outside pitch—and pitches over his head and almost off his shoes, too. This 20-year-old's hand-eye coordination is off the charts. There's just one other thing Ott should know, Gleeson tells the Giants star.

"The Yankees have him under contract," Gleeson says.

"Damn," grumbles Ott, who can already envision Berra's sweet left-handed swing sending one ball after another over the right field fence at the Polo Grounds—the Giants' home field—all of 258 feet from home plate. When the game starts, Ott watches Berra smack a pair of singles off veteran reliever Ace Adams, who has 10 wins and 15 saves this season for the fourth-place Giants. But it's Berra's 400-foot drive to center, hauled in at the wall, which really sticks in Ott's mind after his team's 8–3 loss.

Ott says a hurried goodbye to Gleeson and rushes to catch a train to New York, a plan formulating in his mind. Gleeson finds Berra in the clubhouse after the game and tells him about his conversation with Ott. The Giants manager was disappointed to hear you were Yankee property, Gleeson tells him. "But he was still interested," Gleeson says. "I wouldn't be surprised if you heard from him."

Berra goes back to his job taking tickets at the base movie theater and sweeping it out after shows until the next Raider game. He doesn't mind the work and loves that he sees all the movies for free. Ott returns to New York determined to get "that little catcher in New London" and pitches the idea to Giants owner Horace Stoneham soon after returning home. "He could be worth $500,000 in a few years," says Ott. Fine, the owner tells his star manager, then gives him $50,000 to close the deal.

It's a few days later when Ott visits Yankee President Larry MacPhail in the Yankees' new Fifth Avenue office. MacPhail returned from the war in 1944 after two years of service and put together an ownership team to buy the Yankees for just under $3 million from the trust of Colonel Jacob Ruppert, who built the franchise into a powerhouse before his death in 1939. One partner is Dan Topping, a 33-year-old socialite and heir to a tin-mining fortune who is married to Olympic skater turned actress Sonja Henie, his third of what will be six wives. The other is construction magnate Del Webb, who likes to boast that his booming Southwest-based company built one of the internment camps for the Japanese in America.

Both men loaned MacPhail the money to buy his share of the franchise, agreeing to let the longtime baseball executive run the team and repay his $1 million in loans out of his share of the team's profits.

The blustery MacPhail—who brought night games to baseball when he ran the Cincinnati Reds in the mid-1930s and winning baseball to the Brooklyn Dodgers before the war—was an unlikely choice to run the staid Yankees. And true to his reputation, he came in like a storm. He renovated the stadium with new box seats and a private club for wealthy fans. He put more seats in the bleachers for everyone else and added a host of promotions. He began installing lights in time for the '46 season, convinced night baseball—like all his changes—would hasten his ability to repay his loan.

The Yankee players grumble MacPhail will do anything for a buck, like traveling to Panama to play lucrative spring training games. And there's more than a little truth to their beliefs. So when Ott calls to say he's interested in one of the Yankees' minor league catchers and has $50,000 to spend, MacPhail is happy to take the meeting.

Ott tries a bit of misdirection, pulling a piece of paper out of his pocket and running down a list of names of Yankee prospects. He finally gets around to saying he wants Berra. The Yankee boss has never heard Yogi's name before and is eager to bank a big check. But there's something odd about a smart baseball man like Ott willing to go so high for a kid who's played all of one season in the low minors.

"The little catcher. You like him?" MacPhail says to Ott. "Well, I think we can work something out. I have to check with my farm-system men, but I think we can work out a deal."

The moment Ott is gone, MacPhail bellows for head scout Paul Krichell, who's been with the team since 1920 and discovered Lou Gehrig, among many other Yankee stars. Krichell finds his boss pacing in his office.

"Who's this Berra kid?" MacPhail demands.

Krichell says Berra is a raw but powerful left-handed hitter, perfectly suited for Yankee Stadium's short right field porch—296 feet away with a waist-high wall. The Yankee President instantly decides against the trade. MacPhail inherited an aging team; most of his stars are in their 30s. If Ott likes this Yogi kid so much and Krichell is right, maybe Berra can play an important role in the team's future.

"Let's get Berra up here as soon as you can," MacPhail tells his top scout.

A few weeks later there's a knock on MacPhail's door.

"You want to see me, mister?"

It's Berra, and when MacPhail looks up he's astonished. Yogi's wearing his Navy uniform, which only exaggerates his oddly shaped body, especially the ill-fitting white sailor's cap, which makes his already oversized head look even larger. Years later, MacPhail will tell people he thought Berra looked more like the bottom man of an acrobatic pyramid team than a baseball player, and wondered if he could still make a deal with Ott.

Berra remembers that they had a pleasant 20- to 30-minute conversation about baseball. When MacPhail realizes this kid knows the game, he tells Berra he'll probably send him to Newark, the Yankees' top farm team in the tough International League, when Yogi leaves the Navy. Berra thanks MacPhail, asks whom he should see to get payment for his traveling expenses, and heads back to New London confident that his chosen career—the one he's had to fight so hard for—is right on track.

# CHAPTER 7

# The Longest 12 Miles
## 1945–1946

It's the autumn of 1945, and Yogi Berra—now Seaman 1st Class—volunteers to be the manager for the New London submarine base football team, picking up the Raiders' uniforms and getting them cleaned in the team's oversized washing machines, taking care of helmets and shoulder pads, and repairing and polishing the players' cleats. This is a man who just enjoys sports at whatever level. Picking up after football players is just part of the game.

On Thanksgiving Day, New London travels to Yankee Stadium to play the Tuskegee Army Air Corps Warhawks. The Raiders dress in the Yankee clubhouse, and Yogi strikes up a conversation with Pete Previte, the Yankees' assistant clubhouse man. Berra tells Previte all about his time in Norfolk and how much he's looking forward to moving up to New York as he stuffs a towel into each player's locker.

Previte takes a good look at the kid with thick shoulders and overly long arms. Berra's wearing blue jeans, a T-shirt, and a white sailor cap, and is carrying a big stack of towels. Previte thinks the young man hopes to become a clubhouse man, taking care of uniforms and the rest of the players' needs.

"Oh, no, I'm a catcher," Berra says proudly. "This is a good clubhouse. I think I'm going to like it here when I play with the Yankees."

Previte just shakes his head. No way this kid's ever going to be a Yankee.

It's six months later when Berra takes his next step back to the clubhouse in the Bronx. He receives his honorable discharge from the Navy on May 6, 1946, and rushes home to spend a few days celebrating his survival with family and friends. More than 400,000 Americans were not as fortunate, including 23 young men who never made it back to The Hill; their names will soon be on a bronze plaque that will hang on the back wall of St. Ambrose Church, Yogi's parish.

It isn't long before Berra receives a telegram from MacPhail telling him he's now a Newark Bear and instructing him to meet the team in Rochester, New York. Joe Garagiola will soon make his major league debut with the Cardinals—he gets a single in four at-bats in Cincinnati on May 26—but for the first time in years Yogi feels he isn't far behind his best friend. The Yankees send their top prospects to Newark, New Jersey, a mere 12 miles from Yankee Stadium, and the expectations for the Bears are always high. Indeed, from 1931 to 1945, the Bears won seven International League pennants—winning four postseason titles—and finished second five times.

If he can make it with Newark, Berra figures as he travels to meet his new team, playing for the Yankees is well within reach.

Berra is a bundle of energy as he stands with pitcher Walt Dubiel in a hotel lobby in Rochester, waiting for manager George Selkirk and the Newark players to return from that night's game. But it takes all of two questions from the Bears' manager to turn Yogi's excitement to dread. Selkirk, the man who replaced Babe Ruth in the Yankee outfield and a two-time All-Star for the New York team that won four straight titles, welcomes Dubiel. The big right-hander won 23 games the last two seasons pitching for the wartime Yankees, and Selkirk—whose bonus depends on the success of his team—figures Dubiel can help.

Selkirk knew Dubiel would arrive today. But no one told him about Berra, and he has no idea what to make of the kid standing beside his new pitcher. "Who the hell are you?" he growls at Berra.

"I'm your new catcher," answers Yogi, trying hard to sound confident.

"Bullshit," says Selkirk, who has two veteran catchers he thinks are doing just fine. "Let me see some proof."

Berra nervously digs through his suitcase, finds the rumpled telegram, and hands it to Selkirk. This isn't the first time someone's doubted he was a ballplayer, but given how close Berra is to the major leagues, this time feels the worst. Yogi squirms as Selkirk stares at the paper for a minute or two. Clearly unhappy, the manager instructs the man behind the hotel's front desk to get Berra a room, tells Yogi to make sure he gets to the field on time, and walks away.

Things don't get any better the next day. Berra shows up early and waits until Selkirk appears and tells clubhouse man Jimmy Mack to find the new kid a uniform. Mack picks up on the irritation in the manager's voice. He digs out a well-worn uniform without a number on its back or the word NEWARK across the chest. Mack fishes out a cap, sees that it will never fit Yogi's large head, and slits open the back with scissors before handing it to Berra.

Stunned, Yogi takes the uniform, walks over to a bench, sits down, then pops right back up. He wraps the uniform into a ball, strides angrily over to the clubhouse man, and thrusts it all back to Mack. "Hey, give me a damn new uniform," he says. "I'm not trying out. I play for this club!"

Berra gets his new uniform but not much playing time. Or even time in batting practice. Selkirk, a rookie manager after nine solid seasons as a Yankee outfielder, isn't at all interested in looking at a 21-year-old catcher with one season of minor league experience. For weeks, Yogi is the forgotten man of the Newark Bears.

But Yankee President Larry MacPhail changes all that. Surprised to hear his big investment is riding the bench, MacPhail tracks down Selkirk and tells him to get Berra in the lineup—*now*! Current Yankee catcher Bill Dickey—a future Hall of Famer with a lifetime .313 average and 202 home runs—is 38 years old and in his final season.

MacPhail wants a big bat to replace Dickey and is convinced there's no one else in his minor league system with Berra's potential.

A skeptical Selkirk gives Berra his first start on May 26, and Yogi gets his first hit as a Bear. Selkirk starts Yogi in both games of a May 30 doubleheader, watches Berra slug a grand slam and two singles in seven at-bats, and his opinion about his young catcher begins to change. Another two hits in the next game settles it: but for two injuries—including a chipped bone in his thumb that sidelines Yogi for three weeks at midseason—Selkirk writes Berra's name in the lineup just about every game, 70 times at catcher and another seven in the outfield.

When Yogi is healthy, International League pitchers can barely find a way to get him out. By August 4, Berra is hitting .349 with six doubles and seven home runs in 128 at-bats. Montreal manager Clay Hopper, seeing the powerful Berra pull everything to right field, tries to stack his defense against Yogi, leaving only his third baseman on the left side of the infield and swinging his outfielders around so his left fielder is playing center. Berra smacks five base hits to all fields and Hopper trashes his experiment.

Behind the plate, Berra is agile but unpolished, showing a strong arm with little accuracy. His aim is so bad he hits a runner in the shoulder on one steal attempt and plunks an umpire standing 10 feet from second on another—in the same game. But he's quick around the plate, gobbling up bunts and throwing out lead runners.

And he's surprisingly fast. Almost all catchers are replaced by a pinch-runner in the late innings, especially in tight games when one run can make all the difference. But Berra is fast enough to score from second base or go from first to third on a base hit, so there's no need to pull him for a faster player.

Berra's biggest supporter is Bobby Brown, his roommate and fellow first-year Bear, and no two men could be more different. Unlike Berra, Brown never had anyone doubt his ability or his brains. The son of a liquor industry executive, Brown was a standout shortstop in New Jersey—his father took him to games at Yankee Stadium—and then San Francisco, where the family finally settled. Smart and handsome—he married a beauty queen—Brown went to Stanford with the idea of becoming a doctor.

In 1943, Brown entered the Navy, which sent him to UCLA to finish his pre-med courses and then to Tulane University medical school. He played baseball at both schools, and when he left the Navy in January of '46, the Yankees gave him a $50,000 bonus and a ticket to Newark, agreeing to let him come late to spring training each season until he finished medical school.

There's little Brown needs to tell his roomie about hitting, but he does show Berra a side of life that will help him when they both advance to New York: how to order meals at high-end restaurants, which pieces of silverware to use, how much to tip a waiter, and where to buy a good suit—Yankee management insists their players leave good tips for service and wear suits when traveling. Looking ahead to the time Yogi starts to date, Brown sands down Berra's rough edges, instructing him to open doors for a woman, stand when she leaves the table at dinner, and stand again when she returns.

Like Berra, Brown is hitting well over .300 for Newark, and the two young players talk often about what it will be like to play a dozen miles up the road in the Bronx—"the longest 12 miles in baseball," Brown calls it. And it's Brown who begins telling a story that very well might be the first "Yogi-ism," the collection of sayings and stories that will soon endear Berra to baseball fans everywhere.

It seems Brown spends most of his nights reading medical books and journals. Like many of his other teammates, Yogi is still fond of comic books. One night Brown is ready to shut off the lights when Berra begs for just a few more minutes to finish reading his comic book. Almost gleeful when he turns the final page, Berra reaches for the light.

"Hey, mine was really good," he tells Brown. "How'd yours turn out?"

Brown can't help but love the story a bit more each time he tells it.

There's one other area where Brown's support proves helpful. No sooner does Berra become a star in Newark than he becomes the target of taunts about his looks and ethnicity from opposing players and fans all around the International League. Brown preaches patience, consoling his friend on nights like the one when an especially loud-mouthed fan keeps shouting at Yogi, "Hey, King Kong, who let you out of your cage?"

It doesn't make the insults hurled his way any easier to bear, but Berra knows there is one player suffering through far worse—Montreal's Jackie Robinson. Signed by Branch Rickey in October of 1945 to play this season in the International League—only one of its eight teams is based in the highly segregated South—Robinson performs brilliantly for the Royals under the intense glare of the national spotlight. Knowing his response here will dictate whether he gets the chance to break the color barrier on the major league level, Robinson suffers in silence. Pitchers throw at his head all season long—these are the days before helmets—and runners regularly slide into second base spikes-high, looking to gouge Robinson whenever and wherever they can.

The verbal abuse from players and fans is every bit as bad. On Montreal's first trip to Baltimore, one fan sat behind Robinson's pregnant wife and shouted all game about "that son of a bitch nigger" playing for Montreal. In Syracuse, a player throws a black cat out of the dugout at Robinson while he waits to bat. "Hey, Jackie," the player shouts. "There's your cousin."

Berra can see Robinson is fearless, a great hitter and an aggressive runner who gives him trouble on the base paths all season. There is little doubt Jackie can play on the next level, especially after he finishes the season as the league's top hitter (.349, edging runner-up Brown by eight points), steals 40 bases, and leads the Royals to 100 wins and first place. Berra slumps the final month of the season, dropping his average to .314, but slams his 15th home run in Newark's final regular-season game, an encouraging sign as the Bears prepare to face Robinson and the Royals in the playoffs.

The series is surprisingly hard fought despite the 20-game difference in the standings. The Royals win two close games in Montreal before Berra hits the series' first home run to win Game 3 back in Newark. The Bears win again in Game 4 to even the series, but big right-hander Vic Raschi, a top Yankee prospect, suffers a tough 2–1 loss in Game 5, and Newark is a game away from elimination.

The series shifts back to Montreal, where 19,593 fans pack Delorimier Stadium and anxiously watch the Bears take a 4–3 lead into the home half of the 9th of Game 6. Newark pitcher Herb Karpel retires the first two batters, and Berra thinks he's just caught the third strike against first baseman Les Burge when he hears umpire Artie Gore shout, "Ball." Selkirk comes out to argue—unsuccessfully—which is nothing compared to the scene when Burge hits the very next pitch for a game-tying home run. Selkirk explodes out of the dugout, followed by coaches and players, all shouting at Gore and his fellow umps. When order is restored, Selkirk and several players are ejected, including Karpel.

Veteran Bear right-hander Alex Mustaikis comes in and promptly gives up two hits, the second forcing a play at the plate. Berra thinks he's tagged out the runner, but once again the umpire disagrees. "Safe!" Gore shouts, giving Montreal the series-clinching win.

And now it's pure bedlam. Berra turns and rushes Gore, flinging off his catcher's mask and hurling expletives so crude and so loud he has to be restrained by his teammates. It's a nasty and expensive ending to Berra's season—the league would fine him $500, huge by the day's standards.

But Yogi's aggressiveness hardly disappoints Yankee brass, which later decides to cover the fine. Berra and his teammates are still riled up on the train back to Newark a few hours later when the sports report comes over the radio in the dining car. Silence washes over the players as they hear that four of their teammates—Brown, Raschi, outfielder Frank Colman, and Larry Berra—will be traveling those 12 miles from Newark to the Bronx to spend the last week of the season with the Yankees.

The sports radio announcer didn't know Berra's nickname yet, but there would be time for that soon enough.

★     ★     ★

This is not the typical Yankee clubhouse that Yogi walks into for the team's September 22 doubleheader against the last-place Philadelphia A's. The preseason pick to win the pennant with stars Joe DiMaggio, Joe Gordon, Phil Rizzuto, and Charlie Keller all back from military service, the Yankees are mired in third place in a season full of infighting and disappointing performances. Manager Joe McCarthy, who guided seven Yankee teams to titles in the past 15 years, considered Yankee President Larry MacPhail a loudmouthed showboat—an opinion he shared with anyone who'd listen—and wanted out before the season even began. MacPhail held McCarthy to his contract, but after the team stumbled through six tension-filled weeks, McCarthy quit—by telegram—and MacPhail moved on.

Not many Yankees liked MacPhail's promotions and gimmicks. He dragged the team through Central America for two weeks of big-money exhibition games before spring training opened, and many of the older players are blaming that trip for their subpar performances. He held the team's first Ladies' Day—passing out nylons and free tickets all over town—a gimmick the players considered a tawdry affront to the "Yankee Way." He chartered a team plane and forced the sizable group of players who still feared flying to pay their own way if they chose to travel by train.

As always, the team revolves around DiMaggio, who is closing out the worst season of his career after three years in the military. Joe D limps into the final week of this 1946 season emotionally drained from his failure to rescue his team or his marriage to actress Dorothy Arnold, the mother of his four-year-old son Joe Jr., and physically broken down with a painful bone spur in his left heel and a bum knee from a midseason slide into second base. He's managed just six home runs since mid-August and needs a strong last seven games to avoid hitting under .300 for the first time in his career. He detests MacPhail—*a one-man wrecking ball of Yankee tradition,* DiMaggio tells friends—and feels older than his 31 years.

Dickey stepped in as manager after McCarthy's abrupt departure, and surprises no one by catching only seven games after May 28. But he stuns everyone when he quits September 13—three days after the Yankees are eliminated from the pennant race—resigning over the phone. Everyone soon understands why: MacPhail refused to name him manager for next season. Things were so chaotic that coach Johnny Neun took over for the final 14 games only after MacPhail agreed *not* to consider him a candidate to manage next season.

None of this seems to have bothered the fans, who love MacPhail's promotions and the first season of night games, and come out to the Stadium in droves. The Yankees are the first team in baseball history to surpass two million in attendance and go into the final three home games having already drawn 2,238,086 paying customers. (Final attendance: 2,265,512, a figure most writers agree will never be surpassed. The Yankees will prove them wrong two seasons later.)

Nor does it bother Larry Berra, as the reporters call him in their game stories. (It won't become "Yogi" until well into next season.) He's excited to be in a major league uniform, with NEW YORK across his chest and the number 38 on his broad back. And he understands that a good showing in these seven games could mean a big league contract next season. Nothing is going to take Berra's mind off these games, and sure enough, in his second major league at-bat he belts a two-run homer on a pitch high and outside the strike zone from Philadelphia's Jesse Flores.

DiMaggio sits in stunned silence as the stocky rookie rounds the bases after his first major league home run. DiMaggio thought Berra was a bit of a show-off when he swung three bats instead of the customary two while standing in the on-deck circle. But he's already reevaluating. DiMaggio doubts he could even have hit the pitch Berra walloped—it was *that far* outside—much less yank it into the right field seats. Maybe the Yankees have something interesting here.

Berra homered again in his third game and is hitting .444 when the Yankees head to Boston to play the first-place Red Sox. Word of Berra's hot bat has already reached Beantown. The New York writers took an instant liking to the energetic youngster, so it was without malice that they also began writing less-than-complimentary stories about his looks.

These tales have also reached Boston, where veteran pitcher Mike Ryba eagerly awaits Yogi's arrival. It's during warm-ups at Fenway Park on September 24 when the floppy-eared Ryba, the self-proclaimed captain of baseball's All-Ugly team, strides into Yankee batting practice to find the rookie.

"Kid, I'll have to see you again tomorrow," Ryba tells Berra. "Nobody could look that bad unless he was sick. I hereby appoint you captain of the All-Ugly team. You are the ugliest man I ever saw in my whole life."

Boston's Ted Williams, enjoying an MVP season—he'll hit .342 with 38 homers and 123 RBI—is only slightly kinder when he steps into the batter's box for his first at-bat with Berra behind the plate.

"How ya doing, Ted?" a smiling Yogi says to Williams.

Williams sizes up the newcomer. Berra's shin guards hang loosely from his stubby legs, looking like they'll fall off as soon as he chases a foul pop. His chest protector droops over his knees, and he seems to think a rookie and an All-Star outfielder are on a first-name basis.

"Hey, what are you guys trying to pull here?" Williams bellows. "Is this some kind of joke?"

Berra laughs off both comments and picks up two more hits in two Yankee losses to Boston, then a double and single while catching both games of a doubleheader against the A's in Philly. In his seven games as the Yankee catcher, Berra hits .364 with two home runs, four RBI, and a raft of good reviews. Both MacPhail and GM George Weiss, the man who signed Berra sight unseen four years ago, think the intriguing 21-year-old will be part of a renovated team next season.

Yogi leaves New York for St. Louis soon after the season ends. He can't wait to see his family and his friends on The Hill and tell them all about life with the fabled New York Yankees. He's already forming a bond with Phil Rizzuto, the only Yankee shorter than Yogi, who—just like Berra—was always told he'd never make it in the big leagues. And everyone will want to know about DiMaggio, who remains the most famous athlete in America.

Berra's already got a job lined up in the hardware department at the Sears, Roebuck downtown with his buddy Joe Garagiola, who winds up being one of the stars of the Cardinals' surprising World Series victory. (Almost every player needs an offseason job to supplement his baseball pay.) But mostly Yogi will be counting down the days to spring training. It no longer matters how many clubhouse boys mistook him for a kid trying out. Or that he had to take a quiz to convince a Navy baseball coach that he really was a Yankee minor leaguer.

It doesn't even matter that Branch Rickey told him right to his face he'd never be a major league player. Hell, Mr. Rickey may have done him a huge favor. Sure, it would've been great to play for the hometown team. But Yogi's now a member of the most famous baseball organization in the land. He's dressing in the same locker room as Joltin' Joe! And just before Thanksgiving, newly named Yankee manager Bucky Harris tells reporters that Yogi is one of only eight players New York will not consider trading ahead of next season.

Yogi Berra—an untouchable!

# PART II

# MAKING IT BIG
## 1947–1949

CHAPTER 8

# Dreams Can Come True
## 1947

If 1946 was when Americans took a deep breath after 10 years of the Great Depression and six years of the Second World War, 1947 is a time of great opportunity and optimism. Fueled by the GI Bill, which gives 16 million veterans low-interest loans for college tuition, buying farms, and building new homes, the nation's first true middle class begins to emerge and flourish. America's birthrate—held back for more than a decade—begins to take off. So do the new parents, who migrate to suburbs now beginning to develop outside the nation's major cities.

America is further transformed as farmworkers leave their rural roots for better opportunities in towns and cities. Wages rise and jobs are added as captains of industry struggle to keep pace with demand for their goods. In place of matériel and machines for war, American factories are churning out shoes and clothes, washing machines and ovens, cars and pickup trucks. And for those few who can afford the newest in technology, televisions and air conditioners.

Though there are but 9,000 television sets in the United States in 1947, the broadcast industry will grow quickly and change the country's culture forever. On January 6, President Harry Truman gives the first televised State of the Union address. *Meet the Press*—a news program destined to become television's longest-running show—

brings politicians and power brokers into America's living rooms. *Howdy Doody,* starring a large puppet dressed as a cowboy, holds children spellbound for 30 minutes each day. Interest in Howdy is so great it creates a whole new industry—toys based on television characters.

With their favorite ballplayers back from military service and a little extra money in their pockets, Americans turn to baseball in record numbers. It's hard to overstate baseball's popularity in this rapidly changing country. Opening Day and the midsummer All-Star Game—the latter conceived as a way to bring in fans during the depths of the Depression—are undeclared national holidays. The World Series is just about the only thing Americans talk about for nearly two weeks every fall.

The game has become such a melting pot—the very symbol of America's identity—that the son of Italian immigrants is the game's most popular and admired player. And in the spring of 1947, an African-American will play what is considered a white man's sport even as segregation remains the law of the land throughout the South. It's still more than a decade before the Civil Rights movement truly takes hold, but many more black players will follow Jackie Robinson into the major leagues soon after the Dodger infielder's Rookie of the Year season.

As important as Robinson becomes, the national pastime in 1947 is still very much Joe DiMaggio's kingdom. He's recognized by media and fans alike as the best to ever play the game, and that's been true almost from the first day he pulled on a Yankee uniform in 1936 at the tender age of 21. No player has ever put up the numbers—219 home runs, 930 RBI, a .336 batting average—that DiMaggio did in his first seven seasons. The Yankees won a record four consecutive World Series in Joltin' Joe's first four seasons, adding two more pennants and another World Series in the next three seasons before he left baseball at 27 for three years of military service in World War II.

But DiMaggio is far more than numbers. He's the very embodiment of the Yankee Way: excellence, tradition, and class. He is a true

American hero, as elegant and graceful off the field as he is on it, so popular he can't walk down the street without being mobbed by fans begging for an autograph or hoping to get close enough just to touch his sleeve. Forever withdrawn and distant, he is memorialized by songwriters in pop tunes, and newspapers can't write enough about him. Ernest Hemingway, one of his few real friends, makes DiMaggio a central figure in his Pulitzer Prize–winning novella, *The Old Man and the Sea*.

In mid-February of 1947, as rookie catcher Yogi Berra and the rest of the New York Yankees gather at LaGuardia Field in the early morning hours to depart for a four-week, three-country tour of the Caribbean, there is no man more famous in America than Joe DiMaggio. But as Berra climbs aboard the chartered twin-engine plane for the 1,600-mile flight to San Juan, Puerto Rico, the trip's first stop, he can see DiMaggio is clearly unhappy. And worried—the offseason operation to remove the painful bone spur in his left heel shows no sign of healing.

And that means all of Berra's new teammates are worried, too.

As the Yankees settle into their first week of work in San Juan, there are two stories that dwarf all others. One centers on the absence of DiMaggio, who after three days has yet to emerge from his hotel room, much less interact with his teammates working out for new manager Bucky Harris across the street at Sixto Escobar Stadium. The only person who sees DiMaggio is Mal Stevens, the doctor whose sole responsibility is to tend to the team's most important player.

The other story line is the team's rookie catcher. Yankee veterans and the media aren't quite sure what to make of this kid, but Berra's excitement at simply being in the major leagues is ever-present and endearing. No two players could have more different stories to tell.

DiMaggio is livid with team President Larry MacPhail for forcing him to make this trip just five weeks after doctors removed a three-inch bone spur from his heel. He knows MacPhail is strapped for cash and booked this tour to help pay off loans from his two millionaire co-owners—but DiMaggio doesn't give a damn. He doesn't like MacPhail and hates that the Irishman is using him as a gate attraction when he should be back in New York recuperating.

The spur was discovered a few months ago when DiMaggio complained of pain in his heel while doctors were examining Joe's left knee and ankle, which he injured last season. The operation left a five-and-a-half-inch incision that has refused to heal, and Dr. Stevens spends each day in San Juan slicing away dead skin on Joe's wound and battling a stubborn infection. At 32, DiMaggio is wondering if his career is nearing an end.

That's the question Harris and his players keep hearing before and after each of their workouts in the San Juan sun. Playing with Joe has always had its pros and cons, though his teammates—who hold DiMaggio in nothing short of awe—insist the former vastly outweigh the latter. They see DiMaggio demanding perfection from himself on every play, so they attempt to do the same, becoming better players in the process.

Joyful clubhouse chatter usually accompanies winning, but the Yankee clubhouse is serious and somber, just like the man who dominates the room while rarely saying a word. Win or lose, DiMaggio spends each postgame tucked into his locker, sipping his cup of coffee, dragging on his cigarette, slowly unwinding from the self-imposed pressure. No one celebrates unless Joe does, and that doesn't happen often.

But all this might change this season, for there is nothing somber about Yogi Berra, who within days of the team's first workout has captured the imagination and hearts of his manager, his teammates, and especially the press. While DiMaggio feels the burden of perfection, Yogi exudes the joy of playing a game. He's the kid who just can't stop smiling, and his teammates find themselves smiling, too—especially with Joe nowhere to be seen.

And it's quickly apparent that the kid can play, at least when he has a bat in his hands. Berra, 185 pounds of muscle packed onto a five-foot-eight frame, is still a work in progress behind the plate — "He fields with his bat," writes Dick Young of the *New York Daily News* — but everyone's taking notice of his booming line drives. "He is one of the hardest-hitting rookies I have ever seen," Harris tells the writers after each day's workout.

Then there's what often happens when Yogi opens his mouth. His twisted English and goofy tone give Yankee reporters their first true character to write about since the days of the Babe and his off-the-field antics. "Berra has easily made himself the standout personality in camp," writes the *New York Times'* John Drebinger, dean of the nation's baseball writers, who won't get used to calling the rookie Yogi until late in the season. "Larry exudes good cheer and enthusiasm at every turn."

As much as they all like Berra, neither his manager and teammates nor the media can resist mocking the way he looks, the way he sounds, the trouble he has putting words to his thoughts — even the comic books he reads and shares with many of his teammates. Everything is fair game: his large nose, heavy eyebrows, and dark, leathery skin; his thick neck, almost lost between his oversized shoulders; his low, guttural voice. Names like Nature Boy, Quasimodo, and the Ape are quickly finding their way into what Berra hears from teammates and reporters alike.

Yogi accepts the teasing from teammates with his wide, gap-toothed smile, figuring they wouldn't bother with him if he wasn't good enough to be worthy of their attention. And he still remembers the advice of his old minor league manager Shaky Kain: any protests would only increase the number of insults thrown his way. As for the media, well, it's not like Berra hasn't heard it all before. Besides, he tells one reporter, "I haven't seen anyone who hits with their face." It's a line every writer will repeat for years.

The fascination with Berra is interrupted just twice. The first time comes five days into this trip when DiMaggio finally leaves the hotel. He receives a police escort through the mob of fans as he walks across the street and enters the stadium. But he doesn't play. DiMaggio takes a seat next to the team's dugout, suns himself, and returns to his hotel room.

The second is far gloomier. On February 25, MacPhail announces DiMaggio will be leaving Yankee camp and flying to Johns Hopkins Hospital in Baltimore, where they'll try skin graft surgery in hopes of closing the wound in his heel—and saving the superstar's season. Joe D has missed the first game of the season four of his eight years with the Yankees, so everyone is asking Dr. Stevens the same question: will DiMaggio be ready for Opening Day in Washington, on April 14?

Stevens has no answer.

The man tasked with building the Yankee lineup without its best player does not lack experience. Bucky Harris was the "Boy Wonder" second baseman and manager who led the Washington Senators to their first and only World Series title in 1924, at the age of 27. He managed mostly middling-to-poor teams in four cities over the next 20 years. Last season he was the general manager of the International League's team in Buffalo, where he watched a chunky little catcher called Yogi manhandle his pitching staff. MacPhail brought Harris aboard as a special assistant early last September, then named him the Yankees' 10th manager two months later.

Now 50, the lean, five-foot-nine Harris still retains his boyish good looks and his friendly, easygoing demeanor. He knows the measure of any Yankee manager is Joe McCarthy, who won seven World Series titles in his 16-year run with this franchise. McCarthy put the bar high—anything less than a title is now considered a failure.

Harris has already developed an easy rapport with the beat writers, who are instrumental to any New York manager's success. In 1947, newspapers are still the dominant form of media, and a writer assigned to cover baseball is immediately one of his paper's biggest stars—especially in baseball-mad New York, home to three of the game's 16 teams.

The eight writers who flew with the Yankees to San Juan are almost all veterans with upwards of 20 years or more on the beat.

These are the men who shape the way New Yorkers think about any Yankee manager and player, even DiMaggio—now the Big Dago—who was stung when the writers turned on him during his 1938 contract dispute. There are almost eight million people living in New York City's five boroughs, and at least two million of them read the *New York Daily News* and its Yankee writer Joe Trimble. That's the man Bucky Harris is talking with at a San Juan bar the day Joe D leaves camp.

"Did you see the Ape hit that ball today?" says Harris, talking about yet another day of Berra blasting the ball all over Sixto Escobar Stadium. Harris understands ridicule is part of the game—indeed, there's at least one player on every team whose job it is to rattle opposing players. But Berra, still a few months shy of 22, is taking so much abuse Harris has quietly asked the writers to tone it down. Yet even Bucky slips into insults when Trimble asks him who's going to bat fourth if DiMaggio isn't ready by Opening Day.

"Do you think the Ape could do it?" Harris says, real excitement in his voice. "I bet he could if he didn't get scared."

Actually, Harris is thinking about more than Berra batting cleanup, though he's not ready to share his thoughts with the media. Who knows if DiMaggio will make it back or how good he'll be if and when he returns? And age hangs heavy on this roster: DiMaggio's outfielder running mates Tommy Henrich, the team's next-best player, just turned 34, and Charlie Keller, who led the team with 30 home runs and 101 RBI last season, will be 31 in September. Spud Chandler, his best pitcher, is 39.

Berra's Newark teammate Bobby Brown is also having a strong spring, and young pitchers Don Johnson and Spec Shea look like they will probably help. But it's Berra whom Harris thinks he can build around. Yogi's powerful left-handed swing is tailor-made for Yankee Stadium. And Harris is sure the fans will love this kid in a way they will never love DiMaggio. They'll see his odd-shaped body and his constant smile, and they'll pull for him when he makes a mistake and cheer for him when he smacks the winning hit.

Yes, Harris thinks, Berra has a big future ahead of him. Just not behind the plate. At least not yet.

"Stand at a slight angle when there's a right-handed hitter at the plate," Joe Medwick says. "That way you can see if the ball is going to slice toward the foul line."

Medwick is talking to Yogi Berra, the same kid who used to sell him newspapers back in St. Louis when they were both so much younger. It's the first week of March, and the Yankees are in Caracas, Venezuela for nine days before wrapping up their tour of Latin America with three days in Havana. Bucky Harris had pulled Berra aside soon after they arrived in Caracas and said he was giving Yogi a shot in right field until he learns how to play catcher on this level. And he's asked Medwick, now 35 and finishing out his Hall of Fame career, to be Berra's guide.

So Medwick, a 10-time All-Star for the Cardinals, Dodgers, and Giants, has spent the last few days teaching Berra how to get a jump on a line drive. He instructs Yogi how to play the ball off the wall and set himself before he throws, and how to quickly find the cutoff man for relays back to the infield. He even shows him the right way to flip down his sunglasses without losing track of the ball.

The early results are encouraging. Berra hits a home run in his first game as a right fielder against a local team, then hits three doubles and just misses making a spectacular diving catch in the first of a three-game set against the Brooklyn Dodgers, who were training in Cuba and also touring Latin America. Berra's route to a fly ball is often circuitous, but he is fast enough to make up for it and his arm's strong enough to keep opposing runners honest.

Harris uses Berra behind the plate in batting practice but grows more comfortable with the idea of Yogi playing right field as the Yankees finish up their Latin American tour and fly to spring training camp in St. Petersburg, Florida on March 11. It's the same day DiMaggio has a skin graft, and with catchers Aaron Robinson and rookie Ralph Houk performing well, Harris keeps playing Berra in the outfield.

Best of all: Berra continues to hit. By the time the Yankees are ready to break camp and board their train for the trip north, Berra has hit safely in 14 straight games. "The amazing Yogi continues to astound his skipper more and more with each succeeding day," the *New York Times*' Drebinger writes after Berra has yet another big day. "Blasting him out of that Yankee outfield is going to be no simple task, even after DiMaggio returns to center." The new Yankee manager, Drebinger says, "takes a deep and pardonable pride in the chunky little Yogi who, under the cover of a series of night games in Caracas, was converted from a catcher into a surprisingly fine right fielder."

Not everything written and said about Yogi is positive. Five other teams have their camps in the St. Pete area, and opposing players all take turns taunting Berra. During one game with the Cardinals, outfielder Enos Slaughter—a player Yogi rooted for as a teenager—tells him his face looks like he's been hit with the back of a shovel.

"You're the only player who looks better with his mask on," cracks Slaughter.

That line makes its way to every camp. So does the habit of throwing a banana on the field when Yogi walks up to the plate. As rookie initiations go, Berra sees his will be a tough one.

Yogi lets the insults bounce off him—all but one. It was delivered in the form of a question by Rud Rennie of the *New York Herald Tribune.* "You're not really thinking about keeping him, are you?" Rennie asks Harris. "He doesn't even *look* like a Yankee."

That one stung, but Berra is soothed when Harris tells a group of writers the Yankees are indeed going to keep Yogi. And then Harris goes one step further.

"I'll make a prediction about Yogi," Harris says. "I say within a few years he will be the most popular player on the Yankees since Babe Ruth. I know that Henrich and Rizzuto and DiMaggio have a lot of fans that admire them. They are great ballplayers. But I mean more than that. He's funny to look at and sometimes he makes ridiculous plays. But he has personality and color. That's crowd appeal and it makes people pay their way into the ballpark to see him.

"And don't think he's a dope. Try to remember that he hasn't had much schooling and it is a disadvantage in conversation.

"Just don't sell him short when he is up there at the plate. He's going to kill a few people with that bat and they won't think he's funny at all."

Berra does little to prove Harris wrong in the team's two stops on their way to New York. Yogi blasts a pair of home runs, a double, and two singles, and drives in five runs as the Yankees demolish the minor league Atlanta Crackers of the Southern Association on April 6. A day later, Yogi drives in six runs with a home run, double, and single against his old Norfolk Tars. The home run flew over a high wall, 450 feet away in dead center field. Everyone in the park stood and applauded, save for the Yankees, who have been reacting to Yogi's increasing production with timeworn rookie hazing: sitting in the dugout and giving him the silent treatment.

It's obvious to all they'll have plenty of time to talk to this Berra kid this season.

# CHAPTER 9

# The First Ring
## 1947

The first two weeks of Yogi Berra's life as a full-fledged Yankee in New York are a blur. He quickly finds himself a room at the Hotel Edison on West 47th Street, where many of the younger Yankees stay. It's just $4.50 a night. The added bonus: it's only blocks from more than a dozen movie houses. That's about all the entertainment Yogi can afford since he's sending a good chunk of his $5,000 salary—the major league minimum—back home to Mom.

Berra settles in just in time for the final three exhibition games against the Dodgers—two at Yankee Stadium and one at Brooklyn's Ebbets Field. It's going to take a while getting used to walking into the history-drenched clubhouse in the Bronx, sitting down just a few lockers away from Joe DiMaggio, pulling on a pinstriped jersey with the number 35 on its back. It's also going to take some time to learn New York's subway system, which is why the Yankee PR staff hands out maps to all new-comers in need of directions to Brooklyn for the final exhibition game.

The ribbing from his teammates hasn't stopped when the team arrives in New York, but the writers wonder why the veterans are teasing Yogi about problems getting to Ebbets Field. After all, they saw Berra arrive at the Dodgers' home field in plenty of time. "Oh, I got here on time, all right," he tells them. "I knew I was going to take the wrong train, so I left an hour early."

Everyone has a good laugh when they hear his explanation, and Yogi knows the story is sure to make the rounds. He's discovered playing for the Yankees means just about every comical thing he says and does—and many things that are just made up about him—will appear in newspapers all around the country. But so will everything he does right, including the big home run he hits today over the screen in right field and clear out of Ebbets Field.

Everything about the Yankees seems to make headlines, even their decision to start the rookie Berra in right field. The *Sporting News,* the bible of baseball for decades, celebrates Bucky Harris' decision by running a political-style cartoon of Yogi on the cover of its April 9 edition.

"The newest tenant of Ruthville will be Yogi Berra," the caption reads.

Berra can hardly believe it. The *Sporting News*—published in his hometown of St. Louis—just put his name in the same sentence as Babe Ruth. Not a bad way to start your rookie year.

Berra's first major league season is set to open in Washington on April 14, with President Truman throwing out the first pitch. Rain washes away the game, but Joe DiMaggio is the big news, rejoining the team and announcing he'll be back in the lineup within 10 days. Yogi is in right field and batting fifth for the home opener a day later, when former President Herbert Hoover tosses out the first pitch. Yogi's sacrifice fly drives in the team's only run in a 6–1 loss.

The team is back in Washington on April 18, and this time Senator pitcher Ray Scarborough is waiting for Berra. In the middle of batting practice, Scarborough hangs from the top of his team's dugout with one hand, scratches his armpit like a monkey with the other hand, and loudly asks Yogi how he likes sleeping in a tree. Berra laughs and knows instantly he'll see that stunt repeated in every opponent's ballpark, too. He replies the best way he knows how, rapping out four singles and knocking in a run in a 7–0 Yankee win.

But the major story again is DiMaggio, who says he's ready to play. He pinch-hits against the Senators in Washington on April 19, and Harris pencils Joe into his familiar spots—batting cleanup and playing center field—in the first game of the next day's doubleheader in Philadelphia. DiMaggio sits down with Yogi and tells the rookie how things work in his outfield: If Yogi calls for the ball, it's all his. If not, stay out of the way and Joe will get it. Fly balls don't fall in Joe DiMaggio's outfield—that's what he's always told Yankee pitchers, who've never had any reason to doubt their graceful center fielder's word.

DiMaggio's directions stay with Yogi less than two innings. With two outs and a runner on first in the bottom of the 2nd, A's shortstop Eddie Joost lifts a ball into right-center. It's not clear who calls for the ball, but Joe makes the catch just moments before Berra runs him over, knocking a startled DiMaggio right on his ass. Harris and the entire Yankee team hold their breath until they see Joe get up and jog back to the dugout, the third out safely in his glove.

DiMaggio doesn't say a word. Bobby Brown and George McQuinn open the 3rd with singles, and Joe walks into the batter's box and takes his familiar legs-spread-wide stance. Two pitches later, DiMaggio swings and sends the ball soaring into the upper deck in left field for a three-run homer. Suddenly, all is right with the Yankees, who go on to win, 6–2. Yogi goes hitless but bounces back with a single and double in New York's 3–2 win to sweep the doubleheader.

Berra is just outside the circle of reporters crowding around DiMaggio after the doubleheader, but close enough to hear Joe explain their outfield collision. "I called for the ball, all right," Joe says, "but Yogi was too anxious to help me. He knows all about that bad heel of mine, and he figured he was doing something to save me. He thought I was telling him to make the play. And he did try to pull away at the last minute."

Like everyone, Yogi's heard DiMaggio can be one mean SOB, so he's relieved to hear Joe covering for his mistake. And Berra's even more relieved the next day to see his name on the lineup card on the clubhouse wall. Even a rookie knows crashing into Yankee legends is a good way to lose your job.

Yankee Stadium is something to see when every one of the seats in the lower bowl of the horseshoe is filled, every bench in the bleachers is full, and every seat right back to the last row of the third deck is taken. On April 27, 1947, Berra sees each of the 58,339 fans who've filled the Stadium rise when team officials help Babe Ruth walk up the three steps of the home-team dugout and onto the field. After 14 years of ignoring Ruth, now in the final stages of throat cancer, baseball has declared today National Babe Ruth Day. The audio for the ceremony is being broadcast to every major league park's public address system and every minor league park with the proper equipment. It's even going out to radio stations in Japan and Europe.

Yogi was in the Yankee clubhouse just an hour earlier, watching DiMaggio, Harris, and coach Frank Crosetti hover around the Babe, each of them getting his autograph. Crosetti played three seasons with Ruth, and was in the Yankee dugout when the Babe called his famous home run against the Cubs in New York's four-game sweep of the 1932 World Series.

Berra listens to Francis Cardinal Spellman finish his invocation and watches the Babe walk up to the bank of microphones and address the fans. Ruth's wearing his trademark camel-hair polo coat, and when he takes off the matching camel-hair hat Yogi can see just how gaunt and ghostly the great man looks. He's 52, but three months after his most recent throat surgery he looks more like 80. Still, as the huge crowd's roar welcomes him, Yogi notices Ruth square his shoulders and stand a bit straighter, strengthened by the overwhelming reception.

"Thank you very much, ladies and gentlemen," the raspy-voiced Ruth says. "You know how bad my voice sounds... well, it feels just as bad."

Yogi feels himself fighting back tears, and sees many of his teammates struggling to do the same. The man they're watching grew up in a Baltimore orphanage, then became the larger-than-life performer who rescued the game when a gambling scandal threatened to shut it down. It's nearly impossible not to love the Babe, faults and all.

"The only real game in the world, I think, is baseball," says Ruth, and now Berra is straining to hear as the Babe's hoarse voice grows fainter. "You gotta let it grow up with you, and if you're successful and you try hard enough, you're bound to come out on top.

"There's been a lot of nice things said about me. I am glad I had the opportunity to thank everybody. Thank you."

Ruth waves to the crowd, then staggers a bit when he turns to walk away. Berra and a few of the younger Yankees move to help. "Leave him alone: he knows where the dugout is," comes a voice, low but firm. Yogi doesn't see who spoke, but no one dares to move. The Babe reaches the place near the dugout where Yogi and the Yankees are standing alongside Cardinal Spellman, Commissioner Happy Chandler, and both league presidents. Spellman walks over to the slow-moving Ruth.

"Babe, anytime you want me to come to your house I'll be glad to give you Communion," says Spellman. "No," Ruth tells him. "Thanks just the same. I'll come to your place."

The game with Washington is scoreless until the 8th, when the Senators finally push across a run and take a 1–0 lead. Yogi pinch-hits and pops out to second to end the inning, but Ruth isn't there to see any of it. Tired by the day's events, he left with his wife and daughter before the inning began. Like every Yankee, Berra could see the Babe's days were numbered and wished they could have won this game for him instead of losing, 1–0. Nearly 16 months later, Ruth would be dead, his body lying for two days inside the main gate of Yankee Stadium so baseball fans could pay their final respects.

The Yankees board a train at the end of April for a 15-day, four-city road trip, and Yogi is eager to reach their first stop: St. Louis. But he's also fallen in love with the time the players spend together on the train—36 hours from New York to St. Louis, the game's western-most city—for he's already learning more about baseball on these train trips than he's ever learned in any clubhouse, dugout, or playing field. Sure, he enjoys playing cards on these trips, too—Berra's ability to remember cards makes him tough to beat at gin rummy—but he loves the stories he hears and the knowledge he's soaking up even more.

Like all major league teams, the Yankees have the last three cars on the train—a meal car that also serves as a buffer from the other travelers, then two sleeper cars. Surprisingly, the sleeping quarters of the intensely private DiMaggio is where they all meet, and no one is turned away. It's here the players share what they've learned about opposing hitters and pitchers. And how to play the angles in each stadium, what infield is fast because they cut the grass low, which ones are slow because they constantly wet down the dirt. Which umpires call the outside strike, which ones call anything up in the strike zone a ball.

Yogi hated just about every minute he ever spent in a classroom, but he wouldn't miss these lessons for the world.

He's learned something else, too: where the traveling secretary tells you to sleep translates to your status on the roster. DiMaggio always has the berth in the middle of the car—it's the quietest and smoothest ride on the train. The best players and the next day's starting pitcher have berths on either side of Joe. The farther away from the center of the train, the shakier your status on the team. If the traveling secretary gives you the berth over the wheels—literally the shakiest place on the train—it's entirely possible you'll be demoted to the minors by the time the train makes its next stop.

Yogi makes the rounds on The Hill once the team reaches St. Louis. Everyone wants to know more about DiMaggio. Did Lawdie really bowl over Joe D? What was it like to meet the Babe? Is Bucky Harris ever going to put him behind the plate?

A reporter from the *St. Louis Star-Times* is tagging along with the hometown hero, asking many of the same questions. "I didn't think I was even going to make the team," says Yogi, turning away from another friend he hasn't seen in months to answer the reporter. "It's sure good to be with the Yankees—it's wonderful!"

The reporter asks a few more questions, then ends with this: "How will the American League season turn out?"

"We're going to win the pennant," Berra answers matter-of-factly, as if the outcome is just a question of time.

Berra gets box seats for his parents, his kid sister, and his three older brothers, who watch him go hitless in four at-bats as the lowly Browns drub the Yankees, 15–5. It's part of a slow start for a team that finds itself 8–8 on May 10, when Harris finally gives Berra his first start as catcher. Yogi's struggling at the plate, hitting just .214—he's had but three hits in 22 at-bats since running into DiMaggio—and hasn't driven in a single run. Maybe a change of position will improve his luck.

And Berra's bat comes alive from his first at-bat as the team's catcher, rifling a single up the middle that drives in two runs. He finishes with three hits and four RBI to help his roommate Spec Shea to a 9–6 win. Berra hits his first home run on May 12—his 22nd birthday—and is hitting .290 in his last 11 games when he belts a two-run double off Cleveland ace Bob Feller on the last day of May, giving the Yankees a 4–3 lead in the 4th inning. Yogi's roll ends three innings later when a foul tip off the bat of Cleveland's George Metkovich slams into his right hand, leaving a deep gash that requires three stitches to close and two weeks to heal.

Yankee pitchers appreciate Berra's increased run production after he moved behind the plate, but they're telling Harris that Yogi still has too many shortcomings as a catcher. He can't block pitches in the dirt, he's clueless about what pitches to call, and no one ever knows where the ball is going when he tries to throw out a runner attempting a steal. Yogi knows the pitchers are right—his catching skills are crude, at best—and isn't sure where he'll play when his right hand heals.

The Yankees have moved into first place by the time Berra returns to the lineup on June 15. And he's a bit surprised when Harris starts him behind the plate in the second game of a doubleheader against the Browns. But he quickly repays his manager's faith in him when St. Louis, trailing 2–1, tries a suicide squeeze in the 9th inning. Berra sees the Browns' Jeff Heath break from third just as Yankee pitcher Randy Gumpert releases his first pitch to Johnny Berardino, who drops a bunt right in front of the plate. Berra leaps out from behind the plate, grabs the ball, tags out Berardino, then shoves him out of the way and drops his glove and the ball on the sliding Heath to complete the double play.

Yogi turns around and tags umpire Eddie Rommel for good measure. It's only the 14th unassisted double play by a catcher in baseball history.

The pitchers love Yogi's enthusiasm and warmth—everybody on the team adores this kid—but they continue to bitch to Harris about Berra's catching in the weeks that follow. The Yankee manager has the chance to send Yogi back to the outfield when left fielder Charlie Keller, troubled by a ruptured disk in his back since early June, goes down for the season on June 23. But Harris inserts speedy Johnny Lindell alongside DiMaggio and Tommy Henrich to form what might be the best fielding unit in the league. With Yogi still swinging a hot bat, Harris keeps Berra behind the plate and keeps peace with his pitchers by telling coach Charlie Dressen to call pitches from the bench when the young catcher gets into a jam.

No one realizes it just yet, but Harris has put together a combination that will make history. The Yankees win 28 of their next 31 games after Berra's return, including the last 19 straight—tying the AL record that will stand another 55 years—and the pennant race is all but over by mid-July. Management commemorates the 19-game winning streak with gold watches for every player. Berra (four homers, 12 RBI, a .310 batting average), Henrich (6-29-.323), and DiMaggio (5-24-.339) drive the offense over the 31-game stretch. Allie Reynolds establishes himself as the No. 1 starter with five wins, Shea is 11–2 at the All-Star break, and Joe Page turns into the best relief pitcher in baseball.

The Yankees hold a commanding 11½-game lead over second-place Detroit on July 17, and what worries Berra most now is the speech he has to make when The Hill honors him before a game in St. Louis late next month. Yogi asks Bobby Brown to write something for him, but his friend declines.

"If I write it, you'll forget it," says Brown, who tells Berra to keep it short and simple. "One or two sentences to say thank you," he tells Yogi. "That's all you need."

Yogi continues to play well, and he's practicing his one big line—"I want to thank everyone who made this night possible"—every day when he feels his throat begin to ache in late August. Really ache. The team is in Cleveland on August 23 when Yogi starts to run a fever, too, and he's sent to Cleveland's Lutheran Hospital to see a throat specialist.

He's only slightly better two days later when the doctors tell him he can travel to St. Louis for his big night under one condition: he leaves right after the ceremony and checks into a St. Louis hospital for further treatment.

While their favorite son struggles to regain his health, a committee of businessmen from The Hill raises enough money to buy a new car and golf clubs for the kid they still call Lawdie, a gold wristwatch for his father, and an armful of American Beauty roses for his mother. The Fawns Athletic Club has a diamond ring to give Yogi, too. All gifts are purchased from merchants on The Hill, just as they were on the night they honored Joe Garagiola a year ago.

At 7:15 p.m. on August 26, hundreds of The Hill's residents gather at St. Ambrose Church, where they pile into cars bearing signs celebrating Berra and start the five-mile drive to Sportsman's Park. The ceremony begins with Alderman Louis Berra—no relation; there are lots of Berras on The Hill—praising Lawdie and presenting each of the gifts. And then the moment Yogi has been dreading finally arrives.

Brown nods encouragingly as Yogi, all nerves and an achy throat, steps up to the microphone. "I want to thank the Stockham American Legion Post and the fans and everyone for coming out," Yogi says, "and making this night necessary."

Brown can't hold back his laughter, nor can his friend standing beside him—Browns outfielder Jeff Heath—who damn near falls over he's laughing so hard. Pretty soon everyone is laughing, even Yogi, who walks over to the box seats near the Browns dugout to take pictures with his family. As soon as that's done, he's on his way to the hospital.

It will be another four weeks before Berra gets over the infection in his throat and returns to the Yankee lineup.

His botched line?

That will last forever.

The Yankees clinch the pennant on September 14, doing it for the first time before a television audience. Some in management worried that televising every home game—along with 11 road games—would hurt attendance, and it's true that tavern owners, among the first to buy TVs, draw plenty of customers to watch baseball games on this new technological toy. But the Yankees will draw more than two million fans for the second straight season. If anything, TV is turning even more Americans into baseball fans. And the Yankees are the game's top draw.

Yogi is finally back in the lineup the next day and spends his last 10 games of the season unsuccessfully trying to regain his batting eye—he hits only .212 without a home run. Harris just wants him in shape to face the Dodgers, who won 94 games and the NL pennant with a team built around the speed of Jackie Robinson, Pee Wee Reese, and Pete Reiser, and a young pitching staff anchored by 21-game winner Ralph Branca.

Harris announces he's starting Berra and Shea—the first rookie battery in World Series history in the first televised postseason in history. Reporters ask if he thinks Yogi will be nervous facing the speedy

Dodgers. "Yogi? No way," Bucky says. "He has the emotions of a fire hydrant."

This is one comment that hurts Berra. "Of course I'm nervous—this is the World Series; everyone gets butterflies!" he tells the writers. "I'm human, ain't I?" Truth is, he's scared to death that his throwing problems will be exposed on the big stage.

Reporters badger Berra about his matchup with Robinson, who led the National League with 29 stolen bases—without being caught once—to go with his .297 batting average and the countless insults and opponent-inflicted injuries. Yogi can relate, but this is the World Series, and all anyone wants to talk about is baseball.

"That Robinson is plenty fast," Yogi says, "but he also gets an advantage of having three left-handers following him" who block the catcher's view. "You can never see him."

Robinson has a ready reply. "If I had an arm like his," Jackie says, "I wouldn't talk about it."

The Yankees win the first two games at the Stadium, but Robinson and Reese both swipe bases easily, and reporters joke this could be the first World Series won without a catcher. Harris benches Yogi for Game 3 in Ebbets Field, though Berra hits the first pinch-hit homer in World Series history, a solo blast off Branca in the 7th inning that isn't enough to prevent a 9–8 loss.

Harris comes back with Berra for Game 4 to catch Bill Bevens, who has struggled with his control all season—averaging 4.2 walks per nine innings—and finished 7–13, the only losing record on the Yankee staff. Bevens is wild again against Brooklyn, but he's also unhittable and carries a no-hitter and a 2–1 lead—with eight walks—into the 9th inning. Three more outs and Bevens will have the first no-hitter in World Series history, and the Yankees will own a commanding 3–1 Series lead.

Berra can feel the sweat soaking his uniform as he walks onto the field for the bottom of the final inning. It feels like he can hear every one of the 33,443 Dodger fans screaming for a base hit. Bevens gets the first out on a fly ball to left, then walks the next batter. When Spider Jorgensen, the Dodgers' No. 8 hitter, fouls out, Bevens is one out from history.

Dodger manager Burt Shotton makes two moves that change the game. First he sends Al Gionfriddo to pinch-run. Then he tells Pete Reiser, a tough hitter on the bench with a sore ankle, to pinch-hit for pitcher Hugh Casey. Bevens' first pitch is a strike. Gionfriddo is off on the next pitch, which comes in low, and Berra's throw to second is high. Gionfriddo slides in safely, a play that will haunt Berra the rest of his career. Sure, Gionfriddo got a great jump—something Harris will stress all offseason—but a better throw and this game makes history.

Harris surprises Berra—and everyone—by intentionally walking Reiser, putting the winning run on first. Shotton sends up another pinch-hitter, veteran Cookie Lavagetto, who had all of 69 at-bats in what will be his final season, and only two at-bats in the first three games of the Series.

Bevens throws a strike, and the roar of the crowd grows even louder. His next pitch is a fastball up and away that would have been—should have been—ball one. But Lavagetto reaches out and slaps the pitch to deep right field. The ball crashes off the wall, both runners score, and just like that the Dodgers are celebrating a 3–2 win. Bevens' shot at history is gone, and so is his team's lead in the Series, which is now tied 2–2.

Berra and Bevens sit stunned in a quiet Yankee clubhouse, both fighting back tears. Bevens, his arm aching after throwing more than 140 pitches, numbly mumbles answers to the media's questions. All Berra can think about is his failure to throw out Gionfriddo for what would have been the game's final out.

Yogi, his confidence weakened, watches Game 5 from the bench as Shea dazzles the Dodgers in a 2–1 Yankee win. And he's on the bench in Game 6, too, until he replaces outfielder Johnny Lindell, who cracks a rib in the 3rd inning of what becomes an 8–6 Yankee loss.

Harris puts Berra in right field and bats the rookie third in the decisive Game 7 before 71,548 fans at Yankee Stadium, and Yogi is plenty nervous. He's human, ain't he? The Dodgers grab an early 2–0 lead, but the Yankees are up 3–2 in the 5th when Harris hands the ball to reliever Joe Page to rescue an exhausted pitching staff. Page responds brilliantly, retiring 13 straight Dodgers before allowing a one-out single in the 9th. No matter. Page gets the next hitter to rap into an inning-ending double play to close out a 5–2 victory, and the Yankees have their 11th World Series title, the most in baseball history.

Yogi collected only three hits in six games, but he's thrilled to finish his rookie season with a World Series title. Some men play an entire career and never come close to winning one. Berra and his teammates have only just begun their boisterous clubhouse celebration when Larry MacPhail bursts in and makes more news. He is selling his stake in the team to Dan Topping and Del Webb — which he'd already discussed with his fellow owners — and resigning as President. The second part was news to his partners, who quickly agreed to release MacPhail from his contract.

"This is it," says MacPhail, who leaves as abruptly as he'd entered.

Many of the veterans who have battled MacPhail for the last two years — especially DiMaggio — now have even more to celebrate. For Berra, the news is just part of the immense swirl of emotions at the end of an incredible rookie season. Harris was right — the fans fell in love with Yogi right from the start, forgiving his mistakes while cheering his home runs and hustle.

The writers never stopped writing about him, either, though much of what they wrote he could have done without. All part of playing in the big leagues, Berra figures, and what can be better than getting paid to play baseball? He proved he could perform on this level — hitting .280 with 11 home runs and 54 RBI in just 293 at-bats. Just imagine what he'd have done if he hadn't missed more than six weeks with injury and illness.

Yes, he has to become a better catcher — or outfielder — but he's a

Yankee, he's won a World Series title, and when he gets home, he'll have a $5,830 World Series check—$330 more than his entire season's salary—to show Mom and Pop.

Life can't get much better than this, Yogi thinks as he gets ready to head back to St. Louis.

Oh, but it can.

# CHAPTER 10

# The Girl Who Has It All
## 1947–1948

Julius "Biggie" Garagnani and Yogi Berra have just pulled up to the restaurant on Chippewa Street that bears the nickname of Yogi's new friend. Biggie's Steak House is about four miles and a world away from where Berra grew up on The Hill. This is where the St. Louis elites and wealthy visitors, often decked out in tuxedos and flowing gowns, come to dine before and after a night on the town. Most of the folks on The Hill come to Biggie's to wait on tables, not to eat the filet mignon with mushrooms—the famous restaurant's signature dish—or anything else on the menu that would cost most of them half a week's pay.

Not many on The Hill play golf, either. In the fall of 1947, that, too, is still very much a rich man's game. But Yogi and Biggie have just left the Sunset Country Club, where they played a round of golf with Henry Ruggeri—owner of the city's other nationally known restaurant—and Stan Musial, the 26-year-old Cardinal All-Star outfielder. Yogi's never played golf before, but he's shot a round almost every day since returning home a week or so ago, making good use of the set of left-handed clubs he received on Yogi Berra Night last August.

Yes, life has changed, Yogi can't help but think as he follows Garagnani under the green awning and through the doors of Biggie's.

He's a star now, the Yankee who batted third in the seventh and deciding game of the World Series, the place in the batting order reserved for one of the very best hitters on the team. Sure, he made a few mistakes against the Dodgers, and the writers continue to portray him as a caricature instead of a person. But he just banked a World Series check that doubled his salary, and he has every reason to expect a good raise when the Yankees send out his contract in January. Joey Garagiola says they could probably get jobs at Sears, Roebuck again, but it's been a long season, and Yogi's making more money than he ever dreamed, so mastering this game of golf and hanging out with his friends — old and new — sounds like a much better plan.

Either way, it's great to be home, sleeping in his own bed, eating his mom's terrific cooking. He's the only one of the four Berra boys still living at home, and it's nice to be doted on, too. Paulina can't help herself, and with Momma imploring him, *"Mangia! Mangia!"* — Eat! Eat! — it's going to be tough keeping his weight down. The Yankees mailed out a diet, asking Yogi to stay off fried foods and heavy sauces, but whoever drew up that menu never spent any time on The Hill, where fried mozzarella is just the start of a meal full of pastas — including toasted ravioli, Yogi's favorite — with plenty of meat in a thick red sauce. And a full loaf of bread with every meal.

The Yankees are also talking to Yogi about how to avoid losing weeks at a time with strep throat. The team doctor told the *Sporting News* that Berra's throat infection was due to Yogi's habit of sleeping in the raw. "I just don't like pajamas," Yogi tells *TSN* — but Berra thinks the doc's diagnosis is ridiculous. It turns out Yogi's right — a St. Louis doctor tells him the problem is his tonsils. Remove them, the doctor says, and the throat infections will disappear.

Yogi doesn't mind going under the knife — especially if it means he'll be healthy the entire season — he just doesn't want to pay for it. Once Weiss grudgingly agrees to foot Berra's bill, doctors make a date to remove Yogi's tonsils in early November. Until then, he'll play golf with his new friends and hang out with the old gang, playing gin rummy and poker, drinking beer at Charley's during the day and The Nod at night.

And it's great to be back with Garagiola. The two friends try to play handball as often as they can at St. Louis University. Joe's also got a deal for them to sell Christmas trees, an easy gig for two famous athletes, just to get some extra pocket change.

Joey can still talk with the best of them and is in demand as a speaker despite struggling through much of his second season. Garagiola did not build on his sparkling World Series performance of 1946. He fell to second string, hitting .257 with five home runs and 25 RBI in just 77 games. Garagiola always insisted Yogi was the far better player of the two friends; turns out he was right.

Yogi is also getting banquet invitations but almost always takes a pass. One he can't turn down is from the American Legion—would he even be in the major leagues if Leo Browne hadn't given him the chance to play Legion ball?—and quickly agrees to attend the annual Stockham Post 245 awards banquet. He goes to a few others, but always makes sure whoever is running the show understands he doesn't give speeches. For Yogi, it's a Q&A format or nothing— which remains true the rest of his life.

All this is new to Yogi, and every so often one of the guys from the neighborhood teases him about "going uptown," especially when he complains about having to go to another banquet. But there's little question he's become a celebrity and is living a celebrity's life. He knows he'll never be able to repay Father Koester, Joe Causino, Leo Browne, and his brothers for convincing Pop to give him the chance to realize his dream. Without them, he wouldn't be sitting in a booth sharing a beer with Biggie Garagnani—successful restaurateur, friend to local stars, and a player in the city's Democratic Party—and getting pointers on his nascent golf game.

And that's what Biggie is talking about when Berra abruptly changes the subject. "Who's that?" asks Yogi, who just noticed a beautiful waitress in the main dining room and is finding it hard not to stare.

"That's Carmen Short," Biggie says. "She's got a younger sister Bonnie who works here, too. Great girls."

"You mean you have another one who looks like that?" says Yogi, who is clearly spellbound. He hasn't made much time for women since he started playing pro ball, but there's something about this girl. He can't take his eyes off her while he nurses his beer and talks to Biggie and his partner Charlie Re about golf, the Yankees, life on The Hill—anything to stretch out time so he can keep his eyes on Carmen Short. An hour or so goes by until Yogi finally goes home for dinner, but he can't stop thinking about that waitress.

And the very next day he walks back into Biggie's determined to meet the woman who will change his life.

The young woman who's already captured Yogi's heart is a farm girl from Howes Mill—a hamlet about 120 miles from St. Louis—who couldn't wait to move to the big city. Smart and ambitious, she graduated from her small-town school two years early, took every babysitting job in St. Louis she could find, and made it perfectly clear that farm life was not for her. As headstrong as she is beautiful, Carmen— born four months after Yogi in 1925—moved to St. Louis as a nanny in 1939 and never returned home.

Her parents Ernest and Barbara have a limited education but understand how to live off the land. Ernest is a master carpenter who built his own house on his 300-acre farm in the foothills of the Ozark Mountains. They won't have electricity, running water—rainwater off the roof was collected in a cistern, then pumped by hand for drinking and cooking—or a telephone until well into the 1950s. Ernest, five foot eight, 165 pounds, with powerful arms and hands, raised cows and hogs for market during the Depression, grew grain to feed the livestock and fruit and vegetables to feed his wife and six children. Almost all the meat on their table consists of the squirrels, rabbits, and deer Ernest shot or trapped. When he slaughtered the occasional hog, it was smoked and salted away to last several months.

Barbara, whose grandmother was a Cherokee, is as good with a fishing pole as she is with a sewing machine. She put fish on the table and ran her own business as a seamstress while caring for her growing family. Neither Barbara nor her husband was very religious, but they loved to read the Bible along with *Reader's Digest,* other magazines, and newspapers. They got their news listening to WMOX, the region's biggest broadcaster, on their battery-powered radio. Ernest enjoyed boxing, but any other sport was foreign to him.

It isn't an easy life, but the Shorts never wanted for food, shelter, or clothes, even during the worst of the Depression, when a good year meant having a few extra dollars at Christmastime.

Carmen dreamed of seeing the world—one that didn't include feeding the pigs and chickens before breakfast. She took a job as a receptionist and clerk at the Midwest Pipe Company in 1942, just as everyone was pitching in for the war effort. That included her parents, who sold their farm in late 1944 and moved to St. Louis, where Ernest worked as a carpenter, building the wooden racks that secured the machines of war in ships crossing the Atlantic for delivery to their allies in Europe.

The Shorts moved back to another farm in Howes Mill after the war ended in late 1945. A year later, 17-year-old Bonnie, four years Carmen's junior and almost her twin, joined her sister in St. Louis. The two young women enjoyed the city's thriving nightlife, and before long Carmen, tiring of office work, decided to take a job as a dance instructor—and occasional performer—at one of the town's growing number of dance studios. And that is when fate stepped in.

"If you really want to make some good money," an instructor named Jean told her, "you should think about getting a job as a waitress at Biggie's Steak House. I just started there and the tips are great— a $20 tip is not unusual. I think they're hiring, too."

It wasn't long before both Carmen and Bonnie were working for Biggie, who knows talent when he sees it. Both women are sharp, composed, and beautiful. They're even good at penmanship. That comes in handy when Biggie needs his staff to address invitations for a few special nights at Sportsman's Park honoring two local young men who play Garagnani's favorite sport.

"There's a baseball player over there talking to Biggie at the bar who'd like to make your acquaintance," Charlie Re tells Carmen Short.

Short doesn't know much about baseball. The only player she's even heard of is Terry Moore, and there's only one thing she knows about the Cardinal star center fielder—he has a wife.

"Isn't he married?" she asks, annoyance clear in her tone. "I don't date married men."

Re has to stifle a laugh. "Married? No, Yogi isn't married. Come talk to him."

Short walks over to Berra, who can hear his heart beating as she approaches, and the connection is almost immediate. Short has been dating lots of college boys—hunks, as her sister Bonnie keeps calling them—but there is something endearing about this bashful young man. And when Yogi summons the courage to ask her if she'd like to catch a movie when she gets off work, Carmen agrees.

Neither will ever remember the movie they saw that night, but they do remember holding hands. "He's adorable," Carmen tells her sister that night, and one date turns into another—a night watching the city's minor league hockey team—and then another. Suddenly golf and playing cards don't seem all that important to Berra.

Yogi introduces Carmen to Garagiola, who's just started dating Audrie Ross, the organist at a local skating rink, and the four begin to double-date. Yogi keeps pushing for sporting events and movies. Carmen convinces him to go to burlesque shows but can't get him on a dance floor. That adventure will have to wait.

Carmen gets a crash course in baseball. Her favorite story? Yogi's 23 RBI in two games back in Norfolk. And the World Series, of course. Carmen Short is nothing if not practical, and like many women in the late 1940s, any man she dates must be a good provider. She might not have known much about baseball before she met Yogi, but she's learned enough to understand that this man she's finding more interesting—and sexy—with every date could be a great catch.

And then he stands her up. Teased by his friends that his girl is making all the rules, and a bit nervous they're getting too serious too fast, Yogi doesn't show up for a dinner date with friends. Carmen is furious and all but writes him off. First Christmas and then New

Year's pass without a reconciliation, and that's when Biggie gets involved. "How mad are you at Yogi?" he asks Carmen. Plenty mad, she tells him, but Biggie can sense she misses Yogi, too.

Next he meets Yogi downtown. "Why aren't you coming to my place anymore?" Biggie asks.

"Aw, Carmen is mad at me," says Yogi, admitting he was at fault. "She doesn't want to see me."

Biggie assures Yogi that Carmen isn't all that mad anymore. Eager to patch things up, Yogi goes to the restaurant and apologizes. Carmen quickly accepts and the romance is back on track. Just in time, too, because Berra's life is about to change. He recently received his contract from the Yankees and will soon accept the offer of $9,000—a nice $4,000 raise, the first hint that Yogi might be the team's starting catcher. Finishing 15th in MVP voting couldn't have hurt, either.

The second hint is a big one. On February 25, the team sends veteran catcher Aaron Robinson and two minor league pitchers to the Chicago White Sox for crafty 16-game winner Eddie Lopat. Several minor leaguer catchers will report to camp in five days, but no one carries Yogi's bat or his new contract. The catching job is there for Yogi's taking. And so is uniform No. 8, which he'll get when he reports to camp March 1.

Yogi and Carmen are counting down the days until he leaves for camp when, in a hurry to make the opening face-off of a hockey game, Berra backs his car into a fire hydrant, then speeds off before noticing the geyser of water spraying into the air. He's at his seat with Carmen, Bonnie, and her date when his name is called over the PA system.

"Will Yogi Berra please report to the front office," he hears, and when he arrives there are two policemen waiting for him. Seems a passerby saw him hit the hydrant. Yogi's taken in, charged with careless driving, destruction of city property, and leaving the scene of an accident. He's released on $500 bond.

But Yogi has more than a traffic accident on his mind as he gets ready to leave for spring training. He suggests to Carmen that they get engaged, then make it official when he returns to St. Louis during the season. Carmen is flattered, but demurs. She thinks they should "go steady"—she's already stopped seeing the college boys she was dating—and reevaluate when the Yankees travel to St. Louis the third week of May. Yogi, a bit crestfallen, agrees to wait. Then they promise to write to each other each and every day.

Yankee veterans report to St. Petersburg on March 1 and manager Bucky Harris quickly puts Berra on a diet to work off the extra 8–10 pounds he carries into camp. Harris also goes to bat for Berra, telling reporters the Dodgers exploited an undetected flaw in Bill Bevens' delivery that led to the stolen base so central to the lost no-hitter in last year's World Series. It's all part of building up Berra's confidence so he can perform behind the plate.

"The strain of a first-year catcher working in a World Series is terrific," Bucky tells reporters as spring training gets under way. "To make matters worse, the laxity of our pitcher in holding runners just about sank him. That laxity is going to be corrected this spring."

Harris has Berra behind the plate when the exhibition games start, and on March 11 Berra throws out two Cardinals, prompting reporters to write, "The 1948 model is no longer tossing them as did the Yogi of last October." Six days later, Harris makes it official: Berra is the Yankees' starting catcher. "I figure that Berra can handle the job," says Harris, who knows his pitching staff is not overjoyed with his decision—Berra still has a lot to learn about being a major league catcher. But Harris is confident Yogi will raise his game. "He knows his failings and is working hard to improve himself."

Veteran baseball writer Dan Daniel, whose stories in the *Sporting News* are widely read, sits down with Berra the day Harris makes his announcement. Berra is pleased with Bucky's decision and tells Daniel, a critic of Yogi's catching skills, that he understands what's needed to improve.

"I have to learn to throw better," he tells Daniel. "Giving all my time to catching will make me a better catcher."

Yogi also has a major incentive. "I have got to make the All-Star

Game," Berra says, turning dead serious. "The game is going to be played in my hometown. I want to come to St. Louis for the July 13 game with everyone on The Hill talking about Yogi."

But Daniel picks up on something else. "Is there a girl back home you want to see?" Daniel asks. After a long pause, Yogi finally answers. "Well, could be," he says. After another pause, Yogi blurts out the news. "Garagiola and me have agreed to get engaged on the same day."

So much for waiting to talk things over with Carmen.

# CHAPTER 11

# Hits & Mrs.
## 1948

It's June 11, and the first-place Indians—who hold a three-game lead over the Yankees—are in New York for a big four-game series. A crowd of 67,924 packs the Stadium to see if the defending champs can gain ground, and they're treated to plenty of action. First the Indians score five runs on six hits against pitcher Vic Raschi, who leaves with one out in the 2nd inning. Then Yogi smacks a big three-run homer with two outs in the 3rd inning.

But Berra soon gives the crowd the kind of action that lands him a seat in the Yankee clubhouse. With Tommy Byrne, the Yankees' fourth pitcher, on the mound in the 4th, Yogi starts complaining to umpire Cal Hubbard about his pitch calls. Berra's reputation for chirping good-naturedly to home plate umps is already well established, and the men in blue like Yogi and give him plenty of latitude.

But these words are crossing the line.

"My pitcher is wild enough," Yogi says, "without you calling ball on pitches that are strikes."

Hubbard's reply is quick and pointed. "Yogi, you take care of your job, and I'll take care of mine."

Byrne retires the first hitter, but when Hubbard calls Byrne's next pitch a ball, Berra whirls around to confront the six-foot-five,

265-pound former pro football player. "You missed it!" Berra shouts. "You missed it and you know it!"

Berra pivots, fires the ball to Byrne, and squats down behind the plate. But before the next pitch, Yogi pops back up, turns, and starts shouting again.

"Say you missed it and I'll shut up!" he yells, loud enough for fans in the box seats to hear. "Say you missed it and I'll shut up!"

Now it's Hubbard's turn to flare. The umpire pulls off his mask, throws his right thumb up in the air, and shouts, "You're out of here!"

Bedlam. Berra is screaming and kicking up the dirt at home plate when Bucky Harris and coach Charlie Dressen run out and pull their catcher away. Harris stays to argue with Hubbard as the fans shower the field with beer cans, bottles, fruit, and cardboard boxes. It takes ten minutes to restore order, including removing a fan from the field who tossed an empty beer can at Hubbard.

The Yankees hit two more homers and take a brief lead, but the Indians keep scoring and lead 10–8 in the 9th when New York loads the bases. Bob Feller ends the 3-hour, 15-minute marathon by striking out pinch-hitter Sherm Lollar, dropping the Yankees to third place.

But Harris is more worried that Hubbard will harbor a grudge against his catcher and tells Berra to apologize to the umpire the next day. "You shouldn't take me serious, Cal," says Berra, a sheepish grin on his face. "After all, I'm not really ferocious."

Berra is not ferocious, but he is frustrated. All the Yankees are frustrated. Berra is hitting well, but Yankee pitchers are still complaining about his pitch selection, his inability to block pitches in the dirt, and so much more. The Yankees were the consensus pick to defend their title, but with an aging team and nagging injuries to Berra and Joe DiMaggio, New York hasn't spent a single day in first place.

Another 68,586 Yankee fans watch their team lose a doubleheader and fall a season-high six games behind the front-running Indians. Berra helps the Yankees salvage the final game of the series, blasting a two-run homer off Indian ace Bob Feller in a 5–3 win. But as third-place New York leaves on a 13-game road trip, Yogi and his teammates know the Indians—who finished a distant fourth in '47—will be a headache all season.

Cleveland—and the rest of the American League—is far from the only thing on Berra's mind. He misses Carmen Short. Desperately. Carmen has been good to her word, writing a letter to Yogi every day. He is nearly despondent the odd day or two when a letter doesn't arrive and brightens up when two letters arrive the next morning. Carmen looks forward to Yogi's letters, too, even if they all sound similar.

"Darling, when I'm around you I'm always in the mood for love," Yogi writes in one letter after another. "I love you so much...I'm sure glad that you don't want to go out with any other boys and I don't want to go out with any girls...I mean that. I love you. I love you."

Yogi saw Carmen in May when the Yankees stopped in St. Louis for a quick two-game series, and his ardor only deepened. Berra sees her again on the second stop of this road trip when the Yankees take three of four games from the Browns. Yogi manages just two hits in 15 at-bats, and it's obvious to his family and hometown friends that their boy is distracted. Carmen makes it clear she loves Yogi, but she's coy about getting engaged. She also tells him how much she dislikes the stories portraying him as a lovable buffoon, stories Yogi sees at every stop.

He knows there isn't much he can do about that. Radio announcers in every city book him for their pregame shows, hoping Yogi will be the comic they've all been hearing about, and are disappointed when they interview a quiet, reluctant Berra. Baseball reporters continue to caricature him, and bench jockeys around the league relentlessly mock him. Berra's adept at letting it roll off his back—he's had plenty of practice—especially when the jabs come from his teammates. Still, the banter can be pointed. The Red Sox are at Yankee Stadium in late June when Berra—who's hitting .280 with eight home runs and 41 RBI in 47 games—steps into the cage during batting practice and the insults start to fly.

"Yogi, what tree did you sleep in last night?" asks Boston pitcher Earl Johnson.

"You're not nearly as good looking as Rizzuto," says Red Sox coach Earle Combs, "and he's no bargain."

"Hey, Tommy," Boston's Joe Dobson says to Tommy Henrich. "Do you do Yogi's thinking for him?"

Everyone is laughing and having a good time as Berra sends one ball after another on a line to the outfield, each drive accompanied by a crisp smack upon contact. The sound gets the attention of Boston star Ted Williams. Joe DiMaggio may be the game's most complete player, but Williams is the best pure hitter in baseball. And he knows a good hitter when he sees one.

"Gosh, the ball just flies off his bat," says Williams, who's hitting .412. When Teddy Ballgame talks hitting, everybody listens, and he really likes what he's watching. "They can kid him all they like, but he's a real strong hitter."

On July 7, Harris names Berra to the American League All-Star team, and Yogi is ecstatic. He's an All-Star in just his second season, the game's in his hometown, and Carmen will be there to see him introduced with the best players in the game.

He's also decided he can't wait any longer for Carmen to make up her mind. Phil Rizzuto keeps telling Yogi he knows a jeweler who can give him a good deal on a ring when the time is right. The jeweler is in Washington, D.C., the Yankees' last stop before the All-Star break.

"Find the number for your jeweler," Berra tells Rizzuto. "I'm going to need his help very soon."

Yogi has no idea how to ask the girl of his dreams to marry him. It's the night before the All-Star Game and he's invited Carmen to dinner at his parents' house. The whole family is there. His father, who retired from the hard life at the brickyard to supervise parking cars at Ruggeri's, took the night off. So did John, a waiter at Ruggeri's. Tony and Mike and their wives are here. So is Yogi's little sister Josie, who keeps telling her brother to calm down.

It was just last winter that Yogi and Joe Garagiola agreed to get engaged on the same day. But Joe wants to wait until after the season, and Yogi just can't hold off that long. He's been talking to the media about marrying Carmen for months, even though he never asked if she'd say yes. How could he not be nervous now?

Dinner will be served in the summer kitchen downstairs. There's no air-conditioning in houses on The Hill, and the basement is the coolest place to eat during St. Louis' hot, steamy summers. Yogi's had the box with the ring in his pocket for hours, still trying to figure out when and how to give it to Carmen.

He decides to put the box on her plate while Paulina and Carmen are chatting upstairs. The next few minutes feel like hours until his mother brings Carmen downstairs, and everyone takes their seats. Yogi is already sitting when Carmen pulls her chair to the table and sees the ring box. "Gee!" she shouts as she excitedly opens the box, sees the diamond ring, and puts it on her finger.

A perfect fit.

Suddenly the whole family is standing as Yogi puts his arms around Carmen and kisses her. Then everyone takes turns kissing each other. The Berra family is officially adding a new member, the beautiful auburn-haired Carmen Short. Dinner is as festive as can be.

When dinner is done and dessert is finished, Yogi decides to drive downtown to the Chase Hotel, where the players on both All-Star teams are staying. He wants to show Carmen what life as a baseball player's wife will be like, he tells his family, but he's not fooling anyone. Yogi wants to show off his fiancée. The press and players can call him ugly all they want, but a beautiful woman has just agreed to marry him.

The Yankees start the second half running in place, winning one game then losing the next for the rest of July. The following month doesn't begin much better, and by August 13, the Yankees are in fourth, 3½ games behind the Indians. No one is happy. DiMaggio, this time suffering from a painful bone spur in his right heel, is hitting just .276 in the 20 games since the All-Star break. The pitching staff is grumbling ever louder about Yogi's deficiencies as a catcher. And rumors swirl that Harris, who has waged a battle with GM George Weiss over the laid-back manner in which he runs this team, may soon be fired.

With 50 games left and little to lose, Harris shakes up his lineup, shifting Tommy Henrich to first base, inserting Bobby Brown at third, and sending Berra back to the outfield. The moves pay off instantly. On August 14, the Yankees thrash Philadelphia 14–3. DiMaggio blasts his 25th home run and drives in four runs, and Berra goes 4-for-5 with two RBI. Yankee pitchers are quiet but happy with the decision to make Gus Niarhos their regular catcher.

The Yankees drop the next two, then win 20 of their next 24 as the middle of their lineup turns unstoppable. DiMaggio belts seven homers, drives in 23 runs, and hits .291. Henrich hits .354 with 22 RBI. Berra is the toughest out, hitting .375 and driving in 22 runs. And he's playing right field well enough for Harris to think Yogi's shift to the outfield could be permanent.

On September 24, the Yankees beat Boston 9–6 and find themselves in a three-way tie for first place with the Red Sox and Indians with seven games left to decide the pennant. And that's when the magic runs out. Ten days later, Joe McCarthy and his Red Sox eliminate the Yankees in the season's penultimate game. There will be no World Series check for Berra to share with his bride-to-be this fall.

Instead it's Boston and Cleveland who meet in a one-game playoff to decide the American League pennant on October 4. But there is bigger news for the Yankees. On the same day Cleveland clobbers Boston, 8–3, to meet the Boston Braves in the World Series, Weiss fires Harris. "It feels like I was hit in the head with a lead pipe," Harris says. All Weiss will say about the next manager is he won't choose one of his active players, quickly ending speculation that DiMaggio or Henrich is next in line.

Berra's late-season surge leaves him with impressive stats: 14 home runs, 98 RBI, and a .305 batting average in 125 games. Where the next Yankee manager will play Yogi remains a question, but the splits are telling: Berra hit .271 with 10 home runs and 54 RBI in 63 games at catcher and .349 with four homers and 36 RBI in 47 games as the right fielder. The Yankees were 39–32 with Berra behind the plate and 33–17 when he played right. Indeed, many in the media think Yogi's days as a catcher may well be over.

"You just can't help liking Nature Boy," Dan Daniel writes in the *Sporting News,* using one of Yogi's most derogatory nicknames. "But, as much as we are for Yogi, we hope, fervently, that we will not have to look at him again as a catcher. Berra's short arms and stubby fingers handicap him. He pitches curves to second base. In addition, he no longer likes to catch. Life is much simpler and happier out in right field, and that is where he wants to stay."

But Berra has other things on his mind as he returns to St. Louis.

Yogi has a wedding to plan.

There are two things every young couple on The Hill wants in a wedding.

They all want Father Charles Koester, still the most popular priest among St. Ambrose Church parishioners, to perform the wedding ceremony.

And they all want the reception at the Big Club Hall, the two-story brick building that has been at the heart of this northern Italian community since 1897.

Carmen Short and Yogi Berra get their wishes and set the date for January 26, 1949. That gives the happy couple three months to pull together a reception for 300 guests, complete Carmen's conversion to Catholicism, and prepare for a monthlong honeymoon drive from St. Louis to Palm Springs, Florida, then to Miami Beach, and finally on to spring training in St. Petersburg.

Catering the reception is the easy part. It always is on The Hill. A family member will walk over to Botanical Avenue, where he or she will find one of a handful of women who handle these affairs. Just tell her the date and the number of guests, and she and a crew of teenage girls will be in the Big Club Hall kitchen at 5 a.m. to cook all the pastas, meats, chicken, vegetables, breads, and desserts their guests can possibly eat, all for a few hundred dollars.

Carmen's sister Nadine will be maid of honor, Joe Garagiola the best man, and Joe's girlfriend Audrie Ross one of the bridesmaids. Carmen and Audrie hit it off the first time the two couples double-dated last fall, and it's been sporting events and movies ever since for the four friends, despite every effort by Carmen and Audrie to go to one of the city's many dance halls. Well, Carmen tells them, they'll be dancing at her wedding. And since the wedding is in the morning with the reception to follow, both women insist Yogi and Joe wear morning suits—white tie and vest under a long jacket with tails.

Yogi's baseball life is also changing fast. In mid-October, Yogi and Joe are touring the Midwest with Cardinal star Red Schoendienst's barnstorming team when the Yankees introduce their new manager. His name is Casey Stengel, a former major league outfielder who's managed the Dodgers and Braves, never finishing higher than fifth. A few weeks later, the team brings back Bill Dickey to work with hitters and hires Jim Turner to work with pitchers. And GM George Weiss tells the *Sporting News* he's looking into any trade that will put his team back in the World Series.

But none of that is on Yogi's mind as he stands at the altar in St. Ambrose Church and watches Carmen come down the aisle. Has it only been 15 months since this wonderful woman walked into his life? Father Koester smiles, softly encourages Yogi to relax, and performs a service that is short and touching. The reception is long and happy, very happy. Yogi has already seen a few "Beauty and the Beast" jabs in the press, but anyone looking at this couple right now can see they're in love.

It's just a few days later when the newlyweds pile their suitcases into the Nash the groom received on Yogi Berra Night at Sportsman's Park two summers ago. Yogi slides behind the wheel, starts his car, and heads south beside the woman who will change his life in ways he never dreamed possible.

# CHAPTER 12

# Learning Experience
## 1949

**B**ill Dickey stands at one of the many batting cages at the Yankee spring training complex, his eyes never leaving Yogi Berra as he carries on a conversation with Joe Trimble, longtime Yankee beat writer for the *New York Daily News*. He and Trimble go back to Bill's playing days, and Dickey knows he can talk openly without worrying about what will show up in the next day's paper. It's been a week since Dickey started working with Berra, and he's amazed how quickly Yogi has improved. But he's even more amazed at how little Berra really knows about playing catcher.

"He's been doing so many things wrong," Dickey tells Trimble as Berra catches a pitch, reaches into his glove, and in one smooth motion fires the ball on a straight line to second baseman George Stirnweiss. It's just one of many drills the Yankee coach puts Berra through for two hours after every team workout. "They tell me he threw curves to second base last year. I don't doubt it—he was throwing off balance. He has to learn how to set himself properly and throw directly overhand."

Dickey stops to shout out encouragement, then tells Berra to do it again. And again. "Look, none of the stuff I'm teaching him is really hard," Dickey says. "The only way to learn it is by practicing over and over again. The more you're able to handle the ball, the more you like it."

A lot of players don't want to play catcher, Dickey tells Trimble, his gaze still locked on Berra. Stengel and Weiss have been asking Dickey for a progress report almost every day, wondering if Berra will cut it or if Weiss needs to trade for another catcher. The pitchers have begun to call Berra "The Project," and all the players are surprised just how hard Dickey is working Yogi.

"The Project" is better than a lot of things Berra's been called the last two years. Yogi told Dickey he was especially hurt last season when a rookie would ask if he was catching that day. If Yogi said yes, the player would smile and say, "That's great. I want to see if every-thing they say about you is true."

Fact is, pretty much everything they were saying *was* true, starting with where Berra was setting up to catch—at least two feet too far back. Stop worrying about the bat hitting you, Dickey keeps telling Berra, it's not going to happen. Move closer to the plate and those foul tips that keep hitting you will whiz by instead. And those bad pitches you've been dropping—or missing—will land in your mitt.

Dickey can see Yogi's enthusiasm jump every time he learns some-thing new, and the reluctant student is now an eager pupil. Dickey showed him how to step across the plate and shift his weight to get his body and not just his arm behind his throws. Grip the ball the same way each time, he told him, and those curveballs to second base will disappear. And watch the arc of a throw from your outfielder to gauge where to set up on a play at the plate so the runner barreling in from third doesn't run you over.

Trimble asks Dickey a question every few minutes as one hour turns into another. Dickey listens, then tells Trimble the same thing he's been telling Berra. "The catcher has the most complicated job on the team," he says. "He must be able to throw to the bases, handle bunts and pop flies, and direct pitchers. He has to know where each of his fielders should be stationed and what they all have to do wher-ever the ball is hit. It's a job for which few men are fit and darn few really want."

Dickey pauses to make sure the newsman hears every word he says next. "If Yogi really wants to be a good catcher," Dickey says, "I don't see what's going to stop him."

Dickey asks Stirnweiss to put down a few bunts, and delights in watching Berra pounce on the ball, square up, and fire a strike to a farmhand stationed at first base. Yogi's been out here for hours, Dickey tells Trimble, and he's still fresh. It's just the first week, and Dickey's not prepared to say Yogi is there just yet, but he already thinks Berra has a chance to become a good catcher. Damn, if Berra keeps improving at this pace, he might even become an exceptional catcher.

"Yogi, good work," Dickey shouts. "Let's bring it in."

Berra jogs over, gets a pat on the back from Dickey, and heads to the Yankee clubhouse. Yogi likes Dickey, who seems more like a big brother than a coach, even though they got off to a rough start their very first day. There are some people who say you don't care about becoming a better catcher, Dickey told him. "I do so care," said Yogi, his wounded pride clear in his voice.

But Berra quickly realized "some people" was really Weiss. The Yankee GM had questioned Berra's commitment to catching repeatedly when the two men battled over money soon after Yogi and Carmen arrived in camp. Berra wanted $15,000, Weiss offered $10,000, and after three stressful days, they finally agreed on $14,000, a $5,000 bump from the previous season.

"Prove yourself this season," Weiss told him, making it clear he meant as a catcher, "and you'll get the big raise you want." Berra grunted, signed the contract, and filed away Weiss' words, to be used when they negotiate his contract next winter.

Berra knows he has to impress Stengel, too, but at least Casey hasn't attacked his catching. Just the opposite. The new manager has told reporters he thinks Yogi can be his everyday catcher. No more shuttling between catcher and the outfield. And Stengel has taken to calling him Mr. Berra, which is certainly an improvement over "the Ape."

It turns out Casey is nothing like the clown Berra heard about all winter. Everyone knows the story about Stengel hiding a bird under his cap one game during his playing days, then releasing it when he lifted his hat to wave to the crowd. But there's nothing funny about the rules Stengel spelled out when camp opened on March 1. There will be a practice session in the morning and another in the afternoon, their new manager told them, the first time the Yankees have done two-a-days since 1922. (Stengel allows veterans Joe DiMaggio, Tommy Henrich, Phil Rizzuto, and Charlie Keller to set their own schedules. That's especially important for DiMaggio, who had surgery to remove the bone spur in his right heel in November and is still running gingerly—when he is running at all.)

Stengel also instituted a midnight curfew, which didn't bother the early-to-bed, early-to-rise Berra as it did party guys like Joe Page. But Yogi winced along with most every other Yankee when Casey declared the local dog track off-limits but for Thursday nights. Yogi loves to gamble on the puppies, and like many of his teammates he circumvented the rule by sitting outside the track and using Yankee clubhouse workers to place his bets.

Everyone figured the ban came from Weiss, who's infamous for hiring detectives to follow players he suspects of breaking his rules. The players also know Weiss has repeatedly asked traveling secretary Frank Scott to report back on what they do on the road, a role Scott has refused to play. But there's one player who can't be spied on, and that player showed up at the dog track one Saturday night in white slacks and a loud Florida shirt. Everyone understood DiMaggio was challenging management—less than two months after the Yankees made Joe the game's first $100,000 player—which only makes his teammates admire their superstar that much more. Especially when the ban was quietly dropped.

Rules aside, Berra's focus is on the many things Dickey is teaching him. Or, as he said when one reporter asked about his progress, "It's great—Dickey is learning me all his experience." His personal coach certainly knows the game, and for the first time since he made the big leagues, Yogi is excited about strapping on the catching equipment and getting behind the plate.

"Kid, you can do this—you're going to be a great catcher," Dickey keeps telling him. "Good catchers are scarce. You have a big edge on fellows who are just receivers—you can hit with anyone in the league. Now improve yourself behind the plate, and you'll have a job for years."

Dickey's already picked the brains of the pitchers to learn their problems with Berra. Yogi doesn't know how to frame a pitch, said staff leader Allie Reynolds, or how to sell the umpire on giving pitchers a strike on borderline calls. Dickey often saw Yogi stab at a pitch to catch it, pushing the ball outside the strike zone. "Reach out and pull the ball in," Dickey tells him. "You'll be amazed how often the ump will give you the call—and how much happier you'll make your pitchers."

Once exhibition games began, Stengel quickly saw a flaw in his pitching staff. His pitchers paid scant attention to holding base runners close to first, so he has pitching coach Jim Turner drill them day after day on lowering their leg kicks with runners on base. "Hey, let's give our catchers a chance to throw out base runners," says Casey, who spends much of camp working on fundamentals, something rarely done under Harris. Change is most definitely in the air.

But one thing doesn't change: Yogi is still an easy target for anyone looking for a laugh. When the Yankees play the Detroit Tigers in Lakeland, pitcher Dizzy Trout greets Yogi with a question. "How does your wife like living in a tree?" Trout asks. Casey has quietly asked his players to cut down on their playful jabs at Berra. But there's little he can do about the writers, who ask each other each day if they've heard any Yogi-isms—the label they use for Berra's tendency to mangle words in a comical way. If there isn't anything new, they just recycle old stories—or make up something fresh.

None of that is distracting Berra, who soaks up Dickey's lessons as the rest of the team plays exhibition games. Yogi pinch-hits in a few games, catches a few others, belts a triple and a few hard singles, but Stengel and Weiss know the kid can hit. As training camp draws to a close, they keep asking Dickey if Berra's ready. It's the week before the opener when Dickey finally renders his verdict.

"He'll make it," Dickey says confidently. "And he'll be a pretty good catcher, too. Give him two years and he'll be the best catcher in the American League—by a long shot."

Dickey's positive assessment grows in importance when the Yankee doctors reach their conclusion on DiMaggio's troublesome right heel. All the whirlpools, heat treatments, and special shoes haven't stopped the throbbing pain DiMaggio feels with every step. He'll start the season at Johns Hopkins Hospital instead of Yankee Stadium, and the doctors have no idea when—or if—he'll recover. DiMaggio is again wondering if his career might be over.

He's not alone. Stengel spent the spring telling writers DiMaggio was more about the team's past and Berra was the Yankees' future. He just didn't think the transition would happen so fast. Stengel was hired to win the World Series, but in a preseason poll of baseball writers, 70 pick Boston to win the American League pennant, 42 pick the Indians, and only five choose the Yankees.

For Stengel and the Yankees, the future is suddenly now.

# CHAPTER 13

# Season of Surprises
## 1949

There is no team in the 1949 season more surprising than the New York Yankees, no manager more surprising than Casey Stengel, and no player more surprising than Yogi Berra. The Yankees quickly defy the critics, who picked them to finish a distant third, by grabbing first place on Day 1 and keeping it for all but three days of the season. It gets excruciatingly dramatic at the end, and that makes it all the more surprising.

A good deal of the credit goes to Stengel, whose transformation from bowlegged clown to dugout genius happens almost overnight. Stengel installs a platoon system, rotating players at third base, first base, and all three outfield positions—the last group by necessity, since each of his starting outfielders loses weeks if not months to injuries. Every player Stengel plugs in seems to get the big hit or go on a hot streak.

Casey's almost as good—if not better—with the media. Stengel rarely talks to his players before or after games, preferring to get his message across through the team's regular beat reporters—"my writers," as he calls them—who are soon hanging on his every rambling sentence as the victories pile up.

And Yogi's newfound defensive prowess surprises all those who were certain his days behind the plate were over. Most surprised: base runners, who are startled to see the ball beat them to second base after running with ease on Yogi for two straight seasons. Berra's defensive improvement helps the Yankees' top three starters — Allie Reynolds, Vic Raschi, and Eddie Lopat — start the season winning a combined 25 of 28 decisions.

But the "Big 3," still not convinced Berra sees the game through their eyes, insist on calling their own games. They want Yogi to understand the sequence of pitches they use against every batter in every lineup, and that's still a long way off. Berra is more than agreeable and works out a set of signals so each pitcher can call his own pitches. But if Berra isn't going to call the game, Stengel wants to make the decisions and that doesn't sit well with his pitching staff.

It all comes to a head in an early season game with Reynolds on the mound against the Senators. There are two runners on base, two outs, and two strikes on the batter when Stengel starts yelling for Berra to look into the dugout so he can call the next pitch.

"Berra! Berra!" Stengel shouts.

"Yogi, look at me," Reynolds yells.

"Berra! Berra!" Stengel shouts again.

"Yogi, do not look at the dugout or I will cross you up," counters Reynolds, and the threat carries meaning. Even at 32, Reynolds is still a hard thrower, and if Stengel calls for a curve and the right-hander fires a fastball there's a real chance the unexpected pitch will break one of Berra's fingers.

Yogi, caught in the middle, is unsure what to do, especially when Stengel stands on the top step of the dugout and starts waving dollar bills. "I'll fine your ass if you don't look here!" Casey shouts.

Reynolds repeats his own threat. Finally, Berra listens to Reynolds, who fires a fastball for strike three to end the inning. Stengel smiles wryly and doesn't mention what just happened to either player. The Big 3 feel an important battle has been won: the pitchers, not the manager who never pitched, will call their own pitches. And Berra is now their ally.

No one is surprised by Yogi's production with a bat in his hands.

Batting fifth behind Tommy Henrich, now the team's cleanup hitter with DiMaggio on the sidelines, Yogi drives in four runs three times in May and has seven multi-hit games. He also shows off his speed, stamina, and a flair for the dramatic—sometimes all in one game. On May 28, the Yankees are down 1–0 to Philadelphia with two outs in the 9th inning when Berra clubs a game-tying RBI double. He catches the next five innings, gets a one-out single in the bottom of the 14th, then steams all the way around to score the winning run on a Billy Johnson double.

Six days later in Chicago, Berra doubles in the 7th to give the Yankees an 8–7 lead, then scores an insurance run for a 9–7 win that completes a three-game New York sweep. Casey is holding court with the writers in a happy Yankee clubhouse when he's asked about moving Yogi back to his injury-riddled outfield.

"Nothing doing," Stengel says. "Berra, Henrich, and Rizzuto have carried this team and we're not changing where they play."

Stengel, aware he's within earshot of best friends Rizzuto and Berra, says he now considers Rizzuto the best shortstop in all of baseball. "Phil is one man who is sure to land on the All-Star team," Stengel says.

"Hey," says Yogi from right behind his manager. "How about me?"

Stengel turns to face Berra. "Yogi," Casey says, "you are superlative."

He is indeed. Berra's double extends his hitting streak to five games. He gets two hits in St. Louis the next game, then two more against the Browns a day later, both Yankee wins. He raps out hits in each of the next 10 games, a three-run homer against the White Sox on June 15, stretching his hitting streak to a career-high 17 games. He bats .348 with 13 RBI during his hot streak, which includes catching both games of three doubleheaders.

Berra goes hitless in the next three games, then hits in the next eight—including two more doubleheaders—collecting 13 hits and knocking in 10 runs. In his 39 games from May 15 through June 27, Yogi drives in 37 runs, hits six home runs and 12 doubles, and bats .314. The surprising Yankees are 41–24—the best record in baseball—

and sit 4½ games ahead of Philadelphia and five games ahead of Boston and Detroit.

All without Joe DiMaggio.

And that changes two days later, surprising everyone—especially DiMaggio. On May 23, the Big Dago worked out at Yankee Stadium and could not put any pressure on his troublesome heel without feeling searing pain, and left the ballpark wondering if his season might be lost. But on a morning in mid-June, DiMaggio got out of bed, felt no pain, and proclaimed himself ready to play.

Berra—and every Yankee—won't soon forget what they witnessed next. Playing before 36,228 fans—the biggest nighttime crowd in Fenway Park history—DiMaggio singles in his first at-bat and scores after missing virtually all of spring training and the first 65 games of the regular season. He comes up with Rizzuto on first the next inning and sends the ball rocketing high into the screen above the left field wall, providing the winning runs in a 5–4 Yankee victory. Writers are amazed to see the always reserved DiMaggio laughing and exchanging hugs with Yogi, Rizzuto, and other teammates in the joyous postgame locker room.

Amazement turns to astonishment over the next two days. The Yankees are trailing Boston ace Ellis Kinder 7–1 with two outs and two on in the 5th the following game when Joe pulls another home run over the 40-foot-high Green Monster. The score is tied 7–7 three innings later when DiMaggio sends the ball soaring clear over the 20-foot screen atop the left field wall and onto Lansdowne Street behind the stadium for a solo home run. Yogi, who left the game after a foul tip split the nail on his right pinkie, watches from the bench as the Yankees close out a 9–7 win.

Berra is nursing his bruised finger the next day when DiMaggio dwarfs his first three home runs with a line drive that clears the screen in left field and smashes into a light tower before bouncing back onto the field. The three-run homer is the key to a 6–3 win and a sweep of Boston, which came into this series winning 10 of its last 11 games. DiMaggio's comeback is epic—four home runs, nine RBI in three games, 13 fly balls fielded flawlessly—pushing the reeling Red Sox eight games behind his first-place Yankees.

DiMaggio and Berra form a lethal combination in their first 30 games together. DiMaggio, hitting cleanup, slugs seven homers, drives in 31 runs, and hits .324. Berra, batting right behind Joe, belts five home runs, drives in 15, and hits .286. Six days into August, the Yankees have their best player back in uniform, the best record in baseball, and a four-game lead over a streaking Cleveland team.

And Berra has established himself as the league's finest catcher, hitting 15 home runs with 72 RBI in his first 90 games. Just as important: he is making good use of Bill Dickey's spring training lessons behind the plate.

No home run Berra hits is as telling as the play he makes in the first game of a July 4th doubleheader rematch with Boston at Yankee Stadium, the same day he's named to his second All-Star Game. It comes in the 9th inning after Vic Raschi loads the bases with two singles and a walk. The wind is kicking up a dust storm when Al Zarilla, the next Boston batter, lines the ball to right for what looks like a sure base hit. But Boston shortstop Johnny Pesky, standing at third, can't see the ball clearly through the cloud of dust. When he sees it drop in front of Yankee right fielder Cliff Mapes, Pesky sprints to the plate.

Mapes fields the ball cleanly and fires a strike to Berra, who catches the ball like a first baseman just before Pesky reaches the plate. Umpire Joe Paparella, thinking Yogi has to tag Pesky, makes the safe sign, and the game is tied with the bases still loaded. But Berra spins around, tears off his mask, and confronts Paparella. "He's out, he's out," Berra shouts. "It was a force play. I don't have to tag him. He's out."

Paparella hesitates for an instant, then reverses his call. "By God, you're right," he tells Yogi. "The throw beat him. He's out!"

The Red Sox protest, but Paparella's reversal is correct. Dickey is always telling Berra to think ahead, and this is one time Yogi is way ahead of even the umpire. Raschi gets the final out and the Yankees have their fourth straight win over the Red Sox. The Yankees win the nightcap 6–4, dropping Boston 12 games back with a 35–36 record, their season seemingly in shambles.

The normally quiet Dickey is effusive after the game. "I've been telling you Yogi is going to be the best defensive catcher in the game one day," he keeps telling reporters. "He might be the best right now!"

There's little doubt Berra has grasped what catching is all about. Some of the Yankee pitchers start letting him call their pitches. Even Reynolds, the most stubborn of the lot, begins telling Yogi, "You call the pitches the next few innings." And runners aren't taking the same liberties they once took. "Nobody's running on him," Stengel says. "The way he's throwing, even Ty Cobb couldn't steal on him now."

Yogi feels so comfortable behind the plate he turns up his chatter with both hitters and umpires on every at-bat. "How's the wife and your four kids?" he'll ask a married player right before strike one crosses the plate. "Hey, where's a good place to eat a late dinner in this town?" he'll ask a hitter just before another strike is called. He also has a habit of throwing dirt on a player's shoes, though never when the pitch is thrown. And he has a running commentary on the accuracy of the calls of just about every home plate umpire.

Which is why traveling secretary Frank Scott's frantic search for Berra before an afternoon game at the Stadium ends in the umpires' locker room. "Yogi, this is out of order," a worried Scott says. "You're not supposed to be fraternizing with the umpires!"

Veteran umpire Eddie Rommel erupts in laughter. "Oh, he isn't doing any harm—this bird is a philosopher," says Rommel. "He's also a student. He never misses an opportunity to ask people how to improve himself as a catcher and a hitter."

Rommel pauses, then adds the kicker.

"Actually, Berra is right at home with us," he says with a big smile. "He's not on the payroll of [AL President] Mr. Harridge, but he umpires more than any of us."

Despite his success, Berra remains the butt of many jokes. Yogi is hit by an errant throw in pregame warm-ups in early May, knocked cold, and taken to the hospital for an x-ray. When the doctor reports the tests are negative, the headline in the next day's paper reads, X-RAYS OF BERRA'S HEAD SHOW NOTHING. The *New York Post*'s star columnist Jimmy Cannon writes a scathing piece in late May, dredging up all the old stories while insisting Berra still fits the stereotype of the lovable buffoon. Several less-than-flattering cartoons appear in the *Sporting News* and several of the New York papers.

Berra continues to ignore the insults—at least outwardly—but now he has a new problem. His young wife isn't nearly as forgiving, and he has to keep telling her what he learned a long time ago—responding will only increase the taunts. Carmen is just barely convinced not to confront the writers herself.

Yogi is one of five Yankees chosen for the July 12 All-Star Game in Brooklyn's Ebbets Field, a fitting site for this game. It's the first midsummer classic featuring black players—Jackie Robinson is elected by the fans to start at second base, and Dodger teammates pitcher Don Newcombe and catcher Roy Campanella are added by NL manager Billy Southworth. AL manager Lou Boudreau adds Cleveland's Larry Doby.

Berra goes hitless in three at-bats in the 11–7 AL win but gets off the All-Star Game's best line. In a pregame meeting, everyone is stuck about how to pitch to Yogi's golf buddy Stan Musial, who enters the game with three batting titles and a .344 lifetime batting average.

"You guys are trying to stop Musial in 15 minutes when the National League hasn't stopped him in 15 years," says Berra, adding eight years to the 28-year-old Musial's career. His All-Star teammates break up laughing. And Yogi is right: Musial slams a two-run homer and two singles in four at-bats.

American League pitchers continue having trouble pitching to Berra after the All-Star break. He has his first two-home-run game on July 15 in St. Louis—his first-ever home runs in his hometown—then hits home runs in consecutive games against Cleveland stars Bob Lemon and Bob Feller, batting .312 with four homers and 12 RBI for 24 games in July. He opens August with a three-run homer against

Detroit, then hits home runs in three straight games against the Browns, the last being his career-high 16th on August 7 off Ned Garver in a 20–2 rout of St. Louis.

But that's when the music stops. Batting for the second time in the 3rd inning of the developing rout, Berra takes a Dick Starr fastball off his thumb. X-rays show a bad break, and team doctor Sidney Gaynor says Berra will be out at least three weeks, the team's 50th injury of the season. Henrich is taken to the hospital after getting hit in the elbow later in the same game, with x-rays showing a bad bruise.

Henrich returns to the lineup two games later, and Stengel—Yogi's biggest advocate all season—turns on Berra.

Impatient for his star catcher to lose the cast and return to the lineup, Stengel tells Berra to run the outfield every day and refuses Yogi's request to go to St. Louis, where Carmen, pregnant with their first child, is staying with family. Stengel begins to carp to writers about Berra's lack of toughness as the Red Sox get hot and the Yankee injury toll continues to rise. Henrich stays in the lineup wearing a corset to protect sore ribs. DiMaggio sprains his left shoulder on August 21 but misses only two games.

Dr. Gaynor removes Berra's cast on August 25 and says Yogi should be ready to go when the team arrives in St. Louis five days later. But trouble strikes in a doubleheader in Chicago before the team reaches Berra's hometown. The Yankees win both games, but Henrich crashes into the outfield wall in the first game, cracks two vertebrae in his lower back, and is lost indefinitely. By the time the team arrives in St. Louis on August 29—a much-needed day of rest—Stengel is eager to pencil Berra's name in the next day's lineup card.

But when Berra arrives at Sportsman's Park, there is a lemon wrapped around his left thumb. Seems Yogi spent the off night at his parents' house on The Hill, and when his mother inspected his thumb, she told him it was not fully healed. Paulina promptly went into the kitchen, returned with a lemon slit in half, slid the lemon onto her son's thumb, and wrapped it securely. Her instructions: leave the lemon in place for the next week and your thumb will heal.

Stengel explodes when he hears this story, then complains to the writers that every other manager has a catcher who wears a glove, but he has one who wears a lemon. Berra insists he can't play, and each day brings a sharper barb. "Now, fellas, I'd like you to meet a stranger," he tells his players when Berra walks by. "This is Mr. Berra. Says he's got an ache of some kind."

The Yankees lose two of three games to the seventh-place Browns, dropping their once imposing lead over Boston to just three games, and Stengel gets meaner. He starts telling his players Berra should only get half a World Series share—if they make it that far. More than one player begins repeating Stengel's jab. Yogi's pride is wounded, but his thumb is still sore, he can barely grip a bat, and he remains firm he won't play until he's healthy.

Berra agrees to catch on September 3, then backs out, prompting *New York Times* reporter John Drebinger to write that every Yankee is convinced Berra is healthy enough to play—except Berra. Casey encourages other reporters to write similar stories. When New York loses to last-place Washington the next day—cutting its lead over Boston to 1½ games—Stengel insists Berra will be in the lineup when the Yankees open a three-game series on September 7.

And there Berra is, behind the plate, extra padding in the thumb of his catcher's mitt when Allie Reynolds takes the mound against the Red Sox. The Red Sox have combined the torrid hitting of Ted Williams—37 home runs, 141 RBI, a .353 batting average—and the one-two punch of Ellis Kinder (18–5) and Mel Parnell (21–7) to win a league-best 40 of 56 since the All-Star break. The crippled Yankees are 31–21, and Stengel can feel his first pennant slipping away.

The teams split two games and lose one to a rainout. Berra fails to get a base hit, but every time his bat hits the ball, pain radiates straight up his left arm. It's only slightly less painful when a fastball pounds into his glove, extra padding be damned. But Stengel is going to ride Berra the rest of the way, catching him in back-to-back doubleheaders and just about every other game. The Yankees suffer yet another big blow when DiMaggio, who's hit .345 with 14 home runs and 67

RBI in 74 games, goes down with a virus that turns into pneumonia on September 17. No one knows when he'll return.

It looks certain the season will come down to the last two series between baseball's most bitter rivals. Berra is hitting just .197 since returning 17 games ago when the Yankees arrive in Boston on September 24 for two weekend games, with a makeup game to follow in New York on Monday. The Yankees hold a two-game lead, but the Red Sox show off their power and pitching—Williams hits a pair of home runs, his 42nd and 43rd, and Ellis Kinder and Mel Parnell give up one run and 10 hits between them—and Boston takes both games to draw even. Berra is hitless in four at-bats in the first game, then sits out Sunday's game against left-hander Parnell, who earns his 25th win.

Berra is on the bench against Boston left-hander Mickey McDermott back in New York and watches the Red Sox score four runs in the 8th against relief ace Joe Page to move ahead 7–6. Berra pinch-hits and walks with two outs in the 9th, and gets no further when Hank Bauer lifts a fly ball to center, cementing the team's third loss in three games against the Red Sox before 66,156 disbelieving fans. When Boston leaves town that night there is a new team atop the AL standings for the first time all season. The Red Sox now hold a one-game lead with five games to play.

And that's the way things stand when the teams meet for the final two games in New York. The baseball fan in Berra is just as excited as the player. Everything is on the line: if the Red Sox split, the pennant is theirs. If the Yankees sweep, Yogi's going to the World Series for the second time in three years.

And, as fate would have it, Saturday's game is the long-planned Joe DiMaggio Day at the Stadium. DiMaggio, who's lost 18 pounds while battling pneumonia, leaves the hospital for the Stadium and stands for an hour as he's showered with gifts—from a Cadillac to 300 pounds of ice cream—while 69,551 fans wildly cheer. Dominic comes out and stands next to his brother, and Yogi can see Joe leaning heavily on Dom throughout the ceremony.

DiMaggio, who's missed the last 13 days, tells Stengel he is good for three innings. But Reynolds is hit hard, giving up two runs and loading the bases with one out in the 3rd before Stengel brings in Page—who promptly walks in two more runs. Berra sees DiMaggio hold up five fingers when he enters the dugout at inning's end. Underweight and weak, Joe D will play the entire game.

DiMaggio lines a ground-rule double to right field and scores the first of two Yankee runs in the 4th, and New York is back in the game. Berra drives an RBI single in the 5th to cut the lead to 4–3, and the game is tied when Henrich scores on a double-play grounder. Page is now dominating the Red Sox, striking out four and allowing one hit through the 8th inning, and Berra can feel the team's confidence surging. Their persistence is rewarded when Johnny Lindell drives a pitch deep into the left field stands with two outs in the bottom of the 8th for a 5–4 lead. Three outs later, the baseball season is reduced to one game, winner take all.

Yogi walks into the clubhouse the next day, sees Raschi sitting in front of his locker, his intensity bristling as he waves off anyone who dares comes close, and knows his pitcher is ready. Raschi is at his best when he's angry; some games Yogi will go out toward the pitcher's mound and yell, "Onionhead, get the damn ball over the plate," just to get him focused. It doesn't look like that will be necessary today.

The Yankees jump to a 1–0 lead in the 1st when Rizzuto triples and scores on a groundout. Raschi is pitching brilliantly, and the Yankees boost their lead to 5–0 by the 8th inning. Yogi just needs to get Raschi through one more inning, and the pennant is theirs.

But it's not easy. With one out, Raschi walks Williams, throws a wild pitch, then gives up a single, putting runners on first and third. Second baseman Bobby Doerr, a .307 hitter with 106 RBI, lifts a long fly to center field, the kind of fly ball Yogi has watched DiMaggio run down with ease. But this one sails over Joe's head for a two-run triple, and it's now 5–2. And that's when DiMaggio signals for time. He's hurting the team, so he takes himself out of the game.

Raschi gets another out, then allows a run-scoring single to make it 5–3. Yogi starts to walk out toward Raschi when he sees Henrich coming over from first base. "Give me the ball and get the hell out of here," Raschi says, and Berra smiles as Boston's All-Star catcher Birdie Tebbetts steps in. All Tebbetts can manage is a soft foul pop that Henrich squeezes tightly in his glove. The Yankees are AL champs once again.

Stengel climbs atop a table in the joyous Yankee clubhouse. Berra listens as the old man fights back tears. None of those insults Casey hurled Yogi's way seems to matter anymore. Few people thought Yogi would make it as a major league catcher, but Berra showed he could be one of the best. No one thought this team could survive without DiMaggio playing a full season, and they just beat an outstanding Red Sox team for the pennant. This season was full of surprises, and that made this moment very sweet indeed.

"You men have given me the greatest thrill I've ever had in my whole life," Stengel says. "I want to thank you all. Thank you."

Yogi looks over at DiMaggio, who's drinking a can of beer and smoking a cigarette. He looks across at Henrich, who can't stop smiling, despite the pain of all his injuries. They both look to Yogi like kids who just got what they wanted for Christmas. Sure, the season began with Berra arguing with Weiss over money—and they'll surely do that again soon—but this is when playing ball feels the best. This is when you get to be a kid all over again.

Every World Series is special, but this one—even though it's against the crosstown Dodgers—can't help but feel a bit anticlimactic. Reynolds outduels Newcombe 1–0 in Game 1, giving up just two hits, but Preacher Roe scatters six hits and beats the Yankees by the same score to even the Series. The Yankees then run the table, winning two tight games then blowing out the Dodgers 10–6 for their second championship in three seasons, their 12th overall.

Yogi, his left thumb painfully swollen, manages just one hit in four games, singling and scoring in Game 4. But the same team that ran all over Berra in 1947 has just one stolen base against him in this Series. DiMaggio, still weak from his bout with pneumonia, manages just two hits. Yogi saw Joe's eight-year-old son ask his father to hit a home run for him in the final game. After two long fly outs, DiMaggio pulls one deep into the left field seats.

Yogi sees Joe Jr. waiting for his famous father after the game in the tunnel leading to the clubhouse. Then they walk together, little Joe's arm wrapped around big Joe's waist. "Thanks for hitting a home run for me, Daddy," DiMaggio's son tells his father. Berra's heart just about melts.

There's a big party for the team in the Stadium Club a few hours later; Bob Hope and actors Ray Bolger and William Frawley have flown in to entertain and celebrate with them. The next morning Yogi and Carmen pack up and take the train back to St. Louis with a World Series check for $5,626.74 in hand.

Berra is 24. He has a wife he loves dearly and a first child due in December. He's a two-time World Series champion, a two-time All-Star catcher, and has just led the game's best team in runs batted in. Not bad for a kid who was told he'd never make it to the big leagues.

PART III

# SUPERSTAR
## 1950–1956

# CHAPTER 14

# Main Man
## 1950

It's late in the evening of March 1, 1950, and Yogi Berra is sitting in the back row of seats in the lounge of the Palace Bowl, a popular place on the southwest edge of The Hill to bowl and down a few beers. Outside, a snowstorm is finally coming to an end, an early spring surprise Berra could have done without. Inside are a handful of bowlers, mostly men who just finished the late shift and want to wind down before heading home.

Today was the first day of spring training. But instead of donning pinstripes and playing baseball under the sunny skies of St. Petersburg, Florida, Berra spent the day bundled in winter clothes and shoveling snow. He just had to get out of the house, so he's sitting here alone, dressed in jeans, sweatshirt, and sneakers, wondering how long he'll have to stay in St. Louis before the Yankees meet his contract demands so he can end the first holdout of his young career.

Only a few minutes pass before he sees Bob Burnes, the 36-year-old sports editor of the *St. Louis Globe-Democrat,* stroll through the Palace doors. Yogi waves for Burnes to join him. Every sports fan in town knows Burnes, whose Benchwarmer column is a must-read. He's also the same sportswriter who watched Berra, then 17, play five innings at nearby Forest Park before telling Yogi's American Legion mentor that the kid wasn't much of a prospect.

Yogi and Bob have laughed a lot about that day in 1942. Wary of most sportswriters after serving as the butt of their jokes for years, the 24-year-old Berra has come to trust Burnes. The writer shares Yogi's passion for baseball as well as all things sports at St. Louis University, where Burnes was a soccer star. Burnes often accompanies Yogi to luncheons and dinners, interviewing him in front of audiences so Berra doesn't have to give a dreaded speech.

Burnes plunks down in a seat next to Yogi and silently opens his early copy of tomorrow's newspaper. The pictures of ballplayers swinging bats and throwing balls in Florida almost jump off the page at Berra.

"You going?" Burnes asks Berra, who quickly shakes his head no.

"If I go down there I'll sign, I know it," Berra says. "So I gotta stay here 'til I get what I want."

"How far apart are you?" Burnes asks.

"Not too much—about five, six thousand dollars," Yogi says. "But this is the first time I've ever been tough about a contract. If I give in now, they know they'll never have trouble signing me. I've got to stick it out."

Burnes knows his friend has never forgotten—or forgiven—the delay in receiving his $500 bonus in 1943, his first year with the Yankee organization. Or the days he went hungry that season because his $90-a-month salary couldn't cover the cost of food in Norfolk during the wartime boom. He learned early not to trust management.

Berra knows what he's worth as an All-Star catcher for a World Series champion. And if he didn't, his wife has no trouble reminding him that both Bill Dickey and Casey Stengel were calling Yogi the best catcher in the league by the end of last season. That should mean a big raise.

Burnes also knows Berra and his wife work as a team. First they decide the salary they want, then they agree on the lowest salary they will accept. They're both convinced that Weiss—whose bonus is largely determined by the size of the team's payroll—will lowball them, so Carmen asks Yogi to promise God he won't take a penny less. Yogi still gets up early every Sunday—at home or on the road—to attend Mass, standing behind the back row so no one recognizes him. Carmen knows if Yogi makes a promise to the Lord, he'll never break his word.

Holdout aside, Yogi is like so many Americans in the first year of this new decade: happy, optimistic, and raising a new family. Everything in America is booming: the economy, the suburbs popping up around cities across the country, the size of families. Experts are already calling the rising birthrate a "baby boom." Indeed, Carmen and Yogi—who welcomed Larry Jr. into the world three months ago—are already thinking about another baby timed to the end of next season.

They would have joined the rush to the suburbs of New York City—Berra says they even had a house picked out in New Jersey—if a kid on a bicycle hadn't knocked over Yogi's mother this past fall, breaking her hip. When the doctors went into surgery to repair the damage, they saw Paulina's diabetes had reached an advanced stage, which would slow the healing process. Expect Paulina to spend months in a wheelchair, they warned the family. So once the '49 World Series ended, Yogi and Carmen put off moving east for another year and move back into the basement of his parents' house to help take care of Momma Berra.

Postwar life on The Hill is good. Yogi's heard some of the neighbors talk about the threat of the Soviet Union and Communism and stories about some cranky senator named McCarthy from Wisconsin who keeps saying there are Communists working in the government. Yogi's never paid much attention to politics, and he doubts there are any Communists on The Hill, where he still has plenty of friends. Sure, he'd rather be playing baseball and hanging out with best buddy Phil Rizzuto and his teammates down in Florida. But he's surprised how much he enjoys working as the greeter at Ruggeri's restaurant, chatting about sports with customers as he shows them to their tables.

He also likes shooting pool and playing cards with the guys at his favorite taverns. Yogi doesn't drink much, but he enjoys talking sports for hours on end. And he loves to gamble, so it irks him that some people in this tight community suggest Berra shouldn't be gambling with his friends because he makes so much more money. "I don't hear them complaining," he says when anyone asks him about it. "Anytime they don't want me around, all they gotta do is say so."

Truth is, his buddies love having Yogi around, not because he's a Yankee but because he's still the same guy they grew up with. They enjoy the few stories they coax out of him about the stars he plays with and against, and they relish taking his money when he loses a big hand at cards. "Making expenses," they call it with a laugh. They're going to miss him when he's gone.

But he's not going anywhere until the Yankees meet his price. Yogi and Carmen think he deserves $22,000—$8,000 more than last season—and decide to accept no less than $18,000. The Yankees offered $16,000, so Yogi sent the contract back unsigned and dug in his heels. He knows business is booming for the Yankees, who drew more than two million customers for the fourth straight season. Broadcasters are beginning to pay teams good money, and everyone expects the TV pot will only keep growing.

He also knows co-owner Dan Topping talked DiMaggio into coming back for another year at $100,000. Management gave Tommy Henrich $40,000, and Joe Page signed for $35,000, making him the third-highest-paid pitcher in baseball. *Good for them!* All Yogi wants is his fair share. And that's what Yogi is explaining to Burnes as the two men walk out into the cold St. Louis night.

"They have the idea that I'll take anything they offer me," Yogi says. "Well, I won't. I need the money and I need them. But they need me, too. I've got to stick it out this time."

Burnes offers Yogi a ride home; Berra says thanks, he'd rather walk. As the writer watches the ballplayer trudge off alone through the snow, he can't help but think how the perception of Berra as the happy-go-lucky, none-too-smart slugger is so far off the mark. This is a serious man, one who understands the responsibilities to his family and his true value to the New York Yankees. The Yankees better improve their offer—and fast, Burnes thinks, as he watches Yogi disappear into the night—or they won't see their star catcher any time soon.

It's a few days later when Yogi receives a call from St. Petersburg. It's his boss, and he is not happy. "This is foolish, Yogi—you're not doing yourself or the team any good by staying in St. Louis," Yankee GM George Weiss tells him. "Why don't you get on an airplane and come down here? We aren't so far apart we can't settle it."

Berra is just as blunt. "If I come and don't sign," he says, "who'll pay for the ticket?"

Yogi can feel the GM's anger rise a thousand miles away. "We'll pay your expenses, Yogi," Weiss says. "Just get down here."

Berra flies down to St. Pete on March 5 and walks into Weiss' office the following day. He's soon sorry he made the trip. Weiss immediately starts telling him all the things he does wrong and never moves off his initial offer. "I thought I had a pretty good year," says Yogi, who led the team in RBI with 91 in just 116 games. "But to listen to you, I was a flop."

Negotiations are still at a standstill when Berra walks out of Weiss' office after two grueling hours, and he's immediately surrounded by reporters. Berra tells them he plans to stay in camp and keep talking, but he's not going to cave on his salary demands. "Weiss knows what I want and when he's ready to pay me, I'll sign," says Berra, who cuts the interview short to catch up with his teammates. Yogi enjoys the teasing that comes his way, then stays in the clubhouse and eats sandwiches from the players' spread when his teammates head out to the field for drills.

Berra is back arguing with Weiss the next day, aware that Topping has come to town and is monitoring these talks. It's common knowledge that Berra is the co-owner's favorite Yankee, and the two men have developed a warm relationship. And this time Casey Stengel is sitting in Weiss' office, hoping to get his catcher back in uniform. But it's not long into this session before Weiss accuses Berra of trying to become the richest man in baseball in the shortest amount of time.

That's it for Yogi.

"I'm done talking to you—I want to talk to Topping!" Berra shouts. "He's the boss, ain't he? I want to talk to the boss."

Sensing his invaluable catcher might just be mad enough to leave training camp, Stengel intercedes. He knows what Berra wants and convinces Weiss to up his offer to $18,000. That's good enough for Yogi, who signs and is quickly back in uniform.

"Sure, his feet stick out wrong and he doesn't seem to do anything right," a relieved Stengel tells reporters. "But he murders the ball and when he's behind the plate, my pitchers win. What else can any manager expect of a catcher?"

Stengel likes what he sees from his team in spring training and is convinced this club has a good chance to repeat. Most baseball writers believe otherwise, again picking the Red Sox to win the American League pennant by a wide margin. But the Yankees finish the exhibition season winning their last six games, Joe DiMaggio hit .402, and the offense belted 32 homers in 36 games. Who cares what the writers think?

Stengel has high expectations for his young catcher, too, and Berra delivers right from Opening Day at Fenway Park. The Yankees watch the Red Sox race to a 9–0 lead after four innings, then come roaring back, and Yogi is in the middle of almost every rally. He raps out three singles, scores three runs, and drives in the final run in a 15–10 Yankee win that stuns the Red Sox and the Fenway faithful.

Casey knows Berra gives him a big edge—no team has a good defensive catcher who can also hit like his young star—and he plays Yogi every inning of the first 33 games. Pitching is the real strength of this team, and coach Bill Dickey is soon raving about the new improvement in Berra's game: his ability to call one pitch to set up another and his knowledge of the strengths and weaknesses of every opposing hitter. "I wouldn't trade him for any catcher in the game," Dickey says.

Berra's fielding is impeccable—he'll lead AL catchers in six categories, including most runners thrown out attempting to steal (34), fewest passed balls (7), and the most assists (64)—and his hitting is superb. By the time he has to sit out Game 34 after a foul ball splits a nail on the index finger of his throwing hand, Yogi is hitting .308 with 27 RBI and the Yankees are 24–9, 2½ games ahead of second-place Detroit, three ahead of Boston.

Shortstop Phil Rizzuto is also off to a terrific start, gobbling up every ball that comes his way, hitting .348, and scoring 29 runs. Tommy Henrich is hitting .356 with 16 RBI despite losing a week to a knee injury. About the only player off to a slow start—for him—is Joe DiMaggio. His power numbers are decent—five homers and 30 RBI in 32 starts—but he's hitting .264, almost 70 points below his .331 career average.

DiMaggio's average will be marooned below .300 well into the second half of the season, and it's apparent that age and injury have robbed Joltin' Joe of some of his dazzling talent. But there are milestones to be reached. On June 20, DiMaggio raps a single through the left side of the Indian infield. It's Joe's 2,000th hit, and the ball is retrieved for his trophy case.

After the game, DiMaggio sits at his locker talking to Yogi, who now occupies the locker right next to his—the aging superstar with his heir apparent. "Two thousand hits," says DiMag before taking a long gulp from a bottle of beer. "Have I really been in the league that long?"

There's more than longevity on DiMaggio's mind this day. Now 35, he is staring at his baseball mortality. "I wish I could go up there with the confidence I used to have," he tells Berra. "I used to feel like I could hit any pitcher alive." But that was then. Now it's Berra who strides to the plate thinking there isn't a pitcher in the game who can get him out.

Yogi, whose 25th birthday passed four weeks ago, just nods. DiMaggio is the best player he's ever seen, and Yogi's sure this is just a star player battling a slump. It will be many years before Berra understands what DiMaggio is telling him: this game can be cruel when age catches up to you.

DiMaggio's milestone came right after a four-game series in St. Louis, where Yogi, who has always struggled in front of the hometown fans, finally showed them he's one of the elite players in the game. Berra belted 10 hits in 16 at-bats—including a pair of doubles, a home run, and five RBI—raising his batting average to .309. He even stole a base, his third of the season. Sitting in a box seat near the Yankee dugout for all four games was Pietro Berra, whose opinion of America's Pastime has changed significantly. With Yogi's financial help, Pietro no longer works in the brickyard, and he never misses a game when the Yankees are in town.

Trips to St. Louis are always busy. Parents. Friends. Mass at St. Ambrose. Town folks are constantly asking for his time; this trip he brought Rizzuto, Henrich, and Eddie Lopat to the Hotel York to do a quiz show for a local charity.

He also catches up with Joe Garagiola, who is recovering from the surgery to his right shoulder he needed after colliding with Jackie Robinson in a June 1 game against the Dodgers. Yogi became the star Joe predicted back at the 1946 World Series, but Garagiola never fulfilled the promise he showed in his rookie season. And that's what made this injury so frustrating. Garagiola was hitting .347 when he went down, and now the doctors are telling him he won't swing a bat again until September. He'll never regain his batting stroke, and four years later he'll retire.

Yogi and Joe are still close, more like brothers than friends, but Yankee shortstop Phil Rizzuto is now Berra's best friend. There's almost an eight-year age difference between Berra and Rizzuto, but there are many things that bind these two men. Their Italian heritage, of course. Rizzuto loves when the team plays in St. Louis and he's treated to Momma Berra's lasagna, ravioli, and risotto. And bocce matches with Yogi's neighbors.

Both players are often on the receiving end of pranks—especially Rizzuto. Even Yogi chuckles when a fellow Yankee tosses a rubber snake Phil's way or stuffs a spider or—worse—a dead mouse in his glove and Rizzuto shrieks and runs. Rizzuto shares Berra's passion for movies—on road trips, the two roommates will often throw their travel bags in their hotel room without unpacking and rush off to see the latest movie, preferably a western. Rizzuto likes to play naive, but the 32-year-old from Brooklyn is street-smart and teaches Berra how to handle the media, how to slip questions he doesn't like, and how to deal with demanding fans.

And Rizzuto, godfather to Larry Jr., knows how to take care of his money. It's Phil who convinces Yogi to move to the lucrative New York market to parlay his fame into fortune.

This is the first season the two friends have roomed together, and Rizzuto is discovering the challenges of bunking with Yogi. Rizzuto has convinced his friend to add detective novels to his comic-book-dominated reading list. But to Rizzuto's dismay, once Yogi grabs a book he refuses to sleep until he's finished. It's not uncommon for Phil to chase Yogi into the bathroom so he can turn off the lights and get some shut-eye.

Then there are the times Berra can't sleep and demands his roommate tell him a bedtime story. "Three Little Pigs, Three Bears, anything like that," Rizzuto tells his bemused teammates. "He says the sound of my voice puts him to sleep."

But it's baseball Yogi wants to talk about most, and the two players dissect every game, wins and losses alike. Rizzuto is amazed how much Berra has learned since teaming with Dickey and how often Casey confers with his catcher in private. Rizzuto even thinks Berra could make a good manager someday.

Both players continue their excellent play through June and into July, each earning a starting role in the July 11 All-Star Game in Chicago, the first to be nationally televised. Though Stengel adds six more Yankees to the All-Star roster, much of his team went flat in June—especially reliever Joe Page, who is so ineffective he'll soon be replaced as the team's top reliever by midseason acquisition Tom Ferrick—and New York loses 16 of 32 games to enter the break trailing surprising Detroit by three games.

By then Yogi has a new roomie—21-year-old rookie left-hander Whitey Ford, who arrived from the minors with infielder Billy Martin at the end of June. Stengel doesn't want to room two rookies together, especially two as brash as Ford and Martin, and hopes the well-grounded Berra will be a good influence on his young pitcher.

But Whitey, son of a New York City bar owner, instantly bonds with kindred spirit Page, whose late-night exploits will end his Yankee career this season. Trying hard not to awaken Berra after nights of partying with Page and Martin, Ford changes in the dark, bumping into doors and furniture, before finally dropping into bed. That's when Berra, who has lain awake in silence while Ford fumbled about, turns on the light and insists on talking about the day's game or a movie—anything rather than go to sleep.

The rookie pitcher soon learns he can't rely on his veteran roomie to wake him up. That lesson came before a doubleheader in Chicago, when Yogi, who rises at 6 a.m. no matter what, wakes Ford and asks him to join him for breakfast. "Let me sleep—I'm tired," Ford says. "But wake me up when you leave for the ballpark, and I'll get up and take a cab with you."

Ford rolls over and goes back to sleep. The next voice he hears is Yankee public relations man Red Patterson on his hotel room telephone.

"Where the hell are you?" Patterson shouts. "Don't you know you're pitching today? Casey is really mad."

"What time is it?"

"It's noon. The game is at 1 p.m."

Ford dresses and rushes into a cab from the Hotel Del Prado to Comiskey Park. When he arrives at 12:45, teammates Hank Bauer, Gene Woodling, and Allie Reynolds take turns telling him the same thing every new Yankee has heard for years: "Hey rookie, don't go screwing around with our World Series money." Ford pitches the second game of the day and is awful, allowing three runs on two singles, a triple, and a home run in the first inning, getting just one out before Stengel pulls him. The Yankees rally for a 4–3 win, but it's days before Ford's teammates let him forget his blunder.

When he asked Berra what happened, Yogi had a simple answer.

"I forgot," he tells the rookie.

★   ★   ★

Ford doesn't make many more mistakes, winning nine of 10 decisions, including an 8–1 complete-game gem against the Tigers on September 16 that puts the Yankees into first place to stay. Berra, Rizzuto, and a red-hot DiMaggio each rap out a pair of hits in support, with Joe D slamming his 30th home run. It hasn't been an easy season for DiMaggio, who was embarrassed on July 3 when Stengel played him at first base and he looked lost. Stengel also dropped him to fifth from his cherished cleanup spot in the batting order, then rested him the second week of August, a move that makes national headlines. *Joltin' Joe benched!*

DiMaggio returns to the starting lineup on August 18 in Philadelphia, batting cleanup right behind Rizzuto and Berra, and hits a 9th-inning home run to give New York a 3–2 win. Suddenly the old Joe D is back, turning the top of the Yankee lineup into a gauntlet for opposing pitchers. Rizzuto hits .326 and scores 42 runs in the season's final 43 games; Berra hits .344, clubs 15 homers, and drives in 45 runs. DiMaggio bats .373 with 11 homers and 44 RBI.

The Yankees win 31 of their last 43 games and on September 29 spend their off day before the season's final two games against the Red Sox milling around a room in Boston's Hotel Kenmore. That's where team announcer Mel Allen sits with a special radio setup and relays the play-by-play of the Cleveland-Detroit game. What starts as a tense afternoon eases as the Indians score three runs in the 5th and two more in the 6th. When Cleveland records the final out of a 12–2 rout of second-place Detroit, the Yankees are AL champions for the 17th time.

"Fellows, I consider this pennant an even greater achievement than the one you won for me last year," Stengel tells his players after they finish tossing their 60-year-old manager from one set of shoulders to another. Stengel notes they had to beat four good teams for the pennant this season, praises a few of his key performers, makes sure to thank DiMaggio, then looks over at his catcher.

"Yogi Berra was tremendous," Stengel says. "He caught almost every game for us and never once asked to be taken out for an injury, although he was pretty banged up a number of times. He reflected the spirit of all the players."

It's Berra's third pennant in four seasons, and his performance is one of the finest for any catcher in baseball history. He hit .322 with 28 home runs and a team-high 124 RBI, and scored 116 runs—a total few catchers could ever match and just nine fewer than Rizzuto, the team leader. Still a free swinger, Berra is especially proud of striking out just 12 times, despite the physical toll of catching a league-high 148 games—including 19 of 22 doubleheaders.

The Yankees make quick work of Philadelphia in the World Series, sweeping the young Phillies in four games before 40 percent of each day's national TV audience. Berra manages just three hits, including a home run in Game 4, but his highlights come behind the plate, where he guides a Yankee pitching staff that allows just five runs. Game 1 starter Vic Raschi, once one of Yogi's harshest critics, neatly sums up Berra's vast improvement.

"Yogi, you called a perfect game," says Raschi after tossing a two-hit, 1–0 shutout. "I didn't have to shake you off once. Thank you."

Raschi isn't the only star who appreciates Berra this autumn. Ed Sullivan, whose Sunday night variety show *Toast of the Town* is one of the most popular programs on television, wants Berra to make an appearance once the Series is over. Yogi keeps telling the show reps he'd rather head home to St. Louis, prompting Sullivan, a former sportswriter and a big baseball fan, to visit the Berras at their New York apartment the morning of the final game.

Try as he might, Yogi refuses to change his mind, so Sullivan turns to Carmen. "You would only have to stay an extra day or two," Sullivan says. "I've offered Yogi $1,000. I'm hoping you can get him to change his mind."

"Did you say $1,000?" Carmen asks Sullivan.

Yes, he tells her.

Carmen sees Sullivan's offer as money in the bank and Yogi's appearance on a hit TV show as a down payment on their future. "Don't worry," she says, "Yogi will be there."

Berra has one more thing to do before he leaves town with another World Series check, this one for $5,737.95. His good friend Frank Scott, the team's traveling secretary, has been forced out by George Weiss. The GM continued to ask Scott to report on what players were doing on the road, Scott steadfastly refused, so Weiss fired him over the protests of Stengel and the players.

Scott and his wife are having dinner at the Berras' apartment when Frank asks about the time. He's left his watch at home. "Wait right there," says Carmen, who leaves the room, returns with a box full of watches, and tells him to take one. When Scott asks where all the watches came from, Yogi says he gets one just about every time he makes an appearance.

"You mean those guys don't give you a check?" Scott asks Berra, who just nods, knowing Sullivan's offer was one of the few exceptions. Scott instantly sees his next career. He tells Berra he'll represent him and make sure Yogi gets paid for appearances, keeping 10 percent for himself. The two men will work out the details in the coming months, and the game's first agency for players—Frank Scott Associates—is born. The terms of their deal, one of dozens Scott will quickly make with a host of other stars—DiMaggio, Rizzuto, Willie Mays, and Jackie Robinson among them—will never change. Nor will it ever involve more than a handshake.

Berra is back home on The Hill in late October when word comes that Rizzuto was elected the American League's Most Valuable Player. Sixteen of the 23 members of the Baseball Writers' Association of America cast a first-place vote for Rizzuto, his 284 points a reward for his sparkling defense, 200 hits, and clubhouse leadership. Boston's Billy Goodman, the league's leading hitter, finishes a distant second with 180 points, with Berra (146) third. Yogi is happy for his best friend and even happier when he learns the Yankees gave Rizzuto $50,000 to play next season, making Phil the third-highest-paid Yankee in history behind DiMaggio and Ruth.

It's also a 43 percent raise. That'll figure heavily into the talk Yogi will soon have with his wife about his own contract negotiations. And if the Yankees won't meet his number, well, he's already shown he's ready to wait until they come to their senses.

Yogi is preparing for Christmas when a St. Louis reporter calls and asks about an award Berra just won. The National Association of Women Artists said Yogi has one of the 10 most stimulating faces in America. "They said, 'Yogi has the most down-to-earth face in America,'" the reporter tells Berra. "'It stimulates women's subconscious yearn for the Neanderthal Man.'"

The local papers run with the story, playing it up big with pictures of Yogi. The next night he calls Garagiola. "Joe, have you seen the papers?" Yogi says.

Sure, Garagiola tells him, knowing instantly what story his friend is calling about.

"Well, what does all that stuff mean?" he asks.

"It means the gals go for you," Joe says.

There's a pause.

"Geez," Yogi says. "I hope Carmen doesn't hear about this."

# CHAPTER 15

# Big Money

## 1951

Yogi Berra is sitting in a chair across from J. G. Taylor Spink, one of baseball's most influential men, in the plush lobby of the Hotel Adams in Phoenix. Yogi has a wide grin on his face, and for good reason. It's the second week of March, and he's finally joined his teammates in spring training for the 1951 season. His wife is three months pregnant with their second child, still a closely held family secret.

And in the pocket of his jacket is a Yankee contract for $28,500, making the 25-year-old the highest-paid catcher in team history and one of the highest-paid players in the game.

Berra doesn't like doing interviews, but he doesn't mind talking to the 62-year-old Spink, the editor and publisher of the *Sporting News,* whom he's known for years. Spink was all of 26—the age Yogi will reach this May—when he took over the weekly baseball-centric newspaper after his father died suddenly in 1914. Spink quickly became known for his love of the game, his dedication to detail, and his long hours of work.

The result: his St. Louis–based publication is so indispensable to players, coaches, and the game's fans it's now known as "the Bible of Baseball." Each week, players eagerly await the arrival of the *Sporting News* to check out how their competitors in the minor leagues are progressing. Spink is widely recognized as Commissioner Happy Chandler's unofficial chief adviser, and all news that comes out of the Commissioner's office appears in the *Sporting News* first. This would upset the nation's top newspaper writers more if so many of them didn't freelance for Spink's publication.

Yogi reads the *Sporting News* cover to cover every week. He knows this interview will be a Page 1 story. Last season established him as one of the finest players in the game, the best player on a team that won the World Series for the third time in his four-year career. Now he's ready to answer any question Spink wants to ask.

Spink, long one of St. Louis' leading citizens, starts by telling Yogi he's disappointed the star catcher is leaving his hometown, a decision the Berras announced one day after Yogi signed his new contract. "But I understand," says Spink, acknowledging the opportunities to cash in on fame in New York City.

"I got responsibilities," Berra says. "I got to support my mom and dad. My three brothers are married and have their own financial problems. I support the house. I have a wife and a son.

"And I have to dress like a Yankee, live like a Yankee, act like a Yankee. That takes dough."

Yogi is not the only Berra who has to present well in public. Many of the players' wives come to home games and sit in their own special rows of seats in the loge section. They, too, are expected to dress well, especially Carmen Berra, whom General Manager George Weiss often refers to as "the perfect Yankee wife." Carmen always dresses in the latest style, has her hair done at a top salon in Manhattan, and gets clothes and makeup tips from the fashion-model wife of a close friend.

Well, Yogi tells Spink, all that takes dough, too.

"St. Louis is a great place," Berra says. "The Hill, my friends—it won't be easy to pull up stakes and move east. But if I spend my winters in New York, I believe I can make better connections than I could in St. Louis.

"Carmen likes New York, and I love the place. We're going to buy a home in New Jersey where Larry Jr. can grow up in the country and

I can take the George Washington Bridge to the Stadium in about half an hour."

Berra had to stage another holdout to get the contract he wanted, and this time he did not leave home until Weiss hit his number. Carmen and Yogi wanted $40,000 and were willing to settle for $28,000. The Yankees' first offer—$22,000—wasn't even close. So the Berras wrote a letter to Weiss, telling the GM it was time to stop telling Yogi he was too young to be highly paid and to stop counting the World Series check as part of his salary—as if winning the title each season was a given. Players should be rewarded for winning the World Series, they wrote, not penalized.

If the Yankees weren't going to pay big after Berra turned in a season for the ages, Carmen and Yogi reasoned, when would they? Weiss sent back another offer and a letter of his own. "The club appreciates what you are doing for us and wants to be fair," Weiss wrote. "We hope you will find this adjusted contract satisfactory." The offer was $25,000.

This time Berra responded with a phone call to New York.

"I want $40,000," Berra said.

"No," Weiss said.

End of discussion.

Yogi spends the next few weeks playing golf with Stan Musial and cards with his friends when he isn't going to hockey and basketball games. Sometimes he and Carmen go to her family's farm in Howes Mill; Yogi enjoys getting up early and collecting eggs from the henhouse with Carmen's mother Barbara, then pitching hay later in the day with Carmen's father Ernest Short. Yogi likes the work and loves the anonymity and solitude.

Berra was splitting his time between The Hill and the farm in mid-February when the Yankees opened training camp in Phoenix—co-owner Del Webb traded training sites with Giants owner Horace Stoneham so he could show off his championship team in his hometown. The silence was broken a week or so later when Yankee Assistant GM Roy Hamey flew into St. Louis to see Berra. Meet me at Ruggeri's on The Hill, Yogi told him.

Berra greeted Hamey as if Yogi were still Ruggeri's headwaiter. "I can give you a good seat. Or would you prefer sitting with a few guys who like to talk baseball?" Berra said.

"I don't want to eat," a flustered Hamey said. "I just want to talk to you about your contract."

Yogi didn't blink. "The steak here is good," he said, "and the spaghetti is marvelous." After several more tries, Hamey finally succeeded in getting Yogi to talk business.

"I want $40,000," Berra told Hamey.

"We're not going higher than $25,000," Hamey said.

Sorry, Berra replied, but that wasn't nearly enough.

"Well," Hamey said, "we are at an impasse."

"What the hell is an impasse?" Yogi asked.

Berra stood his ground, and on February 28—a full 13 days after pitchers and catchers reported to training camp—Weiss called again.

"Look, why don't we compromise a little bit?" he said. Yogi said sure, he'd sign for $35,000. Weiss countered with $26,000—almost a $10,000 raise. After some additional discussion—and raised voices—Weiss boosted the offer to $28,500. "Done," said Yogi, who jumped on a plane to Phoenix the very next day.

"You've come along pretty fast financially," says Spink.

"They always told me I would get money if I did the job. Well, I did the job, and I wanted my money," says Yogi, who knew he had plenty of leverage. He's the most popular player for a franchise undergoing a transition, something Joe DiMaggio made abundantly clear the night of March 3, when he told a small group of reporters this would be his last season. The story caught everyone—especially Yankee management—by surprise.

"Joe has not discussed this with any club official," Weiss told reporters who woke him up with the news. "We certainly hope he reconsiders." Stengel also said he hoped his center fielder would change his mind, even though every Yankee beat writer knew Casey was counting the days until he no longer had to endure the big guy's mood swings.

DiMaggio's been walking back his words ever since, insisting he meant this *could* be his last season, but it's been clear in these first few weeks of spring training that Joe's 36-year-old body is betraying him. Yes, he finished last season fast, raising hopes of more good years to come, but so far Joe has never looked so ordinary.

"How many games will DiMaggio play this season?" Spink asks.

"It's hard to predict anything with Joe," says Berra, who's managed to steer clear of the barely concealed feud between Stengel, whom he respects, and DiMaggio, whom he still holds in awe. "He's a great athlete with a lot of determination. He can do anything he puts his mind to."

Both men know that Yankee management is hoping teenage phenom Mickey Mantle, who spent last year playing shortstop and hitting .383 for their Class C team, will soon be ready to take DiMaggio's place in center field. Longtime DiMaggio sidekick Tommy Henrich, who retired right before spring training and signed on as a coach, has been tasked with transforming Mantle into an outfielder.

Berra met Mantle soon after reporting on March 1 and liked him instantly. They're both midwestern boys who are intensely competitive on the field, shy and withdrawn everywhere else. And neither man has much of an education. But that's where the similarities end. Mantle is blond, blue-eyed, and handsome. Berra is still enduring jokes about his appearance. The 19-year-old Mantle launches majestic fly balls—from both sides of the plate—that seem to disappear on the horizon. Yogi's home runs are line drives that rocket over the fence. Berra still has surprising speed; Mantle is the fastest player anyone in this camp has ever seen.

But while Mantle is dripping with star power—and Stengel wants him on his roster for the 1951 season—Weiss insists jumping four levels from Class C to the big leagues is just too much. A decision won't be made until the end of camp.

And there is a great deal at stake behind every decision Stengel and Weiss make—a place in baseball history and the big crowds that go with it. Only one team has won three straight World Series titles—the

Joe McCarthy Yankees, who won four championships in DiMaggio's first four seasons. But the young DiMaggio—who hit .341 from 1936 to 1939 while *averaging* 198 hits, 34 home runs, and 140 RBI—is a distant memory. This DiMaggio is suffering all sorts of aches, pains, and injuries and can no longer dominate a season.

This team's defining star is Berra, the one player who has to produce—both at the plate and behind it—if this team is going to make history. And Berra doesn't have DiMaggio's supporting cast. Sure, Phil Rizzuto should still provide stellar defense at shortstop. And there's every reason to believe the Big 3—All-Star pitchers Vic Raschi, Allie Reynolds, and Eddie Lopat—can duplicate last season's combined 55 wins and 46 complete games.

But reliever Joe Page looks as bad as he did last season; he will be released in mid-May. Left-hander Tommy Byrne is as wild as ever; he'll be traded by midseason. And rookie sensation Whitey Ford, 9–1 after being called up in late June last season, was drafted by the Army this past November for the rapidly escalating Korean War.

With all these questions, Spink says, is it any wonder most baseball writers are calling Boston the team to beat—again—in the American League?

"No question about it," Berra tells Spink, "the Red Sox are going to be really tough."

Spink asks Berra how many banquets he attended this past offseason. About a dozen, Yogi says, and at each one people are disappointed to find out Berra is neither talkative nor funny.

He asks the catcher about his weight. "I'm right where I should be," Berra tells him. "I minded my diet, but it wasn't easy."

How does Yogi explain the exceptional performance he turned in a year ago? "I didn't get hurt so much," he answers. "Maybe because I have more experience."

The two men have been talking for almost an hour, and Yogi has a question of his own to ask before he leaves for the ballpark. He reaches into his jacket pocket, pulls out a newspaper clipping, and shows Spink the headline: BABE RUTH HAD HIS LOU GEHRIG, JOE DIMAGGIO'S GOT HIS YOGI BERRA.

Spink is not surprised to see a headline placing Berra beside the three greatest players in Yankee history. But Berra is puzzled.

"What does this mean?" Berra asks him. "Is it a boost or a knock?"

The journalist assures Yogi the headline is a compliment. "Sometimes it's tough to tell what these guys write about me," Yogi tells Spink. "My wife, she don't like stories which make me out to be a dope. I don't like them myself."

Spink smiles. "Yogi," he says, "anyone who's pulled himself up from five grand to almost $30,000 hardly belongs in the dopey class."

Berra laughs, a look of relief spreading across his broad face. Then he puts the clipping back in his pocket, rises, and sticks the comic book that's been at his side into the back pocket of his pants. It's time to head to the ballpark.

"You know, I like spring training," Yogi says as the writer and the catcher walk toward the door. "I suppose in another 10 years I will be grousing about it like them veterans around here do now. But not yet.

"Baseball is still fun."

# CHAPTER 16

# Passing the Torch
## 1951

The Yankees break their Phoenix training camp in mid-March for a 12-game exhibition tour through California, playing in all the Pacific Coast League parks Joe DiMaggio starred in as a teenager. This is supposed to be a victory tour for DiMaggio, but the fans who pack every stadium to see Joltin' Joe are instead treated to the Yankee superstars of the present and future: Yogi Berra, who rains base hits at every stop, and Mickey Mantle, who belts booming home runs from both sides of the plate. Yogi is hitting better than .400 and is delighted when the team spends a day in Hollywood. Berra tours the studios and chats with Spencer Tracy, Red Skelton, and Greer Garson, a baseball fan who will soon become a pen pal; the two stars will exchange letters for years.

The return to familiar surroundings does little to help DiMaggio find his hitting stroke, and he grows increasingly annoyed when reporters ask him about Mantle at every stop. But there's plenty to discuss. At San Francisco's Seals Stadium, Mickey hits one over the bleachers and clear out of the park. At the University of Southern California, Mantle belts a home run from each side of the plate, one sailing out of the stadium and over an adjoining field house, leading to a new Stengel superlative.

"I have my outfielder, Mr. Mantle," says Casey, "who hits balls over buildings."

Stengel also wins his battle with Weiss. Mantle, who finishes spring training hitting .387 with a team-high nine home runs and 28 RBI, will be the team's starting right fielder for the 1951 season home opener against the Red Sox on April 17. It seems everyone in New York wants to see the teenage star, including Carmen Berra, who can't help but wonder about the player who is stealing headlines from her husband. The writers have described Mickey as an Adonis in pin-stripes, and Carmen is eager to meet the new kid when she arrives at the Concourse Plaza Hotel in the Bronx for the team's annual Welcome Home Luncheon.

Carmen is waiting for Yogi in the lobby when an elevator door opens and out walks Mickey, bashfully staring at the floor as he walks past Mrs. Berra.

"Oh, my God," Carmen says to herself. "Look at this boy!"

The Yankee season opener in front of President Harry Truman in Washington is rained out, but Opening Day at Yankee Stadium is a festive affair, with 44,860 fans watching Casey raise another World Series banner up the flagpole in center field. American League President Will Harridge presents the MVP plaque to Rizzuto. Ford, on leave from the Army, throws out the first pitch three days after marrying his hometown girlfriend Joan Foran, and Vic Raschi shuts out Boston on six hits for a 5–0 win.

Berra, again hitting fifth behind DiMaggio, has a single and a run batted in, then drives into Manhattan with Rizzuto to wave to the audience on Milton Berle's *Texaco Star Theater,* the top-rated show on television. Berle has never paid celebrities to appear on his one-hour variety show, but Frank Scott negotiated a $500 fee for each of his two clients, with the promise of more paydays to come.

It only takes a few games to confirm Yogi is more than able to carry the offense for this team. The Yankees grab the league lead on April 29, the day after Berra begins a 13-game hitting streak during which he hits .407 with four home runs and 12 RBI. Yogi plays 44 of the team's first 45 games as Stengel again leans heavily on the player he continues to call his "assistant manager." Yogi catches both games of doubleheaders against the A's on May 13—the day after he turns 26—and again on May 27. Three days later he catches a doubleheader against the Red Sox—all 15 innings of an 11–10 loss that knocks the Yankees out of first place—then the entire 9–4 second-game loss.

Despite the heavy workload, Berra hits .324 for the month of May and starts June with four homers in eight games. On June 2, Yogi hits a 12th-inning home run to beat Detroit, 8–7, breaking a four-game losing streak. Another homer starts an 8–2 rout of Cleveland and snaps a three-game losing streak. Berra's only real rest comes when he misses three games after suffering a one-inch gash over his left eye on June 7 in a pregame relay-throw competition gone awry.

Berra uses his downtime to sign papers for a house in Woodcliff Lake in upscale Bergen County, New Jersey, a seven-room ranch on a half-acre lot that should be built by the time Carmen, now almost six months pregnant, delivers their second child. All his St. Louis pals who predicted Yogi would never leave The Hill misjudged their friend and his ambitions. The poorly educated kid who used to swipe fruit and vegetables during the Depression will soon be living among New York City executives who are thrilled just to claim they know a famous baseball player.

Berra's new life on the East Coast—and as the prime hitter in the Yankee lineup—is quickly taking shape.

Yogi is back in uniform on June 10 to catch another doubleheader, collecting four hits in a split of the two games against the White Sox. Berra's superior play, the pitching of the Big 3—Vic Raschi, Allie Reynolds, and Eddie Lopat—and Stengel's clever mixing and matching of lineups have the Yankees in second place, just 2½ games behind Chicago. But theirs is an unhappy clubhouse.

One source of discomfort: Mickey Mantle—whose bat goes cold as pitchers learn his weaknesses—reveals an explosive temper. On May 18, Mickey was still the superstar in waiting, hitting .316 with four home runs and a team-high 26 RBI. But he hits just .197 without a homer in his next 21 games, striking out 21 times and smashing dugout bat racks and water coolers as his failures mount. Mantle's problems at the plate lead to defensive lapses in the field, prompting Lopat to corner him in the dugout after one especially bad mistake.

"You want to play?" the veteran pitcher shouted. "If not, get your ass the hell out of here. We don't need guys like you. We want to win."

Berra and Rizzuto, who have befriended the rookie, watch helplessly as writers report Mantle's every temper tantrum and the fans boo his every mistake. And they're relieved when Weiss mercifully sends Mickey to Triple-A Kansas City on July 13 after a three-strikeout game.

Yogi is still convinced Mantle, who won't turn 20 until late October, is destined to be a star. He's less certain that DiMaggio will even make it through this season. DiMaggio misses the first half of May with neck spasms and another two weeks in June with pulled muscles in his legs. On June 16 he learns his ailing mother has slipped into a coma and flies to San Francisco to be at her side when she passes two days later. He returns June 23 and continues his mediocre play, entering July hitting .278.

From his spot in the on-deck circle, Berra sees DiMaggio's problem: Joe just can't get around on a good fastball, which is all pitchers are throwing him. Not that Yogi—or any Yankee—will dare tell Joe, who grows more withdrawn with every poor performance. But how much longer can a Yankee team seeking another World Series title afford a cleanup hitter who hit just three home runs in May and one the entire month of June?

It almost makes Yogi uneasy when he congratulates DiMaggio on the rare day the Big Dago gets a key hit, like his two-run homer that breaks open a tight game against the Tigers on May 24. The hit raises DiMaggio's average to .310. It's the last time Joe's average will be .300 or better.

Still, nothing prepares Yogi for what DiMaggio tells him on an early July afternoon when he finds himself alone in a postgame clubhouse with Joe and Phil Rizzuto. DiMag looks around to make sure the room is empty, then quietly tells his two teammates he's finished.

"This is my final season," DiMaggio says. "I'm done."

"Joe," Yogi says, "you'll never quit."

DiMaggio stares at Berra before replying. "If I play one game with the Yankees next season, I'll give you $500," DiMaggio says. "And you don't have to give me anything if I don't." DiMaggio and Berra shake hands on their bet, and Yogi laughs as the three men leave the clubhouse, secure in his belief that Joe will turn this season around and return next year.

But his certainty vanishes on July 7, when Stengel does the unthinkable: he humiliates DiMaggio before a big crowd at Fenway Park. Yogi is on the bench with a sore back, the last of five games he's missed after a collision at the plate, when the Yankees take the field in the home half of the third. And he's stunned when he hears Casey tell rookie Jackie Jensen to run out to center field and replace Joe D—though not nearly as stunned as DiMaggio. Joe listens to Jensen in disbelief, stands in place for a few seconds, then jogs to the Yankee dugout, down its steps, and straight into the clubhouse.

DiMaggio and Stengel don't discuss the manager's decision—Casey later tells reporters he thought his aging star was limping—but no explanation will satisfy Joe, whose quiet rage will hang over this team for the rest of the season. None of this is lost on the media. The atmosphere around the Yankees, writes Milton Gross of the *New York Post,* "is a frigid one—all because Joe, always a strange man, is now living in a shell that is virtually impenetrable."

The July 10 All-Star Game in Detroit should have served as a temporary respite from the tension-filled atmosphere around his team. But Stengel again insults DiMaggio, adding him to the All-Star team only to keep him riveted to the bench. It doesn't help that Casey told reporters he planned to rest Berra, the fans' overwhelming choice to start at catcher, then plays Yogi the entire nine innings—his sore back wrapped in a corset—in the AL's 8–3 loss.

Allie Reynolds opens the season's second half by throwing a no-hitter against the Indians. Reynolds also supplies a bit of much-needed comic relief. The big right-hander tries so hard to strike out Bobby Avila for the final out that he falls flat on his face after his delivery. Berra rushes out to check on his pitcher, only to find Reynolds, one of the team's most serious men, lying on the ground laughing.

"Get up and let's finish this!" Yogi says. Reynolds strikes out Avila on the next pitch, and this time Yogi runs out to the mound and jumps on his pitcher's back in celebration.

The Yankees move in and out of first place in July and August, with Reynolds, Lopat, and Raschi nearly unbeatable—the three pitchers will combine for 15 shutouts and 51 complete games. While the press continues to write glowingly about Stengel's skillful use of his entire roster—the word *genius* is used liberally—it's Berra who huddles with the starting pitcher before each game to plot strategy. The same pitchers who once mocked Yogi's catching skills now rely on his remarkable knowledge of every hitter in the league and his strategic savvy.

Berra continues his heavy workload through the heat of August, catching all but one game—and five of six doubleheaders—while hitting .301 and driving in 23 runs. He also finds time to appear as a mystery guest on the popular television show *What's My Line?*—in which four blindfolded celebrities try to guess his identity—as well as sit for a photo shoot for the cover story of *Sport,* the nation's most popular sports magazine, and read over copy for a print ad for Prest-O-Lite car batteries.

The prediction Bucky Harris made back in 1947 has come to pass: Yogi Berra is now the most popular Yankee. When people see Yogi on the street, they point, stare, and wave. When headwaiters see Berra and Carmen walk into their restaurants, they promptly escort the couple to the best table, those waiting in line be damned.

Berra opens the final month of the season playing back-to-back doubleheaders, hitting .341 with 10 RBI and five home runs in 12 games. The fifth homer—Berra's team-high 27th—is a grand slam that beats the Tigers on September 14, ending a three-game slide and pulling second-place New York to a half game behind Cleveland with 15 games to play. Mantle is back from the minors and hitting well, but it's rookie infielder Gil McDougald—the eventual AL Rookie of the Year—whose bat supports Yogi, hitting .323 after the All-Star break and driving in 34 runs.

The man still not producing is the team's cleanup hitter. DiMaggio has managed only two home runs in the last 35 games and driven in just 20 runs while leaving almost too many runners in scoring position to count. And when the Yankees drop the next game to Detroit—falling a full game behind the Indians ahead of their crucial two-game showdown at the Stadium—Stengel finally shakes up his lineup. Yogi is now batting cleanup, the spot in the lineup DiMaggio had held for more than a decade. DiMaggio will hit fifth.

Stengel's moves pay off immediately when Berra opens the first game against Cleveland's Bob Feller with a booming, run-scoring triple. The Yankees add two more runs and Reynolds holds the Indians to a single run as the game reaches its turning point in the 5th inning. With Mantle on second and two out, Feller intentionally walks Berra to get to DiMaggio, yet another insult for the aging Yankee great.

Feller, still the hardest thrower in the game, quickly gets ahead of DiMaggio—a ball and two strikes—and decides to throw another fastball to finish off Joe. But this time DiMaggio catches Feller's pitch perfectly and slams a line drive over the head of All-Star center fielder Larry Doby, who chases it all the way to the 457-foot sign, the farthest part of Yankee Stadium. Mantle and Berra trot home while Joe cruises into third with a triple and thunderous applause from the crowd of 68,760. Reynolds makes the four-run lead stand up for a 5–1 win, and now the Yanks are back in first place, .003 percentage points ahead of the Indians.

The Yankees win again the next day, 2–1, with DiMaggio scoring the winning run in the 9th on a daring suicide-squeeze bunt by Rizzuto, and the Yankees take sole possession of first. With 12 games left to play, New York is closing in on history.

★   ★   ★

Berra and Rizzuto are standing in the Yankee clubhouse, cigars clenched between their teeth, as photographers from every New York newspaper snap their picture. Casey Stengel poses across the room, surrounded by Vic Raschi, Allie Reynolds, and Eddie Lopat, a big smile on each man's face. It's September 25, and the Yankees have much to be happy about. They've just received word the White Sox beat the Indians—Cleveland's fourth straight loss—boosting the Yankees' league lead to three full games with just six left to play. Barring a sudden collapse—like the one Berra's friends on the team in Brooklyn are now experiencing—Yogi will soon be playing in the fourth World Series of his five-year career.

Every player has a cigar courtesy of Yankee management, a nice gesture to celebrate the birth of Berra's son Tim, who arrived the night of September 23 as the Yankees were traveling back by train from Boston. The last week of Carmen's pregnancy had taken a toll on Yogi, who managed just four hits in 28 at-bats. The Yankees were off yesterday, giving Berra a chance to visit with Carmen at the hospital and spend time with his growing family.

"Maybe now you'll start hitting again," Stengel shouts over to Berra, who just smiles in agreement. Berra, whose 27 home runs are one shy of his career high, is the only Yankee who will finish with more than 15 homers. And Stengel knows just how fortunate he is that this was only the second time Berra went as many as three games without a base hit all season. Yogi is hitting .291 with 27 home runs and 85 RBI, and is a favorite to win his first MVP award.

Five days later it's Yogi's glove that everyone in Yankee Stadium is focusing on as Berra settles under a pop-up behind home plate off the bat of Boston's Ted Williams. There are two outs in the 9th inning, the Yanks hold an 8–0 lead, and once Berra catches this ball, the team will clinch a tie for the AL pennant in the most extraordinary way—the final out will make Allie Reynolds only the second pitcher to throw two no-hitters in the same season.

And history is all anyone is thinking about as Yogi pounds his glove, ready to make the catch. "Berra's underneath it," announcer Mel Allen shouts into his microphone. "This could be it!" But just then, a sudden gust of autumn wind catches the ball and Berra realizes he's in trouble. Out stretches Yogi's left arm as the ball drifts away, bounces off his glove, and both Berra and the ball fall to the ground.

"Yogiiii!" screams Carmen Berra, who's listening to the game in her hospital bed. Several nurses rush into her room. "My husband dropped the ball," she tells the relieved medical staff.

Reynolds, who made a late dash to catch the ball and wound up stepping on Berra's right hand, reaches for Yogi's arm, pulls up the distraught catcher, and puts his right arm around his teammate's shoulder. "Don't worry about it, Yog," says Reynolds. "We'll get him."

Williams, waiting for Berra at the plate, is not nearly as kind. "You son of a bitch, you've put me in one hell of a fix," the game's best hitter tells Berra. "Even though your man has a no-hitter, I've got to bear down even more than before. You blew it!"

Berra squats down and calls for a high fastball, the same pitch Reynolds just threw. Williams is an excellent fastball hitter, but Reynolds nods in agreement, winds up, and delivers a hard fastball in the same spot as the previous pitch. Incredibly, he gets the same result, as Williams sends a towering pop foul back toward the Yankee dugout. Every Yankee is on his feet, shouting encouragement or instructions to Yogi as the ball descends just a few feet from the New York dugout.

"You got plenty of room, Yogi," Berra hears as he moves perilously close to the edge of the dugout.

*What if I drop this one?* Berra thinks as the foul pop seems to take forever to come down. But there is no gust of wind this time, and when the ball finally hits Yogi's mitt, he squeezes it tightly. This time Reynolds gives his catcher a big bear hug, and soon the entire team is jumping on Reynolds and Berra, excited to be part of baseball history.

The Reynolds no-hitter is the first game of a doubleheader. The

Yankees make quick work of the Red Sox in the second game, winning 11–3 to wrap up the pennant. There's the usual backslapping, hugs, and shouts in the postgame locker room crowded with media, celebrities, and well-wishers. But it is hard not to notice this season's pennant celebration is more subdued than the previous two, the feeling more like relief than excitement.

Berra sits in front of his locker, his first-game blunder still fresh in his mind. A few lockers down he hears reporters peppering DiMaggio with questions about his future. "I honestly don't know about next year," Joe says wearily. "Right now we have some unfinished business—the World Series—and I don't care whether it will be against the Giants or Dodgers."

It's the New York Giants who emerge as the last team standing between the Yankees and another championship. The Giants trailed the Dodgers by 13 games on August 11, then won 37 of their final 46 games to tie Brooklyn for the pennant and force a three-game playoff. Berra is in the Polo Grounds on October 3 for the third and deciding game. He watches the Dodgers take a 4–1 lead in the top of the 8th, then leaves to beat the traffic. He's crossing the George Washington Bridge, listening to the game on the car radio, when the Giants' Bobby Thomson hits baseball's most famous home run, a three-run blast off Berra's friend Ralph Branca that gives the Giants a 5–4 victory and a shot at the Yankees.

Berra will remember this World Series for many reasons, but there are three images he will never forget:

- It's the 5th inning of Game 2 when he sees Mickey Mantle racing after a short fly ball in right-center off the bat of Giants rookie Willie Mays. Even this late in the year, Mantle's speed is breathtaking. But Yogi sees Mantle suddenly drop to the ground as if he is shot. The reason: Mickey tries to pull up when he hears DiMaggio call for the ball at the last second, catches his right foot in a plastic sprinkler cap, and blows out his knee.

There's an ache in the pit of Yogi's stomach as he watches Mickey carried off the field on a stretcher, a shard of bone poking through the side of his leg. Mantle will never possess that blazing speed— or play a single game pain-free—for the rest of his career.

- It's moments before Game 4 when Berra hears Stengel call the team together in the locker room. Yogi has rarely heard Casey give a pregame speech, but the Yankees have looked listless while losing two of the first three games to a Giants team they all think they should beat. "Fellas, I just want to mention one thing to you," Casey says, showing little emotion. "You are not playing these guys 22 games—you only have four left to play. What the hell are you going to do, let them run you out of the ballpark?"

Stengel looks at every group of players standing around him, letting his words sink in, and says simply, "Okay, let's go." Raschi, Reynolds, and Lopat dominate the Giants in the next three games. Yankee hitters pound out 23 runs, and Stengel's team sweeps the next three games to secure their place in history with their third straight title.

The postgame celebration is complete bedlam, and Berra is right in the middle of it. "Ear-splitting yells rent the air," James Dawson of the *New York Times* writes about a Yankee team finally letting loose. It's hard to even move with so many writers, photographers, and well-wishers crammed into the clubhouse.

- What Yogi remembers most happens more than an hour later, when every nonplayer has left the clubhouse and the Yankees are quietly sitting in front of their lockers, letting their accomplishment sink in. Suddenly pitcher Spec Shea walks across the locker room and sits down next to DiMaggio.

"What about it, Joe?" Shea asks quietly.

"I've played my last game," DiMaggio says just as quietly, but every player hears his words.

No one moves for a moment, but soon every Yankee walks over to Joe, each carrying a glove, a ball, a bat, a uniform, all things they ask DiMaggio to sign. Yogi brings over his own collection for Joe and can't help thinking about the bet Joe D made with him way back in July. He wants to keep playing with the best there ever was, but he knows DiMaggio is serious, and that turns this great day bittersweet.

It's late in the afternoon of November 8, 1951, and Yogi Berra is sitting in the den of his suburban New Jersey split-level home, relaxing with one of his favorite comic books. It's an off day from his job as a part-time salesman at the American Shops, an upscale men's clothing store in Newark. And he's already spent two hours at the Seventh Regiment Armory teaching hitting and catching at the American Baseball Academy, the brainchild of Phil Rizzuto. Berra is one of a handful of major leaguers Rizzuto recruited to teach baseball to 1,500 teenagers—two one-hour shifts, five days a week—to pick up a little money for the next three months.

Yogi is one of the best-paid players in the sport—and he figures to get another raise for next season—but owning a nice house in suburbia and raising a family takes more money than all but a select few earn just playing baseball. A week of golf with the guys at the famed Pinehurst courses in North Carolina is about all the offseason Berra can usually afford.

Yogi lifts himself from his chair when he hears the doorbell ring and is surprised to find a group of New York photographers when he opens the door. "Come on in," he tells the half dozen men carrying cameras. "What are you doing out here?"

Now it's the visitors who are surprised. "You don't know?" one of them says. "You're the American League MVP. We're here to take your picture."

Berra is a bit taken aback. No, the news had not reached him yet. "Is this a joke?" he asks. Assured they are serious, Berra quickly calls out to his wife to join them. "Hey, Carmen," says Yogi when his wife appears. "They say I won the MVP!"

"Are you kidding?" Carmen says. Both Berras thought Yogi would get a lot of consideration for the award. But Yogi's bat went cold the final two weeks of the season as he concentrated on guiding the pitching staff to the pennant, and they figured that would cost him too many votes to win. They were convinced Allie Reynolds—with his 17 wins, two no-hitters, and league-high seven shutouts—was almost a lock for the award.

They figured wrong, the photographers explained as they set up their equipment. Berra, Reynolds, and Ned Garver, the Browns' 20-game winner, each received six first-place votes in one of the tightest competitions since the award was started in 1931. But Yogi had more support on the rest of the ballot from the 24 writers—three from each American League city—who decide the MVP.

"I ain't biting the hand that feeds me, but I think they shoulda picked Allie Reynolds," Berra says as the cameras click away. "In the meantime, I ain't gonna throw the award back in the lake. It's big— very big—and I thank the baseball writers for being so good to me."

A few television crews arrive, and Yogi grows silent as they set up their lights and position their cameras for interviews. Suddenly, a different look crosses his face, and he breaks his silence.

"Hey," he says, smiling. "I guess I must of been pretty good!"

# CHAPTER 17

# Big Shoes to Fill
## 1952

Yogi Berra is a few feet from second base at Yankee Stadium, his arms folded across his chest. It's April 25, 1952, and the Yankees are going through a few light drills before a game with the Senators, their tenth of the young season. Berra has yet to play a regular-season game, a big reason for New York's 4–5 start. Berra says his sore left wrist, the result of a wicked foul tip that nailed him in a spring training game back on April 4, prevents him from gripping his bat.

Manager Casey Stengel has a lot to say, too, and little of it good. His Yankees have left 81 runners on base with their best run producer on the bench, and Casey has waged a verbal war to get Berra back in action. And today Berra's best friend is at home plate, hitting ground balls to infielders, playfully imitating one of Stengel's jabs at Yogi.

"Look, Jerry," Phil Rizzuto says to second baseman Jerry Coleman. "Yogi just moved—he blinked his eyes."

"At least that proves he's still alive," Coleman says, trying unsuccessfully not to laugh. Berra pretends he doesn't hear a word.

Rizzuto sends a slow roller toward his friend. "Oops," Phil shouts. "Betcha he doesn't pick it up."

"He has to—what else can he do?" Coleman says.

Berra doesn't change his blank expression or unfold his arms. Instead, he walks leisurely toward the slow roller until it crosses his path, then kicks the baseball in the general direction of coach Frank Crosetti's ball bag.

"Yippee!" Rizzuto shouts. "Hey, if Yog isn't careful he'll work up a sweat. And that could be fatal."

Berra usually smiles at the teasing he gets from teammates—especially from Rizzuto—but the league's reigning MVP is in no mood for jokes. New York's slow start has already sparked talk that these Yankees are wilting under the pressure of pursuing their fourth straight World Series title. Rizzuto's little joke notwithstanding, there hasn't been a lot of laughs around the Yankees these days.

There are plenty of reasons only one team—the 1936–1939 Yankees of Joe DiMaggio, Lou Gehrig, and Bill Dickey—has won four consecutive titles. Veterans begin to break down. Check. Both 33-year-old Vic Raschi (sore knee) and 33-year-old Eddie Lopat (sore arm) are feeling the effects of averaging more than 225 innings each since the Yankee run of three straight titles began in 1949.

Players are called into military service. Check. Jerry Coleman, their slick-fielding second baseman, will rejoin the Marines by the end of April to fly jets in the ongoing war in Korea. Hard-hitting third baseman and med-school student Bobby Brown will leave for the Army hospital in Tokyo in a few months. And Whitey Ford is spending his second year in an Army uniform instead of Yankee pinstripes.

Replacements get hurt. Check. Billy Martin, whose fierce competitiveness made him one of Casey's favorites last year in his first full season, broke his ankle in two places on March 12 while demonstrating how to slide for a TV pregame segment. Others don't rehab after getting hurt. Check. Mickey Mantle, who will never be known as a workout warrior, limped through spring training and much of April, still looking to rebound from last fall's knee surgery.

And superstars get old and retire. A great big check. When Joe DiMaggio—the face of this franchise for 16 years—officially put down his glove and bat this past December, he left a big hole in center field, another hole at cleanup in Stengel's lineup, and a large void in the Yankee clubhouse.

Stengel thinks he can take care of the clubhouse himself—he always wants to be the center of attention anyway. But only two players have hit cleanup for the Yankees since they began dominating baseball in 1923—DiMaggio and Gehrig. On March 6, Stengel anointed Berra—who has more home runs (75) and RBI (303) than any other Yankee the last three seasons—to bat fourth and anchor the team's offense.

The Yankees made their commitment to Berra clear in January, when Yogi walked into the Fifth Avenue office of George Weiss and was surprised when the GM handed him a contract for $32,500—a $4,000 raise. Berra quickly said yes to a salary that is almost 15 times larger than America's $2,300 median income. (In addition, each of Yogi's four World Series winner's checks has been in excess of $5,000, more than what 90 percent of Americans earn in an entire year.) Weiss was so pleased when Berra reported to St. Petersburg on time he threw in an extra $500 the day Yogi sat down to sign the papers in the team's spring headquarters.

Berra's popularity off the field continues to climb. He'll soon be pitching Rheingold beer in a full-page ad scheduled to run nationwide. Publisher Grosset & Dunlap has hired *New York Daily News* Yankee writer Joe Trimble to write a biography of Berra for its Big League Baseball Library series; Yogi will do book signings in every American League city. He'll take a bow on *The Ed Sullivan Show,* one of his three television appearances for the year. Agent Frank Scott continues to line up endorsements for everything from Shelby bicycles for kids to Doodle Oil bait for fishermen.

But right now Berra is missing in action. Yogi's injury problems began when he missed first base on a double-play grounder March 15 and pulled ligaments in his right ankle trying to scramble back to touch the base. Berra returned March 30, hit a three-run homer and a run-scoring single against the Braves, and looked ready to step into Joe D's big shoes. Then Yogi hurt his left wrist in an exhibition game on April 4—x-rays showed several badly bruised bones—and he's been sidelined ever since.

Berra was still hurting when he received his Most Valuable Player plaque from Commissioner Ford Frick before the Yankee home opener against Washington. DiMaggio, reluctantly taking time away from his intense courtship of Marilyn Monroe, was the star of the pregame ceremonies. Joe gave his uniform and glove to a representative of the National Baseball Hall of Fame, then threw a one-hopper to home plate—the ceremonial first pitch—from his box seat beside the Yankee dugout. A few moments later Berra, his left wrist still too painful to swing a bat, took a seat and watched the Yankees hit eight harmless singles in a 3–1 loss to the Senators.

Casey, never patient with players and their injuries, starts pushing hard for Yogi to ignore the pain in his wrist and return to the lineup. Stengel knows each of his team's three pennants was won in the final weekend of the season. The rest of the league is only stronger this year—especially the Indians and White Sox—and a slow start can crush this team's chances of making history. Especially since most observers think this season's Yankees are the least talented of Casey's teams.

Each game counts, Stengel keeps saying, and the Yankees have been giving away games. Case in point: a 3–2 loss in 11 innings to the first-place Red Sox on April 24. The Yankees squandered a two-run lead, left 17 runners on base, and walked in the winning run.

Casey was furious after the loss, and is in no better mood when he arrives at the Stadium for the Friday, April 25 game against the Senators. It's been a full 21 days since Yogi last played, and Berra reluctantly tells his manager he can play—painful wrist and all—if Stengel needs him. But rain starts to fall before the Yankees finish batting practice and officials soon decide to call the game. With downpours in the forecast for the rest of the weekend, it doesn't look like Berra will play his first game of the season any time soon.

The Yogi Berra Era is off to a slow start.

The injury Berra suffered in early April turned out to be more than bruised bones. A second x-ray taken soon after Opening Day revealed a torn ligament, and that takes time to heal. Yogi finally returns to the lineup on April 30, catching both ends of a doubleheader split with the Browns, and it's soon clear it will take Berra some time to regain his swing. By the end of May, he has hit just three home runs and knocked in only 13 runs in 26 games. Not surprisingly, the Yankees enter June in fifth place, 3½ games behind first-place Cleveland.

Nor is it surprising that Stengel is making changes.

Stengel decides the knee Mantle injured in last year's World Series is finally fit enough to shift the 20-year-old from right to center field. When doctors declare Martin's ankle sound after he played second base for the final two weeks of May, Stengel announces Billy's spot in the lineup is permanent and hopes his short-tempered favorite will put an edge on the team's persona.

Stengel also considers replacing Berra as the team's cleanup hitter, but Yogi begs him to wait just a bit longer. Stengel grudgingly agrees, tells his catcher he won't wait much longer, then mentions that he and coach Bill Dickey think Berra is standing a few inches too far up in the batter's box. Berra makes the adjustment and almost instantly begins an assault on American League pitchers.

Yogi warms up with a two-run homer on June 4 that propels the Yankees to a 6–3 win against the White Sox. Six days later Berra starts a streak of 10 home runs in 13 games that carries the Yankees into first place and lifts Berra to the league lead in home runs. No catcher has ever won the home run title in the American League; Berra says he's determined to be the first.

By July 1, when it's announced the fans have again selected Yogi to start the All-Star Game in Philadelphia a week later, Berra has 15 home runs and 41 RBI in 57 games. Despite catching every game since returning to the lineup—he'll get only three games off the rest of the season—Berra is on pace to break Dickey's league record for catchers—29 home runs.

All talk has ended about searching for a new cleanup hitter. So has any question about who will step into DiMaggio's big shoes. Berra has grabbed that role and made it his own.

★   ★   ★

The Yankees have just suffered a tough 10–6 loss in Detroit on July 26 when Yogi gets a phone call every parent dreads. His 2½-year-old son Larry has suffered a badly broken right leg and a deep gash over his right eye in a car accident. Carmen is in St. Louis with their two sons to visit her sister Bonnie, who is recovering from a bad case of peritonitis—inflammation of the abdomen's inner wall. Her brother Norman was driving the family to see Yogi's parents when his car was rammed by a drunk driver.

Carmen is calling from St. John's Hospital, not far from The Hill. She was sitting in the front seat and holding their baby son Tim when the drunk crashed into their car. She's lost part of a front tooth, but Tim is unhurt. Her mother, sitting between Larry and Bonnie's 3-year-old son Steve, suffered a fractured leg. Steve was unhurt, but Larry's leg is broken in several places, and he needed 10 stitches to close the gash on his face, which left streaks of blood all over the back seat.

"Don't worry," says Carmen, who does all she can to shield Yogi from everything outside of baseball during the season. "We'll be all right. Just concentrate on the game."

Berra's focus has been sharp all month. Despite getting just one day off, Yogi hit .316 with six homers and 17 RBI in 34 games in July. He follows that by catching every game in August, hitting seven more home runs—the last coming in a 6–4 win August 30 against Washington that matches his career high of 28. He ties Dickey's American League record two days later against Boston, but the heavy workload is beginning to wear him down.

"I'm 27 years old," Berra tells reporters after the 5–1 win over the Red Sox, "but I feel like I am 36. I'm tired."

Other Yankees are having strong seasons, too. Mantle is still learning how to play center field, but the switch-hitter is crushing the ball from both sides of the plate, belting 12 homers and driving in 43 runs the past two months. Raschi, Lopat, and Reynolds—who's on pace to win 20 games for the first time—are all pitching well.

Yogi Berra was both a Hall of Fame performer and one of the most popular players of his era. In 1959, Berra became only the fourth Yankee to be given a day in his honor while still an active player. Among the 59 gifts: a station wagon, a color télévision, a trip to Italy, dance lessons, model trains, and an outdoor lounger for Yogi to relax on after catching one of his 117 career doubleheaders. *(Ernie Sisto / New York Times / Redux)*

*(Courtesy of The Hill 2000 Neighborhood Association)*

*(Author's personal collection)*

As young boys playing ball on the sandlots of The Hill in St. Louis, Yogi (above, bottom row, far right) and Joe Garagiola (next to Yogi) both dreamed of playing major league baseball. Both made it to the big leagues, where Yogi became a 15-time All-Star and won three Most Valuable Player awards, including in 1954—the year Yankee fans collected this Berra baseball card.

The Berra swing that produced 358 home runs and 1,430 RBI in 19 seasons, and 12 homers and 39 RBI in a record 14 World Series appearances. *(AP Photo)*

*(Courtesy of Quinn Garavaglia)*

Baseball players in Yogi's day were always looking to earn money in the offseason. One popular way was to play on barnstorming teams (top) like the one organized by Red Schoendienst (far right) that included (left to right) Yogi, Howie Pollet, Joe Garagiola, and Clem Labine. In December 1947 (bottom), Yogi and Joe sold Christmas trees on The Hill.

*(Courtesy of Joe Garagiola Jr.)*

Yogi Berra never changed his mind: Jackie Robinson was out on this attempted steal of home in the 1955 World Series. Robinson—and, more important, umpire Bill Summers—disagreed. *(Meyer Liebowitz* / New York Times / *Redux)*

In St. Louis it's

**RUGGERI'S**

2300 EDWARDS ST. · ST. LOUIS 10, MO.

Yogi was surprised by how much he enjoyed being the maître d' at Ruggeri's, one of the finest restaurants in St. Louis, where he would talk to customers about baseball and the establishment's famous steaks. *(Courtesy of Quinn Garavaglia)*

Edition No. 55   CRUSADER CLUB • 5120 Wilson Ave. • ST. AMBROSE PARISH • St. Louis 10, Mo.   June, 194?

**FATHER VINEYARD RETURNS TO ST. LOUIS AFTER NAVY DISCHARGE**

Now home after receiving his discharge from the U.S. Navy during May is Father Vineyard, former Assistant at St. Ambrose, who served almost four years as a Naval Chaplain. He is at present awaiting word of a definite assignment by the Most Rev. Archbishop to some parish, probably in the city of St. Louis. Father served with the 7th Fleet during his 21 months that he served in the South West Pacific, being stationed in New Guinea, the Philippines and the Admiralty Islands. He served for a time aboard the sea-plane tender, the USS Half Moon, and took part in the invasion of Borneo, Leyte and Mindoro, the latter two in the Philippines. He has four battle stars for his Navy record in the recent World War.

While stationed in New Guinea, as reported previously in your CLARION, Father Vineyard received a special letter of commendation from his superior officers: "for courageously facing an uprising among enlisted men and persuading them to disperse peacefully thereby avoiding bloodshed, despite danger of bodily injury." This commendation was given in New Guinea, August 26, 1944.

Father Vineyard returned to the States in December 1945 and was assigned for a time to the Bainbridge, Maryland Naval Separation Center. He received a brief assignment later on to the Navy Department Communication Center in Washington, D. C., before his final Navy assignment out in California at the Long Beach Naval Hospital, where he served as a Hospital Chaplain until his recent discharge. He was originally scheduled to be discharged from the Navy by way of the point system back in April 1946, but decided to spend another year in the Navy to make his service record 4 years in all.

Father had two brothers also in the Service during the war, Glenn, who served in Germany, and his other brother, Bob, who served in the South West Pacific, and met up with Father on one or more occasions during the war. Father Vineyard also met Father Dayer in New Guinea back in December 1945.

**STOCKHAM POST TO SPONSOR 'YOGI' BERRA DAY AT BALL PARK JUNE 6TH**

'Yogi' Berra, Rookie sensation of the New York Yanks will be honored out at Sportsman's Park Friday night, June 6th, with a 'Yogi' Berra Day to be sponsored by the Fred W. Stockham American Legion Post, on whose American Legion Post baseball team he played in 1941 and 1942. There will be no one from the Hill expected to take an official part in this particular 'Yogi' Berra Day. It is expected the Hill however will arrange a 'Yogi' Berra Day of its own later on in the season.

Mr. Leo Browne, of the Stockham American Legion Post, is in charge of the occasion and has arranged for some 400 special reserved seats along the first base line behind the Yankee dug-out, for the Friday evening, June 6th game. The reserve seats are sold at the regular $1.75 price. On the Hill these reserved seats may be bought at Charlie Grassi's tavern, Edwards & Daggett, or through members of the Fawns Club, both of whom are helping to secure a goodly representation from the Hill for this first 'Yogi' Berra Day.

The Stockham Post, according to Mr. Browne, is expected to present to the young Yankee Rookie sensation, a de-luxe traveling bag, bowling ball and other gifts at a pre-game presentation ceremony at home plate. In order to make the presentation as memorable an occasion as possible, the Stockham Post is trying to bring the great 'Bambino', George Herman 'Babe' Ruth, to St. Louis to take part in the 'Yogi' Berra Day. Due to the recent poor health of the Babe, it is not known for certain at this writing if Ruth will be able to attend.

The presentation ceremony in the evening will be preceded by a special luncheon also sponsored by the Stockham Post in honor of 'Yogi', at noon at the York Hotel. Manager Bucky Harris of the Yanks will be present for this luncheon. The Legion Post extends a gracious invitation through the pages of the CLARION to anyone on the Hill who might want to attend this special luncheon -- you are welcomed to attend and honor 'Yogi'.

The *Clarion Crusader*, a newsletter started by a St. Ambrose Church priest to keep The Hill attached to their men in World War II, later kept tabs on the exploits of favorite son Yogi Berra. *(Courtesy of Quinn Garavaglia)*

(Courtesy of Quinn Garavaglia)

Father Charles Koester (top, left) married Carmen Short (center) and Yogi Berra in January 1949, a union that lasted more than 65 years. They were married in The Hill's St. Ambrose Church, the heart of the predominantly Italian community, where a seven-foot bronze statue of Italian immigrants greets parishioners on The Hill to this day.

(Author's personal collection)

*(Courtesy of Quinn Garavaglia)*

Fans flocked to see Yogi Berra, whether it was the day in 2003 he spent signing autographs with Joe Garagiola when the street they grew up on in St. Louis was renamed Hall of Fame Place (top), or at the bowling alley he and Phil Rizzuto built in Clifton, New Jersey in 1959.

But the Yankees can't shake the Indians, who cut New York's lead to a mere four percentage points on September 12 with a nine-game winning streak. New York has a 1½-game lead two days later with a dozen games left when Stengel chooses Lopat to face the Indians before 73,608 fans in Cleveland's Municipal Stadium. Indian manager Al Lopez picks 20-game winner Mike Garcia, who hasn't allowed a run in his last 28⅔ innings, for this one-game showdown.

The Yankees strike early on this sweltering afternoon, and it's Berra who delivers the key hit. With a run in, one out, and the bases loaded, Berra yanks Garcia's pitch down the right field line to drive in two runs. The Yanks are leading 5–1 in the 6th inning when Stengel brings in Reynolds, who yields just one hit the rest of the game. The Yankees leave Cleveland with a 7–1 win, a 2½-game lead, and a pronouncement from the team's leader.

"They had their chance," Yogi tells teammates after reporters leave the clubhouse.

Berra's right. The Yankees win seven of their next eight, setting up the pennant clincher on September 26 in Philadelphia. The Yankees convince the A's to move the game to a nighttime start and televise it back to New York, only their second road game on TV all season. The Yankees jump to an early 2–0 lead, but the A's match that in the 6th. Four tense innings pass before Billy Martin slaps a two-out, bases-loaded single in the 11th that drives in a pair of runs. The Yankees add another run, shut down the A's in their half of the inning, and shortly before midnight the Yankees walk off with a 5–2 win and their record-tying fourth straight pennant.

But there is just one bit of unfinished business, which has Yankee public relations man Red Patterson panicking.

"Yogi, Yogi," he shouts over the celebration in the Yankee clubhouse. "You gotta hit homer number 30 because in the World Series program I have you down for 30."

Berra laughs, but it's a tired laugh.

"You shoulda asked me in June," he says. "I am tired!"

Tired or not, Berra is back behind the plate the next two meaning-less games for a shot at the record. Bill Dickey, whose AL–record 29 homers has stood since 1937, tells Berra how much he'd like to see it broken after Yogi goes hitless in the season's penultimate game. So it's no surprise to see Dickey, the team's first-base coach, jumping up and down a day later when Berra sends a fly ball soaring to right field at Shibe Park. And Dickey is ecstatic when the ball sails over the fence, pumping his prize pupil's right arm as Yogi passes him during his 30th home run trot of the season. Yogi now holds the American League home run record for catchers.

Berra's 30 homers leave him two behind Cleveland center fielder Larry Doby, who becomes the first black player to lead the AL in home runs. Berra's 98 RBI leads the Yankees for the fourth straight season and is fifth best in the league. His .273 batting average is the lowest of his career, a clear result of catching a league-high 140 games, including 20 doubleheaders. Little wonder Berra is tired.

But there is no time to rest. In three days, Yogi and the Yankees will take the field in Brooklyn to start the quest for their fourth straight World Series title. There is more history to be made.

# CHAPTER 18

# Four of a Kind
## 1952

At precisely 7:45 p.m. on the crisp, moonlit night of September 30, 1952, a high-pitched wail blares from 567 air-raid sirens placed throughout the five boroughs of New York City. It is a warning signal—a Soviet B-29 carrying an atomic bomb is closing in on Manhattan, where it will drop its payload over Riverside Drive and West 82nd Street. The sirens sound for a full three minutes before their wailing abruptly ends, then waves of Civil Defense workers wearing white plastic hats and armbands—60,000 workers in all—flood the streets of New York City. There is much work to be done.

"This is a test for the Civil Defense workers only," comes a voice from a loudspeaker atop a van driving the streets near Manhattan's Bryant Park, the main staging area for this drill. The same message is being played by loudspeakers throughout the city. "If there were a real attack you would go to the nearest shelter and wait for the all-clear."

More than 100,000 people are spellbound as they watch many of these workers run into skyscrapers that appear ablaze; pots of colored fire have been placed strategically to create the impression of danger. Other workers rush to repair mock busted water mains, gas lines, and electrical cables. Had this been a real attack, officials estimate 112,409 New Yorkers would have died instantly and another 116,501 would have suffered injuries inside the bomb's kill zone.

America is knee-deep in its Cold War with the Soviet Union, which perfected an atomic bomb three years ago, and everyone is taking the threat of annihilation seriously. Choosing who will have his finger on the button of the atomic bomb will be very much on the mind of every American who goes to the polls in five weeks to elect either Republican Dwight Eisenhower or Democrat Adlai Stevenson as America's next President.

The news of the Civil Defense drill is splashed across the front pages of the city's 10 daily newspapers the next morning. But the previous night's activities are not the center of attention in this town — not even close. All of New York is consumed by only one thought: will the Yankees or the Dodgers win the World Series that starts today in Ebbets Field?

The oddsmakers install the Yankees as 8–5 favorites to win the championship, which would pull Casey Stengel's men alongside the 1936–1939 Yankees as the only teams to take home four straight titles. But Brooklyn fans are positive their team, built around power, speed, and four future Hall of Famers, will end its postseason losing streak at five — the last three at the hands of the hated Yankees. By the time Brooklyn's ace rookie Joe Black throws the game's first pitch, shortly after 1 p.m., the Civil Defense drill will be old news.

Especially to the Yankee star catcher. There are few things that excite Yogi Berra more than playing in the World Series, something he's about to do for the fifth time in his six major league seasons. He loves walking out onto the field and seeing the pennants hanging in Yankee Stadium — this season makes it 19 — along with the 15 world championship banners and the red-white-and-blue bunting on the front rows of box seats up and down both foul lines. He's not a camera bug like many of his teammates, and he doesn't collect autographs, but he's thrilled to see all the celebrities and politicians mill about the playing field before each game. There is no bigger stage in all of sports.

Almost everyone in the country will tune in to the World Series: an estimated 93 million Americans will watch the games on the nation's growing network of local TV stations—68 in 64 cities—and listen in on 700 radio stations, making New York the center of the universe for the next seven days. Workingmen will flock to taverns on their lunch breaks to catch a few innings on TVs mounted over bars. People of all ages will stand at the windows in front of appliance stores whose owners have turned their televisions to face the side-walks and tuned them to the big games. In baseball-crazed St. Louis, Carmen Berra's sister Bonnie and her future husband Peter George, owners of Triangle Appliance, invite city leaders to join them for lunch and baseball in front of their best television set.

They'll all be listening to Yankee announcer Mel Allen, by now a familiar voice across the nation, and his Dodger counterpart Red Barber call the games on television. They'll also be watching and listening to ads for the Gillette Safety Razor Company, which is pay-ing baseball owners a record $1.475 million to be the sole World Series sponsor for both television and radio broadcasts.

Tickets are a tough get in New York, especially in tiny 31,902-seat Ebbets Field. Fire marshals will allow the team another 3,000 standing-room tickets, barely making a dent in the demand.

Ticket requests are always a challenge for Yogi and Carmen, never more than when the opponent is the Dodgers. Not even Willie Mays and the Giants have the passionate following of the team from Brook-lyn, and callers for tickets are relentless, even though Berra's home phone number is unlisted. Yogi writes the Yankees a big check for 60 tickets for each home game before the Series starts. Then it's up to Carmen to keep track of who gets the tickets, who still has to send them money, and how much Yogi will wind up paying for family and close friends.

It's a big headache, but Berra's not complaining. He knows most players go an entire career without getting close to playing in a World Series game. He's already played in 20. And he understands he's part of the first generation of players to perform in the nation's living rooms, which puts him on a first-name basis with America—especially the advertising executives on Madison Avenue. Indeed, Yogi and roomie Phil Rizzuto will do so many television and radio interviews that the American Federation of Radio Artists insists they take out a union card and start paying dues. And that doesn't count any of the post-Series radio and TV gigs Frank Scott is busy lining up.

But most of all, Berra is thinking about his real job—guiding a tired and aging pitching staff to four more victories. Sure, Yogi wants to get his share of hits, but never has the ability to call just the right pitch at just the right time been more important. Or throwing out runners attempting a steal, and blocking pitches with a runner on third to prevent a big run from scoring. Every run in the World Series is big.

The measure of a great World Series catcher is not his batting average or the number of home runs he belts, no matter how much the press focuses on his hitting. Managers, coaches, and players all know a catcher's greatness in the postseason is measured in wins and losses. And Yogi is 12–3 in three World Series since becoming New York's full-time catcher.

Maybe that's why Yogi is standing in the clubhouse after a tough loss in Game 3 at Yankee Stadium—a defeat that gives Brooklyn a 2–1 Series lead—taking the blame for a mistake he didn't make. The play came in the 9th inning, soon after a Berra solo homer in the bottom of the 8th cut the Dodger lead to 3–2. Berra had coaxed Eddie Lopat through eight innings, but the right-hander tired, giving up one-out singles to Pee Wee Reese and Jackie Robinson, prompting Stengel to bring in reliever Tom Gorman.

A 27-year-old bespectacled right-hander from nearby Long Island, Gorman went 6–2 after being called up from the minors on July 14. The Yankees have high hopes for the quiet rookie, one reason Stengel brought him in to face the heart of the powerful Dodger offense with so much at stake. "Hold these two runners on base," Stengel warned Gorman, telling him to expect a double steal.

Stengel was dead right. Reese and Robinson were off and running on Gorman's first pitch to Roy Campanella and stole their bases easily. Casey paced furiously, cursing Gorman for not heeding his directions. But Gorman got Campy to pop up for the second out, then threw two big curveballs to get two strikes on hard-hitting outfielder Andy Pafko. One strike from closing out the inning, Berra called for another curve.

But Gorman saw fastball. And his high, inside pitch handcuffed his catcher, hitting Yogi's index finger, the one he always keeps outside his glove. The ball nearly tore off Berra's fingernail before bouncing off his shin guard and rolling toward the Brooklyn dugout as Reese and Robinson crossed the plate to give the Dodgers a 5–2 lead.

Stengel was irate, convinced Gorman crossed up Berra, and grew madder still when Yankee pinch-hitter Johnny Mize hit a home run that would have tied the score in the bottom of the inning. Instead, the Yankees fell, 5–3, and Berra grabbed Gorman on the way to the clubhouse. "That pitch was my mistake, got it?" Yogi said. Berra knows the Yankees need every pitcher they have to get to four wins; no sense letting this rookie get destroyed by the press. And sure enough, the fateful pitch is all reporters ask about when they flood into the Yankee locker room.

"Gorman didn't do nothing wrong. He didn't cross me up, and don't none of you guys believe him if he says he did," says Berra, almost shouting his words. "I messed up the play. I wasn't crossed up. I got what I called for. Blame me."

A dazed Gorman follows Berra's lead. (He won't let on it was his mistake until next April.) Stengel is convinced the rookie blew it, but he grudgingly defers to Berra, too.

"I dunno about that play," he says. "My ketcher tells me that the other feller don't cross him up, which it looked like to me. But I gotta take Mr. Berra's word for it, don't I?"

The fans in Yankee Stadium give Yogi a big ovation the next day when he comes to bat for the first time in Game 4. There's no question which story they believe to be true. It's a nice gesture by the fans, whose focus soon shifts to Allie Reynolds. Spectacular all season — the Chief went 20–8 with a 2.06 ERA, six shutouts, and six saves — the veteran right-hander overpowers the Dodgers, allowing just four hits and striking out 10 in a 2–0 win that evens the Series.

The Yankees lose a heartbreaker in Game 5 when Duke Snider doubles home the winning run in the 11th inning, and the Dodgers need to win only one of two games on their home field to earn their first World Series title and keep the Yankees from making history. But at least one Yankee is not worried.

"I just hope the next game doesn't go extra innings," Berra tells reporters. "I'm watching the *Gang Busters* series on TV, and they're playing the last episode tomorrow night."

Game 6 is a tight, scoreless affair until Snider hits a home run to put the Dodgers ahead in the bottom of the 6th. Berra matches Duke leading off the 7th, pulling a high, outside fastball over the right field stands and clear out of Ebbets Field. The Yankees score twice more and win 3–2 in a game that is played four minutes shy of three hours. Berra is back in his home in Woodcliff Lake in time to watch his television show.

The Yankee team bus gets a police escort from the Bronx to Ebbets Field for Game 7. Berra doesn't know who his starting pitcher is until he sees Casey has placed a ball in Eddie Lopat's shoe 90 minutes before game time. No matter; Yogi knows today is going to be a real team effort.

The two teams trade a pair of runs and the game is tied 2–2 in the 6th inning when Mantle blasts a solo home run. Mickey singles home another in the 7th for a 4–2 lead, and the Yankees are nine outs from making history. Berra was right about this being a team effort: he guided Lopat through the first three innings of one-run ball. Lopat gave way to Reynolds, pitching for the third straight day, who also threw three innings of one-run ball. Casey goes to Raschi next, but the veteran has nothing after pitching 7⅔ innings in Game 6 and leaves with the bases loaded with one out. With the left-handed Snider up next, Casey calls in tall left-hander Bob Kuzava.

Snider has already hit four home runs in this Series, and Kuzava, 8–8 in the regular season, hasn't pitched since September 27. But Kuzava gets Snider on a weak infield pop-up. Up steps Robinson and out of the dugout pops Stengel, who suddenly changes his mind and takes a seat, leaving the game in the hands of Kuzava and Berra. Mixing fastballs and curves, they get Robinson to a 2–2 count. Yogi calls for another curve, and Robinson hits a towering infield pop-up. Berra jumps out in front of the plate and calls for first baseman Joe Collins to make the catch.

But Collins has lost the ball in the sun. Two runners have already crossed the plate by the time second baseman Billy Martin comes racing through the infield, his hat flying off and the wind pushing the ball away from him. Martin finally reaches down as he passes the pitcher's mound and catches the ball about a foot off the grass. The threat is over, and two innings later, so is the game.

Yogi rushes out and jumps on Kuzava's back, his teammates and coaches all running right behind him. Then they fight their way to the dugout and into their clubhouse as Dodger organist Gladys Gooding plays songs reflecting the mood of Dodger fans everywhere: "What Can I Say After I Say I'm Sorry," "This Nearly Was Mine," and finally "Auld Lang Syne."

Casey is the star of this year's celebration, which includes owners Del Webb and Dan Topping, who must reach over reporters, cameramen, and players to shake Stengel's hand. Fired as manager by both the Dodgers and Braves earlier in his career, Casey is the second manager to win four straight World Series and the only one to do it in his first four seasons with his new team.

Shirts and jackets are drenched in booze as the players try to change clothes, some of which wind up ripped, but no one seems to mind. Not with a winner's check of $5,982.65 to be collected. The only casualty is Berra, who steps on a photographer's used flashbulb on his way to the showers.

Berra sits picking glass out of his foot as he watches the celebration. Only 12 men in this room have played on all four title teams in this run, and there's little question he is the best of the bunch. Yogi doesn't have a lot to say to reporters, and he's not ready to tell anyone what he's really thinking: this team isn't done winning titles yet.

Not even close.

★   ★   ★

Berra's offseason is a crush of activity. Three days after the World Series ends, Yogi and the rest of the Eddie Lopat All-Stars land in Hawaii to play six exhibition games. Lopat's 12-man squad is one of about a dozen teams of major league players who line up games all over America—and some in foreign countries—and play against semipro and military-base teams. Most major leaguers are tired of playing ball by early autumn—especially the ones who have just finished high-stakes postseason games. But what better way to earn extra dough than being treated royally while doing what you do best?

Berra enjoys being with players he isn't allowed to socialize with during the regular season—the major leagues take their no-fraternizing rule seriously in this era and fine players who don't. He bonds quickly with big White Sox first baseman Eddie Robinson, a terrific hitter—he batted .296 with 22 home runs and 108 RBI for third-place Chicago—who knows how to have a good time off the field. And Yogi can't stop talking about the World Series with Dodger shortstop Pee Wee Reese, who takes Berra's playful needling with a smile.

Lopat's team sweeps all six games before appreciative crowds who are thrilled by the major leaguers' display of power—Lopat's hitters average almost 10 runs a game and slug 16 home runs. Robinson leads the team with three home runs, and Yogi hits two. The best part for the All-Stars: the tour clears $32,600 to be split among the 12 players and Frank Scott, who helped Lopat book the tour.

Back home in New Jersey, Yogi tries to hone his golf game before the weather turns too cold, squeezing in 18 holes between speaking engagements, radio and TV interviews—he's a frequent guest on WABD Channel 5—and his Wednesday-and-Saturday shifts selling clothes in Newark's American Shops. Carmen likes to socialize in the city, so Yogi takes her to one of the big-name clubs or restaurants at least once a week. It pays to be a baseball star, too: Yogi never has to wait for a table or search hard for tickets to any hockey, basketball, or football games, where he's now introduced to the crowd. Still shy in public, he'll give a sheepish wave and quickly find his seat.

He especially likes spending time at Toots Shor's, the Manhattan tavern famous as the intersection of stars from sports, entertainment, business, and politics as well as the occasional Mafia boss. It's a place to be seen and not bothered—Toots, himself a larger-than-life character, makes sure of that. Joe DiMaggio has his own table here. So does Frank Sinatra. It was at Shor's a year or so ago that Yogi—one of Toots' favorites—was introduced to Ernest Hemingway. Told Hemingway was a great writer, Yogi replied, "Yeah? What paper you write for, Ernie?" That story circulated quickly.

So did the one about Berra and Phil Silvers a few years later. Yogi and Carmen had just seen Silvers in his hit Broadway play *Top Banana,* for which the comedian won a Tony Award. When Silvers strolled into Shor's and heard the Berras had just seen his performance, he walked over to Yogi's table to hear the baseball star's review.

"It was so funny," Berra told him, "that I almost pissed my pants."

Silvers let out a huge laugh and from then on told everyone it was the best review he ever received.

On November 13, Berra learns he finished fourth in the MVP voting behind pitcher Bobby Shantz and Yankee teammates Allie Reynolds and Mickey Mantle. The diminutive Shantz—all of five foot six, 139 pounds—won 24 of Philadelphia's 79 games and is high on the Yankees' list of trade targets. Berra has now finished third, first, and fourth in the last three MVP votes, the best showing of any player in baseball.

About the only disquieting news is made by Jackie Robinson on November 30, when he appears on NBC's popular television show *Youth Wants to Know.* A young boy asks a question many baseball writers have been quietly asking one another the last few years. "Mr. Robinson, do you think the Yankees are prejudiced against Negro players?"

Robinson's answer is characteristically blunt. "Yes," he answers, stating he was referring to management, not the players. "I think the members of the Yankee team are fine sportsmen and wonderful gentlemen, but there isn't a single Negro on that team now and there are very few in the entire Yankee farm system."

General Manager George Weiss is livid when he's reached for comment. The Yankees will have a Negro player, Weiss says, "when we find one good enough to win a place on the Yankees." Even though Robinson is roundly criticized for his words, the facts support his case. The Yankees have just five black players in their entire system, and none is being considered for next season's roster. Worse, they scouted and passed on Willie Mays and Ernie Banks, two obviously talented players.

Sportswriter Dan Daniel doesn't raise the subject when he sits down with Yogi in the knotty-pine-paneled den of Berra's home the last week of the year to interview him for the *Sporting News*. There are pictures of his Yankee teammates hanging on the walls, bats glued against the den's bar, autographed baseballs nailed to small shelves placed around the room. Daniel accepts a glass of chocolate-flavored wine—"A chocolate malted," Yogi says—and asks Berra about his career-low .273 batting average this past season. Berra admits he was trying too hard to hit home runs the final month of the season to break Dickey's record.

"They tell me the Yankees like to pay for home runs," Berra says. "But I like to hit .300 or better."

And what about your next contract? "George always likes to see us happy," says Yogi, tongue firmly in cheek, and tells Daniel he's already agreed to a deal for the '53 season, news that has yet to hit the New York papers. Did he get a raise? "I want more dough, of course," a laughing Berra says. He is clearly enjoying the conversation—and the holiday wine—he and Daniel are sharing. "This ain't no dime-tipping ball team" is all Yogi will say about his new deal.

But there is one thing he wants Daniel to know before he sends the writer on his way. He wasn't ready to say this when the Yankees beat the Dodgers back in October, but he is now. "Take it from me: we will make it five in a row," Berra says. "Barring injuries, we will do it. Matter of fact, this club of ours could even go on to seven in a row!

"That's what they call long-run predictin'."

# CHAPTER 19

# Simply the Best

## 1953

Yogi Berra is so excited about the 1953 season he formally signs his new contract on January 30—he's bumped to $36,000, worth $337,119 in 2019 dollars. He hires a housekeeper who'll start when Carmen and the kids return from spring training and is the only regular on the field when camp opens in St. Petersburg in late February. The rest of the regulars will sign soon enough; Yogi is not the only Yankee eager to get started. They all think they have a good chance to do what no other team has done—win five straight World Series titles.

Yogi's confidence revolves around three players. He expects Mickey Mantle to become the dominant star everyone expects the kid from Oklahoma to be. He thinks Whitey Ford, bigger and stronger at 24 after two years in the military, will perform as well as he did in his sparkling rookie season, maybe even better.

And Berra, soon to be 28 and at his athletic peak, is confident he'll have a terrific season. If all three stars play up to their potential, the Yankees will be tough to beat. And Berra is right. All it takes is a slight change in Yogi's diet.

Berra is hitting .192 with just two homers and 11 RBI in 21 games when he's forced out of the lineup after taking a pitch on his right elbow on May 9. Yogi usually starts slow, but rarely has he looked this feeble. He's also complaining of being tired after just three weeks, his stomach hurts all the time, and he says he's "itching like a hound dog." Perplexed, Weiss brings in a nutritionist, who discovers the probable cause of Berra's discomfort—the quarts of chocolate milk Yogi drinks before and after each game, which trigger his chronic colitis.

"You should see him down that chocolate milk!" Phil Rizzuto says. "And who knows how much of that stuff he drinks at home?"

Berra returns to the lineup in Washington on May 21 and goes hitless his first two at-bats, dropping his batting average to .183. Maybe that's why he's so annoyed in the 4th inning when umpire Grover Froese says the first two pitches from Yankee pitcher Ray Scarborough are outside the strike zone. American League umpires are used to Berra's running commentary on balls and strikes and most give the veteran All-Star a wide berth. But when Berra turns around and punctuates his remarks by kicking dirt at Froese, the ump gives him the hook.

Things change the very next game when Yogi raps out three hits, including a home run. He goes on a tear when the team starts an 18-game winning streak on May 27, hitting .315 with three home runs and 17 RBI. And yes, he's cut back on his chocolate milk consumption.

The Yankees sweep four games from the Indians at the end of their streak, with Berra delivering the big blows in both games of a June 14 doubleheader before 74,708 dismayed Indian fans at Municipal Stadium. With the Yankees down 2–1 in the 8th inning of the opener, Berra blasts a three-run homer off Indian star Bob Lemon that sends New York to a 6–2 win. In the second game, Berra clubs a two-run triple in the 4th inning and guides Vic Raschi to a three-hit, 3–0 shutout that lifts New York's record to a gaudy 41–11. The Indians, now trailing the Yankees by 10½ games, never recover. And the pennant race, for all intents and purposes, is all but over.

The fans once again select Berra to start the All-Star Game on July 14 in Cincinnati, but this one is special because of a player who is not in a baseball uniform. "Hey, Muscles, how ya' doin'?" Yogi shouts when he sees his good friend Marine Corps Captain Ted Williams on the field before the game. "Well, now I know I'm home," says a smiling Williams, who spent most of the last season and the first half of '53 flying jets in combat in the Korean War.

Captain Williams, who was awarded three Air Medals—the same number of times he was hit by enemy fire—is in Cincinnati to throw out the game's first pitch. He will be officially discharged July 28, one day after a permanent cease-fire goes into effect. The war claimed the lives of almost 40,000 Americans and more than two million Korean civilians. And left the peninsula split into two nations.

"I have a job for you," Yogi tells his friend.

"Yeah, what's that?" says Williams, playing along.

"You can be an intern for our barnstorming team in Japan," says Berra, who's recently agreed to join Ed Lopat's All-Star team on a much-anticipated tour of Japan after the World Series.

"No thanks," Williams says. "I'm in this country to stay."

Williams throws the ceremonial first pitch, poses for pictures with Commissioner Ford Frick, then takes a seat in the American League dugout and watches the National League roll to an easy 5–1 win, the fourth straight All-Star loss for Stengel. Sure, Casey would like to win one of these exhibition games, but as long as his team keeps winning the final game of the World Series, he can handle these midsummer defeats.

Casey received some criticism when he left his own ace off the All-Star roster, but there is no question that Whitey Ford—who was 9–3 with a 2.75 ERA in the first half—is now the Yankees' most important pitcher. Despite always squaring off against the opposition's ace, Ford goes 4–2 against the Indians and 5–0 against the White Sox, including a 3–2 win in Chicago on September 1 that gives the Yankees a 9½-game lead and ends any Chicago hopes for a miracle finish.

The future Hall of Famer has a wide array of pitches—a devastating curveball is his best—and pinpoint control of all of them. And he's savvy enough to let his friend Yogi call the game for him. "I probably throw more of what Yogi calls than any other pitcher," Ford tells reporters. "A batter can't believe the combination of pitches he'll call. He knows what the hitters are looking for. He just has a natural instinct."

Ford instantly befriends Mantle, who may have been the team's best player for the first half of the season, leading the team in home runs (13) and RBI (57) while hitting .314. Mantle carried the team when Yogi struggled in May, hitting .441 during a 14-game stretch. And when Yogi hit his stride, Mantle continued to excel, hitting .394 with four homers and 24 RBI during a 16–1 Yankee run.

Mantle still strikes out too much — 55 times in 75 games before the All-Star break — and fans have become accustomed to watching Mickey vent his frustration by kicking the dugout water cooler. This happens so often that Yogi begins taping a piece of heavy cardboard around the base of the cooler. "Mick, look!" Yogi sings out as soon as he sees Mantle. He kicks the cooler to demonstrate. "It gives ya protection when you kick that thing later on."

It's Berra who carries the Yankees in the second half of the season, getting stronger even as the summer heat and the number of games he catches continue to rise. Berra puts together a 17-game hitting streak in August (five home runs, 20 RBI, .380 batting average) and an 11-game streak to start September (3-9-.383). From his nadir on May 21 to season's end, Yogi is New York's most productive hitter, batting .318 with 25 home runs and 97 RBI in 112 games.

Berra's 25th home run comes in the 4th inning on September 3 against the Browns in St. Louis. As always, Berra's father Pietro is in a box seat to watch his son and the Yankees win, 8–5, but he doesn't have much company. Only 2,330 fans show up to see the four-time defending champions play the home team, and for good reason — the Browns will be playing elsewhere in 1954. Baltimore is the leading candidate to get the team, but Browns owner Bill Veeck is still holding out hope to relocate to Los Angeles.

The Yankees are back in New York 11 days later to face the Indians with a chance to clinch the pennant. Ford has one of his worst outings of the season, giving up five runs — two on bases-loaded walks — before leaving the game after three innings. But the Yankees push across four in the 4th and another in the 6th to tie the score. Then Berra wallops a towering two-run homer in the 7th, Billy Martin gets his fourth RBI of the game, and two innings later the Yankees have won their fifth straight American League pennant.

The postgame celebration is subdued, befitting a team that has just won its 20th pennant in 33 years, and almost all the fuss is just for the cameras. As always, Stengel is the center of attention, taking a seat on a bench between co-owners Dan Topping and Del Webb as players come by to tousle his hair. Berra is the next to get the roughhouse treatment, making sure the photographers and cameramen get all the pictures they need.

The real celebration takes place a few hours later in the Stadium Club, where steaks are served and champagne flows until 11 p.m. The next day there is another pennant in the flag room in Yankee Stadium, and everyone's attention shifts to the Dodgers, whom the Yankees will face in a fortnight. And once again, history is on the line.


Sometimes there are certain plays, coming at just the right moment, that not only alter the outcome of a game but set the tone for an entire World Series. The 7th inning in Game 1 of the 1953 World Series is one such moment.

The backstory: the Yankees have squandered an early 5–1 lead—their last run coming on a long home run by Berra—and are on the verge of blowing the game in the 7th inning with the score tied 5–5, Dodger runners on first and second, and no outs. Up steps Billy Cox, a .291 hitter in the regular season who has already rapped out a single and double in three at-bats.

Dodger manager Chuck Dressen signals bunt, and Cox executes perfectly, the ball rolling into no-man's-land up the third baseline. Almost every one of the 69,734 fans at Yankee Stadium groans, convinced Berra will take the sure out at first, leaving two runners in scoring position with just one out. But Yogi has a different idea. He scrambles up the third baseline, grabs the ball bare-handed, and rifles it to third, getting Gil Hodges by inches.

The fans have barely stopped buzzing about Berra's successful gamble when Dodger pitcher Clem Labine lays down another seemingly perfect bunt, this one rolling just a bit farther than the one before. Berra once again scrambles from behind the plate, scoops up the ball, and throws it to third, this time getting Carl Furillo by a half step. The Dodger rally, so promising just moments ago, is all but dead. It ends, fittingly, when Yogi catches a foul pop off the bat of leadoff hitter Junior Gilliam.

A team that blows a lead should be deflated, especially against a Dodger team that won 105 games in the regular season. Instead, the Yankees come off the field energized by the sparkling defensive play of their catcher. And when first baseman Joe Collins hits a solo homer to retake the lead in the bottom of the 7th, everyone in the Yankee dugout is convinced this game is theirs. Two innings later, the Yankees have a 9–5 victory and the familiar feeling that they will always find a way to win.

Berra's performance even catches the eye of the man completing his first year in the White House. "I received a terrific kick out of Berra's home run," President Eisenhower says the following day to open his first press conference in two months. "That fellow really slammed the ball out of the park."

The teams split the next four games, and Stengel sends out Ford to win Game 6 and the team's fifth straight World Series. Berra enters the game with a hot bat—seven hits in five games—and belts a ground-rule double to right-center in the 1st inning, scoring Gene Woodling and sending Hank Bauer to third. Bauer scores on an error to make it 2–0, and the Yankees add another run in the 2nd inning for a 3–0 lead. With Ford allowing just one run through seven innings, the Yankees looked poised to win yet another championship.

And that's when Stengel decides to tempt fate, bringing in Allie Reynolds to get the final six outs. "I'm not tired!" Ford tells Casey, but his manager isn't listening. He wants his veteran star to close out this game. The move backfires in the 9th when Dodger outfielder Carl Furillo lines a 3–2 pitch into the right field stands to tie the game, 3–3.

But Dodger fans barely have time to celebrate their good fortune. Bauer leads off the bottom of the 9th with a walk, then takes second when Mantle beats out an infield hit. And when Billy Martin belts his 12th hit of the Series to drive in Bauer, the Yankees dance off the field as champions for the fifth straight year—with a place in the history books all their own.

Stengel is the first Yankee to reach the clubhouse and is immediately swallowed in hugs from co-owners Dan Topping and Del Webb. Allie Reynolds, Mantle, and Bauer are next, followed by the usual flood of reporters, cameramen, baseball officials, and celebrity well-wishers. By the time an exhausted Berra trudges in, the path to his locker is blocked, champagne spray is everywhere, and the backslapping and handshaking with teammates is so vigorous Berra wonders if anyone will get hurt.

It is still hard to comprehend what has just happened. Winning one World Series is hard. Winning back-to-back titles is really tough. Winning five in a row? How does that even happen? But there is Stengel, shouting loud enough for all to hear that he is still not content. "I am not going to be satisfied with just five straight championships," Stengel says. "This team of mine is only now growing into greatness and will win again in 1954."

Twelve men played part or all of each of the five championship seasons, and the Yankee front office presents each player with a ring featuring the number 5 in gold, with a large diamond encased in the bottom of the numeral. Berra falls in love with the gift instantly, and it's the only World Series ring he will ever wear. One day in 2015, soon after Yogi passes away, his favorite ring fetches $159,720 when his sons put up most of their father's baseball possessions for auction.

This is also the most lucrative World Series in the game's history. The winner's share of $8,280.68 and the loser's share of $6,178.42—both record-high figures—are the players' cut of $1,779,269 in ticket sales. Berra has collected $32,074.11 in World Series checks the last five years—and that doesn't count the $5,830 he took home as a rookie World Series champion in 1947.

On November 27, Yogi learns he finished second in the MVP voting to Cleveland third baseman Al Rosen, who had a season to remember—leading the American League in home runs (43), RBI (145), and losing the batting title by a single point, .337–.336, on the final day of the season. Rosen received all 24 first-place votes. Despite his slow start, Berra hit .296 and led the Yankees in home runs (27) and RBI (108)—both fourth best in the league—his finest all-around season since 1950.

At 28, Berra is widely considered the best catcher in the game. Only his friend Roy Campanella, Brooklyn's 32-year-old star, is in his class, creating a lively debate among Yankee and Dodger fans about who is the better player. Ebbets Field has the closest fences in all of baseball, Yankee fans argue. Yankee Stadium has the short porch in right field, Dodger fans counter. Both fan bases agree that Yogi and Campy are topflight defensive catchers.

But Berra has now finished first, second, third, and fourth in MVP voting the past four seasons, by far the finest performance in the game. Berra is the best player on the best team in baseball, the key performer on a team that has done something never done before—winning five straight titles—and is destined never to be done again.

# CHAPTER 20

# Most Valuable

## 1954

There is only one word to describe the Yankees' 1954 season. Strange.

It's strange when Yogi Berra—the king of holdouts—walks into the Yankees' Fifth Avenue office in late January, tells GM George Weiss he wants $40,000 to play the upcoming season, and walks out with a signed contract.

It's strange when Vic Raschi, Berra's companion in holdouts, returns the team's first offer unsigned in late February and is promptly sold to the Cardinals for $85,000. Weiss breaks up one of the most successful trios of pitchers in baseball history without warning or so much as a warm body in return. Every Yankee understood the message: crossing management comes with a high risk.

It goes without saying how strange—and long overdue—it is to see a black man wearing a Yankee uniform when spring training opens March 1, given how passionately Weiss fought against integrating his team. But 25-year-old outfielder Elston Howard is just too good to hold back, though accusations of racism are renewed when the Yankees quickly announce Howard will be converted to catcher with Berra still very much in his prime. Howard is shipped back to the minors on April 1 to learn his new position.

And it's odd to watch Yogi, still a few months shy of 29, swinging a lighter bat—33½ ounces instead of 35—and lighting it up in spring training games. "I don't like to waste hits in spring training games," Yogi moans as he compiles a .385 exhibition season batting average. "That's all right for rookies who have to make the team. I'm worried about it—this could mean a bad year."

It's strange to see players carry their gloves to their dugout when the regular season begins—as a new rule dictates—rather than leaving them on the field, a practice in place since organized ball began before the turn of the century. It's even stranger that the St. Louis Browns are now the Baltimore Orioles. There'll be no big Italian dinners for a select group of Yankees at the Berra house on The Hill this season. Or visits with his ailing mother for Yogi.

But nothing is stranger than this: the Yankees win 103 games and spend exactly three days in first place in the American League. And for the first time since 1948, one of those dates is not the final day of the season.

As good as this Yankee team turns out to be—and its 103 victories are the most it will ever win under Casey Stengel—this is the season of the Cleveland Indians, who win a major league record 111 games. Larry Doby, who broke the AL color barrier just three months after Jackie Robinson first took the field in Brooklyn, leads the league in home runs (32) and RBI (126). Another player of color, Mexican second baseman Bobby Avila, leads the league in hitting (.341), and third baseman Al Rosen has 102 RBI and 24 home runs.

But it's Cleveland's pitching that truly sets the Indians apart. Early Wynn and Bob Lemon both win 23 games, and Mike Garcia wins 19 and saves another six in relief. All three have more than 100 strikeouts, allow at least 30 fewer hits than innings pitched, and none has an ERA higher than Wynn's 2.73. Cleveland's Big 3 is so dominant they do the near impossible—overshadow future first-ballot Hall of Famer Bob Feller, now 35, who goes 13–3 as the team's No. 4 starter in his 16th season with Cleveland.

Berra is one of the few hitters to have success against the Indians' pitching staff. Yogi hits .321 against the Tribe, slamming four home runs and driving in 15 runs in 21 games. "Berra is the most dangerous hitter on that team," Garcia tells reporters. "You can even throw the ball over his head and he might hit it out." Wynn agrees, adding, "There is no way to pitch to Yogi."

Certainly not this season. Named the toughest Yankee hitter in the clutch by writers in a preseason *Sporting News* poll, Berra hits .349 with runners on base, driving in a career-high 125 runs. And that despite stomach problems the first month of the season that leave him hitting just .277 with five home runs on May 11. He turns 29 the next day, discovers his stomach woes are gone, and tags Garcia for a pair of hits in a 5–4 win over Cleveland. He hits .310 the rest of the season, finishing at .307 with 22 home runs in 151 games as the team's cleanup hitter.

And with Berra hitting so consistently behind Mickey Mantle, pitchers can ill afford to pitch around the team's 22-year-old center fielder, who recovers from his own slow start—and relentless booing by Yankee fans—to hit an even .300 with 27 home runs and 102 RBI in 146 games. Mantle continues to strike out—he whiffs a league-high 107 times—but there isn't a tougher one-two punch in the game than Mickey and Yogi. Or any other Yankee who knows he'll be in the lineup every day, as manager Casey Stengel continues to mix and match players at every other position to maximize the team's talent.

The same *Sporting News* poll also names Yogi the most popular Yankee, no surprise given the steady stream of newspaper and magazine profiles written about him, the radio interviews at every stop in the league, and a rising portfolio of endorsements and television appearances. He even books a cameo in the upcoming movie version of the Broadway hit *The Seven Year Itch,* starring Marilyn Monroe, now part of the Yankee family after marrying Joe DiMaggio in January.

Sure, the media still pokes fun at Berra's appearance. One staple: when Yogi jumps into the batting cage for pregame batting practice, a writer invariably shouts, "Hurry up, now. Lock the cage. We've captured it alive." It's always good for a laugh, and Yogi plays along as he always has. But he's now the most recognizable player in baseball— and its most admired—and he's popular from coast to coast. Given all that, Yogi can't help but wonder when he'll enjoy the respect he's earned without having to endure the same tired insults, too.

A few weeks before Berra's seventh straight All-Star Game, he sits down with *Sporting News* publisher J. G. Taylor Spink for what has become an annual in-depth interview. Berra tells Spink he and Phil Rizzuto have applied for a liquor license in Clifton, New Jersey, another step toward opening their own bowling alley. He talks about how his father, in New Jersey for a visit, has turned from baseball cynic to box-seat critic, complaining that Yogi is hitting too many ground-ball outs.

"They give you a big stick, and you hit the ball, and what happens? It goes 40 feet!" Pietro says to his son. "Hit the ball harder."

It's a fun interview with the game's most popular player, but it also makes a bit of news: Berra wants to coach when he retires, just like his mentor, newly elected Hall of Famer Bill Dickey. Yes, he tells Spink, he knows some people will laugh when they learn Yogi Berra wants to coach. "Well, Mrs. Berra's boy ain't a dummy," he says. "I've been watching closely, taking notes, studying Dickey, who is the best teacher in the country.

"I am going to be a coach—and a good one, too."

After six World Series championships, one MVP award, and seven All-Star appearances in his first eight seasons, how can anyone doubt anything Berra claims he can do on a baseball field?

The Yankees play good ball after the All-Star break, pulling even with Cleveland on July 20, but they can never quite pass the Indians. Case in point: New York closes out August winning 16 of 20 games but falls another 1½ games behind Cleveland, trailing the Indians by 5½ games as they enter the season's final month. They shave a game off the deficit on September 1 when they beat the Indians 4–1 at the

Stadium behind Berra's two-run homer, two singles, and two runs scored. They win again the next day to pull within 3½ games, but never get any closer.

Earlier the day of the series opener, Berra and pitcher Eddie Lopat were on the field to film their scene in *The Seven Year Itch*. Yogi has worried for days about his three lines of dialogue and begs director Billy Wilder to let him swap roles with Lopat, who has just one line. Wilder, who paid the players $750 apiece, tells Berra to relax, he'll make the change. And when the camera focuses on a relieved Yogi, he delivers.

"No kidding?" he says, right on cue.

The end to the Yankee season effectively comes on September 12, when Cleveland sweeps a doubleheader from New York before 86,563 delighted Indian fans, increasing its lead to 8½ games. The Yankees, who win eight of their last 11 games, can postpone the inevitable only six more days. On September 18, the Indians beat Detroit, 3–2, their 107th win of the season, and clinch the American League pennant.

With the Yankee run of five straight titles officially over, talk shifts to the competition for MVP and what changes Weiss and Stengel will make to retool the Yankee roster. The writers talk of Berra as a prime MVP contender, along with a handful of Indians and Cuban outfielder Minnie Miñoso, the White Sox's first player of color. And the Yankees start talking about shifting the game's best catcher to another position. They test one plan in the season's final game, playing Yogi at third base, with Mantle at shortstop, and rookie first baseman Bill Skowron, who hit .340 in 87 games, at second.

Berra handles two plays in the field flawlessly in an 8–6 loss to Philadelphia and proclaims himself ready to play wherever Casey needs him. But he makes it clear third base would not be his first choice. His reason? "It's too lonesome there," he says after the game. "I like to talk to people at the plate. Third is almost as unsociable as right field."

The Yankees don't lose much time in remaking their team to overtake the Indians, who look a bit more vulnerable after being humbled in the World Series by the Giants' four-game sweep. Step 1: lock up their best player early and set the salary bar for everyone else. And that's why Yogi is sitting in the Yankee office on November 3, posing for photographers with a cigar clenched between his teeth and his feet up on a desk, handing Weiss a contract said to pay Berra $50,000 next season—the highest ever for a catcher.

A playful Berra jokes about the size of his raise—$10,000, more than double what half the nation's 42 million families earn—and again pledges to do his best at whatever position Casey wants him to play. Then he shifts his attention to the Indians. "If we pick up one or two pitchers, we'll be fine," says Berra, who's sure 37-year-old Allie Reynolds, the heart and soul of the pitching staff since Yogi joined the Yankees, is serious about retiring.

So Yogi is not surprised two weeks later when Weiss announces he acquired two young pitchers with great potential as part of a 17-player trade with Baltimore. Yogi and Weiss have had their differences over the years, but Berra admires how Weiss got precisely what the Yankees needed without giving up any of the team's key players. Weiss traded eight players—seven prospects and 32-year-old outfielder Gene Woodling, who hit .250 in 97 games this past season. In return, he got a pair of young, hard-throwing pitchers with high ceilings—Bob Turley and Don Larsen—and slick-fielding 26-year-old shortstop Billy Hunter, who Weiss hopes will replace Phil Rizzuto, now 37 and coming off a .195 season at the plate.

Yogi is excited about both pitchers. Turley has a big fastball, a bigger curve, and racked up a league-high 185 strikeouts. Larsen, a year older at 25, was 3–21 for a team that lost 100 games. But two of those wins came against the Yankees, who privately believe Larsen could turn out to be the better of the two pitchers. The two will complete a rotation that includes Whitey Ford and Bob Grim, the team's Rookie of the Year and 20-game winner. In one deal, the Yankee pitching staff goes from being the league's oldest to one of its youngest. And one of the best.

Berra gets more good news a month later while sitting in the clubhouse at his local golf club waiting for rain to pass. On December 9, Berra is told that he's won his second Most Valuable Player award, finishing just ahead of Cleveland's Doby and Avila. Seven of the 24 voters—three from each American League city—gave Berra their first-place vote, while both Doby, who finished 20 points behind Berra, and Avila each received five. Cleveland fans are irate, insisting Berra only won because their stars split the vote, allowing Yogi to squeeze through.

But while an argument can be made for either Indian star—or for Cleveland's 23-game winners Bob Lemon and Early Wynn—writing Berra off shows an ignorance of the importance of a catcher. Stengel certainly knew how vital Berra's knowledge of hitters was to coaxing 11 or more wins out of five different pitchers, putting Berra behind the plate in a record 149 games—an astonishing 1,271⅓ innings. And despite the heavy workload, Berra still led the Yankees in runs batted in for the sixth straight season, tying Joe DiMaggio for the second-longest streak in team history. Only Lou Gehrig, with seven seasons, has more.

Sure, the vote for MVP was close. And yes, it could have gone to one of the Cleveland stars. But this season established Yogi Berra as one of the most valuable players in Yankee history. And that competition is as tough as it gets.

Berra tries to push aside any thoughts of what position he'll play next season when he and his family spend the year-end holidays in St. Louis, which has developed a complicated relationship with its favorite son. Most everyone is proud that one of their own is now baseball royalty, but more than a few are resentful that he no longer calls St. Louis his home. Carmen says they're just being parochial. Well, Yogi doesn't know what that means, but he does get a little tired of hearing how his good friend Joe Garagiola—who called it quits in October to take a broadcasting job with the Cardinals—never left town when he was traded to Pittsburgh three years ago. Or when he was later claimed off waivers by the New York Giants.

The hint of betrayal is quite clear in the headline above an interview with him in the *St. Louis Post-Dispatch,* which runs Christmas weekend.

### YOGI THE YANKEE,
### ABSENTEE KING OF THE HILL
### BACK AT HOME PLATE

The story reminds readers that "the walking fireplug from The Hill" has not been in his hometown since his last at-bat against the now departed Browns—more than 15 months ago. Yogi shrugs it off, splits his time between family and friends on The Hill and Carmen's folks down on the farm in Howes Mill, and is ready to return to New Jersey when he makes the last stop on this trip—a luncheon at Ruggeri's in his honor. A group of businessmen got together and gave him an inscribed silver tray. *To Yogi Berra, with best wishes from his old friends on "The Hill."*

Berra is touched, mumbles a few words of thanks, and quickly moves into his comfort zone—taking questions from the crowd. The one everyone keeps asking is why he signed so early, since there was a good chance he would have a big bargaining chip once the MVP award was announced.

"I got what I wanted," Yogi says.

How can that be? he's asked, since Yogi has always publicly pegged George Weiss as a real cheapskate.

"Well," Yogi says, a sly smile spreading across his face, "I talked to Dan Topping instead."

It seems, contrary to the story told at the time, Berra found himself sitting across from the Yankee co-owner at a luncheon on October 31 memorializing the late Grantland Rice—one of the nation's leading sportswriters for half a century—at Toots Shor's restaurant. Topping, a big Berra fan, leaned over and began talking about his catcher's next contract.

"What do you think you should get?" Topping said.

Berra knew better than to offer up a number. "What do you think I'm worth?" he asked.

When Topping told him $50,000—a number higher than Yogi and Carmen had agreed upon—Berra reached across the table, shook the owner's hand, and said, "Mr. Topping, you just made yourself a deal."

Everyone in the room applauded when Berra finished his tale.

As Yogi said back in June, Mrs. Berra's boy ain't no dummy.

# CHAPTER 21

# History Lessons
## 1955

Yogi Berra can only wonder as Bill Skowron tells a bunch of his Yankee teammates what happened earlier today when he walked into the Soreno Hotel with Elston Howard.

*What the hell was Moose thinking?*

It's February 28, 1955—one day before Yankee players are required to report to training camp in St. Petersburg, Florida, where Jim Crow is alive and well. Segregation laws call for "white" and "colored" bathrooms and drinking fountains all over this city. Blacks are only allowed to shop on two of four floors of St. Petersburg's biggest department store. Another major store doesn't allow them to use its dressing rooms to try on clothes. Neither establishment serves blacks at its lunch counters. The same is true for every restaurant, hotel, and store on the white side of town.

Howard, who is black, and Skowron, who is white, became good friends when they played minor league ball together in 1953, and Moose, one of several Yankees already in camp, volunteered to pick up Ellie at the train station today. Skowron was an impact player last season as a rookie first baseman. Most of the players figure Howard is a lock to make the Yankee roster after his MVP season for Triple-A Toronto last year. Casey Stengel is already telling Yankee beat writers they'll be writing plenty of stories about Howard this spring.

All the players know Howard will draw plenty of attention if he becomes *the first black Yankee,* but they think the quiet 26-year-old can handle the scrutiny. They care more about his bat—22 homers, 16 triples, 109 RBI, and a .330 batting average for Toronto—and the good reviews they've heard about his strong arm and defensive skills. After missing the World Series last season, the players think Howard can help the Yankees get back to the postseason.

Still, Ellie wondered why Moose was taking him to the Soreno Hotel, one of St. Petersburg's oldest and most luxurious waterfront hotels and the Yankee spring training headquarters for decades. The same Soreno Hotel whose management refused to give Howard a room for spring training last season. Did Skowron know something Howard didn't? Was the Soreno making an exception because Howard was expected to be a Yankee this season?

No, there would be no exceptions. That was clear when the desk clerk told Howard the Soreno does not rent rooms to blacks. Nor would he be allowed to eat in any of the hotel's restaurants.

Embarrassed, Howard left for the south side of town—the black side of St. Petersburg—and the Fifth Avenue South boardinghouse of Bill Williams, who has been renting rooms to black players since Jackie Robinson broke the major leagues' color barrier eight years ago. Just as he did last spring, Howard will watch his teammates pile into a bus and leave Miller Huggins Field for the team hotel after practice and games while he stands on a corner, still in uniform, trying to hail a taxi to take him to Williams' place.

Skowron still can't believe it when he finishes telling the story.

*What the hell was Moose thinking?* everyone else wonders.

Yogi took a quick liking to Howard last spring. They both share a love of movies, an aversion to small talk, and a common heritage—Howard was also born and raised in St. Louis. Yogi, who still keeps track of sports back in his hometown, heard all about the big, strong kid who turned down a dozen football and basketball scholarship offers to sign with the Kansas City Monarchs, the top team in the Negro Leagues. Berra never saw Howard on The Hill, though. And no Italian kid would ever show up where Ellie played—in Compton Heights, just four miles away. Jim Crow is alive and well in St. Louis, too.

Berra was happy when the Yankees signed the kid from St. Louis in 1950 and can see in the first few days of this training camp that the six-foot-two, 195-pound Howard will be his new backup, bumping reliable Charlie Silvera to third string. Yogi is impressed with Howard's work ethic—Ellie's the first player taking batting practice so he can work with Bill Dickey to improve his catching techniques or shag flies to work on his outfield skills. Howard's drive to prove himself also impresses Stengel, who starts calling Ellie his "three-way man"— Howard can play catcher, right field, and left field.

And when exhibition games start, Stengel often has Howard batting cleanup, "which I only do with players who can really hit," Casey says, "and this boy can hit." The only flaw Stengel can find is Howard's relative lack of speed.

"I finally get a nigger," Casey tells the writers jokingly, "and I get the only one who can't run."

Most of the Yankees cringe when they hear Casey's racial slur. The players have worked to make Elston feel comfortable in camp. Berra, Skowron, Phil Rizzuto, Mickey Mantle, and Hank Bauer have grown especially close to their new teammate, and all are upset about their manager's remark. But Howard shrugs it off.

That's evident when he calls his wife Arlene, who's back in St. Louis, pregnant with their first child. "He's 64 years old," Howard tells her. "That's how people of his era talked." If anything, Elston says, he's unhappy Casey called him slow. Sure, he isn't as fast as Willie Mays or Jackie Robinson, but Howard ran track in high school and is proud of his athletic talents.

Yogi tells Ellie he's happy to help hone the young man's catching skills and share his knowledge of the league's hitters. And Berra again tells the writers he is ready to play any position. Yes, he finds it lonely in the outfield. "But no balls are tearing at you," he says, "and no one is trying to run you over out there."

Stengel, however, has other ideas. "Berra's in good shape," Casey says. "I'd say he could catch all the games this year."

Howard looks good wherever Stengel plays him—making plays in the outfield, blocking pitches, and throwing out runners behind the plate. But he truly shines at the plate. After slamming a two-run double in the 8th inning to beat the Cardinals 7–4 on March 17, Howard's batting average is a sparkling .391. He belts his first home run of the spring two days later against the Dodgers, and every Yankee can see Ellie is a major league hitter.

And no one is surprised on March 21 when George Weiss makes it official: Howard is a New York Yankee. After passing on the likes of Willie Mays, Ernie Banks, and other stars from the Negro Leagues, the Yankees finally have a black player on their roster.

The team the Yankees field on a frigid, rainy Opening Day at Yankee Stadium on April 13 is expected to mount a serious run at preseason favorite Cleveland. Berra receives his second MVP trophy in pregame ceremonies and is one of three Yankees to blast home runs in a 19–1 rout of the Senators. Only 11,251 shivering fans show up, the smallest Opening Day crowd in Yankee history. Also a spectator: No. 32, Elston Howard. Stengel, the master of lineup changes, makes just two moves in this rout, putting Jerry Coleman in at second in the 6th and replacing shortstop Phil Rizzuto with Billy Hunter in the 8th inning.

The Yankees are in Boston the following day when Howard gets his first chance, replacing left fielder Irv Noren, who's ejected after bumping the ump while arguing a call at home plate. Howard singles and drives in a run in his first and only plate appearance in an 8–4 loss. It's only one at-bat in the second game of a long season, but given the stature of the Yankees, this is national news.

"Howard's appearance at bat signaled the fall of a dynasty that had been assailed on all sides as being anti-Negro," read the story from the Black Associated Press. "The fans gave Howard a well-deserved round of applause, making his debut on the here-to-fore lily-white Bronx Bombers."

Berra catches every inning of the first 12 games of the season but is forced from a game in Chicago on April 27 when a foul ball badly bruises his right index finger. Howard replaces Yogi in the 5th inning and singles in two at-bats. Ellie gets his first start a day later in Kansas City, catching and batting cleanup behind Mickey Mantle. He bangs out three hits, drives in two runs, and guides sore-armed Don Larsen through eight innings of two-run ball in an 11–4 Yankee win.

Yogi's finger is still sore the next day, so Stengel puts Howard back behind the plate and bats him cleanup again. But Yogi is back in the lineup the following game, and Howard, batting .429 in his 14 at-bats, takes a seat. Many in baseball think Howard would be the starting catcher for more than half the teams in the game, and there's no question he should be the next Yankee catcher when it's time for Yogi to step aside. But it will be 42 more games before Stengel gives Howard another start behind the plate.

"The only thing holding Howard back is that there is a man named Mr. Berra," says Stengel, who is predicting Yogi will repeat as the league's MVP. "Berra is the best player in baseball, except for maybe [Stan] Musial. I count heavily on his judgment. He knows better than I do when a pitcher loses his stuff. He knows the hitters better than anyone."

And there's one more thing.

"All I know," Stengel says, "is whenever I put him in my lineup, we win pennants."

It's a mid-June afternoon at Yankee Stadium, a few hours or so before the start of another game, and a familiar scene is playing out. Casey Stengel is sitting alone on the dugout bench after finishing another entertaining session with "his writers." Yogi Berra, who has caught all but four games this season, is sitting on the dugout steps, his equipment at his feet.

"I ain't feelin' so good," Berra says, loud enough for Stengel to hear.

"Neither am I," Casey answers. "Must be this New York climate."

Berra reaches down, picks up a shin guard, and begins strapping it in place.

"Case, the legs are stiff," he says.

"Yeah?" Stengel says. "Who's pitchin' for them?"

"I think it's the muscle," Berra answers.

"It'll work out," says Casey as he lifts himself off the bench and heads to the dugout tunnel leading to the Yankee clubhouse. "See you after the game. I gotta go change my lineup."

Berra watches his manager disappear as a few of his teammates mill about. "I got sinus real bad," he says, but he knows no one is listening. "Nobody even tells me to take it easy. Nobody cares about me."

Berra can be excused if he goes on about his aches and pains. On May 12, Yogi turned 30, an age when the bodies of baseball players inevitably begin to break down. That should be especially true for Berra, who has averaged an astounding 142 games behind the plate the last five seasons. That's more than 6,000 innings of crouching, running down the first baseline to back up infield throws, taking foul balls off his hands, arms, legs, and head, and blocking the plate.

But Berra, who often wears bandages on his arms and legs because "it makes me feel good," remains incredibly strong. Good thing, too. It appears Stengel wasn't joking about catching Yogi every game this season, no matter how good Elston Howard might be.

Yankee fans forgive Yogi when he gets off to a rough start this season—he's hitting .207 with just two homers and nine RBI while committing six errors through May 3. Six championships, seven All-Star appearances, and an endless stream of endearing stories have bought Berra a lot of goodwill. Yankee fans are far less forgiving of Mickey Mantle, whom they still resent for not being the next Joe DiMaggio, the story line the Yankee PR staff has pushed for the last three years. With their team in fourth place, the fans loudly booed Mickey for each of his 13 strikeouts over the same 18-game stretch.

Berra and Mantle finally go on hot streaks the rest of May, lifting the Yankees into first place. Alternating between the third and fourth spots in the lineup, Berra hits nine home runs—including five in four games—knocks in 29, and bats .370. Mantle slugs seven homers, drives in 23 runs, and hits .368. With Whitey Ford and newcomer Bob Turley pitching like aces, the Yankees win 20 of 25 games to take a three-game lead over the defending-champion Indians by month's end. Suddenly, Stengel isn't the only one talking about Berra winning a second straight MVP.

And Berra remains highly popular off the field. In late April, he joined the ranks of transcendent celebrities like John F. Kennedy, Marlon Brando, and Salvador Dalí when journalist Edward R. Murrow—a huge star in his own right—interviewed Yogi and Carmen at their New Jersey home for Murrow's hit television show *Person to Person.*

On June 3, his teammates tease him about his cameo in *The Seven Year Itch,* starring Marilyn Monroe, which opens to big crowds that same day. A new magazine called *Sports Illustrated* is talking to Frank Scott about putting Yogi on the cover of its All-Star Game issue in early July. And there is usually a stack of comic books several feet high at Yogi's locker before each game, gifts from his adoring fans.

Sure, midway through Berra's ninth season the Yankee star sometimes gets weary of life on the road. Most of the travel is still by train, going to bed in one city and waking up in another. At least each player has his own compartment on the train now, with a pull-down bed and private urinal. They also have management's rules for the road: players must wear a sport jacket to breakfast. A sport shirt is acceptable, but the top button must be fastened. It's dress shirt, tie, and jacket at dinner; the jacket is never removed. And they are to tip 25 cents for breakfast, 50 cents for dinner, and $1 a week for the hotel maid.

Yogi phones Carmen at least once from every city, trying to make sure to call when his two young sons are awake. He knows Carmen spends some of her time alone putting together a scrapbook that Yogi will read at season's end. "I sure am lucky to have such a wonderful wife," Berra says often. "She throws all my bad write-ups away." But

Carmen also has a strict rule about Yogi's complaining about a bad day at the Stadium. "You're the one playing ball, not me," she'll tell him. "Don't tell me about your troubles."

By June of 1955, Berra's Yankee family has been transformed. Only two players on this team were with New York when Yogi came up in 1947—Rizzuto, who's recently lost his shortstop job to newcomer Billy Hunter, and pitcher Tommy Byrne, who spent two seasons with three other teams before rejoining the Yankees last year. Vic Raschi and Allie Reynolds are gone, and in another month the Yankees will trade away Eddie Lopat, erasing all traces of the Big 3 who were so central to their many titles.

Tommy Henrich and Charlie Keller are long gone. So is Joe D, whom Yogi sees at Toots Shor every so often. (It saddens Yogi to see the Clipper moping over the end of his marriage to Monroe after nine tumultuous months.)

Yogi moves easily between the older gang—Rizzuto, Hank Bauer, Jerry Coleman, Gil McDougald—and younger stars Mantle, Ford, Bill Skowron, and Elston Howard. He loves the afternoon poker games at the hotel before night games that help keep the team close-knit. Yogi, Rizzuto, Mantle, Ford, Bauer, and newcomer Eddie Robinson are regulars, and everyone is welcome.

Mantle always seems to be out of money—his nightlife spending sprees are already the stuff of legend—and he usually hits up Yogi for cash before their biweekly paychecks. Berra always agrees to spot Mick $2,000—as long as Mantle pays $2,500 in return. Berra truly likes Mantle, but this child of the Great Depression remains cautious with his money. Indeed, it's a running joke among teammates that Yogi still has the first buck he ever made.

Stengel, whose wise investments have made him financially secure, puts it best. "Money," Casey says, "is the last thing Yogi thinks about before he goes to sleep."

Berra is happy to grab dinner and a movie with Robinson and Rizzuto after day games on the road, content to let Mantle and the younger guys answer the notes passed into the dugouts from pretty young women in one city after the next. "It's not the sex that tires out players," Stengel tells the writers. "It's chasing after the sex that gets 'em tired." But veterans like Berra know better. There are plenty of women who come knocking on their doors at the team hotel, offering a good time to any player who says yes.

One young wife of a Yankee recently asked Carmen Berra how she deals with all the women chasing after the players. "Yogi and I have an agreement," she told the younger woman, who's pretty sure Carmen was joking. "If he ever gets down to one woman, I'm out of here."

"What's the matter, Yog?" St. Louis star Stan Musial says as he steps into the batter's box at Milwaukee County Stadium.

Berra looks at his friend as he bends into his crouch, pulls down his mask, and slowly shakes his head. Musial is the first batter for the National League in the bottom of the 12th inning of an All-Star Game tied 5–5. Berra, once again the American League's leading vote getter, has caught every inning of a game that his team once led 5–0. As this game stretches into its fourth hour, Berra's looking forward to resting his weary legs.

"It's these extra innings, Stan," says Yogi, who has caught 77 of the Yankees' 84 games this season, including both ends of 10 doubleheaders. "It's tough on a guy catching every day."

Umpire Al Barlick, who's crouched before each of the 300-plus pitches thrown in this game, tells both players he's about had enough, too. And one more thing. "It's getting tough to see back here," Barlick says.

Musial, who entered his 12th All-Star Game as a pinch-hitter in the 4th inning, has struck out, grounded out, hit into a double play, and walked. "Yeah," says Musial, at 34 the oldest player on either roster. "I'm getting tired, too."

Berra looks out at six-foot-six Red Sox ace Frank Sullivan standing on the pitcher's mound, doubts Stan can catch up to this kid's heat, and flashes a sign for a fastball. It's the last signal he'll give in this game. Sullivan delivers the ball down the middle of the plate, Musial whips his bat around, and the ball sails over the right field fence, giving the NL a 6–5 win.

Berra is already walking off the field by the time his good friend is rounding first base. He knows Stan will tease him about this home run every time the two men hit the golf course during spring training next season. Oh, well. Berra has better things to think about as the season enters the second half. He's among the league leaders in home runs (15) and RBI (62), a major reason the Yankees are in first place with a comfortable five-game lead.

The Dodgers—who jumped out to a 25–4 start—have all but wrapped up the National League pennant at the break, leading second-place Milwaukee by 11½ games. Berra figures another Dodger-Yankee postseason is inevitable, even when the Yankees stumble to open the second half, losing 11 of 18 and falling out of first place. Order is restored on September 16 when Berra hits a pair of home runs to beat the Red Sox, 5–4, and move back into first. The clincher comes with two games left, a 3–2 win against Boston.

It's the Yankees' 21st pennant, and along the way Berra hits his 203rd home run to pass Bill Dickey for the most homers by an AL catcher. Berra leads the team in RBI for the seventh straight season to tie Lou Gehrig's team record and catches more than 100 games for the seventh straight season, the most of any active catcher.

Berra and Mickey Mantle are the only two regulars in Casey Stengel's platoon system, but Mantle goes down with a torn thigh muscle on September 16, pinch-hits in just two games the rest of the season, and is hobbling when the World Series starts on September 28. Yet the oddsmakers install Berra's team as favorites, and history is on their side. The Yankees have won 16 championships and are five for five in World Series meetings with the Dodgers, who have yet to win a title in their seven trips to the postseason.

But sometimes history is a poor predictor of the future.

# CHAPTER 22

# The Most Popular Player

## 1955

Yogi Berra stares out the window of the *Yankee Special,* one of two propeller-powered airplanes carrying his teammates, Yankee management, and baseball officials from Hawaii to Tokyo. The Yankees have just won five exhibition games against Hawaiian All-Star teams, the first leg of a six-week-long "goodwill and patriotic" tour arranged by the State Department to foster better relations between the United States and Japan. The tour is expected to draw upwards of half a million fans to 16 games in five cities in Japan.

It was a long season, one that did not wind up as Berra had hoped, and he doesn't think playing another six weeks of baseball will help him get over his disappointment. Not after the way the World Series ended.

Especially after the way the World Series ended.

The Yankees will touch down in Japan on October 20—a full 16 days since they lost Game 7 of the World Series to the Brooklyn Dodgers—and Berra is still trying to come to terms with the loss. It was a hard-fought Series—both teams won all three games on their home turf to force the deciding game at Yankee Stadium—and Brooklyn is an outstanding team. But Yogi can still see Dodger out-fielder Sandy Amoros flashing across left field in the deciding game, reaching out as Berra's 6th-inning drive slashed down the left field line. That drive would have—should have—tied the game and left Yogi on second base with no outs and the team's two hottest hitters coming to bat.

Berra was sure the Yankees would win the game right then and there. Instead, Amoros—*who had just entered the game that inning*—made a sensational catch, then wheeled and delivered a strike to shortstop Pee Wee Reese, who threw to first base to double-up Gil McDougald. The Yankee infielder had rounded second base convinced Yogi's drive was a sure double, maybe even a home run, and couldn't make it back to first in time.

*How the hell did Amoros make that play?*

But it wasn't just the Cuban outfielder's speed that saved the Dodgers. Amoros is left-handed, which means he only had to reach out with his gloved hand after streaking across the Yankee Stadium outfield from left center field instead of reaching across his body. It was a play of inches, and the extra inches Amoros had made all the difference.

*Still, how the hell did Amoros make that play?*

It won't be the only play in this Series that Berra and all of baseball will long remember. In Game 1, Jackie Robinson raced down the third baseline in an attempt to steal home. The ball arrived a split second before Robinson slid into home late, and Berra is sure—no, he's absolutely positive—he put the tag on Robinson for the out. But home plate umpire Bill Summers called Robinson safe, sending the Yankees—especially Yogi—into a rage. One thing Yogi knows for certain—Summers was far behind the plate and in no position to make the call.

But that play, though memorable, did not keep the Yankees from winning Game 1. The Game 7 catch by Amoros did prevent the Yankees from winning the World Series, which is why the *Sporting News* is already calling it the greatest catch in World Series history. With young left-hander Johnny Podres pitching brilliantly, Amoros' big play paved the way to a 2–0 win and Brooklyn's first and only title. For the first time in seven trips to the World Series, Yogi will bank a check for the *loser's* share.

After the game, Berra and Phil Rizzuto walked into the Dodger clubhouse to congratulate the winners. Yogi found Podres amid the chaotic celebration and put his arm around the 23-year-old's shoulders. "Kid," Berra said, "you pitched one helluva game."

No one in Japan cares about the World Series loss. "The Yankees are still champions to Japanese baseball fans," proclaimed the lead editorial in *The Mainichi,* the newspaper that published a 24-page supplement about the Yankee visit. Only a decade after their nation surrendered in World War II, more than a thousand Japanese fans are at rain-swept Haneda Airport to greet the Yankees. That includes Prime Minister Ichiro Hatoyama, who wears a Yankee cap, one he rarely takes off in public for the next three weeks.

A 13-vehicle caravan—three convertible sedans for management, 10 Air Force jeeps for the players—takes a full hour to drive the 10 miles to the team hotel. More than 100,000 fans line the streets, and thousands more lean out of office windows and let loose a blizzard of confetti. No sooner does the caravan arrive at the Nikkatsu Hotel than the players are whisked to a ballroom filled with reporters—and translators—eager to ask questions.

"I don't even talk at home," Yogi jokes. "Why should I talk here?"

Baseball is immensely popular in Japan, where the game has been played since the turn of the century, and they hold American players in high regard, none higher than the Yankees. There is a bronze plaque at the entrance of Koshien Stadium in Nishinomiya with an outline of a baseball player and the inscription IN MEMORY OF BABE RUTH (1895–1948) WHO PLAYED AT KOSHIEN STADIUM IN 1934. Hall of Famers John McGraw (manager) and Charles Comiskey (White Sox founder/owner) toured here in 1913. Stengel barnstormed here as a player in 1922, and Lou Gehrig was on tour with the Babe in '34.

The Yankees are the second major league team in three years to visit Japan—the Giants toured in '53—and there is no player more popular than Berra. His unique size and shape—and all his World Series appearances—make him easy for Japanese fans to identify. That's obvious at a reception the first night, when more than 2,000 fans squeeze into the Japan Theater to get a glimpse of the American stars. Yankee infielder Jerry Coleman serves as emcee and calls each player to the stage, where a flower girl hands him a bouquet and a dozen rubber balls to throw to the audience as souvenirs. The theater absolutely erupts as Berra walks onstage, where teenage bobby-soxers shriek and cry as if Yogi were Elvis himself.

All the Yankees receive movie-star treatment the next afternoon at what is supposed to be a closed workout. The guards are overwhelmed by several thousand schoolkids and autograph seekers, some climbing the outfield fences to run onto the field during batting practice, others rushing the gates, running through the stands, and climbing into the dugout to take pictures and get autographs.

The Yankees win four games and tie one in Tokyo—Berra singles and scores in the 9th to secure a 1–1 tie—before visiting the coastal city of Osaka, home to the 16th-century Osaka Castle and many of Japan's oldest shrines. This time the parade through the city streets takes two full hours. More than 70,000 fans pack Osaka's stadium, with millions more watching on TV as the Yankees crush the local team. It is the same scene at virtually every stop on the tour—a parade, a cocktail party, gifts, and another Yankee show of power and grace before sellout crowds.

The team plays each game as if it's playing the Indians or Red Sox, and for good reason—Stengel says he's using these games to evaluate players for next season. That's good news for Elston Howard, who will finish the tour hitting .468. Howard, whose wife is home with their infant son, brought a movie camera and is filming every aspect of this trip, including time the players spend as tourists. The Yankees visit tearooms, shop for kimonos, eat local delicacies—Yogi's stubby fingers are no match for chopsticks—and enjoy the singing and dancing of geishas. Yogi even forgets about Sandy Amoros for a while.

They visit Hiroshima, and this stop is different from any other. Yogi and his teammates are a bit shaken by what they see: a flat city of buildings and streets all made of cement. There are no tall buildings and only a smattering of trees. They are taken to a museum built at Ground Zero; among the exhibits are silver coins inside a bank vault that were fused together from the intense heat of the atomic bomb's blast.

The Yankees are cautioned not to leave their hotel at night out of concern for their safety. Citizens here have not forgotten President Truman's decision to drop the world's first atomic bomb on their city, and the tour organizers fear there could be confrontations. "You'll be safer this way," the tour manager tells them.

The players and wives go their separate ways when the tour stops to play near an American military base in Nagoya. The women stay overnight at a nearby health spa while their husbands win another game, then attend a dance at the officers' club. The players head back to the base hotel after the dance and spend much of the evening at the bar. As the night turns into the early morning, the only players left drinking are Whitey Ford, Billy Martin, and Eddie Robinson.

"Hey, wouldn't it be fun to get everyone back down here?" says Martin, who has a plan. They'll phone their teammates, tell them they're getting their asses kicked in a barroom fight, and say they are in dire need of help. They quickly decide to call Yogi first, figuring the others will believe Berra far sooner than any of them.

Martin and Robinson begin banging chairs and shouting as Whitey calls his catcher. "Yog, come down to the bar!" Whitey shouts. "Billy and Eddie are in a fight. They're outnumbered, and we need your help. Come quick!"

"I'll be right there!" shouts Berra, who flies down to the bar barefoot, dressed in pants and a T-shirt, ready for battle. He turns into the lounge, sees his three teammates calmly waiting for him, and breaks up laughing.

One by one, Yogi calls every Yankee, and they all have the same reaction as Berra when they turn the corner and see a growing number of their teammates drinking instead of fighting. They leave Casey and the coaches alone, and only Bob Cerv and Bill Skowron—two of the strongest men on the team—ignore Yogi's plea for help. It's close to dawn before the party breaks up and the players get a few hours of shut-eye.

The tour ends with three more games in Tokyo. The Yankees sweep them all, crushing an All-Star team 9–3 in the final game before an overflow crowd of 45,000. Berra gives the fans something special to remember, blasting a pair of two-run homers that receive waves of applause, firecrackers, and confetti. When the game ends, both the Japanese and American flags are lowered and "Auld Lang Syne" is played over the stadium sound system. Yogi can feel a lump forming in his throat and tears rolling down his cheeks. Every Yankee and Japanese player feels the same way.

The team will soon fly out of Tokyo to play before American servicemen stationed in Manila and Guam, then fly back home. They depart deeply touched by the warmth of mutual goodwill. And Yogi is no longer thinking about Sandy Amoros every minute of every day.

It's December 3 when Berra receives word that he's been voted the Most Valuable Player in the American League for the second consecutive season and the third time in his career. Only Hall of Famers Joe DiMaggio and Jimmie Foxx have won three MVPs in the AL; Yogi's friend Stan Musial is the only player who's won three MVP awards in the National League. (Dodger catcher Roy Campanella will be awarded his third MVP five days later, five points ahead of teammate Duke Snider.)

Foxx and Detroit pitcher Hal Newhouser are the only other players to win back-to-back MVPs since the Baseball Writers' Association of America instituted the award in 1931. The voting is once again close, with Detroit's Al Kaline—the American League batting champion—finishing 17 points behind Berra and Cleveland outfielder Al Smith another point back.

Berra was a rock behind the plate—catching 145 games, including 18 doubleheaders. His 27 home runs tied him for fourth best in the AL, and his 108 RBI was third. But the key to winning this award is best summed up by *New York Times* columnist Arthur Daley. The Yankee catcher, Daley notes, is the only player who appears on the ballot of all 24 writers tasked with selecting the MVP.

"He wasn't hurt," Daley writes, "by the fact that he is the most popular player in the business."

# CHAPTER 23

# Almost Perfect

## 1956

President Dwight D. Eisenhower stands in front of the presidential box in Washington's Griffith Stadium, a baseball glove on his left hand, a baseball in his right. It's April 17, Opening Day of the 1956 baseball season, and Eisenhower, like any good politician running for reelection, waits for all the photographers to ready their cameras as he prepares to throw out the first pitch of the new baseball season.

Life in America for the last three-plus years under Ike has been good. The economy grew so fast last year—more than 7 percent—that officials are projecting a budget surplus in excess of $4 million. More than 60 million Americans own cars, the GI Bill produced a generation of highly educated workers now earning good salaries, and Europe and Asia are being rebuilt with many of the materials manufactured in the United States. It is the birth of consumerism, and Americans consume a third of all goods and services in the world.

America is also changing. In May of 1954, the Supreme Court, led by Eisenhower appointee Chief Justice Earl Warren, ruled against school segregation in *Brown v. Board of Education*. In December of 1955, Rosa Parks, a black department store seamstress, refused to give up her seat on a Montgomery, Alabama bus. Her arrest sparked the ongoing Montgomery bus boycott, along with sit-ins and demonstrations led by Reverends Martin Luther King Jr. and Ralph Abernathy.

The backlash included the firebombing of four black churches and the homes of King and Abernathy. Undeterred, the movement eventually led to the end of Jim Crow laws in America.

A vaccine for polio, approved almost a year ago to the day, is well on its way to eradicating a disease that afflicted almost 80,000 Americans in 1951–1952 alone, killing more than 2,000. Eisenhower suffered a serious heart attack in 1955, but with the economy going strong, the Korean War settled, and the fever of McCarthyism finally broken, Ike decided to run for a second term. And what better way to show off his health than a strong throw on a sun-drenched day at the ballpark?

The game that follows is an awesome display of power, much of it coming from Yogi Berra and Mickey Mantle. Batting third, Mantle hits two tremendous home runs, the first clearing the 31-foot wall in dead center field at the 408-foot marker. The ball came to rest in an alley across the street, an estimated 465 feet away. The second shot came in the 6th with two runners on. This one clears the fence at the 438-foot mark and rolls another 20 feet into a clump of trees.

Berra, once again batting cleanup, goes 4-for-4, and it's his two-run homer in the 3rd inning that gives the Yankees a 3–1 lead they don't relinquish. Yogi's run-scoring single two innings later pushes the Yankee lead to 4–1, and Berra's two-run double in the 8th puts the game out of reach at 10–4, the game's final score.

The display of power is merely the start of a season-long onslaught against American League pitchers by the two men who will finish first and second in MVP voting. Mantle, in his sixth season at age 24, fulfills the promise long predicted for him, winning the American League Triple Crown. Berra drives in 105 runs, hits .298, and ties his own AL record for home runs by a catcher with 30.

Berra, who often starts slow, is hitting .341 with 12 home runs and 35 RBI on May 31 despite missing seven games with a muscle pull on his right side. He has already caught three doubleheaders despite Stengel's spring training promise to give Yogi more rest. Casey, acutely aware his team has not won a World Series in three seasons, is going to put his best players out there every game. And that means Yogi—who passed his 31st birthday on May 12—is going to be behind the plate even if Stengel has to wheel him out there.

And it's been hard to argue the results. Under Yogi's guidance, Whitey Ford ends May at 7–1 and is pitching like the staff's ace. Johnny Kucks is 6–2, two wins short of his total in his rookie season. The Yankees start June at 29–13, hold a 6½-game lead over Cleveland and Chicago, and have the game's most dynamic one-two punch. Cleveland, Chicago, and Boston all have strong teams, but this Yankee team looks destined to do something special.

If you're listening to a Yankee game on the radio in the summer of 1956, chances are you'll hear an advertising jingle featuring your favorite catcher between innings. "It's me-hee for Yoo-Hoo," Yogi tells you in that familiar gravelly voice. And then an announcer delivers the kicker. "Yoo-Hoo—Yogi Berra's favorite drink. The chocolate drink of champions."

If not quite Yogi's favorite drink—a shot of vodka will always top Berra's list of liquid refreshments—Yoo-Hoo is a close second. But one thing is certain: Berra's investment in the chocolate-flavored soft drink, produced not far from the Berras' home in Woodcliff Lake, New Jersey, is the crown jewel of his rapidly growing financial portfolio.

Berra's association with Yoo-Hoo is the result of one of two chance meetings on the White Beeches golf course in the waning days of 1955, two bits of serendipity that change Yogi's life in ways big and small. The small: on a warm day in November, Yogi found himself paired with Tommy DeSanto, one of the country club's best players. After watching Yogi struggle through 10 agonizing holes, DeSanto suggested the left-swinging Berra try hitting the ball from his other side. "Here," said DeSanto, who plays right-handed. "Use my driver and see how you make out."

Yogi took DeSanto's club and smacked his best drive of the day. Yogi finished the round using DeSanto's clubs—for everything but wedge shots and putts—and by round's end he was a right-handed golfer. Just as surprising: there was a noticeable improvement in Yogi's golf game.

The other chance meeting came in the same month when Yogi landed in a foursome with Natale Olivieri, the 41-year-old former owner of a small soda fountain who discovered a way to make a chocolate drink that would stay fresh in a bottle or a can. Olivieri started marketing the drink he called Yoo-Hoo with decent results, but he was looking for a high-profile celebrity who could lift the sales of the Yoo-Hoo Chocolate Products company's signature drink.

After spending a few hours together on the links, Berra and Olivieri began a friendship that would last a lifetime and profit them both handsomely. Thinking Berra possessed the winning combination all advertisers want—he's likable and trustworthy—Natale asked Yogi if he would do some commercial work for Yoo-Hoo. But after talking it over with Carmen, Berra came back with a counteroffer.

Berra was already earning good money. On January 26, 1956—his 11th wedding anniversary—Yogi was in the Yankees' Fifth Avenue office to sign a contract for $58,000, a nice $8,000 bump for his MVP season. Yankee General Manager George Weiss made sure reporters understood that Berra has received a raise after every season since joining the team in 1946 and is currently the highest-paid Yankee, the third-highest-paid player in baseball behind Ted Williams ($100,000) and Stan Musial ($80,000), and the highest-paid catcher in major league baseball history.

The loser's share for last season's World Series was $5,598.58, bringing Berra's total for seven postseasons to $43,502.72. His agent Frank Scott says Yogi is pulling in another $15,000 a year or more in endorsements. And plans for the 40-lane bowling alley in Clifton, New Jersey he's building with Phil Rizzuto are well under way.

In short, Yogi Berra is quickly becoming one of the richest men in baseball.

So Berra told Olivieri he wasn't interested in doing the usual commercial gig for Yoo-Hoo. Yogi was looking for something bigger. His pitch: instead of salary, he wanted to be paid in company stock. He would be a Vice President, using his fame and connections to recruit investors to Olivieri's company while convincing many of his Yankee teammates to promote the chocolate drink on TV, on radio, and in print.

Olivieri agreed, signed Berra to a 15-year deal, and Yogi threw himself into the job, pitching the soft drink over the airwaves and in person at supermarkets and neighborhood groceries. It's not too long before Mickey Mantle, Whitey Ford, Elston Howard, and a handful of their teammates are touting Yoo-Hoo as "the drink of champions." New York soon is one of several teams stocking its clubhouse refrigerators with the chocolate drink.

The Chicago Match Company prints Yoo-Hoo matchbook covers: open one, and inside you can check a box next to the name of any of six different Yankees—Berra and Mantle included—and get the player's autograph on a hat for 50 cents or a regulation baseball for $2.00. Olivieri prints Yoo-Hoo baseball cards featuring Yogi, Mickey, Whitey, and other Yankees, including first baseman Bill Skowron, who decides to invest in the company.

In typical fashion, an apocryphal story of Yogi and a Yoo-Hoo customer surfaces. Berra, who frequently visits the Yoo-Hoo bottling plant in Carlstadt, New Jersey, is standing in an executive's office when the phone rings. Yogi, or so the story goes, answers the phone. A woman asks him if "Yoo-Hoo" is hyphenated.

"No, ma'am," Yogi tells her. "It isn't even carbonated."

Berra says the phone call never happened. But it's good for a laugh, and Yogi really doesn't mind. Just more publicity for his newest investment, one that takes off with Yogi as the face of the company. Yoo-Hoo will be distributing 600,000 bottles a year by 1960 and close to two million bottles by 1964.

The Yogi Berra brand has never been stronger.

There's always that one bump in the road, that one stretch of games in baseball's 154-game season that knocks a team off stride. For these

Yankees, it comes on a late June trip into Chicago, and it's quite unexpected: New York enters the Windy City on June 22 riding a seven-game winning streak. Mantle (27-64-.380) and Berra (17-45-.332) are battering pitchers and will finish one-two in fan voting when the All-Star Game results are announced in another week. The Yankees hold a 5-game lead over the second-place White Sox, and writers and opposing team executives are complaining about a Yankee romp to another American League pennant.

But just three days later, the Yankees have dropped four straight games to the White Sox, their lead is down to a single game, and no one is talking romp. Instead, some reporters are beginning to wonder if all those days and nights behind the plate are catching up to Berra. An 0-for-19 stretch drops his batting average to .308 in what feels like a blink.

Suddenly it's the White Sox who have the hot hand, especially outfielder Larry Doby, who came over from Cleveland in a big trade last October to provide power to the Chicago lineup. And power is just what Doby gives the White Sox in the four-game set with the Yankees. He hits a big home run in the first game, which Chicago wins 5–4 in 12 innings. After Jim Wilson pitches a 2–0 gem in the second game, Doby blasts a three-run homer in both games of a doubleheader sweep.

Comiskey Park is aglow with postgame fireworks celebrating Chicago's big day. Reporters fan out across the clubhouse to ask about the Yankees' disappearing lead over the White Sox, now suddenly down to .004 percentage points. A few of the boldest reporters ask if perhaps Chicago might be the better team.

Berra sits quietly at his locker, listening to these questions, his look of annoyance discouraging reporters from even approaching him. But when he hears a few of them say the White Sox are talking confidently about overtaking the Yankees, Berra has heard enough. "Look, this is silly!" Yogi almost shouts. He wants his teammates to hear this. "The White Sox ain't going to win the pennant. We are."

Berra knows what he's talking about. The Yankees make quick

work of the White Sox's hot streak, rolling to 18 wins in the next 20 games. Among the victories: a doubleheader sweep of the White Sox and a three-game sweep of the Indians. When Johnny Kucks blanks the Tigers 4–0 for his 14th win on July 17, the Yankees are 58–26. They hold a 10½-game lead over the now second-place Indians and an 11½-game lead over Boston.

The White Sox? They're in fourth, 13 full games behind the Yankees. Yes, this race is now over. All the most interesting story lines will be coming out of New York the rest of the season.

Two of them revolve around two of Yogi's best friends, and their stories could not be more different. Mantle is waging war on Babe Ruth's home run record while shooting for the Triple Crown. He stays ahead of Ruth's ghost the entire summer, entering September four homers ahead of the Babe's 60-home-run pace. But Ruth slugged 17 home runs the final month of the season. Mantle, feeling the effects of several minor injuries, hits just five more and finishes with 52. He falls short of the Babe but finishes 20 ahead of Cleveland's Vic Wertz, his closest American League competitor.

The other story focuses on Phil Rizzuto, who begins to almost disappear as the season progresses. The 38-year-old shortstop, a Yankee since 1941, starts seven games in June, one in July, and one final game on August 2. A few days later he announces this will be his last season, after which he hopes to find a job managing. His next appearance is as a pinch-runner on August 16, and questions begin to surface about whether he will make the postseason roster.

The answer comes on August 25 — Old-Timers' Day at Yankee Stadium — when Weiss and Stengel call Rizzuto into Casey's office. They're looking for a player to cut so they can sign veteran outfielder Enos Slaughter off waivers, they tell him, and they want his opinion. After going through more than half the roster, Rizzuto realizes this meeting was called to give him his release.

Dazed, he walks out of Stengel's office and bumps into infielder Jerry Coleman.

"Where are you going?" Coleman says.

"Home!" Rizzuto replies. "I've just been cut."

Several teams call Rizzuto immediately, offering him a chance to play, to coach, or to join their broadcasting team. The Yankees, quickly realizing they've made a public relations blunder, offer Phil a job in their broadcasting booth for next season. Rizzuto, who sees the game through a fan's perspective, will become an instant hit and a fixture on Yankee broadcasts for the next 40 years.

Yogi is angry with Casey for embarrassing Phil, especially in front of so many old friends and teammates. Berra takes this episode as a sharp reminder that as much as he loves playing baseball, this game is a business. He's glad Phil has the bowling alley to look forward to and tells his friend he'll be great in the broadcast booth.

Everyone, meanwhile, wonders when Stengel is going to give Berra some rest, especially after Yogi hits a pedestrian .274 with five home runs in July and August. Other than the seven games Berra missed in May with a pulled muscle, he's caught all but four games heading into the season's final month. Yogi keeps asking for time off, and Casey keeps writing his name in the lineup card.

Casey has his reasons. Berra's work with this young pitching staff—nine of New York's 10 top pitchers are between 23 and 27 years old—is a major factor in the team's success. On the rare occasion a Yankee hurler shakes off more than a few of Yogi's calls, Berra simply stops calling pitches and lets the man on the mound make his own decisions. When a series of hard-hit balls inevitably follows, the pitcher will politely ask Yogi to resume calling pitches.

Tired or not, Yogi turns it on in September, which features a 19-game hitting streak, two more milestones, and one inspirational telegram. On September 14, he sends a pitch from the Tigers' Jim Bunning flying over the right–center field fence, more than 400 feet away. It's his 29th home run of the season and the 237th of his career, one more than former Cubs catcher Gabby Hartnett's major league record. How big is this accomplishment? Hartnett, elected to the Hall of Fame last year, hit 236 home runs in 20 seasons. Berra sets the record in his 10th full season.

Berra hits a robust .361 for the month with seven home runs and

26 RBI, and the Yankees coast to their 22nd pennant, clinching on September 18 with almost two weeks left to play. Stengel, who gives Berra two games off after the clincher, starts him in the season's final game with Yogi one shy of his own league home run record for catchers. But even after Berra slams No. 30 in the first inning, Stengel plays him all 10 innings of a meaningless loss to the Red Sox. Casey's Yogi habit dies hard.

Yogi also took time out earlier in the month to send a telegram to Al Grosch, the coach of Stockham American Legion Post 245 in St. Louis. Grosch, whose team was in Nebraska to play New Orleans Post 345 for the American Legion World Series title, called his teen-agers together and read Berra's Western Union message aloud.

AS A FORMER MEMBER OF THE STOCKHAM POST TEAM I'M SURE PLEASED TO LEARN THAT YOU ARE IN THE NATIONAL FINALS. WILL BE PULLING FOR YOU ALL THE WAY. LET'S GRAB ANOTHER CHAMPIONSHIP. BEST WISHES.           — YOGI BERRA

Properly inspired, Stockham defeated New Orleans, 8–3, to win St. Louis' first American Legion title. The best part of their reward: an all-expenses-paid trip to attend the first two games of this fall's World Series and meet the players. Berra is genuinely excited for his hometown team, the one he played for all those years ago after Branch Rickey told him he'd never reach the major leagues.

The Dodgers, Braves, and Reds battle for the NL pennant down to the final days of the season. No Yankee will admit it publicly, but every one of them wants another shot at Brooklyn. And they get their wish on the final day of the season when Brooklyn ace Don New-combe beats the Pirates for his 27th win and the NL pennant, setting up the fourth Dodger-Yankee World Series in the past five years.

But there's a question whether the field leader will be on the field.

"How is Carmen feeling?" Pietro Berra asks his son, whose wife is almost seven months pregnant with their third child.

"She's good, Pop, she's good," Yogi Berra tells his father over the telephone. It's the evening of September 30 and in three days the Yankees will open the World Series in Brooklyn. With much of America riveted to the rematch of last season's dramatic seven-game affair, President Eisenhower—his bid for reelection now just five weeks away—will make a campaign stop at Ebbets Field to throw out the first pitch.

But it's also the night before Paulina Berra will have major surgery at St. John's Hospital in St. Louis, and her youngest son is wrestling with a difficult decision. Diabetes, which has already robbed Yogi's 63-year-old mother of most of her sight, is blocking the circulation of blood into her right leg. Doctors will remove her dying limb tomorrow morning to save Paulina Berra's life.

There is a brief silence before Yogi speaks again.

"Pop, I think I should come home," Yogi says. "I think I should be there."

Pietro's reply is quick and firm. "Lawdie," says Pietro, "your brothers and sister are here. You stay in New York. You play good for your team. That is what will make your mother the happiest."

Father and son agree. Yogi will travel to St. Louis soon after the World Series, and if the oddsmakers are right, that day won't be far off. The Dodgers have baseball's best pitcher in Newcombe, who won nine of his last 10 decisions and almost single-handedly carried Brooklyn to the pennant. But no other Dodger pitcher won more than 13 games, Roy Campanella has injuries to both hands and hit only .219 this season, and Jackie Robinson's 37-year-old knees have reduced him to a part-time player. This Dodger team is not as strong as it was a year ago.

Sure, the Dodgers have the confidence of defending champions, but Yogi is feeling confident, too. He's on a hot streak and Mantle is as healthy as Mick ever gets, giving the Yankees the game's best one-two punch. Young Bill Skowron has become a true home run threat, and old hand Hank Bauer slugged 26 homers and knocked in 84 runs. Ford and Larsen are pitching lights-out, so the Yankees just need one

or two other pitchers to step up for New York to win the championship Yogi thought they should have won a year ago.

The oddsmakers install the Yankees as 3–2 favorites, but after two
games, the Yankees will have to do it the hard way. New York loses
both games at Ebbets Field, running its losing streak in Brooklyn's
bandbox of a stadium to five. And they lose in embarrassing fashion,
with Ford lasting only three innings in a 6–3 loss and Larsen failing
to get out of the 2nd inning in a 13–8 defeat.

The second loss really hurts. Yogi hit a grand slam in the 2nd
inning, giving Larsen a 6–0 lead and driving Newcombe out of the
game to thunderous boos. But Larsen allowed a single, two walks,
and a run on a sacrifice fly in the bottom of the 2nd, and Stengel
pulled him with two outs for Johnny Kucks. Larsen was furious with
Casey's quick hook, and even madder when Kucks gave up a two-run
single. Then Tommy Byrne came in and coughed up a home run to
Duke Snider and—*poof!*—the six-run lead was gone.

Yogi thought Casey was a bit too quick to yank Larsen, but it was
hard to argue—this was not the same pitcher Yogi boasted about to
the kids on the Stockham American Legion championship team.
"You watch him," Berra had told the young players while sitting in
the Ebbets Field clubhouse before Game 2 was rained out. "He's
changed his delivery. I think he's going to do something special."

Turns out Berra was right—he just had the wrong game.

Ford rebounds in Game 3 at the Stadium, taming the Dodger bats
in a 5–3 win. Berra continues his hot streak with a pair of hits; his
RBI double in the 8th gives Whitey some breathing room to close
out the game. Tom Sturdivant also goes the full nine in a 6–2 Game
4 win. With the Series even, Stengel plays it coy about his starting
pitcher, telling the media he'll wait until the next day to announce his
decision.

Many of the writers think it will be Larsen, but the big right-
hander doesn't agree. He complained vehemently about being taken
out so early in Game 2 and doubts Casey will give him the ball. So he
does what he usually does in Manhattan—spends the night partying.

Larsen is seen by a few writers at daybreak the morning of Game 5, entering the lobby of his Bronx hotel with a pizza and the morning paper in hand.

Yogi arrives at Yankee Stadium midmorning and sees the ball in Larsen's cleat, the sign Casey has picked Gooney Bird to pitch. The players hung the nickname on Larsen a year ago for his big ears, his big hands and long arms, and his pear-shaped six-foot-four frame. Or to reflect his oddball personality. Or both. Yogi thinks Larsen could be an excellent pitcher—maybe even a great one—if he took better care of himself. Today he just hopes the big guy has the overpowering fastball he was missing in his last start.

Yogi sees right from the start that Larsen's fastball is electric—coming in hard with a late downward or sideways break. Berra will mix in Larsen's slider and slow curve—both look good today—to keep the Brooklyn hitters off balance. But Yogi's going to call for that fastball until the Dodgers prove they can hit it.

They couldn't in the 1st inning, with Larsen getting a pair of called third strikes. Jackie Robinson hits the ball hard in the 2nd inning, a hot smash to third that deflects off Andy Carey's glove and right to shortstop Gil McDougald, who throws out Robinson. Larsen makes easy work of the Dodgers the next two innings, then Mantle makes the play of the game in the 5th, speeding into left-center for a back-handed catch of Gil Hodges' 400-foot drive.

Veteran Dodger pitcher Sal Maglie keeps the game tight, allowing only a solo homer by Mantle in the 4th inning and a run-scoring single from Bauer in the 6th. Larsen gets three more outs in the 7th and is sitting next to Mantle in the dugout when he looks out at the scoreboard. All he sees are zeros. "Hey, Mick, look at that," Larsen says. "Two more innings to go. Wouldn't it be something?"

Mantle gets up immediately and walks away. Baseball tradition dictates no one speaks to a pitcher throwing a no-hitter. Talking to a pitcher tossing a perfect game in the World Series? Not even Yogi is talking to Larsen.

Yogi keeps calling for fastballs in the 8th, refusing to change his call the two times Larsen tries to shake him off. When Mantle tracks down a long fly to center by Sandy Amoros to end the inning, Larsen is three outs away from making baseball history.

Larsen, sitting off by himself in the Yankee dugout, can feel his legs shaking and whispers a little prayer. When it's time to take the field, Yogi walks over to his pitcher and slaps him on the rear. "Let's get the first batter out," Berra tells Larsen, as if this is just another game.

Everyone in the crowd of 64,519 is standing as Larsen gets the first batter—power-hitting outfielder Carl Furillo—on a routine fly ball to Bauer in right field. One out. Roy Campanella hits the second pitch he sees slowly to Billy Martin at second base, who makes the easy play. Two outs.

Veteran Dale Mitchell—a lifetime .312 hitter ending his career this season with Brooklyn—comes in to pinch-hit for Maglie. Carmen Berra, seven months pregnant, is sitting with her sister Mary in the stands and tells Mary she'll name the baby Dale if Larsen retires Mitchell. Her husband's mind is somewhere else. He can still remember Bill Bevens standing on the mound with the same 2–0 lead in the 1947 World Series, one out away from pitching a no-hitter. And he can still see the double that cost Bevens both his no-hitter and the victory. Berra is determined not to let that happen again.

Yogi calls all fastballs and Larsen gets ahead of Mitchell, a ball and two strikes. Mitchell fouls off the next pitch, and Berra signals for yet another fastball. Larsen's 97th pitch comes in chest high. Mitchell starts to swing then holds up, and home plate umpire Babe Pinelli jerks up his right hand and shouts *STRIKE!* Larsen has just retired the 27th straight hitter he's faced.

"Yippee!" shouts Yogi, who jumps from behind the plate, holds up the ball in his right hand, and rushes toward Larsen. He can see tears in Larsen's blue eyes as he jumps into the pitcher's arms and gives him a bear hug, a picture destined to become one of baseball's most iconic images. The rest of the team is right behind, all trying to pound on Larsen's back as the pitcher pushes his way to the dugout and the clubhouse, which is every bit as crazy.

The Yankees mob Larsen, shaking his hand and babbling on about making history. Dodger owner Walter O'Malley squeezes through to congratulate the 27-year-old Yankee pitcher. So do Jackie Robinson and Dodger pitcher Ralph Branca. Pinelli, who's retiring after this Series, gets inside the mob. "Greatest pinpoint control I've ever seen," the home plate umpire tells Larsen.

Yogi pulls away from the crowd to talk with reporters. A big smile never leaves his face, but he's also relieved. Berra knows Bevens would have won that game in '47 had he thrown out a Dodger stealing second in the 9th inning. "I wanted to win the game, that's all I wanted to do," Yogi says. "I've never caught a greater pitcher than Don was today."

Yogi looks over at the crowd around Larsen and knows Gooney Bird is going to be standing there for hours answering questions. Yogi finishes up with these reporters, dresses, shakes the hands of a few more teammates, and heads out to New Jersey. He has other things on his mind.


The hospital operator asks Yogi to wait one moment, finds the right number, and directs the call to his mother's room in St. John's Hospital. Yogi's brothers and sister Josie have taken turns visiting their mother while making sure their father has plenty to eat at home on The Hill. Yogi finds his mother in good spirits. She knows about today's perfect game—she watched with her eldest son Tony and a cousin from Detroit—and wants to hear all about it from her Lawdie.

Yogi wants to know how she is feeling and says he can't wait to see her when the World Series is over. Hopefully with another Yankee title. When he senses Paulina is tired, Yogi has one last question. "Momma, is there anything I can do for you?" he asks.

"Can you hit a home run for me tomorrow?" she asks.

"Sure, Mom, sure," Yogi says.

There are no home runs from anyone in Game 6, and for nine innings there are no runs at all, despite the shift back to Ebbets Field and its easy-to-reach fences. Yankee starter Bob Turley gives up only four hits while striking out 11 to hold Brooklyn scoreless. Dodger veteran Clem Labine gives up seven hits—including two more to Berra—but is never in real trouble. Despite the high stakes—a Yankee win ends the Series—Larsen's historic moment seems to have drained most of the emotion from this day's game.

The Dodgers finally push across a run in the 10th, and for the second straight year the Series goes to a decisive Game 7. And Stengel is again agonizing over the selection of his starting pitcher. Berra keeps telling him Johnny Kucks is the right choice. Yes, Kucks is just 24, and yes, he lost his spot in the postseason rotation with a poor showing in September.

But he's a sinkerball pitcher, Yogi keeps repeating. "He'll make them hit the ball in the dirt," Berra says to his manager, "and they won't get any pop fly home runs."

After a sleepless night, Stengel tells Kucks the start is his when the Yankees meet at the Stadium. And as the team walks out to board their bus to Ebbets Field, Yogi catches up to the young pitcher. "Johnny," Yogi says, "today you have the chance to be the hero or a bum."

Berra applies pressure, and then he takes it off in the game's very first inning. Down two strikes with Hank Bauer on second, Yogi slams Don Newcombe's next pitch over the right field fence for a two-run homer. "That's for you, Mom," Yogi says to himself as he rounds third base.

Newcombe stares incredulously as Yogi trots home. His third pitch was chin high and outside, a pitch out of the strike zone designed to entice a hitter to chase something he won't be able to hit hard—if he hits it at all. But Newcombe had been warned that strategy doesn't work with Berra. And now he just got burned.

Kucks gives up a one-out walk and a single in the bottom of the 1st with Jackie Robinson up next, and Stengel has two pitchers warming up. Berra calls for a sinker, Kucks throws a good one, and Robinson hits the ball on the ground right back to the pitcher, who starts an inning-ending double play. Berra is right about Kucks—the Dodgers will hit only three fly balls all game.

Yogi comes up again in the third inning, right after Newcombe strikes out Mantle for the second time with a man on first. This time Newcombe runs the count to 2–2. Newcombe's next pitch is a low strike on the outside corner, a pitch most batters hit weakly to second if they try to pull it. But Berra is right on it and sends the ball sailing over the fence in right center field and out of Ebbets Field for another two-run homer.

Knowing Newcombe is devastated, Berra shouts to him above the loud boos from the Brooklyn fans. "It was a good pitch, Newk," he yells as he rounds second base. "Really, it was." A 4–0 lead is never safe in this tiny ballpark, but Yankee players can see a look of defeat etched on their opponents' faces. Elston Howard opens the 4th with a home run, and Newcombe leaves the field to even louder boos. Kucks is cruising, and when Bill Skowron belts a grand slam in the 7th for a 9–0 lead, the rest of the game is a formality.

The Yankee clubhouse is once again a madhouse, a crazy mix of celebrating players and management, with the media, celebrities, and politicians piling in. Larsen wins the *Sport* magazine MVP award and the Corvette that goes with it, but Berra is the best player in this seven-game Series. He hit .360 to lead all hitters, and his 10 RBI topped the record held by Lou Gehrig.

"Gosh, is that right?" Yogi says when told about the RBI mark. "I am right proud of that."

Yogi's two home runs were the decisive blows in the 9–0 Game 7 victory, and he coaxed five straight complete games from a pitching staff shaken by two awful performances to start the Series. How good was Yankee pitching? The Dodgers managed just three runs in the final four games.

Robinson walks into the Yankee clubhouse to congratulate the winners, and the first player he seeks out is Berra. The TV cameramen rush over just as Jackie puts his arm around Yogi's broad shoulders. "This guy is a great competitor," Robinson says. "He is one of the greatest clutch hitters who ever lived."

When Robinson leaves, Berra tells reporters of the promise he made to his ailing mother before Game 6 and how he had failed to deliver. "I tried my darnedest, but I just couldn't do it," Yogi says. "So I got two today. I hope I made her happy."

The Yankee players, management, and their families celebrate the team's 17th World Series title with several hundred guests at a party in the Waldorf Astoria's famed Starlight Room. Don Larsen is kept busy signing ticket stubs for Carmen's sister Mary and everyone else who had the presence of mind to save the Game 5 ducat. The festivities stretch until dawn.

Yogi rests for a few days, picks up $1,000 for waving to the *Perry Como Show*'s studio audience, then flies out to St. Louis. He arrives the day Paulina is released from the hospital and spends the week in his childhood home, making sure his mother is healthy and comfortable. His sister Josie and her husband live with Paulina and Pietro, and Yogi is comforted knowing his mother is in good hands.

The Professional and Business Men's Club of The Hill honors Yogi at a luncheon at Ruggeri's on October 19. And that's where Yogi is on a sunny Friday afternoon, sitting on the dais as the master of ceremonies tells the 200 guests—including his father and friends Stan Musial and Red Schoendienst—that Yogi has joined Columbus and Marconi as "one of the three best-known men in the world."

The club's Vice President Fred Giacoma tells the guests there is now a scholarship in Yogi's name to help the neediest kids on The Hill. The club also plans to help pay Paulina Berra's medical bills. Giacoma then hands Yogi a scroll of honorary membership—only the second the club has ever granted.

"You are the same natural, unassuming Yogi Berra who knows the real meaning of humility," Giacoma says. "You have the respect and admiration of all of St. Louis."

December is a happy time for the Berra family. Yogi and Phil Rizzuto break ground for their big bowling alley early in the month and are hoping to open a year from now. Yoo-Hoo sales are growing, and more teammates have agreed to help promote the chocolate drink. Yogi is talking about paying some of the players a few hundred dollars to wear T-shirts with the product's slogan printed across the chest. Agent Frank Scott is hard at work putting together advertising deals and TV appearances like the spot on the *Phil Silvers Show* that will run next fall. That one features Yogi playing opposite a rising young comedian named Dick Van Dyke.

On December 13, Carmen delivers another son, whom the couple promptly names Dale. Yoo-Hoo Chocolate Products owner Natale Olivieri, who's become a close family friend, is Dale's godfather. A wire service photographer is at Valley Hospital in Ridgewood, New Jersey two days later and snaps a picture of nurse Phyllis Bohack holding Berra's newborn son that will run nationwide. Yogi sports a big grin and a small sign that reads:

SCORE

BOYS + GIRLS

3 + 0

Carmen will soon be looking for a bigger house with more land for their growing family.

A week later Yogi drives into Yankee Stadium in his new rose-pink Cadillac for a press conference: he and Whitey Ford have agreed to contract terms for the 1957 season. Ford got a $5,500 bump to $34,000. Yogi signed for $65,000—a healthy $7,000 increase—and he is once again the third-highest-paid player in the game behind Stan Musial and Ted Williams.

Berra sips the champagne the Yankees put out for this event and tells reporters he doesn't want any part of the prediction business—"It sounds like boasting"—then makes two exceptions. Yogi predicts Mickey Mantle's Triple Crown '56 season is just a stepping-stone to even bigger things for the Yankee star. And he expects to bring home another World Series title. "We will win again," he says matter-of-factly.

And why not? Yogi, who'll turn 32 next May, and Hank Bauer are the only key players in their 30s. Mantle looks like the best player in baseball, there's a core of young stars supporting him, and a handful of exciting rookies like Bobby Richardson are ready to break in. The winner's share for this season's title is $8,714, running Berra's career postseason winnings to $52,217.48, second only to Joe DiMaggio's $56,940.

Another title will make him No. 1 in postseason earnings, and there are plenty of reasons to believe that number will grow as long as Berra is in a Yankee uniform.

# PART IV

# YOGI, INC.
## 1957–1963

# CHAPTER 24

# The Tipping Point
## 1957–1958

**Y**ogi Berra is standing at the front door of the new home he and Carmen bought in July of the 1957 season, a nine-room split-level on two hilltop acres in affluent Tenafly, New Jersey. It's a cold day in late January of 1958, and Yogi has a long list of things to do with spring training in St. Petersburg just a few weeks away. But he agreed to allow a writer from *Sport* magazine to come to his house and talk with him and his wife today. It's the final interview for what will be a major story in the nation's premier sports magazine, and Berra is waiting impatiently for writer Irv Goodman to arrive.

Yogi sees Goodman pull into his long driveway, opens the front door, and points to his watch. This is the third time in the past six years Goodman has written a profile of Berra, but Yogi still does not remember the man's name. What he does remember is the time he told the writer to arrive, and Goodman is 20 minutes late.

"Hi," says Goodman, who understands why Yogi is pointing to his watch.

"I'm going to have to leave in the afternoon," says Yogi as he walks with Goodman to his large, well-furnished den. "Got an appointment down at the bowling alley in Clifton."

Berra and Goodman take seats and exchange just a few pleasantries before the interview begins. Yogi is a man on the clock, and he has the business of bowling on his mind. He tells Goodman the bowling alley, a 40-lane establishment he built with his best friend Phil Rizzuto in nearby Clifton, New Jersey will have one opening in March and then another a few weeks later.

"What's the difference?" Goodman asks.

"The opening is going to be while I'm in St. Pete," Berra says. "So Phil will do it. First four days free bowling, that sort of stuff. The grand opening is for when I'll be back. That'll be a six-day opening. I'm going to bring the Yankees down for it."

Berra told Goodman in an earlier interview that he asked his brother John, who'd been a waiter at Ruggeri's on The Hill for the past 20 years, to move east and manage the cocktail lounge. Berra is very proud they paid a high-end designer to fashion the lounge to resemble Yankee Stadium. Freddy Rizzuto, one of Phil's brothers, will manage the front end.

"Your brother settled in yet?" Goodman asks.

"John sold his house in St. Louis a year ago, figuring we'd be ready to open, and all he's been asking ever since is when it's going to happen," Berra says. "You know, we can seat 54 people in the lounge. We're going to have to figure out what people drink around here. I figure the bowlers and the whatchacallthem, the stiff-shirts? Uh, white-collar people. The bowlers will go for beer. But them, I don't know. What do you think—not beer, huh?"

Goodman shrugs and asks Berra how the bowling idea got started.

"Bowling is really growing fast, and some guys came around and wanted us to front an alley for them," Yogi says. "But we figured why not do it ourselves? So we put in only our money. If it don't go, Phil and me take a beating. We're 50-50. But we stand a chance to make a good buck, too."

Goodman turns the conversation to baseball. The 1957 season is almost a sore subject for Berra, who posted several firsts he'd like to forget. Berra drove in 82 runs in '57, the first time in five seasons he hasn't passed the magic century mark in RBI. It was the first time he failed to find his hitting stroke—his .251 batting average was a full

43 points below his average for the previous 10 seasons. And it was the first time in eight seasons he did not finish in the top four of MVP voting.

It is also the first time he's ever taken a pay cut. Goodman attended the January 8 press conference at the Yankees' office in Manhattan when the team announced Berra had signed a contract for the '58 season, telling the media its star catcher had agreed to a cut in pay. No other details were given. And though Berra said all the right things that day—"I deserved the cut," he said. "I plan to get it back"—he was clearly steamed about losing $5,000 from the career-high $65,000 he earned in '57.

It wasn't just that his 24 home runs, 82 RBI, and .995 fielding percentage topped all catchers in the American League. Or that he masterfully guided six Yankee pitchers to 10 or more wins—a major factor in winning yet another American League pennant, the eighth in the nine seasons since Berra became the team's starting catcher. The Yankees lost the Series to Milwaukee in seven games, but Berra hit .320, one of only two Yankees to top .300 against the tough Braves pitching staff.

Nor was it that he did all this while suffering a horrific injury on June 5 when a foul tip broke the lower bar of his face mask, pulling it apart from both ends and fracturing the bridge of his nose. He left the field in Cleveland that day with blood gushing from the gash made by the crushed catcher's mask, thankful the metal bar hit his nose rather than one of his eyes. He missed three games, played left field for six, pinch-hit twice, and was back behind the plate 11 days later. He still caught 121 games, once again the most in the league.

And it wasn't the indignity suffered when the front office, looking for an answer to Berra's season-long batting slump, ordered him to wear glasses—which he dutifully wore and quickly discarded.

No, what bothers Yogi most is this: the 1957 season was his first poor performance—by *his* standards—after 10 sterling seasons. Why couldn't management just give him the same salary as last season? He'll be 33 come May, and manager Casey Stengel is still playing him at the game's most taxing—and important—position more than any other catcher in baseball. The fans again voted him to start the All-Star Game. And he remains the Yankee most in demand for public appearances.

And this is how the organization repays him?

Sure, the pay cut bothers him. And yes, he's determined to earn it back this season. Goodman wonders aloud how Berra explains his slump last season.

"I struck out only 24 times all year. The rest of the time I hit the ball, but nothing went," Berra says. "I tried a lighter bat. I'm a funny guy. If I'm not hitting, I don't blame me, I blame the bat."

But honestly, Berra doesn't feel there is a reason to assign blame.

"It was just one of those years," he says.

Goodman hears the rumble of feet coming from the hallway leading to the den. Berra's live-in housekeeper Julia has finished giving lunch to Berra's three sons—8-year-old Larry, 6-year-old Timmy, and Dale, who passed his first birthday last month—and they all are soon in the den, rolling on the floor, looking for attention. Yogi reaches down, picks up Dale, and changes the focus of his conversation with the writer.

"I go to some affairs in the neighborhood, Communion breakfasts, places for the local Little League," Yogi says. "You get so many calls from people, I could go somewhere every night if I wanted to. I do these things when a friend asks, not because somebody wants to pay me."

The two men are talking about the 15-minute commute from this plush suburb to Yankee Stadium when Carmen walks in and joins them. They talk about golf—Yogi's other true passion—and the challenges of the course at the White Beeches Golf and Country Club, where the Berras are members. Carmen tells Goodman she knows a surefire way to annoy her husband—tell him that Mickey Mantle, who took up the game just a year ago, is already as good as Yogi, who's been playing for eight years and has seen scant improvement in his game.

"He gets so mad," says Carmen, who started playing golf this past year and says she now understands the hold the game has on her husband. "He wants to master the game, but he can't."

Yogi tells Goodman they see a lot of Broadway plays — they enjoyed the hit musical *My Fair Lady* and want to see *The Music Man,* but tickets have been hard to come by, even for a baseball star. They leave the kids home and drive into the city for dinner about once a week, which is more than enough for Yogi. "I'd rather eat home," he says. "I have enough of that restaurant food when we're on the road."

Carmen enjoys going to nightclubs with other Yankee couples, but Yogi says catching takes too much energy for them to stay out late too often. Their night out at the Copacabana last May 16 is another memory from '57 Berra would rather forget. A handful of Yankees and their wives went to the Copa, one of the city's most exclusive clubs, to celebrate Billy Martin's birthday that night. Yogi, hitting just .188 in May and .200 for the season, did not want to go. But Carmen thought a night out with the Mantles, the Fords, and other friends would be good for her moody husband and convinced him to go.

What happened that night was splashed over newspapers all across the nation. A bunch of bowlers at tables on both sides of the Yankee table began heckling headliner Sammy Davis Jr., and several players took exception. Stories differ about who did what next, but a few of the bowlers and Yankees wound up in the men's room, punches were thrown, and Yankee outfielder Hank Bauer was accused of breaking the jaw of one of the bowlers, who filed a $250,000 suit against Bauer and the Copa. (The suit was later dropped.)

Every Yankee there was fined, several — including Yogi — were benched for the next night's game, and the scandal left Berra deeply embarrassed. "If the Yankees had as much punch on the field as they did at the Copa..." was the running joke in game stories the rest of the season. Carmen felt terrible for months, knowing Yogi would have been in his bed at home in Tenafly, sound asleep, when the late-night fight broke out had she not pushed him to join his friends.

Nightclubs have never been Yogi's thing. No, what Yogi likes best about living so close to New York City are the many sporting events—hockey, basketball, and football games, the big prizefights—he attends in the offseason. He's taken his two older sons to basketball and hockey games at Madison Square Garden, but not before they passed a test of Yogi's making. "First time, I have someone watch them and see if they behave," he tells Goodman. "If they run around and make noise, I'll hold off taking them to another game. If they're not gonna behave, it wouldn't be any fun taking them."

With that story, Yogi gets up to find his coat. It's time to head over to the bowling alley; Goodman can finish his interview with Carmen. Yogi's wife needs little prompting to pick up the conversation once her husband leaves the house. She tells Goodman that Yogi knows everything there is about sports and never has to write anything down. Once he reads or hears a result—no matter what the sport, no matter how much time has passed—it's locked in his mind.

"I don't know how or why," she says. "Friends are always calling him to settle bets. He can tell you how many fights a boxer has had in his career, including the names of the fellows he fought."

Just don't ask Yogi about much of anything else. "He is as unaware as can be about other things," Carmen says. "What he has to know, he knows. But nothing about world affairs, for instance. I was talking to him about the [Soviet] missiles, and he didn't know what I was talking about."

Carmen pauses, and a slight smile crosses her face. "It didn't concern him," she says.

Goodman shifts subjects again, asking Carmen why her husband is investing in a bowling alley, and is surprised when she replies, "So he doesn't have to go to Washington." Asked to explain, Carmen says Yogi doesn't want to hang around as a washed-up player in need of a paycheck, probably getting traded to a losing team that hopes his fame will be enough to attract fans. He wants to walk away on his own terms.

"And then what?" Goodman asks.

"Yogi would like to coach," she says. "But never manage, though I think he would be good at it. Yogi would be happy coaching, but you have to be able to afford it. It can't be your total livelihood; it's not enough [money]."

"Yogi feels it would be a good life. He'd get satisfaction out of teaching kids, and being with the ball club, and living the life—but only as a coach."

Carmen gets up to show Goodman the rest of the house, and the question of why Berra does not want to manage is never asked. Or is it that Carmen doesn't want Yogi to manage? That question is not asked, either. Carmen takes Goodman up and down the three levels of the house, telling him she has yet to get used to the layout after moving here a year ago and is already thinking about relocating. There's a large ranch-style house just a few blocks away that has caught her eye.

It's late afternoon by the time the tour is complete. Goodman is all but done asking questions and Carmen walks the writer out to his car. As they cross a large patio to the driveway, Goodman has one more question. "Yogi isn't what most people have made him out to be," he says. "What do you think he is?"

Berra's wife doesn't answer immediately. After a minute or so, she has an answer that Goodman will use to end his nine-page story, which his editors will title "The Other Yogi Berra."

"Yogi is a man happy in baseball, but moody in almost anything he does," Carmen says. "But it isn't because he has something against people. Not at all. It's just the way he is."

Goodman takes a few steps toward his car, satisfied his questions have been answered and convinced he has a better understanding of one of baseball's most celebrated—and complex—players. But Carmen stops him. She has one more thing to add.

"In your story you should say that Yogi has learned to take care of himself and his family," she suggests. "He is happy, mostly, and he's easygoing.

"And he is good."

Yogi is sitting in his home in New Jersey, enjoying a rare springtime off day in the Yankee 1958 schedule, when he picks up the receiver of a ringing phone.

*Happy birthday to you,*
*Happy birthday to you,*
*Happy birrrrthdaaay, dear Yogi,*
*Happy birthday to you.*

It's May 12, 1958, and he can barely keep from laughing before Joe Garagiola finishes singing to Berra from his hotel room in Chicago, where he'll broadcast the Cardinals-Cubs game in a few hours. Yogi, who turns 33 today, sang the same song for Joey's birthday three months ago to the day. It's a ritual the two old friends started a few years back, and it's one they will repeat for the rest of their lives.

It doesn't matter if the two men from The Hill talked to each other yesterday or haven't spoken in a month—Yogi and Joe fall into an easy conversation, catching up on their families and each other's careers. Joe likes to tell people he turned to broadcasting at 28 when he realized he wasn't going to be the best catcher on his block. Yogi always laughs at that line. Carm and the boys are fine, Yogi says. He and Phil finally opened the bowling alley in late March. Yes, his brother John misses Ruggeri's—where Joe's brother Mickey is still a waiter—but likes his new life in New Jersey.

"And let me know if you need any more Yoo-Hoo T-shirts," says Yogi, who makes sure everyone he knows is helping him sell the chocolate drink.

Yogi asks about his mother. Joey always checks in on Momma Berra when he visits his parents, who still live in the same house on Elizabeth Avenue right across from the Berras. Joe knows Paulina hardly ever misses a Cardinal broadcast—that's when Joe lets her know how her youngest son is faring. *I know you're listening, Momma Berra,* Cardinal fans are used to hearing. *Yogi's hit a home run, and the Yankees are winning.*

"Joe, how is she doing?" says Yogi. By the spring of 1958, diabetes has robbed Paulina Berra of much of her sight as well as her right leg, and the insulin shots just don't help as much as they used to. "Please be honest," Berra says. "I gotta know."

Garagiola can hear the pain in Berra's voice. The best he can do is tell Yogi his mother has good days and bad days. What he doesn't say is the bad days outnumber the good, and Yogi doesn't ask. Garagiola is sure Berra's heard it all from his sister or one of his two brothers who still live on The Hill.

The conversation turns to baseball. Yogi always wants to know how his friend Stan Musial is doing. "He's still hitting," Joe says. Musial, now 37, is off to a great start, hitting .483 in 22 games. "When are you going to get going?" Garagiola asks. Berra has six hits in his last 10 games, and on his birthday is hitting .203 with just five extra-base hits for the season. Considering Yogi's age and all the miles on his legs, it's not unreasonable to wonder if Berra will ever again be the impact player who won three MVP awards in five seasons.

"You know me—this slump isn't my fault," Yogi says. "It's the bat's fault. I just gotta find a bat with hits in it."

Berra won't find the right bat until well into July, but Casey Stengel still pencils him in at catcher for just about every game of the season's first half for two simple reasons.

Stengel remains convinced putting Yogi behind the plate gives his team its best chance to win. Elston Howard, now in his fourth full season with the Yankees, is a fine catcher and a terrific hitter, but there is still no one better at handling a pitching staff than Berra.

And Casey knows he has to win. Not just the pennant but the World Series, too. He'll be 68 at the end of July and his team has won only one World Series title in the last four years. Toss out the three wartime seasons, when many ballplayers were wearing a soldier's uniform, and you have to go back to the 1932–1936 seasons to find a Yankee dry spell like this one. Without another title, Casey knows he'll lose the best job he ever had.

This is the first season the Yankees have New York to themselves— the Dodgers and Giants are now playing in California—so all the attention is focused on Stengel and his players. They are again the favorites to win the American League pennant—every key player who took Milwaukee to the seventh game of the World Series last season returned, all hoping to get a second shot at the Hank Aaron–Eddie Mathews–Warren Spahn Braves.

The Yankees are loaded with stars, none bigger than Mickey Mantle. The Mick followed his Triple Crown season with 34 home runs and a .365 batting average in '57, winning his second straight MVP award. But like Berra, the injury-prone 26-year-old is off to a slow start in '58, and Yankee fans have been unforgiving, booing Mickey every time he fails to produce when the game is on the line. The boos are especially loud after a strikeout, and Mantle—who has been in the American League's top three in strikeouts in seven of his eight seasons—has already struck out 17 times in the Yankees' first 17 games. (He'll lead the league with a career-high 120 strikeouts.)

Yogi cannot understand why Yankee fans treat Mantle so poorly, especially with the team doing well despite poor production from its two best power hitters. The Yankees grabbed first place after the fourth game of the season and never let go; by July 3 they hold a double-digit lead and aren't threatened the rest of the season. The only thing the boobirds do is make Mantle kick the dugout water cooler more violently with every strikeout.

Berra never hears boos—at home or on the road—but this is the first time since 1950 that he doesn't hear his name called when the All-Star Game starters are announced in late June. It's the first season the players, managers, and coaches do the voting, and Yogi—who reaches the All-Star break hitting just .228 with 13 home runs—finishes a distant third behind Baltimore's Gus Triandos and Chicago's Sherm Lollar, both former Yankees.

Yogi tells Stengel it's fine to leave him off the roster when Casey chooses the rest of the team, but Stengel insists his catcher belongs. And sure enough, there's Yogi in Baltimore, catching the last three innings of the AL's 4–3 come-from-behind win. Old habits die hard, and the old man is most at ease with Berra behind the plate.

But with his Yankees opening the second half of the season with a comfortable 11-game lead on the rest of the league, Stengel finally begins to give Berra more time in right field, where the strain on his body is so much less. And sure enough, Yogi's bat comes alive. In one seven-game stretch in late July, Berra belts a pair of doubles and three homers while batting .400 and driving in nine runs. He's in right field on August 2 when he drives in all New York's runs in a 6–1 win against Chicago that gives the Yankees a 17-game lead over the second-place Indians, their biggest of the season.

Stengel splits Berra's playing time between right field and catcher the rest of the season, and plenty of opposing players say they miss Yogi's chatter when they come up to bat and he's not there. Yogi hits a robust .311 with nine home runs and 50 RBI for the second half, finishing the season hitting .266 with 22 homers. His 90 RBI is good for sixth in the AL. With Mantle also having a terrific second half—21-53-.330—the Yankees clinch the pennant on September 14. A week later, they get their wish for a second shot at Milwaukee when the Braves win their second straight NL pennant.

Both teams finish 92–62, but the oddsmakers favor the Yankees to unseat the defending champions. That forecast quickly looks foolish when the Braves win the first two games in Milwaukee, then split the first two in New York to take what is surely an insurmountable 3–1 lead. Only one team—the 1925 Pirates—has ever come back from a 3–1 deficit to win the Series. And the Braves make it clear they think this Series is over.

"I wish the Yankees were in the National League," says Braves pitcher Lew Burdette, who won Game 2 after beating them three times in '57. "They'd be lucky if they finished fifth." Shortstop Johnny Logan declares the Yanks are "over the hill," while Braves left-hander Warren Spahn predicts "the last two games at County Stadium won't be necessary."

Berra, who is back behind the plate for every game in this Series, has never seen a Yankee team as fired up as the one that walks into Yankee Stadium for Game 5. Their season—everything they've worked for since February—is on the line. And they are all certain they will have to prove themselves for a new manager unless they run the table in the next three games.

And that is exactly what they do. First, Bob Turley throws a five-hit, 10-strikeout masterpiece for a 7–0 win that makes Spahn's prediction look a bit foolish. The games in County Stadium are necessary after all. Next, the Yankees win Game 6 in 10 innings, with Berra tying up the game at 2–2 with a sac fly in the 6th, then a Gil McDougald homer to open the 10th and a Bill Skowron RBI single leading to a 4–3 Yankee win. Fellas, Berra tells his teammates in the Yankee clubhouse, there is no way we lose Game 7 tomorrow.

Absolutely no way.

Yogi is so confident that he delivers the very same message to the Braves in batting practice. "It's all over," he tells Hank Aaron, Eddie Mathews, and every Milwaukee hitter as each one steps into the batting cage. "We got this one. No way we lose today."

And it's the same message he delivers each time a Milwaukee hitter comes to the plate, first against Don Larsen, then against Turley, who smothers the Braves for the final 6⅔ innings. The game is tied 2–2 with two outs in the 8th inning when Berra drills a double off the right field wall, missing a home run by a foot. He scores the go-ahead run on a Howard single. When Bill Skowron slugs a three-run homer two batters later, Yogi knows this game—and the World Series—is over.

The Yankees are calm in the postgame clubhouse, as if to underscore just how they felt about their opponent's premature celebration. That all changes on the charter flight home, where one champagne cork after another is popped, the sound drowned out by the whoops, hollers, and songs coming from every section of the plane. Whitey Ford, whose sore left elbow limited him to 15 innings in three games, appoints Berra "wing commander" and tells him he's in charge.

"Whitey," says Berra, who broke six World Series records this time around, including most career postseason hits with 61, "the only thing I'm taking charge of is the filet mignon in front of me and as many martinis as I can drink before we reach New York."

Ford starts burning the champagne corks and using the blackened ends to draw on the faces of his teammates as the Yankees' plane approaches their home city, saving his best and biggest artwork for Stengel: a huge dollar sign on the old man's right cheek. The winner's take for this World Series is $8,759—almost $3,000 more than the average salary in America. Yogi watches as Stengel shows off Ford's handiwork for the photographers and fans who greet them at LaGuardia Airport.

Yogi is confident they saved their manager's job, and sure enough, Stengel soon signs his sixth two-year contract extension. Rumor has it that Casey will bank $80,000 per season. Stengel is coy about his new deal—"I certainly didn't take a cut," he says at his press conference—but he doesn't hesitate when asked about all the men he's managed to seven championships in 10 years. The greatest player? Joe DiMaggio, of course.

The next best?

"Yogi Berra," Stengel says.

It's almost Christmas, and Yogi is back in the old neighborhood on The Hill in St. Louis walking up to Grassi's, one of his favorite taverns. Carmen and the kids are back at his parents' house on Elizabeth Avenue. They'll head out to Howes Mill after gifts are exchanged on Christmas Day and spend another week with Carm's parents on the farm, one of Yogi's favorite trips. The quiet and calm on Barbara and Ernest Short's farm—even with three young boys running around all day—is soothing after a long, arduous baseball season.

"Oops, we got a live one here," shouts bartender John Prachelli as soon as he spies Yogi walking through the door of Grassi's. Berra quickly buys a round for all his friends, who immediately start tossing friendly insults his way. Yogi smiles broadly and laughs.

Hey, the jabs could have been worse—the Yankees could have lost to the Braves again—though he does flinch a bit when someone teases him about Yogi Bear, a new cartoon character dreamed up by the fledgling animation studio Hanna-Barbera. The character debuted during the World Series as part of the new *Huckleberry Hound Show,* and Berra is annoyed enough to consider filing a defamation suit, an idea that quickly fades. But the cartoon character is a big hit and will once again serve to reinforce Berra's own cartoonish image, which persists even this late into his career—much to his dismay.

Yogi loves his life in New Jersey, but he'll always have a soft spot for The Hill and the friends he left behind. Many of them have bought the same shotgun-style houses their parents own on The Hill, which remains a solidly Italian enclave. There are some who still have a lingering sense of betrayal over Yogi's moving east, but even they admit Berra would not be hawking Yoo-Hoo on television or getting paid to regularly appear on the Ed Sullivan, Milton Berle, and Jackie Gleason shows if he stayed true to his St. Louis roots.

Yogi earned this time at Grassi's by taking his three boys to morning Mass at St. Ambrose Church. Carmen, Yogi's sister Josie, and the other women of his large family are back home in his mom's kitchen cooking enough food for a small army. It's good to hang out with the guys who—unlike the management of the Cardinals and the since-departed Browns—always figured Yogi would make it big in baseball.

After a few drinks, it's time to say his goodbyes and head back home. "Yogi," Prachelli says, "this is for your folks," and hands Berra a bottle of wine.

Yogi's brothers—Tony, Mike, and John—are already in the house on Elizabeth Avenue, mixing martinis and Manhattans when he returns. There are platters of cold meats, cheeses, and Yogi's favorite—toasted ravioli, a specialty of The Hill. Carmen reminds him not to make a whole meal out of the ravioli, and before long Yogi sits down with the entire family for a Christmas turkey dinner. Yogi can't help but think of all the lessons he learned in this little house—it's probably small enough to fit into any one of the three levels of his house back in Tenafly.

It's several hours later, dinner and the kitchen cleanup are done, and most everyone is moving into the living room. And that's when a large group of kids—the St. Ambrose choir—knocks on the door.

They walk in, 20 in all, somehow fitting into this tiny space. They are here to sing Christmas carols for Paulina, who can no longer make it to church.

Yogi stands next to Paulina's wheelchair, holding her hand, as the choir begins. It's not long before she squeezes Yogi's hand, and he leans down to hear her speak. "I wish," she says softly, "that I could see them." Her sight is almost a memory now, and her cheeks are wet with tears. But Yogi knows she is happy, sitting there in her home, surrounded by her family, with 20 children singing beautiful songs.

Paulina has always been thankful for what she has, and this is pure joy.

# CHAPTER 25

# Season of Losses
## 1959

The phone call Yogi Berra has been dreading comes at 6 a.m. on May 4, 1959. It's from a doctor at St. John's Hospital in St. Louis, where Paulina Berra is fighting for her life. "Yogi, you better get here right away," the doctor says. "She is going fast."

Berra is stunned, but he is not surprised. Paulina Berra went into the hospital last week to have her one remaining leg amputated in another attempt to stave off the ravages of diabetes.

Yogi has called her every day since, first from Chicago, then Cleveland, and again yesterday from Detroit, after the Yankees lost a doubleheader to the Tigers. He knew the outlook was dire and had already asked and received permission to go to St. Louis while the team went to Kansas City. He had booked a noon flight, but now he throws his clothes into his suitcase and arrives at Detroit Metro Airport in time to catch the 7 a.m.

Berra arrives in St. Louis by late morning and rushes to St. John's, where his father, sister, and three brothers have been sitting vigil since before daybreak. His mother is still alive, they tell Yogi, but she's in a coma. Yogi leans over the bed and speaks softly to his mother.

"Mom, it's Lawdie," he says. "It's me, Mom. Lawdie."

Yogi thinks he sees his mother's body move ever so slightly, and is hopeful that she hears him. It's only a matter of moments before a priest appears to administer Extreme Unction, one of the three sacraments that constitute the last rites in the Catholic Church. As the priest says the prayers, Yogi and his family begin to accept that this is the end.

"Yogi, it was a miracle that Mom didn't slip away before you got here," his sister Josie tells him, and several nurses tell him the same. "I think she waited for you."

A few hours later, Paulina Berra, just 64 years old, is gone.

The Calcaterra Funeral Home guides the Berras through the next three days. The funeral is Friday morning at St. Ambrose Church, where a healthy Paulina Berra started almost every day with 5 a.m. Mass. Yogi holds the rosary that was in his mother's hands in her final hours. The family says their last goodbyes at Resurrection Cemetery, where Paulina is laid to rest.

There is now a hole in Yogi's heart—a big one—that will never be filled. Writers have been speculating for weeks that Yogi's poor early season performance—he's driven in all of four runs and has yet to hit a homer in 16 games—was linked to his concern about his mother's health.

But it will be only a matter of days before the beat writers pose a new question: is this the beginning of the end of Berra as a star?

Berra returns to New York in time to go hitless in a 7–0 loss to the Washington Senators on May 9, just another bad day in what has thus far been a frustrating season. Yogi was the first Yankee star to sign a contract despite taking another cut, this one to $57,500, still one of the top salaries in the game. Casey Stengel finally makes good on his promise to cut down on Berra's workload behind the plate, but it comes with a twist. Instead of returning to the outfield, Casey wanted to try Berra at first base.

Yogi knows that age—he turns 34 in three days—and catching all those games have robbed him of some of his speed. But he's confident he can still handle either of the corner outfield positions. Berra also remembers how awkward Joe DiMaggio looked in the one game Casey forced him to play first base and wants no part of it.

Stengel was still pushing the idea on a day early in the season when Yogi brought Larry Jr. to the Stadium. Father and son were in the clubhouse before the game when a few teammates began teasing Yogi about his reluctance to play first base. Larry Jr., now 10 years old, heard all the chatter, looked into his father's locker, and had a question.

"Daddy, you have two kinds of gloves in your locker now," he said. "Why don't you get a first baseman's mitt?"

Yogi was quick to reply: "You mind your own business," he said, "or I won't bring you to games no more."

Larry also spends a lot of time at the Rizzuto-Berra Bowling Lanes, which has been an instant hit. More than 5,000 people showed up for the official opening in April, helped greatly by the presence of Mickey Mantle and Stengel. Many of the Yankees who live in Jersey—Gil McDougald, Ralph Houk, Bill Skowron, and more—bowl here in several leagues. They are all on the same team in one league; another league has one Yankee on each team.

Business is so good that two armed men show up just before closing at 3 a.m. on April 27. One of the men put a gun to the 21-year-old night clerk's head and ordered him to lead them to the manager's office. As two unaware bowlers finished out their games, the night clerk opened the door to the manager's office, where the assistant manager was counting the weekend's take. The two men took the money—$6,000 in all—cut the phone line, and ordered the two workers to lie on the floor as they walked out. Police never found the robbers.

It's been that kind of year.

Berra belts his first two home runs of the season in the eight games following the loss to Washington. But the Yankees—everyone's pre-season pick to win their fifth straight pennant—lose five of the eight games and fall to 12–18 on May 19, a far cry from their 24–6 record after 30 games just one year ago. *New York Journal-American* reporter

Barney Kremenko asks newly appointed Tiger manager Jimmy Dykes what other AL managers have told him about the Yankees' miserable start.

The first thing Dykes says he's heard: "Yogi Berra is over the hill."

Dykes probably thinks his rivals are nuts when he watches Berra club a pair of home runs against his Tigers on May 20. But the Tigers still beat the Yankees 13–6, a loss that drops New York .007 percentage points behind Detroit—and into last place. It's a big story, one that runs on the front page of the *New York Times* the next day—YANKEES LOSE AND FALL TO CELLAR—right below the report that the Soviet Union strongly opposes the reunification of East and West Berlin.

It's the first time the Yankees have occupied the bottom rung of the American League since May 25, 1940. "There is no place to go but up," Yogi says when the writers enter the hushed clubhouse and make their way to Berra's locker. A couple of teammates repeat the line, but that's all the talking the Yankees are going to do this day.

The Yankees spend the next 10 days in last place, then rally to win 9 of 11, and on June 10 they are just 2½ games behind the first-place White Sox. But the two stars who carried New York through most of this decade go cold in June—Mantle hits a pedestrian .279, Yogi a dreadful .209—and the Yankees slide back. As July melts into August, the Yankees are 49–51 and 10½ games out of first place.

About the only nuggets of good news are a few Stadium innovations and the milestones that begin to pile up for Berra. He set the record for consecutive errorless games behind the plate at 148 on May 10. The streak ends two days later, Yogi's birthday. Berra's already received his annual call from Joe Garagiola when the Yankees tell the crowd it's Yogi's birthday on their new scoreboard featuring the game's first message board—eight lines of eight characters each. The crowd sings "Happy Birthday" when Berra comes up to bat in the 5th inning.

Berra drives in his 1,200th run on June 19; only two active players in the American League—Ted Williams and Enos Slaughter—have more RBI. Casey adds him to the All-Star roster, Yogi's 12th straight

All-Star team. This is the first of four seasons with two All-Star Games—a decision designed to bring in more money for the players' pension fund—and Berra is named the best player of the second game when he hits a two-run homer off Don Drysdale in a 5–3 American League victory.

Individual honors are nice, but Berra knows that winning pennants and World Series titles are the only trophies that matter. On September 8, the Yankees, 17½ games out of first place, are officially eliminated from the pennant race. With 16 games left on the schedule and little to play for, it's clear to every Yankee that some of them will not be in a New York uniform next season.

It's September 19, and Yogi Berra is standing in his spacious new home in Montclair, New Jersey, going over the four lines he has to repeat today at Yankee Stadium. Carmen never did like the house in Tenafly, and she fell in love with a 15-room Tudor on a two-acre corner lot in Montclair so quickly that she bought it for $60,000 before Yogi had even seen the place. "You should see it," he told his teammates after moving in two months ago. "It has nothing but rooms."

But his new home is not what's on Yogi's mind right now. He's obsessed with the four lines he has to say at Yogi Berra Day, which will be held before today's matchup with Boston at the Stadium. He's only the sixth Yankee to receive a "day" while still an active player—joining the ranks of Lou Gehrig, Babe Ruth, Joe DiMaggio, Charlie Keller, and Phil Rizzuto—and the first when the team is not battling for the pennant. The Yankees are 74–73, a stunning 16½ games behind first-place Chicago, and fighting to hold on to third place with seven games left to play.

Cynics have suggested the team scheduled this day to boost attendance—today's ticket sales of 24,800 are far from a sellout though double what the team could have expected without the special promotion. But no one suggests Yogi, now in his 13th season, doesn't deserve a day in his honor. He hit his 300th home run last month—the first catcher to reach that milestone—and is closing in on 2,000 hits. Though 34, he'll finish second to Mantle in home runs (19) and tied for third in RBI (69) for the season, and remains a big fan favorite.

Carmen tells Yogi it's time to leave for the Stadium and rounds up their three boys. Yogi's father Pietro and his sister Josie have come in from St. Louis and will sit in the family box with Carmen, the kids, and Yogi's brother John. Yogi is happy Red Sox star Ted Williams is here for his special day. The tall, well-sculpted Williams and the short, rumpled Berra are quite the odd couple, but the two men have developed a warm relationship over the years and can sit and talk about hitting all day.

Yankee broadcaster Mel Allen is the master of ceremonies and will call the presenters as soon as a truck and trailer deliver the 58 gifts to home plate. Joe DiMaggio, the honorary chairman of Yogi Berra Day, is first up and receives thunderous applause as he presents Yogi with a watch. Pitcher Art Ditmar hands Yogi a silver tray inscribed with the signatures of every current teammate.

Yankee management gives Yogi a station wagon and a set of trains for the boys. There's a slate pool table, a color television, dance lessons for Yogi and Carmen, and dance lessons for the boys, too. There's a year's supply of coffee, pizza, and candy, plus 50 pounds of sirloin steak.

Ted Williams gives Yogi a fishing rod, and Allen reads a letter from American League umpires proclaiming him a "player-umpire," drawing laughs from Yogi, his teammates, and the crowd. Allen hands him a letter from Francis Cardinal Spellman. Yogi reads it in silence, then tells the crowd he'll put the letter in a safety-deposit box.

The Yankees collected more than $9,000 for the Yogi Berra Scholarship at Columbia University. The first winner is James Cleven, a catcher from Lynbrook, Long Island, who is presented with a check for his first semester. There's a set of the *Encyclopedia Americana,* airfare to Bermuda for two, and much, much more.

When Allen is done announcing all Yogi's gifts, it's Casey Stengel's turn to talk. It's clear from the start of his rambling address that this is an emotional day for the 69-year-old manager. No one will ever accuse Casey of coddling his players; indeed, he can go days without speaking to any of the men who play for him. But there's a special bond between Berra and Stengel, who have been so vital to each other's incredible success these past 10 seasons.

Would Stengel have become a Hall of Fame manager without Yogi's bat and—far more important—his uncanny ability to coax the best from an ever-changing pitching staff? Would Berra have become a star—and a household name—if Stengel hadn't brought in Bill Dickey to teach the young man how to be a catcher? This relationship has produced one of the most sustained periods of excellence the game has ever seen.

Stengel praises Berra's prowess at the plate, his World Series titles and MVP awards, and the fine family he's raised in that big house in New Jersey. It's a typical Stengel talk, going off in one direction and then another. But his closing line is crystal clear. "In my 10 years with the Yankees," Casey tells the crowd, "outside of DiMaggio, the man at the plate, Berra, is the greatest player I ever had to manage, which is a great thing to enhance my career."

Casey usually loves to milk his moments in the spotlight, but not on this day. As soon as he finishes talking, he doffs his cap and walks quickly to the dugout, where he loses his battle to hold back his tears. Yankee players are shocked; not a man among them has ever seen the old man cry.

And now it is finally Yogi's turn to talk. A few days ago, he told Dan Daniel of the *New York World-Telegram* that he would rather go to the electric chair than speak before a crowd. Everyone in baseball still remembers how he flubbed his one line when his friends on The Hill honored him at Sportsman's Park in St. Louis his rookie year. It was one of the very first of what are now simply called Yogi-isms.

Sportswriters and his close friend Joe Garagiola have embellished—or flat-out made up—many of Yogi's most famous sayings ever since. "I didn't say half the things I said" is without question the most accurate of all Yogi-isms.

Berra doesn't mind these stories, especially the ones that come from Garagiola. Joey has used his extensive store of Yogi anecdotes—often adding a bit of his own imagination for comic effect—since quitting baseball for show business in '54. His Berra stories always elicit big laughs and have stamped Garagiola as a rising star on radio, television, and the banquet circuit. And Yogi is more than happy he can help Joe.

Now Yogi steps to the microphone, his cap in hand, and clears his throat. "Until now, everything was fine," says Yogi. "I was enjoying myself and I hope you were, too. On behalf of myself and my family, I wanted to thank you…[gulp]…not for the gifts but for showing up. I'm grateful to the wonderful organization, the Yankees, and to my many friends. God bless you all."

All that's left is for photographers to take pictures of Yogi and some of his gifts before the 35-minute program is over and a relieved Berra is behind the plate against the Red Sox. As often happens on a player's "day," Yogi goes hitless in four at-bats, but the Yankees still win, 3–1. After the game, Berra and his family are invited to visit Dan Topping for drinks in his private lounge. When Yogi introduces his father to General Manager George Weiss, Pietro has a question.

"You the man who gives my boy all that money?" Pietro asks. Yogi rushes his father away from his boss, afraid Pietro might give Weiss an excuse to cut his salary.

The Yankees win four of their remaining six games to finish 79–75—the team's worst record since 1925—and clinch third place. For the first time in Yogi's career, New York did not spend a single day in first place.

Berra sits at his locker after the final game of the season, a 3–1 loss to the Orioles. He can't help but think of all the changes he's seen in his 13 full seasons in this Stadium. He likes to sit in the postgame locker room, drinking a beer and talking with teammates when the writers are gone. But it seems this generation of players is in a hurry to dress and leave as quickly as they can. He misses the camaraderie of those postgame beer-and-bull sessions.

Yogi caught 116 games this season, but he'll be 35 next May and is sure this is the last time he'll catch 100-plus games. Elston Howard will be the starting catcher next year. Berra knows there will be plenty of other changes, and he's heard all the rumors that one major change could be the man who occupies the manager's office. As Berra gets up to leave for the last time this season, he hopes Stengel will be in charge when he returns next year. There isn't another manager for whom he'd rather play.

Yogi Berra is walking on a street near the ancient Forum in Rome in early December when he runs over to a tree and shouts back to his wife Carmen. "This is it," he says. "This is the tree I stood by in 1944 when another GI took my picture." It's been 15 years since then 19-year-old seaman Larry Berra spent a day walking through this city, a break from the war he'd been fighting in for almost a year, and all the memories are rushing back.

Today he's here on behalf of Baseball for Italy, Inc., a nonprofit organization that asked Berra to come to Rome and hand out $1,000 worth of balls, bats, and mitts to the country's one baseball league. But customs officials had no idea what the equipment was, or who Yogi was, and it would be a full day before the equipment was released. Alitalia airlines, another sponsor that gave Yogi and Carmen free tickets for this trip, steps in, provides the Berras with a bus and a guide, and tells them to go and have a good time.

Yogi marvels at the sights of this city and listens intently as the guide explains the history behind it all. He enjoys a big lunch of macaroni, two helpings of tripe, salad, bread, ice cream, and a bottle of Italian wine. Baseball for Italy even arranges a brief audience with Pope John XXIII, who is far more familiar with the baseball star standing before him than the customs officials were.

"Hello, Yogi," the Pope says.

"Hello, Pope," Yogi says.

Customs releases the baseball equipment the next day, and Yogi tours the league's handful of fields, hands out the equipment, takes a few turns in the batting cage, and poses for pictures. There are barely any instructors who know the game. And the siestas—the two-hour midafternoon naps favored by many Italians—make it difficult to practice or attract many fans to games. Baseball won't be competition for soccer in Italy any time soon.

Once his job as baseball ambassador is done, Yogi and Carmen spend three more weeks in Europe, visiting Paris, Naples, and Milan, from which Yogi makes a 25-mile trip out to Malvaglio, the village of his parents. Dozens of relatives come to greet them—five of his mother's sisters, one brother, and almost too many nieces, nephews, and grandchildren to count. One aunt rides three miles on a bicycle to see him. He is taken to the local cemetery, which is filled with Berras, and is deeply touched to see a gravestone for Paulina. The visit ends with a home-cooked dinner in a local hall with more than 40 of his relatives. He truly feels at home.

The Berras arrive stateside on December 20, and Yogi learns the Yankees have made major changes for next season. No, it wasn't Casey, though management did offer the job to White Sox manager Al Lopez. Stengel and Lopez have been friends for years, and Lopez quickly turned down the job. Instead, the team fired pitching coach Jim Turner, who's been with Casey since his first season in New York. Many think Turner is the best pitching coach in the league, and Yogi considers his firing a mistake.

The big deal is with Kansas City and involves seven players. GM George Weiss traded 37-year-old veteran Hank Bauer, pitcher Don Larsen, promising outfielder Norm Siebern, and young first baseman Marv Throneberry to Kansas City for 25-year-old Roger Maris, infielder Joe DeMaestri, and first baseman Kent Hadley. Yogi is sorry to see Bauer leave—Berra is now the only Yankee left from Stengel's first team in 1949.

Maris was the key to the deal for New York. Like Yogi, the kid from North Dakota has the kind of left-handed power swing that is perfect for Yankee Stadium's short right field fence. But his three-year career has been marked by ups and downs, and his three-season career marks—58 home runs, 203 RBI, a .249 batting average—are mediocre.

Berra, who knows hitters as well as anyone in the league, thinks Maris will be a better player in New York than he had been in Kansas City.

A much better player.

# CHAPTER 26

# Beginning and the End
## 1960

The first year of the new decade is one of great change and challenge for America. On February 1, 1960, four black college students sit down at the lunch counter at Woolworth's department store in Greensboro, North Carolina and order coffee. They are refused service. The next day 30 students show up, then 60, then 300. Media attention grows as peaceful sit-ins and boycotts of Woolworth's spread across the South and last for months. On July 25—after sustaining more than $200,000 in losses in the Greensboro store alone—Woolworth's begins serving blacks at most of its stores, and the nonviolent Civil Rights movement builds.

Still, many black baseball players carry *The Negro Motorist Green Book*—a listing of hotels, guesthouses, service stations, drugstores, and restaurants known to be safe for African-Americans—as they travel to Florida or Arizona for spring training. And Elston Howard, who will soon be named the starting catcher for the New York Yankees, still cannot stay or dine at the Soreno Hotel, the team's headquarters in St. Petersburg, Florida.

The USSR shoots down an American U-2 spy plane over the Soviet Union and captures pilot Francis Gary Powers; he will be traded for a Russian spy two years later. The number of American military advisers in Vietnam increases to 900, a total that rises to

16,300 within three years, laying the groundwork for America's next war.

More than 90 percent of US homes have a television set, and 70 million Americans tune in on September 26 to watch Massachusetts Senator John F. Kennedy and Vice President Richard M. Nixon in the nation's first televised presidential debate. Six weeks later, Kennedy narrowly defeats Nixon to become the country's first Catholic President. One key campaign promise: Kennedy pledges he will not take orders from the Pope.

In sports, baseball fans are waiting to see how the nation's most prominent team will respond to its first truly mediocre season in decades. Some sportswriters—perhaps a bit too gleefully—write that the Yankee dynasty is dead. Casey Stengel disagrees and soon announces his first major change: after automatically writing the name Yogi Berra in his lineup card for 10 seasons, the player Stengel has long called his assistant manager is now a role player.

Any doubts that Stengel means what he says are erased on Opening Day in Boston. Just moments after Yogi ambles onto the field at Boston's Fenway Park for batting practice, he quickly hears a familiar voice.

"Hey, you playing today, Yogi?" bellows Ted Williams.

"Naw," says Berra, who tries to hide his disappointment with a joke. "I can't make the team."

A Boston sportswriter is standing nearby and expresses surprise at Yogi's news. This is the first time that a healthy Berra—who will turn 35 in another month—isn't in New York's starting lineup to open the season. "I never played sometime before," says Yogi, who quickly tries to correct his latest Yogi-ism. "I shoulda said this ain't the first time I haven't played."

Nor will it be the last time this season there's a seat on the bench for Berra. Troubled with a bit of the flu, Yogi doesn't make his first appearance until the team's sixth game, when he has three hits and three RBI playing right field in a 15–9 rout of the Orioles. Berra doesn't start his first game at catcher until May 3, a 10–3 win against

Detroit. He's now part of Stengel's platoon rotation, playing left field, right field, and catcher, and serving as the team's top pinch-hitter.

Berra, who signed for the same $57,500 he earned a year ago, excels in his new role. On May 22, Yogi starts behind the plate and bats cleanup in a 9–7 win in Kansas City, knocking in three runs with two homers and a single to raise his average to a team-high .343. A week later he records his seventh three-hit game of the season, the last a two-run homer in the 8th to beat the Senators, 3–2. He's hitting .326 on June 18 after collecting a pair of singles and three RBI in a 12–5 win in Chicago, part of a four-game sweep of the White Sox that lifts the Yankees within a half game of first place. Three days later they retake first place, where they'll stay for all but 20 games of the rest of the season.

And he is still delivering Yogi-isms. The favorites among baseball writers:

On Pirate star Dick Groat: "He's the main *clog* of the Pirate machine."

On a home run Yogi says is a lucky hit: "Come on—the ball *chromed* off the foul pole."

A question Yogi asks a stewardess from Denmark: "Does it get this hot in *Danish?*"

Yogi is hitting .291 with seven homers and 27 RBI by the end of June. And despite playing catcher in only 23 of his 37 starts, AL players vote him their All-Star catcher by a wide margin—161–31—over Chicago's Sherm Lollar. Joining Yogi as starters for the two mid-July games—the first in Kansas City, the second in New York—are teammates Bill Skowron, Mickey Mantle, and Roger Maris, who is excelling as a Yankee, just as Yogi predicted. The newcomer ends June leading all of baseball in home runs with 25, to go with 64 RBI and a .326 batting average.

Berra sits down with Dan Daniel a few days before the July 11 All-Star Game in Kansas City to discuss playing on his 13th straight All-Star team. "I honestly wasn't sure I would be picked this time," Yogi tells Daniel, who's interviewing Berra for the *Sporting News* annual All-Star issue. "Don't think I don't appreciate getting on the team. I ain't so loaded with baseball honors that I don't get excited over being selected.

"They pick you and you're still Yogi Berra. They ignore you and you say to yourself, 'Hey, what's going on here. Are they trying to show me the door?'"

Berra readily admits he enjoys playing more games in the outfield this season. He tells Daniel this is the best he's felt at midseason in years and has an interesting theory to explain why: the offseason time he spent at the Rizzuto-Berra Bowling Lanes. "The customers want me to bowl with them," Yogi says. "So I kept pretty busy, melted off weight, and slept hard."

That said, Berra concedes he's wondering just how many years he has left as a productive player. Sure, Ted Williams is still playing well and is again an All-Star at 41, but the Red Sox star has announced this will be his last season. And when Berra's ready to call it quits, he tells Daniel, "I hope to stay with the Yankees as a coach."

His interview with Berra done, Daniel checks in with Stengel, asking the Yankee manager if he thinks Yogi would make a good coach. Absolutely, Casey says, but he has another idea about Berra's future. "I think Berra is managerial timber," Stengel says.

The National League wins both games; Berra goes hitless in four at-bats. But it's Stengel's idea about managing that sticks in Berra's mind as the Yankees resume battling Baltimore and Chicago for the pennant.

The idea becomes even more intriguing when both leagues soon announce intentions to add two teams each, and by the fall the cities are set. In 1961, the American League will add teams in Los Angeles and Washington, D.C., with the current Senators moving to Minnesota. Even better, the NL will put expansion teams in Houston and New York in 1962, when Yogi will be 37.

"I think I would be a good manager," he begins telling teammates and writers alike. "Don't you think I'd make a good manager?"

The Yankees begin to overpower the White Sox and Orioles as the teams make the turn into September. New York takes sole possession of first place on September 10 and clinches its 25th pennant 15 days later. Both games are part of a historic season-ending run. New York wins 19 of its last 21 games, including the last 15 straight. No team has ever entered the postseason as white-hot as these Yankees.

Or with as many home runs. Yogi finishes the season with 15 homers and plays in 120 games — 63 as catcher, 36 in the outfield, and 32 as a pinch-hitter. He's one of six Yankees who reach double digits in homers as the team sets the home run record with 193. Maris belts 39 homers and 112 RBI and will be voted MVP. Mantle hits a league-leading 40 home runs, and Skowron hits 26 homers, knocks in 91 runs, and hits .309.

Is it any wonder the Yankees are heavy favorites to beat the Pirates and win their eighth championship in 12 seasons under Stengel when the World Series begins in two weeks?

Sometimes, you just can't explain the game of baseball. That's what Yogi Berra is telling reporters in the hot and steamy Yankee clubhouse after his team crushed the Pirates to force a deciding Game 7 the next day in Pittsburgh. The Yankees have outhit the Pirates 78–49, setting a World Series record for hits, and outhomered them 8–1. They've won their games 10–0, 16–3, and 12–0 — their 38 runs also a World Series record. The Pirates have won their games 6–4, 3–2, and 5–2.

Yet somehow, everything comes down to one game, winner take all.

Yogi puts his arm around the shoulders of Associated Press writer Joe Reichler and whispers in his ear. "Don't write this," says Yogi, who had three hits and two RBI in the Game 6 win, "but even if they beat us tomorrow, we've got a much better club."

A surprised Reichler asks Berra why he shouldn't write what Yogi just whispered.

"I dunno," Yogi says. "It just doesn't sound right for me to say it." Berra turns to Mantle, who is sitting right next to him and heard what Yogi told Reichler. "Hey, Mick, what do you think? Should he write what I just told him?"

Mantle doesn't hesitate for a second. "Hell, it's true, isn't it?" he says. "If you don't want to be quoted on that, he can quote me."

"Okay," says Yogi, turning back to Reichler. "Go ahead and quote me. Anyway, I don't think I am saying anything critical about the Pittsburgh fellas. They deserve a lot of credit sticking in there with us. Look at them and look at us. There is no comparison. Yet here we are even, and we might even lose the thing.

"It just don't figure."

Nothing that would happen the next day would help Berra or any of his teammates come to terms with the result of the 1960 World Series. Yogi starts the game in left field, batting fifth, and watches the Pirates jump out to a 4–0 lead after two innings. Like everyone, he still wonders why Casey Stengel didn't start Whitey Ford—the team's best big-game pitcher—in Game 1, which would have made the left-hander available today. Instead, the Yankees are using their third pitcher—veteran Bobby Shantz—by the 3rd inning.

But the Yankees rally and trail 4–2 in the 6th when Yogi comes to bat with two runners on base and one out. Berra fouls off the first pitch from Pirate ace relief pitcher Elroy Face, then jumps on the next pitch and sends a towering fly ball down the right field line. For a moment it looks like the drive would drift foul, but the ball stays fair and Berra hops in the air as he sees it land in the upper deck for a three-run homer and a 5–4 Yankee lead. Berra now has seven RBI on seven hits and stands an excellent chance to be the hero of this World Series.

The Yankees add two more runs in the 8th inning to go up 7–4, and now they're just two innings from another world championship. And that's when fate steps in. Shantz allows a leadoff single in the bottom of the 8th, then gets Pirate center fielder Bill Virdon to hit a perfect double-play grounder to shortstop Tony Kubek.

But the ball hits a pebble just before it reaches Kubek, takes a bad hop, and hits the shortstop square in the throat, knocking him to the ground and putting runners on first and second. Kubek's windpipe is so badly bruised he's spitting up blood. He's quickly pulled from the game and sent to a local hospital with a possible fractured larynx.

Given a reprieve, the Pirates don't stop hitting until they score five runs. Now it's the Pirates, leading 9–7, who are three outs from an improbable championship.

But this drama is not over yet. Mantle drives in another run in the 9th to cut the deficit to one run with runners on first and third and one out. Berra follows with a hot smash over the first-base bag that looks like a run-scoring double. Instead, Pirate first baseman Rocky Nelson snares the ball, steps on first, and starts to throw to second base to try to nab Mantle for the game-ending out. But Mantle stops, dives back to first safely, and Berra's eighth RBI of the Series ties the score.

Ralph Terry, who got the final out in the 8th, walks to the mound to start the 9th. Stengel had Terry warming up several times throughout the game, and the right-hander is tired. He is also having trouble getting the ball low in the strike zone. Up steps Pirate second baseman Bill Mazeroski, a high-ball hitter who has one thought on his mind: end the game—and the Series—with a home run.

Mazeroski, the No. 8 hitter in the Pirate lineup, takes Terry's first pitch for a ball. Terry's next pitch is a slider he hopes will break down and away. Instead, it stays high and flat, and Mazeroski sends it rocketing high in the air to left field.

Berra immediately sees this ball will sail over his head and turns to position himself for the carom off the wall. Mantle races from center field to back up Berra. But when Yogi looks up, he sees the ball fly over the fence for a home run, a 10–9 win, and a Pirate championship. Berra turns and looks at Mantle with a grimace on his face. He slowly shrugs his shoulders, and the two Yankees jog in while Pittsburgh fans mob the field in a wild celebration.

Yogi has never seen a more distraught Yankee clubhouse. Mantle sits in front of his locker, crying freely. He is not the only Yankee overcome by tears. And Berra is uncharacteristically bitter when the writers are allowed in the clubhouse.

"We didn't lose this one, it was taken away from us—that dirty, lousy infield beat us," Yogi says, trying hard to restrain himself but losing the battle. "This was one of the most exciting games I ever played in, but we were the better team. I mean, I just can't believe it."

The Yankees fly home in almost total silence, lost in their own thoughts. Berra still can't understand how this team, one he firmly believes is the far better team, could have lost this World Series. He also knows co-owners Dan Topping and Del Webb not only share this belief but will hold Stengel accountable. Everyone knows it. And soon after the game, New York City Mayor Robert Wagner tries to give Casey a lifeline.

Wagner sends a congratulatory telegram to Pittsburgh's mayor and another telegram to Stengel. "Our city is solidly behind you," Wagner writes, "and hope that you will stay with the Yankees and win the Series next year."

Unfortunately for the Yankee manager, Wagner has little say in Stengel's fate.

The Casey Stengel Era officially comes to an end on October 18 at the Savoy Hilton Hotel. Almost 150 members of the print and electronic media jam into the hotel's Le Salon Bleu and listen as Topping explains the Yankees' new mandatory retirement age, which they've set at 65, making Casey—whose final résumé in New York includes seven world championships and 10 pennants in 12 seasons—five years past due.

"I wish Casey was 50 years old," Topping tells the disbelieving press corps.

Several reporters ask if Stengel was fired. Topping simply ignores the question. Then it's Casey's turn to address the room.

"Mr. Topping and Mr. Webb have paid me up in full and told me that my services no longer were desired," says Stengel, who insists he's leaving the Yankees on good terms even if it's earlier than he planned. But the grim look on Stengel's face tells a different story. Reporters keep pressuring Stengel to tell them if he was dismissed, and before long someone tells Casey that the Associated Press is reporting he was fired.

Stengel finally goes off script. "Quit. Fired. Write whatever you please, I don't care," Stengel says. "I'll never make the mistake of being 70 again."

Two days later the Yankees hold another press conference at the same hotel for an announcement almost everyone expects: 41-year-old Ralph Houk is the new Yankee manager. Elston Howard is the lone player present at Houk's press conference. A few weeks later, GM George Weiss, who is 65, is pushed upstairs to make way for his assistant Roy Hamey.

Out in Montclair, New Jersey Yogi Berra is struggling to make sense of firing a man who came within two innings of winning an eighth World Series title, the one manager who insisted Yogi could be a terrific catcher when everyone else thought Berra belonged in the outfield. In Casey's place is a man who spent eight seasons riding the Yankee bench, blocked from ever showing if he had big league talent because he played the same position as Berra.

Yogi never believed the whispers that Houk resented his success. But Stengel is gone, Berra does not understand why, and Yogi recently asked to be considered for the manager opening in Detroit. He had a productive 1960 season, but he knows the game is a business and has never forgotten the way the Yankees cut his best friend Phil Rizzuto less than four years ago.

No one can blame Yogi, soon to be 36, if he's wondering exactly what his future holds.

# CHAPTER 27

# Last Hurrah

## 1961

Yogi Berra looks up into the Florida sun searching for the pop fly launched from a bazooka-like machine, locks onto the ball, and watches it fall safely into his catcher's mitt. New Yankee manager Ralph Houk stands nearby, barking out orders for drills taking place in every corner of the Yankee spring training camp. It's February 22, 1961, only 10 days since the official start of the post–Casey Stengel Era, but Berra is already convinced this season will be nothing like the dozen he played under the man who helped make him a star.

There's a whole new feel to Berra's 15th training camp. Stengel's camps were organized chaos, with players tossing the ball around at their leisure or just shooting the breeze until Casey ordered some of the team into action. Bucky Harris, his first manager, ran a relaxed camp where players pretty much set their own pace, joining drills when they wanted to hone whatever skills they felt needed work.

This camp is running with military efficiency, befitting the man who entered the Army as a private in World War II and left as a decorated major. Houk's brought in two new coaches — Wally Moses for the hitters and Berra's old teammate Johnny Sain for the pitchers — to run a bundle of new drills. There's no aspect of the game that isn't getting serious attention.

"How many scoring chances have you seen wasted by a big fella lumbering into a base and tagged out standing up?" Houk asks his players as he introduces them to the camp's sawdust-filled sliding pit. Berra can't remember the last time he saw a Yankee use the pit for anything more than a place to rest. Houk has scheduled sliding drills for every player, no matter his age, size, or fleetness of foot.

There are new rules for curfews—midnight ahead of day games, 2 a.m. before night games. There is a new rule against drinking hard liquor in public and another that bans playing card games for high stakes. Nickels and dimes a point for gin rummy, pinochle, and hearts are just fine. Poker games with pots in the hundreds will get you fined. And the money confiscated.

But there's one new rule that has many of the players—especially Yogi—absolutely thrilled: the Yankees can now play golf on off days during the season, a big no-no under Casey. Yogi's golf game hasn't improved much over the years, but his passion for the links has only increased with every passing season.

There's also a new menu for the training table. The heavily breaded sandwiches of ham, bologna, and tuna that Yogi enjoys so much are gone. So are the platters of cake and cookies for dessert. Now the choices for the team's midday meal consist of soup—tomato or chicken—cottage cheese, sticks of celery and carrots, apples, oranges, milk, and coffee.

"We are here to get in condition—and stay in condition," Houk tells his players, and no one is arguing with the Major. At least not to his face—or to reporters.

Berra knew things were going to be very different the day he signed his 16th contract—breaking a tie with Babe Ruth for the most in Yankee history—back on January 12. Berra was expecting new General Manager Roy Hamey to push a pay cut after a season in which Yogi played in the fewest games, hit the fewest home runs, and drove in the fewest runs in more than a decade. Yankee beat writers were openly speculating about a cut of at least $5,000.

Instead, Hamey offered Berra the same $57,500 Yogi has earned the last two seasons, keeping him one of the game's top-paid players.

Yogi accepted in a heartbeat. He was just as surprised by what Hamey told the media once the annual guessing game over Yogi's salary was done: the Yankees were not going to cut the salary of *any* player. Hamey added that management would make very generous offers to top stars Mickey Mantle, Whitey Ford, and MVP Roger Maris.

Indeed, Mantle—a perpetual holdout—flew into town three days later, met with Hamey, and then flew back to Dallas the same night. The Yankees gave Mantle a $10,000 raise, bringing the 29-year-old star to $70,000 for the coming season. By the time Berra flew down to Florida in early February for the annual players golf tournament, Hamey had every Yankee's name on a contract, something that never happened under Weiss.

It's clear management is doing all it can to hand Houk a happy, well-compensated team. No surprise, since the Yankees have been grooming the 41-year-old Houk for this moment for years—maybe as long ago as 1948, when the Major, then the team's third-string catcher, was sent back to the minor leagues because the new kid Berra was the No. 1 catcher. Houk refused to go, insisting he was better than the catchers on a half dozen other teams. He'd rather quit, he told Yankee management, and help run a construction business back home in Kansas.

But team officials convinced Houk they had a plan for him, and he soon followed orders. Management brought him back in 1950; he played 30 games in parts of four seasons, then took over as manager of New York's top farm team in 1955. Three successful seasons later, he was back in New York coaching under Stengel and biding his time.

And now that plan is taking shape in St. Petersburg. Houk has already announced he's dumping Stengel's elaborate platoon system in favor of a set lineup—with one notable exception. Berra will rotate with Elston Howard and Johnny Blanchard at catcher and Hector Lopez and Blanchard in left field. "Whether it's behind the plate or in the outfield, Yogi will play at least 100 games this season," Houk tells the media as exhibition games get under way in March. "Is he my idea of a defensive outfielder? No. But he gives me a lot of flexibility."

The Major is also going from a five-man to four-man pitching rotation for the American League's new 162-game season. And one more major change: Houk has already doled out more praise in the first four weeks of training camp than Stengel did in an entire season. "You won't hear me blasting a player in public," says Houk, a clear reference to Stengel's tactic of criticizing his players in the media.

The chief beneficiary of Houk's approach is Mantle, who never met the high standard Stengel set for him. Yogi and many other players thought Stengel's constant criticism—eagerly reported by the press—was the major reason Yankee fans have been so hard on Mantle, who takes the constant booing he hears like punches to his gut. Houk is going out of his way to praise his star, and Mantle is responding with the best training camp of his life.

With all the praise has come one request: the Major says it's time for Mickey to become the team's on-the-field leader the way Joe DiMaggio once was. Berra considers this a fine idea—he thinks the world of Mickey—but he can't help but wonder if his new manager believes the Yankees have been without an on-the-field leader since DiMaggio retired. Maybe there is some truth to the rumors that Houk has long been jealous of Berra's popularity after all.

Yogi's never been a force in the clubhouse—he's always been more of an observer than a leader before and after games. But each and every Yankee team of the '50s knew its star catcher was the man in charge once they stepped onto the field. His slightly bruised feelings aside, Yogi hopes Mantle can become the team's leader, a role that may help his friend deal with the demons that lead him to drink.

There is only one real controversy in this camp, and it's one that is much bigger than the New York Yankees. On January 31, Dr. Ralph M. Wimbish, who like Bill Williams has opened his home or found other spring training accommodations for black players on the Yankees and St. Louis Cardinals, announced he and other African-American homeowners would no longer provide this service. Wimbish, the director of the St. Petersburg chapter of the NAACP, instead called on the Yankees and Cardinals to persuade the hotels used by their white players to also house and feed their black players.

"This business contradicts my active fight against discrimination," Wimbish said in a story the *New York Times* buries on page 44, "and I can no longer participate in it."

Yankee co-owner Dan Topping responded the next day, asking the management of the Soreno Hotel—the Yankees' spring headquarters of 36 years—to change its policy on segregation. Topping said the Yankees' three black players—Howard, Lopez, and catching prospect Jesse Gonder—are full-fledged members of his team and entitled to the same accommodations and services as any other player. It took the hotel management all of one day to flatly decline. Topping told the media his team would be moving to Fort Lauderdale as early as 1963—sooner if the hotel released the Yankees from the last two seasons of its three-year contract.

On March 20, Topping announces the Yankees' spring training home next season will indeed be in Fort Lauderdale, on the more liberal east coast of Florida. It is widely—and accurately—assumed that every Yankee player will stay at the team hotel if he so chooses.

The team that will replace the Yankees at the Soreno Hotel? The Mets, the National League's new team in New York next season, which a week earlier hired former Yankee executive George Weiss as team President. The hotel management says it looks forward to serving the needs of the expansion team's players in 1962—as long as the players are white.

Yogi sits at his locker in the visitors clubhouse in Los Angeles on June 28, a plate with an uneaten slice of cake perched on a stool right beside him. He's answered the final question from reporters about the sharp single he lined over second base in the 4th inning of a 5–3 loss to the expansion Angels. It was the 2,000th hit of Berra's career. Umpire Joe Linsalata called time and presented him with the ball as a fan climbed up the steps of the Yankee dugout and wheeled over a cake for Yogi, a remnant of which now sits beside him.

Yogi has waited for this moment for the last few weeks, and now that it's here, he can't help but ask himself where all the years have gone. It's the same question Joe DiMaggio asked when he and Yogi sat together the day Joe got his 2,000th hit in Cleveland, 11 long seasons ago. Yogi can still picture Joe taking a gulp from a bottle of beer and telling him to savor every moment of every game, that a baseball career goes by way too fast.

"Have I really been in the league that long?" DiMaggio asked him that day. He was 36 years old, the same age Yogi turned in May.

And now it's Berra, this team's oldest player, who shakes his head and wonders the same thing. Oh sure, he's thrilled to be the first catcher to collect 2,000 hits and the fourth Yankee to reach that mark, trailing only Babe Ruth (2,873), Lou Gehrig (2,721), and DiMaggio (2,214). The two home runs he hit against these Angels two weeks ago in New York gave him 329 for his career; no other catcher is even close to 300. And he just played his 1,903rd game in a Yankee uniform—only Gehrig and Ruth have played more.

If he stopped playing the game today, he would soon join these baseball immortals in the Hall of Fame.

*But where did all the time go?*

*And when will my time in this game come to an end?*

Given his age and all those innings spent crouching behind the plate, no one quite knew what to expect from Berra this season. But he's emerged as a key player in Ralph Houk's plan to win a pennant in his first season as Yankee manager. Houk surprised everyone—including Yogi—when he started Berra at catcher 15 times in the team's first 34 games. But Houk finally decided Ellie Howard—who was hitting .375 and calling a great game—should be behind the plate every day and shifted Yogi to the outfield permanently.

And that's when both Berra and the team—off to a pedestrian 18–15 start—finally took off.

Yogi, batting fifth in the powerful Yankee lineup, hit .298 with seven home runs and 16 RBI in his next 28 games. He had two or more hits in nine of those games, including back-to-back three-hit games against the tough Cleveland pitching staff. Now it's June 28, Berra is hitting .290 with 11 homers and 31 RBI, and in a few days he'll be named to his 14th consecutive All-Star team—this time as an outfielder. And it is no honorary selection.

Today's loss to the Angels ends a 16-game road trip—the longest of the season—and the Yankees return home in second place at 44–27, just 1½ games behind the front-running Tigers. Berra is not the only veteran having a terrific season. Whitey Ford, thriving in Houk's four-man rotation, is 13–2 with 100 strikeouts in 136 innings. Screwballing reliever Luis Arroyo, who seems to close every one of Ford's games, has 16 saves. Howard is among the league leaders in hitting at .348, and his work behind the plate is superb.

There are others on this team having a terrific year, too, but as the 1961 baseball season pushes into July, there are only two players every baseball fan is talking about: Roger Maris and Mickey Mantle. The M&M boys, as the press has dubbed them, are stalking the ghost of Babe Ruth and his record 60 home runs in a season, and their fame has already transcended sports. "Did they hit one today?" seems to be the question on the lips of every American. Fans mob hotel lobbies, restaurants, airports, and any other place they can catch a glimpse of the men of the moment.

Even Berra, the only Yankee old enough to remember seeing the Babe play, has been caught up in the heroics of his two teammates. Every Yankee has. The eight home runs Mantle hit in the team's first 16 games were enough to jump-start talk of breaking Ruth's 1927 record. "He's eight days ahead of the pace set by Babe Ruth," the *New York Times* wrote after Mantle's fourth home run.

Maris starts slowly, then hits 24 home runs in 38 games and passes Mantle in late June. Pulling ahead of Mickey also puts Roger squarely in the crosshairs of both the fans and media, who see Maris as the villain of this two-man drama. Mantle, the whipping boy for the last nine years for not becoming the next Joe DiMaggio, is now the hometown hero.

Yogi doesn't know Maris all that well, but what little he does know he likes very much. All the quiet 26-year-old wants to do is play base-ball and win—he'd be a perfect fit for the teams of DiMaggio, Bill Dickey, and Tommy Henrich, the men who taught Berra the mean-ing of being a Yankee. But none of those old-time Yankees heard jeers from fans on the road *and* in the Stadium. Fans seem to resent Roger for chasing Babe Ruth's ghost.

The press is even worse. Yogi cringes when he hears reporters ask Maris, "Roger, how come a .260 hitter like you manages to get more home runs than Babe Ruth?" And he cringes even more when Maris replies, "What are you, a newspaperman or a goddamn idiot?" Yogi learned a long time ago not to fight the barbs he received from the press, a lesson the stubborn Maris resists.

Yogi can see the strain wearing on Maris. The dark circles under Roger's eyes began forming weeks ago. Now there are empty patches on his scalp where his hair has fallen out. Yogi's told Maris to stop read-ing all the stories they're writing about him, but Roger can't help him-self. Yogi has leaned on a few of the writers to back off Maris but wonders how Roger will cope as the pressure builds with every home run.

Mantle is enjoying the adulation Yankee fans have never shown him, but the constant attention is wearing him out, too. Mantle has always hated dealing with fans and the press, and by July the endless questions are making him surly, too. And Yogi knows exactly how Mickey will cope: he'll hit the bottle, hard. Both Yogi and his wife Carmen adore Mickey and have spent many nights urging Mantle to cut back on the booze.

"Mickey, all this drinking is killing you," Yogi keeps telling his friend. "Yog, if I can't have a drink I'd rather be dead" is Mantle's ready reply.

Mantle's drinking problem is hardly a secret, and in a society that lionizes the hard-drinking man—as long as he can perform at a high level like the hotshots on Madison Avenue—this problem is roman-ticized as a virtue.

But few people know about the night Mickey and his wife Merlyn were having dinner at Carmen and Yogi's home a few years back.

The four of them enjoyed food and drink, but after Yogi hit his limit of four vodkas on the rocks and stopped, and Carmen knew when she'd had her last glass of wine, both Mickey and his wife drank 'til they were drunk. Yogi and Carmen asked Mickey not to drive, then begged Merlyn not to get in the car when her husband insisted on getting behind the wheel.

Don't worry, Mickey told them, our house isn't that far away. We'll be fine. But they hadn't gotten very far when Mantle hit a telephone pole at 70 miles an hour, sending Merlyn through the windshield. It took 70 stitches to close all her wounds. A police report was filed, and Mantle paid $400 for the pole. No mention of alcohol appeared in the report, and the story never made the press.

But Yogi knows what happened, and he knows his friend is drinking every night these days to relieve this season's stress. There are no safe havens, not with every newspaper in the nation carrying a chart plotting Mantle and Maris performances against Ruth's immortal season.

On July 17 Commissioner Ford Frick ratchets up the tension. The Commissioner—a former sportswriter and Ruth's good friend and biographer—mandates that any player attempting to break the Babe's record must do so within 154 games—the schedule Ruth played—not the new 162-game American League schedule adopted in this first year of expansion. If the record is broken after Game 154, Frick says, it will carry a special designation in the record book to indicate it was done under a different schedule.

Yogi underscores the absurdity of Frick's decision with a simple question. "What happens if one guy breaks the record inside 154 games," he says, "but the other guy ends up with more home runs after 162 games? Then who has the record?"

Maris wonders aloud why the Commissioner made his decision at midseason instead of when the expanded schedule was implemented in the spring. Mantle publicly endorses Frick—"If I broke the record in the 155th game, I wouldn't want it," he says—but privately he seethes. And drinks.

Yankee players are used to seeing Mantle arrive at the ballpark hungover—and then go out and slug a pair of home runs—but now he's arriving hungover every day, and his teammates are worried. Carmen and Yogi suggest an intervention at their house, and Houk gives his approval. A handful of players arrive, and they all take turns voicing their concern for Mantle's well-being to him.

"Stay here for the next five days," Yogi says. "We have plenty of room. Just give it a rest." Mantle reluctantly agrees and spends a sober night at the Berras' stately house. But by the next day, he is gone.

# CHAPTER 28

# Witness to History

## 1961

**O**kay, that's a wrap!" shouts Delbert Mann as he pops up from his director's chair on the set of his movie *That Touch of Mink*. "Good job, everyone. Thank you."

And with that, the moment everyone on Mann's set has been eagerly waiting for finally arrives. Crew members, extras, and dozens of their children surround Roger Maris, Mickey Mantle, and Yogi Berra as the three Yankees emerge from the mock dugout Universal Studios built for this scene. Everyone is carrying gloves, bats, balls, jerseys, or just slips of paper they hope all three baseball stars will sign. Even executive producer Robert Arthur is standing with the crowd; he's under orders from a nephew back in New York to get autographs from his three heroes.

It's noon on August 23, a day after the Yankees lost the opener of a three-game series to the expansion Los Angeles Angels, 4–3, cutting their lead over second-place Detroit to just two games. But the big news in last night's game was the two-run homer Maris blasted high over the center field fence of LA's Wrigley Field, his 50th of the season. Maris, by far the most nervous of the three Yankees during their 90-minute movie shoot, now has 29 games left to hit 11 home runs and break Babe Ruth's record in the 154-game time frame set by Commissioner Ford Frick.

Mantle, who trails Maris by four home runs, was only slightly less nervous when he delivered his one line to Doris Day, America's Favorite Virgin, who's being wooed by co-star Cary Grant in this will-she-or-won't-she romantic comedy. Grant plays a tycoon ready to do whatever it takes to bed the lovely Doris. In this scene, Grant fulfills Day's dream of watching a Yankee game in the dugout alongside Maris, Mantle, and Berra.

Only Berra appears comfortable with his role, even going off script to shrug his large shoulders, shake his head, and wave his right hand dismissively when umpire Art Passarella throws him out of the game. "I didn't suggest any of those things to Berra," Mann tells a reporter. "He's just an outgoing type."

Indeed, Yogi's come a long way from the frightened thespian who six years ago begged the director of *The Seven Year Itch* to give his three lines to teammate Eddie Lopat, leaving Berra just one line of dialogue in the hit Marilyn Monroe movie. Yogi has spent plenty of time in front of cameras since then. Last month, he was the mystery guest on the popular game show *What's My Line?* He turned out to be too famous and the blindfolded panel guessed his identity almost immediately. He's the public face of the popular Yoo-Hoo soft drink, so important for TV ads and public appearances that when BBC Industries bought the franchise this past March, it insisted Berra's 15-year contract be part of the deal.

Yogi's autobiography, which debuted in February and sold 18,000 copies in the first two months, is a national bestseller. He's done book signings in every American League city. Savoy clothing has been added to his growing list of endorsements. And while the producers of the popular *Huckleberry Hound Show* laughably continue to deny Huck's "co-star" Yogi Bear is based on Yogi Berra, it's hard to argue the cartoon character hasn't benefited from the similarity in name and manner to the popular Yankee star. No one was surprised when the producers spun off the Berra clone as a new show in January. (And yes, the best way to get a rise out of Yogi is to call him Yogi Bear.)

The M&M boys may be the biggest baseball stars of 1961, but the

Business of Being Berra has never been better. In a profession where only the truly special players are remembered for more than a few seasons, Yogi Berra remains a household name 16 years after slugging a home run in his second major league at-bat.

And right now he is holding court on a movie set with his two teammates, dressed in their Yankee uniforms, signing whatever these show business people and their kids put in front of him. The only person paying attention to Day and Grant is Bobby Houk, the Yankee manager's son, who explains he can always talk to baseball players. For everyone else, this is a very special day.

The time for autographs is almost up—the Yankees have another game with the Angels tonight and seven more games on this road trip, which runs through the end of August—when one of the crew asks Yogi how he likes the movie business. Neither the studio nor the players have revealed what kind of paycheck the three stars are getting for this movie, which will become the fourth-highest-grossing film the following year. But Berra, a tough negotiator and a real movie buff, makes it clear he's quite content with his compensation for 90 minutes of work.

"This," says Berra, smiling broadly, "is like stealing money."

It's the first day of September, and the 65,566 fans in Yankee Stadium are nervously watching Detroit's Al Kaline walk to the plate. There's a runner on first and one out in the 8th inning of a scoreless tie. A Detroit win in this game, the first of three between the top two teams in the American League, would put the Tigers just a half game behind the first-place Yankees with 29 games left to play.

Kaline, at 26 already a seven-time All-Star, rifles the second pitch he sees down the left field line. Everyone in Yankee Stadium thinks it's a sure double—everyone except left fielder Yogi Berra, who takes a sharp angle to the ball. Yogi is gambling the ball will hit the section of the wall that juts out before it reaches the outfield fence, then bounce into his waiting hands. If Berra's wrong, the runner on first will score easily and Kaline will be standing on third with a triple.

But Berra plays the angle perfectly. He scoops up the ball, pivots, and throws all in one motion—more like a catcher than a left fielder—and his throw is straight and true. All Yankee second baseman Bobby Richardson has to do is catch the ball and drop his glove on the sliding Kaline for the second out. Kaline, certain he had doubled, stands up, dusts himself off, and stares at Berra in disbelief as he jogs off the field.

The Tigers fail to score, and the game is still scoreless in the bottom of the 9th when Berra comes to the plate with two outs and Elston Howard on first. Berra, still at his best with the game on the line, shoots a line drive single into the right–center field gap, sending Howard to third base. When Bill Skowron follows with a base hit, the Yankees have a 1–0 win and a 2½-game lead over the deflated Tigers.

The Yankee lead grows to 3½ a day later when Maris belts a pair of home runs—his 52nd and 53rd—to power a 7–2 victory. The Yankees complete the three-game sweep when Mantle hits two homers—his 49th and 50th—and Yogi hits his 19th for an 8–5 win. The Tigers exit New York 4½ games behind the Yankees and know this race is over. Indeed, Ralph Houk's men reel off another 10 straight wins, the last two a doubleheader sweep of the Indians at the Stadium on September 10, pushing their lead to a season-high 11½ games.

As the Yankees board a train to Chicago the next day to begin their final road trip of the regular season, there is just one question left to answer.

Will Mantle or Maris—or both—break the Babe's home run record?

So much happens on this 13-game road trip. On September 14, Mantle tells reporters he has sent a telegram to Ruth's widow, informing her he could not break Babe's record. A day later, Berra hit his 20th home run—his best showing since 1958—in the first game of a doubleheader in Detroit. Berra's homer is the team's 221st of the season, tying the record for team home runs held by the Giants and Reds.

The Yankees hit two more home runs while splitting the double-header to own the record outright; they will finish the season with 240.

On September 20, Maris hits homer No. 59 in the 3rd inning against Baltimore, a high arching fly ball that easily clears the 14-foot wall at the 380-foot sign in right field. Berra follows with his 21st homer, and the Yankees have all the runs they need for a 4–2 win that clinches the pennant in the season's 154th game. Maris fails to connect in three more at-bats, and just like that, the months-long pursuit of Ruth's ghost is all but over.

The Yankee postgame locker room is a mixture of celebration and relief. Houk is the 11th manager to win a pennant in his first season; his team's 104 wins are already one more than any Yankee team won under Houk's legendary predecessor. It's Berra who adds history to this day: this is his 12th pennant, breaking a tie with Joe DiMaggio for the most in a career. At 36, he played an integral role in this team's success, and Yogi once again indulges with gusto in the ritual pouring of champagne and then beer over the heads of his teammates. Some things never get old.

It's almost hard to remember there are eight games still on the schedule. Even Maris feels a sense of finality. "Now that it's all over, I'm happy with what I got," Roger says. "I feel free and relaxed." If Maris passes the Babe now, there will be an asterisk in the history books.

The Yankees are back at the Stadium four games later when Maris rifles his 60th home run into the right field seats. Maris asks to sit out the next game, a request Houk honors. The 27-year-old star has rashes on his arms and bald spots on his scalp where tufts of his hair have fallen out, all from the stress of chasing the most cherished record held by the most popular player the game has ever known. Emotionally and physically exhausted, Maris has to be coaxed back into the lineup for the final three games.

Maris manages just one single in the next two games, leaving him one more chance to set the home run record, asterisk or no asterisk. There are 23,154 fans in Yankee Stadium on the cloudy afternoon of

October 1 when Maris comes up in the 4th inning of a scoreless tie. Berra, once again batting cleanup, is kneeling in the on-deck circle as Roger digs in against Red Sox rookie Tracy Stallard.

Berra watches Maris take the first two pitches, both balls, and listens as boos rain down from the crowd. Stallard's next pitch is belt high, and Yogi knows from the sound of Roger's bat meeting the ball that Maris has just made history. The record 61st home run sails 10 rows deep into the right field bleachers, where it is caught by 19-year-old truck driver Sal Durante from Coney Island.

The earsplitting ovation seems far louder than a crowd of this size should be able to make. Maris lopes around the bases, his head down until he reaches home plate, where he shakes hands with Berra and jogs into the dugout. Maris did not come out of the dugout to acknowledge the fans when he hit No. 60. But this time Yogi waits outside the batter's box as Yankee players and coaches refuse to let Maris take a seat. Once, twice, three times, and finally a fourth time Maris comes out of the dugout, lifts his hat, and waves to the fans, who refuse to sit down.

It's October 5, and Casey Stengel is doing what he does best — bantering with several dozen sportswriters on the field before a game on a sunny autumn day at Yankee Stadium. But for the first time in 12 years Stengel's uniform is a suit and tie, with a spiffy green Tyrolean hat sitting atop his head. It's almost two weeks shy of a year since he lost his job as manager of the Yankees — and just seven days since he was formally named manager of the expansion New York Mets. Casey's in town to watch his former team play the Cincinnati Reds in the first two games of the World Series and prepare for the player draft to stock his new team when the Series ends.

Stengel sees the first Yankee walk onto the field for batting practice and shifts his attention. "Well, I do declare — there's Mr. Berra, which used to help me manage," says Stengel, loud enough for Yogi to hear him. "Hi, Yogi. I saw you yesterday with the bases loaded and whadja do? Pop up!"

Everyone laughs, including Berra, who ambles over to greet the 71-year-old Stengel. Yogi enjoyed playing for Ralph Houk this season, and hitting in the heart of a Yankee lineup setting home run records was truly a treat. But Casey was the first manager to really believe in Yogi, to trust his judgment, to treat him with respect. Playing for Stengel will always be special.

"How long you going to manage the Mets?" Berra asks his former mentor.

"I signed for a year," says Stengel, who will earn $65,000 to manage New York's newest team next season.

"Stick around," Yogi says. "When I get done here I'll come over and give you a lift."

Stengel waits a beat, allowing Berra to start his walk to the batting cage before offering a reply. "I can't wait that long," Stengel says. "You'll be here until they retire you at 65."

After 109 wins and months of making history, this World Series feels almost anticlimactic. The young Reds are a fine team built around the power and speed of outfielders Frank Robinson and Vada Pinson—Cincinnati's first black stars—and a deep and talented pitching staff. But no one thinks Cincinnati has much of a chance against these Yankees, even with Mickey Mantle still recovering from an operation to clear up an infection in his hip. Mantle will get just one hit in six at-bats, but it takes just five games to finish off the Reds.

Yogi has a solid if not spectacular Series, hitting his 12th World Series home run in Game 2, the one game the Yankees lose because of three costly errors. Yogi slaps a run-scoring single in Game 3 to tie the game 1–1, a hit the Sporting News calls the turning point of the Series. The Yankees win the game 3–2 on a Roger Maris home run in the 9th, and the Reds turn lifeless.

The Yankees cruise to a 7–0 win the next day. The highlight: Ford tosses five shutout innings to run his scoreless streak to 32 innings, breaking Babe Ruth's World Series record of 29⅔ innings. The lowlight: Yogi dives and misses a line drive in the 6th inning, suffering a gash over his right eye when his glasses break as he hits the left field turf.

Berra jams his right shoulder diving into third base trying unsuccessfully to go from first to third on Bill Skowron's RBI single in the 7th inning, and when his shoulder stiffens overnight, he takes a seat next to Mantle for Game 5. But the Yankees hardly miss their second- and fourth-leading home run hitters. New York bangs out four doubles, a triple, and three home runs to crush the Reds, 13–5, and win its 19th title in 26 World Series. Mantle doesn't even wait for the final out before he changes and heads to the airport and a flight home. Berra and the rest of the Yankees shower and change in the cramped locker room and rush to make a special train for their trip back to New York. It's the quietest—and quickest—title celebration Berra has ever witnessed.

The Series may have been lacking in drama, but the Yankees set 42 World Series records, nine by Berra alone. No one has played in as many World Series games (72) or had as many at-bats (256). His three hits lift his own World Series career record to 71, and his three RBI pushes his record to 39. The two runs he scored raise his record total to 41.

The record he's most proud of is the one he just tied. This is Berra's ninth championship, pulling him even with Joe DiMaggio for the most career titles in baseball history. Yogi feels good after playing 88 games in the outfield and catching just 15, and has no thoughts of retiring. The Yankees will be heavy favorites to win again in 1962, and if that comes to pass, the kid from St. Louis will be the sport's biggest winner.

But a few weeks later Berra is left wondering where and how much he will play in 1962. The uncertainty comes when Ralph Houk tells a handful of beat writers that Yogi, who turns 37 in May, will see more time behind the plate. "Yogi will continue to play left field, but not as often as in '61," says Houk, whom the Yankees rewarded with a two-year contract and a big raise to $50,000 a season on October 12. "If Johnny Blanchard proves he is entitled to seniority, Yogi will return to his old catching specialty. He is 36, true, but a lively, active, and valuable 36."

Houk's goal is clear: he wants to find more playing time for 28-year-old Blanchard, who hit .305 with 21 home runs and 54 RBI in just 93 games. Blanchard came up in 1959 as a catcher, but five-time All-Star catcher Elston Howard just turned in an outstanding season handling the pitching staff while hitting .348—third best in the majors—with 21 homers and 77 RBI. At 32, Howard is going to play almost every day, so Houk is clearly planning to cut into Berra's playing time to make room for Blanchard in left field.

But before Berra can give next season much thought, he is on his way to St. Louis. His 75-year-old father has been battling advanced heart disease and watched the entire World Series from a bed in St. Mary's Hospital, where he's been for most of the last two months. All those years working in the brickyards, breathing in the dust and dirt for at least eight hours a day, finally caught up with Pietro Berra. On November 7, Yogi, his three brothers, and their sister Josie have a funeral to plan.

# CHAPTER 29

# Taking Charge
## 1962–1963

There comes a time in every baseball player's career when he can no longer outrun his athletic mortality. When recovering from an injury takes weeks instead of days. When he can't catch up to a good fastball or pick up the spin on a curveball when it leaves the pitcher's hand. When fly balls he once caught drop in front of him or sail over his head and his throws bounce once, maybe twice, before reaching the cutoff man.

For Yogi Berra, that time is 1962. And even though the season ends in another pennant and a World Series title, Berra can't help but feel a bit embarrassed by what he does—or doesn't do. He hits just 10 home runs and drives in 35 runs—both career lows. He bats a meager .224, a full 64 points below his career average. At 37 years old, Berra appears in 86 games, only 55 as a starter, by far the fewest of the 16 full seasons of his career.

Sure, there are days when Yogi stops the hands of time. There's the pinch-hit three-run homer he slugged on June 9, the one that put the Yankees ahead in a 7–3 win against the Orioles. It was Berra's 2,000th game; only Lou Gehrig and Babe Ruth have played more games wearing a Yankee uniform.

On June 24, he catches all 22 innings in a 9–7 win over at Tiger Stadium, guiding rookie Jim Bouton through the final seven of 16 consecutive shutout innings. Teammates and writers tease Berra after the game, saying it will take a derrick to get him out of bed the next morning after he crouched behind the plate in this seven-hour marathon. But there's Yogi in the hotel dining room the next morning, eating a hearty breakfast before most Yankees—all his junior—even wake up.

There's a four-hit game against Boston on July 18—a single, two doubles, and a home run with three RBI—his best day at the plate all season. Two weeks later Berra appears in his 18th and final All-Star Game, his selection based on his popularity rather than a sterling season. No one quarrels with Houk's decision to add Berra for the second of two games—the last time there will be two All-Star Games in a season.

On August 22, he hits a big two-run homer in the 8th inning against Los Angeles to give New York a 4–3 win and knock the surprising Angels into third place, six games behind the Yanks. And there's Berra's 10th and final homer of the season in Detroit on September 11—two nights after catching all 16 innings against Boston in New York—a solo shot in the 10th inning that beats the Tigers, 8–7.

But mostly Berra sits and watches, feeling like a spare part. While Tony Kubek spends most of the season in the Army, Yogi watches switch-hitting rookie Tom Tresh step in comfortably at shortstop, hitting 20 homers and driving in 93 runs to win Rookie of the Year. He sees Ralph Terry blossom and win 23 games once pitching coach par excellence Johnny Sain teaches him to throw a slider. He has nothing but sympathy for Roger Maris, who listens to boos all season and is criticized endlessly in the media for not producing another record-setting season. Somehow, 33 home runs and 100 RBI are no longer good enough.

The team again revolves around Mickey Mantle, and the Yankees slump in mid-May when their superstar misses 25 games with a torn thigh muscle. Berra still marvels as he watches the Yankee trainer wrap both of Mickey's legs in bandages from hip to ankle before

Mantle can even walk onto the field. Mantle returns and hits .321 with 30 homers and 89 RBI, leading the Yankees to yet another pennant, their 12th in the last 14 seasons. Maybe that's why the clubhouse celebration is subdued when they clinch on September 25. Berra and Mantle do the obligatory interviews, pour some champagne over the heads of their younger teammates, then slip off to watch the Sonny Liston–Floyd Patterson heavyweight title fight on closed-circuit TV.

The Dodgers and the Giants finish tied at the end of the regular season, and while the two rivals play a best-of-three series to determine who will oppose the Yankees in the World Series, New York writers speculate on Berra's future. In late August, Berra stated emphatically that he was not considering retirement. "When I don't have it anymore," he said, "I'll be the first to admit it."

But Berra's name has been linked to several managing jobs, most prominently with the Red Sox. The *Boston Globe* reports that Berra is Red Sox owner Tom Yawkey's top choice to manage his team next season. But the Yankees refuse to release Yogi from his contract, and Boston hires its second choice, former Boston star shortstop Johnny Pesky.

The *Sporting News* calls Berra the "No. 1 active player most likely to become a star manager," and he has plenty of support. White Sox manager Al Lopez, the only skipper to beat the Yankees in a pennant race since 1949—with Cleveland in '54, then Chicago in '59—says if Berra wants to manage "he will do it superbly." Paul Richards, a manager and general manager with a knack for building teams, agrees.

"Berra's deadly serious, even though he gives the impression of kidding around, and he's smart," Richards says. "He will make a fine manager."

And there's the enduring endorsement of Casey Stengel, who still calls Berra his assistant manager whenever he talks about his dozen years with the Yankees.

Berra's thoughts? Yes, he's interested in managing—when he's done playing, and under the right conditions. "I don't want anybody giving me the starting lineup and things like that, and I've gotta have some pretty good players," says Berra, who hasn't ruled out coaching. But he has ruled out managing in the minors to get managerial experience.

"I've been catching and handling pitchers for 16 years," he says. "That's plenty of experience right there."

It's the hard-hitting Giants who win the third and final game of the NL playoff, setting up one of the most memorable World Series in years. The two teams alternate wins in the first six games—all but one game being decided in the final few innings—setting up a decisive Game 7 in San Francisco. The Series also features the longest rain delay in baseball history, with heavy rains putting five days between Game 5 in New York and Game 6 in San Francisco.

Berra, who extends his record of World Series appearances to 13, sees action in just two games. He's a last-minute addition to the Game 2 lineup when Elston Howard's right wrist swells up after he hurt it sliding into third base in Game 1, and Yogi goes hitless in two at-bats with a walk in the Giants' 2–0 win. He pinch-hits in Game 4 against former teammate Don Larsen on the sixth anniversary of Larsen's perfect game, drawing a walk in a 7–3 loss to the Giants.

Berra's on the bench when Ralph Terry takes the mound for the Yankees in Game 7 against Jack Sanford. Both pitchers are 1–1 in this Series, both are hard-throwing right-handers, and both have their best stuff working for them on this sun-drenched day. Terry—ever mindful of the 9th-inning home run he coughed up in Pittsburgh to lose the 1960 Series—faces the minimum 15 hitters through his first five innings. Sanford is almost as good, giving up three singles and one run, the lone Yankee crossing the plate on a double-play grounder.

The Yankees are still clinging to their 1–0 lead with runners on second and third in the bottom of the 9th inning, just one out away from another World Series title. Houk comes out to ask if Terry wants to pitch to the left-handed Willie McCovey—who tripled to deep center field in the 7th and homered off him in Game 2—or right-handed Orlando Cepeda, the next batter, who hit 35 home runs and drove in 114 in the regular season.

Terry, who doesn't want to load the bases, chooses McCovey, and Houk returns to the Yankee dugout knowing the media will slaughter him if McCovey delivers the winning hit. The Yankee manager is barely in his seat when McCovey drives Terry's first pitch deep down the right field line. But it curves foul for a loud strike.

McCovey laces Terry's next pitch on a line toward Richardson, the kind of hard-hit drive that usually takes off like a golf shot. All the Giants leap up from their seats in the dugout, thinking for a split second they have just won the game. But the ball dives instead of rising, and Richardson snags it chest high, the force of the blow pulling his glove toward his ankles, and the game is over. The Yankees have won the game, their second straight title, and their 20th championship.

The Yankees carry Terry off the field on their shoulders and shout and holler the whole way from the field to the clubhouse. "This is the greatest thrill of my life," Terry repeats over and over for reporters who surround him for at least an hour. "The toughest game I've ever managed," says a much-relieved Houk.

Sitting quietly off to the side is Berra, who's seen this kind of celebration nine times before in his long career. But it's the first when he's barely moved off the bench, much less failed to make a significant contribution. And when reporters congratulate Berra on advancing eight World Series records, each related to his longevity, Yogi says, "Don't congratulate me — I didn't do anything out there."

A week later Houk and GM Roy Hamey meet the media to discuss their plans for next season. Both men are confident this team has enough young talent to dominate for years to come. Then a reporter asks where Berra fits into the Yankees' plan, and Houk makes a bit of news: Yogi's days in the outfield are over. "He is now a catcher — period," the manager says. "He can still hurt the opposition with his bat, and I can see no inkling that he is over the hill as a catcher."

When reporters call Berra at his home in Montclair, Yogi's not sure how to respond. Elston Howard had a terrific season — 21 homers, 91 RBI, his sixth straight All-Star berth — and Yogi knows his friend will be behind the plate for most games next season. Yogi also knows the Yankees are thinking about offering him a coaching job, a role Berra would rather not play just yet.

"I want to play if the Yankees want me back," Yogi answers, "and I'll do whatever Ralph asks me to do."

What Berra doesn't know: Houk had a secret meeting with Hamey and Yankee co-owners Dan Topping and Del Webb during one of the rainout days in San Francisco. And Yogi figured prominently in their discussion.

Berra, who'll be 38 in May of 1963, is well prepared financially for the pay cut he'll take as a coach when his playing days are over. He earned $57,500 for the 1962 season—his fourth straight year at that lofty level—and the $9,882.74 World Series check pushed Yogi's postseason winnings to a record $89,069.15. Lawyers for Berra and Phil Rizzuto are working on the final details for the sale of their bowling alley to Lence, Inc., which operates 23 bowling alleys in New Jersey. The deal is expected to net the two friends a bit more than $1 million, and Yogi is already talking about opening a cocktail lounge his brother John will manage.

And sales of Yoo-Hoo have increased so dramatically after Berra became the face of the chocolate drink company—officially, he's the Vice President of Promotions—that parent company BBC Industries is opening a new bottling plant in Carlstadt, New Jersey. Yogi's playing time might have diminished, but he's never been more popular.

How popular? That's what the executives of Quaker Oats are asking hotshot adman George Lois, whose innovative advertising campaigns would later turn Tommy Hilfiger, ESPN, and MTV into household names. In the summer of '62, Quaker Oats executives hired Lois to create an ad campaign for their cat food brand Puss'n Boots. Their only guidance: it's women, they told Lois, who buy cat food. Lois returned with a revolutionary idea centered on a talking cat and Yankee star Yogi Berra.

*We told you that women buy cat food, not men,* the company officials again told Lois.

"And I'm telling you my wife knows who Yogi Berra is, and so do yours," Lois responded. His client was still not convinced, so Lois conducted a series of focus groups with two hundred women. More than 180 said they recognized Berra. Even more important, the women called Berra trustworthy, and that's advertising gold.

Lois got his man.

Lois agreed to pay Berra $5,000 and shoot the commercial in one day at Manhattan's Regis High School gym in late autumn. Berra arrives in a dark suit and tie, his lines committed to memory. The film crew shoots a cat running down a track, leaping over a hobbyhorse, and bouncing on a trampoline. Lois will splice in shots of Yogi watching, smiling, and whistling during the workout. Finally, the cat leaps onto a stool set up across from Yogi.

With the camera shooting from behind the cat, Yogi says, "Gee, champ, you're in great shape."

"Yogi, I like to work out every day," says the cat, the voice coming from someone in Lois' crew offstage.

"What do you eat to keep yourself goin'?" Berra asks.

"I always eat Puss'n Boots. Fish flavor or meat flavor, both terrific."

"After all," says Berra, smiling into the camera while holding up a can of the cat food, "who knows more about cats than Puss'n Boots?"

Lois calls Berra's agent Frank Scott when the ad is done and invites both men up to his Manhattan office for a viewing. Lois had used an unknown young actor named Alan Alda to voice the cat when showing the idea to the people at Quaker Oats. Alda nailed it, but Lois wanted another sports celebrity, so he offered Whitey Ford $1,000 for the gig under one condition: he couldn't tell Yogi about it.

Lois shows Berra and Scott several replays of the 30-second spot.

"Boy, I did good!" Yogi says.

"You were sensational," says Lois, who then asks Yogi if he recognizes the voice of the cat. Berra says no, and Lois shows the ad one more time. But Yogi still doesn't recognize the voice.

"It's the Chairman of the Board!" says Lois, using one of Ford's most famous nicknames.

Yogi thinks for a moment.

"Really?" he says. "Which company?"

The ad is a big hit, which doesn't stop Yogi's teammates from teasing him every time they see him. But Berra doesn't mind. "Who do you know," Yogi replies, "who got paid pretty good for talking to a cat?"

Yankee co-owner Dan Topping is guiding his yacht out of the marina and toward the ocean off the east coast of Florida. It's a sunny day in mid-February of 1963, just a few days after the opening of the Yankees' spring training camp, and Yogi Berra's life is about to change. Ralph Houk had asked to meet with him at the team's spring training hotel, and when Berra arrived this morning, Topping and General Manager Roy Hamey were already there. Topping, who practically lives on his yacht, invited them all to enjoy a day of sailing.

A lot has already changed for Berra since the end of last season. The Yankees did, indeed, want him back, but as a player-coach, with a $5,000 pay cut and an undefined role. The day Berra signed, Hamey said Yogi would "break in gradually as a coach." Berra will soon be 38, and he's coming off the least productive season of his career. With Elston Howard, the team's No. 1 catcher, at his peak and Johnny Blanchard firmly entrenched as Ellie's backup, it's hard to see where Berra's playing time will come from.

Some in the media have written that coaching this season is Berra's first step toward becoming a manager, but the truth is, he doesn't want to leave the Yankees. Houk is just 43 and has won two World Series titles in his first two seasons, so he's not going anywhere. Berra figures if he's going to stay in pinstripes, it will be as a coach. But after a couple of days of spring training Yogi has no idea what his coaching duties entail.

Now he's about to find out.

"Yogi, I have a question for you," Houk says. "How would you like to manage next season?"

"Manage who?" Berra asks.

"Here," Houk says. "The Yankees."

Stunned, Berra blurts out the first thing that comes to his mind. "Where the hell are you going?"

Houk tells Berra he will be replacing Hamey as GM. Hamey jumps in and explains he wants to retire after this season to spend time with his wife. What neither man says: elevating Yogi is Topping's idea. Topping has always liked Berra, and when Houk and Hamey couldn't agree on a manager, the Yankee President decided Berra was the best man for the job.

It wasn't Yogi's potential as a field general that most intrigued Topping. All Yankee management was surprised—and concerned—with the warm reception the expansion Mets received in their inaugural season. It certainly wasn't the new team's performance—the collection of a few aging stars, castoffs, and misfits lost a record 120 games in 1962. But the team attracted plenty of fan interest and headlines, much of it attributed to the popularity of one Casey Stengel and the manager's skillful handling of the press.

Who better to challenge Stengel's undeniable grip on the media, Topping reasoned, than the most popular player in the game? Is there a player in baseball more quotable than Yogi? Hell, is there anyone in America quoted more often than Berra?

So what if Yogi lacks managerial experience? This team has won three straight pennants and practically runs itself. At least that's what Topping and co-owner Del Webb believe. Not that they shared this view with the man they want to be their next manager. Berra will learn on the job, they figure, and Houk will be right there to help Yogi's transition.

And now they are waiting for an answer from Yogi, who is still digesting the question he just heard. Yes, this is what he wanted. But he never thought it would happen so fast. Once he regains his footing, Berra tells the three men he has to talk it over with his wife.

"If Carmen agrees," Yogi says, "I'll take it."

"Talk to your wife, take the day to think it over, and let us know," says Topping, confident Carmen Berra won't object. And Topping is right; Berra will come back and accept the job a day later.

Just one more thing, Topping says. "We need to keep all this quiet this season," he tells his three top baseball men. "It will be our secret."

They all agree and enjoy a few hours of sailing with their boss, secure in the knowledge that there is now a concrete plan of succession for the sport's most successful team.

What the three baseball men don't know: Topping has one more secret, and this one is bigger than the management merry-go-round they just set in motion. Topping and Webb, who bought the Yankees for just under $3 million in 1945 and have known nothing but success, have quietly been talking with investment bankers. Their goal: sell the New York Yankees by the time Berra takes over as manager.

Yogi Berra's last season as a player ends in the same fashion as all but three of the 16 previous seasons—with his team playing in the World Series. The Yankees win 104 games, clinch their fourth straight pennant with more than two weeks left to play, and finish a whopping 10½ games ahead of the pack.

But this team is different from the others in so many ways. With both Mickey Mantle and Roger Maris missing large chunks of the season with injuries and Bill Skowron traded to the Dodgers in the offseason, these Yankees don't have the big home run bats in the middle of the lineup.

These Yankees win with strong pitching, great defense, and a balanced offense led by catcher Elston Howard, who hits a team-high 28 home runs, drives in 85 runs, and earns his first Gold Glove. In early November, with America still reeling from the September 15 bombing of a black church in Birmingham, Alabama, which kills four girls and injures 22 others, Howard will be the first black player to be named MVP in the American League.

The Yankee infield—third baseman Clete Boyer, shortstop Tony Kubek, second baseman Bobby Richardson, and rookie first baseman Joe Pepitone—is the league's best defensive unit. The Yankees boast two 20-game winners—Whitey Ford (24) and Jim Bouton (21)—for the first time since 1951, and Ralph Terry has another fine season, winning 17 games with little run support. The Yankees promote left-hander Al Downing in early June, and the team's first black starting pitcher dazzles. The 22-year-old strikes out 171 in 175⅔ innings while winning 13 games, giving the Yankees the best four-man rotation in the league.

Berra spends most of the first half of the season coaching first base, getting just 46 at-bats in the team's first 72 games, hitting a meager .196. And when the American League announces its All-Star roster, the name Yogi Berra does not appear for the first time since 1947.

Unfazed, Yogi finds his stroke when the calendar turns to July, rapping out 12 hits in 23 at-bats. His 10th-inning double against the Indians on July 7 leads to a 7–4 win and a five-game lead on second-place Chicago. On July 12, Berra hits a three-run homer in the 6th inning—the 355th of his career—to beat the Angels in Los Angeles. Two days later he knocks out two singles and a double in an 11–6 win in Kansas City, raising his season average to .304.

More noteworthy, it's the 2,085th game of Berra's Yankee career, moving him past Babe Ruth and behind only Lou Gehrig (2,172) for most games played as a Yankee. "I don't feel like an old guy—not lately, anyway," he says. "I'd like to break the record, but I don't play that much anymore."

Berra pauses.

"Maybe next year," he says with a sly grin only Houk understands.

Berra gets more playing time in August, hitting .333 in nine starts as the Yankees begin to pull away from the field. But Yogi's real star turn comes on the studio lot for the new soap opera *General Hospital,* where he plays Dr. Aloysius Sweeney, brain surgeon. Yogi is doing the gig as a favor to the soap's star John Beradino, a friend and former infielder for the Browns, Indians, and Pirates who left baseball after 11 seasons, removed an "r" from his last name, and entered show business.

The Yankees are in LA to play the Angels when Yogi shows up on the set early on August 9. He's instantly met by a young female staffer who asks him to sign a form and give her $15. Seems Berra has done enough acting to owe dues to the Screen Actors Guild. Berra, dressed in a doctor's white coat and wearing a stethoscope, discovers his non-speaking part is now a three-line scene, which he pulls off flawlessly. Asked why Berra's part changed, casting director Pam Polifroni says, "Because he has the hands for it."

Beradino, who will win three Emmys in his several decades on *General Hospital,* is thrilled with his friend's performance. "Yogi should consider a change in career," Beradino says.

"I haven't sunk that far yet," replies Berra, who earns $155 for the day's effort.

The Yankees sweep three games from the Angels and leave LA with a nine-game lead over Chicago. By the time Yogi belts a two-run double in the 8th to beat Boston in New York on August 27, the Yankee lead is 12½ games, and the countdown to the pennant officially begins. The clincher comes on September 13, a 2–0 win against the Twins that gives the Yankees a 14-game lead over the Twins and White Sox with 13 left to play.

Unlike last season, this pennant celebration is raucous. Old hands like Mantle, Maris, and Ford exchange joyous shouts with the kids—Pepitone, Boyer, Bouton, Downing, and more—knowing how hard they all worked to overcome injuries and run away with the AL title. And Yogi has a different perspective, too. Last season he felt like a spare part. Now he looks out into a clubhouse and sees a fine blend of veterans and young stars, an excellent team that will be his to manage after they take care of the Dodgers in the World Series.

Berra's final two weeks as a player are filled with intrigue. On September 13, Hy Goldberg of Newark's *Star-Ledger* gets wind of the changes to come from an unlikely source. Seems a former Yankee PR man bumped into Berra's lawyer, who told him he was headed to the Yankee offices to sign a contract that would make Yogi the next Yankee manager. The Yankees deny the story, but more than a few players are already wondering why Berra was spending so much time talking over strategy with Houk during and after most games, and a few are starting to suspect the change to come.

On September 21 — one day short of 17 years since a 21-year-old rookie named Berra homered in the 4th inning of his first game as a Yankee — Yogi smacks a two-run homer in the 4th inning at Yankee Stadium. Yogi will play two more games this season, but this home run — his eighth of the year and 358th of his career — is Berra's last hit as a New York Yankee.

Yogi will not remember the 1963 World Series fondly. None of the Yankees will. They score just four runs in the Dodgers' four-game sweep, the first time Berra's lost a World Series without a decisive seventh game. It starts on October 2 with Sandy Koufax striking out a World Series–record 15 hitters and ends four days later with a 2–1 Dodger victory, the winning run the result of an error on a routine throw to first base.

"Best pitching we've seen all year," Berra says.

As if to wipe the slate clean, the Yankees call a press conference at the Savoy Hilton 17 days later to announce that Houk is the team's new general manager. Few of the writers are surprised. The Yankees have won a pair of World Series titles and three pennants under Houk, the manager is in demand, and the Yankees want to keep him. Outgoing GM Roy Hamey explains health problems led to his resignation, and Houk says the promotion came with a four-year contract and a significant raise.

Houk's promotion was so expected that most of the questions are about the identity of the next manager, and they are all but rhetorical. Everyone figures it will be Yogi, so it's no surprise when Dan Topping introduces Berra as the 18th manager of the New York Yankees two days later. "We are losing a great player," Topping tells more than 100 writers and cameramen, "and getting a great manager."

No one doubts the first part of Topping's statement. Berra, who officially retires as a player today, walks away as arguably the best catcher in the game's history. The numbers—358 home runs, 1,430 RBI, 2,148 hits, and a .285 batting average—barely do justice to the impact Berra had in a career spanning 17 full seasons that included 10 World Series titles, three MVP awards, and 15 All-Star appearances.

And, of course, unparalleled popularity. Yogi and his Yogi-isms are well known far outside the realm of major league baseball.

Whether his ability to handle a pitching staff will translate to handling an entire team is something Berra himself is eager to find out. That's one of the reasons he accepted a one-year deal instead of listening to Hamey, who told Yogi he had the leverage to demand a two-year contract, since several other organizations wanted him to manage their teams. He also accepted $35,000, the same starting salary as Houk and Casey Stengel but a big cut from the $52,500 he earned last season.

"If I'm not capable of doing the job, I'll quit. If I am capable," Berra says, shooting a sly glance at Topping, "I'll stick around a while and we can talk about a new contract."

Berra has a good first day at the microphone, looking surprisingly relaxed as he answers a long series of questions. Berra's ability to communicate is one of the two big questions about his promotion. He makes solid contact today, giving short, direct answers mixed with a few Yogi-isms.

What does he think will be his biggest challenge? "Finding out if I can manage."

What makes a good manager? "Having good ball players."

What are his expectations for next season? "I just hope I can stay in the same shoes as Houk did."

Berra talks about the year spent watching Houk and talking over the Major's decisions. "You can observe a lot by watching," he says. He thinks being a catcher for all these years will make him a good manager. "I didn't spend all those years behind the plate without learning nuttin'."

The media is not bashful about questioning Berra's ability to handle the men he's called his teammates—and friends—for more than a decade. No one mentions any players by name, but everyone understands they're talking about Mantle and Ford, two of Yogi's pals who have long treated policies like curfews as suggestions rather than hard-and-fast rules.

"I'm a softie to a certain extent," Berra says. "But I know their habits, and I know how to handle them. Of course, you have to put your foot down sometimes."

As if on cue, he is handed a telegram, which he scans, smiles, and reads to the press. "Our congratulations on your new job. We would appreciate it if you would give us our unconditional release so we can become pro golfers," Berra says. "It's signed Whitey and Mickey."

When Berra finally finishes answering questions, he thanks everyone for coming and rushes off to find a phone. The call is to Jimmy Gleeson, his old coach at the naval station in New London, Connecticut. Gleeson, 51 and a baseball lifer, has been coaching in the Yankee farm system and has a good handle on every prospect. Berra plans to keep all Houk's coaches but wants his former manager to replace him at first base. Gleeson happily agrees.

The next stop is the Waldorf Astoria a few blocks away, where Joe Garagiola is the master of ceremonies for a Topps company banquet honoring the best rookies of 1963. Rusty Staub, Pete Rose, and Gary Peters are among the 400 people in attendance, and they all rise to give Berra an ovation when he walks into the banquet room. Garagiola calls for his old friend to join him at the podium.

"A funny thing happened to Yogi on his way to the luncheon," Garagiola says.

"What's new?" says Berra, who gets a big laugh in his first official appearance as the Yankee manager. "The greatest thrill of my life happened today when I was named manager of the great New York Yankees."

The reviews across baseball are overwhelmingly positive. Stengel, who will now share a stage with his former protégé, gives Berra a hearty endorsement. Roger Maris says he's looking forward to playing for Yogi. Bobby Richardson assures reporters the man who gave him a room in his house when the second baseman was a lonely rookie will be successful. "He'll have the respect of the team," Richardson says, "and be able to get the most out of the players."

One columnist, summing up the general feeling inside baseball and out, writes, "No man begins a career with more fervent wishes for success than Lawrence Peter Berra." One of the few skeptics turns out to be Berra's 13-year-old son Larry, who upon hearing the news blurts out, "You? The manager?"

As Yogi and Carmen sort through the reaction across baseball, two stories jump out. Both focus on the public's perception of Yogi versus the person he really is, and both remind Carmen why she hoped her husband would never take a manager's job. "There are two misconceptions the public has about Yogi—that he talks all the time and that he's a buffoon—you know, dumb," says young Yankee third baseman Clete Boyer, speaking to 600 Indiana college and high school athletes at a banquet in Indianapolis.

"Well, he hardly talks at all. And that clown picture is good newspaper copy, I suppose, that Joe Garagiola did a lot to build up. But Yogi is a real serious guy about baseball. Yogi will make a good manager, you can believe me on this."

*New York Times* columnist Robert Lipsyte makes the same point in terms that make Carmen cringe.

> The hydrant-shaped folk hero called Yogi Berra is a cuddly noble savage who lusts after comic books, innocently scratches himself in public, loves children and dogs, exudes natural humor and swings down from his tree house to excel in a game he would happily play for nothing. . . .
>
> The man named Lawrence Peter Berra, however, was once a poor little boy taunted for his stumpy ugliness, . . . a coal-yard laborer who saved money with banana-and-mustard sandwiches.
>
> The myth and the man are never very far apart: . . . Both have hit a lot of home runs, caught many fine games, earned

a great deal of money and made reams of comical remarks. But like all myths, the one called Yogi was created by the needs of other people....

Yogi the man is not a lovable teddy bear. He is slow to respond because he is relatively inarticulate, filled with the innate suspicion of the slum kid, prone to bits of sudden crudeness when he thinks he is being put on the spot or conned....

Yogi the myth is funny, egged into grammatical mistakes and non sequiturs by those who record the mouthings of the famous. But the man's words, separated from their delivery, usually make sense.

Houk sets up a series of meetings with Berra to review their minor league players when a big decision pops up suddenly. Coaches Frank Crosetti and Jim Hegan quickly agree to return, but pitching coach Johnny Sain is demanding a two-year contract with a $2,500 raise. Houk refuses. Sain won't budge, and Houk tells his manager they need to replace the best pitching coach in baseball.

"I want Whitey," says Berra, who sees no reason Ford can't coach while remaining the ace of the staff. A surprised Ford takes one night to think it over, and agrees to terms—$60,000 to pitch and coach—the next day.

"I picked Whitey because he's just about the smartest pitcher I ever saw," Berra says at a hastily called press conference on November 15. "I know it's never been done before, but there's always a first time."

In an offseason of surprises, the choice of the 35-year-old Ford could be the biggest—and riskiest. It was Houk who brought Sain on board in 1961, and almost every Yankee pitcher flourished under his tutelage. No one doubts Ford's ability, and he's often been seen talking about pitching with younger pitchers. But how can Whitey give others his undivided attention when he's the staff ace, pitching every fourth game for a team expected to win another championship?

Some observers think making Ford part of management will

sideline Mantle's running mate and all but eliminate Berra's problem of dealing with the team's most prominent rule breakers. One writer went as far as calling the move a stroke of genius, arguing that making Whitey one of Yogi's lieutenants "clamped an effective silencer on him."

A dissenting view comes from a man who knows all three men very well: Billy Martin, now a scout with the Twins and a man with managing aspirations of his own. Martin wonders why Houk would weaken a rookie manager's staff by removing Sain and asking Ford to do double duty. When Houk replaced Casey Stengel three years ago, the Yankees went out of their way to sign every player early. Not a single player took a cut in pay, and many players received salary bumps. Why wouldn't Houk spend the extra $2,500 on Sain and do the same for Berra? The question would loom even larger by season's end.

And no one knows the nighttime habits of Ford and Mantle better than Martin, who spent many late nights with his two friends during his almost seven seasons in New York. Billy says it's hard to see Ford changing his ways, regardless of his new responsibilities. And Martin thinks it will be even more difficult for Yogi to change his own ways. That, says Billy, will make it difficult for Berra to control his team.

"Yogi is going to have to get mean at times," Martin says.

"I just don't know if he can do that."

# PART V

**SOMETHING TO PROVE**

1964–1985

# CHAPTER 30

# It's Over Before It's Over

## 1964

There are so many questions swirling as 1963 ends and 1964 begins. Americans wonder why someone named Lee Harvey Oswald assassinated John F. Kennedy, their vibrant young President, in November of 1963 and whether he acted alone. When will violent reactions to the ongoing Civil Rights movement abate? And why are more of their sons going to fight a new war in Vietnam?

Women are wondering whether it's safe to use the birth control pill even though it's still illegal in 27 states. Why are audiences of American girls screaming for four boys from England called the Beatles? And who is this brash young boxer named Cassius Clay who is boasting he'll beat the brooding Sonny Liston for the heavyweight title?

Americans have a lot on their minds in early February of 1964, but Yogi Berra can be excused if there are other issues that preoccupy him. He'll soon board a plane for Fort Lauderdale to start his first spring training camp as manager of the New York Yankees. He long ago answered all the doubters—from Branch Rickey to the players and baseball beat writers—who thought he'd never make it as a major league ballplayer. Indeed, he will soon take his place among the all-time greats in Cooperstown.

But he no longer has a bat or glove in his hands. Now he has to win games with his mind and his words. At 38, Yogi Berra knows he has to prove himself all over again.

And that is why Berra walks through the tunnel that connects the Yankee clubhouse to Dowdy Field in Hollywood, Florida—home to the team's minor league camp—in the early morning hours of February 17. Always an early riser, Berra routinely arrives at the ball field well ahead of everyone else. But today is different. Today is his first official workout as manager of the Yankees and he is trying to burn his nervous energy. It's the third—or maybe the fourth—time he's made the trip this morning.

Clipboard in hand, a pen dangling from a buttonhole in his jersey, and a notebook stuck in the back pocket of his uniform pants, Berra steps onto the field, squinting as he looks from one foul line to the other. Then he walks back to the clubhouse, sits down in his office, and reviews the stack of note cards he wrote out last night when sleep never came. Then he's up again, taking another walk to the field.

A few hours later he leads 50 of the organization's top minor leaguers and a handful of young veterans through the same tunnel out to center field for the first team meeting of his new career. Whitey Ford, Frank Crosetti, spring training instructor Joe DiMaggio, and the rest of the coaching staff are surprised. Meetings like this are always held in the clubhouse, away from the eyes, ears, and cameras of the baseball press, but Berra has something different in mind. In fact, he has many different things in mind.

"Listen up," he says, the media a respectful distance away but still within earshot. "I want to go over the rules for this camp." Berra looks down at his note cards and starts to rattle off a list of don'ts.

Don't arrive late for workouts. We begin promptly at 10:30 a.m.

Don't play golf before or after workouts.

Don't gamble.

Berra ticks off a few more don'ts before he gets to his final rule.

"Don't break curfew," he says. "It's midnight, and that's going to stick even when the veterans show up."

Berra looks at his players and can feel his body begin to relax. He looks over at backup outfielder Jack Reed and nods. "Everyone up," Yogi shouts. "Reed here is going to lead you all in calisthenics." He walks slowly toward the media as Reed barks out orders for jumping jacks. None of the reporters can remember seeing baseball players doing calisthenics and rush to ask Yogi why the change.

His answer is simple.

"Exercises never hurt anybody," says Berra.

The squad soon breaks up into smaller groups as Berra takes up a position behind the batting cage, a field general watching his troops. There's Ford on the pitcher's mound, talking to 20 pitchers in his first day as coach. DiMaggio, once again wearing his No. 5, is instructing a handful of starstruck outfielders in left field. Crosetti is working with infielders at second base and Johnny Neun is happily telling a few young players about the day in 1927 he made the last unassisted triple play by a first baseman.

Ralph Houk is there, too, wearing slacks and a button-down shirt instead of a Yankee uniform for the first time in 25 years. The Major is walking from one station to the next, absorbing everything, and there's a satisfied look on his face. "Most orderly first day of training camp I've ever seen," Houk says.

DiMaggio agrees. "I learned a long time ago not to underestimate Yogi," he says. "I think he's going to do just fine."

Berra's ascension makes Yankee camp a must-stop for baseball writers, just as Yankee management hopes. Despite all Houk's success, Yankee attendance fell 400,000 during his three seasons as manager. Worse, the last-place Mets, losers of 111 games last season, drew 1.08 million fans, just 228,000 fewer than the Yankees. And there's the show Casey Stengel is still putting on, stealing more than his share of headlines and back pages.

Who better to counter the man they fired three years ago than the lovable Berra? Any lingering doubts that management sees Yogi as counterprogramming are erased when Dan Topping addresses the media early in training camp. "Yogi is unique, and we've told him we don't want him to change one bit," the co-owner says. "We want *nothing* about him to change."

Berra respects Topping's judgment, but Yogi knows he has to change in one very important way or he will most certainly fail. Almost every player on the 1964 Yankees has been his teammate, most for many years, and now he is their boss. It's a difficult transition for anyone, even more for a good-natured player who has been a favorite target of playful clubhouse jokes—and some that were not so playful.

And that's why Berra is visiting Bobby Richardson and his wife Betsy the evening of March 3. Yankee veterans will report to camp the next morning, and Berra has asked the team's well-respected second baseman and his wife to listen and critique what he plans to say.

"Okay, this is a new season," says Yogi, nervously pacing the floor of Richardson's spring training cottage. "We'll put 1963 behind us. We are going to have new rules: no swimming, no tennis, no playing golf, no fishing, no cocktails before dinner, no staying out late."

Yogi pauses on his next "no." He acts as if he is looking around a stunned clubhouse.

"Then I'll say, 'I'm kidding. We'll play hard, we'll play together, we'll be relaxed. And we'll win.'"

He stops pacing and looks at Richardson, who understands better than most the many challenges Berra faces. The popular veteran, who runs a weekly Bible study group for a handful of teammates, played four full seasons for Stengel and three for Houk and was an All-Star under both. He knows Berra was Stengel's favorite, while almost everyone else hated playing for Casey. He also knows many of the players still wonder why Houk left for the front office—"abandoning us," some are saying.

Worse, many Yankees don't think Yogi is smart enough to manage or tough enough to discipline the hard partyers—especially the two most prominent rule breakers, who are also Berra's longtime friends.

Not that Bobby is going to share any of this with Yogi, who is nervous enough already. If Berra's going to succeed, he'll have to figure out these things for himself.

"How does that sound?" Yogi asks.

"It sounds great," Richardson says. Betsy agrees. "You'll be fine," she assures him.

Yogi thanks them both and heads back to his room, where he'll practice his lines a few more times before trying to get a few hours of sleep.

The next morning, a nervous Berra calls the team together in the clubhouse. He looks around at all the familiar faces, takes a deep breath, and tells them he wants to go over the rules for this camp. Berra launches into his script but gets through only the first few lines before Mickey Mantle, sitting in the back of the group, stands up and throws his bat on the concrete floor with a dramatic flourish.

"That's it—I quit," shouts Mickey, who strides out of the room as the whole team breaks into laughter.

An experienced manager might have played off Mantle's stunt, but Yogi is dumbstruck. Mantle's act was meant as a joke, the same sort of jab he's given Yogi for years. But it ruins Berra's carefully planned icebreaker and he's embarrassed.

Not exactly the way Yogi hoped the first meeting with his veterans would go.

The Yankees' biggest star was always going to be Yogi's biggest challenge. They are friends, but Mantle doesn't think Berra commands the instant respect—more like fear—the position demands or the forceful personality a manager needs to succeed. When the *New York Journal-American*'s Jimmy Cannon interviewed Mantle soon after the announcement and asked whether Berra would have the respect of his players, Mickey's words were less than reassuring.

"You know as much about that as I do," said Mantle, who sat in a hospital room recovering from surgery on his left knee. "We'll have to wait and find out. But I really like Yogi and will do whatever he asks."

Problem is, Berra doesn't ask Mantle and Ford to stop making jokes at his expense. Or to stop drinking heavily and breaking curfew when the season begins. Mantle's first joke already cost Berra a measure of respect, especially among the players who harbor doubts about their new manager. Mantle told Cannon his new manager had his respect, but Mickey's actions will soon tell another story.

And sadly, Berra is not getting the same Mantle who played for Stengel, the one who was an annual Triple Crown threat. Or even the scaled-down version who played the last three seasons for Houk. The injury that cost him almost 100 games last season left Mantle with two knees almost devoid of cartilage—the buffer between bones—turning every step on the field into a battle with pain.

His teammates can see him grimace with every swing in the batting cage throughout the spring. Opposing catchers hear him grunt in pain when he swings and misses in exhibition games. His many operations have robbed Mantle of the speed to beat out a bunt, take an extra base, or outrun a long fly ball to center field, all things he once did routinely. At 32, Mantle still has the shock of blond hair and matinee-idol good looks of his youth, but just watching him walk tells a very different story.

Mantle is far from Berra's only problem. His team hits just nine home runs in its 12–17 exhibition season, at one point failing to score a single run in 25 straight innings. Roger Maris, who missed 53 games after last season's All-Star Game with a bad back, hit .172 with one homer and six RBI. Shortstop Tony Kubek also has back trouble and will start the season on the disabled list. Pitcher Jim Bouton, a 21-game winner last season, had a long contract battle with Houk and suffered a sore arm in his rush to catch up.

And the vaunted Yankee farm system has yet to produce the next big star. Catcher Elston Howard is the team's best all-around player. But Ellie's 35 and the team has so little depth that Yogi frequently catches batting practice to stay sharp should he have to jump back on the active roster. Carmen is pleased that he's exercising, but that's the only silver lining.

Berra's first team is suddenly old and injury-prone. Yet everyone still assumes Mantle and his teammates will turn it on once the bell rings and the Yankees enter the season as the overwhelming pick to win a record-tying fifth straight American League pennant. The Vegas bookies even make the Yankees a stunning 1–3 favorite. In the *Sporting News* poll of writers, 178 of 232 name the Yankees to finish atop the AL.

What do the Yankees think? When the beat writers ask Mantle for his predictions at the end of spring training, he has a ready answer.

"We're going to win," says Mickey, a wide smile on his handsome face, "despite Yogi."

Every Yankee sits in the visitors locker room in the bowels of Metropolitan Stadium, and no one is happy. It's June 2, and they've just lost to Minnesota, 6–2. Mantle is once again missing from the lineup with sore legs — he's done nothing more than pinch-hit three times in the last six games, four of them losses. Bouton couldn't get past the 3rd inning and Yankee hitters left 12 runners on base. With his team now 21–18 and sitting in fifth place, 5½ games behind the surprising Orioles, manager Yogi Berra has called his first team meeting.

Berra's been upbeat throughout the team's slow start, one that's seen the Yankees bounce between first and fifth place the entire month of May. Injuries have been a big factor, especially on the pitching staff, where Bouton is just one of several pitchers battling sore arms. Yogi, who's refused to be rattled, wants his team to know it's far too early to start worrying.

"Everyone just needs to relax," says Berra, whose great strength has always been understanding a baseball season is a marathon. This is no time to panic. "The world ain't come to an end. There's a long way to go and we're going to be just fine."

The players simply nod and say nothing as Berra finishes up and signals to open the clubhouse to the media. The writers head straight for Mantle, all with the same question: when will he play again? When Mickey just shrugs, the writers rush off to talk to Berra and his dispirited players.

Mantle threw no bats in jest in today's meeting, but he's wondering if old friend Billy Martin was right last fall when he told reporters Yogi isn't mean enough to manage. Berra has yet to come down on a single player for making a bonehead mistake—and there have been plenty—or use the media to criticize a slumping player, something Casey Stengel did all too well.

And he hasn't enforced his own rules, even the ones that are easy to follow. Just for laughs, Mantle decided to test Berra when the team was on the road a few weeks back. Berra made it clear from Day 1 that when they're on the road, every player should be on the team bus to the ballpark promptly at 5 p.m. So Mantle waited in the lobby until 5:10 p.m. before strolling out to the bus, the rest of the team in their seats, waiting and watching.

"Hiya, Yogi," Mantle said as he walked past Berra, who stood by the bus waiting for his star.

"By the way," Mickey said over his shoulder, "do you know what time it is?"

"You mean now?" asked Yogi.

The players were still laughing as Berra climbed the steps of the bus and took the manager's customary seat in the first row.

Meanwhile, more than a few players have been running to GM Ralph Houk to complain about their new manager. Yogi can't communicate, they say. Worse, he can't control the players who break the rules. And more: Yogi is leaving the starting pitchers in too long. Or he's taking them out too soon. He has relief pitchers warming up too early—or too often—and the bullpen is already exhausted.

And on and on.

Berra didn't know his players were going to Houk behind his back, but he's not naive, either. He knows there are Yankees who revered Houk and wish the Major hadn't been promoted. And he's known from the start he couldn't really win. "If we win again, everyone will say that Mickey Mouse could win with this team," Berra told a friend early in spring training. "And if we lose, everyone will say it was my fault."

But Yogi is used to a clubhouse that policed itself, a place where veterans like Allie Reynolds and Vic Raschi, Tommy Henrich, and Charlie Keller—tough men who thought winning and breathing were one and the same—kept the younger players in line. And everyone was afraid of disappointing DiMaggio. A player going to management? Behind the manager's back? Unthinkable.

None of the current Yankees ever takes a complaint to Berra. They all gripe to Houk, to one another, even to the beat writers—but never on the record. Indeed, when the season is over and the postmortems are written, Yankee players will admit there was a steady procession to Houk's office, but no one will ever take responsibility or identify which of his teammates undercut Yogi.

That also includes Houk, the former military officer who understands the importance of the chain of command. The Major never tells his players to take their gripes to the manager. Or to stop bitching and start playing better. Nor does he sit down with his rookie manager and tell him about the problems brewing in his clubhouse, as both Topping and Webb clearly expected. Instead, Houk watches silently to see whether this team will start playing to win.

They do, especially when Mantle is in the lineup. Mickey returns on June 9 and hits .345 with five home runs and 11 RBI to fuel a 13–4 run. By June 22, despite all their problems, the Yankees are in first place, a half game ahead of the Orioles and 3½ ahead of the White Sox. As Berra told them, it was way too early to panic.

The Yankees are accustomed to watching their rivals wilt when they go on a hot streak. But these Orioles and White Sox aren't going anywhere this season. Both Baltimore and Chicago are young, aggressive teams with deep pitching staffs. The three teams will bounce in and out of first place all summer.

"Just my luck to take over when both Baltimore and Chicago have good teams," Berra starts telling the writers, always with a smile. Turns out Yogi enjoys being a manager, even if it once again means spending so much time away from his three sons, now 15, 13, and 8 years old.

Berra doesn't start feeling comfortable in his new role until July's

All-Star Game, but he does a good job juggling his lineup and winning with a team plagued by injuries and inconsistency. Roger Maris,
whose unhappiness playing in New York grows by the day, misses 19
games with sore legs and can't find his power stroke. Switch-hitting
outfielder Tom Tresh, an All-Star his first two full seasons, fights
through several long slumps. Tony Kubek misses 32 of 101 games
through July with a bad back and is hitting just .230 while slick-
fielding third baseman Clete Boyer has struggled all season to keep
his batting average above .200.

Berra is also doing a lot of juggling with his pitching staff, especially when Whitey Ford begins to experience a mysterious pain in
his right hip. Ford opened the season winning 10 of his first 11 decisions—six of them shutouts—but the pain in his hip prevents him
from throwing his curve effectively and he's won only two of eight
starts since June 20. Ford pitches seven innings in agony in a 5–1 loss
to Kansas City on August 4, lasts just two pain-filled innings in his
next start, and banishes himself to the bullpen.

It's Jim Bouton who keeps the starting rotation afloat. The young
star lost six of his first 10 decisions, but Berra kept telling him to
relax, things would turn around. Bouton rewards Yogi's patience,
going 8–2 with a 1.77 ERA from June 21 to August 2. With Bouton
at the top of his game and rookie Pete Mikkelsen developing into a
reliable relief pitcher, the Yankees move back into first place on
August 6, four percentage points ahead of the Orioles, their opponent
for the next four games in Yankee Stadium.

Berra has Bouton ready to open the big series and is relishing matching wits with former teammate Hank Bauer, the Oriole first-year
manager. It was Bauer who told writers early in March that he didn't
envy his old teammate's challenge. If the Yankees finish a close second,
he predicted, Yogi will be in trouble. If the Orioles finish second,
Bauer said, Baltimore would consider him a conquering hero.

Bauer is right, but there is a secret in New York: Yankee management has already decided the Berra experiment is a failure.

"I think we've made a mistake," Ralph Houk started telling

co-owners Del Webb and Dan Topping in late July. Seems keeping his team in the pennant race did not satisfy Berra's critical players or stop them from sharing their grievances with Houk. Grievances that only grew sharper as the season progressed.

There were games like a loss to Baltimore on June 23 that several players blamed on Berra's decision to shift Boyer from third base to shortstop to replace the injured Kubek, with backup infielder Phil Linz playing third. The Orioles, trailing by five in the 8th inning, scored seven times to win 9–7, with several key hits coming on balls hit past Linz—hits the critics thought Boyer would have turned into outs. They seemed to forget that Houk started Boyer at shortstop in nine games last season and Linz 11 times at third.

And there were reports of wild parties, like the one in Hollywood when the team was in Los Angeles in late July. It attracted more than a few Yankees and lasted well into the wee hours. The Yankees won two of three games against the Angels that trip, leaving the West Coast in first place, 24 games above .500—just three games off the pace set by Houk's team last season. But that wasn't good enough to win the GM's confidence.

"Yogi can't control the players," Houk kept telling Webb and Topping, who never ask why Houk isn't helping his rookie manager as expected. "He's in over his head."

Berra certainly wasn't getting any help from Mantle, Ford, and other Yankees who were often blatant about breaking curfew on the road, drinking to all hours in the team hotel's bar or a bar nearby. It wasn't as if Mantle & Co. were teetotalers under Stengel or Houk, but both those managers let it be known that drinking at team hotels would not be tolerated. Yogi knew—hell, he often saw them in the act—and did nothing.

As July became August, Houk had yet to sit down with Berra to discuss any problems. But he had made up his mind. "I think we're going to have to make a change," he told his two bosses.

It didn't take much to convince Webb, who had been reluctant to give Berra the job, fearing he wouldn't be able to discipline his former teammates. He also thought Berra should have managed in the minor leagues, as Houk did, before taking over the major league team. Webb liked Yogi but quickly agreed they'd made a mistake.

Topping, who had conceded Yogi would be learning on the job, expected Houk would help Berra grow into a solid manager by season's end. But attendance was down and Houk was undercutting Berra, not helping him. By the second week of August, before the Oriole-Yankee showdown, Topping pulled his support and all three men agreed: Yogi had to go.

But when? And who would replace him? None of them thought the team was destined to win the pennant. Firing Berra was going to be a public relations fiasco whenever they announced it, so waiting until season's end made the most sense. By then the pool of available talent would be larger. Their top pick is Cardinal manager Johnny Keane, whom Houk knew and respected when they were opposing managers in Triple-A ball.

Like Berra, Keane is on a one-year contract. Unlike Berra, Keane and his team have spent most of the season in the bottom half of the NL standings, and the word inside baseball is the Cardinal manager may not last the season. None of that diminishes Houk's interest. And there are other men who would be a good fit for this team, the GM tells the two owners. Start putting out feelers, they tell Houk, but quietly.

The co-owners have another secret, one they aren't yet ready to share with Houk. On August 13, Webb and Topping will announce they are selling 80 percent of the team to CBS for $11.2 million, effective November 2. Assuming the deal is approved by at least seven of the other nine American League teams, the franchise so often compared to U.S. Steel for its arrogant dominance of major league baseball will be part of one of the best-known corporations in America.

Berra isn't the only Yankee in for a surprise.

# CHAPTER 31

# Surprise Ending
## 1964

The bus carrying the Yankees from White Sox Park to Chicago's O'Hare Airport is stuck in traffic on the hot, humid afternoon of August 20. And with each stop and start, Yogi Berra can feel his emotional control slip. Just a few hours earlier, the Yankees lost to the White Sox, 5–0, a game that dropped his slumping team into third place, 4½ games behind Chicago, and prompted reporters to ask Berra if he feared for his job.

"No," he told reporters, a clear edge to his voice. "We're going to win this thing." It wasn't the questions about his job that made Berra angry—truly angry—for the first time as Yankee manager. What angers Berra is the sloppiness and distractions of the past two weeks— easily the worst of his 18 seasons as a New York Yankee.

Presented with a chance to take charge of the American League pennant race with two weeks of games against their top two rivals, the Yankees lost 10 of 15 games against the Orioles and White Sox, including all four just played in Chicago. Every one of Berra's key players is failing and flailing. Ford lasted all of three innings today, giving up five runs and nine hits. The pain in his right hip and now his left arm is worse, and the team's ace looks lost.

Maris hits two important home runs in this stretch, but Roger's legs keep cramping. He collects more strikeouts (14) than hits (11), and he's still telling anyone who'll listen how much he hates playing in New York—only louder. First baseman Joe Pepitone, already a two-time All-Star at 23, hits one home run, drives in a mere two runs, and jokes after every loss.

Mantle is just worn-out. He sits out two of the first 11 games and racks up as many strikeouts—nine—as hits in the games he does play. He pinch-hits in the first of the four games in Chicago—a harmless pop out—then misses the next three games. He also got a lecture—or a plea—from Berra, who finally sat down with Mickey and Whitey a week ago, told them the season was on the line, and asked them to cut down on their late-night adventures.

But Mantle has decided this is a lost season and leads a few of his teammates to the Playboy Club their first night in Chicago. Berra learned of it, rushed to the club, and saw Mantle staggering down a stairway, clearly drunk. "What the hell are you doing here?" Berra shouted at his star. "You better get the hell back to the hotel."

Berra saw several more players, and ordered them all to leave. Everyone obeyed, and nothing was said the next day. Nor was anyone fined. Berra still can't bring himself to discipline his players.

The only bright spot: Berra finally convinced Ralph Houk to bring up pitching prospect Mel Stottlemyre, a tall sinkerball pitcher who is 13–3 with the organization's top minor league team. Stottlemyre beat the White Sox at Yankee Stadium in his first start on August 12 behind two booming home runs by Mantle.

But any good feeling from that game was wiped away one day later when Webb and Topping announced the sale of the team to CBS. Several American League owners quickly spoke out against the deal, and a handful of politicians said they wanted to investigate the sale—it is, after all, an election year. But no one expects the deal to collapse, leaving *every* Yankee wondering about his future.

Right now, all Berra wonders is when the damn bus carrying his team will pull free of traffic and get to O'Hare, where they'll catch a flight to Boston. And that's when he hears it. First it's just a couple of notes from what sounds like a harmonica. Then the sound becomes clear: someone in the back of the bus is playing "Mary Had a Little Lamb" on a harmonica.

Coach Frank Crosetti looks at Berra. "Are you going to take that?" he says. Berra, reaching a boiling point no one on this team has ever seen, shouts over his shoulder, "Take that harmonica and shove it up your ass!"

The party gang—Mantle, Ford, Pepitone, Phil Linz, and a few others—is sitting in the back of the bus, and it's Linz who's playing a harmonica he bought only yesterday.

Linz stops. "What did he say?" he asks.

No one is sure whether Linz heard Berra or not, but it doesn't matter. They all had a few beers while they waited for the bus, sneaking more beer onto their ride, breaking another of Berra's rules. They're all tired, disgruntled, and feeling little pain.

"He said to play louder," Mantle replies.

Linz pauses, then starts playing again.

"I said to shove that harmonica up your ass!" Berra roars, but this time he's rushing down the aisle, his right arm raised, his hand clenched into a fist. Red-faced as he reaches the back of the bus, Berra sees the culprit. "Linz, I told you to shove that thing up your ass," he shouts. "And I mean it!"

Linz tosses the harmonica to Berra, who swats it away, the instrument bouncing off Pepitone's knee and tearing his trouser leg. Pepitone starts rocking in mock agony, "My leg, my leg," he cries out. A Band-Aid would cover the small cut the harmonica left.

"We lose four straight and you act like we just won the pennant!" Berra yells as every player turns to watch what will happen next.

"Why are you getting on me?" says Linz. "I give a hundred percent out on the field. I try to win. I should be allowed to do what I want off the field. Playing this relaxes me."

Berra stares at his player coldly. "Play it in your damn room," he says.

The bus is silent now, every eye locked on the manager, who turns and walks back to his seat, muttering "I'll take care of you" loud enough for many of the players to hear.

Every player watches a Berra they barely recognize. Including Mantle, who realizes an important line has just been crossed. All season, he's watched Yogi stroll through the clubhouse, smiling and nodding, patting players on the back and encouraging them to play and win.

Even after today's loss, Yogi told the players not to worry, there was still plenty of time to win the pennant. The team—Mantle included—thought Yogi was clueless and mocked him as soon as he left the room.

But they've just seen Berra's tough side. He's lost his temper and—in the arrested-adolescent world of professional sports—regained much of his authority. In Mantle's mind, it was the first time Yogi showed leadership, and he felt the difference. He could already sense it in the back of the bus. It was time, Mantle decides, to stop joking and make sure his teammates played hard in each of the 43 games the Yankees have left.

"Ralph, I'm calling to let you know what happened before you read it in the papers," Berra tells Houk from his hotel room in Boston. Houk had been with the team in Baltimore and Chicago but returned a day early to take his family to Boston for the four games against the Red Sox. He listened intently as Berra described events on the bus.

"Yogi, do whatever you think is right, and I will back you," says Houk. "This is between you and Linz."

"Thanks, Ralph," Yogi says. "I just wanted you to hear it from me. I'll take care of it."

Every Yankee beat writer had been on the team bus in Chicago, and they all wrote the story, making headlines across the country. Berra, they wrote, "betrayed a sense of panic." The team was "cracking up," and Yogi's job was "in serious jeopardy." Joe Trimble of the *New York Daily News* declared the Yankee season all but over.

"Color them black for mourning," the veteran reporter wrote. "There will be no pennant for the Yankees."

Linz walks into Berra's office at Fenway Park the next day, clearly embarrassed. "I'm sorry. I know I was wrong," he tells Berra. The two men shake hands, then hug. There will be no grudges, Berra says, but this time Yogi knows he has to take action.

"Phil, you know I gotta fine you," he says. "The writers are coming. How much do you think I should fine you?"

"Whatever, Yogi," Linz says. "I was wrong."

"How about $250?"

"That's fair," says Linz, who will soon be surprised when the Hohner harmonica company gives him $10,000 to endorse its product.

An hour later the two men are sitting in the visitors dugout, posing for pictures, smiles all around. There is no panic, and the team is not cracking up. Of course, Berra has already lost his job, but no one knows that yet. Yogi is having a good time with the media, talking about all the headlines his team has garnered.

"A Yankee fan called me this morning at the hotel and wanted to know what song Linz played," a smiling Yogi says. "I told him 'Yankee Doodle' and hung up." And then he laughs, a relaxed laugh the media hasn't heard in months.

Yogi tells them Houk, who arrived right after Linz's fine was announced, said he heard a local radio announcer urging fans to bring harmonicas and kazoos to Fenway for tonight's game. And sure enough, a group of early arrivals stands behind the Yankee dugout, musical instruments in hand. The serenading soon begins.

"This is exciting, isn't it?" says Berra, clearly enjoying himself. "We're getting the publicity, aren't we? And maybe it'll wake us up, too."

After losing the next two games in Boston, the Yankees do more than wake up. Mantle returns to the lineup ahead of schedule, Stottlemyre excels, Ford learns to pitch in pain, and veteran right-hander Pedro Ramos arrives in a trade to rescue a thin and tired bullpen. The result: the Yankees win 23 of their next 30 games.

On September 4, Berra permanently shifted Mantle to left and right field to cut down on the running Mickey has to do on defense.

The Yankees moved into a tie for first with Chicago and Baltimore on September 17, the same game Mantle singled in the 6th inning to join Yogi, DiMaggio, Gehrig, and Ruth as the only Yankees with 2,000 hits. One inning later, Berra jumps up from his seat in the dugout to watch the ball Mantle crushes land deep in the right field stands. It's Mickey's 450th home run—only six players in baseball have hit more—and Yogi has seen every one of them.

When Stottlemyre blanks the Senators on two hits on September 26—the Yankees' 11th straight win—the team pronounced dead four weeks ago is now in first place, four games ahead of the Orioles and White Sox with just eight to play. With a record-tying fifth straight pennant in sight, the media is suddenly praising Berra's calm demeanor and sound game strategy. All seem to agree—except Webb, Topping, and Houk, who privately have begun contacting candidates to replace Berra. "Did the incident in Chicago turn things around for us?" Berra says. "I certainly don't think so, but how can anybody ever really tell?"

It was Mantle who launched the hot streak, despite a right knee that buckles on almost every swing the switch-hitter takes from the left side. He had a pair of key homers in the first two wins of this streak, but it's his sheer determination that lifts the performance of the entire team. Mantle's finally become the leader Berra needs.

Stottlemyre has the poise of a veteran, rarely showing any emotion while winning nine of his 11 starts. The rookie has taken some of the pressure off Ford, who learns the pain in his hip is the result of a calcium deposit; x-ray treatments wear it down by late August. By then, he'd become adept at using a small blade in a ring on his left hand to slice the ball, giving more break to his curve. When the umpires caught on, Elston Howard started nicking the ball with a sharpened buckle on his right shin guard. The Yankees go 6–2 in Ford's last eight starts of the season.

It's Topping who made the deal for reliever Pedro Ramos on September 5 over the objections of Houk, who insisted it was too late for the flamboyant right-hander to make a difference. Houk could not have been more wrong. Ramos replaced a tired Pete Mikkelsen as Berra's first choice out of the bullpen and saved five games and won another. The Yankees are 15–3 since Ramos arrived.

The Yankee streak ends with a 3–2 loss to Washington, but they sweep a doubleheader against the Tigers the next day—Ramos saves both games and Mantle hits his 35th home run—and now it's just a matter of time. The clincher comes October 3, the penultimate game of the season, when the Yankees score five runs in the bottom of the 8th inning to take an 8–3 lead over Cleveland. When Ramos gets the Indians' third and final batter in the 9th to foul out to Howard, Yogi and all the Yankees rush the field to celebrate like little boys, jumping up and down, leaping on top of one another, shouting and laughing.

There's the usual sloshing of champagne in the clubhouse before television cameras, with a horde of reporters trying to get to the Yankee stars. "Frankly, I thought we were out of it," says Mantle, who will sit out tomorrow's game and finish with 35 homers, 111 RBI, and hitting .303 in what will be his last big season. "When we lost those four in Chicago, I gave up on it. But then we all started playing better—I don't know why—and it all came out fine."

Berra spends enough time in the clubhouse to get soaked from head to toe—including standing still while Linz pours champagne over his head for the cameras—then walks into his office, now filled with reporters. He knew managing would be tough but quickly discovered there was so much he didn't know. He made plenty of mistakes, but he observed a lot by watching, corrected what he was doing wrong, and won 99 games—more than Hall of Famers Casey Stengel and Joe McCarthy won in their first seasons as Yankee managers.

He's asked to grade his own performance. "Will it sound too cocky to say I thought I managed all right once I got into it a little?" he says.

And working with Houk?

"He kept telling me not to get panicky when things weren't going too good," says Berra. "He cooperated with me in all ways. And he never got panicky, either." Berra wouldn't learn the truth about Houk until much later.

With one game left to play, St. Louis and Cincinnati are tied for first in the National League. Berra says he doesn't care which team wins—he's just happy his team made it into the World Series. A reporter remarks that he looks relaxed. "It may not show outside," Yogi says, then points to his gut. "But it's in here. I mean, I've been through winning before, but this being my first year and all—well, it's just good, that's all."

Berra rests every Yankee starter in their meaningless final game the next day, a 2–1 loss to Cleveland that stretches over 13 innings. By then he knows the Yankees will face the Cardinals in the World Series, which starts in three days in St. Louis, and he's happy for all his friends in his hometown. "It will be good to go home," he says.

Yogi knows the two teams took similar routes to the postseason, both coming from behind to win the pennant, both managers supposedly fighting for their jobs. And he thought it a bit funny that the press is now writing that Yogi and Keane saved their jobs by making it to the postseason. He knows what it was like to hear all the rumors about his own job and can't help but wonder how Keane, a veteran manager, handled the rumors about his.

If Berra only knew.


Yankee Al Downing has just thrown the pitch exactly where he wants it and gets exactly the result he wants: a ground ball to Bobby Richardson, his Gold Glove second baseman, who will surely turn it into an inning-ending double play. Once the double play is turned, Downing will walk off the pitcher's mound in Yankee Stadium with a 3–0 lead in the bottom of the 6th inning in pivotal Game 4 of the World Series.

His manager is thinking much the same thing. And as Richardson corrals the ball, Yogi Berra's mind is already going over his pitching options to get the next nine outs and take a commanding 3–1 Series lead over the St. Louis Cardinals. *Let's go, Bobby, turn that double play.*

Downing is pitching a gem. The young left-hander has allowed only a single and a walk through the first five innings, striking out four. The Yankees gave him three runs in the 1st inning—three runs that looked big until Downing allowed a pair of singles to open the

6th. But he got Lou Brock to fly out, and now Richardson is about to start a tailor-made double play. The inning is all but over.

But...

But...

But Richardson grabs once, twice, three times at the ball in his glove before finally tossing it to shortstop Phil Linz. The ball, Linz, and Cardinal base runner Curt Flood all collide at second base. The ball bounces off Linz's glove—right before the sliding Flood upends him—and rolls toward Richardson, who angrily grabs it. Flood is safe at second, the slow-footed batter Dick Groat is safe at first, and now the bases are loaded. Downing, shaken, has to shift gears in a hurry.

Up steps cleanup hitter Ken Boyer, whose 119 RBI led the National League. Berra has six-foot-six reliever Steve Hamilton warmed up and ready. Hamilton hasn't pitched since tossing a scoreless inning in the final game of the regular season and is fresh, but Berra decides to stay with Downing. Boyer, the older brother of Yankee third base-man Clete, has struggled all Series, hitting just one single in 13 at-bats. Berra likes this matchup.

But this time he's wrong. Boyer sends Downing's second pitch on a long arc to left field, and the only question is whether the ball stays fair. When it lands fair by no more than six feet, 30 rows deep, Boyer has a grand slam and the Cardinals have a 4–3 lead. It's their first lead in 19 innings.

Everyone in the Yankee dugout is stunned. So are the 66,312 fans in Yankee Stadium. The Yankees now trail in what only moments ago looked like a sure win. Downing retires the next two Cardinals, but the shift in momentum is tangible. Berra watches 12 of the next 13 Yankee batters go down meekly—only Mantle reaches on a two-out walk—and Berra is soon in his office explaining how his team blew a game that would have put them in control of this Series.

"Except for that one pitch, Downing was great," says Berra, who agrees when reporters say the blown play in the 6th inning changed everything. "If the ball is handled right, we're out of the inning. That's all I'm going to say about that."

Is Ford ready to pitch Game 5, the last game of this Series at Yankee Stadium? Everyone knows Ford was battered in New York's Game 1 loss. But the Yankees have a secret: Ford's told Berra his arm hurts too much to pitch again. "Mel Stottlemyre is my pitcher," says Yogi. "When will Whitey pitch again? I wish I knew."

Stottlemyre pitches well, but Bob Gibson is better. The Cardinal ace strikes out 13 in 10 innings, winning 5–2 when Yankee reliever Pete Mikkelsen, in his third inning of work, gives up a three-run homer to Cardinal catcher Tim McCarver in the 10th to break a 2–2 tie. If only Houk had not stood in the way of acquiring Ramos early enough to qualify for the postseason.

The Yankees decide to hold practice at the Stadium the next day before leaving for St. Louis. Berra is in his office after the workout, packing up a few last-minute things from his desk. Two writers who date back to Yogi's rookie season are chatting idly with him when Berra suddenly opens up.

"Players are different today," he says. "You can't make them play by threatening their job. The only way to do that now is to pat them on the back. They're all college men, and if they don't like what is happening, they will just pack up and go home. It was a lot better in the old days when you had to play well or someone else got your job."

Back in St. Louis, the Yankees crush the Cardinals 8–3, setting up a decisive Game 7. Berra knows there's nothing quite like playing a Game 7—the entire season riding on the outcome with the whole country tuned in. Yogi played in eight of these games, feeling the wild excitement of winning five times, the misery of losing three.

But this is the first time he understands what Casey Stengel and Ralph Houk experienced when they made out their lineup cards and chose their starting pitchers. He knows every decision he makes will be analyzed now and for years to come. The first is a big one: he picks the rookie Stottlemyre, pitching on two days' rest, to go up against Gibson, as intense a competitor as there is in baseball, who'll pitch on the same short rest.

Both Stottlemyre and Gibson start strong, but the Yankee defense falters again, and their first mistake takes a heavy toll. After Stottle-myre yields a single and a walk to open the 4th, McCarver hits a sharp grounder to first baseman Pepitone, who fires to Linz covering second to begin what looks to be a sure double play. But Linz's throw to Stottlemyre, covering first, is offline, pulling Mel off the bag as one run scores. Stottlemyre falls while reaching for the ball, crashing hard on his left shoulder, which stiffens immediately. Another run scores when the Yankees throw wildly on both ends of a double steal, and a third comes in when Mantle makes a poor throw from right field.

Stottlemyre gets the next two outs, but his shoulder is throbbing and this is his last inning. The Cardinals score three more runs in the 5th, and it's just a question of whether a tired Gibson can hold a 6–0 lead through the next four innings. Mantle cuts the lead in half, smashing a three-run homer—his 18th in World Series play—in the 6th inning. Ken Boyer gets one back in the 7th with another home run, and now Gibson is firing as hard as he can for as long as he can. Working fast to disguise his fatigue, grunting loudly from pain on every pitch, he retires Mantle on a fly ball, strikes out Elston Howard, and gets Pepitone on a pop fly.

St. Louis fails to score in its end of the 8th, and Berra's team has one inning left to pull out this game. Clete Boyer hits a long home run with one out, and now the Yankees trail 7–4. One out later, Linz sends another Gibson pitch deep into the left field seats.

It's 7–5, but Johnny Keane is sticking with his ace. Up steps Rich-ardson, who already has a World Series–record 13 hits, with Maris and Mantle waiting behind him. A comeback like this is the stuff of Yankee lore. But not this time. Richardson lofts a pop-up to second baseman Dal Maxvill, who makes the easy catch, then throws his arms up in celebration. Bedlam erupts in Busch Stadium, and hun-dreds of fans flood the field to celebrate with their Cardinals as the Yankees slowly walk to the clubhouse.

"It was a good Series; we fought back, damn it," Berra says before even one reporter asks a question. The press always treads lightly after a loss like this, and Berra doesn't get many tough questions. Yes, the botched double play in the 4th inning was the key to the game because he had to pull an injured Stottlemyre. But give St. Louis credit. "Every time we made an error," he says, "they scored."

"But we'll get them next year," says Berra. And he means it. He worked through a slew of injuries to key players, an August controversy that went national, and his own rookie mistakes to win a pennant. He lost his starting shortstop before the Series and his best pitcher after Game 1 but still came within three runs in Game 7 of winning a title.

Sure, he's disappointed, but Yogi feels there is reason to be optimistic about next season. It's with that in mind that he turns to Ford a few hours later on the charter flight back to New York and asks him to return as pitching coach. "What makes you think you'll be back?" says Ford, a wide smile telling Berra the question is a joke. "Sure, Yogi, I'll do it again."

The flight is closing in on New York when Berra sits down next to Richardson and his wife Betsy, again seeking advice. "I'm meeting with Topping and Houk tomorrow morning," Yogi says. "Do you think I should ask for a two-year contract?"

Betsy Richardson answers before her husband can say a word. "Absolutely," she says. "Why, if it hadn't been for Robert making that error in Game 4, Boyer doesn't hit the grand slam and we'd have won the World Series. You deserve a two-year contract."

It's just the thing Berra needs to hear. And as the charter jet carrying his team approaches New York, Yogi has his mind made up. Betsy Richardson is right: there is no reason not to ask for a two-year deal.

Yogi walks into the Yankee offices, says hello to the secretaries, and makes his way into Dan Topping's office. His mood is upbeat until he sees Topping and Ralph Houk waiting solemnly. Any catcher worth his shin guards can read the body language of men stepping up to the plate, and this doesn't look good.

It's Houk who speaks.

"Yogi, we've decided to make a change at manager," Houk says, and that's when Berra's ears begin to ring. He thinks he hears Houk say something about being very sorry, and he hears Topping's voice, but one word just blurs into the next. All he knows is he's just been fired.

*Fired?*

Time seems suspended when he hears Houk suggest that he sit down. Yogi finds a chair and sits to clear his head. "Like I said, Yogi, we feel it's better for all concerned if we make this change," Houk says. "You're a Yankee, and there'll always be a place for you. We're offering you a job as a special field assistant. You'll do some scouting, evaluate our minor leaguers, and anything else I need done."

Yogi looks at Topping, who looks away. It was Topping who told reporters this spring that he didn't want Yogi to change. And Yogi didn't. He knew Topping thought making him manager would bring fans to Yankee Stadium, but this season's attendance hit a 19-year low. Was that Yogi's fault? Only 14,879 fans showed up the night the Yankees clinched the pennant after a tight, exciting race. Wasn't that the responsibility of the smart guys who sell the tickets? He won a pennant and almost won the World Series with an aging and oft-injured team. Wasn't *that* enough to keep his job?

Houk is talking again.

"We'll give you a two-year contract and pay you $25,000 a year," Houk says. "If you want to take another job, you can break the contract. And there'll be some money for you — probably $25,000 — if you decide to leave."

Yogi remains quiet.

"Is that a deal you will accept?"

Berra blinks. He's never made a big decision without Carmen since the day they married. "I want to call my wife," he says.

It's only a few moments before he hears Carmen's voice on the other end of the phone line. "Carmen, I have some news," says Yogi, who quickly tells her what details he remembers.

"Yogi, whatever you want to do is fine with me," Carmen says. "I'll support whatever decision you make."

Houk's offer is $10,000 less than he made this season, but Berra's outside businesses are all doing well, so this decision isn't about money. What Yogi wants is a job in baseball—he's nowhere near ready to leave this game—and this is a baseball job. So Yogi says he'll accept their offer, says goodbye quickly, and walks out of Topping's office for the last time.

Berra stops home, hugs Carmen, then gets his golf clubs—he has a golf date with three friends and damn if that isn't what he wants to do now. Carmen understands. She never wanted Yogi to manage. But being embarrassed like this is heartbreaking. And it will be awful when Yogi tells their three boys and when the boys get teased about it at school. Life as a celebrity, as wonderful as it can be, has its drawbacks.

But Carmen knows her husband can handle it, just as he's handled adversity all his life—with a mixture of stoicism, humor, and grace. And she's sure he'll soon make a phone call to Casey Stengel to see if there is a way for him to get back into uniform. It's a move she won't mind at all.

Yogi is on the golf course when Houk gets word from St. Louis that Johnny Keane has officially resigned. He hastily calls a press conference for 2 p.m. at the Crystal Room of the Savoy Plaza Hotel. The ballroom, the same one the Yankees used to announce Berra as their manager almost exactly a year ago, is once again packed as Houk walks in.

And once again, the news Houk delivers catches much of the media by surprise. Indeed, most of the writers here wrote that winning the pennant vindicated Yogi after a tough season. Now Houk is telling them they got it all wrong.

"This decision was first discussed in August, and we made the final decision before the World Series," says Houk, who will soon look foolish when co-owner Del Webb tells the *Sporting News* that Yogi was out by mid-August. "Losing Game 7 had nothing to do with it,"

Houk says. "We believe this move will be beneficial to all concerned. We've offered Yogi a job with the organization, and he has accepted."

The questions come fast and furious, but mostly they just ask why.

"When Dan Topping and I discussed the situation with Yogi this morning, he seemed very satisfied with the decision and the future opportunities offered him," says Houk, ducking the question.

But why was Berra fired? Houk is asked repeatedly.

"Look, we think this is better for all concerned," he repeats, then finally gives in.

"Let's just say that I don't think Yogi was cut out to be a manager," Houk says. "It was my mistake. I miscalculated his ability to manage. I could say more, but I won't. It serves no purpose."

What will Yogi be doing in his new role? "Most anything I ask him to do," Houk answers.

The writers finally ask about the identity of the next Yankee manager, their fourth in the last six years. Houk confirms he's been talking to Alvin Dark, the recently fired manager of the Giants, and says there are at least two others on his list.

"What about Johnny Keane?" someone shouts.

"He's not available, is he?" Houk says. He's told Keane handed his letter of resignation to Cardinal owner August Busch just 30 minutes before a press conference called to announce Keane's contract extension, stunning the beer baron.

"I didn't know that when I came into this room," says Houk, who will fly out to Keane's home in Houston this weekend to close their deal. "But if that's so, then I would add him to the list. He would certainly be considered."

A handful of writers and TV reporters catch up with Berra as he's walking off the White Beeches golf course. Berra's hair is windblown, and he's wearing a yellow polo shirt, brown slacks, and a look of bewilderment. Only one day earlier, Berra was telling reporters he planned to do some things differently next season. Now there is no next season, but he's ready to talk about the sudden turn of events and the new job he just accepted.

"Where can you get a job like this?" Berra says. "I don't have to sign in or punch a clock and the pay is good. My contract is nonbinding, and if another offer turns up I'm free to take it."

Yogi tells them he enjoyed his year as manager and he learned a lot. And he insists he harbors no bitterness. "I understand what had to be done," Berra says, "and there are no hard feelings."

But the words sound forced. Far more telling: Yogi never once looked into the cameras when he spoke. The reporters walk away knowing that Berra is hurt—deeply hurt—but is too much of a team player to tell them.

The media has no such reluctance, unleashing an avalanche of negative stories about both management and the players. That very night, the *New York Daily News* reports Johnny Keane has already agreed to become the team's next manager. The decision to fire Yogi, the paper says, was made in July. Syndicated columnist Jimmy Cannon says his sources are telling him management soured on Yogi much earlier—before the team even finished spring training.

There are several reports about a "Malted Milk Rebellion" led by Bobby Richardson and Tony Kubek, telling readers the team's nondrinkers complained to management that Yogi allowed the team's hard drinkers to break curfew regularly. "These reports are ridiculous. I've always been Yogi's friend," Richardson tells every reporter calling for comment. Kubek issues the same response.

"In retrospect, Berra couldn't win," writes Leonard Koppett of the *New York Times*. "If a player didn't hustle, didn't stay in shape, didn't find his own way out of a slump, it was Yogi's fault. If anything turned out right, the players believed it was because they were good enough to overcome the handicaps put in their path."

Dick Young, considered the city's top baseball writer, puts much of the blame on Yogi's two old friends. Mantle and Ford gave Berra everything they had left in their battered bodies, he wrote. But instead of using their immense influence with their teammates to ease their friend's transition to manager, they undermined his authority with their overactive nightlife and their scornful jokes.

"Yogi would still be there if he clamped down on his friends," Young writes. "But he was too nice a guy to do it, and nice guys finish where Yogi did, which is outside looking in."

Harold Rosenthal of the *New York Herald Tribune* gives this angle a sharper point. "The oddest part is that Berra seemed to generate so little loyalty among the men he was called upon to lead," Rosenthal writes, "even though his sometimes superhuman bat had lined their pockets through timely homers over the years."

Given all that, one can only wonder what goes through Yogi's mind when he and Carmen meet the Fords and the Mantles for dinner the very day he was fired. Whitey walks up to his friend sporting a sly smile.

"So, Yogi," Ford says loudly. "What's new?"

Yogi does, indeed, call Casey Stengel at his home in California the next day, and the Mets manager is more than interested in adding Yogi to his coaching staff. And maybe even as a pinch-hitter. Casey, now 74, knows the press will instantly assume Yogi will be groomed as the next Mets manager, so Stengel will have to knock down that story as quickly as he can. No reason to stick Yogi with a team as bad as these Mets, who despite their growing popularity have lost more than 100 games in each of their three seasons.

It will take several weeks for Berra to decide to leave the only organization he's known for all his 22 years in baseball, then a week or so to work out the contract details. Houk works much faster to sign up Johnny Keane. Just four days after firing Berra, Houk is back at the Savoy Plaza to introduce his new hire. But instead of celebrating his latest move, Houk spends most of the press conference fighting off questions about when Keane was contacted. "It's not fair to baseball or to Johnny to imply that we spoke with him before the World Series," Houk says.

George Weiss lets the media know he wants Yogi during a luncheon at Shea Stadium the day before Halloween, telling reporters he hopes the Mets "will be lucky enough to get him." Berra is also quietly talking about a coaching job with new Cardinal manager Red Schoendienst and Senator manager Gil Hodges, two old friends. Yogi is eager to stay in uniform but is reluctant to uproot his family or leave them behind in New Jersey. If he leaves the Yankees, he already knows it will be to join Casey and the struggling Mets.

Berra's decision to join the Mets is announced on November 16. Yogi and Weiss are both beaming as they lay out the details. Berra has signed a two-year deal to coach—probably first base, Weiss says—for $35,000 a year, the same salary he earned to manage the Yankees. He'll also serve as a pinch-hitter if he shows he can still hit in spring training. Yogi says his desire to remain in uniform is the reason he's leaving the Yankees for the Mets. And he wants everyone to understand he's not bitter about the way he left the Yankees.

"I don't feel I was wronged," says Berra. "They hired me off the St. Louis sandlots when the Browns and Cardinals didn't want me, and I was happy there for 18 years. They never did me any wrong."

Does he think he'll regain his batting eye at age 39 after taking off a full year? "We'll have to wait and see," he says. "You never know."

Does he want to manage again?

"Right now I'm only going to be a coach," he says. "But if I do want to manage again, I'm under a good man in Casey. I learned a lot from him in 10 years, and I can learn a lot more."

Berra answers a few more questions before someone asks if he's informed the Yankees of his decision yet.

"Yes," he says, "I sent Houk a wire."

When?

"About an hour ago."

Bitter? No.

But Berra's nobody's fool, either.

# CHAPTER 32

# A Second Chance
## 1965-1972

**C**armen and Yogi Berra are visiting with friends in Miami on April 2, 1972—Easter Sunday—trading stories about their children, talking about the depiction of Italians in Marlon Brando's new movie *The Godfather,* wondering if President Nixon will ever end the war in Vietnam. This visit was on short notice, since the baseball players voted overwhelmingly just two days ago to strike for improvements to their pension plan—the first strike in baseball history—making this a rare day off for a baseball coach.

No one is happy about this strike, but there could be one silver lining for the Berras: Yogi, soon to turn 47, might actually get to see his 15-year-old son Dale, the youngest of his three boys, play baseball for Montclair High School. Carmen Berra has been the one sitting in the stands for years—baseball, football, hockey, and more—watching their sons mature into fine athletes. If there's one certainty in baseball it's this: fathers do not see much of their children growing up.

And if a baseball player becomes a manager or a coach like Yogi— this is his eighth season coaching with the Mets after one season managing the Yankees—well, an entire family lifetime can fly by before Dad realizes it. Larry Jr. is in spring training with one of the Mets' rookie league teams. Tim, a star wide receiver at the University of Massachusetts, will be home for the summer before heading back to school for his senior year. And Dale, a three-sport star at Montclair High School, is still at home.

Yogi has always kept close tabs on how the kids are playing, but his offseason TV gigs, personal appearances, and other moneymaking opportunities leave little time to attend many of their games. Spring training begins in early February, and teams are on the road more than half the time until October. Even when the Mets play home games, Berra is driving to Shea Stadium no later than 2 p.m. to beat the traffic. Going to a high school baseball game—or even enjoying a family dinner—just isn't possible.

Carmen always keeps Yogi's off days clear in season: no shopping, errands, or chores around the house. (She tries to keep his days clear in the offseason, too.) Yogi's never been the kind of guy who resets a fuse when it pops. Carmen doubts her husband even knows where the fuse box is.

And after the rare day game, Yogi wants to spend his evening enjoying two of his favorite things: the Italian dishes Carmen still cooks from Momma Berra's recipes—among the few meals Julia, their longtime live-in housekeeper, doesn't prepare—and his favorite television shows. Everyone in the Berra household knew not to bother Yogi during *Sanford and Son, Hogan's Heroes,* or *Mission: Impossible.*

Yogi truly cherishes time off during the season, even as a coach, and he often keeps to himself unless he's on the golf course. He'll take the boys to the occasional movie, but he prefers to relax at home. So Carmen wasn't surprised the day Dale asked his father to play catch only to have Yogi turn him away. "That's what you have brothers for," Yogi told his son.

Disciplining the children usually falls to Carmen, too, though Yogi can occasionally holler at them. These days, the length of his sons' hair seems to bother Yogi most. The boys have always known it takes a lot to get their old man mad, but as Larry says, you don't want to be around when it happens.

Tim learned that lesson the hard way. As Larry tells the story to family and friends, his brother was about eight years old when Dad brought them to a game at Yankee Stadium. Yogi was still in his prime, and both young boys were excited to see their father and the Yankees play. It was one of those days when Mickey Mantle struck out three times and New York lost. In the clubhouse after the game, young Timmy approached Mantle—whose locker was right next to Yogi's—with a simple message.

"You stink," he said.

Larry's eyes grew wide as Yogi smacked Timmy across the mouth for insulting Mantle. "Tell Mickey you are sorry, sit down, and shut up," Yogi said that day. "We will talk about this when we get home."

The offspring of celebrities rarely have it easy, and being the sons of Yogi Berra—superstar catcher for the New York Yankees, an advertising icon with a goofy cartoon namesake—was always going to be tough. Larry can still remember the endless teasing when they moved to New Jersey—first to Woodcliff Lake, then to Tenafly, and finally to their big house in Montclair. He remembers being grateful the family settled in Montclair long enough—almost 13 years now—for the teasing to subside.

The burden of having a famous father grew heavier once the boys competed at sports. Carmen tried to broaden their interests, giving them piano lessons and taking them to museums and Montclair's library. But the lessons stopped when the piano teacher told Carmen the boys were offering her money to let them go play ball.

Tim still played piano on occasion, and Larry was an avid reader, especially about the Civil War. But sports came first. Yogi has stayed neutral about their preferences, but his presence was huge. Whenever one of the boys excelled, they heard "Yogi Berra's son Tim Berra scored three touchdowns." Or "Yogi Berra's son Larry hit two home runs today." Or "Just like his famous father, hockey star Dale Berra has learned a lot by observing." Yogi might only be five foot eight, but he cast a very long shadow in athletics.

Which is why Tim decided to quit baseball and concentrate on football, even though his father—a keen judge of talent—thinks his second son has enough ability for the major leagues. "But he thinks the game is too boring," Yogi tells people, though that's not Tim's story. Tim Berra knows baseball is his best sport, and maybe his father is right. "I just didn't want to be compared to my dad," he tells curious friends.

Playing professional sports has always been on the minds of the Berra boys, which led to conflict between Larry and his parents in 1968. Larry, who once dreamed of being a pro bowler when his father co-owned the Rizzuto-Berra Bowling Lanes, switched to baseball and became a star catcher for Montclair High. As a senior, Larry was named All-State and drew interest from a handful of major league teams.

But players under 21 had to have parental permission to apply for the professional baseball draft in '68. And Carmen refused.

"You're our only son I'm sure will graduate from college," she told him. Passing on college would also have left Larry eligible for the military draft and deployment to Vietnam, where 549,500 American soldiers were fighting an escalating war in 1968. "You can keep playing baseball in college," Carmen said, "but we want you to get a degree." Yogi just nodded.

So Yogi's oldest son attended Montclair State—a short drive from the Berras' handsome Tudor house—where Larry studied business and played baseball. His father arranged for him to be a bullpen catcher for the Mets, and Larry even took a few road trips. He turned 21 in December of 1970, quickly applied for baseball's draft, and was disappointed not to be selected.

Larry signed with the Mets as a free agent and hit .150 in 15 games for their rookie league team in 1971. He's in spring training now as March turns into April of 1972. But already 22 and destined for a league where many players are still in their late teens, the oldest Berra son is wondering whether the window of opportunity on his dream has closed.

Yogi's youngest son Dale has just made Montclair High's varsity as its starting shortstop. Since he's 15, any talk about turning pro is still another three years away. And with the major league players voting 663–10 to strike two nights ago, Yogi hopes he'll have the chance to see Dale play a game or two after the Mets management and coaching staff fly back to New York.

The visit with their friends and all the talk about their kids is interrupted by a phone call for Yogi from Mets GM Bob Scheffing, and the news is stunning. Gil Hodges, Yogi's good friend and Mets manager the last four seasons, has just died of a heart attack. He was just two days shy of 48. Tears are already on Carmen Berra's cheeks when her husband says Scheffing wants to meet him tomorrow along with Donald Grant, the chairman of the board.

"I think," says Yogi, his words catching in his throat, "they're going to offer me the manager's job."

It's almost 11 a.m. on April 6, and Yogi and Carmen Berra are sitting near the front of the red brick Our Lady Help of Christians Church. The small Roman Catholic church is filled with big names: Tom Seaver and Sandy Koufax, Jackie Robinson and Pee Wee Reese, New York City Mayor John Lindsay and Police Commissioner Patrick Murphy, Mets owner Joan Payson and chairman Donald Grant. Baseball people fill more than half of the 600 church seats, all of them full.

Outside, upwards of 10,000 people line the streets of this middle-class neighborhood in Brooklyn where Gil and Joan Hodges raised their four children. Yogi still can't believe his friend died four days ago. A former chain-smoker, Hodges had played 27 holes of golf with his three other coaches when he suffered a massive heart attack and collapsed on their walk back to the hotel. It all happened so quickly, and now Yogi is sitting in a church, listening to Gil's parish priest eulogize the man Berra will replace as manager of the Mets. He's going to miss his friend dearly.

Carmen and Yogi attend Hodges' burial at Holy Cross Cemetery, then drive to Shea Stadium. The Mets have called an afternoon press conference to introduce Berra as their next manager, the job Carmen and others close to Yogi tried to convince him to turn down.

"You already have a good job," Phil Rizzuto told him. "The Mets aren't expected to do anything this year. Why do you want all the headaches?"

Joe Garagiola, now a cohost of the *Today* show after coming east in '65 to broadcast Yankee games, had the same conversation. "Why take it? You've got the best job in baseball," Garagiola said. "Managers come and go, but you could be a coach forever."

No one urged him to reject the job more than Carmen, and no one better understood why Yogi accepted it almost immediately. Though he hides it well, Yogi still chafes at being fired by the Yankees in '64 and disputes the charge that his players turned on him. Carmen can still remember the phone call soon after Yogi was fired from Tony Kubek, one of the players most frequently accused of going behind Berra's back to GM Ralph Houk. When Carmen said Yogi was too upset to come to the phone, Kubek told her he'd only talked to Houk once, and it was Ralph who had initiated the conversation.

And Carmen knew Yogi was stung when Casey Stengel retired and Mets management gave the manager's job to Wes Westrum, even though Berra swallowed hard and told reporters it was the right move. And he was hurt again when the Mets turned to Hodges after Westrum quit—before he was fired—in the final days of the miserable '67 season.

Yogi's friendship with Gil dated back to the days of the Yankee-Dodger postseason battles of the 1950s. Berra admired and respected him as a player and manager and offered to resign as coach if Gil wanted a clean slate. Absolutely not, Hodges replied, asking him sincerely to stay. It wasn't long before Yogi was calling Hodges the best manager he'd ever worked with, Stengel included.

Carmen understood Yogi felt he still had something to prove, but these last seven seasons as a coach have been some of the best years of their shared life. It was good to see her husband relax, no longer bearing the pressure of being the team's star or its manager. They both knew the Mets' invitation in 1965 was motivated in part by publicity, especially the attention generated by Yogi's brief return to the playing field. Regardless, Yogi worked hard to get in shape and played four games that May before retiring for good two days short of his 40th birthday.

It hurt both of them when some of the writers asked where Berra's pride had gone when he didn't leave the Mets after being passed over not once but twice. One especially critical columnist wrote that Yogi was nothing more than a "paper cone on which the media has spun a cotton-candy legend about a dumb and lovable child-man."

But Yogi has dealt with insults his whole life. He loved coaching for Gil, whose stern professionalism immediately put an end to the "lovable losers" image Stengel had made synonymous with being a New York Met. Berra truly enjoyed teaching young catchers how to call a game, explaining to pitchers what hitters are thinking, and demonstrating the intricacies of hitting to the Mets' growing cadre of good young players.

Carmen will always treasure the day this past January when Yogi received the news he'd been voted into baseball's Hall of Fame. And nothing can match the sustained high of the 1969 season, when the 100–1 shot Miracle Mets won 100 games—the team's first winning season—swept away Hank Aaron and the Braves in the National League Championship Series, then defeated the heavily favored Baltimore Orioles to become World Series champions.

"I've played, managed, and now coached in a World Series," a happy Berra said that season. "I've done it all."

But Berra still longs to manage a team to a World Series title. At the end of his long conversation with Garagiola about managing the Mets, his boyhood friend asked to speak with Carmen.

"We have no right to ask him not to take this job," Joe told Berra's wife of 23 years. "He's got to find out if he can manage."

Yogi and Carmen are in the home-team locker room at Shea Stadium just three hours after Hodges' funeral, listening to Donald Grant address the media. The team's chairman apologizes for holding a news conference the same day as the large funeral for their deeply admired manager, explaining that news leaks and the possible end of the play-ers strike—now in its sixth day—forced his hand. Indeed, Dick Young of the *New York Daily News* broke the big news about Berra's selection last night.

"We have signed Yogi Berra to a two-year contract as manager," Grant says while TV cameras roll and dozens of reporters take notes, "and we're going to deliver a good team to him. My other announce-ment is that we have made a trade for Le Grand Orange."

The Mets' pursuit of Rusty Staub, the 28-year-old redheaded out-fielder, has been in the rumor mill for weeks. The Mets gave up three good young prospects to get Montreal's five-time All-Star outfielder. "We like to train our own young men, and it tore our hearts out to give up these young players," says Grant. "But we need a man who can knock in runs."

The Mets have already sent a package of four young players—including 25-year-old pitcher Nolan Ryan, 29–38 in five seasons with the Mets—to the Angels in December for shortstop Jim Fregosi, a six-time All-Star. Fregosi, who turned 30 on April 4, missed the entire exhibition season with a broken thumb but will start at third base when the strike finally ends. Berra will have options Hodges never had the past two seasons, when the Mets finished third with identical 83–79 records.

When it's time for Yogi to talk, he stands before the microphones of the city's many TV and radio stations flanked by coaches Rube Walker, Eddie Yost, and Joe Pignatano, who all came to the Mets with Hodges five years ago. Berra, who insisted on a two-year deal with a $60,000 annual salary, asked Gil's coaches to stay, and all three agreed.

"We left a good man today," Yogi tells the media. "I hope I can fill his shoes. I was honored when Mrs. [Joan] Payson and Mr. [Donald] Grant offered me the job. I talked it over with my wife and we decided, let's do it."

Yogi is peppered with questions about where Staub will bat (cleanup), if he will go with a set lineup (yes), and if he knew about the big trade before taking the job (no). Yes, he has long wanted to manage again. No, he hasn't received any offers since leaving the Yankees.

And now that he finally has another shot at managing, one writer says, what did he learn in his time with his former team?

Berra thought a moment before responding. The Yankees have fallen on hard times since the day he left, finishing sixth in 1965, then dead last the next season when Houk had to step in for Johnny Keane after only 20 games. The Yankees have finished higher than fourth just once since Yogi's exit, even after the leagues expanded in 1969 and split into two divisions composed of six teams each.

Berra felt little joy when the Yankee collapse vindicated his leadership in '64, and he chuckled when writers began calling him a good luck charm after the Mets won it all in '69 with Yogi coaching first base. Yogi has been quiet all these years about what happened in 1964, and now that he's about to embark on his second tour as a manager, he wants to make a few things clear.

"I thought I did a good job over there," says Yogi with a hint of defiance. "And I didn't have all the problems people said I did."

While the city's baseball writers and fans debate whether the Mets should have named Hodges' successor on the day of his funeral, union chief Marvin Miller and the players settle with the owners. On April 13, baseball announced the strike's end. The owners will add another $500,000 to the pension fund, all missed games are canceled—some teams will play as few as 153 games—and there will be no back pay for the players. The owners also agree to salary arbitration, a decision destined to greatly increase player salaries.

Berra is just happy to have one day of workouts before his team opens the season on Saturday, April 15. Pitchers Tom Seaver and Jon Matlack are the first to arrive, walking into Shea around 8:30 a.m. Yogi is there to greet them. "You ready?" he asks Seaver, who will start the first game against the defending world champion Pirates.

"Do I have a choice?" replies Seaver, the team's most important and, at $120,000, its highest-paid player. Yogi takes Seaver's smile as affirmation.

Berra's first Opening Day as manager since '64 is a cold, rainy afternoon, and only 15,893 fans brave the wet 40-degree weather. Seaver is indeed ready, throwing six scoreless innings and leaving with a 4–0 lead. Reliever Tug McGraw finishes off the Pirates with three hitless innings, giving the new manager his first victory.

"I was as nervous as I was the day I played my first major league game," says Berra, whose first postgame interview session is interrupted by a call to his office phone. It's Casey Stengel, calling to congratulate his old "assistant manager" after watching the nationally televised game from his home in California. Berra is happy to simply smile and nod as Stengel talks almost nonstop for 10 minutes.

Unlike Berra's season at the helm of the Yankees, the Mets get off to a terrific start. On June 3, Seaver wins for the eighth time in 10 decisions. McGraw closes the game, earning his eighth save to go with a 3–1 record and 1.24 ERA. Staub is hitting .313 with seven home runs and 27 RBI—all team bests—and his bat in the middle of the lineup has helped Tommie Agee (.296), John Milner (.297), and Cleon Jones (.280) get off to fast starts. The win lifts the first-place Mets' record to 31–12, the best in baseball, and gives them a five-game lead over the Pirates.

Still, comparisons to Hodges are inevitable. If Berra makes a move that backfires, there are players who think Hodges would've made the right decision. And some of the players listen to their manager mangle the English language and consider him bumbling. But not every Met enjoyed the strict environment set by Hodges, or his aloofness, and those players appreciate Berra's more relaxed style. And it's hard to argue with many of Yogi's decisions when his team has won more games than any other in baseball.

The winning also helps Berra through two family setbacks and one profound professional challenge. The first happened a few weeks back. His son Larry was catching an early season game in the Florida

State League in a light rain when an opposing hitter lifted a high infield pop-up. Both Berra and his pitcher gave chase, and Berra shouted, "I got it."

But the pitcher was running hard, the grass was wet, and instead of stopping, the pitcher slipped on the grass and barreled into Larry's knees. The blow severed tendons and ligaments, requiring major surgery that will cost Berra the season. Given the severity of the injury, Berra's oldest son may never play pro baseball again.

On May 4, Yogi's brother John, 3½ years his elder, surrenders to cancer. The third of Paulina and Pietro's four sons was only 50 and managing a bowling alley in Paramus, New Jersey, before becoming ill. Yogi flew to St. Louis, where John was buried near their parents in Resurrection Cemetery.

It was a week later when the Mets announced a big and long-discussed deal that would test their new manager—or any manager. On May 11, Willie Mays officially returned to New York, where he had been a huge star with the Giants in the '50s. Yogi had argued against the deal. At 41, Mays was a shell of the superstar he'd once been, and he had turned bitter when San Francisco's fans failed to shower him with the adulation he received in New York. The last thing Berra wanted was a sour, aging star who had dictated when and where he played in his last seasons with the Giants.

But owner Joan Payson has long been a big Mays fan and told GM Bob Scheffing to make the deal when the Giants made Willie available. Scheffing complied, sending a little-used pitcher and $50,000 to the Giants, who were happy to be rid of their biggest headache. Trying to protect his manager, Scheffing met with Willie before he put on a Mets uniform and explained Yogi—not Willie—would decide how often and where Mays played.

Willie said he understood and is a model citizen while contributing to the Mets' hot start. Mays hits .333 with a pair of homers and five RBI in his first nine games, acquitting himself nicely in the outfield, too. The fans, of course, erupt every time they see Mays take the field. Berra ignored chants for Mays in Willie's first game as a Met, but if Mays keeps producing, Berra will happily listen to the fans chant Willie's name all they want.

Scheffing's heart-to-heart with Mays is not the only time the GM gives Berra the kind of support he never received from Ralph Houk, whose Yankee team is 17–20 at the end of May. "Yogi has been a hell of a manager since he took over, and he couldn't have done it under worse conditions," Scheffing told reporters after a Mets victory on May 18. "He might not sound too good when he talks, but his actions tell you something, and the players are responding to him. He's even got Cleon Jones hustling.

"I'm impressed with the way he has handled everything."

But the fast start isn't sustainable, not when a tidal wave of injuries obliterates their first-place status and optimism for a championship season. Staub is the first to go down after he's hit by a pitch on his right wrist in that June 3 win over the Braves. He's in and out of the lineup until mid-July, when another set of x-rays reveals he has a chip fracture that can only be repaired by surgery. Berra's best player won't reappear until mid-September.

It's not long before other Mets fall. Outfielders Tommie Agee and John Milner suffer badly pulled muscles. Jones hurts his elbow. Jim Fregosi injures his shoulder and catcher Jerry Grote has bone chips in his right elbow and can't throw. Gold Glove shortstop Buddy Harrelson struggles all July with a bad back before finally going on the disabled list for three weeks in August.

"I've never seen anything like this," says Berra, who in one week loses his entire outfield, his top outfield reserve, and the left side of his infield.

The result is predictable. After spending all of May and the first half of June in first place, the Mets slide into second behind Pittsburgh on June 13, pull even with the Pirates on July 1, then slip back again. By the time Yogi and his family head to Cooperstown on August 6 for the next day's Hall of Fame Induction Ceremony, his Mets are eight games behind the Pirates.

A season that started with such promise is in serious jeopardy.

★ ★ ★

When Yogi Berra was just a boy playing baseball on the sandlots of The Hill in St. Louis, he dreamed of making it to the major leagues. When Berra grew up and found a place in the starting lineup of the New York Yankees, he allowed himself to dream of becoming a star. And when Berra became one of his era's best players, he dared to dream of the day he would be inducted into baseball's Hall of Fame.

That day is a warm, muggy August 7, the time is 10 a.m., and the place is a platform built in front of the National Baseball Library, right behind the National Baseball Hall of Fame and Museum in picturesque Cooperstown, New York. The Induction Ceremony is a two-day celebration of America's Pastime, and there's a record crowd of 3,500—family members, friends, and fans—stretching out past the library's front steps into the surrounding fields of Cooper Park to welcome the eight newest members of baseball's most exclusive club.

Berra looks at the sea of faces from his seat on the platform, nervously checking the inside pocket of his plaid sport jacket where he put the short speech he and Carmen rehearsed the last few days. Those being honored will be called to speak in alphabetical order, so Yogi is batting leadoff in a lineup that includes Lefty Gomez, Sandy Koufax, Buck Leonard, and Early Wynn, all sitting to his left. Three family members of other inductees who have passed away are also waiting nervously in their seats.

Only 126 men have bronze plaques memorializing their achievements hanging in the main room of the museum behind him, and Yogi listens intently as Commissioner Bowie Kuhn reads the names of the 22 Hall of Famers who have returned for this year's ceremony. Old friends Stan Musial and Joe Medwick are here. So are Bill Dickey and Casey Stengel, and Bob Feller and Roy Campanella. Cooperstown is tucked away in the hills of central New York State, a four-hour drive from New York City. But every living member of the Hall of Fame tries hard to attend every year.

"We come now to the heart of the ceremony," says Kuhn, and Berra checks his pocket again as the Commissioner introduces him, reading from the plaque that will soon hang in the Hall. "Lawrence Peter Berra. Yogi.... He played on more pennant winners, 14, and world champions, 10, than any player in history.... He had 358 home runs and a lifetime batting average of .285...." Berra waits for Kuhn to read a few more lines before stepping to the podium, his heart thumping hard.

Berra puts on his glasses, takes a deep breath, and gives the crowd what it wants: the very first Yogi-ism. "I guess the first thing I should do is thank everybody who made this day necessary," says Berra, relieved when the crowd laughs and applauds his now famous line. Yogi allows himself a smile, takes the sheet of paper from his pocket, and turns serious. "This is the most important day of my life and I want to get it right," he says, "so that's why I'm gonna read it."

One more deep breath. "I'm really happy to be here today. Thank God I made it," he says. "I always loved the game of baseball. I hope my being here will be an inspiration for every boy in America.

"I can't begin to thank everyone who helped me achieve this goal...but I have to mention Bill Dickey, who put me on the right track, and Casey for having enough faith in me to play me every day, and also George Weiss, who gave me my first contract with the Yankees. Being with them was a dream come true, and now the Hall of Fame."

He thanks Carmen—"a perfect baseball wife," he says—and she beams when Yogi reads the names of their sons and asks the three boys to stand up. His voice catches as he continues.

"My only regrets are for those who didn't live to see this day—my mother, my father who died several years ago," he says haltingly, "my brother John and Gil Hodges, who died this year." Joe Garagiola, sitting a few rows from the front, wipes away tears as his friend takes another deep breath.

"I want to thank the Yankees and the Mets, the only two organizations in baseball I worked for. I would like to thank all of my loyal fans who supported me all these years. And last of all I want to thank baseball. It has given me more than I could ever hope for.

"I hope that when I am through with this game I will put something back."

Berra flies to St. Louis soon after the Induction Ceremony, and much of the joy of Cooperstown evaporates in his team's performance against the Cardinals. The Mets suffer a morale-crushing loss when left fielder Cleon Jones tries to make a shoestring catch on a short fly ball hit by Ted Sizemore in the bottom of the 13th inning. Not only does Jones fail to reach the ball, he also stumbles and falls as the ball rolls all the way to the wall. While Jones lopes to retrieve the ball, Sizemore races around the bases for an inside-the-park home run and a 3–2 Cardinal win.

The pitchers in the Mets locker room grumble afterward about Jones' lack of hustle. Grumbling becomes a constant as the Mets lose 12 of their last 20 games in August, scoring more than four runs just five times—and two of those come in losses. The Mets slip into third place by the end of the month, 13 games behind the Pirates, and chatter about player trades is rife in the season's final five weeks.

And, as always, speculation is intense about the fate of the manager. Once again, there are complaints that Berra should have run the team with a firmer hand. Jones was not the only player who failed to hustle once the season went sour, and while Yogi talked about fines, he imposed none. Other players grew overweight, which Berra also let pass.

But General Manager Bob Scheffing remains in Berra's corner as the Mets finish third for the third straight season. "I think Yogi definitely did a good job," he tells reporters at season's end, pointing out that even with all their injuries, the Mets finished 83–73, the second-best record in the team's 11-year history.

And they did it with almost no offense. Not a single Mets hitter reached 100 hits, something that's never happened in the National League's 96-year history. Rookie John Milner led the team with a mere 17 home runs, and Jones' team-best 52 RBI was a franchise low.

Berra is heartened by Scheffing's support, vows to impose more discipline next year, and looks ahead to his second season with guarded optimism. Yogi thinks back to what his team did when it was healthy and sees a pennant winner. No team can lose its best player for 90 games, its All-Star shortstop for 41, and its starting catcher for more than half the season and expect to contend. Virtually every player in Berra's lineup was lost for weeks at a time.

There is no way his team will get hit with this many injuries again, he tells the media in his final interview session of the season. Unfortunately for Berra, he's right.

# CHAPTER 33

# Ya Gotta Believe
## 1973

A ll in all, Yogi Berra enjoys his first offseason as manager. The highlight: watching Tim catch a 17-yard touchdown pass to spark the University of Massachusetts to a 35–14 victory over UC Davis in December's Boardwalk Bowl in Atlantic City. Yogi still thinks Timmy's best sport is baseball, but his son has turned into a quality football player. Though undersized, Tim still dreams of playing for an NFL team.

Berra is intrigued by the news in early January of '73 that CBS is selling the Yankees to a group headed by George Steinbrenner, a shipbuilder from Cleveland. The geniuses at CBS sold the team for less than they paid in '64. Yogi chuckled when he read that Steinbrenner vowed he'd be an absentee owner. Berra's been around rich owners his entire adult life and has yet to see one of them resist nosing into Yogi's business. The Yankees just signed a deal to play at Shea Stadium for two seasons starting in 1974 while the city renovates Yankee Stadium, so he'll have a ringside seat from which to watch the team's new owners.

Carmen is still trying to get Yogi interested in something other than baseball—more books, more Broadway plays, even the opera, all with minimal success. But he was able to tell her a few things she didn't know about Richard Nixon, who was reelected President in a landslide. Nixon's politics are mysterious, but he is such a huge base-ball fan that in 1965 baseball owners all but begged the former Vice President to become Commissioner. Nixon kept declining but con-tinued to attend Yankee and Mets games, where he often sought out Yogi to talk baseball strategy.

The opening of spring training camp is delayed 18 days when the owners lock out the players before agreeing on salary arbitration rules and a new three-year deal. Berra is eager to see pitcher George Stone and second baseman Felix Millan, the two players GM Bob Scheffing picked up in an offseason trade with the Braves. He is especially excited about Millan, a Gold Glove second baseman and a contact hitter who rarely strikes out, giving Berra much-needed flexibility to scratch out runs. With the Mets' strong pitching staff, Berra figures they only need four or five runs a game to contend for the NL East crown.

But they have trouble reaching even that low bar when the season starts on April 6, placing a large burden on Berra's pitching staff. The Mets average 3.5 runs in Jerry Koosman's first four appearances, but the veteran left-hander gives up just four earned runs in 34 innings and wins all four starts. Tom Seaver gives up just five runs in five games, but the Mets give him only six runs, and the team's biggest star enters May at 2–2. Thanks to their superior pitching, the Mets still end April in a first-place tie with Chicago.

But it's soon déjà vu all over again for Yogi and his Mets.

With little offensive margin for error, Berra starts losing one key player after another. When Cleon Jones hurt his right wrist making a sliding catch against the Cubs on April 19, he was only expected to miss a game or two. Wrong. Jones strained several ligaments in his wrist and is out indefinitely. A week later first baseman John Milner, stretching to catch a ball at first base, felt a tug in his thigh. The tug turned out to be a pulled hamstring, and the Mets lose their best home run hitter until mid-May.

On May 8, pitcher Jon Matlack is struck in the forehead by a hard-hit line drive. The sound is so sickeningly loud that Berra, running to the mound, fears Matlack might be dead. But Matlack, dazed but alert, leaves the game with a fractured skull. Miraculously, he's back pitching 11 days later against the Pirates, strong as ever, leaving the game after striking out six in six scoreless innings.

But the team playing behind Matlack upon his return is not the same. On May 11, both right fielder Rusty Staub and catcher Jerry Grote leave a game against the Pirates after being hit by pitches. The third and fourth fingers of Staub's right hand are badly bruised, and he leaves the hospital with them taped together. He will play that way the rest of the season. Grote is not nearly as lucky. The pitch that hit his right wrist fractured a bone. One of the game's best defensive catchers has his right arm in a cast and won't be back on the field until mid-July.

The bad news doesn't stop. Millan, whose fielding at second base was as good as—if not better than—expected, twists his ankle in mid-May and is lost for two weeks. Jones returns on May 11, plays half of the next 12 games in pain, and goes back on the disabled list, this time with a cast on his right arm from wrist to elbow. He won't be in the lineup again until early July.

Then comes the killer blow. On June 4, slick-fielding shortstop Bud Harrelson, the glue that holds this infield together, is upended while turning a double play against the Reds. Harrelson reflexively puts his glove hand out to cushion his fall and breaks a bone along the knuckles. He'll miss 33 games.

By now Berra is either unbelieving or stunned. What remains of his team plays hard and is 19–17 on May 22, still clinging to second place. But they lose nine of their next 12 on a road trip out West and return to Shea on June 6 in fifth place, 7½ games behind the Cubs. Three weeks later, slumping relief pitcher Tug McGraw gives up a run-scoring single in the bottom of the 10th that hands the Cubs a 4–3 victory and drops the Mets into last place.

Berra's postgame interview is noticeably tense.

Reporter: "What's happened to your team?"

Berra: "We're losing a lot of games by one run."

Reporter: "Would things be different if the guys were healthy?"

Yogi: "I don't know."

Reporter: "What would it take to change things?"

Yogi: "Wins."

Dissatisfied with the questions he's receiving, Berra wants to make one thing clear. "I still think we can win this thing," he says. "There's still plenty of time."

Berra knows he has the pitching to compete. He knows a baseball season is a test of endurance, of overcoming injuries and sustaining focus for nearly nine months. And he knows if his pitchers can hold steady, the Mets can break out when their hitters return.

What Berra doesn't know is whether he will still be managing this team by then.

The headline shouting from the top of *New York* magazine's cover in early July is as sizzling as a Bob Gibson fastball: THE LAST DAYS OF YOGI BERRA. The story, written by TV and magazine journalist Dick Schaap, himself a New York sports personality, isn't quite the funeral notice the cover suggests. More like describing a manager on life support.

If Yogi isn't a dead manager walking, he is — according to Schaap — a manager who has lost the respect of his players. Schaap's story is crafted around two losses to the Cubs at Shea in late June. In one passage, Schaap tells about taping a TV segment in which he asks several Mets for one dramatic event that could turn around their season. The answers are predictable. We need players to get healthy. We need players to get hot. We just need a few big breaks.

When taping is done and the camera off, one player offers a different take. "One dramatic event?" he says to Schaap. "How 'bout fire the manager?" The player requests anonymity.

Another anonymous player tells Schaap incredulously how Yogi makes a move on the field. "He turns to the players and asks *us* if he did the right thing," says the player. The comment, Schaap says, was said with pity, not anger. Imagine — a manager asking his players what they think.

Speculating on Berra's future is all the rage this summer, with

George Steinbrenner came to the Yogi Berra Museum & Learning Center in January 1999 to apologize to Yogi for the way he fired Berra as Yankee manager. The apology ended Berra's 14-year boycott of Yankee Stadium and started a deep friendship between the two men. *(Photo by Arthur Krasinsky)*

Yogi's museum chronicles his career as an advertising sensation and sharp businessman. One of his biggest success stories: recruiting Yankee stars like Mickey Mantle to help him make chocolate drink Yoo-Hoo a top seller. *(Courtesy of Clean Sweep Auctions)*

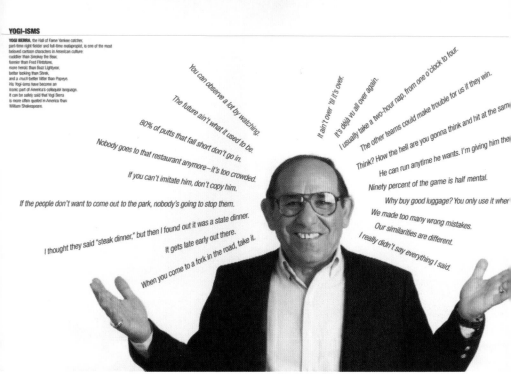

Spreads like this one helped establish "Yogi-isms" as part of American culture. *(Courtesy of Luke Lois)*

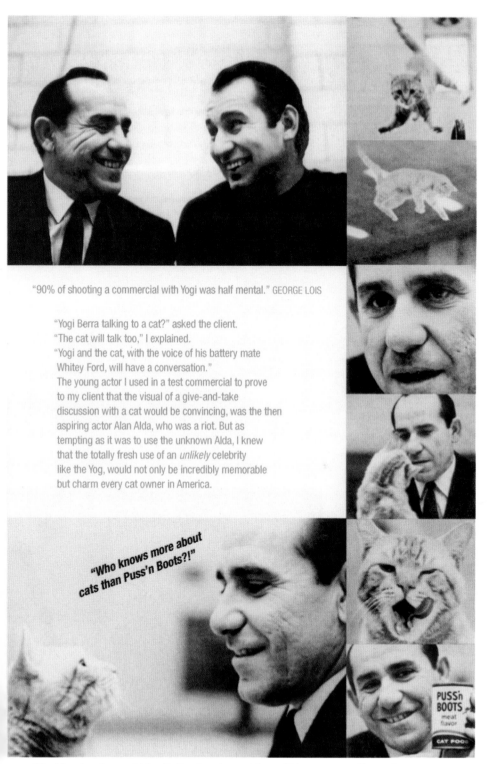

"90% of shooting a commercial with Yogi was half mental." GEORGE LOIS

"Yogi Berra talking to a cat?" asked the client.
"The cat will talk too," I explained.
"Yogi and the cat, with the voice of his battery mate Whitey Ford, will have a conversation."
The young actor I used in a test commercial to prove to my client that the visual of a give-and-take discussion with a cat would be convincing, was the then aspiring actor Alan Alda, who was a riot. But as tempting as it was to use the unknown Alda, I knew that the totally fresh use of an *unlikely* celebrity like the Yog, would not only be incredibly memorable but charm every cat owner in America.

"Who knows more about cats than Puss'n Boots?!"

PUSS'n BOOTS
meat flavor
CAT FOOD

Yogi broke the mold in 1962, chatting with a talking cat to sell Puss'n Boots cat food. Berra couldn't peg the man who voiced the cat: it was good friend Whitey Ford. *(Courtesy of George Lois)*

Yogi shows his good buddy Ted Williams the display of Joe DiMaggio at the dedication of the Yogi Berra Museum & Learning Center in October 1998 (top). Williams would pretend to be mad when Berra called DiMaggio the "best player I ever saw." Yogi also toured his museum that night with then–New York City Mayor Rudy Giuliani (left), who rarely missed a chance to celebrate with the Yankees.

Visitors looking through the exhibits at the Yogi Berra Museum & Learning Center would often stop and have a chat with Yogi, too. (© *2015 Montclair State University*)

Joan and Whitey Ford (far right), and Cora and Phil Rizzuto (center), were on hand to help Yogi and Carmen dedicate the Yogi Berra Museum & Learning Center. *(Courtesy of Rose Cali)*

Tim Berra, who spurned baseball for football, was honored at halftime of his final home game at the University of Massachusetts, along with Yogi and Carmen Berra, on "Salute to Yogi" day. *(University of Massachusetts, Special Collections and University Archives)*

Yogi's other sports passion: playing golf. *(© 2015 Montclair State University)*

One of Yogi's favorite activities: interacting with the students who attended educational programs at the Yogi Berra Museum & Learning Center. (© *2015 Montclair State University*)

Granddaughter Lindsay Berra helps Yogi cut the red ribbon to celebrate both his 90th birthday and the restoration of the display of championship rings and MVP plaques, which were stolen in a museum burglary in 2014. (© *2015 Montclair State University*)

reporters checking on Yogi's status almost daily. One such query yields a rather bizarre response from Donald Grant, the Mets' chairman of the board, who tells reporters on July 5 he has no desire to fire his manager. But the decision, he says, is not in his hands.

"We would not consider doing it unless forced to by public opinion," Grant says. "That hasn't happened, and we hope it doesn't."

Not willing to wait for the fans to vote, the *New York Post* quickly asks its readers who they think is most responsible for the Mets' woes. Their choices: Grant, GM Bob Scheffing, and Berra. And it's abundantly clear whom the respondents blame: 1,488 point their fingers at Grant, 1,207 at Scheffing, and only 611 select Berra.

The fans also put their money on Yogi. The Mets draw 100,751 fans for their three-game series with Atlanta following Grant's comment, well above the season average of 25,000 a game. The man at the center of these stories remains unchanged. Berra still comes to work smiling, still tells his players "Don't worry, we'll get them tomorrow" after a tough loss, and still tells a player who strikes out with the go-ahead runs on base that no one is a .300 hitter every day.

And even as his team hits the halfway mark in last place at 35–46—its worst midseason record since 1967—Berra insists there's plenty of time for his team to win this division. "It ain't over 'til it's over," he tells reporters, a line duly noted in the press but not fully understood or appreciated until much later.

As for support from the front office—or lack thereof—Berra remains philosophical. "It's up to the owners," says Berra. "If they fire me, they fire me. I can't tell them what to do. I've been in baseball since I was 17, and I know all you do is the best you can."

What Berra thinks about is the return of his players from the disabled list. And he sure would like to solve the mystery of Tug McGraw. His 28-year-old relief pitcher has always been considered a flake, the rare player who speaks freely. So Yogi isn't surprised in mid-July when Grant holds an impromptu team meeting to tell the players to keep believing in themselves and McGraw jumps up, flexes his muscles like a pro wrestler, and shouts, "Ya gotta believe!"

What does surprise Berra: McGraw, one of the game's best relievers the past five seasons, can't seem to get anyone out. After a solid first month, McGraw has been hammered, his performance getting worse with each outing. He blew three saves in May—after blowing only five all of last season—giving up 13 runs in 19⅔ innings. In June, teams hit a robust .306 against him.

Things hit rock bottom on July 3 in an inning as ugly as anyone can remember. After loading the bases on a single and two walks, McGraw gave up seven runs the hard way—on four pitches. The first was ball four, forcing in a run. McGraw's next pitch was hit for a grand slam. The third pitch turned into a double, and the fourth was another home run. Yogi mercifully pulled McGraw from the game. McGraw's ERA, a minuscule 1.32 on May 4, stood at 6.07. His confidence? Shattered.

With the game's highest-paid relief pitcher slumping badly, the losses piling up, and the chatter about Yogi's fate, it's easy to miss that several of Berra's most important players are returning to the playing field. Cleon Jones is finally in left field on July 7. Bud Harrelson returns at shortstop on July 9, and catcher Jerry Grote is in the lineup four days later. Rusty Staub's two injured fingers are still taped together, but he's hitting with authority again.

And on July 11, GM Bob Scheffing does a little addition by subtraction when he concedes the trade of pitcher Nolan Ryan—now an All-Star with the Angels—for Jim Fregosi was a bust. Scheffing sells the infielder's contract to Texas, removing an unhappy player from the clubhouse and boosting the confidence of replacement Wayne Garrett.

Berra knows he still needs to straighten out McGraw and decides to give the struggling reliever a few turns as a starting pitcher to clear his head. The first try on July 17 is a disaster: McGraw gives up six runs to Atlanta on 10 hits—three of them homers—in six innings. Yogi sits his star until July 30, and this time the strategy works: McGraw gives up just one run on four hits while striking out five in 5⅔ innings. The success restores McGraw's confidence and Berra sends his best relief pitcher back to the bullpen, where he's soon pitching like a star again.

Berra has one more player to straighten out, and that happens at the team hotel in San Diego in mid-August when he knocks on the door of Cleon Jones' room. The 31-year-old outfielder is startled to see his manager standing in the entryway. "Can I come in?" Yogi says. Jones nods, then Berra walks in and pulls a sheet of paper out of his jacket pocket. It's Cleon's stat sheet since returning to the lineup, and the numbers are not pretty: in 35 games, Jones is hitting .256 with just two home runs and 16 RBI.

"I still think we can win this thing," Berra tells Jones. "But I need you to hustle, to play all out, to give it your best."

Jones has always been an enigma. There's no question he has talent: he hit .340 when the Mets won the title in '69 and hit .319 two seasons ago. But he can be moody and has stretches when it looks like he just doesn't care. "Look, the team needs you, and I need you," says Berra, pausing to let the words sink in. Jones sits silently, staring at his manager.

"What are you trying to do?" Yogi says. "Get me fired?"

Berra can see alarm in Jones' eyes. He wants to inspire Cleon, not alienate him, so Yogi smiles his toothy smile and reassures Jones that he's joking. But, he adds quickly, he meant the rest of what he said. You can carry this team, Yogi tells him, and Cleon promises to work harder. Jones gets four hits in the three games against San Diego, and Berra guesses—accurately—there's more quality play ahead.

The Mets endured another setback on August 3 when Bud Harrelson was sidelined with a break in his sternum, an injury suffered in a collision on the base path. At 5 foot 11, 160 pounds, Harrelson is not built for a long season, but the kid is a great shortstop. When Harrelson returns on August 18, Berra feels the Mets are poised to make their move.

His Mets are still in last place, and it's tough jumping over five teams. But every team in the NL East has turned cold—the Cardinals are the only division rival with a winning record at 62–60. Yogi stays on message when the Mets clobber the Reds 12–1 in Harrelson's first game back, the win putting them 6½ games out of first with 42 games left to play. "Like I've said all along," he says, "there's plenty of time left."

And the breaks start to come. The Mets take two games from the NL West–leading Dodgers on August 21–22 at Shea, winning both times in the bottom of the 9th. The Mets are also beginning to believe in their patient manager, whom many had mocked for insisting this season wasn't lost. After tossing 10 shutout innings to beat the Giants 1–0 on August 24, veteran Jerry Koosman tells reporters, "It's starting to feel like 1969."

It certainly feels that way three nights later when Rusty Staub belts a grand slam and McGraw strikes out three straight Padres in the 9th to lock down a 6–5 win. "Ya gotta beeee-lieve!" McGraw shouts as he reaches the clubhouse, and this time every Met shouts it right back. These three words are now the team's official battle cry, one that is showing up on posters all over Shea Stadium.

"We're the only team in the division that hasn't had a hot streak," Berra tells the media. "Maybe we're going to have ours now."

Indeed they do. Berra's team wins three of their last four games in August, stepping out of last place on August 31. They win 11 of their first 16 games in September, and suddenly Yogi—dead manager walking two months ago—is making all the right moves. His team is in fourth place, just 2½ behind first-place Pittsburgh, their opponent for the next five games.

The teams split two games in Pittsburgh, with the Mets scoring five times in the 9th inning of the second game for another 6–5 win. The battle shifts to Shea Stadium, where Jones slugs two home runs and drives in five in the series opener. McGraw pitches three more shutout innings, and the Mets win, 7–3. Berra's team is now in third, 1½ games out.

The next game is decided in the 13th in bizarre fashion. Pirate right fielder Richie Zisk is on first base with two outs when rookie Dave Augustine hits a rocket to left field that looks like a certain home run. Jones races to the wall, stops and looks up, expecting to watch the ball sail into the stands.

Instead, the ball hits the top of the fence and takes a perfect bounce back to Jones, who catches it, pivots, and throws a strike to cutoff man Wayne Garrett. Then Garrett whirls and fires another perfect strike to catcher Ron Hodges, who tags a stunned Zisk for the third out.

The Mets score the winning run in the bottom of the 13th when Hodges—who entered the game in the 10th as a defensive replacement—shoots a run-scoring single to left field. The improbable win boosts the Mets into second place, half a game behind Pittsburgh, with Tom Seaver ready to pitch the series finale.

The Mets ace is very good the next night—allowing just two runs and five hits—and gets plenty of help. Jones doubles in two runs in the 1st inning, Grote doubles in two more for a 4–0 lead, and the Mets never look back. The 10–2 win evens the Mets' record at 77–77. More important, Berra's team now sits atop the NL East, a half game ahead of the Pirates.

Most of the season-high crowd of 51,381 remains at Shea to celebrate. Groups of happy fans take turns dancing atop the Mets dugout, chanting "We're No. 1!" while the players shout "We beee-lieeeve!" in their noisy clubhouse. In the relative quiet of his office, Berra sits behind his desk, calmly assessing the division race. Just 2½ games separate his team from the fifth-place Cubs with eight games to play. "We've been hot since August 17th," he says, "but it's still wide open."

Berra knows he holds the hot hand. His team's won 24 of its last 35 games, his big hitters are back, and he has the best pitching in the division. The NL East is theirs for the taking. And sure enough, on a cold, windy, and wet October 1 in Chicago, Jones homers for the sixth time in the last 10 games, McGraw pitches three more flawless innings, and the Mets beat the Cubs in the first game of a doubleheader to clinch the title.

The celebration is muted inside the tiny Wrigley Field clubhouse until the umpires call off the second game. The official reason: wet grounds. The real reason: the Mets' 6–4 win renders the final game moot. "Let's get that champagne out here!" Berra bellows upon hearing the news. McGraw climbs atop a trunk, calls everyone to attention, and shouts, "One, two, three..."

"Ya gotta bee-lieeeve...ya gotta bee-lieeeve," every Met shouts while spraying champagne in all directions.

Berra escapes to the manager's office and is surrounded by many of the reporters who not too long ago were writing his professional obituary. "It's been a long year—it feels more like 10 years," says Berra. "I was on 14 Yankee teams that won, but this is a big thrill because we had to jump over five clubs.

"We were 12 games back and hurt. But I never gave up, and neither did the players."

And now everyone believes.

It's late in the morning of October 2, and Yogi Berra is in his office in Shea Stadium, still feeling a bit groggy. It was a joyous flight back from Chicago, and when the team plane arrived at LaGuardia at 11:08 p.m., more than 500 Met fans were there to greet his team with cheers of "We are No. 1! We are No. 1!" and "Yo-gi! Yo-gi!" Then there was the ceremony with the city's Chief of Protocol Walter Curley, who handed Yogi a gold key to the city.

In four days the Mets will open their best-of-five series in Cincinnati against the Reds, who are overwhelming favorites to advance to the World Series. Makes sense. The Big Red Machine overtook the Dodgers to win the powerful NL West with a 99–63 record. At 82–79, the Mets would have barely finished fourth in the West. If they somehow beat the Reds, they will have the lowest winning percentage—.509— of any pennant winner in baseball history.

But none of that matters to Berra, whose team won 29 of its last 42 games—the best record in baseball—once Bud Harrelson returned to the lineup and his team played at full strength. In a few minutes they'll take the field for a light workout, but as he walks out of his office, he asks the team to gather around him.

"It's been a long season, but this is where we all wanted to be when we came together in spring training," he says. "I just want to thank everyone for working so hard. Boy, I think they were going to fire me if you had not won this thing. I really appreciate you doing that."

And with that, Berra and his team take the field, where a gaggle of writers has gathered, waiting to talk to the Mets manager. They're all wondering about the status of Tom Seaver, who slumped at the end of the season and is complaining about a tired right shoulder. It will be Seaver against the Reds in Game 1 if he's ready, Berra tells them, and Jon Matlack if Tom's shoulder still hurts.

Dick Young of the *New York Daily News* shifts gears and asks if the Mets have talked to Berra about a new contract yet. "Nope," Yogi says. "Haven't heard a thing."

*New York Times* columnist Dave Anderson jumps in. "You'll probably win it and then get fired anyway," says Anderson, and the reporters chuckle.

"Don't laugh," Berra says quickly. "It's happened before."

Seaver is on the mound Saturday afternoon in Cincinnati, and it's obvious from the start that his shoulder is just fine. He strikes out 11 and holds the powerful Reds scoreless through seven innings. The Mets maintain a 1–0 lead on an RBI double by Seaver, who talks often about the toll of pitching so many high-stress innings in all these low-scoring games. And the stress catches up to him in the final two innings.

First Pete Rose, the league's leading hitter, ties the game with a solo home run in the 8th inning. And then Johnny Bench hits a one-out homer in the 9th, giving the Reds a 2–1 win. "That's only one game," Berra says. "What the hell—we still got to lose two more."

Matlack pulls the Mets even, holding Cincinnati to just two hits in a 5–0 win. The series shifts to Shea, and the Mets blow open Game 3 early with two homers by Staub, leading 9–2 by the 4th inning. And that's when the hometown fans—not the Reds—almost steal this game from the Mets.

It starts in the top of the 5th inning when Rose slides hard into

Harrelson as the Mets shortstop throws to first to complete a double play. Harrelson, tired of being knocked down all season long, shoves Rose, who outweighs him by a good 40 pounds. When shoves turn into punches, players and coaches from both sides rush in, more fights break out, and the umpires need 15 minutes to restore order.

But that's just the warm-up. When Rose returns to left field, Mets fans pelt him with food, cans, paper cups, and anything else they can throw. Soon an empty whiskey bottle whizzes by Rose's head, prompting Reds manager Sparky Anderson to pull his team from the field. Chaos reigns.

NL President Chub Feeney confers with the umpires, then asks Yogi to talk sense into the fans in left field. Yogi brings Willie Mays with him and sends Seaver, Staub, and Jones to walk the sidelines and talk to their fans. "Please, please, look at the scoreboard!" Berra yells to the fans in left field. "We're winning 9–2. If you keep doing this, we will forfeit the game."

The field is cleared of debris, and the Reds return to loud boos but no more flying objects. A few innings later, Koosman finishes the 9–2 win, and the Mets are one game from the World Series.

Rose exacts a measure of revenge the next game, belting a home run in the top of the 12th to give the Reds a 2–1 win, tying the series.

But the Mets give Seaver six runs in the first five innings of Game 5, and their ace holds the Reds to two runs before Yogi hands the ball to Tug McGraw in the 9th with the bases loaded and one out. Two batters later, the Mets have a 7–2 victory. Berra is the second manager ever to win a pennant in each league, and delirious Mets fans confront 340 special-duty policemen hired for crowd control.

The police have no chance. Hundreds, maybe thousands of Mets fans race onto the field, where they pull up and run off with home plate and all three bases, along with chunks of infield turf. Some even rip off pieces of the padding on the outfield walls. Things are less crazed in the Mets clubhouse, where the manager is admitting that even he is a little surprised at how far his team has come.

"Whoever figured we'd win it and wind up in the World Series?"

says Berra, who knows exactly why the Mets won: his pitchers never allowed more than two runs in any game, and his hitters outscored Cincinnati, 23–8. And his team is finally healthy. "They've really played great baseball since we got them all together again."

Next up: the defending champion Oakland A's, a team with a deep pitching staff and powerful offense. The Mets are again decided underdogs and lose the first game 2–1. The two teams split the next two games before Mets pitchers hold the A's to a single run in two games at Shea, both New York victories. With the Series shifting back to Oakland, Berra's surprising team needs to win just one of the next two games to claim the World Series title.

Berra is ready to gamble. He wants to start Seaver, his best pitcher, in Game 6 on three days' rest, one short of his normal routine. If Seaver falters, it means gambling that Matlack can come back on three days rest and win Game 7. Berra's always had a chilly relationship with the cocky Seaver, but he's never questioned the pitcher's talent or desire. He asks Seaver if he's ready to pitch Game 6.

"I want the ball," Seaver tells him.

That's all Berra wants to hear, and it's Seaver who faces off against Oakland ace Catfish Hunter. And that's when the miracles end.

Seaver pitches well, giving up two runs in seven innings, each run scoring on a double by Reggie Jackson. But Hunter is better, giving up just one run. McGraw yields a run in the 8th, and the A's even the Series with a 3–1 win. Berra's dream of managing a team to the title now rests on Matlack, who hasn't allowed an earned run in 23 postseason innings.

The A's, who hit 147 home runs in the regular season, enter Game 7 without a Series homer. That changes in the 4th inning, when first shortstop Bert Campaneris and then Jackson slug two-run homers. The Mets offense manages just an RBI double by Rusty Staub until the final inning, when they score another run to make it 5–2 and have two runners on base with two outs.

Mets third baseman Wayne Garrett, a star of the team's September surge, steps in against reliever Darold Knowles. Garrett has already hit two home runs in this Series, and as he digs in, Berra is hoping his young third baseman can keep the Mets' season alive. But all Garrett can muster is a little pop-up. And when it falls safely into the glove of Campaneris for the final out, the Miracle Mets of 1973 come up one miracle short.

In a quiet Mets clubhouse, the players balance their disappointment with an appreciation for their accomplishment. "If you told me two months ago that we'd even be in the World Series, I'd have told you that you were crazy," Seaver says.

Staub agrees. "You can never feel bad about losing a World Series," the outfielder says. "I'm really proud of what we did."

It was the same message his manager had delivered right before they took the field. "I told our players before the game that we had a great year and I was proud of them," Berra says, "whether we won or lost." He's disappointed and can't help looking at pivotal moments. After all, his team left 72 runners on base in seven games, a World Series record no manager wants.

"If Milner's shot off the wall in the third game is six inches higher, he has a home run and Seaver wins in nine. Instead we lose it in the 11th," Yogi says, briefly yielding to what-ifs. "I could mention other things, but I ain't gonna." Because, despite the disappointment, he's grateful.

"Who thought two months ago we'd even be here?" Berra says.

A few hours later, the team is flying back to New York when GM Bob Scheffing sits down next to his manager. "Take a day or two off to rest up," Scheffing says. "Then Mr. Grant would like to see you at the team's suite at the Mayfair House."

Berra heard a similar request in 1964, but he's confident this meeting will be different. He learns just how different two days later. The 9:30 a.m. meeting lasts 30 minutes, long enough for Berra to make a request. Carmen told Yogi to insist on a three-year deal this time. And he does.

"Would you accept two?" Grant asks.

When Berra says he prefers three, Grant replies he'll check with the team's board of directors. By the time Yogi drives home and then to White Beeches Golf and Country Club, the deal is done—three years at $75,000 a season, the highest salary of Berra's long career. "We are just showing Yogi that we'd like to have him around for a while," GM Bob Scheffing says.

Berra didn't get the ring he so desperately wants, but he's 48 years old, has a young, talented team, and has just been given three seasons to win a title.

"Now I'm going to relax," Berra tells reporters who track him to the golf course. "I'm finally going to get to see Timmy play football this Saturday."

# CHAPTER 34

# Going Home
## 1973–1975

Tim Berra takes the Vermont kickoff three yards deep in his own end zone and dashes up the middle of the field. The University of Massachusetts star sees a lane to his right and slices through the Vermont defenders, reaching midfield. Berra has one man to beat, with two more Vermont defenders pursuing. He slows crossing the 40-yard line to wait for a block, and that's when a Vermont defender pulls even and shoves Berra out of bounds.

The run electrifies the Alumni Stadium crowd on the sunny, windswept afternoon of November 3, 1973. This 64-yard return isn't Berra's longest this season. He ran one back 93 yards for a touchdown against Villanova in the season's second week. He ran another back 97 yards two weeks ago, getting knocked out of bounds right before the Rhode Island goal line.

But his father wasn't in the stands for either of those games; he was managing the Mets to an improbable pennant. Both Yogi and Carmen Berra are here today.

And neither of those contests was the final home game of Tim's glittering three-year career as the Minutemen's record-setting wide receiver and kick return man. Nor did either feature a halftime "Salute to Yogi Berra," the school's tribute to the famous father of one of its stars.

Tim has an uncharacteristically rough first quarter. After his kick return, he leaps for a high pass but cannot hold it when he hits the turf. Later in the drive, a pass hits Berra squarely in his chest and bounces away. Yogi cringes after each mistake.

The Minutemen hold a 13–7 lead in the waning moments of the first half when a UMass staffer comes to collect Carmen and Yogi and take them to the field for their halftime ceremony. "Don't make the speech too long," shouts his friend Frank Tripucka, who along with his wife carpooled here from New Jersey with the Berras.

"What speech?" Berra shouts on his way to meet his son.

The three Berras stand at the 50-yard line as the UMass marching band serenades Yogi. Then Athletic Director Frank McInerney hands Yogi a portrait of Berra painted by a local artist along with a thick scrapbook filled with his son's football exploits.

The timing couldn't have been better. When these plans were forming, Yogi seemed on the verge of losing his job. Instead, UMass honors the man who engineered baseball's miracle season of 1973. "We not only want to congratulate Yogi on such a fine season," McInerney says to the crowd, "we wanted to thank him for being a loyal supporter of UMass sports."

Tim can't compete with his father's fame, but he's hoping to catch the eye of pro scouts who've traveled to the Amherst campus to watch games this season. At five foot eleven, 186 pounds, Tim Berra is neither especially big nor especially fast, but he has good hands and knows how to elude the two defenders he sees on almost every play. He's already garnered an invitation to play in the North-South Shrine Game, a showcase for some of the country's best college players, on Christmas Day in Miami.

The Minutemen beat Vermont 27–7, then split the next two games and finish Tim's senior season 6–5. There is no bowl game, but Berra finishes the season with 62 catches for 992 yards and scores 12 touchdowns—all Minutemen records.

Perhaps Tim Berra chose the right sport after all.

Yogi is standing on the set for his latest TV commercial, his arms pulled behind his back, surrounded by his three grown sons. Dad—his craggy face clean-shaven, his wavy black hair neatly trimmed—is wearing a white T-shirt with the words JOCKEY WHITE UNDERWEAR in three block-letter lines across his chest.

Larry, Tim, and Dale all sport long hair—24-year-old Larry also has a thick black mustache—and all three of Yogi's sons wear different-colored T-shirts. Across their chests is the brand's new message: JOCKEY COLOR UNDERWEAR.

Jockey International—founded in 1876 as Coopers, Inc. to cater to the needs of lumberjacks—decided to make a bold move in 1973: break tradition and market men's underwear in an array of colors to complement its traditional whites. The company's advertising agency was looking for a traditional man and quickly settled on Yogi Berra.

Even better, Yogi's three sons—ages 24, 22, and 17—fit the target demographic for its new product line. The admen had only one concern: the commercial would be shot over the summer for fall airing. Would Yogi be fired before the campaign hit the airwaves?

We don't care about that, Jockey executives told Levine, Huntley & Schmidt. The agency, which made Subaru a household name and broke ranks with the big Manhattan agencies by hiring Italians and Jews, was pleasantly surprised to hear Jockey's take. Yogi, the company executives told the admen, transcends sports.

Anyone traveling with Berra can attest to that. People in airports routinely stop Yogi, stare for a moment, and say, "No—you can't be Yogi Berra!" It happens so often that Yogi sometimes can't resist having some fun. "You're right, I'm not Berra," he'll say. "But a lot of people tell me that I look like him."

The Jockey ad hits the right themes: in the rapidly changing America of the early 1970s, fathers everywhere are dismayed by their sons' hair, mustaches, and beards and wonder why they're making choices very different from their own. Berra, surrounded by his three sons, nails the everyman role.

"I'm Yogi Berra, and I believe in haircuts," Yogi says stoically.

"We're Yogi Berra's sons, and we believe in hair."

"I believe in tradition," Yogi declares.

"We think things need a lot of changing," his boys counter.

"Jockey brand white underwear," says Yogi, looking to his left at Dale.

"Jockey brand colored underwear," the boys answer.

"White!" grunts Yogi, looking to his right at Tim.

"Colored!"

"White!" insists Yogi, now looking directly at the camera.

"Colored!" the boys shout.

"Where did I go wrong?" asks Yogi wearily, shaking his head.

Dad's look of serious puzzlement never changes. The boys all laugh, and Jockey has a hit TV ad campaign.

Baltimore Colts fans can be excused if they know more about Tim Berra the pitchman for Jockey underwear than about Berra the wide receiver–kick returner chosen by their team in the 17th and final round of January's National Football League draft. The University of Massachusetts football team doesn't receive much national coverage or TV time, so there's little reason Colts fans would know much about him.

And there is little doubt why dozens of writers, TV and radio anchors, photographers, and cameramen gather at the Hunt Valley Inn hotel in suburban Baltimore in early February: Yogi Berra joins his son at the press conference announcing Tim's signing with the Colts. Events like these are typically reserved for the franchise's No. 1 draft pick, but when your team has won just nine of 28 games the past two seasons, you don't pass on a little publicity.

"What a great guy," Colts PR director Ernie Accorsi tells a reporter about the elder Berra. "I was leery of calling him, but he acts like we're doing him a favor."

Tim Berra stands at the front of the room, Colts General Manager Joe Thomas is on his right and his father is to his left. Thomas presents Tim with a Baltimore jersey marked No. 8. Photographers ask Yogi to place Baltimore's iconic white helmet with the blue horseshoe on Tim's head, which the proud father does as cameras click.

"My whole life has been wrapped up in sports," Tim says. "I played a little baseball in high school but concentrated on football when I went to college."

Thomas tells reporters two Baltimore scouts took long looks at Berra, and both thought he had terrific hands but was too slow. He says their opinions changed when they timed him during practices for the North-South Shrine Game. "We asked him where he got his speed," Thomas says. "He told us he got it from his mother."

But the writers focus far more on Yogi. He tells them he never pushed any of his sons to play sports, says his knowledge of football is limited, then promises to come to Colts games in Baltimore if his son makes the team.

One reporter asks how he feels about the Yankees playing in Shea Stadium the next two seasons. "Should be interesting," he says. Another asks him to list his favorite Yankee Stadium memories. "First has to be Don Larsen's perfect game," he says, with Allie Reynolds' second no-hitter of the 1951 season a close second. "I remember almost blowing that," Yogi says. Despite a heavy cold, Berra keeps talking until the writers run out of questions.

His son watches Yogi while answering questions for a smaller group of writers. Many of the questions are variations on the same theme: what's it like to be the son of a famous athlete? And Tim delivers his stock answer: "People tend to make a bigger deal of his fame than I do."

Not much has gone right for the Mets since Yogi signed his three-year deal in October of 1973. The team turned down a host of offers for their top three starting pitchers after the World Series and paid a steep price in the '74 season. Another wave of injuries to key players crippled Berra's team, which fell into last place in mid-June and never recovered. Their 71–91 final record was the franchise's worst showing in seven years.

One ingenious fan combined the misery of Mets fans with the suffering all Americans felt living through five months of the Watergate hearings. IMPEACH YOGI read one of the 2,682 banners at the team's annual pregame Banner Day parade at Shea the first day of August. Berra survived all the speculation he'd be fired by season's end. Richard Nixon did not fare as well, resigning his presidency on August 8 when Republican senators told him he'd otherwise be impeached.

The 1975 season isn't going much better for Berra, despite the addition of 34-year-old Joe Torre and young home run hitter Dave Kingman. There is the shouting match at the end of spring training with Rusty Staub, who was hurt and out of shape most of last season. There are persistent rumors that pitcher Tom Seaver, the team's best player, is complaining to the front office about how Yogi handles the pitching staff.

Then comes the first of two scandals involving perpetual problem child Cleon Jones, who remained in Florida after spring training to rehab his surgically repaired left knee. On May 4, St. Petersburg police find Jones and a woman who isn't his wife sleeping naked in a van and arrest them for indecent exposure. Worse, the woman has marijuana. Charges against Jones are dropped, but Mets chairman of the board Donald Grant fines him $2,000, forces him to make a public apology, and insists his wife is by his side.

Berra is able to push his team to play through the controversies, and his Mets are 30–23 and in second place on June 13, a half game behind the Pirates. But Yogi once again loses key players to injuries, and by July 18 the Mets have fallen to third, 10½ games out.

And then things turn ugly.

Trailing the Braves 3–1 at Shea Stadium in the bottom of the 7th, Berra sends Jones to pinch-hit. Jones lines out softly to shortstop, stomps back to the dugout, and throws his helmet at the water cooler. When the inning is over, Berra tells Jones to play left field. Jones refuses. Yogi tells him once more to take the field, and Jones again refuses.

Berra never publicly criticizes his players, but this is blatant insubordination, and Yogi orders Jones to leave the dugout. Jones goes to the clubhouse, changes, and leaves Shea by the time the Mets finish a 4–3 loss.

There's a tense meeting with management after the game. "Jones has to go," Yogi says. When Donald Grant pushes back, Yogi tells the team's chairman he has a choice: "Either Jones is gone or I quit," he says. When Grant pressures Berra's coaches to change their manager's mind, Yogi stands firm.

Another meeting to clear the air does nothing but pull Carmen Berra into the fray, with rumors emerging that she not only attended the meeting but also spoke for Yogi. It takes Grant four days to suspend Jones, during which time the situation begins to take on racial overtones. Jones exercises his contractual right to block several trades, leaving the Mets no choice but to grant Cleon's request for his unconditional release on July 26.

Yogi won the battle, but the Mets manager is pretty sure he will soon lose his war with Grant if the Mets don't start winning consistently.

Carmen has seen the toll this has taken on her husband and is thankful for all the good news at home. Tim Berra defied the odds last summer and made the Colts roster as a punt and kickoff return man. The Colts finished a dismal 2–12 in 1974, but management is saying Tim will play wide receiver this coming season.

In June, the Pirates drafted Dale Berra in the first round of the baseball draft—YEP, IT'S YOGI'S SON read the headline in the *Pittsburgh Post-Gazette*—then offered the high school senior a $50,000 bonus to decline several scholarship offers to play football or hockey. Carmen and Yogi let their 18-year-old son decide, and Dale is now the starting third baseman for the Niagara Falls Pirates.

The Mets win 12 of 17 games after Jones refused to take the field, but Berra can feel management just waiting for a reason to fire him. And he's pretty sure they have it when his team drops a doubleheader to the last-place Expos the evening of August 5, losing both games by identical 7–0 scores. The two losses extend the most recent Mets losing streak to five games and drop their record to 56–53, 9½ games out of first place.

Yogi and Carmen are driving to their New Jersey home soon after the doubleheader, the dimmed lights of Shea Stadium still in the rearview mirror, when Yogi breaks his normal silence. Berra can interpret signs in baseball, and this is an easy read. "I think I'll be getting a call in the morning," he says.

Carmen sighs. She's been a baseball wife her entire adult life. They've been living with speculation about Yogi's job for months, and after all the tension of the past two seasons, being fired would almost be a relief.

The call Yogi anticipated comes at 9:15 the next morning, exactly as expected—Yogi is finished as Mets manager. Roy McMillan, one of his coaches, is the new manager. "We just felt we needed to make a change," says first-year GM Joe McDonald, who tells Yogi the team will find a place for him in the organization if he wants to stay.

Berra—who is owed the balance of his $75,000 for this season and another $75,000 for next year—already has other thoughts. Just four days ago, the Yankees fired manager Bill Virdon, whose team wasn't meeting the expectations of the increasingly vocal George Steinbrenner, and hired old friend Billy Martin. Yogi has a hunch he'll be coaching in pinstripes next spring.

But first things first. Yogi calls his four coaches, congratulating McMillan and informing the other three of the change. Phone calls finished, Yogi and Carmen drive around Montclair, a town they both have come to love. "I think you should take the next year off and relax," says Carmen, but she knows better. Yogi's a baseball lifer.

Yogi is besieged with phone calls once they return home, the deluge a mix of comforting friends and inquiring media digging for the gory details. Dale calls, too, telling his father he got a raw deal. "What the heck," Yogi says to his son. "I have nothing to complain about."

Yogi tells reporters he doesn't know what the future holds—except for spending today with Carmen. "You won't see me tonight," he says. "But I'll be at Shea tomorrow to see the players and say goodbye."

Berra walks into the Mets clubhouse the next day at 9:30 a.m., as always the first to arrive. Reporters come soon after, knowing this is their shot at talking to Yogi before players trickle in. The questions flow, and Yogi is ready to talk. But if the reporters hope for fury, they are disappointed.

"I had an inkling this would happen—it comes with the game—but I'm not sad," he says. "What do I have to be sad about? I've got two acres of land and a 15-room house I never thought I'd have when I started out. I never thought I'd be in the Hall of Fame, either."

Several reporters have already sought out Yankee management, and Steinbrenner, Martin, and GM Gabe Paul all indicated they'd welcome Yogi when they reopen Yankee Stadium next season. "Billy hasn't called me yet," Yogi says. "I don't want to get a job just because I'm Yogi Berra." But it's clear he's interested in going home.

Did Berra think he was fired for forcing the Mets to release Jones? "You'll have to ask Mr. Grant, but sure, that might have blown the fuse," Yogi says. "But I still wouldn't do anything differently."

Yogi sees McMillan walk in and rushes to greet him. He calls to the photographers. "Hey, get the handshake picture," he says. The photographers follow orders, and shutters snap as Berra shakes the hand of his replacement. "Good luck, Roy," says Berra, his grip tightening so McMillan knows he's sincere.

The two men walk into the manager's office followed by a trail of writers. It's McMillan who sits behind the desk with Yogi grabbing a chair and chatting away as if it's just another day at the ballpark. It's not long before the phone rings and McMillan answers. "Oh, hello, Carmen," McMillan says. "I'm doing fine, thank you."

McMillan listens intently for a minute or so. "Yogi? Yes, he's right here," he says. McMillan turns to Yogi, handing him the phone. "It's your wife."

Berra smiles as he listens to Carmen. "You have a lot of calls there?" Yogi says. "Well, I have a lot of guys waiting for me here, too. Okay, I'll be home around 12."

Now the players are filing in, and Berra walks into the clubhouse to greet them. Most are surprised, some awkward and awed as their now former boss shuffles from player to player in slacks, a polo shirt, and loafers instead of a Mets uniform and cleats.

There is no pretense as Berra thanks each man for playing hard and wishes him luck. Everyone watches as he approaches Seaver, who they all know had hectored Grant for months to replace Berra. But if Yogi holds a grudge, it's not evident as he shakes Seaver's hand, thanks Tom for leading the team to the World Series in '73, and wishes him success.

When the players drift to the field for batting practice, Berra tells the reporters it's time to meet his wife. A reporter quickly asks him if he has any regrets. "Well, I made it to the World Series twice in four [full] seasons [as manager]," he says. "My only regret is not getting that World Series ring.

"But I have no complaints. I have a great life. And now I'm going to be able to play golf on Sunday in the summer for the first time in 33 years."

A handful of Mets remain in the clubhouse as Berra walks out for the last time. One left watching is Ed Kranepool, once a highly sought high school star who signed with the fledgling Mets in 1962 at 17 and is now a veteran of 13 major league seasons. For someone just 30 years old, Kranepool's seen a lot. He knows how great the game can be when you win and how cruel it is when you lose.

"Yogi is a good baseball man and a good man—he'd never hurt anyone," Kranepool says as Berra walks away from life with the Mets.

"He's just too nice a man to be a manager."


Yogi did play golf on Sundays—and the rest of the week, too— though he's frustrated his game never improves. He and Carmen took an extended road trip to upstate New York to watch Dale play. Yogi can remember seeing just two of Dale's high school games, so this was a treat. The one disappointment: Ted Marchibroda, the Colts' new head coach, cut Tim three weeks before the team's season opener.

After two months of media speculation about Yogi rejoining the

Yankees—with many stories calling Berra "a national folk hero"— the team announces the reunion at a well-attended press conference on December 5. "I'm happy to be back," says Berra, who signed a one-year deal to coach under Martin. "I love baseball. That's all I've known my whole life."

Martin says he wants Yogi to be a "bumper" between him and the players. Berra's not exactly sure what Martin means, but he's not asking today. He's going home again and could hardly be happier.

"Whatever Billy wants me to do," Yogi says, "I'll do it."

# CHAPTER 35

# The Bronx Zoo
## 1976–1983

**H**ow do you survive life with George Steinbrenner's Yankees?

That's the question Yogi Berra hears throughout his eight years as the "complaint" coach in his second tour with the New York Yankees. Whenever anyone asks what it's like coaching a team routinely called "the Bronx Zoo," he smiles wryly. "It's not as bad as the media makes it out," he answers. "No one has punched anyone in the face yet."

One thing is certain: despite the chaos that envelops these Yankees, Berra's return solidifies his credentials as the biggest winner in baseball history. Yogi never liked hearing he was a "good luck charm"—as Casey Stengel so often called his star catcher—but that sobriquet is repeated endlessly in 1976 as the Yankees play in their first World Series since Berra's single season as the team's manager a dozen years ago.

Berra even finds himself managing an inning in the fourth and final game of the 1976 World Series against Cincinnati, taking over when Billy Martin is ejected. Berra receives a loud and lengthy ovation when he walks to the mound to change pitchers. New York is one inning away from being swept by Cincinnati, but seeing the 51-year-old Berra back on the field in pinstripes is a thrill for Yankee fans, no matter the circumstances.

The Yankees win back-to-back championships the next two seasons, and Yogi is in the first car of the parade down Manhattan's Canyon of Heroes after each World Series. They're titles No. 12 and 13 for Berra, who tells friends that riding in a ticker-tape parade never gets old. And when the Yankees win the American League pennant again in 1981, it's the 21st time Yogi walks onto the field for the World Series. That burst of excitement before introductions in a packed Yankee Stadium never gets old, either.

But being a Yankee is different now. These are not the dignified DiMaggio Yankees of Berra's youth. Or the perennial Casey Stengel winners of Berra's prime. Or even the mischievous Mantle-Ford Yankees who dominated baseball at the end of Yogi's playing career.

These are the three-ring-circus Yankees of George Steinbrenner–Billy Martin–Reggie Jackson, the men who command headlines and produce championships, crises, and chaos. It is each man's constant, competing need for attention and affirmation that has turned this franchise into the Bronx Zoo.

And they are the reason Yogi's calm, patient demeanor—mistakenly considered a liability in his four seasons as manager—has never been more essential. There are some people—and Berra is clearly one of them—who have an elevating effect on a team, even when they are not in charge. They project dedication, joy, and confidence in the talents of teammates as well as genuine humility and a fundamental respect and empathy for others. He reminds players they can work hard and have fun, too.

Simply put, Berra's example helped these Yankees find joy amid the chaos.

Berra learns almost immediately what it means to be Billy Martin's "bumper." It happens in Yogi's first Yankee spring training after an exhibition game loss to the Mets—a sin in Steinbrenner's book. Steinbrenner is irate with Billy for not taking the players bus back to Yankee headquarters in Fort Lauderdale. Martin explains that he drives with his coaches to evaluate player performances more freely.

"That's ridiculous," bellows the Boss, who summons Berra to set his manager straight. But Steinbrenner is disappointed. "When I managed, I drove back in a car so I could talk to my coaches about the players," Berra says. "Just like Billy does." Steinbrenner says nothing, then stomps away.

The situation is more serious the following March after another exhibition loss to the Mets in St. Petersburg. Steinbrenner has been poking at Martin for weeks, second-guessing his manager's lineup decisions, complaining loudly after spring training losses that matter only to him. This time he confronts Martin in the trainer's room, his General Manager Gabe Paul in tow. Martin, sitting in a corner of the room with spring training instructor and drinking buddy Mickey Mantle, snaps back at George. The exchange grows so heated that Paul steps between the two men just as Martin swings his fist into a bucket filled with ice, dousing the 67-year-old GM with freezing water.

Martin and Mantle leave first. George, with Paul in tow, charges into the coaches' room and finds Berra. "You're taking over as manager," Steinbrenner says to Yogi. "Billy's gone."

"Uh-uh," Yogi says calmly. "This is Billy's club, George."

Steinbrenner explodes again and tells traveling secretary Bill Kane he wants Martin in his Fort Lauderdale office at 9 a.m. the next day. Kane can't locate Martin and instead finds Yogi at the team's hotel. "I'll take care of it," says Berra, asking for a key to Martin's room, where he spends the night waiting. Billy walks in at 5 a.m., bleary-eyed and wasted from another night of drinking.

"Shower up and get some rest," says Yogi, who delivers Martin as required. The owner and his manager call a truce, and Martin's job is safe — for now.

The next eruption occurs three months later in a nationally televised game in Boston. Expectations are high in 1977 for the defending American League champions after Steinbrenner signs Reggie Jackson and pitcher Don Gullett, the two biggest stars in baseball's first-ever class of free agents. But the Yankees have just fallen out of first place — behind the hated Red Sox — when they take the field at Fenway Park on June 18.

The Yankees are trailing 7–4 in the 6th inning when Boston's Jim Rice lifts a short fly to right that drops between Jackson and second baseman Willie Randolph. Jackson is slow getting to the ball, Rice takes second base, and Martin's short fuse is lit. Billy changes pitchers, returns to the dugout, then sends Paul Blair to replace Reggie, intending to embarrass his star. Berra and fellow coach Elston Howard watch carefully as Jackson reaches the dugout and engages Martin in a shouting match.

Yogi and Ellie stand between the two combatants, who appear to settle down as they walk to opposite sides of the dugout. But then Reggie shouts at Billy—every Yankee has a different version of the exact words, none of them good—and Martin charges the bigger, younger Jackson. And that's when Yogi grabs Martin, his two strong hands locked onto the screaming manager, unyielding, until Howard and others usher Jackson into the clubhouse.

Martin somehow retains his job, and the next day he's showing reporters the bruises on his arm and chest where Berra had grabbed him. "That damn Yogi," a smiling Martin says, "picking on a 160-pound guy."

There is real affection between Yogi and his friend with the hair-trigger temper. Yogi's always been impressed with Martin's grasp of the game and dismayed by his self-destructive nature. Billy calls Berra his "morning newspaper," the man who tells him how the players feel about their manager on any given day. He's also the man Martin vents to about the constant criticism from the team's owner.

Which is exactly what Martin should have done in July of 1978 after yet another problem with Jackson. On the 17th, Martin suspends Jackson indefinitely for disobeying a sign while batting against the Royals. The suspension is quickly reduced to five days and Jackson rejoins the team in Chicago on July 23 but doesn't play in the third-place Yankees' 3–1 win, their fifth straight. When the team arrives at O'Hare for its flight to Kansas City, Martin pulls two reporters aside and unleashes a torrent of criticism about Jackson, walks away for 45 minutes, then returns for another round.

But the second assault is also aimed at Steinbrenner, whose fondness for Reggie bothers Billy enormously. "The two of them deserve each other," Martin tells the two reporters. "One's a born liar, the other's convicted."

Both reporters know Martin is alluding to Steinbrenner's conviction for illegal contributions to Richard Nixon's reelection campaign. When they reach Steinbrenner by phone, the Yankee owner is stunned. When word of Billy's outburst circulates on the flight to Kansas City, Yogi just shakes his head. Martin will certainly be fired. Instead, Martin resigns in tears the following day before Steinbrenner can act.

"We haven't seen him," Yogi tells reporters when the news breaks. "He'll get a job again; I know it."

Berra is right, but even he's stunned by what happens five days later. It's Old-Timers' Day at Yankee Stadium, and Berra's just been introduced to a huge ovation from the crowd of 46,711. Yogi stands next to his old teammates and waits for PA announcer Bob Sheppard to bring on Joe DiMaggio, always the final player called. But instead of Joe D, it's Martin jogging onto the field and waving as the crowd applauds wildly.

And the cheers grow even louder as Sheppard announces that Martin will return as Yankee manager for the 1980 season, almost two seasons from this day.

Current Yankee manager Bob Lemon, who will lead this team to its second straight title, stares in disbelief. And he has plenty of company. Just another day at the Bronx Zoo.

But the stunning announcement turns out to be inaccurate. The Yankees are 34–31 and in fourth place on June 17, 1979, when Steinbrenner fires Lemon and reinstates Martin almost a half season early. Just not for long. Steinbrenner fires Martin in late October, this time after Billy punched a marshmallow salesman in a barroom argument, then hires and fires six managers in the next three seasons.

Not once is Berra's name raised as a possible manager.

And Yogi isn't sure whether he's upset or relieved.

To be sure, there are wonderful, memorable moments during these years. Reggie's three home runs on the first pitch from three different pitchers in Game 6 of the '77 World Series, which clinched the Yankees' first title in 15 years. Left-hander Ron Guidry's 25–3 record in 1978, and his 18-strikeout game—a Yankee record. And the Bucky Dent home run that beat the Red Sox in their one-game playoff for the AL title that same season.

Yogi won't forget helping out at Double-A Nashville during the 58-day players strike in 1981 and the 19th-round draft pick who caught his eye there. He told the team's manager that the kid—a 20-year-old named Don Mattingly—was going to be a big star. And he kept telling Steinbrenner, notorious for trading good young talent for washed-up veterans, never to let go of Mattingly.

He treasured all the time spent on the road with his good friend Ellie Howard—all the meals shared, all the times their wives, also close friends, laughed at the clothes their husbands bought on long road trips. Yogi never tires of telling a story about Ellie and Reggie. The two friends both admire Reggie's enormous talent, but neither could stomach Jackson's giant ego. One day early in '78, Reggie approached Yogi and Ellie during pregame drills and asked where he would have fit on the great Yankee teams of the '50s.

"Fifth outfielder," Howard answered without missing a beat. The two old Yankees howled with laughter as Jackson stormed off.

And there are the tragedies Yogi will never forget, too.

The day team captain Thurman Munson died when his Cessna jet crashed and burst into flames on his final practice landing on August 2, 1979. The whole team attended the funeral in Canton, Ohio four days later. The emotional charge when Munson's best friend Bobby Murcer drove in five runs later that night at Yankee Stadium—including the game winner in the 9th—was almost tangible.

So was hearing the news from Howard in February of 1979 that he had myocarditis, a serious, sometimes fatal heart disease. He'll never forget the phone calls and hospital visits, or carrying Ellie's casket along with Mickey, Whitey, and three other baseball stars, at Howard's funeral in mid-December of 1980. Ellie was only 51.

Myocarditis is an inflammation of the heart muscle. But Arlene

Howard told Carmen Berra her husband really died of a broken heart. It was Elston's dream to manage, Arlene told Carmen, and the first black Yankee was bitterly disappointed he never got the chance.

Carmen understood. She is sure her husband wants to manage again and is thankful Steinbrenner hasn't offered him the job.

Not in late 1979, when George picked former coach Dick Howser to replace Billy.

Not in November of 1980, when Steinbrenner forced out Howser—whose team won 103 games but lost to Kansas City in the playoffs—and hired Gene Michael, then fired Michael with 25 games left in the '81 season and brought back Bob Lemon.

Not in 1982, when Lemon, Michael, and Clyde King all took turns sitting in the manager's chair.

Yogi's been there through it all—coaching first base, working with the catchers, telling stories about the old days. Yogi feels blessed he's still in uniform. And on this team he's the calm center in the unstable world of George Steinbrenner.

And that's what he'll be again in 1983, now that George has announced he's bringing back Billy Martin to manage the Yankees for the third time.

Yogi never had a chance at the job.

And for that, Carmen Berra is grateful.

Yogi is in Los Angeles for the third game of the 1977 World Series when his life once again changes. On October 14, 1977, Lindsay Berra, the baby daughter of Francine and Larry Berra, enters the world. It's not long before Carmen and Yogi understand a grandparent's joy. They are both 52—though Carmen smiles and contends she's four years younger—they both enjoy good health, and their smart investing has made them financially secure. They can dote on their grandchildren in ways they couldn't with their three sons.

Indeed, Lindsay is only a few years old when the Berras start a tradition in their beautiful colonial house on Highland Avenue with the big backyard and views of the Manhattan skyline. Every Thanksgiving morning Carmen and Yogi rent a horse-drawn open-air carriage and driver to give their grandchildren and the neighborhood kids a ride up and down their street. There's champagne for the parents, and Carmen and Yogi never stop smiling.

The eight years Berra spends as a coach under Steinbrenner's constantly rotating cast of managers are golden years for the Berra family. Larry and Tim are both married, and by the end of 1983, Grammy and Grandpa Berra have three grandchildren to spoil with another on the way. Larry is Vice President of Sales for a local flooring business; one day he will have a flooring company of his own. Tim is managing a racquetball club built in 1978 by Yogi and a group of investors in nearby Fairfield.

And Yogi is as popular as ever, the humble Hall of Famer who connects Yankee fans with their team's celebrated past. And as a Yankee coach and resident folk hero, Berra is well positioned for the sudden boom in the sports collectibles market that begins in the late '70s. He has his pick of baseball card and memorabilia shows, where he can earn several thousand dollars—or more—in each appearance.

With her two older sons out of the house and starting families of their own, and her youngest off playing in the Pittsburgh Pirate organization, Carmen volunteers time with local causes. The Salvation Army and the town's vibrant library are two favorites, and she becomes a prized fund-raiser for the local Republican Party. A Berra fund-raiser almost always opens with Yogi greeting the crowd, then introducing Carmen, who closes the deal with grace and charm.

They both love their adopted hometown of Montclair, which has evolved from a pre–World War II summer home for the rich and powerful to a diverse community with a thriving middle and upper middle class. And celebrities looking to stay close to Manhattan, 19 miles to the east. Among the most active: actress Olympia Dukakis and her husband actor Louis Zorich, who moved to Montclair in 1970 to rear their children and opened the Whole Theater Company. Carmen joined the theater's board and helped raise money to stage five plays a year. Among the actors who appear: Dukakis, Samuel L. Jackson, Blythe Danner, and Colleen Dewhurst.

Montclair is also hometown to astronaut Buzz Aldrin. The town anointed him "Montclair's Man on the Moon" and placed a plaque in front of his childhood home. Former NBA star and future Senator Bill Bradley settled here in 1977. Larry Doby, Yogi's old friend and the first black player in the American League, raised his family in Montclair.

The town is becoming a media hamlet, especially for dozens of writers and editors at the *New York Times*. There are numerous authors, playwrights, and artists here, too. And a growing number of bankers and industrialists, many of them living in the mansions that line Upper Mountain Avenue.

One of the best and brightest is Montclair native John McMullen, who graduated from the United States Naval Academy and MIT, became a naval architect and businessman, and built one of the largest naval architecture companies in America. He and his wife Jacqui are close friends with the Berras, and John shares Yogi's passion for sports. A limited partner with the Yankees—"There is nothing more limited than being George Steinbrenner's limited partner," he's fond of saying—McMullen cashed out his stake in New York in 1979 and bought the Houston Astros.

Three years later he bought the Colorado Rockies hockey team and moved them to New Jersey with a new name: the Devils. McMullen, seven years Yogi's senior, enjoys inviting his friend—still a big hockey fan—to his arena suite to watch the Devils play. They walk together or work out most mornings at the team's training facility in West Orange, New Jersey.

The two men also enjoy playing golf and dining at the Montclair Golf Club, the social hub for the town's elite. Inevitably, a crowd forms around Yogi, hoping to chat with the Hall of Famer.

Yogi is just as comfortable driving to blue-collar Jersey City with Phil Rizzuto for a morning of coffee and baseball talk with old friend

Ed Lucas, a blind sportswriter who writes often about the Yankees. Rizzuto befriended Lucas in 1951 when he heard the 12-year-old from Jersey City had lost his sight playing baseball—a batted ball struck him between the eyes. Phil and Yogi became the young boy's friends and benefactors, raising funds to help him attend a special-needs school, supporting his dream of becoming a journalist.

Carmen and Yogi are always in demand for dinner parties in town and are often seen in one of the cafés and restaurants in downtown Montclair. Carmen likes the tables near the window. Town residents who catch Yogi's eye will usually get a wave. Catch Carmen's attention, and she'll wave you in to say hello and chat.

Ask Carmen about Dale, and the conversation might take a while. Dale starred in the minors and made his major league debut in 1977 at age 20—a year younger than his dad. He split his time between the minor and major leagues the next two seasons, getting enough big hits in 44 games with the Pirates in 1979 for his teammates to vote him a three-quarter share of the winner's pot when they went on to win the World Series.

Dale, a lanky six feet and 180 pounds, stays with the big league team for two seasons as a reserve infielder before taking over as the starting shortstop in 1982. His teammates all call him Yogi—he says he doesn't mind—and the organist plays "Here Comes the Sun" when Dale comes up to bat. And by now the Pirate clubhouse man is used to getting calls from Dale's father during the game to check on how his son is playing.

Father and son talk after some of Dale's games, too. At the end of every conversation, Yogi always says, "How are you doing?"

"I'm all right, Dad," Dale replies.

"That's all I wanted to know," Yogi says.

When George Steinbrenner was asked in January of 1983 why he brought back Billy Martin to manage his team—with the security of a five-year, $2 million contract—the Yankee owner pointed to Martin's résumé: five division titles, two pennants, and one World Series championship. "You need a winner to win," Steinbrenner said. "Billy has taken teams who have had no right to be winners and won with them."

And asked if he was at all concerned about the big storms that accompany Martin, Steinbrenner turned to his shipbuilding background. "A sailing ship with no wind goes nowhere," Steinbrenner said. "Sometimes you have to have a little turmoil."

What Steinbrenner gets for his money in 1983: not enough wins and way too much turmoil in what might be the most excruciating season of Martin's long, rocky managerial career. The chip on his shoulder is as large as ever, his fuse as short as ever. The 55-year-old Martin spends the entire season fighting with umpires, the media, a revolving cast of Yankee players and coaches, his league's President, and one clubhouse urinal.

And, of course, the team's owner, whose laughable promise to step back and let Martin run the Yankees ends well before the All-Star break. And that's why Yogi Berra finds himself surrounded by reporters before the team's June 14 game against the Indians in Cleveland. They all want to talk about a story in the *New York Daily News* that hints Berra might soon become the Yankee manager.

"Steinbrenner to fire Martin" stories, which have been circulating for weeks, intensified when the owner scheduled a meeting with Martin and his agent for June 15 in Cleveland. *Daily News* writer Bill Madden called Steinbrenner on June 13 and was surprised when George answered. Madden then listened intently while the Boss rattled off all the reasons he might fire Martin. When Steinbrenner was done venting, he had a question for the veteran writer.

"What would you think about Yogi as manager?" he asked. "That's who I am thinking about. He'd be perfect, I think."

Caught off guard, Madden paused before answering.

"If that's what you think you have to do," Madden said, "what's not to like about Yogi?"

Now every other Yankee beat reporter wants to hear Yogi's thoughts about replacing Martin. But there's not much to tell, since this is news to Berra.

"Nobody's told me nothing," he keeps repeating. "I don't know anything about it."

Berra does know Martin thinks he'll be fired, and the stress is getting to his friend. Just a few hours after fielding questions about the *Daily News* story, Yogi sees another reason to worry about Billy. The Indians score six runs in the 1st inning, and the tension in the dugout is palpable. The score is 8–2 after five innings when Berra sees Martin suddenly jump off the bench, grab a bat, and head toward the bathroom behind the dugout. Once inside, Martin repeatedly smashes the bat against a urinal, sending pieces of white porcelain flying.

Billy won his battle against the urinal, but the Yankees lost to the Indians 9–6, dropping the fifth-place team's record to 29–30. Martin knows that's not what Steinbrenner expects from a team with the highest payroll in baseball.

It pains Berra to watch his friend unravel, and he's silent about Madden's story after the team's latest loss. Steinbrenner's offered Berra the manager's job twice over the last seven seasons, but both times it was rage talking, not a real job offer.

Truth is, Steinbrenner is leery of hiring Berra—and for good reason. Yogi's immense popularity would make it difficult to publicly berate him—George's preferred method of motivation—or fire him. Steinbrenner's heard the ovations for Berra on the field. And he's been in the clubhouse before Old-Timers' Games and seen how all the players—today's stars and yesterday's—gravitate toward Berra. Even Mantle and DiMaggio.

But with his team floundering and the Mets making headlines with rookie sensation Darryl Strawberry and a big trade for former MVP Keith Hernandez, it might be worth the risk. Just not in mid-June. Steinbrenner gives Martin a reprieve, instead firing Art Fowler, Billy's longtime pitching coach and drinking buddy, as punishment for the team's poor play.

The Yankees finally start winning consistently in July, but there are almost as many player complaints about life with Billy as there are wins, and several agents tell Steinbrenner their clients will leave if

Martin returns next season. Martin's last chance to save his job slips away when the first-place Orioles win three of four mid-September games at the Stadium, ending any hopes of a division title. Billy's third tour ends with 91 wins and a third-place finish.

Steinbrenner refuses to comment on Billy's status at season's end, but Martin is clearly done. Steinbrenner's first target is Dodger manager Tommy Lasorda, who leverages George's interest to get a big raise and a three-year contract from Los Angeles—the first multiyear deal for a manager in Dodger history. And when Steinbrenner fails to talk former Oriole manager Earl Weaver out of retirement, he warms to the idea of giving Berra another shot.

The two men talk at a Boy Scouts dinner in West Orange, New Jersey on December 1. After dinner, *New York Times* columnist Dave Anderson, a friend, asks Yogi if Steinbrenner offered him the manager's job. "Well," Yogi says, "a little bit." When Anderson presses Yogi to explain, Berra admits the Yankee owner "said I was the No. 1 choice. He asked if I'd be interested, and I said I'd have to think about it."

Berra has already made up his mind to take the job—it's Carmen who requires convincing. All three of Berra's sons urge him to accept. "What do you have to lose?" they say, forgetting the loss of dignity—if not sanity—suffered by every one of the seven men who held the job under Steinbrenner. It is the woman of the family who sees the risks.

"I like your coaching job," Berra's wife of 35 years tells him. "I just don't think this is a good idea. You've done everything in baseball. Why do you want to manage now?"

Carmen doesn't have to wait for an answer. She knows her husband has quietly resented the jokes made at his expense for so many years, all those barbs insulting his intelligence. And she knows he wants to prove, once and for all, that the jokers were wrong. Dumb men don't lead baseball teams to championships.

Berra could have taken managing jobs in Atlanta and Texas—and with other teams, too, if he'd lobbied for them. But he never wanted to leave his adopted home state, and he never wanted to prove himself anywhere but in New York. And now he has another chance.

"I've done a lot, but I haven't done everything," Yogi tells Carmen. "I haven't won a World Series."

Carmen offers her reservations for several days, but her husband knows this team, and he thinks he can win. When Carmen acquiesces, it's just a matter of finalizing the details.

The announcement comes in a Yankee Stadium news conference on December 16, a full 19 years after Berra retired and was named to manage this franchise under very different circumstances. "Managing my teammates won't be a problem this time," he tells the media jammed into Steinbrenner's office. He's 58, with 20 years of managing and coaching experience. Berra has a two-year contract—with a big raise to $225,000 a season—and the solid support of his players.

"Yogi has helped us all over the years," says second baseman Willie Randolph, who was a rookie when Berra returned in 1976. "I want to give something back to the man. We all do."

Randolph, catcher Rick Cerone, and outfielder Steve Kemp are at the Stadium representing the Yankee players and greet the news with a mixture of relief and excitement. The moody Martin ignored or embarrassed his other coaches, but he listened to Yogi. And the players knew talking to Berra was their best shot at getting through to Billy.

"I understand it's different when you're a manager," Randolph tells reporters, "but I still believe I could go up and talk to Yogi and he would listen. People change, but I don't think Yogi will. You can always talk to Yogi."

Much about baseball has changed since Yogi's first stint as a manager, most of it revolving around the game's finances. The minimum salary in 1964 was $6,000. This year it will be $40,000. The average salary in 1967—the first year records were kept—was $19,000. This year it will be $300,000. Next month, the Pirates will sign Yogi's son Dale to a five-year, $3.05 million contract. Dale will make more in his final season of the deal—$820,000—than the $685,600 Yogi earned in his entire career.

"Yeah, the salaries are so much more than they used to be, and guys have guaranteed deals, which we never had in the old days," Berra says. "But players still want to play and win. That never changes.

"And I think this team can win it all."

Every manager who preceded Berra thought he could win, too. Some did, some didn't, but every one of them was fired by Steinbrenner, who is changing managers for the 12th time in 11 seasons. Berra is the fifth in the last three years.

Berra has seen it all up close for the past eight seasons, staying steady inside the chaos. He understands he's in the line of fire now, but on this day he shows the confidence he'll need to survive.

"I don't get mad too quick. I'll listen to what George has to say, but that doesn't mean I have to do what he says," Yogi tells the media. "And I think he'll listen to what I have to say."

"Will you argue with Steinbrenner?" he's asked. Of course, Yogi replies.

"Who'll win?" he says. "I guess I'll find out."

# CHAPTER 36

# Sixteen Games
## 1984-1985

It doesn't take long for Yogi Berra to find out if he can win an argument with George Steinbrenner.

The answer: no.

That is made abundantly clear the night of April 6, soon after a tough loss to the Rangers in Arlington, Texas—the season's fourth game. The Yankees battled back from a 6–0 deficit to tie the score, only to lose in the 8th inning when Bobby Meacham, a promising 23-year-old shortstop, bobbles a two-out grounder then throws wildly to first, allowing what becomes the winning run to score.

Soon after the loss, the team's third in four games, the phone rings in the visiting manager's office. Yogi picks up the phone, and George starts in immediately. "I want Meacham sent down to the minors," Steinbrenner shouts. "He cost us the game tonight. He's not ready."

"George, I think that's a mistake," says Berra, knowing how a decision like this can shatter a young player's confidence. "It's just one game."

"I don't care what you think," Steinbrenner says. "Just tell him he's going down to Nashville."

Berra waits until the next morning to deliver the bad news, calling Meacham to his hotel room at 9:30 a.m. He gives the rookie his new assignment and tells him to keep his head up. "You're a good player," Yogi says. "You'll be back in New York."

Berra is far more tight-lipped when the media asks for an explanation. "It's not my doing and I don't want to talk about it," says Berra, grim determination locked on his face.

Who made the decision to banish Meacham?

"I don't want to talk about it," Berra repeats.

Other Yankees make clear it was Steinbrenner's call, and several wonder how much longer Berra will want to remain manager.

After four games.

"Yogi's upset," says one player, insisting he remain nameless. "Everybody's staying away from him."

The team has played just one week of the regular season and Steinbrenner's constant meddling—he reversed several of his manager's personnel decisions the final week of spring training—has already begun to weigh heavily on Berra. The two men could not be more different. Steinbrenner is reactive, thinks every mistake is fatal, and sees every loss as a betrayal of the high salaries he pays. He pits players against each other to spark competition, rages against them, and famously craves attention and respect that is neither earned nor deserved. George generates high drama and seems rarely to have a feeling without acting on it—loudly.

Yogi is his opposite almost completely—his singular achievements have made him a superstar, but he remains modest, centered, and generous in attention to others. He is frank, patient, and encouraging. And most of all, he understands that a baseball season demands strategic stamina: no single bobbled ball or game or even series of games is unrecoverable, so long as everyone on the team is learning and solving problems.

Writers, players, and coaches all thought Steinbrenner would be more careful with Berra than he was with previous managers in deference to Yogi's popularity. And at first Steinbrenner was hesitant to criticize the Yankee legend. But that changes when the Yankees' slow start lands them in last place while the Mets rocket to the top of the NL East and their 19-year-old strikeout artist Doc Gooden becomes the new media darling.

By early May, the "Berra in trouble" stories start appearing on a regular basis. *New York Times* columnist Dave Anderson writes that Berra is smoking again after kicking the habit two years ago. Another writer watches Berra walk alone down the right field foul line before a game at the Stadium, his head down, trying to ease the tension that rises as the Yankees end May at 20–27, a staggering 17½ games out of first place.

The only saving grace: everyone in the American League is looking up at the Detroit Tigers, who win 35 of their first 40 games and are never seriously challenged. Still, Steinbrenner drags Berra and his coaches into meeting after meeting as May turns into June, demanding to know why his team is not in contention. Berra says little at these meetings, just trying to wait out George's wrath.

But Steinbrenner finally finds Berra's breaking point. It happens at the Stadium after a loss to Detroit in mid-June that pushes the Yankees 19 games out of first. With his manager and staff sitting around the large oak table in the middle of Steinbrenner's office, the Boss goes off on a tear, directing most of his ire at Yogi.

"You guys have really let me down," Steinbrenner says. "I gave you what you wanted. Everything you wanted! This is your team, and look at it. Look what's happening!"

Steinbrenner continues blasting away, repeatedly claiming these are the players Yogi wanted, they aren't performing, and asking Berra what he plans to do. Berra listens to the tirade with his head down, staring at his fists, which he keeps clenching, then opening, trying to keep his anger from boiling over. But Steinbrenner says "this is your team" once too often, and suddenly Berra jumps up and fires a pack of cigarettes in George's direction. The package takes one bounce and hits Steinbrenner in the chest.

Nobody moves.

Except Yogi.

"If you don't like it," Berra says, "get another manager."

"Are you quitting?" Steinbrenner says.

"No!" Berra says. "If you want to get rid of me, you'll have to fire me."

Steinbrenner looks poised to renew his tirade when Berra truly opens fire.

"This isn't my fucking team, it's your fucking team," Yogi shouts. "You make all the fucking decisions. You make all the fucking moves. You get all the fucking players that nobody else wants."

Berra takes a quick breath, and everyone remains silent. "You put this fucking team together," Berra shouts. "And then you just sit back and wait for us to lose so you can blame everybody else because you're a chickenshit liar!"

Yogi storms out of Steinbrenner's office, and everyone left behind sits still, not quite knowing what to say. Before they can decide, Berra returns and once again launches into another obscenity-filled diatribe against Steinbrenner, each sentence punctuated with the word *liar*. When Yogi is finally yelled out, he stalks off, this time not to return. Steinbrenner, who sat calmly through both verbal assaults without uttering a word, finally breaks his silence.

"Well," George says, "I guess the pressure of losing is getting to Yogi."

End of meeting.

With the Tigers running away from the field—they'll win 104 games and a World Series title—Steinbrenner decides to wait until the end of the season before firing Berra. It's a decision he'll regret. The Yankees promote several players from their farm clubs—including Meacham—and the injection of youth transforms the team. Riding the kids' enthusiasm and the hot bats of Don Mattingly and Dave Winfield—who battle for the batting title right down to the final day of the season—Berra's boys go 51–29, the best second-half record in baseball. It creates great optimism for next season, and George's hands are tied.

The atmosphere around the team, so tense in the season's first three months, improves dramatically as the players adjust to Yogi's relaxed style. Berra believes it's his job to decide who plays and where, and it's the players' job to play well and win. He'll keep the Boss off their backs—as best as he can—so they can concentrate on baseball.

The players generally enjoy this arrangement, though at times they think Yogi could be more hands-on. One example: the Yankees have a 1–0 lead with two runners on late in a game and Ron Guidry looks over at Yogi, wondering if his manager will call for a sac bunt or a hit-and-run to set up an insurance run. But it's clear Berra, standing behind the bat rack with arms folded across his chest, isn't planning to call a play.

"Hey, Skip," Guidry calls to Berra. "Don't you think you might want to make a move here?"

Berra glances over at Guidry, then moves two steps to his left.

"How's that?" Berra says.

The team is loose enough now for everyone to enjoy a good laugh on September 21 when a reporter tells Yogi he's mentioned in *Bartlett's Familiar Quotations*—and has been since 1980.

The following appears on page 903, he's told.

> Yogi (Lawrence Peter) Berra
> "The game isn't over 'til it's over."
> Attributed.

"Hey," says Berra, "I said that one."

It's also the day the Yankees beat the Tigers to move within a game of second-place Toronto. Winfield goes hitless while Mattingly singles to grab the lead for the batting title—.346 to .344—with 10 games to play. Yankee fans clearly favor Mattingly, and the issue of race has entered the conversation, something Yogi keeps out of his clubhouse. Indeed, Mattingly and Winfield are openly rooting for each other.

The Yankees can't catch Toronto, but the season ends with a 9–2 win against Detroit at the Stadium, their 87–75 record good for third place. Mattingly singles in the 8th inning—his fourth hit in the season's final game—raising his average to .343 and clinching the batting title. When Winfield, hitting next, reaches on a force out to finish at .340, Berra quickly sends in a pinch-runner, and the two players jog off the field together to thunderous applause from the 30,602 fans.

"This isn't announcement day," Steinbrenner says when asked about Yogi's status after the game. He has to see who's available, he tells reporters, before making his decision. Steinbrenner, who hasn't talked to Yogi since their explosive meeting in June, is still hoping to lure former Baltimore manager Earl Weaver out of retirement. "I don't know where to rate Yogi as a manager" is all he tells reporters about Berra.

Steinbrenner lets Yogi dangle for another month. He toys with the idea of promoting Lou Piniella, his hitting coach, but keeps remembering Piniella's answer when he asked him about Yogi late this season. "I think Yogi has rebuilt the pitching staff," Piniella told him. "Yogi got more aggressive as the season progressed. He's in better control of the team and turned the place around."

After an unsuccessful run at Weaver, Steinbrenner releases a statement on October 25, saying Berra will return. "Yogi did a very creditable job blending all of our fine veteran players with some outstanding young talent," was the best Steinbrenner could say about the first Yankee manager since Billy Martin in 1977 to return after working a full season.

But four days later, Steinbrenner elaborates on Berra's true status. If the Yankees get off to another slow start next season, George says, he would strongly consider firing his manager.

The year 1984 was one of mixed blessings for Yogi's youngest son. Coming off another solid '83 season at shortstop for the pennant-contending Pirates—and a new five-year, $3.05 million contract in his pocket—both Dale Berra and Pittsburgh management expected big things. But Berra didn't lift his batting average above .200 until mid-June, and he made so many errors both fans and the media began calling him Boo-Boo of Yogi Bear cartoon fame. The nickname stuck.

Berra suffered his first real injury, bursitis in his right elbow, and missed 22 games in September. The Pirates, five years removed from a World Series title, lost regularly and were booed roundly by their fans, who singled out Dale for extra abuse. The fans' treatment of Dale was so harsh and Berra's performance so poor—he hit .222 and committed a league-high 30 errors at shortstop in 136 games—that the Pirates decide trading Berra is in everyone's best interests.

Berra's personal life is a different story. Dale marries Leigh O'Grady, a local Jersey girl, on December 1, 1984. The newlyweds buy a house in upscale Glen Ridge, a five-minute ride from Carmen and Yogi. By midmonth there is serious talk that the Pirates might trade Dale to the Yankees, and a slew of stories about how Yogi will manage his son quickly follows.

"I know the both of them, and I am sure they will work it out," Carmen says. Her husband agrees. "If he plays well, he plays," says Yogi, who plans to move his son back to third base and platoon him with left-handed hitter Mike Pagliarulo if the trade goes through. "And if he doesn't play well, he sits. It's that simple."

Dale Berra knows the spotlight in New York will be far greater, but he feels the atmosphere in Pittsburgh is toxic. The Yankees, who earlier this month acquired Rickey Henderson—the best leadoff man in baseball—are contenders with a real chance to reach the World Series. So he's thrilled when a five-player deal sending him to New York is completed.

"Playing for my father," Dale tells the media when the trade's announced, "is like a dream come true."

But only days after the trade, that dream takes a dark turn. There were rumors all over Pittsburgh this season of a major investigation into cocaine use by baseball players. A few players were rumored to have cooperated with authorities, but no one in baseball knows for sure. That is about to change. Dale Berra is one of several players who have been subpoenaed to appear before a grand jury to testify about drug trafficking in Pittsburgh.

Berra knows plenty about that. He and several teammates have been buying coke from a group of seven men around the team—including a clubhouse caterer, Curtis Strong, and Kevin Koch, the man inside the team mascot costume—for at least the last four years. Dale started using cocaine at a friend's 1979 New Year's Eve party in Montclair, snorting off the end of a car key, then began using it about once a month in Pittsburgh. This is the 1980s, when cocaine is the hip drug for young and wealthy city dwellers, and it is being used—openly—in clubs and bars in cities all over the country. Pittsburgh is no exception.

Berra was using two to three times a week by 1983, and though confident his drug use was under control, he knew he'd lost a split second off his reflex time—the micro instant that's the difference between a major leaguer and a player in the minors. Losing that split second rarely happens at 27, a player's prime. When Berra got hurt last summer, his use of cocaine increased, though he remained convinced he still had a handle on the whole thing.

Now he has to tell all this to a grand jury in a federal courthouse in Pittsburgh in early January of 1985. But first he has to tell his parents. They sit in stunned silence as he goes through his story, stopping frequently to insist his drug use is under control. It's recreational, he tells his parents. He's not an addict. They don't have to worry.

And they don't have to be concerned about his grand jury appearance. He's a witness, he says, not the target. Don't worry, Dale repeats. It's going to be all right.

Yogi stares at his son for a few moments when Dale is done talking. Then he speaks. Mom and me care about you and want to help, Yogi says. Tell us what we can do. Dale reiterates his drug use is not a problem.

Finally, Yogi asks the one question he's always asked Dale.

"How are you doing?" Yogi says.

"I'm doing all right, Dad," Dale says. "Everything is fine."

★　　★　　★

The man George Steinbrenner wants to fire is sitting at the head table of the White House state dinner honoring King Fahd of Saudi Arabia, listening to President Ronald Reagan regale his guests with stories of his days as a radio announcer for the Chicago Cubs. Announcers did not travel with teams back in the 1930s, Reagan tells those at his table, and his job was to re-create the game from reports coming over the telegraph. But when the wire went dead in the 9th inning of a game against the St. Louis Cardinals of Berra's youth in 1934, Reagan had to improvise.

It's a story Reagan tells often, and at this state dinner on February 11, 1985, the President is telling it well. "I had [Billy] Jurges hit a foul ball, then I had him foul one that only missed being a home run by a foot," he says. "I had him foul one back in the stands and took up some time describing the two lads that got in a fight over the ball. I kept on having him hit foul balls until I was setting a record for a ballplayer hitting successive foul balls and I was getting more than a little scared."

He pauses. "Just then my operator started typing," Reagan says. "When he passed me the paper I started to giggle. It said, 'Jurges popped out on the first ball pitched.'"

The anecdote gets a big laugh. Berra enjoys the story, and the meal—salmon and sole mousse, chicken supreme, asparagus mimosa, lemon soufflé with raspberry sauce, and champagne. He gazes around the room, searching for familiar faces. Norman Vincent Peale is there. So are Pearl Bailey and Rita Moreno. Yogi is the only athlete on the guest list.

King Fahd speaks up, saying soccer is becoming a popular sport in his country. "I played that game as a kid," Berra says as Reagan beams. The President loves baseball players, and he has one of the best ever at his table.

Nellie Connally, the wife of former Texas Governor John Connally, is sitting to Yogi's left. She leans over and quietly tells Berra her husband very much wants to switch seats with her. "But I told him no," Nellie says with a smile.

When the last course of dinner is finished, Reagan signs autographs and insists on getting a signature from everyone at his table. Drinks and dancing to the music of an orchestra follow. It's not the first evening Berra has spent at the White House, but sitting at the head table and talking sports with a President and a king is one night he and Carmen will always treasure.

The day after the story appears, a newspaper reporter asks whom among the many interesting people at the dinner Yogi had spoken with. Yogi looks perplexed. "It was hard to have a conversation with anyone," he says. "There were so many people talking."

A week later, Berra is having a much different conversation in the Yankee spring training compound in Fort Lauderdale. He's called his coaches together five days before training camp officially opens on February 20 to outline everyone's roles and responsibilities. Yankee fan favorite Lou Piniella is retired now and will concentrate on his role as hitting instructor. Former manager Gene Michael is back to coach third base. Stump Merrill, the minor league manager Yogi worked under during the 1981 strike, is getting his shot to coach in the big leagues after winning six titles in seven seasons in the Yankee farm system. He'll take over at first and work with infielders.

Once business is done, it's time to play golf and get in some fishing before a leisurely dinner. It's a relaxed afternoon and evening, and everyone seems content. One day later, Steinbrenner makes an announcement. "Yogi will be the manager this year," Steinbrenner tells the media at Fort Lauderdale Stadium. "I said the same thing last year; I'm saying it again this year. A bad start will not affect Yogi's status.

"I have put a lot of pressure on my managers in the past to win at certain times. That will not be the case this spring."

It's the same message he gave Bob Lemon in 1982; Lemon was fired when the Yankees lost eight of their first 14 games. And it's the same message he gave to Berra in their first meeting of the spring. Asked by the writers what he thinks about George's endorsement, Berra says, "You don't think it means anything, do you?"

As if on cue, the big story the day after camp opens is about who will follow Yogi as Yankee manager. "Lou Piniella will probably be the next manager, but I don't know about next year," Steinbrenner tells a writer from his home in Tampa. "It's not in the cards right now. Yogi's going to be the manager this season.

"At the end of the year, we'll sit down and see how Yogi feels. He's 61. [Actually, Yogi will be 60.] We don't know if he'll want to retire. Someday Lou will be the manager. I think everybody realizes that."

No one is fooled by Steinbrenner's timetable. Everyone, especially Yogi, recognizes the reminder to pay attention to what George does, not what he says. Berra's team hasn't even made it to the exhibition season and he's already answering questions about his job status.

Yogi is sitting in his underwear in his office early the next morning when Piniella, looking as if he hadn't slept, knocks on the open door.

"Yogi, I'd like to talk to you," Piniella says.

"Sure, Lou, what's up?" Yogi says.

"This manager thing that has been in the papers—"

"Aw, don't worry about that crap."

"Yogi, I'm sorry this thing ever happened. The last thing I would do is undermine you. If you don't want me on your coaching staff, if you think it would be easier without me, I'll pack my bags now and go home and get out of your way."

"Hell, no," Yogi says. "You just stay here and do what you are doing. You work well with the hitters. I want you to stay. I'll teach you whatever I can. You just watch and listen and do your job."

Piniella follows Berra's orders, but it's hard to work with hitters when they can't suit up, and the Yankees have a bundle of players sidelined with injuries most of the spring. Don Mattingly is still recovering from arthroscopic surgery on the knee he injured just before training camp. Mike Pagliarulo, slotted to be the left-handed hitting side of the third base platoon with Berra's son Dale, has a hyperextended elbow. Willie Randolph plays with an injured foot all spring. Dave Winfield and Rickey Henderson hurt their backs on successive days in late March: Winfield is back in the lineup as Opening Day nears, but Rickey will miss the season's first 10 games.

Steinbrenner keeps Berra and his coaches busy with endless meetings after practices and games, and they're on edge when their season opens April 8 in Boston. Everyone can feel George's eagerness to get rid of Berra, and the drumbeat starts when the Yankees lose the season's first two games in Boston, 9–2 and 14–5. Steinbrenner says the next game—the season's third game!—is "crucial," and the Yanks lose that one as well, 6–4.

Worse, the team travels to Columbus, Ohio the next day to play their top farm club and loses 14–5, looking sloppy and uninterested. Steinbrenner rips the entire team but singles out the manager's son. "Dale Berra is out there laughing," Steinbrenner says. "I don't like to see anything taken lightly. Columbus is taking it to us, and he's out there laughing."

Steinbrenner's choice of players was obvious, if not ironic. The father-son story has run its course without incident, and Dale, a starter at shortstop with the Pirates, has taken to platooning at third base without complaint. Yogi could see his son was having trouble fitting in with his new teammates, but Dale was playing well. The Yankees win their next four games, all with Berra playing third base and hitting .300. Steinbrenner is silent. Yogi even delivers a Yogi-ism before the Yankees' home opener.

"A home opener is always exciting," Berra says, "no matter if it's at home or on the road." Everyone laughs.

But the Yankees follow their four-game winning streak with four losses in five games and the owner's silence ends. After the Red Sox beat New York in 11 innings to drop the Yankees to 5–6, Steinbrenner tells reporters Yogi's immediate future is unclear. So much for getting a whole season.

"I haven't made any decision," says Steinbrenner, who reveals he's been back in touch with Earl Weaver. "But I'm not going to be deterred. What I think is best for the team is what I'm going to do."

What can Yogi say? He's sure he doesn't have many games left. "He must think we don't have feelings," Berra says. "We don't like to lose, either. It's tough to manage when every move you make, you're wondering what he's going to say about it. The players are uptight and you can't play this game when you're uptight."

When the writers leave, Berra turns to Piniella. "If they want to get me, why in hell don't they get it over with?" he says. "Why do they keep hunting me down?"

The Yankees split the next two games with Boston, and the beat writers are on high alert. When the Yankees lose the first two games of a three-game series in Chicago, falling to 6–9, Steinbrenner calls GM Clyde King, who is traveling with the team. We're making a change, he tells King. Yogi is out! Billy is coming back and will meet the team in Texas, the next stop after Sunday's game against the White Sox.

"Give Yogi the news after the game," Steinbrenner instructs King.

The Yankees lose Sunday's game to the White Sox, who score the winning run on a bases-loaded walk in the 9th inning. Berra is talking to the media when King enters his office and asks the reporters to leave. Everyone knows what comes next. King tells Yogi this is the hardest thing he's ever had to do, then gives him the news. "He's the boss," says Berra, shrugging his shoulders, a look of relief washing over him. His ordeal is over after 16 games. "He can do whatever he wants."

While King is talking to Berra, Yankee publicity man Joe Safety is handing a four-paragraph statement from Steinbrenner to the media. It's April 28, and the Yankees are changing managers. Again. "This action has been taken by the Yankees, and we feel that it is in the best interests of the club," Steinbrenner's statement reads.

The clubhouse is silent until designated hitter Don Baylor picks up a large trash can and tosses it across the room, garbage flying in every direction. Suddenly almost every player is cursing loudly, upset that

Yogi is gone, angry that Billy is coming back. Dale Berra is walking out of the shower, a towel around his waist, when he sees pieces of trash coming his way. "What's going on?" he asks Mattingly.

"They just fired your dad," answers Mattingly, who stalks into the trainer's room and is soon flinging metal containers against the walls. Ashen-faced and still wrapped in a towel, Dale opens the door to his father's office, walks in, and closes the door behind him. He doesn't have to say a word.

"Don't you worry about me," Yogi tells his son. "I've done everything in baseball there is to do. So don't worry. I'll be all right."

Father and son embrace, and Dale is sobbing. His father doesn't deserve this.

"Look, you're still young—you have a future," says Yogi, who pulls back and puts his meaty hands on his son's shoulders. "Billy's a good man; you've known him since you were a kid. Play hard for him."

The father forces a smile for his son. "I'll be watching you."

Dale hugs Yogi and leaves the office, his eyes red from crying. One by one, Berra's players come in to talk to their suddenly former manager. Most shake Yogi's hand, several embrace him, more than a few emerge with tears rolling down their cheeks. Berra walks out to talk to the rest of his players and coaches. Mattingly simply hugs Yogi, unable to speak. Gene Michael, twice fired as Yankee manager, leans over and whispers, "I know how you feel."

The writers stand and watch as the emotional scene plays out. They've all written too many "Yankee manager is fired" stories, but none involved tears. Now they're in Yogi's office, listening to a man who does not sound bitter or angry. "He's the boss," says Yogi. "I'm used to this. This is the third time I've been fired."

Someone says 16 games is a pretty short season. "Did I have a chance?" Berra says. "He [Steinbrenner] must have thought so.

"Look, I had an inkling. If it happened now or later, what's the difference? I still think this is a good club, and they'll turn it around. Me, I'm going to play some golf."

He's asked if he'd work for Steinbrenner in another role. "I don't know," Yogi says. "He hasn't asked me. My contract doesn't say I have to. But I'll still be at the Stadium to see Dale play."

His final interview session over, Berra collects his things and reaches for the phone. He needs a cab to take him to the airport for his trip back to New Jersey. But King convinces him to ride with the team, so there is Yogi, sitting in his customary seat in the front row of one of the two team buses, the players sitting silently behind him. The Yankee buses stop at the United Airlines terminal, and the players clap loudly as Yogi ambles down the steps and begins his walk to the terminal.

"Good luck, Yog," one player shouts, and now the players and coaches are all shouting out encouragement. Yogi turns, gives them a small wave, then continues his walk to the terminal, a short, slump-shouldered, soon-to-be 60-year-old man carrying a small bag, on his way home to talk over the future with his wife.

Carmen Berra is not nearly as calm about the day's events when her husband arrives home. She's never forgiven Ralph Houk for firing Yogi after he took the Yankees to a World Series as a rookie manager in 1964. But this? Steinbrenner hounded Yogi for weeks, then fired him after 16 games, most of them played without several of his best players? This is just ludicrous.

"Yogi, don't you ever step foot in that stadium again," she tells him. "Not as long as *that man* owns the team." Yogi knows not to argue when his wife is this upset, but she's asking a lot. And she keeps repeating it all night. At least one member of this marriage is fuming, and that isn't going to end any time soon.

Murray Chass of the *New York Times* reaches Berra the next day, and Yogi is not ready to cut all ties with his team. He tells Chass he expects to talk to Steinbrenner in the next week and discuss what George might have in mind. He quickly says he's unsure if he would accept any role.

Berra says it would have been good to see what this team could do at full strength. "We only had my full starting lineup in five of 16 games," he says, adding he wished he could have talked about this team with Steinbrenner. But the two men still haven't spoken since their blowup at the Stadium last June. All communication since has been through Clyde King.

Yogi is still mulling over Carmen's words when he finishes his conversation with Chass. "Steinbrenner paid my salary," Berra says. "He gave me a chance to manage. Right now I don't feel good about being fired, but I'll get over it. Sure, I would've liked more time. But I beat Lemon by two games."

Berra chuckles and hangs up, but the longer he thinks about Carmen's stand, the more sense it makes. His good friend John McMullen is giving him the same advice, and the salty language Mac uses makes it clear how he feels about what his former partner has done.

By July, Yogi's position has shifted: he's not going back to Yankee Stadium as long as George owns the team. He makes no announcement, but the Yankees begin to get the idea when Berra declines an invitation to the Old-Timers' Game on July 13, saying he would be out of town. Everyone knows the Old-Timers' Game might be Berra's favorite day of the season. This will be the first one he's missed since he managed the Mets a decade ago.

Yogi's stance is made clearer when a reporter decides to call Berra's home the day of the game. Carmen answers, and the reporter, who is not at all surprised that the Berras are not out of town, asks if Yogi is in. "No, he's playing golf," Carmen says. "We were going to go away, but we decided not to go, so he's playing golf."

Yogi and Carmen are in Cooperstown two weeks later for the induction of Lou Brock, Hoyt Wilhelm, Enos Slaughter, and Arky Vaughan to the Hall of Fame. This is another chance to catch up with old friends, and Yogi loves every minute of his time here. Berra is signing autographs under a large tent on Main Street when *New York Daily News* writer Bill Madden walks over and stops at the table where Yogi is stationed.

"Have you gotten over it yet?" Madden says. No need to explain what "it" is.

"Would you?" Berra says. "Sixteen games."

Madden sees Berra is more upset now than he was the day he was fired.

"I hope we'll be seeing you around the park," the writer says.

"Not as long as he's there," Yogi says. No need to explain who "he" is, either.

Berra is right about his former team. It takes some time, but the Yankees do put it all together. And on September 12, they beat first-place Toronto in the first of four games at the Stadium to pull within 1½ games of the Blue Jays. But the Yankees lose the next three, the beginning of an eight-game losing streak that effectively ends their season. And Martin's fourth tour as Yankee manager is all but over in late September when he gets into a late-night brawl with New York pitcher Eddie Whitson in the team's hotel bar in Baltimore.

Three weeks after leading his team to a 97–64 record and a second-place finish, Martin is replaced by Lou Piniella. The rookie manager soon asks Yogi to join his coaching staff, but Berra turns him down. He's not working for Steinbrenner again. Ever. Instead, he takes his friend John McMullen's offer to be the bench coach in Houston, helping another rookie manager, Hal Lanier, the son of Yogi's old friend Max, a former St. Louis Cardinal pitcher. For the first time since joining the Yankees in 1947, Yogi Berra will not be wearing the home uniform of a New York baseball team.

Things have not worked out as well for Dale Berra, and his parents are worried. And it's not related to Dale's poor season—he played only 37 games under Martin, hitting a meager .176. They realize he's used cocaine for at least four years and fear for his future and reputation. It's painful to watch reporters and cameras follow Dale into a federal courthouse for witness testimony in a public criminal proceeding, forced to describe purchasing cocaine and how it made him feel. It's a sickening, helpless nightmare for his parents.

On September 9, Dale Berra sat on the witness stand in the federal courthouse in Pittsburgh, dressed in gray slacks, white shirt, red tie, and blue blazer, and talked for two hours. He was the fourth player to testify in the government's case charging clubhouse caterer Curtis Strong with 16 counts of cocaine distribution. In the same courtroom three days earlier, Mets All-Star first baseman Keith Hernandez admitted he used cocaine for three years while playing for St. Louis, using "massive amounts" in the second half of the 1980 season.

"I think it was the love-affair years," Hernandez said about the use of coke inside baseball. "It was pretty prevalent."

Like every player in this case, Berra had been granted immunity in exchange for his two days of testimony. Yes, he bought cocaine from Strong when the Pirates played in Philadelphia. "I handed him $100....He handed me a gram....I used it in my room and in Lee Lacy's room," Berra testified. "It made me feel euphoric; it sharpened my senses. It made me feel good."

Dale admitted he snorted cocaine with Pirate star Dave Parker and got amphetamines from team leader Willie Stargell—who only hours later would insist Berra's claim about him was untrue. Dale called his use of cocaine "sporadic" and "occasional" until he was hurt last season and used the drug more frequently. "I just thought it was an opportune time to do something," he said.

Berra insisted he "absolutely did not" use cocaine after the Pirates traded him to the Yankees. The packed courtroom grew especially quiet when Strong's defense attorney asked Berra to describe his father's reaction when he learned his son had a drug habit. "He was very supportive of me," Dale Berra answered. "Obviously it wasn't an easy thing to do. But he's been such a good father to me his whole life. He accepted it and stood behind me."

His father was still processing everything when he got another surprise. Soon after Berra's court appearance, Steinbrenner revealed a conversation he had had with Dale about drugs before the season, a talk kept secret from Yogi. If you do anything to embarrass your father—you're gone, Steinbrenner told Dale, who agreed to be drug-tested twice during the season. Dale is clean, Steinbrenner told reporters, and his job here is safe as long as he stays clean.

The Berra family knows all about the perils of listening to anything Steinbrenner says.

Now they are wondering whether they can believe everything Dale tells them, too.

# PART VI

## SAINT YOGI
### 1986–2015

# CHAPTER 37

# Different Stripes
## 1986–1989

**Y**ogi Berra, tanned and spry at almost 61, walks into Osceola County Stadium in Kissimmee, Florida. It's a late March morning in 1986, and for the first time in his 40 seasons in major league baseball, Berra isn't wearing a Yankee or Mets uniform. This one reads ASTROS in large white block letters hovering over a white star. It's the workout jersey of the Houston Astros, Berra's new team.

But neither the jersey nor the new team matters to the legion of fans lined up along the wire-mesh fence hours before Houston's exhibition game this afternoon. They are here to glimpse the squat, knock-kneed Hall of Fame catcher. And, if they're lucky, maybe score his autograph.

"Yogi, Yogi, our Yogi," shouts a middle-aged woman the moment she spots Berra emerging from the dugout. His gold-framed sunglasses gleaming in the Florida sun, Berra walks over to her, a bat with the familiar inscription NO. 8 tucked under his left arm. He smiles and signs the first of many autographs.

"Yogi, can I get a picture of you with my kids?" a man asks. Berra pushes his blue cap back on his head and smiles as the father clicks off several pictures. "Uh-oh," Yogi says to Astro infielder Craig Reynolds as he moves to sign his next autograph. "I had a toothpick in my mouth."

A fan hands Yogi an old baseball card to sign, and Berra is intrigued. "Gee, I was young there," he says. Reynolds looks over and seems almost stunned to see Yogi in his younger years. "How old were you there?" says Reynolds, a 33-year-old entering his 12th season.

"This is about 1951," answers Berra, who won the first of his three MVP awards that season at 26.

"Heck, I wasn't even born then!" teases Reynolds, playfully jabbing Yogi in the ribs. Berra's been an Astro coach for little more than a month, but the team already feels comfortable poking fun at their new old man. "I'm just happy to be in a uniform," Berra tells a writer from New York.

Yogi's next stop is the Astro dugout, where he answers the New Yorker's questions before practice. Yes, having the summer off last year—his first summer off in 43 years—was strange, but he tried to enjoy his break. He and Carmen took a cruise and he played lots of golf, including a bunch of charity golf tournaments. "There are so many," he says. "You can play in one just about every day."

Berra confirms he declined an offer from his friend Astro owner John McMullen to manage his team this season. "We are good friends, and I want it to remain that way," says Yogi with a smile and a wink. He agreed to become a coach only after Hal Lanier, the team's rookie manager, came to Montclair to insist he wanted Berra on his staff.

"You'll be a big help," Lanier emphasized, so Yogi has spent five weeks hitting fly balls to outfielders, loading the pitching machine in the batting cage, working with catchers and the younger Astros— anything Lanier asks. "I've been doin' this since I was 14 years old," he tells the writer. "I don't know what else to do."

Just then a voice interrupts the conversation. "Hi, Yogi," says Bert Blyleven, a veteran pitcher with the Twins, the Astros' opponent this afternoon. "How's Dale doin'?"

"Okay," Berra says. "Okay."

Blyleven walks past the Astro dugout and Berra returns to the writer. "That's one of the old Pirate guys," says Yogi, somber now. Dale, identified as one of 21 MLB players using cocaine, has just taken a deal Commissioner Peter Ueberroth offered in late February to the seven most involved users: instead of serving a one-year suspension, Dale chose to donate 10 percent of this season's salary—$51,500 for Berra—to drug programs, perform 200 hours of community service in two years, and agree to career-long random drug testing. (The other 14 players received lesser penalties, with all agreeing to random drug testing.) In exchange for their trial testimony against a dealer, Berra and the other MLB players face no criminal charges. Despite all this, Dale hopes new Yankees manager Lou Piniella will give him a real shot at playing time this season.

And Dale's told Carmen and Yogi he's kicked his cocaine habit.

"I didn't understand why he did it," Berra says. "I guess, you know, you go to parties and everyone's having a good time. But you gotta be able to say no. I said if he wants to stay in the game he'd have to kick it. I hear it's like alcohol. You just gotta be able to stay away from it."

Berra pauses.

"I think he's all right now," Yogi says. "I gotta call him tonight. We talk on the phone about every 10 days."

Yogi enjoys training with his new team, and on April 8, Opening Day, he wears the Astro home jersey—white with large orange and yellow horizontal stripes. The Astros lose their opener but win 10 of their next 13 to jump into first place in the NL West, where they spend most of the season. They win 96 games and the division title— the second in franchise history—and face the New York Mets in a best-of-seven series for the NL pennant. Every New York paper runs a story about Yogi's magic touch, but the magic ends in Game 6, a postseason classic that goes 16 innings before the Astros fall, 7–6.

Even so, Houston is optimistic. The Astros lost two games to the Mets in extra innings and three games by a single run. And with Cy Young winner Mike Scott, ageless Nolan Ryan, and a good young nucleus— and Yogi on their side—a return to the postseason looks almost certain.

Tom Villante and Yogi Berra have been friends since the late 1940s, when Berra was a rookie catcher and Villante, a former Yankee batboy and infield prospect, was a student at Lafayette College. Villante, who quit baseball and went on to an ultrasuccessful career in advertising, has always been fascinated with his friend's love of movies. And he's long been intrigued by how much Yogi's teammates enjoyed his reviews—and relied on his judgment. In the early days of 1988, Villante has an idea: he wants Yogi to do 30-second movie reviews, which he will sell to a sponsor and syndicate around the nation.

"We'll see," Yogi tells Villante, who knows "We'll see" is Yogi-speak for "No." So Villante makes another run at his friend in the den of Berra's home in Montclair. And this time Carmen, who handles the couple's business matters, is sitting in. "All you have to do is sit in a chair and answer a few questions," Villante says. "We'll shoot about a dozen or so for the year, a few of them at a time. And I think I can get you about $100,000."

Yogi is still unconvinced, but Carmen perks up.

"How much did you say we'll get paid?"

"About $100,000," Villante repeats.

Carmen looks at her husband. "I want a new kitchen," she announces. Then, turning back to Villante: "He'll do it."

The format is simple: Berra summarizes a movie in one sentence, then answers three or four questions from Villante, who's offstage. After a commercial break, Berra is back on air with "Yogi's Scoreboard," the segment in which he rates the movie a single, double, triple, or home run. If he thinks the film is a clunker, he calls it a strikeout. Villante sells the package, which will run in 64 markets across the country, to the Stroh Brewery Company.

The initial session is in a studio in Manhattan. First at-bat: *Fatal Attraction.*

"Was it a thriller, Yogi?"

"A thriller? You should see the last 15 minutes of that movie. I couldn't even see it!"

"Yogi, did you get scared?" Villante asks.

"No, I didn't get scared, you know," he says, "until it came to the part where you get scared."

Villante wants Berra's take on the movie's star, Glenn Close. But Yogi keeps calling the actress "Glen Cove"—a Long Island suburb near Whitey Ford's house—and that footage hits the cutting-room floor.

And how does Berra rate the movie? "I give it a home run," he says.

Yogi slowly adjusts to his new gig. Just before a session at his home in Montclair, he sits on a stool, twisting the two big rings he's wearing, one from his induction to the Hall of Fame, the other from the Yankees' fifth straight World Series title in 1953. He's reviewing the action movie *Above the Law* and Villante asks his opinion of the film's star, Steven Seagal.

"He could be another Cliff Eastwick," says Yogi, conflating actor Clint Eastwood with former relief pitcher Rawly Eastwick—and someone named Cliff. The technicians are laughing so hard Villante has to stop taping. But Yogi's blooper is the one-minute spot's highlight, just as Villante expected.

Some of Yogi's instant classics:

"Hey, Yogi, whaddya think of *Biloxi Blues*?" Villante says.

"It reminded me of being in the Army—even though I was in the Navy."

"Did you guess the ending in *Masquerade*?"

"No, I couldn't," says Berra. "Towards the end you could."

"Hey, Yogi, what'd you think of Cher in *Moonstruck*?" Villante asks.

"She did a good job," Yogi says. "She got the Golden Glove Award."

Villante titles the segment *Yogi at the Movies* and TV sports anchors nationwide can't resist doing a spot on Berra's new gig. Like most of Berra's projects, the ads are a hit. They run for two seasons—Yogi earns a big payday and sportswriters get new Yogi-isms for their stories.

And Carmen gets her new kitchen.

As Yogi prepares for his fourth Astro spring training in February of 1989, he privately expects this to be his last season in a major league baseball uniform. He'll turn 64 in May, and he's tired of all the airports, hotel rooms, and restaurant food. Most of all, after three years as an Astro coach, he's tired of living six months away from home. He has six grandchildren, with a seventh on the way. He missed much of his three sons' childhoods and he's determined not to do the same with his grandchildren.

He won't announce until fall, and he's hoping for a good final season. But the Astros are in Atlanta on April 20 when expectations for a pleasant final year fade. The team is about to leave for the ballpark when Astro director of public relations Rob Matwick tells Yogi he's just received bad news about Dale: Berra's youngest son was arrested early this morning in a big cocaine bust.

Berra is stunned. He knew the years since his son's last brush with cocaine had been tough on Dale. The Yankees released him on July 27, 1986, and in what was widely seen as a favor to his father, the Astros signed Dale to a minor league contract eight days later. When Dale was called up to Houston late in the '87 season, Yogi could see his son—who at 30 was still in his prime—no longer possessed the quick reflexes that once made him a hot prospect. Dale moved to Baltimore's top minor league team in 1988, but he was released at season's end and called it quits. It was also the final year of Berra's five-year, $3.05 million contract.

And now Dale Berra is one of 23 people arrested after a six-month investigation into cocaine distribution and use in northern New Jersey. Two police officers arrested him at home at 8 a.m. and searched the house in the presence of his shocked wife Leigh while their two-year-old daughter slept.

After finding two vials containing traces of cocaine, officers drove Dale to the Morristown police station, where he was charged with conspiracy to violate New Jersey narcotics laws. Berra was fingerprinted, photographed, held until his $5,000 bail was posted, and was home in Glen Ridge at 3 p.m.

Yogi finds out shortly after, and reporters soon swarm. "I'm sorry, but Yogi will not be talking to the media," says Astro Assistant GM

Bob Watson. The team, Watson says, "is going to give Yogi all the moral support we can."

Watson, who has fond memories of Yogi from playing with the Yankees in 1980 and '81, knows the next few days will be rough. DALE BERRA ARRESTED IN DRUG PROBE reads one headline on the ubiquitous story, and every report mentions that the 32-year-old Dale is Yogi's son.

It takes several months for Dale's case to wind through the justice system. Meanwhile, the Astros have a solid season under new manager Art Howe—they'll finish 86–76—and Yogi finds a new project in the team's rookie catcher Craig Biggio. He likes Biggio's bat and athleticism, and wonders if the kid's speed is wasted behind the plate. Think about shifting the 23-year-old to a different position, Berra suggests to Astro officials, adding that Biggio could become a big star.

A week before season's end, Berra announces he's retiring. The media conference is understated, as Berra desires, and barely noted outside Houston and New York. Yogi will help out in spring training for a few more years and advise his friend Astro owner John McMullen. But his days of coaching a 162-game season are over.

"I've got seven grandkids, and I want to see more of them," Berra tells reporters. "I want a chance to travel a little bit before I die."

But first he wants to know what's ahead for Dale, whose case is unresolved. The two spent time together when Yogi was home for the All-Star break, and Dale swore he was finished with drugs. He makes the same assurances to prosecutors, who have evidence that Berra met three times with the drug dealer at the investigation's center. They also have recordings of the two men discussing a cocaine transaction.

Prosecutors recommend a pretrial intervention program. If approved by a judge, writes Morristown's *Daily Record,* Dale would submit to regular drug tests, pay a fine of $1,095, and give 72 one-hour antidrug lectures. He must also agree to testify against co-defendants arrested with him in the drug raid, and tour the Morris County jail. If all goes well for three years of supervision, the felony charges will be dismissed and removed from his record.

On October 27, Dale Berra is in a Morristown courtroom, about a half-hour drive from his parents' home, where Judge Reginald Stanton says he has accepted the prosecutor's recommendation. But Stanton has reservations about the former major league shortstop delivering antidrug lectures to high school kids. "It's sometimes better for people like Mr. Berra to shut up and be quiet," Stanton says.

Dale Berra assures the judge he can have a positive effect. "When a kid hears it from me it has an impact," he says. "I can tell them what drugs did to me, did to my career, and did to my family."

Yogi, who has publicly stood by his son, is pleased with Dale's response to the judge.

And he prays Dale listens to himself.

# CHAPTER 38

# Filling the Void
## 1990–1995

After a rainout, a snow-out, and an owners' lockout, the New York Yankees open the 1990 season on April 12, beating the Cleveland Indians 6–4 before 50,114 fans. Whitey Ford is there for a touching Opening Day ceremony—Billy Martin Jr. throws the first pitch in honor of his father, who died in a car crash this past Christmas Day. Phil Rizzuto is starting his 34th season in the broadcast booth. Both old Yankees had asked their friend and former teammate to end his boycott and join them at Yankee Stadium. And both received the same answer.

"No way!" Yogi Berra vowed.

Berra hasn't been to an Opening Day, Old-Timers' Day, or any other day at Yankee Stadium since George Steinbrenner fired him by messenger after 16 games in 1985. Even the opportunity in 1988 to stand beside his mentor Bill Dickey when the Yankees affixed plaques for both men at Monument Park couldn't change his mind. Instead, Berra spends his first Opening Day in 44 years out of an MLB uniform playing golf and watching the Yankees on television.

Rizzuto and Ford are far from the only ones wondering when Yogi will relent, a situation Yankee players, officials, and fans all blame on Steinbrenner. Joe DiMaggio remains the greatest living Yankee, and Mickey Mantle is still the idol of the baby boom generation. But there's little question Berra is the most beloved Bronx Bomber, and his every absence from the Stadium is a story.

It happens again on July 15, when the Yankees honor Rizzuto on his 50th year with the team as both player and broadcaster. Joe D is there. So are old friends Whitey, Bill Skowron, and Tommy Byrne. Berra, who received an invitation, replied he would be on the aircraft carrier USS *Enterprise* off the Virginia coast with his friend John McMullen, a former naval commander.

"I had dinner with Yogi about three weeks ago," the 72-year-old Rizzuto says. "He told me he'll never set foot in Yankee Stadium as long as George Steinbrenner owned the team. I told him I respected how he felt."

There is speculation Yogi will return a few weeks later when news breaks that Steinbrenner has accepted a lifetime ban imposed by Commissioner Fay Vincent on July 30, George's punishment for paying $40,000 to a gambler to dig up dirt on Yankee star Dave Winfield. Berra dismisses that, too.

"To me, I don't think he's out of it yet, so I don't know when I'll come back," Berra tells a reporter in late August, a week after Steinbrenner resigned as managing partner of the Yankees. Has he had any communication with the Boss? "I waved at him in a [winter] meeting once," acknowledges Berra. "But speak? Nope."

Berra says it hurts watching his good friend and six-time All-Star Don Mattingly endure this awful Yankee season—the team will finish 67–95, its worst record since 1913—but insists he's enjoying his first year of retirement. He's busy playing in charity golf tournaments nationwide, running the family racquetball business, and spending time with his grandchildren.

"Carmen hasn't thrown me out of the house yet," he says. "So it's been all right."

Berra again refuses an invitation to the Yankees' Opening Day in 1991, this one delivered by GM and good friend Gene Michael. It's the first question Claire Smith of the *New York Times* asked him in late March during Yogi's second season as an Astro spring training coach. Smith, who reported on the Yankees for the *Hartford Courant* in 1983, was the first African-American woman to cover any baseball beat. Claire was smart, savvy, and fair, and Yogi liked and trusted her.

Does he miss being at the Stadium? Smith asks.

"Sure," he tells her. "Heck, I played there 17 years."

Smith probes: Will he go to this season's Old-Timers' Game?

"You mean on July 17?" says Yogi, who's missed the date by 10 days. "Nope."

Sure, he'll miss being with Mickey, Whitey, Moose, and the rest of the old gang. That's the tough part, he agreed. But at least he sees them at charity golf tournaments, including one he started in New Jersey in June of 1991 for Boy Scouts with special needs.

And Yogi sees some of his former teammates — as well as old opponents like Ted Williams and Bob Feller — at Cooperstown for the annual induction of new entrants to the Hall of Fame. Now that he's no longer working during the baseball season, Induction Weekend highlights Berra's summer. The next one, on July 21, is special: Joe Garagiola has been honored by the media with the Ford C. Frick Award for baseball broadcasting.

The two men's paths have not crossed often in recent years. But their bond endures, even though Garagiola still occasionally uses Yogi as a good-natured punch line. "Joe is not the only one who has used me as a stooge," Berra says in a second autobiography, *Yogi: It Ain't Over,* written with friend and author Tom Horton in 1989. They used one chapter to distinguish the Yogi-isms Berra actually said from the ones concocted by others — including Garagiola. "It was good for him to say all he has said about me," Berra wrote, "and it has been good for me, too."

Yogi understands Garagiola's stories have helped to make him a beloved national personality, so he's not surprised this summer when he's told *The New Yorker* magazine wrote, "Hardly anyone would quarrel that Winston Churchill has been replaced by Yogi Berra as the favorite source of quotations." Garagiola and Berra still call each other on their birthdays, and when they get together, they are suddenly back on The Hill, nagging their parents about playing baseball.

On the sunny third Sunday of July, Berra is one of 31 Hall of Famers on a platform before the National Baseball Library in Cooperstown as Garagiola delivers his acceptance speech. "I don't remember ever not knowing Yogi," Garagiola tells the audience. "And when I called Yogi, I said, 'Yog, I'm going to get the Ford Frick Award.' And as only Yogi would put it, he said, 'What took you so long?'"

The audience loves it, and Garagiola tells more Yogi stories before replying to the question his friend had asked.

"Well, to answer him, I don't know, Yog. We're in different buildings, but we're in Cooperstown together," says Garagiola, choking up a bit. "I can bet you that Poppa Peter and Momma Paulina Berra, and Poppa John and Momma Angelina, are pretty proud.

"And we can both say, we told you not to worry about us. Look who we're hanging around with now."


It's the cold early weeks of 1992, and Yogi Berra is preparing for his final season as an Astro spring training instructor. And that's when the family gets word from friends that Yogi hoped—prayed—he'd never hear: his son Dale is using cocaine again. He and Carmen knew Dale was going through a tough time. His marriage to Leigh had fallen apart almost two years ago—Dale admits his drug use drove them apart—and their divorce was made official on January 8. And he still hasn't found his niche after leaving baseball more than three years ago.

But going back to drugs? Again? That just isn't acceptable—indeed, it's time for the family to have a very serious talk with its youngest member. The Berras' two older sons are alerted and on their way to the big house on Highland Avenue when Yogi picks up the phone and calls Dale.

"Get up and get over here" is the first thing Yogi says. "I want to talk to you" are his only other words. Dale doesn't ask any questions. He hasn't heard this tone in his father's voice in a very long time, but he knows Yogi is angry and that can only mean trouble.

Dale walks into his parents' house and finds his father, mother, and two brothers sitting quietly in the living room. Larry and Tim talk first, telling their little brother they all know about his drug use. There are words of support from his family, but words of disappointment, too. When Dale looks back on that day, he'll remember his brothers looking grim, his mother crying, and his father telling him something he never thought he'd hear.

If this continues, Yogi said, Dale would no longer be part of the family.

Dale knows how stubborn his father can be, and can tell from the tone of his voice and the expression on his face that this is no idle threat. His father, who has supported him through all his troubles, has just drawn the line. Dale, shaken, swears he'll never use cocaine again, and years later said publicly it was a promise kept.

Yogi and Carmen are grateful their friends spoke up. No one in the Berra family ever discussed it with friends again and none of their friends asked. They knew Yogi and Carmen were crushed to learn Dale was using cocaine in 1985. And their devastation was again evident when Dale was arrested and faced a judge four years later.

The friends are happy — and amazed — that news of Dale's relapse doesn't leak to the press or law enforcement. Montclair is a small town, and tales of trouble — especially involving the town's most famous residents — tend to travel fast. But the only news comes several months later from the *New York Times,* which reports Dale's court-ordered supervision has ended on June 25, 1992. The original charges have been dismissed and the record of his arrest has been expunged.

A chapter in the Berras' life closes.

Another opens when Carmen calls an old friend. Concerned about Dale's future, she phones Tom Villante and asks whether the advertising exec can meet with Dale and Tim. Of course, responds Villante, who meets the two Berras in his Manhattan office. After a handful of questions, Villante suggests Tim and Dale form a company to market their father, handling everything from card shows to commercials to all the hundreds of requests for autographs.

The Berra family loves the idea and by early 1993, Larry, Tim, Dale, and Tim's wife Betsy form LTD Enterprises. The selling of Yogi Berra is now a family business.

Yogi will one day tell his good buddy Ron Guidry that the half dozen years following his last spring training with the Astros in '92 were just about the worst time of his life. He missed the game—the clubhouse banter, sharing his knowledge with younger players, even the smell of the perfectly cut grass as he walked onto the field. Mostly he missed seeing his old teammates and competitors. He only had to return to Yankee Stadium to fill that void, but as long as George Steinbrenner owned the Yankees, that path was closed.

Still, there is plenty of happiness in his life. His grandchildren are a joy. He loves playing golf at Montclair Golf Club and looks forward to his Wednesday night poker game in the club's Grill Room; Carmen knows never to schedule anything for that night. His circle of friends grows wider, and couples like makeup executive Bobbi Brown and her husband Steve Plofker, a real estate developer, become regulars at their dinner parties. Carmen loves to entertain, and an invite to a Berra party is a prized possession.

Yogi becomes a member of the Hall of Fame's Veterans Committee and has the joy of telling Phil Rizzuto on February 25, 1994, that the Scooter will finally enter the Hall. "Did Yogi call collect?" Rizzuto asked his wife upon learning Berra was calling with important news.

And he continues to see some of his former teammates at card shows, which become considerably easier to manage beginning in 1993 when his sons recruit Kevin McLaughlin—a young collector and Yankee fan—to organize the long autograph sessions. McLaughlin becomes Yogi's trusted assistant and friend for life.

After two seasons, Steinbrenner's lifetime ban from baseball is commuted on March 1, 1993, and just after midnight that evening George tells New York sports radio host Suzyn Waldman and her WFAN audience that he wants Yogi back. "I'm planning to work through Yogi's wife," he says, "to get Carm to intercede for me." But nothing changes.

Berra sees Steinbrenner from time to time at somber occasions. Some of Yogi's teammates and baseball friends have begun to die: Eddie Lopat and Sandy Amoros in 1992. Roy Campanella and Bill Dickey in 1993. Allie Reynolds in 1994. On August 13, 1995, Yogi is playing at the Bob Hope Desert Classic in Palm Springs when he learns Mickey Mantle has surrendered to liver cancer at age 63. Dolores Hope offers Yogi her husband's private plane to attend the funeral in Dallas and serve as pallbearer. Steinbrenner attends, leading Yankee officials.

The two men see each other again at the funeral of fabled Yankee announcer Mel Allen in June 1996, where they exchange a few words. "I talk to him when I see him," Yogi tells reporters.

Has he ever said "Please come back?" they ask.

"No," Yogi says. "He's never said that."

Berra's boycott endures.

When Yankee manager Joe Torre, a longtime friend, asks Yogi to present him with his first World Series ring on Opening Day of 1997, Berra declines. Don Mattingly implores Yogi to come when the team retires Mattingly's number later in '97, but he demurs again. "You deserve to be there," Mattingly insists. Yogi is unmoved: "I said no to Phil, and you'll have to do with that, too."

Little did Berra—or any of the Yankees who miss him dearly— know that plans are spinning to bridge the Yogi–George divide.

# CHAPTER 39

# As Good as It Gets

## 1998–1999

It's twilight on a late September day in 1998, and Yogi Berra is on his 73-year-old knees beside the freshly poured cement walkway surrounding the soon-to-open Yogi Berra Museum & Learning Center at Montclair State University. Standing beside him are his wife Carmen and close friend Rose Cali, the driving force behind the museum. Berra, dressed in a blue blazer, white shirt, dark tie, and khaki pants, leans over and plants his palms firmly into the cement. Next, he picks up a large wooden pencil and carefully writes his name.

He grins getting to his feet, glances at the museum that bears his name, and turns to Carmen and Rose. "Ya know," he says, "you usually have to be dead before you get one of these things."

It's a line Berra has used many times in the two-plus years since he and Carmen went to dinner with Cali, her husband John, and then MSU President Irv Reid and his wife Pamela in early '96. The Berras assumed the university wished to award Yogi an honorary doctorate in May, which was indeed planned. But Rose, a Montclair State trustee, had more news.

Former Kmart CEO Floyd Hall is spending $10 million to build an ice arena and, most important, a new baseball stadium, hoping to attract a minor league team, Rose told the Berras. "We want to name the stadium after Yogi," Rose said that night. "And we want to use one of the skyboxes on the upper rim of the stadium for an exhibit to pay homage to Yogi's career and his life."

Yogi was blown away. Getting an honorary degree was cool—*Dr. Lawrence Peter Berra*! But having his name on a baseball stadium in his adopted hometown? And an exhibit to honor his career *and* his life? Rose says Yogi's values—his humility, the kind and respectful way he treats people—should be celebrated. *Damn.* Carmen and Yogi quickly agreed, and Carmen ordered champagne for the table to celebrate.

The next two years are almost nonstop activity, much of it overseen by the 56-year-old Cali. Rose and her husband John have been good friends with Carmen and Yogi ever since they bought the Berras' first Montclair house in 1976. Soon after their dinner, Carmen drove Rose to Cooperstown to gather ideas, and when they returned, Cali was as driven as any ballplayer Yogi has ever known. The skybox morphed into a freestanding museum on the rim of the stadium overlooking the field. Rose formed a board—Carmen was treasurer for the first year—hired the architect who'd revamped the Hall of Fame to design the interior and exhibits, and added a Learning Center with the help of MSU professors. The university contributed the land rent free.

Cali formed the Friends of Yogi, Inc.—a 501(c)(3) charity—and negotiated the politics of fund-raising for a project that would cost almost $3 million. Her husband signed for a $1 million loan to cover early construction costs, and friends like John McMullen, Bobbi Brown, and venture capitalist turned philanthropist Ray Chambers each contributed $25,000 or more.

Rose also worked with lawyers to allow Yogi's sons to operate their marketing business from a shop and office in the museum for $10,000 in rent, payable at the end of each year. Yogi was thrilled. Instead of driving to a storefront in a strip mall and sitting in a cluttered room to sign memorabilia, he could soon use the skybox at the back of the museum overlooking Yogi Berra Stadium.

Yogi drove the 15 minutes from his home a few times a week to visit Rose in the project's construction trailer, where Cali oversaw every detail. As the museum took shape, Yogi saw life-size photos of himself as a young Yankee catcher in action and others chronicling his days on The Hill and his Navy service during World War II. There was an exhibit featuring one of his three MVP trophies he'd lent the museum and other awards from his long career.

There were times Yogi barely believed the work others, especially Rose Cali, were devoting to honor him—an immigrant's son—as a baseball player and man of principle. "The mission of the Yogi Berra Museum & Learning Center," the museum's literature stated, "is to sustain and promote the values of respect, perseverance, sportsmanship and excellence through inclusive, culturally diverse sports-based educational exhibits and programs." That put a lump in Berra's throat.

Which is exactly what happened a few weeks ago. Rose had invited New Jersey's own Toms River East American Little League team, fresh off their victory in the Little League World Series, to visit the museum. The 12-year-old boys, including future major leaguer Todd Frazier, rushed off the bus and down to the field for batting practice with the independent minor league team who shares the stadium with the university's team. After that, they met Yogi and Carmen in the museum.

New MSU President Susan Cole, who quickly embraced the museum project when she arrived in September, also attended and spoke first, congratulating the boys on their championship. Then it was Yogi's turn. But as he started talking, tears welled in his eyes and his throat tightened. He managed a few lines, thanked them, and rushed away.

"Don't ever put me in front of kids like that," he told Dave Kaplan, the museum's new executive director and former Sunday editor at the *New York Daily News*. Carmen saw Kaplan's bewilderment and reassured him. "He gets that way when he has to talk to people," she told him. "He'll be fine."

Yogi is more than fine after writing his name in cement. In March, LTD Enterprises published *The Yogi Book*—pictures of Yogi through the years with teammates and family and short explanations and/or Yogi-isms—and it's a bestseller. George Steinbrenner, whose Yankees are having a record-breaking season, keeps talking about how much he wants Yogi to return, and the media is celebrating Berra for standing firm. Yogi made a hole in one at his charity golf tournament in August. Ted Williams is among many guests who have already accepted invitations for the museum's gala opening night in late October.

Yogi has his health and nine grandchildren, and he and Carmen will celebrate their 50th wedding anniversary in January. And soon the doors will open at the Yogi Berra Museum & Learning Center.

Yes, life is good.

It's the cocktail hour at the dedication of the Yogi Berra Museum & Learning Center on October 23. Berra, who greets many of the 125 guests at the door, walks beside a wheelchair-bound Ted Williams—whose mind and wit are still sharp at 80—pointing to one picture after another. Some of the players in these pictures—Phil Rizzuto, Whitey Ford, Larry Doby, Ralph Branca—are also here. So is good friend and former football star Frank Tripucka along with Arlene Howard and many of the Berras' Montclair friends.

New York Mayor Rudy Giuliani also attends. Earlier in the day he presided over another parade for the New York Yankees, who two days ago beat the San Diego Padres in four games for their second World Series title in three years. There is plenty of talk tonight about how these Yankees, who won a record 125 games, compare to Berra's Yankees, who won five straight titles. "They still have a ways to go," Yogi tells one of the many reporters present.

Yogi and Williams stop to examine a big photo of Joe DiMaggio, under which is a quotation from Yogi in large letters—one of many that adorn the museum—calling DiMaggio the best baseball player he ever saw. Williams reads the quotation about his former archrival, makes a face, and laughs. This is a night to retell stories and enjoy old friends. And pay tribute to Yogi, the somewhat embarrassed man of the hour.

Soon guests enter a large tent enclosed by clear plastic overlooking the 3,784-seat Yogi Berra Stadium, its beautifully manicured field, and the circle around Yogi's signature in big white letters behind home plate. President Cole welcomes everyone to her campus, expressing her pleasure with the museum and its Learning Center.

Carmen and Yogi take the podium. "I want to thank everyone for coming here tonight and for all you have done to turn the dream of this museum and Learning Center into a reality," says Carmen. "Yogi and I are humbled and grateful."

Carmen speaks eloquently for several minutes, then calls Rose Cali to the podium to publicly thank her for all she's done. Yogi and Carmen stand on opposite sides of Rose, and all three close friends beam as cameras click. Cali leans to the microphone and invites everyone to visit the museum when it officially opens on December 1.

But Cali remains mum about a major news event, still in nascent talks, that may occur at the museum—if the handful of planners can actually pull it off.

Yogi sits in the theater of the Yogi Berra Museum one morning a few weeks later, listening intently to Rose Cali's proposal. John Cali stands to the side, museum director Dave Kaplan sits near Yogi, and both look anxious but hopeful. This is important.

George Steinbrenner wants to come to the museum to apologize for the way he fired you, Rose tells Berra. He's willing to come to you. You only have to agree to this meeting and your boycott of Yankee Stadium can end.

"No! No way!" says Yogi, staring straight ahead at the replica of the scoreboard in Yankee Stadium mounted at the front of the theater.

It's been 14 years since Steinbrenner axed Berra as manager of the Yankees after 16 games. George didn't even have the decency to fire Yogi himself, instead delegating the task to his GM. Berra told reporters that day he'd return to see Dale play, but once he talked with Carmen, he decided never to set foot in Yankee Stadium as long as Steinbrenner owned the team.

And Berra hasn't budged—if anything, he's dug in deeper. But Rose Cali and Dave Kaplan have secretly been contacted by Suzyn Waldman of WFAN about bringing Yogi back into the Yankee fold. Waldman, who is close with Steinbrenner, has been blunt with the Yankee boss: if George truly wants Yogi back, she told George, he would have to apologize. On Yogi's turf.

It took time, but Waldman got Steinbrenner's word he would apologize to Berra at Yogi's museum. The two men would then do a live broadcast on-site with Waldman. George insisted on just one condition.

"No advance publicity," said Steinbrenner, concerned that Berra might reject him. "Not a word, or the deal is off."

Waldman delivered the offer. Now the Calis and Kaplan are trying to convince Yogi he should accept.

"Yogi, think about—" Cali starts to say before Berra cuts her off.

"This is just another of George's gimmicks," Yogi says. "I'm not doin' it!"

John Cali steps in. "Yogi, think about your grandchildren," he says. The tall, 80-year-old Cali—seven years Berra's senior and co-owner of one of the largest commercial real estate firms in New Jersey—has been Yogi's friend and confidant for more than 20 years. "Your nine grandchildren have never seen you in the Stadium or heard the crowd cheer for you."

"The hell with it—he ain't coming here!" says Berra as he rises from his seat. "That man is a liar and can't be trusted!" And Yogi walks out of the theater.

Rose, John, and Kaplan are dumbfounded. They expected Yogi to be wary but not this stubborn. "I've never seen Yogi act like that," John Cali says. "Not in all the years I've known him."

It's not long until Dale Berra enters the theater. Dale and his brother Tim had been working in the LTD Enterprises office when Yogi walked in distraught and angrily shared the news. "Dad is really upset," Dale tells them. "But I'm all for it. Give us a few minutes."

Only a few moments later, Dale pokes his head back into the theater. "Round 2," he says, smiling. Inside the LTD office, the two brothers are working on their dad. They're repeating what so many of Yogi's old Yankee friends have told him: it's time. Even Carmen has lately been telling Yogi this feud should end.

Berra's sons know their father still considers himself a Yankee. And it must kill him not to be at the Stadium, especially when the team is winning the way Yogi's teams did. "Dad, none of your grandchildren has seen you in the place you became famous," Dale says. "Why continue to deny them?"

Yogi's sons keep pushing until their father relents. "Okay, okay, but your mother has to be there," Yogi says. "Whatever George has to say, he has to say to her, too."

Yogi walks into the theater a few moments later. "Okay, Ro," says Yogi, using his nickname for Rose Cali. "I'll do it."

After several phone calls with Waldman, the date for détente is set: December 16. Everyone is sworn to secrecy. Sometimes in the following weeks the museum staff sees George's limo driver circle their parking lot, timing various routes from Newark Airport to Montclair State—and they can't help laughing.

No one laughs when the plan hits a snag: Steinbrenner has to attend the funeral of Florida Governor Lawton Chiles, who died of a sudden heart attack. Chiles will be laid to rest on December 16, the date of George's planned trip to Montclair. Yogi grouses but agrees to a new date: January 5, 1999.

Somehow, the day arrives without a single leak. Only two journalists are tipped to the 5 p.m. meeting: one from the *New York Times,* the other from the *New York Daily News,* both Montclair residents.

The Berras and their sons, Rose and John Cali, Dave Kaplan, a few board members, and a few friends of the Berras are at the museum along with a very nervous Suzyn Waldman and the WFAN tech crew.

It's 5:10 p.m. when the town car carrying Steinbrenner and his public relations man Rick Cerrone arrives. Yogi stands at the back door as he watches the 68-year-old Steinbrenner exit the car and walk to the museum. George isn't dressed in his trademark power uniform: blue blazer over a white turtleneck and sharply creased gray slacks. Instead, the Yankee owner is wearing a camel-colored blazer, a tan turtleneck, and brown pants.

And he's visibly nervous.

"Hello, Yogi," George says at the door.

Berra looks at Steinbrenner, then taps his wristwatch.

"You're late," Yogi says.

The ice is broken.

"Yogi, give me a break," George says with mock exasperation. "I came all the way from Florida."

They shake hands, and there are small smiles on both men's faces when they walk down the hallway and into the museum. Cali suggests they speak in private in the small office she shares with Kaplan, and Carmen—carrying a bottle of champagne—joins the two men as they walk into the cramped space. George gets right to the point. Putting his hands on Yogi's shoulders, he looks him straight in the eye.

"I know I made a mistake by not letting you go personally," says George, who begins to weep softly, just as he did when he accepted the World Series trophy on national television last fall.

Berra has heard what he needed to hear. "I made a lot of mistakes in baseball, too," Yogi says.

Carmen pops the cork on the champagne, and their toasts and laughter are loud enough for the anxious people outside to think they might be shouting. But when the door opens and all three are smiling, the summit's planners relax.

"Show me your museum," Steinbrenner says to Yogi.

The two men walk through the displays. They stop before a large blowup of Berra at home plate during a World Series game against Brooklyn. Then again to admire a picture of Joe DiMaggio, Tommy Henrich, and Lou Gehrig. Steinbrenner is especially taken with the exhibit on Larry Doby, who broke the color barrier in the American League playing for Cleveland, George's hometown team.

The two reporters interrupt Yogi and George, squeezing in a few questions before rushing off to file stories.

Yogi, does this mean your boycott of Yankee Stadium is over?

"I told him what he needed to do," says Yogi, a smile on his face. "He apologized. We'll see."

Steinbrenner doesn't wait for a question. "If I could get Yogi to come back, I'd bring him over the George Washington Bridge in a rickshaw."

Berra's tour winds up in the museum's theater, and soon the two men sit down with Waldman, who tells listeners this is a special night. She then introduces her guests. "Mr. Steinbrenner, you know Mr. Berra," she says. "Mr. Berra, Mr. Steinbrenner." Everyone laughs, and soon the stories start to flow. And the phones ring. Ted Williams calls in, and so does Joe Garagiola.

Before long, there is a line at the museum door. People who were tuned to WFAN heard the news and rushed to the museum; the staff is admitting them a couple at a time. At one point, Waldman looks up, stunned to see the 65-seat theater completely full, with more people lining the walls and sitting in the aisles. It was hard to tell who felt more pleasure, the lucky fans or the two men who had just broken a 14-year feud.

Waldman finishes her show, and Steinbrenner prepares to leave. On his way out, George gives Carmen a big hug. "He's got to forgive me and come back," he tells her. "You did the right thing coming here," she tells Steinbrenner.

The Yankee owner clutches a copy of *The Yogi Book* and a museum

T-shirt as Yogi walks him to the door. "Thank you for inviting me, Yogi," says George. "I'll talk to you soon." The two men embrace, and Yogi stands in the entranceway and watches Steinbrenner amble to his limo and drive off. The door closes as Berra turns to his family and friends standing in the hallway.

"Fourteen years," Yogi says with a wide smile. "It's over."

# CHAPTER 40

# Perfect Timing
## 1999

Yogi Berra sits nervously in the Yankee Stadium dugout he hasn't occupied for what seems like forever as the defending world champions are introduced to 56,583 Opening Day fans. Each player taps Yogi on the leg for good luck before trotting into a cold, steady April rain. When the last uniformed player is introduced, a roar starts to build as longtime public address announcer Bob Sheppard raises his familiar voice to signal something important.

"Let's welcome back a very special guest," says Sheppard. And now the crowd rises, waiting to welcome the big little man in the blue blazer, gray slacks, and Yankee cap perching on the dugout steps. Sheppard quickly lists highlights from Berra's many achievements before giving the crowd, the players, and the man standing and applauding in the owner's box what they've wanted for so long.

"A true leader. A man of conviction and a source of strength to his teammates. Let's welcome back No. 8, Yogi Berra. No. 8."

Berra walks to the pitcher's mound, where Yankee starter David Cone claps into his glove. The crowd cheers as Yogi shakes Cone's hand and walks several steps in front of the mound. The 73-year-old Berra takes a short windup and tosses the ball high and wide to catcher Joe Girardi, and the crowd's roar spikes as Girardi, ball in hand, rushes to the Yankee icon.

"Thanks, Yogi," the Yankee catcher says. "This is a real thrill."

"Thank you," Berra says.

His Opening Day work almost complete, Yogi half waves to the crowd and strolls off the wet field to chants of "Yogi! Yogi! Yogi!" It's raining hard, but Berra feels only the warm embrace of Yankee fans he's missed for so long.

Sitting soon afterward at a table alongside Whitey Ford in the Yankee clubhouse, Yogi tries to share his feelings with the media. "Sure, I was a little nervous out there," says Berra, who will watch the Yankees beat the Tigers, 12–3, in George Steinbrenner's box with museum director Dave Kaplan and Carmen but without their three sons, who did not attend. "It was like any Opening Day," he says. "I don't care how long you've played. You're always a little nervous."

But this was not just any Opening Day. He had been hoping to share first-pitch honors with Joe DiMaggio, but the best player Yogi ever saw succumbed to lung cancer in March. DiMaggio's death shifts the title of Greatest Living Yankee to Berra, who instead points to either Ford or Phil Rizzuto. Rizzuto and Ford raised the 1998 championship banner today in the pregame ceremonies and received a warm welcome. But the crowd's roar made it obvious that Berra is first in Yankee fans' hearts.

"Being away 14 years... it was a very happy moment," Yogi says. "I came in with my wife; she was very happy." He pauses, a wide smile crossing his famous face. "I'm glad it's over with, that's the thing! It feels great."

Weather aside, the timing of Berra's return couldn't have been better. Interest in baseball—spurred by last season's McGwire-Sosa home run race, peaking when McGwire broke Roger Maris' record—is the highest in decades. The Yankees have won two of the last three World Series, and with players like Derek Jeter, Mariano Rivera, and newcomer Roger Clemens, they are once again the most popular team in sports. And now the most popular living Yankee is back where he belongs.

And in demand. He's already done a commercial promoting Amtrak and touting tourism in New Jersey. In May, he'll be featured in a TV ad for Nike, and he has his choice of radio and TV spots for many

New Jersey businesses. PBS has been shooting a documentary on his life scheduled to run later this summer. *The Yogi Book* has already sold 300,000 copies and LTD's mail-order business is thriving.

"There has always been an interest in Yogi Berra because he has a strong and colorful personality," Nova Lanktree, President of Lanktree Sports Celebrity Network in Chicago, tells the *New York Times*. "He just has those charismatic qualities that transcend time. Even the younger people get him."

The Yogi Berra Museum & Learning Center is already a hit. In February, Yogi and board President Rose Cali went to the New York Mercantile Exchange to accept a gift of $5,000 for the museum. Yogi signed 36 pictures and other memorabilia, which earned another $3,500. On April 5, Mayor Rudy Giuliani delivered the 1998 World Series trophy to the museum, where it was displayed until Opening Day. It was returned shortly afterward to the museum, where George Steinbrenner intends to leave it for several months. Indeed, the museum is doing so well there's already talk of expanding the building and the educational partnership with Montclair State, a growing university of more than 13,000 students.

When Joe Garagiola calls to sing happy birthday on May 12—Berra's 74th—Yogi tells him New York Waterway just renamed one of its 79-foot commuter and tourist ferries the *Yogi Berra*. Nine days later he is inducted into the Brooklyn Dodgers Hall of Fame. And later this summer Yogi's museum will display 10 of McGwire's and Sosa's home run balls from their historic duel.

Steinbrenner can't do enough for the museum. After replacing the large bronze plaques for DiMaggio and Mickey Mantle displayed in the Stadium's Monument Park, George donates the originals to Berra's museum.

On July 13, Yogi is one of 100 players nominated for baseball's All-Century Team—the best players in baseball's first 100 years—to be selected by fans and announced before Game 2 of the 1999 World Series. (With more than two million votes eventually cast, Berra was a shoo-in for the 30-man team.)

The summer's highlight is Yogi Berra Day on July 18 at Yankee Stadium. The museum rents the *Yogi Berra* ferry to take Berra, his family—including his sister Josie and nephew Larry from St. Louis—and about 100 friends to the Bronx. It stops on the way for Mayor Rudy Giuliani, who rarely misses a celebration with his favorite team.

The Stadium is packed on this hot, humid day. There are 22 white chairs and a podium behind home plate. More than two dozen photographers wait for Yogi, who sits atop the back seat of a 1957 white Thunderbird convertible in right center field, eager to begin. Yankee announcer Michael Kay, today's master of ceremonies, speaks from the podium.

"It's a pretty good time to be a Yankee fan," Kay tells the crowd. "You get to root for the world champions. Your team is in first place. And Yogi Berra is back."

With that Yogi begins the slow ride around the outfield and down the left field line while the fans cheer and a collage of great moments in Yogi's career scrolls across the scoreboard's large video screen. Every Yankee stands and applauds, as do the day's opponents, the Montreal Expos. After Berra's ride, Kay escorts Yogi to his seat, then introduces today's guests. Carmen Berra, looking youthful in white blazer, skirt, and blouse, leads their whole family, followed by teammates and friends. The crowd gives Phil Rizzuto a huge ovation and erupts for Don Mattingly. Whitey Ford is here, of course, and so is Don Larsen. The last man introduced hasn't known a day without his friend Yogi—Joe Garagiola.

The gifts are lavish: Rizzuto awards tickets for a trip to Italy, which includes an audience with the Pope. Joe Torre presents a 1998 World Series ring. Mattingly hands Yogi a complete set of World Series rings from his 10 title seasons. Steinbrenner watches from his box as Kay describes three gifts from George for Berra's museum: a framed No. 8 Yankee jersey, the original 1951 World Series banner won in Yogi's first MVP season, and a big cardboard check for $100,000.

And now it's Berra's turn. Yogi breathes deeply as he stands before the microphone. There will be no jokes or malaprops this time. "You know, my mother used to say, the two most beautiful buildings in the world," he says, his voice trembling with emotion, "were St. Peter's in Rome...and Yankee Stadium. This is a tremendous honor, and I am thrilled to share it in this beautiful building with my whole family, my friends, and you fans. You're great.

"You know, I was proud to be a major league ballplayer and proud to be a Yankee. A lot of good things have happened to me since I first put on the pinstripes more than 50 years ago. I got married to Carm and raised a wonderful family. I played on great championship teams. And the Yankees ultimately became my family."

Yogi pauses, straining over emotion to speak his final lines. "I want to thank you all for making me feel right at home. God bless you. Thank you."

Happy and relieved, Berra takes his seat to thunderous chants of "Yogi! Yogi! Yogi!"

When the field is cleared, he has one last duty. Larsen strolls out to the mound next to Cone, waiting for Yogi and Joe Girardi at the plate. It was 43 years ago when Larsen and Berra produced the only perfect game in World Series history. "Are you going to jump into Yogi's arms?" Cone asks Larsen. "Kid, you have it wrong," says Larsen, two weeks shy of 70. "He jumped into *my* arms."

Girardi and Berra are having their own history talk. Yogi used a smaller glove than the one catchers use now, and Girardi has a smaller model in his locker. He asks if Yogi wants him to fetch the smaller one, but Berra tells him the glove Girardi holds is just fine. "Would you put a blessing on it?" Girardi asks just before Yogi catches Larsen's ceremonial pitch.

Yogi is far more relaxed an hour later in a private suite, laughing with his family and playing with his grandchildren while trying to track the play on the field. David Cone is the starting pitcher, and though the Expos have some good young hitters, everyone expects the Yankees to win this game for Yogi. After all, the Yankees are 53–36—first in the tough AL East—and the Expos are 33–54, 21½ games behind Atlanta in the NL East.

But when Cone retires the Expos in order in the 7th inning, something extraordinary is brewing: the Yankee pitcher is throwing a perfect game. The laughter and chatter in Berra's box disappear as Cone, with a 5–0 lead in the 8th, retires three more Expos. The Yankees add another run in their half of the inning, and the crowd rises as Cone walks from the dugout, three outs from perfection.

Cone takes a deep breath, then strikes out the first batter swinging. He gets the next hitter to lift an easy fly ball to left.

Up in his box, Yogi strategizes along with Cone and Girardi about what Cone should throw to Orlando Cabrera, the 27th batter at the plate. With the count 1–1, the Yankee right-hander throws a sweeping slider and Cabrera hits an easy pop foul behind third base. When Scott Brosius catches the ball for the final out Cone drops to his knees and is mobbed by teammates. Staring down at the celebration, Berra is stunned: a perfect game!

Berra and Larsen, who watched the drama from Steinbrenner's suite, meet in the hallway and hustle to the clubhouse, where they take pictures with a euphoric Cone. The Yankee pitcher threw only 88 pitches to complete the 16th perfect game in baseball history. "All the Yankee legends here, Don Larsen in the park, Yogi Berra Day," says a wide-eyed Cone. "It makes you stop and think about the Yankee magic and the mystique of this ballpark."

Berra agrees. "My day, and Don Larsen's here—this was great," Yogi says. "Those pinstripes make you do something."

Berra is a bundle of emotions as he leaves Yankee Stadium for the ferry ride home. There are drinks and food on the boat, joyful laughter, and amazement at Cone's performance. Several of the men start explaining the extraordinary rarity of a perfect game to museum President Rose Cali, who had never attended a baseball game before this one. Suddenly Rose can't spot the man everyone wants to see and begins looking for him. Her search ends in the captain's cabin, where Berra sits to one side, alone, lost in thought. Berra sees Cali and smiles.

"Ro, what are you doing up here?" says Yogi, still overwhelmed.

"I guess this is the only time you've really had to relish all that happened today," she says. "Don't worry—enjoy it all. Come down whenever you want."

The two hug and Cali leaves her friend to his thoughts. Berra eventually returns to the main deck and is immediately the center of attention. Isn't he always? No matter how many times they all review the day's events, no one can believe what they witnessed on Yogi Berra Day.

Which is exactly what Yogi thinks as his large party leaves the ferry for the buses back to the museum. Carmen and Yogi kiss their kids and grandkids and climb into Carmen's red Jaguar for their 15-minute ride home.

"Can you believe it?" Yogi says as Carmen heads home. "A perfect game on my day!"

# CHAPTER 41

# Friends of Yogi

## 2000–2008

### The Collector

Yogi Berra and Kevin McLaughlin are chatting in the lobby of the Otesaga Hotel, the historic luxury resort in Cooperstown, New York. It's July 22, 2000, and the two men and Carmen Berra are waiting for the bus to the Saturday night cocktail party at the National Baseball Hall of Fame and Museum. It's Induction Weekend, and 45 Hall of Famers have gathered to welcome their newest members.

Yogi has traveled to this village in upstate New York every year since 1991, and he's pleased to see old friends: Whitey Ford, Larry Doby, Al Kaline, Willie Mays, Brooks Robinson, and many others. It's the biggest gathering of Hall of Famers since it opened in 1939.

Suddenly McLaughlin pokes Yogi. Sandy Koufax has just entered the lobby. The Dodger left-hander posted six of the greatest seasons in baseball history—averaging 22 wins, 286 strikeouts, and a 2.19 ERA; winning three Cy Young Awards in four seasons; throwing four no-hitters—the last a perfect game. Then Koufax listened to the pain shouting at him from his arthritic left arm and retired in 1966 at age 30—one year after Kevin was born.

Koufax and Berra entered the Hall together in 1972 and have been fast friends ever since. Yogi hasn't seen Sandy here often; the reclusive

Koufax has been back to Cooperstown only twice in the past 10 years. And now McLaughlin is begging Yogi to introduce him.

"Sure," Yogi says, walking over to Koufax. "Sandy, this is Kevin McLaughlin. He wants to meet you."

"Nice to meet you, Kevin," Koufax replies.

Almost speechless, McLaughlin returns the greeting and pushes himself to ask for a photo with both Berra and Koufax.

"I don't know," says Koufax, winking at Berra. "What do you think, Yogi? Should we take a picture with this guy?"

Yogi can see Kevin's embarrassment. "Sandy, he's my guy," Yogi says. "He takes care of me."

And that does it.

"Okay, then," Koufax says. "Let's get this picture taken."

It was only a few hours earlier that McLaughlin was taking care of Yogi, who, like dozens of other Hall of Famers, signs autographs in makeshift booths up and down Main Street. Thousands of fans come to Cooperstown from all parts of the country for this weekend every summer, and collecting autographs from their heroes is a major draw. In 2000, a player of Yogi's stature gets $50 or more to sign photos, programs, and baseballs—$125 for a bat or a jersey.

The line of autograph seekers leading to Yogi's booth is always long, and it's McLaughlin's job to organize them—find out what fans want signed, give them a color-coded ticket, and collect the money. He also matches tickets to items and keeps the line moving. Baseball fans of all ages—male and female—will stand for an hour or longer on a sunbaked sidewalk in 90-degree heat and stifling humidity to have a quick chat with Yogi and get his autograph.

Yogi always signs in front of TJ's Place, a restaurant whose owner—Ted Hargrove—is credited with starting these autograph sessions on Main Street. McLaughlin keeps a watchful eye over Berra, making sure he has enough water and takes breaks inside Hargrove's air-conditioned restaurant. Kevin's been by Yogi's side so long that Induction Weekend regulars sometimes ask if he's a Berra.

It was in 1993 when Tim Berra—McLaughlin's friend and former co-worker at a small investment firm—was just launching LTD Enterprises with his wife and brother Dale. Tim had asked Kevin whether he'd like to help at the 20 or so autograph shows Yogi did each year. Kevin, then 28 years old and a big baseball fan, leaped at the chance.

And for the past seven years he's been Berra's volunteer companion at memorabilia shows once or twice a month from April through December. Yogi concentrates on shows in the tri-state area, often teaming with Whitey Ford, Phil Rizzuto, Ralph Branca, and other former players who live close by. Don Larsen is a regular partner—thanks to their perfect World Series performance—flying in from his home in Hayden Lake, Idaho. Big stars like Willie Mays, Hank Aaron, and Brooks Robinson enjoy doing shows with Yogi, too. The venues are usually shopping malls, hotels, and colleges—places that can accommodate large crowds.

And the money is good—$15,000 to $50,000 a show, depending on crowd size, Yogi's stamina, and whether LTD has negotiated an appearance fee. McLaughlin has never asked to be paid and protests to Carmen every summer in Cooperstown when she wants to cover his hotel room. In Kevin's mind, he's holding the winning lottery ticket. How many people become friends with Yogi Berra and gain entrée to the world of baseball royalty?

McLaughlin still gets a kick out of watching Yogi, who enjoys meeting his fans—especially the kids—and listens intently when older fans tell him about their favorite moments of his career. But the part Yogi loves best is spending time with former players, which makes the trip to Cooperstown a reunion.

Yogi is always the first player to tell Jeff Idelson, the Hall of Fame's communications director, that he and Carmen will attend, and he's always the first to arrive, ready to greet all the other players. Friday includes an autograph signing before a private dinner for Hall of Famers given by chairman Jane Forbes Clark, whose family's philanthropic foundation founded the Hall of Fame here in 1939. Saturday offers a golf tournament and more autographs on Main Street before the cocktail party Saturday evening with Carmen and Kevin.

And on Sunday, Berra, Koufax, and the 43 other Hall of Famers are on the big platform set up for the Induction Ceremony, now held on the rolling meadow of the Clark Sports Center. More than 20,000 baseball fans gather to watch the pinnacle of the weekend—Boston catcher Carlton Fisk, Cincinnati manager Sparky Anderson, and Reds first baseman Tony Perez accept their Hall of Fame plaques.

It all ends Monday morning. Sometimes Yogi will spend an hour or so on Mondays signing autographs, but this time he's ready for home. There is just one more thing he'd like Kevin to do: please ask Jeff Idelson for the date of next year's Induction Weekend.

## The Ready Companion

Dave Kaplan is driving his dark gray minivan across the George Washington Bridge toward Yankee Stadium for Game 4 of the 2001 World Series. Sitting beside him is Yogi Berra, still talking about the previous night's game. Baseball's exciting postseason has been a balm for the grief-stricken country after the September 11 terrorist attacks, but Kaplan and Berra can see smoke still rising from the fallen towers—15 miles away on the southern tip of Manhattan—as they cross into the Bronx.

Game 3 of the Series between the Arizona Diamondbacks and the Yankees had been full of drama. Kaplan and Berra watched from Steinbrenner's box as President George Bush strode confidently to the pitcher's mound, dozens of snipers stationed along the Stadium's roof. Bush gave the 55,820 fans a thumbs-up and threw the ceremonial first pitch to chants of *"USA! USA!"* The Yankees won it, 2–1, behind the overpowering pitching of Roger Clemens and Mariano Rivera.

But it's this game on a cool October 31 night that sets this Series on the path to greatness. Last night's Game 3 win cut the Yankees' Series deficit in half, but Yogi's team is in deep trouble in the closing moments tonight, trailing 3–1 with two outs and a man on first in the

9th inning. Only five teams have ever come back to win a World Series title after trailing three games to one, the last doing it 16 years ago.

And that's when the Yankee first baseman Tino Martinez slams the first pitch he sees for a two-run homer to deep right center field, tying the game and setting off a wild celebration. It gets wilder still one inning later when Derek Jeter slices the game-winning homer just over the fence into right field, evening the Series at two games apiece.

By that time, though, Yogi and Kaplan had left Steinbrenner's suite, departing as always in the 6th inning to watch the excitement from their Montclair homes. No one knows better than Yogi that the game isn't over 'til it's over, but Berra has his routine. Kaplan always takes him to the Stadium hours before the first pitch—sometimes early enough to turn on the lights in manager Joe Torre's office so Yogi can make his rounds, talking to Torre and his coaches, the trainer and assistant trainer, the clubhouse men and the security guards—anyone connected to baseball. No one is beneath his notice.

He'll check in with the players, who enjoy Berra's visits—part baseball talk, part friendly jabs. Yogi especially loves teasing Jeter, the face of this Yankee team, which has won four of the last five World Series. Everyone within earshot remembers the day Yogi asked Jeter why he'd struck out on a pitch far out of the strike zone, ending the game with the winning runs on base.

"Why not?" Jeter said. "You did!"

"Yeah, but I hit those pitches," Yogi replied. "You don't."

Yogi's next stop is always the opposing clubhouse, where he seeks out players he coached with the Yankees, Mets, and Astros and the coaches and managers whose fathers he knew back in his playing days. When Yogi arrives in George Steinbrenner's suite 40 minutes before game time, the bartender knows to serve him exactly four ounces of vodka—his daily limit in his mid-70s. Berra talks a bit with George—a former adversary, now a good friend—calming the owner's nerves.

Celebrities invariably fill the suite—Billy Crystal, Barbara Walters,

Tom Brokaw, Donald Trump, Henry Kissinger, and Mayor Rudy Giuliani, among others—all but Trump wanting time with Yogi. Berra, unfailingly polite, shakes hands and chats but soon finds a corner where he can watch the game.

And like clockwork he asks Dave Kaplan to leave by the 6th inning, beating the traffic to watch the game's end in his comfortable den. His oldest son Larry, soon to be 52, moved back home in 2001 and is Yogi's baseball companion there. Only a Series-ending game will hold Berra until the final out so he can congratulate the winners and console the losers.

At his side for every game at Yankee Stadium is Kaplan, the executive director of the Yogi Berra Museum & Learning Center. Once Yogi realized upon returning to the Stadium on Opening Day in 1999 just how much he had missed it—and how much the fans missed him—he started calling Kaplan about attending games together.

So now Yogi routinely parks his tan Jaguar at the museum at 1 p.m. and jumps into Kaplan's minivan for the short drive to the Stadium, making the trip at least once for every home series. Kaplan, at Berra's side throughout, is with him so often people frequently ask whether he is one of Yogi's sons.

The two greatly enjoy each other's company, and last season during their drives Kaplan asked questions for the first of four books they eventually wrote together. (*When You Come to a Fork in the Road, Take It!*—a collection of Yogi-isms and vignettes from Berra's life— published in the spring of 2001.) One night Yogi grew irritated by the constant queries as they traveled.

"Why are you asking me so many questions today?" Berra grumbled. "What are you doing, writing a book or something?"

Yes, Kaplan reminded Yogi. "With you!" The book is a *New York Times* bestseller.

Kaplan moved to Montclair in 1989, attracted by good schools and proximity to the city. Like most Montclair residents, he'd seen Yogi and Carmen shopping and dining downtown and took pride that an American icon lived there. A sports journalist who rose to be the Sunday editor of the *New York Daily News* sports department, Kaplan knew plenty about Berra's career. But the two men hadn't met until museum board President Rose Cali invited Kaplan to a fund-raiser at Berra's home in early 1998, soon after hiring him as executive director.

The first few months with Yogi were revealing. Kaplan discovered a private and quiet man — not at all like the funnyman image crafted by others. Berra, he saw, embodied the values the museum wanted to promote — he was deeply kind, respectful of others, humble about his accomplishments. Dave learned both Yogi and Carmen were wary of favor seekers and discovered how forcefully Carmen protected her husband.

Kaplan saw firsthand how much Yogi enjoyed children — whether at Learning Center classes, tours of the museum, or the weeklong baseball and softball summer camps for 8- to 12-year-olds. Berra told the kids about the insults he'd endured in childhood and was often asked how he responded.

"I always figured I must be doing something right," he told the kids, "if they're paying attention to me."

Kaplan also saw a man determined to remain healthy and busy as he approached 80. Berra was in the museum most days to sign photos, bats, balls, and most anything arriving at the LTD Enterprises office. It's true that Yogi occasionally wondered aloud why he was in the LTD office autographing memorabilia while his sons golfed, but he understood the family business. When a close friend once asked Berra whether he ever minded that his sons earned a living from his fame, Yogi replied, "Well, it beats a life insurance policy."

Over the years, Kaplan watched Yogi improve his diet and stop chewing tobacco and smoking. Berra started most days working out with John McMullen at the New Jersey Devils' gym in West Orange, attending morning Mass at Our Lady of Lourdes, having coffee and a bagel at Henry's in Verona, and spending several hours at the museum — all inside a 10-mile radius, comfortable for a man who was never a terrific driver.

Berra and Kaplan, after the thrilling victory in Game 4 of the

Diamondback-Yankee World Series, arrive early the next day at the players parking lot for Game 5. The winning team would return to Arizona needing only one more victory to become world champions.

Berra, of course, is pulling for the Yankees. But whatever the score, he and Kaplan would leave in the 6th inning so Yogi could watch what turns out to be another classic from his favorite chair in Montclair.

## The Driving Force

Rose Cali stands backstage in the ballroom of Philadelphia's Bellevue Hotel watching Yogi Berra enter to rising applause from more than 200 startled partners of the Pepper Hamilton law firm. Yogi ambles toward Jim Murray, the firm's prominent outgoing executive partner, and shakes the astonished 62-year-old's hand. Murray, in the presence of his boyhood hero, is starstruck.

It's November 20, 2002, and Yogi's appearance is a surprise gift to Murray, a former college catcher and die-hard Phillies fan, whose favorite player smiles beside him. Only three members of Pepper Hamilton knew about Berra's appearance, including Joe Del Raso, who sits on the board of the National Italian American Foundation with Cali. It was Del Raso who asked Cali if Yogi would consider coming to the meeting to honor Murray.

Cali, still running the day-to-day operations of the Yogi Berra Museum she founded in 1997, thought Berra would agree if the firm donated $10,000 to the museum's Learning Center. Yogi would surprise Jim, sign a few autographs, and take questions for 30 minutes.

And that's what Yogi is doing now. Rose, watching Berra's charming performance, appreciates the irony. Yogi, once mocked for his lack of education and inarticulate English, turns a roomful of lawyers into little kids.

One wants to know what it was like to play with Joe DiMaggio. "Best player I've ever seen. He did everything right." Was Berra worried that Don Larsen would drop him when he jumped into the arms of the only man to pitch a perfect game in World Series history? Yogi laughs heartily—he's never heard the familiar question asked this way—and Cali can see her friend is truly enjoying himself. "No— Don's a big guy. I knew he could handle it."

And then there's the one question about the 1955 World Series that always revs up Yogi. "Was Jackie Robinson safe when—"

Berra interrupts, shouting, "He was out, he was out, he was out." Delighted, they all laugh. Standing next to his hero, Murray sees the competitive fire—the passion that made Berra the game's biggest winner—still burning brightly at 77.

Yogi does a very different Q&A a bit later. Pepper Hamilton supports a reading program for second and third graders from inner-city schools, and none of them has even heard of Yogi, which delights Berra. The easier to enjoy their company. After lunch with Murray and a few of the partners, Berra and Cali are on the train back to New Jersey by late afternoon. "Ro, this was a really great day, a really great day," Yogi keeps telling Rose.

Cali's already warm friendship with Yogi and Carmen Berra has deepened with the museum's success. She's traveled with him for events like today's in Philadelphia, and Yogi often spends downtime at the museum telling Rose how much baseball has changed since his playing days. "Hey, Ro, we never dove into the bases," he tells her. "That's how you get hurt." The Calis often socialize with the Berras and John and Jacqui McMullen, regularly entertaining at their homes, attending dinner parties together, or dining at one of the area's many restaurants.

Rose and Carmen meet regularly for dinner and marvel over the museum's growth and success. Indeed, talk of expansion began almost immediately, and the New York media has made the museum a regular spot for broadcasts. Joe Torre, Whitey Ford, and Arlene Howard are among the many celebrities who have held book-signing events at Yogi's museum. Award-winning documentarian Aviva Kempner screened a film at the museum ahead of its New York premiere—a profile of Hank Greenberg and the anti-Semitism the Hall of Famer encountered in the 1930s and '40s. Ted Williams flew from Florida to promote the event in January of 2000. *Meet the Press* host Tim Russert conducted the first of several interviews from the museum in July of 2000.

Yankee perfect-game pitchers Larsen and David Cone attended a museum fund-raiser, along with Yankee catchers Joe Girardi and Jorge Posada. "Perfect Night" tickets sold for $1,500 and $1,000 and netted $60,000 for the museum and several other charities. Yankee first basemen Don Mattingly, Joe Pepitone, and Tino Martinez have also signed up for a fund-raiser featuring first basemen.

More than a few visitors who pay the nominal admission fee—$4 for adults, $2 for children—are surprised to find Yogi strolling through the museum and thrilled to spend time chatting with him. Cali soon engaged a local event planner, and the museum was host to its first bar mitzvah late in 1999.

Fellow Hall of Famer, close friend, and Montclair neighbor Larry Doby has told Yogi he'll "do anything" for the museum and frequently speaks to groups of kids from Paterson, New Jersey, his hometown. Yogi was one of the first opposing players to speak to Doby when they were both rookies in 1947, and Larry delights in telling a story about their days as rivals. "As a catcher, Yogi talked to everybody. I finally had to tell the umpire: 'Please tell him to shut up. He asked me how my family was back in the first inning.'"

Cali has watched Yogi bring baseball royalty to the museum with just a phone call. And she's pleased that many former players come just to sit in the LTD office and share old stories—and maybe a shot of vodka—with Yogi.

But there are also a few warning signs Cali missed along the way. In November of 2000 Richard Ben Cramer was set to appear at the museum for a discussion and signing of his new biography of Joe DiMaggio. Berra did not hear about Cramer's visit until the morning of the event, but he'd heard the book was critical of DiMaggio. "Ro, he can't come to my museum, no way," Yogi told Cali, who scrambled to shift Cramer's appearance to Montclair State's campus.

The storefront for LTD, the family's memorabilia business, was frequently closed, even during events at the museum. The museum staff felt awkward when visitors asked for store hours. "Tell them to go to the website," Tim and Dale responded.

And in early 2002 Cali realized LTD had not yet paid its rent. The museum had received the rent check for $10,000 in December the previous two years. When Cali asked Tim Berra in January of 2002 when she could expect the next payment, Tim said LTD decided it had already met its obligation. Since Yogi's appearances on behalf of the museum garnered more than $10,000, LTD would not be making any further payments. If she disagreed, Tim told her, speak with Carmen.

Cali, taken aback, advised the board to avoid a fight. The board reluctantly agreed, even though the museum, which continued as a 501(c)(3) nonprofit organization, was $170,000 in debt at the end of 2001.

Still, all involved remained hopeful about the museum's future. Berra's friend John McMullen donated $1 million from his foundation, one of three grants of at least $500,000 the museum received in 2001. The Yogi Berra Celebrity Golf Classic moves under the museum's umbrella in 2003; Rudy Giuliani chairs the '03 event, while Joe Torre, Andy Pettitte, football star Michael Strahan, music legend Meat Loaf, and other celebrities attract a full field of golfers.

After seven years as the uncompensated full-time President of the museum, Cali decides to step down from day-to-day operations in late 2003, remaining as board President and concentrating on fundraising. The board votes unanimously to hire Beth Sztuk, the chief financial officer of the New Jersey Economic Development Authority, as its new executive director, effective January 1, 2004. Among her priorities: bring more structure and discipline to museum operations and increase the number of school programs, an obligation of its state educational funding and a great source of pride for Yogi.

Both Yogi and the museum have big years in 2004. All the slots in Berra's golf tournament are sold by February. A month later, Yogi is inducted into the National Italian American Foundation's Hall of Fame alongside Academy Award–winning actor Ernest Borgnine and NFL Commissioner Paul Tagliabue. Bob Feller appears at the museum, an event that earns $11,000. Documentarian Ken Burns holds an audience spellbound talking about the intersection of baseball and immigration. And despite a dip in attendance, Sztuk delivers the year under budget, receiving high grades from the board.

But trouble is brewing behind the scenes. The small museum staff, which the Berras treated like family, felt torn between personal affection for and service to the Berras and the obligations of running a professional museum. The Berras have their own issues, especially Carmen, who finds Sztuk insufficiently warm. She was embarrassed by the whistle Beth used to call for attention before speaking at the golf tournament players' reception and confided in some close to her that she no longer wanted Sztuk to represent the museum.

None of this was shared with Sztuk or any member of the board until Carmen Berra calls Rose Cali the first Thursday of March in 2005. "I'm going to the museum tomorrow to fire Beth," Carmen told Cali. "She has to go." Stunned, Cali explains that only the board can hire and fire staff, then asks Carmen to explain the problem. Berra does not elaborate — "She needs to be fired," she repeats — and continues to insist she is going to fire Sztuk the following day.

"Give the board a couple of months to look into the situation," says Cali. Berra is unmoved and ends the conversation with her mind unchanged.

The next 24 hours are the beginning of the end for Cali and the Yogi Berra Museum. She informs the board of her conversation with Carmen Berra at an emergency meeting. There is no way Sztuk can continue without the Berras' support, she reasons, and recommends they pay the final two years of Sztuk's contract. No one disagrees, but the board is dismayed. Two resign in protest. As one board member succinctly observed, Beth thought she was the executive director for the museum, not the executive director for Carmen and Yogi.

Cali asks to meet with Sztuk the next morning. Like Cali and the board, Sztuk is stunned. But she, too, understands the situation. Without the Berras' backing, she can't function. Sztuk soon agrees to resign if the board pays her the two years remaining on her contract.

Cali accepts the board's request that she act as interim executive director but serves only a handful of weeks. Rose's relationship with Carmen has withered since protesting that Berra couldn't and shouldn't fire the museum's executive director. On April 27, Cali reads the board a letter resigning as acting executive director of the museum and president of the board—affirmative about the museum's past and future, but definite in her departure. "I want to thank my fellow Board members for your service to the Museum, your support and most important your friendship," says Cali in her last line.

Several board members walk over and thank her warmly for her eight years of work for the museum. Carmen Berra, attending as an adviser, says nothing.

On her way home, Cali stops at the museum to retrieve the personal tools she used for small repairs. Yogi and the staff have already heard the news. "Hey, Ro, what are you doing?" Yogi calls from the LTD office.

"Just getting my tools and going home," answers Cali, knowing her friendship with Yogi and Carmen Berra would never be the same.

## Driving Mr. Yogi

Ron Guidry knows Yogi Berra is nothing if not a man of habit.

He's known it ever since the first time he picked up Berra at the Tampa International Airport in March of 2000. It was Yogi's first season as a Yankee spring training coach, and Guidry was there with his big white pickup truck to greet him. Guidry took Berra to his hotel, the grocery, then to camp. Later, he took Yogi to dinner.

"Yogi is your responsibility," Yankee manager Joe Torre had told Guidry, one of his spring training pitching coaches. "When Yogi is here, he is more important than working with the pitchers."

That has been true ever since. For about four weeks every spring for the last three years, Guidry becomes Berra's driver, golf partner, and daily companion. And the former Yankee wouldn't have it any other way. Guidry may bristle when people say he's become like a son to Berra—"I have a father; Yogi is my good friend," Guidry answers sternly—but there's little question these two men, born 25 years apart, have grown very close.

And Guidry knows keeping Yogi happy is pretty simple: just follow Berra's routine.

But on this day in late March of 2003, Guidry is determined to break one of Yogi's habits. Every spring Guidry, whose nickname "Gator" springs from his Louisiana-Cajun roots, brings something special to camp: seven or eight dozen frog legs to fry in his special sauce for fellow coaches. Pitching coach Mel Stottlemyre is a big fan. So is third base coach Willie Randolph and spring training coach Goose Gossage.

And every spring Guidry asks Yogi if he wants to try one.

And every spring Yogi declines.

But now Guidry is giving his friend a tough choice.

"Yogi, if you don't try one, we're not going out to eat tonight," Guidry says. "If you don't try one, you're eating in your room. Alone."

Yogi has always told his good friend he wants to be treated like everyone else, and Gator is now taking him at his word. But for all the others at spring training, treating Yogi like "everyone else" is impossible. He's a Hall of Famer, a 15-time All-Star, a three-time MVP. These Yankees understand how hard it is to win a World Series and know the exhilaration of winning often. But Yogi won 10 titles, and no one but Berra knows what that feels like.

The young Yankees want to hear details of his stunning achievements as a player, but he deflects. Ask him how it felt to hit two home runs off Brooklyn ace Don Newcombe in Game 7 of the 1956 World Series, and Yogi will describe Joe DiMaggio's grace, Mickey Mantle's power, or the blazing speed of Bob Feller's fastball.

He's here to help them improve, not talk about himself. In 2000, Steinbrenner hired him as a senior adviser and spring training coach, giving Berra a contract worth just north of $100,000, and Yogi's determined to earn it. His first project was to help catcher Jorge Posada, a power at the plate, become just as formidable behind it. Berra advised Posada to stop calling so many fastballs with runners on base and gave him tips for blocking the plate.

Yogi is happy to help anyone who asks, and he loves talking baseball. A stadium is home, and even if Yogi will be 78 in May, his energy and focus excite the group. Just as he did when he was a young Yankee, Yogi talks about the game with such passion, confidence, and joy that it lifts the entire team. The boldest players will tease him, and when Yogi laughs, he lights up the clubhouse. So the team is excited when they see Yogi's golf clubs arrive in Joe Torre's office, knowing that means Berra isn't far behind.

By now, Guidry has Yogi's schedule down pat. He picks up Berra at the hotel at 7 a.m., and by 7:30 Berra is on the treadmill at the ballpark. At 8:15 Yogi is on the massage table, and by 9 he's showered and eating breakfast with Torre. At 9:30 he's working the clubhouse, developing bonds with players, especially the new guys. The team workout is 10:30–11:30 a.m.; then he's in the coaches' room, getting ready for that day's game. A couple of nights each week Yogi will slip out early to attend evening Mass.

Yogi and Gator use an off day—or a distant away game—as their time to golf. Berra and Guidry have a standing invitation at the MacDill Air Force Base course—Yogi's favorite—courtesy of Brigadier General Arthur "Chip" Diehl. The base commander is a baseball fan who grew up thinking Yogi Berra represented the best of America—proof that anyone from any background can succeed with discipline and determination.

Guidry told Diehl there's only one rule for playing with Berra: when Yogi gets the ball on the green, it's as good as in the hole. Diehl, happy to comply, shouts, "That's good—you're done!" whenever Yogi hits the green. It's a convivial outing, and Diehl loves talking with Berra as they ride in a golf cart together.

After a ball game or round of golf, Yogi and Gator eat dinner at one of five local restaurants, and Berra never strays from having a chopped salad with his favorite dish at each eatery. Everyone recognizes Yogi in public places, and Guidry does his best to protect Yogi's privacy. Fans who manage to approach Yogi receive a polite but firm declination. "Sorry," Berra says. "I've been told I'm not allowed to sign anything. It's business."

Every fourth night they eat in their respective rooms, and Guidry makes sure Yogi has a good sandwich with a side of veggies. And that is what Yogi is facing this mid-March evening of 2003, Guidry tells him, if Berra doesn't at least try one of Gator's signature frog legs.

"Forget going to the Bahama Breeze tonight," Guidry says, "unless you taste one of these."

Berra grunts, pulls one leg from the tray, and bites. Then a bigger bite, and the meat disappears. Then, smiling wryly at Gator, Yogi silently takes four more legs.

"When are we going to have these again?" he asks when the tray is empty.

"You're going to have to wait until next spring," Guidry replies. "This was the last batch."

Another grunt. "Okay. Just don't forget."

## The Old Friend

It's midmorning in late July of 2007 when Yogi Berra walks into Phil Rizzuto's room at the Green Hill assisted living facility in West Orange, New Jersey. Yogi has been coming to see Phil once or twice weekly for the last year, and he's pleased to find Rizzuto awake. "Hi, Yog," Phil says softly as Yogi sits down by the bed and takes his friend's frail hand. Some days the two men play cards or bingo, but Rizzuto is too tired for the game room. Today Yogi will look for a movie on TV while they talk.

Both men know these are the last few months, maybe weeks, of the 89-year-old Rizzuto's life. A few years earlier Phil had surgery to remove part of his stomach, and—given the steroid scandals dogging baseball—he joked about having to take the drugs. Problems with his esophagus began last fall, and now he's battling pneumonia.

They both love reminiscing. After all, it was almost 60 years ago when Rizzuto—then an All-Star shortstop with the Yankees—urged the team's promising young catcher to leave St. Louis and move east. New York is where the money is, Rizzuto told Berra, eight years younger. New York is for stars.

Berra listened and has never regretted taking Phil's advice. Sure, there was a little grumbling from some folks on The Hill who felt Berra had left them behind. Yogi sensed it four years earlier when he and Joe Garagiola attended a ceremony changing the name of Elizabeth Avenue—the street where both lived as boys—to Hall of Fame Place. Some whispered it was the first time they had seen Yogi in years—unlike Joe, who visited often.

In truth, Yogi did go home, although he preferred to stay with Carmen's parents in quiet, rural Salem. But Ernest Short died in 1984, Carmen's mom Barbara in 2000. Yogi's sister Josie came to visit him in New Jersey fairly often, so there were fewer reasons to spend time in St. Louis.

Home for Yogi was Montclair, about a 20-minute ride from the house Rizzuto had bought in Hillside in 1949 and never left. That's where he and Cora, his wife of 65 years, raised their four children. The two families grew up together, and Yogi and Phil became as close as brothers. Phil is the godfather of Yogi's oldest son Larry, and lately they've recalled good times on the beach with their families during spring training in St. Petersburg, Florida.

Phil had been right about opportunities in New York. They both made plenty of money from their bowling alley as well as public appearances and commercials. And both have profited in the lucrative memorabilia market. Sometimes they complain—then laugh—about fans who think of Phil as the man from the Money Store, the finance company he represented on TV for almost 20 years, and of Yogi as the Yoo-Hoo guy.

Phil slowed down by the end of the '90s, but Berra is still going strong. After the terrorist attacks of September 11, 2001, Berra starred in a classic public service ad for New York City. Dressed in a tux, he conducted the New York Philharmonic before a cheering audience. Ending with a leaping flourish, he deadpanned, "Who the heck is this guy Phil Harmonic?" A year later he had a smash hit pitching for the Aflac insurance company opposite the Aflac duck. "If you get hurt and miss work, it won't hurt to miss work," Berra says in the most popular segment of the long-running campaign.

You know, he's told Phil many times, that duck doesn't really talk, and they always laugh. And they laughed at the VISA commercial Berra did with Yao Ming, the seven-foot-six NBA star from China. Phil still hasn't caught up with the three books Berra has published since 2001.

Today, neither man is paying much attention to the movie on TV, just enjoying each other's company. It was the diminutive and gregarious Rizzuto, affectionately nicknamed Scooter, who did most of the talking in their younger days. *Yogi doesn't talk much,* Phil would tell people. *He listens and makes noises, but I know what he means.* And now it's Yogi who carries the conversation.

They reminisce about DiMaggio, Whitey, the Mick, and so many others. Eating Momma Berra's pasta when the Yankees played in St. Louis. Buying cannoli from their favorite Italian bakery in Jersey City after visiting their friend Ed Lucas, the blind sports reporter. And golf, always golf. So many great times together.

Yogi stops talking as Phil falls asleep, then kisses Rizzuto on the forehead. "I'll see you soon, buddy," he whispers, then tiptoes out.

It's a sunny Tuesday, August 14, when Dave Kaplan drives Yogi to the Stadium to see the Yankees play the Orioles. As always, they arrive many hours early. Yogi is in the clubhouse chatting when Kaplan learns that Rizzuto has passed away in his sleep late the night before, a month shy of his 90th birthday. Kaplan knows this will be a big story for the dozens of reporters covering the game, and everyone will seek Yogi's reaction. He finds Yankee manager Joe Torre, tells him the news, and asks Berra's good friend if he can help Yogi during the unavoidable interview session.

Soon Torre is sitting with Berra on the Yankee bench, his right arm draped around the shoulders of a grieving man. At least two dozen reporters surround them with microphones and tape recorders, jostling with photographers and cameramen.

Berra takes a deep breath.

*Yogi, can you tell us how much you will miss him?*

"I'll remember him the rest of my life.... He's my son's godfather, you know." His voice breaks as Torre's large hand squeezes Berra's shoulder. "I'm going to miss him."

*What has the last month been like?*

"It's been pretty bad," Yogi answers, his voice low but steady now. "He got an infection—they were feeding him through the stomach. He was gradually going down. But I'd come in and he would recognize me."

*What are some of your best memories?*

"What can I say? Geez, there are a lot of good memories," he says, his mind flooded. But then he smiles.

"When he made that long speech when he got in the Hall of Fame, and he said if nobody wants to stay they can leave," says Yogi, laughing a bit as he tells the story. "So Johnny Bench and I got up and walked off the stage."

*Did you do a lot of reminiscing?*

"If he was awake," says Yogi, his head down. "He wasn't awake a lot of the time, you know."

Yogi looks up again. He turned 82 in May, and friends have begun to die. Ted Williams passed away in 2002, Larry Doby in 2003. John McMullen died in September of 2005.

And now the Scooter.

"Phil was one of the greatest people I ever knew," Yogi says. "I'm really going to miss him."

## The New Man

Yankee manager Joe Girardi is sitting in his office at Legends Field in Tampa in early March of 2008, and he's anxious. In a few moments Yogi Berra will walk in to begin another four-week stint as a spring training instructor. And Girardi, whose four seasons as a Yankee catcher ended before Berra rejoined the team's spring coaching staff, has no idea how Yogi feels about Joe's new position.

He does know Yogi is close to former manager Joe Torre, who departed unhappily when management, now led by 38-year-old Hal Steinbrenner, refused to give him more than a one-year contract. Torre won four World Series, six pennants, 10 division titles, and the hearts of Yankee fans in 12 seasons and is headed to the Hall of Fame. Girardi also knows the man he beat for the job, former Yankee star and fan favorite Don Mattingly, is also great friends with Berra.

Girardi, like General Manager Brian Cashman, advocates using data-based scouting reports, an approach that irritated Torre, who believed in observation and instinct over statistics. And Berra, Girardi knows, managed like Torre when he took two of his teams to the World Series. All these potential resentments and frictions account for the knot in Girardi's stomach.

Girardi played 15 seasons for five different teams, then coached with the Yankees in 2005 before managing an awful Florida Marlins team to a surprising 78–84 record. Despite good reviews as a rookie manager, he was fired after constant disputes with the Marlins front office, then took a job in the Yankee broadcast booth. The first few weeks of this camp have gone smoothly, but Girardi felt butterflies when Berra's golf clubs appeared recently in his office, heralding the Yankee legend's arrival.

He followed Ron Guidry's advice—a bottle of Ketel One vodka, Yogi's favorite, is in his desk drawer. And now Berra stands in the doorway of Girardi's office wearing a blue Yankee blazer and Yankee cap. "Hey, Skip," Berra says. "Can I come in?"

"Sure, Yogi," says Girardi, who scrambles from his seat to greet Berra. "Come in, please. Sit down."

Berra sits down and quickly asks his primary question. "So, Joe," he says, "what do you want me to do? I'm here to help."

Girardi can feel his tension melt. If Yogi harbors hard feelings about the acrimonious split between the Yankees and Torre, he clearly holds no ill will toward Girardi. Indeed, within minutes, Joe feels Yogi's reassurance for *him*.

The two old catchers talk about the 2008 Yankees. How to handle Jorge Posada's probable transition from starter to reserve catcher. What they could expect from Jason Giambi, now 37 and no longer using steroids. How to pace a team whose three best pitchers are 36, 38, and 39, with seven position players who are 32 or older.

Girardi, a Northwestern grad with a quick, curious mind, could spend all day picking Berra's brain for sharp observations, but the day's workout approaches. Yogi has just two questions left for Girardi.

"What do you want *me* to do?" Berra repeats.

"Anything you want," Girardi answers. "Obviously, working with the catchers would be great. But just let me know what else you want to do."

Berra nods.

"Also...I was wondering if I could leave early on Saturdays when we have night games," Yogi says a bit sheepishly. "I like to go to evening Mass."

"Yogi," says Girardi, a bit stunned Yogi is asking permission to do *anything,* "you can leave to go to church whenever you want."

# CHAPTER 42

# Immortal
## 2010–2015

A table sits in the glass-enclosed lobby of the Yogi Berra Museum &
Learning Center, a brace of microphones set up in front of the
middle of three chairs facing reporters and cameramen. Yogi Berra
enters and slowly slides in behind the microphones, and Carmen and
their son Dale sit on either side. It's the early afternoon of July 13,
2010, and Yogi, in a white button-down shirt and blue Yankee cap,
looks sad and older than his 85 years.

A Steinbrenner aide had called a few hours earlier to tell Yogi that
George had died, and Berra is still shaken. He knew George was battling
a form of Alzheimer's disease and it was in an advanced stage. But they'd
spoken just nine days earlier, and Steinbrenner was having a fine day.

It was July 4, George's birthday, and Yogi called to wish him well,
as he'd done every year since Steinbrenner's apology in 1999. The
two men have grown old together in the years since, and a warm
friendship replaced their celebrated acrimony. So George was excited
to receive Yogi's 8 a.m. birthday call.

"How's my girlfriend?" he asked, referring to Carmen. "I'm in
great shape, Yogi. I'm feeling fine. I feel good."

He'd been chipper and making jokes. Nine days ago. And now,
gone.

Museum director Dave Kaplan tells the assembled reporters what a great friend "Mr. Steinbrenner" has been to the Museum & Learning Center. Then he cedes to Yogi and the media.

*Are you going to miss him?* shouts a reporter.

"Yeah, you're darn right I will," Yogi says. "Are you kidding? He was a good man. When I go to Florida for spring training he called me all the time to come up to his box and watch the game with him. He became a good man, a nice man."

It pained Yogi to remember the last few times he saw his friend in Yankee Stadium. During the 2008 All-Star pregame ceremonies, the scoreboard screen showed Steinbrenner weeping behind dark glasses as he rode in a slow-moving jeep from the outfield fence to the infield. It sobered Yogi to watch this once powerful man reduced to tears. A little more than a year later, a frail, wheelchair-bound George, at the Stadium for Game 2 of the 2009 World Series, barely recognized Berra.

"He tried to get a winner the best he could," Berra tells reporters. "Heck, I wish I could have played for him. He was very generous. The only thing I didn't like was the way I was fired as manager. I didn't like the...way...he...did it," says Berra, fighting tears. "That's why I didn't come back all those years."

Carmen reaches over to touch her husband's arm. "When I called him he sounded good, good," repeats Berra. He shakes his head ever so slightly, his jaw moving as if he's about to say something, but the words fail.

*Can you talk about coming back after 14 years?* another reporter asks.

"We went through some tough times like everyone else did, but he was a wonderful man," Yogi says. "Talked to him on his birthday... He sounded real good. He said, 'Maybe I'll see you on Old-Timers' Day.'

"I was wishing that would happen."

Yogi's own plan to attend his favorite game ends just 24 hours before Saturday's event. Leaving his house on July 16 for a haircut and manicure, he trips on the front steps and falls face-first on the brick pathway. Berra is in excellent health for a man his age, but he takes a blood thinner for an irregular heartbeat, so there is blood everywhere.

Determined to be properly groomed for the Old-Timers' Game and for Induction Weekend in Cooperstown the following weekend, Berra forges ahead. He changes clothes and, keeping pressure on the bleeding, drives one-handed. Denise Duke, his stylist, pleads with him to go to the hospital, but he refuses. A worried Duke gives him a haircut and manicure while assistants try to stop the bleeding.

It isn't until Duke accompanies Berra home that she reaches Larry Berra, who calls Carmen. She's stunned when she sees Yogi and insists that he go to the hospital, where doctors treat and release him. But Berra wakes up sore and stiff the next day and consents to return to the hospital. This time, fearing complications and perhaps a concussion, the doctors admit him.

Berra does not leave the hospital for almost two weeks, missing the Old-Timers' Game and his annual trip to Cooperstown. This fall has taken a large toll. Yogi can walk without pain, but his pace is slower now, his gait just a bit unsure, even with a cane or walker. And when he talks, his voice is softer. Carmen takes his car keys.

There is more hard news just a few months later. Yogi's sister Josie, who was still living in the family's house on The Hill in St. Louis, passes away at 80 on November 6. Carmen and Yogi travel to St. Louis for the funeral and stay with Carmen's sister Bonnie. Carmen has told her sister all about Yogi's fall, but it's still a shock for Bonnie to see this once graceful, athletic man—the brother-in-law she's loved for more than 60 years—now unsteady on his feet.

Yogi's two oldest brothers—he still talks appreciatively about all the extra hours at work they put in so he could have the chance to play baseball—have long since passed, Tony in 1977, Mike in 1995. Now his little sister is gone, too. At age 85, Yogi is Pietro and Paulina Berra's last living child.

Josie is laid to rest at Resurrection Cemetery, where Yogi's mother and father and two of his three brothers are buried. After a few days of visiting relatives and friends, the Berras are back on an eastbound flight.

It's the last time Yogi and Carmen will see their home state.

*     *     *

Yogi and Carmen begin to slip from public view over the next few years. Yogi flies to Tampa for spring training in March of 2011, and Yankee coaches and players are surprised by the frail version of the friend whom they all adore. He decides against getting into uniform, watches games from the owner's box, and usually asks Ron Guidry to drive him to the hotel well before game's end.

Yogi is disciplined with his rehab, but he almost falls again at Joe Torre's golf tournament in June. A few weeks later, Kevin McLaughlin catches Berra when he slips in a bathroom at a card show. Carmen has battled her own health issues, including a minor stroke, and can no longer care for Yogi.

The family makes arrangements for Yogi to enter Crane's Mill, an assisted living facility a few miles from their home, in early 2012, and Carmen joins him soon after. Yogi flies to spring training in March but stays just a few days. He all but vanishes from his two cherished clubhouses—Yankee Stadium and the Yogi Berra Museum. One of his few visits to the Bronx comes on May 12, when the Yankees present him with a pregame birthday cake at home plate. Ron Guidry elates Yogi as the surprise guest. Soon after the ceremony—with "Happy Birthday" sung by the crowd—Dave Kaplan drives Yogi, now 87, back to Crane's Mill.

Yogi attends the Old-Timers' Game in a wheelchair on July 1, and Guidry is once again by his side. Berra brightens noticeably at the sight of his former teammates. Old friends Mel Stottlemyre, Bobby Richardson, Bobby Brown, Stump Merrill, and more engulf Berra. The Yankees honor their Hall of Famers, Yogi and Whitey Ford, driving them from the outfield to the infield in a golf cart to ovations from the crowd of 48,324. And soon after the pregame ceremony, Kaplan again shepherds Yogi back to Crane's Mill.

Three weeks later Carmen and Yogi surprise their doctors and make the long trip to Cooperstown, where they attend all the dinners and ceremonies, though Yogi begs off the induction stage after 30 minutes in stifling heat. He loves seeing Sandy Koufax and Bob Gibson, Al Kaline and Willie Mays, Brooks Robinson and George Brett. And Red Schoendienst, now 89—the same Red who pitched to Yogi in their tryout for Branch Rickey so many years ago. To all the 44 Hall of Famers here this weekend, Yogi and Carmen are still the king and queen of the prom.

Yogi even spends an hour or so signing autographs at TJ's Place under the watchful eyes of Kevin McLaughlin, Ron Guidry, and Goose Gossage. When Monday comes, McLaughlin, who's been taking care of Yogi in Cooperstown for almost two decades, ushers Carmen and Yogi into their limo for the four-hour ride to Montclair. Being with them in Cooperstown this year had been as unexpected as it was heartwarming, and as McLaughlin watches the car pull away, he doubts Carmen and Yogi will grace Cooperstown again.

Both Carmen and Yogi celebrate their 88th birthdays in 2013—Yogi in May, Carmen in September. There are health challenges, but wonderful moments, too. Yogi calls Joe Garagiola on February 12 to sing "Happy Birthday" and laugh. And he makes two appearances at Yankee Stadium, one at his final Old-Timers' Game, the star of the event, and another at Yogi Berra Bobblehead Night. He still watches most Yankee games, analyzing plays, in his room at Crane's Mill.

He appears at his museum with San Francisco's star catcher Buster Posey in January, giving the 25-year-old National League MVP a tour and doing a Q&A with Posey for several dozen elementary school students from nearby Bloomfield. More than 20,000 students now attend seminars here each year.

And Yogi and Carmen are in the front row of the sold-out museum's theater in mid-November for a managers roundtable with former and current managers Tony La Russa, Jim Leyland, Buck Showalter, Joe Girardi, and Don Mattingly, manager of the Los Angeles Dodgers, who wears No. 8 to honor Yogi.

The five managers spellbind the audience with stories of high-pressure games, favorite strategies, and the management challenges that come from dealing with highly paid big league players. As the evening draws to a close, the 69-year-old La Russa, who will learn he's made the Hall of Fame a month later, tells the audience he has another thought. "The opportunity to be here tonight, to be at your museum," La Russa says, looking directly at Yogi, "is one of the nicest things I have ever been involved in. I thank you for inviting me, and if you ever need me for anything, I will be here with bells on."

Yogi and Carmen quietly celebrate their 65th wedding anniversary on January 26, 2014, but soon after, Carmen suffers a serious stroke. She loses most of her ability to swallow and sees only family now. Then one day her granddaughter Lindsay calls Dave Kaplan. "Gram wants to see you and Naomi," Lindsay says. Kaplan and his wife visit the next day for a tender, teary conversation.

Soon after, Carmen stops eating, and on March 6, after a day with Yogi and her sons, Carmen dies peacefully in her sleep. For the first time in almost 70 years, the pretty young waitress from Biggie's on The Hill, the woman who profoundly and devotedly shaped Yogi's life, is no longer by his side.

The saddest year of Yogi Berra's life gets a little sadder when his memory-filled house on Highland Avenue—where he watched late-night reruns of *Seinfeld* and *Sanford and Son* with his son Larry for a decade prior to entering Crane's Mill—is sold in July for $988,888. Larry had tried to move out several times after returning in 2001, but Carmen always convinced him to stay. "Your father really looks forward to watching TV with you," she told him.

There's a bittersweet moment when Yogi, now 89, surprises a huge Yankee Stadium crowd on August 23, riding in a golf cart with Joe and Ali Torre the day the team retires their former manager's uniform number. Berra sits a bit slumped in his blue blazer and Yankee cap, occasionally raising his right arm a foot off his lap to wave slowly as the cart makes its way from the outfield to the podium and chairs flanking the pitcher's mound. He remains seated in the golf cart while Torre speaks to the crowd for himself and his old friend.

When Torre finishes to loud applause, he walks back to Berra, leans over, and kisses him on the head.

"I love you, my man," Torre says.

And there's a shocking moment in early October of 2014 when thieves break into the Yogi Berra Museum & Learning Center and steal Yogi's 10 championship rings and two MVP plaques. Local, state, and federal law enforcement authorities investigate, offering a $5,000 reward for information, but the case goes unsolved.

Thankfully, many of the rings were replicas. Berra's third MVP plaque rests safely in the Hall of Fame in Cooperstown—along with the glove he used in Don Larsen's perfect game—and insurance covers most losses. The Yankees soon announce they will present the museum with rings for all 27 of their championships, the Mets say they will donate rings for the 1969 World Series and the 1973 National League pennant, both won under Berra, and Major League Baseball will deliver replicas of all three MVP plaques.

Berra is touched by this generosity, but most touching of all is his response to the theft. Pointing to his head, he says, "It's all up here."

Berra battles congestive heart failure in 2015 but still loves to get out by wheelchair. One of those rare moments comes on May 12, when Yogi celebrates his 90th birthday at the museum. Joe Torre is there, along with former Yankees Willie Randolph, Mickey Rivers, and Rick Cerone. So are friends Arlene Howard, Marty Appel, and Jeff Idelson, now Hall of Fame president. The entire Berra clan attends, save Nick, one of Yogi's 11 grandchildren, who is serving in the Army overseas.

Governors Chris Christie (New Jersey) and Andrew Cuomo (New York) proclaim May 12 Yogi Berra Day, and the Hillside Elementary School's Drums of Thunder provide entertainment. There is a cake, of course, and a red ribbon–cutting ceremony to mark the reopening of the championship ring and MVP plaque exhibits. Yogi is not quite strong enough to wield the scissors, so granddaughter Lindsay holds his hand and they cut the ribbon together.

All the local TV stations are filming the event, and Lindsay asks the public to support nominating Yogi for the Presidential Medal of Freedom, the nation's highest civilian honor. "He is the embodiment of the American dream," Lindsay summarizes, appealing for the 100,000 signatures needed in the next 30 days.

Yogi, sitting in his wheelchair and wearing a white Museum & Learning Center hat, doesn't speak. But he beams over the gathering with deep appreciation.

Yogi grows weaker in the following month. On September 22—the same day Berra played his first game as a fledgling Yankee 69 years earlier—museum director Dave Kaplan, sportscaster Russ Salzberg, and granddaughter Lindsay Berra visit Yogi together. Kaplan leaves first, giving Yogi a hug and telling him he loves him. Salzberg follows, kissing his old friend on the head as he leaves.

Lindsay and others in the family take turns at Yogi's side, leaving him to rest as the day ebbs. Later that evening, the hospital staff calls Larry Berra, and the family rushes to hold Yogi's hands as his breath fades. Tim arrives just in time; Dale walks in moments after his father passes.

He's lived a long, grand, even heroic life, and it's hard to imagine a world without Yogi. "A punch to the gut," Dave Kaplan says when the museum staff gathers to craft its statement. Larry Berra calls Joe Garagiola in Scottsdale, Arizona. Garagiola, battling health problems of his own, immediately calls his son Joe Jr. "I just lost my best friend," he says.

The response to the loss of Berra, both sadness and honor, flows from every national corner and lasts for days. Governor Christie orders flags to half-mast, and the Empire State Building is lit blue and white to evoke Yankee pinstripes. Moments of silence precede every Major League Baseball game.

The Yankees hold a heartfelt pregame ceremony, with four catchers—Joe Girardi, Brian McCann, Gary Sanchez, and Austin Romine—laying a large white wreath shaped as a number 8 in the box behind home plate. President Obama issues a statement, offering condolences.

"Yogi Berra was an American original," Obama says. "He epitomized what it meant to be a sportsman and a citizen."

Newspapers and magazines publish photos of the arc of Yogi's life: from The Hill to D-Day, from star catcher to American folk hero. Television networks broadcast clips of the many iconic moments of his two careers—the catcher leaping into the arms of perfect-game pitcher Don Larsen, the pitchman upstaging the Aflac duck. Former teammates and opponents call radio and TV stations to recount favorite Yogi stories and reflect.

"To those who didn't know Yogi personally, he was one of the greatest baseball players of all time," Derek Jeter says. "To those lucky ones who did know him, he was an even better person."

Every opinion and headline writer searches for words to capture the magic of the man's 90 years—70 of them on the national stage.

YOGI BERRA, YANKEE WHO BUILT HIS STARDOM 90 PERCENT ON SKILL AND HALF ON WIT, DIES AT 90 reads the headline on the front page of the *New York Times*.

"As long as people talk about the game of baseball," says legendary Dodger announcer Vin Scully, "whenever they mention the name Yogi Berra, they will smile."

"Baseball legend Yogi Berra, whose humorous quotes made him one of America's most beloved sports icons, has died," the BBC tells its readers in England.

Yogi's many quiet acts of kindness explain much of the outpouring. Sportswriter Moss Klein first met Berra in 1976 as a green reporter covering the Yankees for the *Newark Star-Ledger*. The veteran coach eased Klein's nerves by chatting about sports and their mutual love for New Jersey. And when Klein missed four straight games early in the 1980 season, Berra noticed. He learned the writer was recovering from minor surgery, and soon the phone rang at Klein's home.

"Hey, it's Yog," Berra said. "How are you feeling?"

No Berra story feels complete without a Yogi-ism, and there are many—eight in *Bartlett's Familiar Quotations* alone.

The most famous is his insight about discipline: *It ain't over 'til it's over.*

Some are observant, if a bit fractured: *If people don't want to come out to the ballpark, nobody's going to stop them.* Or *It's déjà vu all over again.*

Others are goofy: *Never answer an anonymous letter.* And this one: *You better cut the pizza in four pieces; I'm not hungry enough to eat six.*

One is simply spot-on: *I really didn't say everything I said.*

Few are as sweet as his tribute to his wife: *We have a good time together, even when we're not together.*

And none more apropos at this moment: *You should always go to other people's funerals. Otherwise, they won't come to yours.*

The streets surrounding the Church of the Immaculate Conception in Montclair are closed on September 29 for Berra's funeral, which looks like a ceremony for a head of state. More than 100 servicemen and servicewomen from two New Jersey naval stations circle the church, a tribute to Yogi's combat naval service. The funeral, broadcast live on local television, is also amplified for crowds standing behind police barriers.

Timothy Cardinal Dolan, the Archbishop of New York, presides over the one-hour service for 400 invitation-only guests. More than a dozen Yankees, past and present, attend: Derek Jeter, Alex Rodriguez and CC Sabathia, Reggie Jackson, Bernie Williams, and Ron Guidry. Managing partner Hal Steinbrenner is here, as is Commissioner Rob Manfred, Jackie's widow Rachel Robinson, and Rudy Giuliani. So are Sandy Koufax and Bill White, Yogi's longtime friends.

Every speaker mixes tender memories with lighthearted humor. The family chose Dale to speak so Yogi's youngest son could publicly thank his father for his support in tough times. Joe Torre speaks next. After recounting many of Yogi's accomplishments, Torre tells the congregation that those statistics and stories don't capture "what Lawrence Peter Berra was all about."

He shares a story from Joe Garagiola Jr., attending for his family. "He said his dad used to call Yogi his 3 a.m. buddy," says Torre, who had asked Joe to explain. "He said, 'Well, Dad says they might not talk for six months, and he could pick up the phone at three in the morning and say I need to see you. And Yogi would be right over.'"

An honor guard concludes the service: a bugler plays taps and two others smartly fold an American flag and present it to Larry Berra. The ashes in an urn will be interred at the Gate of Heaven Cemetery in East Hanover, New Jersey, next to Carmen.

As the church empties, a gray-haired woman of 56 listening behind the barrier approaches Spencer Ross, a local sportscaster, as he leaves the church. Her name is Mary Anne DeVarti, from a town an hour away. She had always hoped to meet Berra but never did, she tells Ross, and wonders whether he would be kind enough to part with the service program as a memento, which he does.

"Standing out here," DeVarti tells Ross as tears run down her cheeks, "I felt as if I could see through the bricks, as if I was inside. I've been a Yankee fan since I grew up, but I always believed that Yogi Berra was much more than a ballplayer."

So does everyone. Because the proud and humble man behind the mask was more than a baseball player.

Much, much more.

# Epilogue

arry Berra is sitting in the second row of seats in the East Room of the White House with 16 other men and women who will all soon be standing, one at a time, beside the man who is speaking at the podium before them. It's November 24, 2015, and President Barack Obama is extolling the virtues of the 17 women and men who are about to be awarded the Medal of Freedom, the highest civilian honor in America.

Berra listens as Obama tells the audience about 97-year-old mathematician Katherine Johnson, sitting in the front row, a couple of seats down from Larry, the African-American woman who calculated the flight path that put Neil Armstrong on the moon. The President talks of Steven Spielberg taking us from Jurassic Park to the beaches of Normandy and about the essential work of Bill Ruckelshaus, the nation's first Administrator of the Environmental Protection Agency, who is now battling climate change.

Obama is relaxed and smiles as he praises the lifework of these civilian masters. "This is an extraordinary group," he says, "even by the standards of Medal of Freedom recipients." He nods toward Barbra Streisand and tells everyone of the young Barbra who saw her first Broadway show at age 14 and just knew she could walk onto the stage and play any role she wanted with no trouble at all.

"That's what's called chutzpah," Obama says.

And then the President comes to Larry Berra's namesake.

"What can be said about Lawrence 'Yogi' Berra that he couldn't say better himself?" Obama asks, getting a nice laugh. "The son of an

Italian bricklayer, he was born to play baseball. But he loved his country," Obama says. He talks about a young man who joined the Navy and performed bravely in the invasion at Normandy. "After he returned, Yogi embarked on a career that would make him one of the greatest catchers of all time....He had, as one biographer put it, 'the winningest career in the history of American sports.' Nobody has won more than this guy.

"He lived his life with pride and humility, and an original, open mind. One thing we know for sure, if you can't imitate him, don't copy him." It takes the audience a half beat to recognize the Yogi-ism and respond. "It took everybody a while," Obama says with a sly grin.

Which is fitting, for it took a while to gain enough momentum to collect the 100,000 signatures required for the nominating petition. It even appeared it was going to get late a bit early—the petition was almost 30,000 signatures short in the final weekend of the 30-day window for submission. And that's when Yogi's granddaughter Lindsay beat the drum on just about every New York–area TV station, radio station, and sports website to get out the vote. By Day 30, there were 113,450 names on the petition, and when the Obama Administration saw Yogi's name on the list of candidates, the only question Obama had was why Berra hadn't already received this honor.

The President finishes the last of his introductions, and now it is time for the day's honorees to "get some hardware." Obama signals a military aide to call the roll, and first up is Yogi. "Larry Berra, receiving on behalf of Lawrence Peter Berra," says the aide as Larry makes his way to the podium. Another military aide stands at attention, holding open a large flat case so the audience can see the Medal of Freedom—a dark blue circle with 13 stars in the middle of a large white star, all set in a circle of five golden eagles.

"One of our nation's most beloved and quotable sports heroes, Lawrence Peter 'Yogi' Berra was a world-class baseball player and a great spirit," the first aide says as Larry Berra and the President stand side by side. "As the manager of the New York Yankees, he guided his team and the sport he loved with a wisdom that lives in our national consciousness, and taught us all that we can observe a lot just by watching."

The aide hands Obama the medal, and the President presents it to Larry, puts his right arm around Berra's broad, round shoulders, and points to the photographer. Pictures are taken as the crowd erupts in applause.

Lindsay Berra is one of six family members in the audience, applauding with a smile and a few tears. She kept her grandfather updated on the progress of the petition, and along with the rest of the family hoped their patriarch would live long enough to enjoy the honor. Sadly, Berra passed away just eight weeks before the White House announced the 2015 award winners.

But Yogi would be pleased at how it all turned out. The medal is now displayed in the front atrium of the Yogi Berra Museum & Learning Center, along with a video of Obama extolling Yogi's virtues. The message is clear: work hard, be a good person, respect others, and even a poor kid with an eighth-grade education can earn the nation's highest civilian honor.

It's September 13, 2016, a little more than a week shy of the one-year anniversary of the passing of Yogi Berra, and on this day, you can buy a piece of the baseball legend's legacy—especially if you have very deep pockets. This is the date when 108 pieces of Yogi Berra memorabilia—from his 1972 Hall of Fame induction ring and the No. 8 jersey he wore in the 1961 World Series to his Social Security card and an expired driver's license—go up for auction on Brandon Steiner's auction website.

The biggest prize: Yogi's 1953 World Series ring, the only championship ring he wore. Steiner set the opening price for Berra's ring—given to the 12 players on the Yankee teams that won five straight World Series titles—at an even $100,000. "His '53 championship ring is a real collector's item because it has a diamond 5 on it," says Dale Berra of his father's favorite piece of personal history. "It was given to the few players like Dad and Phil Rizzuto. That's a very special piece."

Dave Kaplan and others at the Yogi Berra Museum make sure to tell reporters that none of the handful of Yogi's personal memorabilia on display at the museum will be sold. The museum has just a small slice of Yogi's huge trove of memorabilia, but what is there will stay.

The auction is part of a deal the Berra family signed in April with Steiner that grants Steiner Sports exclusive rights to market Yogi's name and likeness. Steiner, who had marketing deals with Yogi that predated LTD Enterprises, is only putting a portion of the memorabilia he purchased from the Berra estate in this auction. The Berra collection is the centerpiece of what Steiner is calling the "Fall Classic Auction," which will also include items from Don Larsen. Berra's partner in the only perfect game in World Series history is selling his collection—including his 50th anniversary ring commemorating the perfect game—to help finance his grandchildren's college education.

This is not the first time the Berras are auctioning family heirlooms. Four months after Carmen's death, scores of her possessions—from mink stoles and evening gowns to china and antiques—were offered for auction with a different online auction house. Items ranged from a Sarouk-style carpet, which went for $4,620 after drawing 14 bids, to a Pendleton wool blanket that sold for $60. Carmen Berra's three surviving sisters didn't learn about the auction until several years later, much to their deep dismay.

There is plenty of publicity surrounding the sale of Yogi's memorabilia, the auction previewed by local media as well as industry publications and websites. "It is a pleasure and honor for the Berra family to share Dad's history with his many followers," Dale Berra repeats for most every reporter handling the story, "because they are responsible for his legacy."

The online auction ends October 24, and as expected, Yogi's 1953

World Series ring is the top seller: $159,720, offered by an anonymous bidder. Berra's 1972 Hall of Fame ring goes for $90,000, and his game-worn 1961 World Series jersey brings in $71,874.

There is a big market for the more obscure pieces of Berra history. Sixteen collectors bid for three of Yogi's passports (winning bid: $7,530), a dozen bid for a signed Mastercard ($1,435), and eight bid for a $10,000 check to Dale Berra from his father ($720). All bore Yogi's signature.

In all, 81 of the 108 pieces are sold, bringing in $493,855. The rest of Berra's memorabilia will be sold in later auctions or as separate pieces by Steiner, who is betting Yogi's name will endure for years to come. There is reason to believe: in the 2016 Davie-Brown Index, which measures a celebrity's influence on consumers, Yogi's name is as recognizable as those of Olympic stars Usain Bolt and Mia Hamm.

"We're trying to see what's still there," Tim Berra tells the *New York Times*. "But he has some advantages: He's a great Yankee, he's well known outside the athletic genre, and he's beloved by everybody.

"Our main goal is to keep my dad's name around."

How do you keep an icon museum afloat when it loses its icon?

That's the question the board of the Yogi Berra Museum & Learning Center hires new executive director Eve Schaenen to answer early in 2017. And that's why Schaenen is in a middle school in Rome, Georgia a few months later, sitting across from a retired schoolteacher, listening to the story that shaped this man's life.

Schaenen, a Montclair resident with extensive nonprofit experience, was going through the mail in her first few weeks on the job when she came upon a donation for about $30 from a man named Therian Smith. It was the return address that caught her attention: *Rome,* Georgia. How appropriate, she thought, given Yogi's Italian roots. She sent Smith a thank-you note, as she does for every contribution.

When Eve saw another contribution from Smith the next month, and then again the following month, she asked the staff what they knew about this man. Not much, they said, other than Smith has sent in a monthly donation—sometimes as much as $100, sometimes as little as $10—religiously since late 2012.

Schaenen could not find a trace of Smith on the internet, so this time she wrote and asked Therian to contact her. The call came a week later, and it didn't take long for Eve to decide she needed to speak to Smith in person.

"My father left his wife and five kids when I was 11, and we were destitute," Smith tells Schaenen. "We survived on what our church gave us and what little money the rest of us could earn. I had a paper route."

He also cleaned the cafeteria after lunch, and that's what he was doing when he heard a commotion from the kids surrounding a TV set brought in for the 1953 Dodger-Yankee World Series. Smith had never seen a game but was curious enough to walk over in time to hear the announcer say Yogi Berra was coming to bat.

"Yogi hit a home run and there was this surge of electricity all over my body—I can't explain it," he tells Eve. "That was it. I became a Yogi Berra fan for life. I didn't pick Yogi as much as he picked me."

Schaenen is moved and very glad she has a videographer with her. Smith talks about reading everything he could find about Yogi, learning he was as good a person as he was a ballplayer. And when Therian graduated college and came back to Rome to teach English literature and grammar to middle school students, Yogi's life and his Yogi-isms became a big part of Smith's lesson plans.

Schaenen flew home with an idea. She had created the first Yogi Berra Museum Awards Gala to raise money and the museum's profile. They have already sold all 300 tickets—at $1,000 per ticket—for the May 12, 2017, event at the Plaza Hotel in Manhattan, and recruited former NFL star Boomer Esiason and actor Robert Wuhl to serve as emcees. Awards are going to Jennifer Steinbrenner, Ron Guidry, and the John McMullen family. The night's entertainment is set: New

Jersey's Southside Johnny and the Asbury Jukes, and former star Yankee Bernie Williams, who will display his considerable skill as a guitarist.

But the video interview with Smith will be her centerpiece. And the 75-year-old Therian and his nephew will be her guests and share a table with the Berra family.

Smith barely knew what to say when he learned he was going to New York. He is even more astonished the night of May 12—what would've been Yogi's 92nd birthday—as he sits with the Berras in the Plaza's Grand Ballroom, listening to Eve address the audience of family, friends, and celebrities. Schaenen talks about the new exhibits, the outreach to the military to honor Berra's service to his country, and new programs with Montclair State University.

"But tonight isn't only about *what* we're doing at the museum," she says from the ballroom's podium. "Tonight is also about *why* we're doing it." And that's when she tells the story of Therian Smith, his monthly donations to the museum, and why she thought it so important to meet him. "I'd like to think I can make the most eloquent case for the Yogi Berra Museum now that Yogi is no longer with us," she says. "But I couldn't possibly make the case better than Mr. Therian Smith. So I invite you all to listen to him now."

The lights are dimmed as the video of Smith plays on giant screens on each side of the podium. It opens with Therian talking from behind a desk in a room filled with pictures of Berra. He tells the story of Yogi's home run, and clips of Yogi are threaded throughout the three-and-a-half-minute video: Yogi hitting a home run, Yogi playing with his three sons, Yogi embracing the woman he loves, scenes from the Berra Museum.

"Throughout my career in education, I was committed to instilling in my students the values I so admired in Yogi," Smith says as the video draws to a close. "That's why I was drawn to supporting the Yogi Berra Museum & Learning Center. The world needs a place where our children can be inspired to carry on the qualities that made Yogi my hero."

Smith ticks off the qualities, which are in big bold letters on display cases at the Berra Museum. Soon the scene shifts to kids of all ages standing in the museum, talking about the same virtues: loyalty, respect, and honor; acceptance, cooperation, and community.

"The world will never have another Yogi, but the values that made him my hero live on at the Yogi Berra Museum," Smith says. "When it comes to Yogi's legacy, it ain't over."

The video ends, the room brightens, and in an instant everyone is standing and applauding. Most people in this room have their own Yogi stories, but rarely does one so perfectly encapsulate the man they are honoring than this modest, warm schoolteacher from Rome, Georgia, who appears to share with his hero those very qualities of character he so admires.

The awards are presented, the food is served, and stories are exchanged. The night goes by in a flash; the Asbury Jukes rock, and Bernie Williams amazes. The event is everything Schaenen hoped it would be for the Yogi Berra Museum. It's an experience Therian Smith will bring back home and never forget.

The news is not as good 17 months later. Smith was involved in a traffic accident in October and died from the injuries he sustained on November 2, 2018, at the age of 76. The obituary for Therian Hester Smith on the funeral home website is short and poignant. It tells of a man who taught for 30 years and worshipped at Second Avenue Baptist Church for 47 years, a man who loved to fish and considered himself a coffee connoisseur. And, of course, a lifelong New York Yankee fan—a Yogi Berra fan.

His devotion to Yogi was obvious from the picture accompanying the obituary. It was taken when Smith and his nephew traveled to New Jersey in the fall of 2012 and watched the first game of the World Series with a small crowd in the theater of the Yogi Berra Museum. The picture shows the tall, angular Smith wearing a Yankee jersey and a Yankee cap. The smiling man standing beside him is his idol, Yogi Berra.

The final lines of the obituary are instructions to his family and friends. In lieu of flowers, memorial contributions should be sent to the Yogi Berra Museum & Learning Center, 8 Yogi Berra Drive, Little Falls, New Jersey.

When it comes to Yogi's legacy, it ain't over.

# Acknowledgments

This story starts, as many baseball stories do, with a mitt. More specifically, a catcher's mitt. That's what my father handed to me to play Little League Baseball. I wanted to be a catcher, the same position my father played in his fastpitch softball league. Why catcher? My father's favorite player was Yogi Berra, one of the best and most interesting players he'd ever seen. That's why he played catcher, and I followed my father's path.

Tall, thin, and fast, I was later shifted to center field, which might be the more glamorous position but does not provide the unique view of the game one gets behind the plate. The catcher is the only player to see the entire field—nothing happens until he puts his fingers down to call the pitch, and no one but the catcher is required to know what every player has to do once the ball is hit. It's the catcher who pulls together the eight other players on the field and makes them into a team.

You don't win a championship without a good catcher. And you don't win multiple championships without a great one, as Yogi proved during his Hall of Fame career.

You don't write a book without a team, either, and the people who helped me write *Yogi* are exceptional. It's hard to overstate the influence Marty Stansell-Gamm had on this book. Her intelligence and boundless curiosity helped me work past the caricature of Yogi and understand how he affected everyone in his orbit: his family, his teammates, his friends. Marty brought many skills to our long talks, but I am grateful for one thing above all else: she never let me stop reporting or thinking about a story until I got it right. She knows when to push, when to nudge, and when to back off, and our talks truly helped shape the characters in this book.

Many others shaped *Yogi* as well, no one more than David Black, who again showed me how valuable an exceptional agent truly is. David's no-nonsense approach means you always know you are getting the truth—even if it is hard to hear. He knows when to deliver a stern lecture and when to be supportive. David goes far past being an advocate for the book—he is a friend, and that is invaluable.

Barry Geisler and my older son David were essential members of this team, reading the first drafts of chapters and responding quickly with the big-picture take. Both tough critics—neither Barry nor David sugarcoat their assessments—I knew if they gave a chapter the thumbs-up, I was on the right path. Yes, their critiques made for more work, but it was always worth the effort.

I was blessed with a roster of terrific researchers who led me to many of the anecdotes in this book, helped sort through the multiple versions of Yogi stories, added their ideas, and were always there to help me think through this narrative. Andy Werle, who researched my first book, *The Game,* laid an early organizational foundation until he left for MLB.com. My younger son Steve researched and edited the first part of *Yogi* before demands of a new job pulled him away. Nick Zararis put in two solid years of work researching and organizing the book as it grew. And my dear friend Craig Winston came in at the end when I needed a strong journalist, helping me sharpen the book and also hunt down the photos to illustrate Yogi's life.

A special thanks to the National Baseball Hall of Fame, which opened its archives to me, and HoF researcher Matt Rothenberg, who put together several terrific packages of clips for the book's major characters as well as found the needles in the haystack when I needed to track down obscure stories. Matt left the Hall of Fame in 2019 but remained in touch with the project, and fact-checked the final version of the book. I also need to thank Helody Dorvilus, who came in at the end to help fact-check as well as calm down a nervous author.

No one was a better friend to this book than Ron Wade, a news editor at the *St. Louis Post-Dispatch* who decided to be my guide in St. Louis. A student of local history, Ron took me through one neighborhood after another, giving me the historical background for the many ethnic sections of his adopted city. And he knew the best places for barbecued ribs in town. Ron—a big man with an even bigger heart—died far too young on January 25, 2017 of pancreatic cancer. He was 62. Ron has gone on to his next game, but his influence on this book is undeniable.

At Little, Brown and Company, I owe great thanks to publisher Reagan Arthur for green-lighting this book and waiting patiently for me to finish it, and to executive editor John Parsley, whose immediate embrace of the idea of a definitive Yogi biography gave me the confidence needed to tackle this project. When John left to be editor in chief at Dutton in the spring of 2017, Phil Marino stepped in without missing a beat. Phil's excitement about where the book was headed, as well as his excellent suggestions and guidance, were always a boost to my morale. He encouraged me to take the risks that, hopefully, made this book a good read.

Karen Landry and her production team—Barbara Clark, Barb Jatkola, Jeffrey Gantz, and Kay Banning—were, as always, invaluable. There's no question that Barbara's many suggestions made this book better. No one brought more good cheer—and was more flexible to my needs—than Karen. All I had to do was refrain from mentioning the plight of her beloved Red Sox in 2019 and all went smoothly.

Well more than a hundred sources helped shape my view of Yogi and the world in which he lived, from suffering the poverty of the Great Depression to attending school, going to war, playing American Legion ball, performing for the New York Yankees, and becoming a cultural icon. No one was more helpful than three men from The Hill in St. Louis who grew up with Yogi: Quinn Garavaglia,

Charlie Riva, and Vince DiRaimondo. Our two three-plus-hour sessions at The Hill Neighborhood Association brought out tales from the 1930s and '40s they hadn't revisited in years and years. We had plenty of phone conversations that filled in many a blank. Sadly, Quinn and Charlie passed away in recent years. The joy Quinn, Charlie, and Vince brought to their stories also flows through this book.

The Hill 2000 Neighborhood Association, director Lynn Marie Alexander, and board president Chris Saracino opened their archives to me, helped set up interviews on The Hill, and gave me the benefit of their memories about the early days of life in St. Louis' Little Italy. I am in their debt.

Two other sources must be mentioned: Bonnie Morse and Rose Cali. Both women spent long hours explaining the lives of Carmen and Yogi Berra to me. Bonnie, one of Carmen's four sisters, shared intimate memories of growing up on Barbara and Ernest Short's family farm, the early years with her sister and Yogi, and what it was like when Carmen married the famous ballplayer. I will never forget Bonnie's reply to one of my many email questions: "Jon, you are asking me to remember things that happened 70 years ago!"

But Bonnie always dug deep into her memory to answer my questions. So did Rose Cali, a longtime resident of Montclair who bought the Berras' first home in one of New York City's first suburbs in 1976, and later became the driving force behind the Yogi Berra Museum & Learning Center. Her help with other interview subjects was much appreciated, and Rose's insights and stories about the Berras from the 1970s to the years her two friends passed are treasures.

No author can write a book without a strong network of family and friends who remain supportive, interested, and full of helpful ideas despite several years of being asked the same questions and hearing the same stories. Special thanks go to Shirley Cohen, Kody Kurfien, Kathleen Pessah, Enid and Dennis Skahill, Phil and Lisa Jacobs, and, of course, Little Sammy; Shareeda Allen, Dr. Chris Cesa, Claire Smith, Bob Sansevere, and Kris Fitzgerald.

And finally, there is simply no way to adequately thank the one person most responsible for this project going from idea to finished book: my wife Suzi. Knowing full well the toll this project would take on our lives after enduring the five years it took to write *The Game,* Suzi did not hesitate to tell me to go for it again—just as she's always done as I've jumped from one career challenge to the next. Muse, supporter in chief, superlative sounding board, and proof-reader, Suzi held my hand when I was filled with doubts and kicked me in the rear when I needed a push. I am so very thankful she is always by my side in whatever we do.

# Notes and Sources

*Yogi: A Life Behind the Mask* is the result of hundreds of hours of interviews with more than 150 people conducted during a more than four-year span. The sources come from a wide spectrum: The Hill in St. Louis—Berra's boyhood neighborhood; Major League Baseball; the New York Yankees; the people of Montclair, New Jersey; and more. Many sources agreed to multiple interviews—some more than a dozen times over a span of several years—as well as lengthy email communication. Following is a list of many of my sources.

The book is written as a narrative, relying on events and anecdotes to tell the story of a boy growing up in an Italian enclave in St. Louis who became Yogi Berra, one of the most famous athletes and celebrities in the world right up until his death at the age of 90 in 2015. To re-create these scenes, I drew on a wide-range of material, especially Berra's two autobiographies: one written in 1960, when he was 35 and at the tail end of his Hall of Fame playing career, the other written in 1989, when he was 64 and leaving his second baseball career as a manager (seven seasons) and coach (19 seasons). To sort through multiple versions of the same story, I relied heavily on interviews with people involved or those who had direct knowledge of the events, and I reconstructed dialogue and events based on the recollection of my sources, direct quotations, and reporting from the print and electronic media.

I also relied on notes from meetings, personal correspondence, court and government documents, the Major League Baseball basic agreement, videos and documentaries, and the work of other reporters as cited in these notes. Several websites were of particular importance: the *Sporting News* archives, the *New York Times* archives, BaseballReference.com, and the Society for American Baseball Research biography project. Coverage of baseball salaries evolved from the pre-union contracts that bound players to their teams when Yogi broke into baseball in 1947 to the beginning of the Major League Baseball Players Association and free agency, when Yogi was a manager and coach and his youngest son, Dale Berra, was an active player in the 1970s and '80s. News outlets reported various salaries for a given season. For consistency in Berra's yearly salary, this book cites the figures for each season found in BaseballReference.com.

## Sources

Jean Afterman, Lynn Marie Alexander, Tom Amico, Dave Anderson, Marty Appel, Harvey Araton, Don Baylor, Joel Berenson, Larry Berra, Lindsay Berra, Ralph Branca, Bobbi Brown, Bobby Brown, Mary Frances Brown, Ray Bueneman, Father Frank Burla, Rose Cali, Brian Cashman, Rick Cerrone, Bob Cerv, Jim Coates, Dr. Susan Cole, Len Coleman, Eric Davis, Joe Del Raso, Al Downing, Stacy Fishman, Joan Ford, Joe Garagiola Jr., Quinn Garavaglia, Holly Gera, Joe Girardi, Peter Golenbock, Goose Gossage, Ron Guidry, Arlene Howard, Jeff Idelson, Al Kaline, Dave Kaplan, Bill Katz, Tom Kean, Dan Knowles, Jerry Koosman, Don Larsen, Randy Levine, Robert Lipsyte, George Lois, Chris Lucas, Ed Lucas, Bill Madden, Steve Mahfood, Jill Martin, Jon Matlack, Don Mattingly, Tim McCarver, Kevin McLaughlin, Stump Merrill, Bonnie Morse, James Murray, Sweeny Murti, Phil Niekro, Marty Noble, Betty Lou O'Dell, Phil Pepe, Joe Pepitone, Mark Porter, Willie Randolph, Tom Reich, Betsy Richardson, Bobby Richardson, Charlie Riva, Betty Robinson, Eddie Robinson, Russ Salzberg, Chris Saracino, Eve Schaenen, Red Schoendienst, Bobby Shantz, Roy Sievers, Claire Smith, Therian Smith, Rusty Staub, Brandon Steiner, Steve Swindal, Beth Sztuk,

Ralph Terry, Frank Thomas, Dick Tofel, Tom Villante, Ron Wade, Suzyn Waldman, Finn Wentworth, Bill White.

## Books

Appel, Marty. *Casey Stengel: Baseball's Greatest Character*. New York: Doubleday, 2017.

———. *Pinstripe Empire: The New York Yankees from Before the Babe to After the Boss*. New York: Bloomsbury, 2012.

Araton, Harvey. *Driving Mr. Yogi: Yogi Berra, Ron Guidry, and Baseball's Greatest Gift*. New York: Houghton Mifflin Harcourt, 2012.

Baldassaro, Lawrence. *Beyond DiMaggio: Italian Americans in Baseball*. Lincoln: University of Nebraska Press, 2011.

Barra, Allen. *Yogi Berra: Eternal Yankee*. New York: W. W. Norton, 2009.

Baylor, Don, with Claire Smith. *Don Baylor: Nothing but the Truth—A Baseball Life*. New York: St. Martin's, 1989.

Berra, Dale. *My Dad, Yogi: A Memoir of Family and Baseball*. New York: Hachette Books, 2019.

Berra, Yogi. *The Yogi Book: "I Really Didn't Say Everything I Said."* New York: Workman Publishing, 1999.

Berra, Yogi, and Ed Fitzgerald. *Yogi: The Autobiography of a Professional Baseball Player*. New York: Doubleday, 1961.

Berra, Yogi, with Tom Horton. *Yogi: It Ain't Over*. New York: McGraw-Hill, 1989.

Berra, Yogi, and Dave Kaplan. *Ten Rings: My Championship Seasons*. New York: HarperCollins, 2003.

———. *What Time Is It? You Mean Now?: Advice for Life from the Zennest Master of Them All*. New York: Simon & Schuster, 2002.

———. *When You Come to a Fork in the Road—Take It: Inspiration and Wisdom from One of Baseball's Greatest Heroes*. New York: Hachette Books, 2001.

———. *You Can Observe a Lot by Watching: What I've Learned About Teamwork from the Yankees and Life*. Hoboken, NJ: John Wiley & Sons, 2008.

Bevis, Charlie. *The New England League: A Baseball History 1855–1949*. Jefferson, NC: McFarland & Company, 2007.

Bradlee, Ben, Jr. *The Kid: The Immortal Life of Ted Williams*. New York: Little, Brown, 2013.

Branson, Douglas M. *Greatness in the Shadows: Larry Doby and the Integration of the American League*. Lincoln: University of Nebraska Press, 2016.

Burk, Robert F. *Much More Than a Game: Players, Owners, and American Baseball Since 1921*. Chapel Hill: University of North Carolina Press, 2001.

Cateura, Linda Brandi. *Growing Up Italian: How Being Brought Up as an Italian-American Helped Shape the Characters, Lives, and Fortunes of Twenty-Four Celebrated Americans.* New York: William Morrow, 1988.

Cramer, Richard Ben. *Joe DiMaggio: The Hero's Life.* New York: Simon & Schuster, 2000.

*Daily News* [New York]. *Joe DiMaggio: An American Icon.* Daily News Legends Series. Champaign, IL: Sports Publishing, 1998.

———. *Yogi Berra: An American Original.* Daily News Legends Series. Champaign, IL: Sports Publishing, 1998.

DeVito, Carlo. *Yogi: The Life and Times of an American Original.* Chicago: Triumph Books, 2008.

Elson, Aaron. *A Mile in Their Shoes: Conversations with Veterans of World War II.* Maywood, NJ: Chi Chi Press, 1998.

Forker, Dom. *The Men of Autumn: An Oral History of the 1949–53 World Champion New York Yankees.* Dallas: Taylor Publishing Company, 1989.

Garagiola, Joe. *Baseball Is a Funny Game.* Philadelphia: J. B. Lippincott, 1960.

Gittleman, Sol. *Reynolds, Raschi, and Lopat: New York's Big Three and the Great Yankee Dynasty of 1949–1953.* Jefferson, NC: McFarland & Company, 2007.

Golenbock, Peter. *Dynasty: The New York Yankees 1949–1964.* Englewood Cliffs, NJ: Prentice Hall, 1975.

———. *George: The Poor Little Rich Boy Who Built the Yankee Empire.* Hoboken, NJ: John Wiley & Sons, 2009.

Halberstam, David. *The Fifties.* New York: Villard, 1993.

———. *October 1964.* New York: Villard, 1994.

———. *Summer of '49.* New York: William Morrow, 1989.

Heaphy, Leslie A, ed. *Black Ball: A Negro Leagues Journal.* Jefferson, NC: McFarland & Company, 2012.

Kahn, Roger. *The Boys of Summer.* New York: Harper & Row, 1972.

Leavy, Jane. *The Last Boy: Mickey Mantle and the End of America's Childhood.* New York: Harper, 2010.

Madden, Bill. *Pride of October: What It Was to Be Young and a Yankee.* New York: Warner Books, 2003.

———. *Steinbrenner: The Last Lion of Baseball.* New York: Harper, 2010.

Madden, Bill, and Moss Klein. *Damned Yankees: Chaos, Confusion, and Craziness in the Steinbrenner Era.* Chicago: Triumph Books, 2012.

Mills, Dorothy Seymour, and Harold Seymour. *The People's Game.* Vol. 3 of *Baseball.* Oxford, UK: Oxford University Press, 1990.

Mormino, Gary Ross. *Immigrants on the Hill: Italian-Americans in St. Louis, 1882–1982.* Champaign: University of Illinois Press, 1986.

Palmer, William Howard, Jr. *We Called Ourselves Rocketboatmen: The Untold Stories of the Top-Secret LSC(S) Rocket Boat Missions of World War II at Sicily, Normandy*

(*Omaha and Utah Beaches*), *and Southern France*. Atlanta: LitFire Publishing, 2018.

Pepe, Phil. *The Wit and Wisdom of Yogi Berra*. New York: Hawthorn Books, 1974.

Pessah, Jon. *The Game: Inside the Secret World of Major League Baseball's Power Brokers*. New York: Little, Brown, 2015.

Reed, Thomas J. *America's Two Constitutions: A Study of the Treatment of Dissenters in Time of War*. Teaneck, NJ: Fairleigh Dickinson University Press, 2017.

Richardson, Bobby, with David Thomas. *Impact Player: Leaving a Lasting Legacy on and off the Field*. Carol Stream, IL: Tyndale House, 2012.

Rizzuto, Phil, and Tom Horton. *The October Twelve: Five Years of Yankee Glory, 1949–1953*. New York: Forge, 1994.

Robinson, Eddie, with C. Paul Rogers III. *Lucky Me: My Sixty-Five Years in Baseball*. Dallas: Southern Methodist University Press, 2011.

Schoor, Gene. *The Story of Yogi Berra*. New York: Doubleday, 1976.

Seidel, Michael. *Ted Williams: A Baseball Life*. Chicago: Contemporary Books, 1991.

Simon, Lojo, and Anita Simons. *Heartland: A Historical Drama About the Internment of German-Americans in the United States During World War II*. Social Fictions Series 9. Rotterdam: Sense Publishers, 2014.

Spatz, Lyle, ed. *Bridging Two Dynasties: The 1947 New York Yankees*. Lincoln: University of Nebraska Press, 2013.

Terry, Ralph, with John Wooley. *Right Down the Middle: The Ralph Terry Story*. Tulsa, OK: Müllerhaus Legacy, 2016.

Trimble, Joe. *Yogi Berra*. New York: Tempo Books, 1965.

Tygiel, Jules. *Baseball's Great Experiment: Jackie Robinson and His Legacy*. Oxford, UK: Oxford University Press, 1983.

White, Bill, with Gordon Dillow. *Uppity: My Untold Story About the Games People Play*. New York: Grand Central, 2011.

Wind, Herbert Warren. *The Gilded Age of Sport 1945–1960*. New York: Open Road Integrated Media, 2016.

## Newspapers and Magazines

"1963 Attendance at Stadium Lowest in 18 Years." *New York Times,* December 10, 1963.

Ackerman, Jan, and Carl Remensky. "Berra's Drug Tale: Ex-Pirate Used It Most When on Disabled List." *Pittsburgh Post-Gazette,* September 10, 1985.

"Albert V. Olivieri, 70, Founder of the Yoo-Hoo Beverage Co." *New York Times,* February 25, 1984.

"All Jokes Aside, Berra Is Back on Top." *New York Times,* February 13, 1984.

"All-Stars Win in Hawaii; Reese, Eddie Robinson, Berra Star in 15–4 Triumph." *New York Times,* October 15, 1952.

Anderson, Dave. "The Last Days of Willie Mays." *New York Times*, May 6, 1973.

———. "You Gotta Believe Mets Feel Frustrated." *New York Times*, October 22, 1973.

———. "The Patience of Yogi." *New York Times*, June 23, 1974.

———. "'Yogi Will Communicate Very Well.'" *New York Times*, December 6, 1975.

———. "Yogi, Coach and World Series Perennial." *New York Times*, October 17, 1976.

———. "Face on the Scoreboard." *New York Times*, August 4, 1979.

———. "Berra No. 1 for Now." *New York Times*, December 5, 1983.

———. "Billy Martin's Back Room." *New York Times*, December 17, 1983.

———. "Another Cigarette for Yogi Berra." *New York Times*, April 4, 1984.

———. "Day 'Dad' Let Koosman Hit." *New York Times*, February 10, 1985.

———. "On Pinch-Hitting for Your Son." *New York Times*, April 21, 1985.

———. "Yogi's Future: Assume Nothing." *New York Times*, April 26, 1985.

———. "'They Just Fired Your Dad,'" *New York Times*, April 30, 1985.

"Another Yogi for TV." *St. Louis Post-Dispatch*, August 11, 1963.

Araton, Harvey. "There's Room for More Than One Local Hero." *New York Times*, April 27, 1997.

———. "On the Other Side of the River, Another Hailing of Champions." *New York Times*, October 25, 1998.

———. "Yogi and the Boss Complete Makeup Game." *New York Times*, January 6, 1999.

———. "For Berra and Guidry, It Happens Every Spring." *New York Times*, February 23, 2011.

———. "A Yankee's Forgiveness Won't Be Forgotten." *New York Times*, September 23, 2015.

"Baird, Like the Mets, Turns to Yogi." *New York Times*, May 6, 1965.

"Ball Players Robbed." *New York Times*, April 28, 1959.

Barnes, Bart. "Joltin' Joe Has Gone Away." *Washington Post*, March 8, 1999.

"BBC Industries." *New York Times*, December 2, 1960.

Berger, Jerry. "Costas Heads for Hill for Garagiola Feature." *St. Louis Post-Dispatch*, May 11, 1994.

Berkow, Ira. "Some Words from Berra." *New York Times*, December 6, 1984.

———. "St. Patrick's Filled to Honor a Slugger." *New York Times*, December 24, 1985.

———. "For Yogi Berra, a Happy Return." *New York Times*, March 24, 1986.

Berman, Zach. "Yankee Stadium Welcomes Berra for His 87th Birthday." *New York Times*, May 12, 2012.

"Berra Back on Witness Stand." *New York Post*, September 20, 1985.

"Berra in Batting Drill." *New York Times*, September 4, 1949.

"Berra Clouts No. 30." *New York Times*, September 29, 1952.

"Berra Dispute Reported." *New York Times,* June 20, 1984.

"Berra, Home Again, Says Italy Prefers 3-Hour Nap to Baseball." *New York Times,* December 20, 1959.

"Berra Injured." *Philadelphia Inquirer,* June 1, 1947.

"Berra Jumped the Gun on Pal Joe." *Sporting News,* August 24, 1949.

"Berra to Keep Yank Job." *New York Times,* February 21, 1985.

"Berra Leads Way, Setting 14 Marks." *New York Times,* October 14, 1960.

"Berra as Manager: A Cliff-Hanging Tale." *New York Times,* August 10, 1975.

"Berra and Mantle Pace Bomber Drive." *New York Times,* March 10, 1953.

"Berra Misses Tough Catch, Maris Makes Easy One." *New York Times,* October 9, 1961.

"Berra to Motor to Miami." *New York Times,* October 9, 1955.

"Berra Picks Yankees to Win Again in '59." *St. Louis Post-Dispatch,* December 28, 1958.

"Berra to Return to Line-Up Today." *New York Times,* April 30, 1952.

"Berra Says Move Is 'Not My Doing.'" *New York Times,* April 8, 1985.

"Berra Says Yanks Worked Hard to Regain First Place and Intend to Keep It." *New York Times,* September 18, 1964.

"Berra's Blow Is Decisive." *New York Times,* September 28, 1949.

"Berra Set to Catch for Yankees Tonight." *New York Times,* April 25, 1952.

"Berra Shatters 6 Records, Extends 4 He Held and Equals 3 Others." *New York Times,* October 10, 1958.

"Berra Stars in Triumphs." *St. Louis Star-Times,* August 25, 1942.

"Berra's Thumb Swollen." *New York Times,* October 6, 1949.

"Berra Takes His Place with Columbus, Marconi." *New York Times,* October 19, 1956.

"Berra Vindicated as Tactician After Bumpy Road to Pennant." *New York Times,* October 4, 1964.

"Berra Voted A.L.'s Most Valuable Player for the Second Time." *St. Louis Post-Dispatch,* December 10, 1954.

"Berra of Yankees Granted Salary Increase." *New York Times,* February 27, 1949.

Beschloss, Michael. "DiMaggio and Sinatra: The Feud Between Two Italian-American Pathbreakers." *New York Times,* June 13, 2014.

Best, Neil. "TIMEOUT: Yogi Berra." *Newsday,* December 18, 2005.

"Big Crowd Greets Yankees in Tokyo." *New York Times,* October 14, 1955.

Bingham, Walter. "That Old Yankee Soap Opera." *Sports Illustrated,* September 10, 1962.

Bleth, Alex. "Yogi Berra, American Original and Yankees Immortal, Dies at 90." *Sports Illustrated,* September 23, 2015.

Blount, Roy. "Yogi: What Did Berra Say, When Did He Say It and What Does It All Mean?" *Sports Illustrated,* April 2, 1984.

Bolvin, Paula. "Garagiola Crushed by Loss of Close Friend Berra." *Arizona Republic,* September 23, 2015.

"Bombers' Victory Ill-Timed One for Scheduled Train-Catching." *New York Times,* September 19, 1956.

Borgi, Augie. "Yogi Says So Long…Did Best with What I Had." *Daily News* (New York), August 8, 1975.

"Bowling Alley Started by Baseball Stars Sold." *New York Times,* May 22, 1962.

Bracker, Milton. "7 in Theatre Balk at All Questions on Communist Ties." *New York Times,* August 16, 1955.

Bradley, Laura. "The Relationship Between Yogi Berra and Yogi Bear, Explained." *Slate,* September 23, 2015.

Briordy, William J. "Berra's Four Hits Pace 10–4 Verdict; Yanks Get 16 Blows as Ford Goes Route Against A's for His 6th." *New York Times,* July 31, 1957.

———. "Collins, Berra and Martin Slam Homers as Bombers Win, 3 to 1." *New York Times,* May 28, 1953.

———. "Mantle Heads Both Leagues in Homers, Runs Batted In and Batting Percentage." *New York Times,* October 1, 1956.

———. "Yankees and Dodgers Win Pennants in Final Games." *New York Times,* October 3, 1949.

Broeg, Bob. "Yogi the Yankee, Absentee King of the Hill, Back at Home Plate." *St. Louis Post-Dispatch,* December 26, 1954.

———. "From Banana Sandwiches to Top Banana." *St. Louis Post-Dispatch,* October 25, 1963.

———. "Hall of Famer Berra Way Ahead of Game." *St. Louis Post-Dispatch,* January 20, 1972.

Broun, Heywood Hale. "Bombers' Ball-Riding Berra Balks at Walks." *Sporting News,* April 16, 1947.

Buckley, Steve. "Yogi Berra Saved Best Words for His Wife." *Boston Herald,* September 23, 2015.

"Bunts and Boots." *Sporting News,* February 26, 1947.

Burns, Bob. "Berra Passes Up Broadway to Barber on Hill." *Sporting News,* January 10, 1951.

Burns, Jimmy. "Allie, Scooter, Yogi, to Swing Golf Clubs in Miami Tourney." *Sporting News,* February 13, 1952.

———. "Yogi Hardest Worker on Any Field." *Sporting News,* January 25, 1956.

———. "My Friend Yogi." *Sporting News,* November 6, 1957.

Caldera, Pete. "Yogi Berra Gives Tour of the Museum Named for Him." *Montclair Times,* December 24, 2009.

Cannon, Jimmy. "Sure, Berra Raps Bad Balls—Hard to Pitch Him Strikes." *Sporting News,* May 25, 1949.

————. "Yanks Soured on Yogi in Spring Training." *Chicago Daily News,* October 17, 1964.

Chass, Murray. "2 Homers Help Mets Subdue Phils, 3–2." *New York Times,* September 13, 1973.

————. "When Bottle Flew from Shea Stands, Rose, Anderson, Other Reds Saw Red." *New York Times,* October 9, 1973.

————. "Colts Acquire Fan for Jet Game — Yogi." *New York Times,* October 17, 1974.

————. "Martin Raps Steinbrenner, Jackson and Jeopardizes Job." *New York Times,* July 24, 1976.

————. "Reds Triumph, 7–2, and Complete 4-Game Series Sweep of Yankees." *New York Times,* October 22, 1976.

————. "Engine Failure Cited by Investigator as Apparent Cause of Munson Crash." *New York Times,* August 4, 1979.

————. "Berra Offer Likely if Martin Leaves." *New York Times,* December 3, 1983.

————. "Berra Delays on Relief." *New York Times,* February 17, 1984.

————. "Yanks Shuffled by Steinbrenner." *New York Times,* March 27, 1984.

————. "Steinbrenner's Team: A Week in the Lives." *New York Times,* April 8, 1984.

————. "Hot Play Helping Berra." *New York Times,* August 7, 1984.

————. "Winfield Makes the Season Another Learning Experience." *New York Times,* September 23, 1984.

————. "Steinbrenner Says Berra Will Return for '85." *New York Times,* October 26, 1984.

————. "Berras Are Hoping They'll Join Forces; Father, Son Favor Trade." *New York Times,* December 19, 1984.

————. "Kemp for Berra Is Called Final." *New York Times,* December 20, 1984.

————. "Kemp-Berra Deal Opens a Loophole." *New York Times,* December 21, 1984.

————. "No Date for Piniella Takeover." *New York Times,* February 25, 1985.

————. "Yanks Routed, 14–5; Steinbrenner Upset." *New York Times,* April 11, 1985.

————. "Martin Institutes Changes, but He Loses in Debut; Steinbrenner Lost Faith in Berra." *New York Times,* April 30, 1985.

————. "Baseball and Cocaine." *New York Times,* August 19, 1985.

————. "Piniella Asked to Manage Yankees." *New York Times,* October 27, 1985.

————. "Berra Will Not Return." *New York Times,* November 5, 1985.

————. "Berra to Be Coach in Houston." *New York Times,* November 19, 1985.

————. "Dale Berra Working Hard to Forget Shattered Season." *New York Times,* January 5, 1986.

————. "Berra and Scurry Accept Punishment." *New York Times,* March 2, 1986.

————. "Billy Martin of the Yankees Killed in Crash on Icy Road." *New York Times,* December 26, 1989.

————. "On Day Made for Legends, Cone Pitches Perfect Game." *New York Times,* July 19, 1999.

"City Sirens to Sound at 7:45 p.m. in a Test for Civil Defense Staff." *New York Times,* September 30, 1952.

Coffey, Wayne. "Yogi's Kid Finds Contentment Telling Others of Drugs' Perils." *Daily News* (New York), October 22, 1989.

————. "'She Was an Angel': Yogi Berra's Wife, Carmen, Laid to Rest in Emotional Funeral." *Daily News* (New York), March 12, 2014.

"Colts Draft Tim Berra." *New York Times,* January 31, 1974.

"Congress Declares War on Japan, 1500 Killed in Attack on Hawaii." *St. Louis Post-Dispatch,* December 8, 1941.

"Conzelman Looks for a Postwar Sport Comeback." *St. Louis Post-Dispatch,* August 21, 1943.

Creamer, Robert. "Casey Puts It on Ice." *Sports Illustrated,* July 23, 1956.

————. "The Name Is Yogi." *Sports Illustrated,* October 22, 1956.

"C.Y.O. Honors Berra Here as Sportsman of the Year." *New York Times,* January 10, 1964.

"Dale Berra Arrested in 'Coke' Raid." *Asbury Park Press,* April 21, 1989.

"Dale Berra Arrested in Drug Probe." *Indianapolis News,* April 21, 1989.

"Dale Berra: From High School Kid to Major League Man." *Wilmington Star-News,* July 7, 1975.

"Dale Berra Indicted." *Morristown Record,* August 26, 1989.

"Dale, Coke Make Me Sharp." *Daily News* (New York), September 10, 1985.

"Dale Next Berra to Bear Watching." *New York Times,* May 1, 1975.

Daley, Arthur. "Short Shots in Sundry Directions." *New York Times,* March 27, 1947.

————. "Waiting for the World Series." *New York Times,* September 30, 1947.

————. "It Happened in Brooklyn." *New York Times,* October 4, 1947.

————. "Overheard at the Stadium." *New York Times,* April 25, 1948.

————. "Overheard at the Stadium." *New York Times,* July 1, 1948.

————. "Overheard at the Stadium." *New York Times,* July 4, 1948.

————. "Casey at the Bat." *New York Times,* October 14, 1948.

————. "Overheard in St. Pete." *New York Times,* March 14, 1949.

————. "Nature Boy." March 20, 1949.

————. "Return of the Yankee Clipper." *New York Times,* June 30, 1949.

——. "Stars Among Stars." *New York Times,* July 15, 1953.

——. "The Strange Vic Raschi Deal." *Sporting News,* February 24, 1954.

——. "Flatbush Fantasy." *New York Times,* October 5, 1955.

——. "In Mild Dissent." *New York Times,* December 4, 1955.

——. "Notice for Ted." *New York Times,* April 20, 1960.

——. "A Venture into Literature." *New York Times,* February 5, 1961.

——. "Overheard at the Stadium." *New York Times,* September 3, 1961.

——. "Nothing but the Best." *New York Times,* March 3, 1962.

——. "Yogi." *Boys' Life,* April 1963.

——. "Yogi's Little Helper." *New York Times,* November 18, 1963.

——. "The Peerless Leader." *New York Times,* March 1, 1964.

——. "What Was the Hurry?" *New York Times,* April 9, 1972.

——. "Yogi, Willie and Other Met Problems." *New York Times,* March 6, 1973.

——. "Overheard in St. Pete." *New York Times,* March 12, 1984.

Daniel, Dan. "Roundup of Major Leagues' Outstanding Rookie Performers: Larry Berra." *Sporting News,* April 9, 1947.

——. "Outfield Out for Berra as Yanks' No. 1 Backstop." *Sporting News,* March 17, 1948.

——. "Yogi Berra Likely to Stay in Right Field." *Sporting News,* September 1, 1948.

——. "Yanks Invite 'Reasonable' Deal Offers." *Sporting News,* November 10, 1948.

——. "Young in Early Warmup Under Florida Sun for Yank First Base Race." *Sporting News,* February 2, 1949.

——. "Phil and Yogi…Close as Ham and Eggs." *Sporting News,* January 10, 1951.

——. "Scott Quits as Road Sec to Become Player Agent." *Sporting News,* January 10, 1951.

——. "Yanks, Still Hoping for Deal, Keep Two Roster Spots Open." *Sporting News,* January 10, 1951.

——. "Yogi Berra Completes Double When BBWA Names Him MVP." *Sporting News,* November 14, 1951.

——. "Berra Basks in Most Valuable Player Award." *Sporting News,* November 21, 1951.

——. "Stengel Trying to Put Burr Under Berra as a Blocker." *Sporting News,* June 11, 1952.

——. "Little Bobby High on A.L. Valuable List; Rosen, Yogi in Running." *Sporting News,* July 9, 1952.

——. "Writers Give the Low-Down on Big Names." *Sporting News,* January 6, 1954.

———. "Pulled Muscle Sends Yogi Berra to Bench for Rest." *Sporting News,* January 11, 1956.

———. "Yogi to Catch Less and Howard More, Casey's Winter Tale." *Sporting News,* January 11, 1956.

———. "Yogi Grabs $50,000, Mantle Gets 30-Grand Pact." *Sporting News,* February 1, 1956.

———. "Backstops Golden Boys of Game; Yogi, Campy at Receivers' Record High." March 14, 1956.

———. "Rizzuto, Yankee Since '41, Stunned by Release on Old Timers' Day." *Sporting News,* September 5, 1956.

———. "Berra Fulfills His Promise to Mother with 2 Homers." *Sporting News,* October 17, 1956.

———. "Yogi $ees a Better $eason for Mickey." *Sporting News,* January 30, 1957.

———. "Ol' Perfessor Maps Rugged Slate for Yogi." *Sporting News,* February 13, 1957.

———. "Ol' Case Would Breathe Easier If Yanks Had Ten-Game Lead." *Sporting News,* June 17, 1957.

———. "Ball Players, Glasses and Yogi Berra." *Sporting News,* June 24, 1957.

———. "Yogi Enjoys Big Time as Yak-Yak Yankee Flyhawk." *Sporting News,* July 30, 1958.

———. "Ditmar Halts Yankee Skid as Yogi Hits Two Homers." *Sporting News,* August 27, 1958.

———. "Casey Plans to Platoon Berra at First Base in '59." *Sporting News,* October 1, 1958.

———. "Still No New Yogi, Stengel Finds in Rating Catchers; Berra, Near 34, Likely to Play at Three Positions." *Sporting News,* November 19, 1958.

———. "Yogi Chokes-Up and Casey Cries at Day for Berra." *Sporting News,* September 18, 1959.

"Dan Topping Dead at 61; Yankee Owner 22 Years." *New York Times,* May 10, 1974.

Davids, L. Robert. "Iron Man Yogi Trains Sights on Mitt Full of Mask Marks." *Sporting News,* March 27, 1957.

Dawson, James P. "DiMaggio Accepts Salary Put at $42,500 to End Yankee Holdout." *New York Times,* March 13, 1942.

———. "Noisy Celebration Marks Cards' Record-Equaling Batting Feat in Boston Game." *New York Times,* October 11, 1946.

———. "Berra's Debut as Catcher Today." *New York Times,* May 6, 1947.

———. "Yanks' 7 in First Two Frames Set Back the Red Sox, 9–6." *New York Times,* May 11, 1947.

———. "Keller's 2 Homers Help Yankees Win." *New York Times,* June 1, 1947.

———. "Bombers Topple Browns by 10–4, 2–1." *New York Times,* June 16, 1947.

———. "Yankees Bow to Indians, 4–3, 6–1; Feller 4-Hitter Takes Nightcap." *New York Times,* August 23, 1947.

———. "Yankees' 17 Blows Over Indians for Reynolds, 13–6." *New York Times,* August 24, 1947.

———. "Browns Win in 9th from Bombers, 4–3." *New York Times,* August 27, 1947.

———. "Berra Predicts Another Flag." *New York Times,* February 17, 1948.

———. "Berra's 3-Run Double in 7th Lifts Yanks to 8–4 Victory at St. Louis." *New York Times,* May 20, 1948.

———. "Stengel Threatens Disciplinary Action Against Yanks for Dog Track Violations." *New York Times,* March 12, 1949.

———. "Henrich Home Run in Ninth Beats Senators; Berra Hit Ties Score." *New York Times,* April 20, 1949.

———. "Berra Is Big Star." *New York Times,* May 29, 1949.

———. "Yankees Beaten, 7–6, by Browns." *New York Times,* June 6, 1949.

———. "Ford, Berra and DiMaggio Are Besieged in the Clubhouse After Series Triumph." *New York Times,* October 8, 1950.

———. "Berra's Acceptance of Yanks' Terms Makes Him Best-Paid Backstop This Year." *New York Times,* February 28, 1951.

———. "DiMaggio Plan to Quit After '51 Stuns Yankee Players, Officials." *New York Times,* March 4, 1951.

———. "Berra on Casualty List." *New York Times,* May 3, 1951.

———. "Happy Yanks Heap Praise on Stengel, Mantle, Woodling, Berra and Martin; Victory Sets off Explosion of Joy." *New York Times,* October 8, 1952.

"A Day for Phil." *New York Times,* September 17, 1955.

Deford, Frank. "Cliffhanger for Yogi and Crucial for July." *Sports Illustrated,* July 27, 1984.

Delano, Hugh. "Yogi's Not About to End Yankee Stadium Boycott." *New York Post,* February 1, 1992.

Demetri, Justin. "Italians in America: From Discrimination to Adoration (or Almost)." *Life in Italy,* April 26, 2018.

Dickson, Terry. "Yogi Berra—Baseball's Incredible Kid." *St. Louis Post-Dispatch,* July 3, 1949.

Di Ionno, Mark. "Yogi Berra's Latest Honor Marks Heroism Beyond Baseball in the Bronx." NJ.com, October 22, 2013.

"DiMaggio to Enter Home Run Contest." *New York Times,* June 22, 1949.

"DiMaggio to Join Yanks in Florida." *New York Times,* January 12, 1964.

Dodd, Mike. "Berra, Garagiola Are Kings of 'The Hill' in St. Louis." *USA Today,* July 14, 2009.

Donnelly, Frank. "Yogi Berra Museum Break-In Helped Crack Ninja Burglar Case." *Staten Island Advance,* April 22, 2016.

Dorman, Larry. "Berra Calls 'Em as He Sees 'Em." *New York Times,* January 19, 2010.

Dougherty, Philip H. "Sport Trustables." *New York Times,* November 21, 1973.

Drebinger, John. "3 Yankee Rookies Star at San Juan: Berra, Catcher, and Pitchers Hiller and Don Johnson Catch Harris' Eye." *New York Times,* February 18, 1947.

———. "DiMaggio Will Leave San Juan Camp Today to Be Treated at Johns Hopkins." *New York Times,* February 26, 1947.

———. "Yanks' Pitching, Except One Lapse by Chandler, Encourages Harris." *New York Times,* March 20, 1947.

———. "Yankees' 15 Blows Rout Red Sox, 13–5, at St. Petersburg." *New York Times,* March 23, 1947.

———. "Harris Admits He Hasn't Decided Yankees Opening Day Line-Up." *New York Times,* April 5, 1947.

———. "Bombers Overcome Hassett Tars, 19–5." *New York Times,* April 8, 1947.

———. "Yankees Are Turned Back by Athletics in Opening Baseball Game at Stadium." *New York Times,* April 16, 1947.

———. "Jubilant Bombers Hail Victory News." *New York Times,* September 16, 1947.

———. "Yankees Turn Back Browns, 8–3, Then Drop 8–2 Contest to Zoldak." *New York Times,* September 17, 1947.

———. "Dodgers Beat Yanks, 9–8, with Casey Stopping Rally." *New York Times,* October 2, 1947.

———. "Yanks Win Series, Page Taking Final from Dodgers, 5–2." *New York Times,* October 7, 1947.

———. "More Medical Matters." *New York Times,* November 6, 1947.

———. "'Rehabilitation' of Catcher Berra on Program." *New York Times,* March 4, 1948.

———. "Yogi Berra Sprains Foot, May Be out of Action for a Week." *New York Times,* March 16, 1948.

———. "Berra and Reynolds Slightly Hurt." *New York Times,* March 27, 1948.

———. "Optimistic Yankees Start North with Regulars Ready for Opener." *New York Times,* April 8, 1948.

———. "Berra Out with Split Finger." *New York Times,* April 13, 1948.

———. "Yankees Celebrate Babe Ruth Day in Typical Fashion." *New York Times,* June 20, 1948.

———. "Lindell, Berra Connect." *New York Times,* June 26, 1948.

———. "Yanks Overwhelm Athletics by 14–3." *New York Times,* August 15, 1948.

———. "Shea Beaten by 4-Run Second in Nightcap Despite Berra and Henrich 4-Baggers." *New York Times,* August 16, 1948.

———. "Bombers Capture Seventh Straight; Berra Bats in 4." *New York Times,* September 5, 1948.

———. "DiMaggio Smashes His 33rd Homer—Henrich and Berra Shine." *New York Times,* September 6, 1948.

———. "Yankees Now Are Game from the Top." *New York Times,* September 20, 1948.

———. "Yankees Beat Red Sox, Gain Triple Tie for Lead as Indians Lose to Tigers." *New York Times,* September 25, 1948.

———. "Yankees Crushed in Finale 10 to 5." *New York Times,* October 4, 1948.

———. "Stengel Signs as Yanks' Manager with 2-Year Contract for Undisclosed Sum." *New York Times,* October 13, 1948.

———. "Berra Wallops His 12th." *New York Times,* July 20, 1949.

———. "Berra's Thumb Healing." *New York Times,* August 26, 1949.

———. "Yankees Lose Lead for First Time." *New York Times,* September 27, 1949.

———. "Yanks Whip Red Sox in Season Finale to Win 16th American League Pennant." *New York Times,* October 3, 1949.

———. "Yanks Win Series, Beating Dodgers in Fifth Game, 10–6." *New York Times,* October 10, 1949.

———. "Raschi and Berra Sign Contracts with Yankees After Stengel Acts." *New York Times,* March 8, 1950.

———. "Berra Leads Drive in Victory by 13–6." *New York Times,* August 23, 1950.

———. "Jubilant Yankees Stage Rip-Roaring Celebration in Hotel Rooms at Boston." *New York Times,* September 28, 1950.

———. "Rizzuto Signs $50,000 One-Year Pact." *New York Times,* December 1, 1950.

———. "Yankees' Reynolds Hurls No-Hitter." *New York Times,* July 13, 1951.

———. "Berra Leads 15-Hit Bomber Drive in 8-to-5 Victory over Senators." *New York Times,* August 16, 1951.

———. "Yanks Lose Twice, Yield Lead to Indians; Berra Wastes Two Homers." *New York Times,* September 12, 1951.

———. "Yanks Clinch Flag, Aided by Reynolds' No-Hitter." *New York Times,* September 29, 1951.

———. "Yanks Win Series as Bauer's Triple Tops Giants, 4 to 3." *New York Times,* October 11, 1951.

———. "Berra Clean-Up Man in Yankee Batting Order for First Exhibition Tomorrow." *New York Times,* March 7, 1952.

———. "Berra Hits Homer; 3-Run Drive in the Sixth Wins Game Called in Seventh by Rain." *New York Times,* August 17, 1952.

———. "Berra Belts No. 28." *New York Times,* August 31, 1952.

———. "Yankees Clinch Fourth Straight Pennant." *New York Times,* September 27, 1952.

———. "Dodgers Win by 5–3 for 2–1 Series Lead; 2 Runs Cross in 9th on Passed Ball." *New York Times,* October 4, 1952.

———. "Yanks Win, 3–2, Tie Dodgers." *New York Times,* October 7, 1952.

———. "Berra Signs as Yankees Raise Salary to About $37,000." *New York Times,* January 30, 1953.

———. "69,374 See Yanks Beat Dodgers, 9–5, in Series Opener." *New York Times,* October 1, 1953.

———. "Yanks Take 5th Series in Row, Record." *New York Times,* October 6, 1953.

———. "Rosen Unanimously Named American League's Most Valuable Player for 1953; Yanks' Berra Next at 167 in Most Valuable Vote." *New York Times,* November 28, 1953.

———. "Yanks Tally 6 Times in 4th, Then Win on Berra Homer in 9th at Kansas City." *New York Times,* July 25, 1955.

———. "Yanks Beat White Sox on Berra's Homer." *New York Times,* July 27, 1955.

———. "Berra Home Run Beats Tigers, 3–0." *New York Times,* August 6, 1955.

———. "Yanks Overwhelm Red Sox with 18-Hit Attack." *New York Times,* August 17, 1955.

———. "Bauer, Berra Hit Homers to Win, 5–4." *New York Times,* September 17, 1955.

———. "Yankees Win 21st Pennant, Their Sixth in Last 7 Years." *New York Times,* September 24, 1955.

———. "Dodgers' Pitching Superiority over Yanks Not Clear-Cut." *New York Times,* September 27, 1955.

———. "Yanks Win First; Collins' 2 Homers Beat Dodgers." *New York Times,* September 29, 1955.

———. "Dodgers Capture 1st World Series; Amoros Catch Thwarts Bombers." *New York Times,* October 2, 1955.

———. "Berra Is Named Most Valuable Payer in the League Again." *New York Times,* December 4, 1955.

———. "Dodgers, Yankees Picked for Flags." *New York Times,* April 15, 1956.

———. "Larsen Clouts Grand Slam; Collins, Berra Also Hit Homers for Yankees." *New York Times,* April 23, 1956.

———. "Cleveland Infielder Injured as Yanks Win 6th in Row—Berra, Mantle Play." *New York Times,* July 13, 1956.

———. "Berra Takes Catchers' Big League Mark for Homers with 237th in Fifth." *New York Times,* September 15, 1956.

———. "Berra Wallops Grand Slam for Bombers." *New York Times,* October 6, 1956.

————. "Larsen Beats Dodgers in Perfect Game." *New York Times,* October 9, 1956.

————. "Yanks Champions; Berra Has Pair of Two-Run Homers and Skowron Gets Grand Slam in Finale." *New York Times,* October 11, 1956.

————. "Yogi Pay Sets Catchers' Record; Berra Accepts Third Highest Salary in Yank History." *New York Times,* December 21, 1956.

————. "Berra, First Yankee to Sign, Agrees to 'Slight' Decrease for 1958 Season." *New York Times,* January 10, 1958.

————. "Foul Tip Sidelines Yanks' Berra." *New York Times,* March 31, 1958.

————. "Yogi Hits Homer as Yanks Open Stand Against West." *New York Times,* April 30, 1958.

————. "Yankees Win, 4–3, in Tenth and Tie Braves in Series." *New York Times,* October 9, 1958.

————. "Yanks Beat Braves, 6–2, and Win Series." *New York Times,* October 10, 1958.

————. "Bomber Players Keep Making Money at Varied Off-Season Enterprises." *New York Times,* October 20, 1958.

————. "Berra Signs Pact for $5,000 Rise." *New York Times,* January 29, 1959.

————. "Berra's 4-Bagger Trips Ramos." *New York Times,* September 4, 1959.

————. "Pirates Win, 10–9, Capturing Series on Homer in 9th." *New York Times,* October 14, 1960.

————. "Whither the Yankees? Club's Top Brass and Fans Are in Dark About Future of Stengel and Weiss." *New York Times,* October 15, 1960.

————. "Stengel, 70, Is Let Go by Yankees." *New York Times,* October 19, 1960.

————. "Houk, Yankees' New Pilot, Assured of 'Free Hand' at Helm by Topping." *New York Times,* October 21, 1960.

————. "Everything Except Bugles." *New York Times,* February 23, 1961.

————. "Yank Spring Ends in St. Louis Rain." *New York Times,* April 10, 1961.

————. "Great to Be Yankee? Keeping Up with Cross-Country Slate Is Nightmare of Planes, Trains, Buses." *New York Times,* May 10, 1961.

————. "Yanks Clinch Pennant; Maris Hits 59th Homer but Misses 154-Game Mark." *New York Times,* September 21, 1961.

————. "Maris Hits 61st in Final Game." *New York Times,* October 2, 1961.

————. "Yanks Defeat Reds, 13–5, in Fifth Game and Take World Series for 19th Time." *New York Times,* October 10, 1961.

————. "Berra Says He Insisted on a Short Contract So He Can Quit If Unsuccessful." *New York Times,* October 25, 1963.

————. "Howard of Yanks Named American League's Most Valuable Player." *New York Times,* November 8, 1963.

————. "Yogi Lays Down Law in Inaugural Address." *New York Times,* February 18, 1964.

———. "Berra Has a Style All His Own and It Appears to Make Sense." *New York Times,* March 9, 1964.

Durso, Joseph. "Cards Win World Series, Defeating Yankees, 7 to 5." *New York Times,* October 16, 1964.

———. "Houk Denies 'Tampering' in Obtaining Manager." *New York Times,* October 21, 1964.

———. "Stengel Steps Down as Manager of Mets; Westrum, Berra Possible Choices." *New York Times,* August 31, 1965.

———. "Hodges, Manager of Mets, Dies of Heart Attack at 47." *New York Times,* April 3, 1972.

———. "Quiet but Forceful Hodges Changed Club into Champions in 2 Seasons." *New York Times,* April 3, 1972.

———. "Yogi Berra Is Named Manager of Mets." *New York Times,* April 7, 1972.

———. "Staub Is Here, Eager for Hits and Dollars." *New York Times,* April 9, 1972.

———. "Berra Congratulated by a Familiar Voice." *New York Times,* April 16, 1972.

———. "Mays Back in Town and Mets Have Him." *New York Times,* April 16, 1972.

———. "George Weiss Dies at 78." *New York Times,* August 14, 1972.

———. "Most N.Y. Yankees Call N.J. Home." *New York Times,* August 20, 1972.

———. "Mets Lose by 7–3, Fall 16½ Behind." *New York Times,* September 7, 1972.

———. "Requiem for Contender: Mets Dismantling Due." *New York Times,* September 15, 1972.

———. "C.B.S. Sells the Yankees for $10-Million." *New York Times,* January 4, 1973.

———. "Mets Sign McGraw for $75,000, Record Contract for Relief Pitcher." *New York Times,* February 1, 1973.

———. "Mets Raise Seaver to $140,000." *New York Times,* February 27, 1973.

———. "Mays Has His Way, and Yogi Has His Way." *New York Times,* March 2, 1973.

———. "Mets Sign Staub in $330,000 Deal." *New York Times,* March 6, 1973.

———. "Mays Fined by Berra." *New York Times,* March 12, 1973.

———. "Matlack Is Flattened; Pitcher Struck on Head by a Line Drive." *New York Times,* May 9, 1973.

———. "Mets Defeat Pirates, 4–3; Grote's Wrist Is Broken." *New York Times,* May 12, 1973.

———. "Reds Beat Mets, 5 to 0; Harrelson Hurt." *New York Times,* June 5, 1973.

———. "Berra Is Safe at Home for the Time Being." *New York Times,* July 1, 1973.

———. "Mets Say Berra's Job Is Safe—Unless Fans Say Otherwise." *New York Times,* July 6, 1973.

———. "Mets Attain .500 Mark and First Place in East as Seaver Defeats Pirates, 10–2, Before 51,381." *New York Times,* September 22, 1973.

———. "Club Can Win Title with Sweep and a Pirate Loss." *New York Times,* September 23, 1973.

———. "Mets Need One Victory to Clinch Tie; Pirates Bow." *New York Times,* September 30, 1973.

———. "Mets Split and Clinch Tie for East Title." *New York Times,* October 1, 1973.

———. "Mets Win East Title." *New York Times,* October 2, 1973.

———. "Mets Win, 9 to 2, as Fight Erupts." *New York Times,* October 9, 1973.

———. "Mets Defeat Reds, 7–2, for Pennant and Enter World Series." *New York Times,* October 11, 1973.

———. "Mets Get 4 Runs in 12th to Beat A's, 10–7, and Even Series at 1–1." *New York Times,* October 15, 1973.

———. "Mets Beat A's, 2–0, Lead World Series, 3 Games to 2." *New York Times,* October 19, 1973.

———. "Mets Look to Seaver to Finish World Series Today." *New York Times,* October 20, 1973.

———. "A's Top Mets, 5–2; Win Series Again." *New York Times,* October 22, 1973.

———. "Berra Gets Reward: A 3-Year Contract." *New York Times,* October 24, 1973.

———. "Mets Dismiss Berra and Name McMillan." *New York Times,* August 7, 1975.

———. "Berra Back with Mets for a Good-by." *New York Times,* August 8, 1975.

———. "Yogi and the Snipers." *New York Times,* August 12, 1975.

———. "Stengel's Death at 85 Widely Mourned." *New York Times,* October 1, 1975.

———. "Stengel Gets a Farewell at St. Patrick's." *New York Times,* November 5, 1975.

———. "The Return of Billy the Kid." *New York Times,* July 30, 1978.

———. "Martin's Future as Manager Is in Doubt." *New York Times,* June 19, 1983.

———. "Berra Replaces Martin as Yankees' Manager." *New York Times,* December 17, 1983.

———. "Off Season for Baseball Isn't What It Used to Be." *New York Times,* January 11, 1998.

Eck, Frank. "The Berra Dream May Be Over." *Courier-News* (Bridgewater, NJ), September 22, 1972.

Effrat, Louis. "Raschi, Rookie Pitcher, Wins League Debut." *New York Times,* September 24, 1946.

———. "Dodgers Purchase Robinson, First Negro in Modern Major League Baseball." *New York Times,* April 11, 1947.

———. "Truman and Crowd of 28,579 See Yankees Capture Opener in Washington." *New York Times,* April 19, 1947.

———. "58,339 Acclaim Babe Ruth in Rare Tribute at Stadium." *New York Times,* April 28, 1947.

———. "Berra's Grand Slam Homer in 5-Run First Big Blow of Stadium Thriller." *New York Times,* June 22, 1947.

———. "Berra's Four-Run Homer in Third Marks 8–5 Triumph for Bombers." *New York Times,* July 31, 1947.

———. "Champions Subdue Mackmen by 4 to 2." *New York Times,* April 27, 1948.

———. "Berra Eviction Irks Fans; Missiles Fly at Umpire Before Rain Interval—Yogi, McQuinn and DiMaggio Hit Homers." *New York Times,* June 12, 1948.

———. "DiMaggio's 2 Triples, Homers by Berra and Rizzuto, Win as 49,641 Watch." *New York Times,* June 14, 1948.

———. "Harris Dropped as Manager of Yankees After Two Years in Post." *New York Times,* October 5, 1948.

———. "Four Homers for Yanks; Keller, DiMaggio, Henrich, Berra Connect, Yogi with Three on Bases." *New York Times,* August 6, 1949.

———. "Berra Hurt, Out 3 Weeks; Catcher's Thumb Is Broken by a Pitched Ball." *New York Times,* August 8, 1949.

———. "Yankees Check White Sox at Stadium on Berra's Two-Run Double in 7th." *New York Times,* July 18, 1950.

———. "Yogi Berra Hurt in Play at Plate at the Stadium." *New York Times,* July 25, 1951.

———. "Berra Paces Drive." *New York Times,* August 5, 1951.

———. "Berra's 2 Big Blows for Yankees Help Reynolds Trim Tigers, 8–0." *New York Times,* June 20, 1952.

———. "Yankees Take Two from Indians." *New York Times,* July 17, 1952.

———. "Berra Wants to Play Nine Positions in One Game." *New York Times,* April 4, 1953.

———. "Yankees, Using 19 Players, Rally to Beat Senators—Berra, Martin Ejected." *New York Times,* May 22, 1953.

———. "Yankees Lift Victory Streak to 18 by Beating Indians Twice Before 74,708; Berra's Bat Paces 6–2, 3–0 Triumphs." *New York Times,* June 15, 1953.

————. "Indians Sink Yanks Twice Before Record 86,563; Berra Wastes Homer." *New York Times,* September 12, 1954.

————. "Yankees Crush Senators in Stadium Opener." *New York Times,* April 14, 1955.

————. "Berra, Martin and Carey Hit Homers to Help Southpaw Gain Ninth Victory." *New York Times,* June 27, 1956.

————. "Berra Joins List of Injured Stars." *New York Times,* July 11, 1956.

————. "Turley Is Cheered by Return of Confidence Despite His Defeat by Dodgers." *New York Times,* October 10, 1956.

————. "Maris Hits No. 19." *New York Times,* June 19, 1960.

————. "Mantle and Berra Connect." *New York Times,* September 18, 1960.

————. "Berra Replacement Studied by Yank Pilot." *New York Times,* October 8, 1960.

————. "Author Berra Signs Yankees' Pact." *New York Times,* January 13, 1961.

————. "Yankees Rout Senators for Ninth in Row as Mantle and Maris Hit Homers." *New York Times,* August 12, 1961.

————. "Yankees Sign Berra for 17th Year." *New York Times,* January 17, 1962.

"Eisenhower Sees Opener on TV, Finds Berra Blow Impressive." *New York Times,* October 1, 1953.

"Elston Howard Highest Paid Catcher." *New York Amsterdam News,* February 27, 1965.

"Emotion Bests Yogi at Hall Ceremonies." *St. Louis Post-Dispatch,* August 7, 1972.

"Ernest Borgnine, Yogi Berra and Paul Tagliabue to Be Inducted into Italian American Hall of Fame." NIAF.org, April 20, 2004.

Eskenazi, Gerald. "Cleon Jones Is Arrested in Florida." *New York Times,* May 6, 1975.

Evans, Howard. "Elston Howard: He Never Caused Waves." *New York Amsterdam News,* December 20, 1980.

"Father Takes Berra's Homers in Stride, but Yankee Outs on TV Set Provoke Him." *New York Times,* October 11, 1956.

Ferdenzi, Til. "Yogi Flawless Fielder in Quiz Session." *Sporting News,* November 9, 1963.

————. "Berra Fired as Manager." *New York Journal-American,* October 16, 1964.

————. "Yanks Decision to Dump Berra Came Last July." *Sporting News,* October 31, 1964.

Fink, David. "Yep, It's Yogi's Son; Pirates Pick Dale Berra." *Pittsburgh Post-Gazette,* June 5, 1975.

Fitzgerald, Ed. "The Fabulous Yogi Berra." *Sport,* August 1951.

Fletcher, Jeff. "The Boys of the Summer of '42." *Los Angeles Times,* August 9, 1992.

"Former Ball Player Sold." *New York Times,* March 4, 1961.

Fuchs, Marek. "Yogi Gets 100% Emotional, and Then Some, for a Pal." *New York Times,* February 19, 2005.

"Funeral Monday for John Berra." *St. Louis Post-Dispatch,* May 5, 1972.

"Garagiola and Friend Berra Handle Strikes in Bowling Just as in Baseball." *St. Louis Post-Dispatch,* January 6, 1949.

Gietschier, Steven P. "Yogi Berra, Rocket Man." *St. Louis Post-Dispatch,* October 1, 2015.

Gildea, William. "Nation, Baseball Mourns as DiMaggio Dies at 84." *Washington Post,* March 9, 1999.

Goldaper, Sam. "Flatbush Faithful Pay Last Respects to Gil Hodges." *New York Times,* April 5, 1972.

———. "Houk Out as Yanks' Manager." *New York Times,* October 1, 1973.

Goldberg, Hy. "Yogi's Punch Line: 5 Seasons, 2 Pennants." *Miami Herald,* December 25, 1983.

Goodman, Irv. "The Other Yogi Berra." *Sport,* May 1958.

Goodwin, Michael C. "Dale Berra Admits to Use of Cocaine." *New York Times,* September 10, 1985.

———. "Baseball Orders Suspension of 11 Drug Users." *New York Times,* March 1, 1986.

Goodyear, Sarah. "When Being Italian Was a Crime." *Village Voice,* April 11, 2000.

Goold, Derrick. "'One That Got Away': When Yogi Tried Out for the Cardinals." *St. Louis Post-Dispatch,* September 23, 2015.

Graczyk, Wayne. "Tale of Two Trips: 1955 Yankees Here Weeks, 2004 Team Days." *Japan Times,* April 14, 2004.

Gross, Jane. "Yanks Won't Start Mattingly." *New York Times,* March 13, 1984.

Gross, Milton. "Behind the Berra Firing." *Sport,* February 1965.

———. "They're Watching You, Yogi, and You're Managing Up a Storm." *Boston Globe,* May 19, 1972.

Grossfeld, Stan. "At Age 90, Yogi Berra Is Still Going Strong." *Boston Globe,* May 17, 2015.

Hageman, Bill, and Steve Nidetz. "Berra's a Big Hit in His New Role as a Movie Critic...Even Glenn Cove Would Love Him." *Los Angeles Times,* June 21, 1988.

Hall, Don. "Return to Form of Ex-GIs to Lift Yankee Fortunes, Larry Believes." *Sporting News,* December 25, 1946.

Hann, Christopher. "It Ain't Over." *New Jersey Monthly,* February 1, 2008.

Harvin, Al. "Faithful Few Welcome Team." *New York Times,* October 2, 1973.

"Hats Off: Yogi Berra." *Sporting News,* August 29, 1956.

"Hey, Gals! Here's Yogi's Advice on How to Wear a Girdle: Put It On, Forget About It." *St. Louis Post-Dispatch,* July 31, 1951.

"The Hill Honors Yogi Berra; He Talks of Pitches and Putts." *St. Louis Post-Dispatch*, October 19, 1956.

Holland, Gerald. "All Hail the Hero: Mighty Mickey." *Sports Illustrated*, March 4, 1957.

———. "The Laughing Season." *Sports Illustrated*, January 14, 1963.

Holmes, Tommy. "Yogi Polishes His Irons, Ponders Job." *St. Louis Post-Dispatch*, October 30, 1964.

Holtzman, Jerome. "Yogi, on Yoo-Hoo Pitch, Spills Yarn About Cardinal Bid." *Sporting News*, November 21, 1964.

"Howard Accepts Terms." *New York Times*, January 31, 1964.

"Howard Is Shocked at Ouster of Berra." *New York Times*, October 17, 1964.

"How the Mets Did It: Healthy Arms." *New York Times*, September 23, 1973.

Hummel, Rich. "Hall of Fame Catcher Yogi Berra Dies at 90." *St. Louis Post-Dispatch*, September 23, 2015.

———. "Catcher, Broadcaster and Hill Icon Joe Garagiola Dies at 90." *St. Louis Post-Dispatch*, March 24, 2016.

"Hurt Back May Keep Berra off All-Stars." *New York Times*, July 7, 1951.

"'I Never Gave Up, and Neither Did the Players,' Says Berra About How the Mets Won the Eastern Title." *New York Times*, October 2, 1973.

"It's Official: Yogi Yankee Manager." *St. Louis Post-Dispatch*, October 24, 1963.

Izenberg, Jerry. "The Day When a Bunch of N.J. Kids Made Yogi Berra Cry." *Star-Ledger* (Newark, NJ), September 24, 2018.

Jackson, David. "Obama Honors 'Extraordinary' Medal of Freedom Recipients." *USA Today*, November 24, 2014.

Jacobson, Steve. "Berra's Appeal Still Ain't Over." *Newsday*, March 29, 1989.

———. "The Day It Was Almost Over for Yogi Berra." *Newsday*, June 7, 1994.

"Joe DiMaggio." BaseballinWartime.com.

"Jones Disobeys Berra." *New York Times*, July 19, 1975.

"Jones to Stay a Met?" *New York Times*, July 25, 1975.

Kaulessar, Ricardo. "Sons of Famous Athletes in the Spotlight." *Bloomfield Life*, October 2, 2016.

Kernan, Kevin. "Why Yogi Berra, 90, Is the Most Beloved Player Alive." *New York Post*, May 12, 2015.

———. "Bobby Richardson's Fondest Yogi Memories: One Came After Brutal Series Loss." *New York Post*, September 23, 2015.

King, Joe. "Berra, with 237, Sets All-Time High Total of Homers Smashed by Catcher." *Sporting News*, September 26, 1956.

———. "Yogi Yanks' Series' Dean—Has Chance to Be Most." *Sporting News*, October 25, 1956.

———. "Café Society Yanks Draw Casey's Fire." *Sporting News*, May 22, 1957.

———. "Lack of Berra's Big At Bat Slowing Up Bang of Mantle." *Sporting News*, May 22, 1957.

———. "Scare over Yogi's Face Injury Helps Fire Up Bombers." *Sporting News*, June 12, 1957.

———. "Yanks Set New Sock Mark—$5,500 Night Club Tab." *Sporting News*, June 12, 1957.

———. "Yogi Eyes Okay, Docs Find After Winning Bingle." *Sporting News*, June 25, 1958.

———. "Lefty Bats Control Series Homer Derby." *Sporting News*, October 1, 1958.

———. "Vet Yogi Reigns as Yankees' King of Clutch." *Sporting News*, October 3, 1961.

Klapish, Bob. "Dale Finally Joins Dad in Pinstripes." *New York Post*, December 21, 1984.

Klein, Moss. "The Day I Met Yogi Berra." *Star-Ledger* (Newark, NJ), September 23, 2015.

Klein, Willie. "Teammates Find Rookie Berra Easy to Rib, but Yanks' Belter Can't Be Fooled by Pitchers." *Sporting News*, February 19, 1947.

Koegel, Dick. "Eager Dale Berra Leaves Comedy to Pop." *St. Louis Post-Dispatch*, September 15, 1977.

Koppet, Leonard. "Berra, Once a One-Room Man, Finds Executive Suite Too Noisy." *New York Times*, April 22, 1964.

———. "Yanks, Once 'Dead,' Regain First Place." *New York Times*, September 18, 1964.

———. "Yogi, a Losing Winner." *New York Times*, October 17, 1964.

———. "Berra Expected to Sign 2-Year Pact with Mets Today as Player and Coach." *New York Times*, November 17, 1964.

———. "Berra Signs Two-Year Contract as Coach with Mets at $35,000 a Season." *New York Times*, November 18, 1964.

———. "New Yank: Garagiola, Yogi's Pal Joey." *New York Times*, December 19, 1964.

———. "A Legend of the Game: Lawrence Peter Berra." *New York Times*, October 3, 1973.

———. "Yogi Fingered as Fall Guy." *Sporting News*, August 30, 1975.

Lancaster, Marc. "Before Yankees Career, Navy Gunner Yogi Berra Was Part of D-Day Invasion." *Sporting News*, September 23, 2015.

Landauer, Bill. "The Pitch Man." *Lafayette Magazine*, Spring 2017.

Lang, Jack. "Mets Paid Stiff Penalty for Stand-Pat Policy." *Sporting News*, August 24, 1974.

———. "Pilot Yogi Stands Firm as Mets Release Jones." *Sporting News*, August 9, 1975.

————. "Fill-In McMillan Likely to Lead Mets in 1976." *Sporting News,* August 23, 1975.

"Larsen Hits the Strike Zone on 71 Delivers." *New York Times,* October 9, 1956.

Lauro, Patricia Winters. "One of Baseball's Most Colorful Figures Finds He Is in Demand Again." *New York Times,* April 30, 1999.

Leggett, William. "Trouble Sprouts for the Yankees." *Sports Illustrated,* March 2, 1964.

————. "In Front with a New Look." *Sports Illustrated,* September 28, 1964.

"Legion Baseball Dinner." *St. Louis Post-Dispatch,* September 11, 1941.

Lennon, Dave. "Joe DiMaggio: 'You Followed Whatever He Did.'" *Newsday,* March 8, 1999.

"Leo Browne Gives Parish Soccer Cup." *St. Louis Post-Dispatch,* December 28, 1939.

Leonard, Tom. "Joe DiMaggio Made a Poor Soldier, Military Records Show." *The Telegraph* (UK), August 3, 2010.

Lieb, Frederick G. "Stan, Ted, Spahn and Yogi Eligible for L.A. Spectacle." *Sporting News,* July 29, 1959.

Lipsyte, Robert. "Yogi Berra Works Out with a Management Team." *New York Times,* November 17, 1962.

————. "The Man and the Myth: A View That Berra Is a Bit of Each—A Lovable Myth and a Sensitive Man." *New York Times,* October 25, 1963.

"Little Potatoes at Sportsman Park." *St. Louis Post-Dispatch,* July 11, 1940.

Litzky, Frank. "Frank Scott, 80, Baseball's First Player Agent." *New York Times,* June 30, 1998.

Long, Gary. "Dale Berra Making It His Own Way." *Miami Herald,* January 29, 1984.

Lucas, Ed. "For D-Day Tomorrow, Remember War Heroes Like Yogi Berra." *Jersey Journal,* June 5, 2014.

————. "Farewell, Yogi Berra, a Friend When I Needed One Most." *Jersey Journal,* September 25, 2015.

Lupica, Mike. "George Steinbrenner Fires Yogi Berra as Yankees Manager: Lying Boss, Thy Name Is Dirt." *Daily News* (New York), April 29, 1985.

Madden, Bill. "Billy Martin Replaces Fired Yogi Berra: Yankees Players Infuriated by George Steinbrenner's Move." *Daily News* (New York), April 29, 1985.

————. "Yogi Berra Dead at 90." *Daily News* (New York), September 23, 2015.

Madden, Bill, and Filip Bondy. "Break in at Yogi Berra Museum and Learning Center, Priceless Memorabilia Linked to Yankees Legend Stolen." *Daily News* (New York), October 9, 2014.

Madden, Bill, and Nathaniel Vinton. "Yogi Berra's Wife of 65 Years, Carmen, Dead at 85 Following Complications from Recent Stroke." *Daily News* (New York), March 7, 2014.

"Major League Flashes: Red Explains Close N.L. Race." *Sporting News,* November 6, 1946.

"Man of Bomber Crew; Yogi Quiet and Shy, but His Bat Is Noisy." *New York Times,* October 11, 1956.

Manning, Gordon. "Yankee Yogi: 'I'm Human, Ain't I?'" *Collier's,* August 13, 1949.

"Mantle's Teammates Say Goodbye." *New York Times,* August 16, 1995.

"Maris and Berra Pace 5–1 Triumph." *New York Times,* June 8, 1961.

"Maris Lost to Yanks for Week." *New York Times,* July 11, 1963.

Martinez, Michael. "Steinbrenner Irked at Exhibition Loss." *New York Times,* April 13, 1985.

———. "Berra Dismissed by Steinbrenner; Martin Rehired to Manage Yanks." *New York Times,* April 29, 1985.

"Martin Will Return as Yankee Manager in 1980." *New York Times,* July 30, 1978.

"Matlack Loose and Confident for Seventh-Game Assignment." *New York Times,* October 21, 1973.

McAlary, Mike. "Those Fabulous Berras Ready for Bronx Debut." *New York Post,* March 8, 1985.

———. "Boss: I've Tested Dale for Drugs." *New York Post,* August 20, 1985.

———. "Billy: I Knew About Berra 2 Years Ago." *New York Post,* September 10, 1985.

McCulley, Jim, and Joe Trimble. "Yogi Ousted but Stays as Houk Aide." *Daily News* (New York), October 17, 1964.

McGowen, Roscoe. "Branca Eager for Another Try." *New York Times,* October 1, 1947.

———. "Sun Fields Bother Reiser, Hermanski." *New York Times,* October 2, 1947.

———. "Contracts Signed by Lindell, Berra." *New York Times,* February 14, 1948.

———. "Bombers Crush Indians, 8 to 2, DiMaggio Smashing 2,000th Hit." *New York Times,* June 20, 1950.

———. "Bombers Trip Tigers, 8–7, on Berra's Homer in 12th." *New York Times,* June 3, 1951.

———. "Berra and McDougald Sign Yankee Contracts for Higher Salaries." *New York Times,* January 24, 1952.

———. "Yanks' Berra Hurt in Game Cut Short by Rain at Miami." *New York Times,* March 16, 1952.

———. "Berra Signs Yanks' Contract Making Him Highest-Paid Catcher in Baseball." *New York Times,* November 4, 1954.

"Mets Get Shot from Ol' Yogi." *St. Louis Post-Dispatch,* May 5, 1965.

"Mets Name Stengel as Manager for '62." *New York Times,* September 30, 1961.

"Mets: No Comment on Jones." *New York Times,* May 7, 1975.

"Mets Release Jones." *New York Times,* July 26, 1975.

Michael Berra obituary. *St. Louis Post-Dispatch,* August 8, 1995.

"Midget Title." *St. Louis Post-Dispatch,* July 10, 1940.

Miller, Norm. "Mets Skip Yogi's Son, Draft Catcher First." *Daily News* (New York), June 5, 1975.

Montgomery, Paul. "Martin and Jackson Argue in Dugout in 10–4 Loss." *New York Times,* June 19, 1977.

Moore, Gerald. "The Ordeal of John Cali." *Reader's Digest,* January 1975.

Morrow, Art. "DiMaggio Clouts Homer." *Philadelphia Inquirer,* April 21, 1947.

Moser, Whet. "When Jackie Robinson Tried Out for the White Sox." *Chicago,* April 11, 2013.

"Mrs. Berra Dies; Services Friday." *St. Louis Post-Dispatch,* May 5, 1959.

Munz, Michelle. "Elizabeth Avenue Is Renamed Hall of Fame Place for Former Residents Yogi Berra, Joe Garagiola and Jack Buck." *St. Louis Post-Dispatch,* June 2, 2003.

Murray, Brian. "Berra Pleads Innocent to Cocaine Allegations." *Daily Record* (Morristown, NJ), September 16, 1989.

———. "Berra Vows to Lecture Against Drugs; but Judge Fears Opposite Effect." *Daily Record* (Morristown, NJ), October 28, 1989.

"MVP: Mickey Duplicates Rosen's Grand-Slam of '53; Berra Runner-Up, Kaline Third." *Sporting News,* November 21, 1956.

"Newark Wins in 9th." *New York Times,* June 23, 1946.

Nightengale, Bob. "The World Loved Yogi." *USA Today,* September 23, 2015.

"Ninth Championship for Stengel Ties League Mark Set by Mack." *New York Times,* September 15, 1958.

Noble, Marty. "Dale Disgraces Father's Name." *Newsday,* April 23, 1989.

"O'Connors, Brocks Take Titles in Young Ballplayers' League." *St. Louis Post-Dispatch,* July 11, 1940.

Olson, Carolyn. "Yogi Berra Comes Home: The Making of a PBS Documentary." *St. Louis Post-Dispatch,* August 10, 1999.

O'Neill, Tom. "New Center on The Hill Creates Exhibits and Archives on the Neighborhood." *St. Louis Post-Dispatch,* March 19, 2016.

"Pacific Tour Approved; Lopat All-Stars to Leave Shortly After the World Series." *New York Times,* July 14, 1953.

Pepe, Phil. "Mets Tell Yogi They Believe via 3-Year Contract." *Daily News* (New York), October 24, 1973.

———. "Yogi Comes Out Ahead." *New York Post,* April 30, 1985.

"Phil Rizzuto." BaseballinWartime.com, May 13, 2007.

Phipany, Michele. "Yogi Berra Museum Shares Baseball Memories with Community Kids." *The Montclarion,* December 14, 2000.

"Pirates' Berra Ready for Career." *Pittsburgh Press,* June 5, 1975.

Povich, Shirley. "Houk's Admission: 'Yogi My Mistake.'" *New York Journal-American,* February 28, 1965.

Prendergast, Curtis. "Yanks Capture Japan." *Sports Illustrated,* November 14, 1955.

"President Cheered at Ball Game, but Few Line Route to and from Park." *New York Times,* October 4, 1956.

"Presidential Greetings Are Received by Yogi." *New York Times,* May 16, 1964.

"President Opens Baseball Season." *New York Times,* April 18, 1956.

Radford, Rich. "Navy World Series: In World War II, Norfolk Hosted Baseball's Best." *Virginian-Pilot,* July 24, 2011.

Radosta, John. "His Fellow Parishioners Pay Respects to Gil Hodges." *New York Times,* April 6, 1972.

"Rebuild the Yankee Champs? Yes, It's Job Ahead of Weiss." *St. Louis Post-Dispatch,* October 9, 1947.

Red, Christian. "The Mayor of Montclair: Everybody Loved Humble Yogi Berra in Jersey Town He Called Home for 50-Plus Years." *Daily News* (New York), September 26, 2015.

———. "A Sitdown with Oldest Living Yankee Eddie Robinson, 95, and Yankee Great Bobby Brown, 91, as They Talk Friendship, Joe DiMaggio and Baseball's Golden Era." *Daily News* (New York), April 24, 2016.

"Red Sox Get Six All-Star Berths, Yankees and Indians Five Apiece." *New York Times,* July 5, 1949.

Reel, Ursula. "At Last—Berra and Boss Bury the Hatchet." *New York Post,* January 6, 1999.

Reichler, Joe. "'We Flatten Them, Yet We're Only Tied'—Berra." *Pittsburgh Post-Gazette,* October 13, 1960.

Rendon, Ruth. "Yogi Berra Keeps Swinging as He Takes Job as Irreverent TV Critic of Movies." *Los Angeles Times,* July 16, 1988.

"Reynolds, Berra Balking at Terms." *New York Times,* January 21, 1950.

Rhoden, William. "Deja Vu All Over Again: Berra's Magic Day." *New York Times,* July 19, 1999.

Rickart, Paul. "Berra Again Swat Leader with .360." *Sporting News,* October 17, 1956.

"Rizzuto, Shocked by Release, Says Club Offered Reinstatement After Sept. 1." *New York Times,* August 27, 1956.

"Robinson Says Summers Call on Steal Was Correct." *New York Times,* October 14, 1955.

Rogers, Thomas. "Esteemed Guest Is Honored." *New York Times,* February 15, 1985.

"Rookies to Start Series for Yanks." *New York Times,* September 29, 1947.

"Roosevelt Orders Navy to Strike First at Axis Raiders." *St. Louis Post-Dispatch,* September 12, 1941.

Rosengren, John. "Elston Howard Became the Yankees' Jackie Robinson 60 Years Ago." *Sports Illustrated,* April 13, 2015.

Rosenthal, Harold. "Berra Adds Shatter-Proof Glasses on Order of Brass." *Sporting News,* June 17, 1957.

Ruddy, John. "Berra Became a Heavy Hitter Playing for Sub Base in 1945." *The Day* (New London, CT), September 23, 2015.

Ruhl, Oscar. "They Laughed on Berra's Bow." *Sporting News,* September 14, 1949.

————. "Yogi's Profile of George Weiss." *Sporting News,* January 23, 1952.

Safire, William. "Mr. Bonaprop." *New York Times,* February 15, 1987.

Samedy, Maureen. "Yogi Berra Museum Slated to Open Dec. 1." *The Montclarion,* November 25, 1998.

Sandomir, Richard. "For Yoo-Hoo and Yogi, It's Deja Vu All Over Again." *New York Times,* April 20, 1993.

————. "Phil Rizzuto, Yankees Shortstop, Dies at 89." *New York Times,* August 15, 2007.

————. "Carmen Berra, Yogi's Wife, Dies at 85." *New York Times,* March 7, 2014.

————. "Sons Make Marketing Deal to Perpetuate Yogi Berra's Legacy." *New York Times,* April 26, 2016.

Schacht, Beulah. "A Pork Chop, a Ring, an Engagement." *Sporting News,* August 24, 1949.

Schumach, Murray. "Mantle, Maris and Berra to Be Seen in 'Touch of Mink.'" *New York Times,* August 3, 1961.

————. "Fans Jam Movie Set to See Mantle, Maris and Berra." *New York Times,* August 24, 1961.

————. "Triumphant Yankees Revel in Unabashed Adulation." *New York Times,* October 20, 1977.

Sheehan, Joseph M. "Berra Connects in Fourth, Yanks Take Fifth in Row." *New York Times,* May 15, 1948.

————. "Berra and Henrich Hit Homers as Bombers Move Within 1½ Games of Lead." *New York Times,* August 26, 1948.

————. "Berra's Homer Caps Uphill Battle Carrying Bombers to 5–4 Triumph." *New York Times,* September 1, 1948.

————. "Rizzuto of Yanks Most Valuable; Berra Third." *New York Times,* October 18, 1950.

————. "Bombers Display Quiet Self-Satisfaction Rather Than Wild Joy at Clinching." *New York Times,* September 15, 1953.

————. "Berra and Byrne Pace 3–2 Triumph." *New York Times,* June 17, 1955.

————. "Indians Contend Berra Interfered with Avila at Plate." *New York Times,* June 17, 1955.

———. "Whooping and Shouting Follow Wallop of High Fast Ball by Berra—Yogi's Aim to Cut at First Pitch Paid Off." *New York Times*, September 17, 1955.

———. "Berra Will Be Rested More Next Year." *New York Times*, December 31, 1955.

———. "Mantle Hits 19th and 20th Homers to Help Yankees Defeat Senators Twice." *New York Times*, May 31, 1956.

———. "Berra's 16th Home Run and Bauer's 13th Help Yankee Pitcher Top Athletics." *New York Times*, June 8, 1956.

———. "Yankees Make Houk Executive; Yogi Berra Due to Be Manager." *New York Times*, October 23, 1963.

Smith, Claire. "Yogi Puts Yankees at Ease." *Hartford Courant*, March 25, 1984.

———. "Allie Reynolds, Star Pitcher for Yankees, Is Dead at 79." *New York Times*, December 28, 1994.

Smith, Red. "Remembrance of Things Past." *New York Times*, June 26, 1972.

———. "Things Are Tough All Over, Yogi." *New York Times*, April 16, 1975.

———. "The Sad Case of Cleon Jones." *New York Times*, July 27, 1975.

———. "Yogi Berra." *New York Times*, August 7, 1975.

———. "On Howard, a Class Guy." *New York Times*, December 15, 1980.

Snyder, Cameron. "Yogi Arrives for Hoopla as Colts Sign Last Round Pick Tim Berra." *Baltimore Sun*, February 11, 1974.

Spink, J. G. Taylor. "Looping the Loops." *Sporting News*, November 13, 1946.

Stahl, Jeremy. "Yogi Berra Wasn't Trying to Be Witty." *Slate*, September 23, 2015.

Stearn, Jess. "Two Boys from The Hill." *Daily News* (New York), June 10, 1947.

"Stevens Ousts Yogi in Japan, but Lopats Triumph, 15–1." *New York Times*, October 31, 1953.

Stewart, Barbara. "DiMaggio Leaves for Home After 99 Days in Hospital." *New York Times*, January 19, 1999.

"Stockham Legion Nine Is Largely a Beaumont Team." *St. Louis Post-Dispatch*, July 17, 1941.

"Stockham Nine Faces Berwyn After Winning from New Orleans 6–5." *St. Louis Post-Dispatch*, August 26, 1941.

"Stockham Nine Regional Title." *St. Louis Star-Times*, August 17, 1942.

"Stockham Opposes Augusta Legion Nine." *St. Louis Post-Dispatch*, August 27, 1941.

"Stockham Post Honors Players at Banquet Here." *St. Louis Star-Times*, September 12, 1941.

"Stockham Qualifies for State Legion Tourney by Routing Wellston, 27–1." *St. Louis Post-Dispatch*, July 17, 1941.

"Stockhams Advance to Legion Sectional." *St. Louis Post-Dispatch*, August 15, 1941.

"Stockhams Beat Indiana Champions." *St. Louis Post-Dispatch*, August 13, 1941.

"Stockhams Capture State Title." *St. Louis Star-Times*, August 5, 1941.

"Stockhams Eliminated by Coast Teams, 13–6 in Western Legion Final." *St. Louis Post-Dispatch,* August 31, 1942.

"Stockhams in Final Round of Regional Championship Tourney." *St. Louis Post-Dispatch,* August 14, 1941.

"Stockhams Play St. Joseph in Legion Tourney." *St. Louis Post-Dispatch,* August 1, 1941.

"Stockhams Routed in Title Play." *St. Louis Post-Dispatch,* August 28, 1941.

"Stockhams, State Legion Champions, Honored Here." *St. Louis Star-Times,* August 8, 1941.

"Stockhams to Depart Tonight for Nebraska." *St. Louis Post-Dispatch,* August 27, 1942.

"Stockhams Win Regional Meet, Qualify for Eastern Zone Finals." *St. Louis Star-Times,* August 15, 1941.

"Stockham Takes State Title." *St. Louis Star-Times,* August 4, 1942.

"Stockham Wins from St. Joseph." *St. Louis Post-Dispatch,* August 1, 1941.

Stockton, Ray J. "Speed the Deciding Factor in Cardinals' World Series Triumph." *St. Louis Post-Dispatch,* October 4, 1942.

Strauss, Michael. "Berra Considers Job with Mets After Talking with Weiss." *New York Times,* October 30, 1964.

Talese, Gay. "Mantle—The 'King' Whose Homage Is Catcalls." *New York Times,* June 1, 1958.

———. "Toots Shor Opens 52nd St. Tent." *New York Times,* October 8, 1960.

———. "Fans Score Stengel Dismissal as 'Error' for Yankee Owners." *New York Times,* October 19, 1960.

———. "The Silent Season of a Hero." *Esquire,* July 1966.

Taylor, David A. "During World War II, the U.S. Saw Italian-Americans as a Threat to Homeland Security." *Smithsonian,* February 2, 2017.

Teague, Robert L. "Berra Hits Homer." *New York Times,* July 30, 1961.

"Ted Williams." BaseballinWartime.com, January 11, 2007.

"Too Much Yogi Berra for East Chicago Nine." *Courier News* (Bridgewater, NJ), August 19, 1942.

Trimble, Joe. "Yogi Ends Playing Career, Takes Cut for Pilot's Job." *Daily News* (New York), October 25, 1963.

Tuckner, Howard M. "Berra Makes Pitch to Sell Book, but He Strikes Out as a Speller." *New York Times,* February 11, 1961.

"Turley Twinkles on Mound as Howard Clouts Clincher." *Sporting News,* October 15, 1958.

Vaccaro, Mike. "War & Remembrance: Some Memories Die Hard for an Old Sailor Like Yogi Berra." *New York Post,* February 24, 2003.

Vecsey, George. "Yogi's Back in Style." *New York Times,* December 17, 1983.

———. "The Real Villain in Yankee Drama." *New York Times,* June 5, 1984.

————. "The Boss Is Back." *New York Times,* October 1, 1984.

————. "Greenwade Knew the Territory." *New York Times,* August 22, 1986.

————. "Whitey Ford, a Six-Time Champion, Can Add a Title: Greatest Living Yankee." *New York Times,* September 24, 2015.

Vergara, John. "The Yogi I Know." *Daily News* (New York), April 7, 1974.

"Victory Today Would Give Stockham Title." *St. Louis Post-Dispatch,* August 4, 1941.

"Villanova Overcome by UMass." *New York Times,* September 15, 1973.

"Virus Hits McDougald, Carey, Berra." *New York Times,* April 23, 1960.

Waldstein, David. "An Incubator of Baseball Talent." *New York Times,* October 20, 2011.

Ward, Robert. "Reggie Jackson in No-Man's Land." *Sport,* June 1977.

Warner, Ray. "The Berras and the Tripuckas, or the Games Some People Play." *New York Times,* January 23, 1973.

"Warning to American League: The Berra Era Is About to Start." *New York Times,* April 13, 1964.

"Weiss Spikes Players' Plot to Grab DiMag's $90,000." *Sporting News,* February 13, 1952.

"Welcome in Tokyo Stirs Lopat Stars." *New York Times,* October 23, 1953.

"Westrum Taking Calculated Risk." *New York Times,* September 5, 1965.

White, Gordon S. "No Strikes for Yogi." *New York Times,* November 4, 1958.

Wilner, Paul. "Yogi Berra: At Bat in Montclair." *New York Times,* January 8, 1978.

Wind, Herbert Warren. "From the Hill to the Hall." *Sports Illustrated,* March 2, 1959.

Wolff, Craig. "Carmen and Yogi Berra: A Love Affair for the Ages." *Star-Ledger* (Newark, NJ), March 8, 2014.

————. "Yogi Berra Was an American Original, a Baseball Legend and a Yankee for the Ages." *Star Ledger* (Newark, NJ), September 23, 2015.

Woodward, Steve. "Stargell: I Didn't Give Berra Pills." *USA Today,* September 11, 1985.

Wray, Louis. "Mr. Browne Dreams of a Title." *St. Louis Post-Dispatch,* August 13, 1942.

————. "Junior League a Good Investment." *St. Louis Post-Dispatch,* August 21, 1943.

————. "This Yogi's Religion Is Baseball." *St. Louis Post-Dispatch,* January 26, 1947.

Wright, Alfred. "Look Out! Here Comes Case." *Sports Illustrated,* March 14, 1955.

Wulf, Steve. "Oh No, Not Again; Fired Seven Times as a Manager, Billy Martin Hired for the Fourth Term by the Floundering Yankees." *Sports Illustrated,* May 5, 1985.

"Yankee 'Nature Boy,' Bride-to-Be." *Sporting News,* January 26, 1949.

"Yankee Party Departs on Six-Week Tour of Orient." *New York Times,* October 9, 1955.

"Yankees Appear in a Class Alone." *New York Times,* February 16, 1964.

"Yankees' Head Expects to Be Charged with 'Insubordination' and Indicates Desire for Showdown with Commissioner." *New York Times,* April 30, 1947.

"Yankees' New Find to Be Feted by Home-Folks." *St. Louis Star-Times,* April 29, 1947.

"Yankees Pay Tribute to Guidry." *New York Times,* August 24, 2003.

"Yankees Seek an End to Segregation of Their Players in St. Petersburg." *New York Times,* February 2, 1961.

"Yankees Who Will Play with the All-Stars in Chicago on Tuesday." *New York Times,* July 9, 1950.

"Yankees Will Lose Their Outfield Ace." *New York Times,* January 14, 1943.

"Yanks Celebrate Until Dawn on Waldorf's Starlight Roof." *Sporting News,* October 17, 1956.

"Yanks Eye Berra." *New York Times,* August 21, 1975.

"Yanks' Homer Derby Goes West and Berra Ponders a New Pitch; Yogi Asks: What Happens If One Star Hits 61 in 154 Games but the Other Finishes with More in 162?" *New York Times,* August 22, 1961.

"Yanks' Staff Sent to Minors." *New York Times,* June 17, 1981.

"Yanks Win, Close Tour of Japan Without Loss." *New York Times,* November 14, 1955.

"Yanks Woo Cabbies with 20,000 Tickets." *New York Times,* June 20, 1964.

"Yogi Berra." BaseballinWartime.com, January 13, 2007.

"Yogi Berra Buys Home, Yankee Catcher to Live at Woodcliff Lake, N.J." *New York Times,* June 9, 1951.

"Yogi Berra Caught in a Squeeze Play." *St. Louis Post-Dispatch,* February 9, 1948.

"Yogi Berra Changes Yankee Uniform for Tux—to Greet Diners." *St. Louis Post-Dispatch,* November 7, 1949.

"Yogi Berra a Father." *St. Louis Post-Dispatch,* December 9, 1949.

"Yogi Berra Makes an Error; Leaves Scene of Accident." *St. Louis Post-Dispatch,* February 23, 1948.

"Yogi Berra: Philosopher of the Diamond." Achievement.org, June 1, 2005.

"Yogi Berra's Father Dies in Hospital." *St. Louis Post-Dispatch,* November 8, 1961.

"Yogi Cave 'Em In!" *St. Louis Post-Dispatch,* December 6, 1950.

"Yogi Gets New Post—Yanks Consider Keane and Dark." *New York Times,* October 17, 1964.

"Yogi Now a Classy Clouter in Golf—He's a Switch-Hitter." *Sporting News,* February 29, 1956.

"Yogi Pitches Fresh Malaprops in AFLAC Campaign." *Brandweek,* May 27, 2002.

"Yogi's Not the Only Yank Who Likes Comic Books." *Sporting News,* January 10, 1951.

"Yogi Sprains Ankle." *Sporting News,* March 26, 1952.

"Yogi Tells Legion Champs Yanks Will Repeat." *St. Louis Star-Times,* November 29, 1947.

"Yogi to Be All-Year New Yorker." *Sporting News,* March 4, 1951.

"Yogi Top N.J. Pro Athlete." *Sporting News,* January 13, 1954.

"Yogi Traces Yearly Raises Since He Got $5,000 in '47." *Sporting News,* February 3, 1954.

Yollin, Patricia. "A Secret History / The Harassment of Italians During World War II Has Particular Relevance Today and Serves as a Warning of What Could Happen." *San Francisco Chronicle,* October 21, 2001.

Young, Dick. "George: Players Blew It for Berra." *New York Post,* April 30, 1985.

Zernike, Kate. "A New Jersey Township Mourns Yogi Berra, Its Civic Treasure." *New York Times,* September 23, 2015.

## Multimedia

"Yogi Berra: Déjà Vu All Over Again." Public Broadcasting System, August 1999.

"Tino's Two-Run Shot Ties the Game." MLB.TV, October 31, 2001.

Yogi Berra interview. *Dan Patrick Outtakes.* ESPN.com, December 6, 2001.

"Yogi Berra on the Loss of Phil Rizzuto." YouTube.com, posted by YESNetwork, August 14, 2007.

"Mickey Mantle: How I Became a Yankee." YouTube.com, posted by Lewearly, November 17, 2008.

"Mickey Mantle: The Fight at the Copacabana Nightclub." YouTube.com, posted by Lewearly, February 27, 2009.

"65 Year Anniversary of D-Day—Yogi Berra Feature." YouTube.com, posted by YESNetwork.com, June 8, 2009.

*"Brown v. Board of Education."* History.com, October 27, 2009.

"Yogi at the Movies: Moonstuck" [*sic*]. YouTube.com, posted by Mike Gardner, October 12, 2010.

"Yogi Berra Falls, Released from Hospital." ESPN.com, March 10, 2011.

"Joe Torre, Bob Costas Help Yogi Berra Reopen His Montclair, NJ Museum." CBS.com, June 24, 2011.

"The Navy World Series: WWII Baseball in Norfolk, July 21, 2011." YouTube.com, posted by VirginiaPilot, July 11, 2011.

"1955 World Series Dodgers Win Game 7." YouTube.com, posted by MyFootage.com, August 18, 2011.

"Yogi Berra on Baseball and Business." CNBC.com, April 4, 2012.

"Big Think Interview with George Lois." YouTube.com, posted by Big Think, April 23, 2012.

"When Italian Immigrants Were 'the Other.'" CNN.com, July 10, 2012.

"Funny Yogi Berra Clip, Talking Cat Commercial!" YouTube.com, posted by CourtsideTweets, August 29, 2012.

"Pete Rose & Bud Harrelson Brawl, 1973 NLCS!" YouTube.com, posted by CourtsideTweets, September 13, 2012.

"The Yogi Chronicles, 1940s–2012." PopHistoryDig.com, October 21, 2012.

"1955 World Series Highlights / Brooklyn Dodgers vs New York Yankees." YouTube.com, posted by YamaMX, March 26, 2013.

"What's My Line?—Yogi Berra; Martin Gabel [panel] (Jul 2, 1961)." YouTube.com, posted by What's My Line?, April 19, 2014.

"What's My Line?—Yogi Berra; Louis Jourdan; Steve Lawrence [panel] (Apr 26, 1964)." YouTube.com, posted by What's My Line?, April 26, 2014.

"Yogi Berra's NJ Home Ready for Next Inning." Today.com, April 30, 2014.

"What I Learned from Rose Cali." Interview with Bobbi Brown, YahooBeauty.com, August 14, 2014.

"Phil Rizzuto 1994 Hall of Fame Induction Speech." YouTube.com, posted by National Baseball Hall of Fame and Museum, September 25, 2014.

"Dugout Scene Yankee Stadium from *That Touch of Mink* (1962)." YouTube.com, posted by RF88, March 6, 2015.

"The Yogi Berra Museum Celebrates Yogi's 90th Birthday." YouTube.com, posted by YESNetwork, May 26, 2015.

"This Day in 1918: MLB Season Ends Due to World War I." AOL.com, September 1, 2015.

"1956 WS Gm7: Berra Hits a Pair of Home Runs." YouTube.com, posted by MLB.com, September 23, 2015.

"Remembering Yogi Berra." CTV News, September 23, 2015.

"Yogi Berra Mingles with the Stars in 1962." YouTube.com, posted by NJ.com, September 23, 2015.

"Yogi Left Indelible Mark on the 1956 World Series." MLB.com, September 23, 2015.

"Yogi Berra on Catching Don Larsen's Perfect Game (June 8, 2001)." YouTube.com, posted by CharlieRose, September 24, 2015.

"Yankees Pay Tribute to Yogi Berra." YouTube.com, posted by MLB.com, September 25, 2015.

"Yogi Berra Day, July 19, 1999." YouTube.com, posted by BigTimeEmpire, September 30, 2015.

"Yogi Berra United States Navy Funeral Honors Detail." YouTube.com, posted by Matthew Oden, September 30, 2015.

"Joe Torre on Yogi Berra Funeral." YouTube.com, posted by Mark Schilling, October 3, 2015.

"President Obama Awards Yogi Berra, Willie Mays the Medal of Freedom." CBSSports.com, November 24, 2015.

"The History of Baseball Broadcasting: Early Television." BaseballEssential .com, December 19, 2015.

"I Was There When: David Cone's Perfect Game." YouTube.com, posted by New York Yankees, December 21, 2015.

"Joe Garagiola Delivers Ford C. Frick Award Speech." YouTube.com, posted by MLB, March 23, 2016.

"Thrill of a Lifetime." Legion.org, June 13, 2016.

"World Series Television Ratings." BaseballAlmanac.com, 2017.

Evan Andrews. "The Green Book: The Black Travelers' Guide to Jim Crow America." History.com, February 6, 2017.

"Hiroshima: Dropping the Bomb—Hiroshima—BBC." YouTube.com, posted by BBC Studios, March 14, 2017.

"Yankeeography: Casey Stengel." YouTube.com, posted by Yankee Classics, July 19, 2018.

Therian Hester Smith obituary and tribute movie. DignityMemorial.com, November 5, 2018.

"June 18, 1977—Billy vs Reggie (WPIX Clips)." YouTube.com, posted by epaddon, February 17, 2019.

"Yogi Berra's Son on Baseball, Family and Overcoming Hardships." NPR.org, May 4, 2019.

"Nagasaki Marks 74 Years Since US Atomic Bombing." YouTube.com, posted by RT, August 9, 2019.

## Websites

Baseball-Almanac.com
BaseballHall.org
Baseball-Reference.com
En.Wikipedia.org
MLB.com
NorfolkTides.com
SABR.org

## Undated

"What Really Happened in 1963: The New York Yankees," ThatsBaseball.org

"Buzz Aldrin Rock," RoadsideAmerica.com

George Weiss profile, National Baseball Hall of Fame

"Naval Station Norfolk," *Wikipedia*

Baseball Labor History, SI.com

"WWI-Great Depression-WWII timeline," Timetoast.com

"The Hill, St. Louis," *Wikipedia*

"Great Depression," History.com

"Franchise Timeline," St. Louis Cardinals, MLB.com

"Franchise Timeline," New York Yankees, MLB.com

"Franchise Timeline," Los Angeles Dodgers, MLB.com

"Franchise Timeline," New York Mets, MLB.com

"Norfolk Naval Base," SalutetoFreedom.org (National WWII Museum)

"Japanese Relocation During World War II," National Archives

"1942: The Home Grown Champions," ThisGreatGame.com

"Prohibition," Britannica.com

"The War: 1940 Timeline," PBS.org

"Italian American Racism During the WWII Era," Wishaw.50megs.com (Wishaw, PA, Historical Society)

"Robinson Steals Home 09/28/1955," MLB.com

## SABR Biography Project

"Yogi Berra," SABR.org

"Bill Bevins," SABR.org

"Spud Chandler," SABR.org

"Bill Dickey," SABR.org

"Joe DiMaggio," SABR.org

"Gil Hodges," SABR.org

"Eddie Lopat," SABR.org

"Mickey Mantle," SABR.org

"Roger Maris," SABR.org

"Joe McCarthy," SABR.org

"Joe Page," SABR.org

"Vic Raschi," SABR.org

"Allie Reynolds," SABR.org

"Phil Rizzuto," SABR.org

"Spec Shea," SABR.org

"Bill Skowron," SABR.org

"Ralph Terry," SABR.org

"1947 Yankees Ownership," SABR.org

## Documents

President Roosevelt's Green Light Letter, National Baseball Hall of Fame, January 15, 1942

Notice to Aliens of Enemy Nationalities, Archives.gov, February 9, 1942

General Dwight D. Eisenhower's Order of the Day, OurDocuments.gov, June 6, 1944

MLB Collective Bargaining Agreement, 1973

Policy of Title Insurance, Sale of Berra house in Montclair, NJ, to John J. Cali and Rose L. Cali, February 24, 1976

Lawrence Berra vs. Francine Berra, Judgment for Divorce, March 24, 1986

Leigh O'Grady Berra vs. Dale A. Berra, Judgment for Divorce, January 23, 1992

"Report to the Congress of the United States: A Review of the Restrictions of Persons of Italian Ancestry During World War II," Schino.com, November 2001

Rose Cali, President of the Board and Acting Executive Director, Yogi Berra Museum and Learning Center, Letter of Resignation, April 27, 2005

# Index

# About the Author

Jon Pessah is the *New York Times* bestselling author of *The Game,* a critically acclaimed examination of the power brokers who built Major League Baseball into a multibillion-dollar business. A founding editor of *ESPN the Magazine,* where he ran the investigative team, Pessah has also managed the sports departments for *Newsday* and the *Hartford Courant.*